Monetary Theory and Policy

Major Contributions to Contemporary Thought

Edited with Introductions by **Richard S. Thorn**

University of Pittsburgh

New York RANDOM HOUSE

1969

FIRST PRINTING / © *Copyright, 1966, by Random House, Inc.*
THIRD PRINTING/*July, 1969*

To my parents

Foreword

In the past decade and a half, there has taken place an intensive re-examination and rethinking of prevailing doctrines of monetary theory and policy, the results of which will mark this period as a significant one in the history of economic thought.

In making the selections for this book, I have been guided by the principle of presenting to the reader the most important new work in the field of monetary theory and policy that has taken place during this fifteen-year period. The collection of articles assembled here constitutes, in fact, a textbook of contemporary monetary thought.

While I would have liked to include all of the significant contributions of recent years, in a book of manageable length final choices must be somewhat personal. While difficulty and length were not primary criteria used in making the selections in some cases they were the factors that ultimately influenced the final decisions. The article by John R. Hicks although written earlier than the other articles has been included because of its widespread influence on the monetary thought of the period. Similarly the article by William Fellner and Harold M. Somers also lies somewhat outside the fifteen-year period but inasmuch as it gave rise to ideas and problems that caused considerable debate, I felt it useful to include it in this volume.

Though the selections have been placed under six conventional divisions of monetary economics, it should be mentioned that many of the articles cut across the subject matter of several or all of the sections. The introductions that appear at the beginning of each division are to provide the reader with some background to the central issues as well as to maintain continuity in the exposition.

Due to the limited space available, personal acknowledgments by the authors have been omitted and four of the articles have been slightly shortened where indicated. In many instances the authors have made minor revisions in their articles eliminating errors or misprints.

Page references in footnotes referring to articles reprinted in this volume are followed by a number in parentheses indicating the corresponding pages in this book.

The preparation of this book required the cooperation of many people. I am grateful to the authors and publishers for their kind permission to reprint the articles appearing herein and wish to thank Professor Jacob Cohen of the University of Pittsburgh, Professor Edgar Feige of the University of Wisconsin, Professor William Fellner of Yale University, Dr. Juan Giral of the Comitee of Nine, Pan American Union, Professor Robert Mundell of the University of Chicago, Professor Boris Pesek of Michigan State University, and Dr. William H. White of the International Monetary Fund for their helpful comments and suggestions. I should also like to thank Mr. Theodore Caris and Mrs. Miriam Z. Klipper of Random House for the interest they have taken in the preparation of this volume, and Miss Margaret Tierney for her help in preparing the bibliography. Finally, special appreciation goes to my wife for her great patience.

RICHARD S. THORN
New York City
September 1, 1965

Contents

Part **I**

Introduction

The intellectual impact of Keynes' *General Theory of Employment, Interest and Money* (1936) with its persuasive arguments for the wider use of fiscal policy in the circumstances of the great depression was overwhelming, and the subsequent absorption of economists with the problems of wartime finance and postwar reconstruction was so intense as to result in a virtual neglect of monetary theory and policy in the immediate prewar and postwar periods. It was not until the 1950's that monetary problems once again attracted the attention of a large number of economists. This renewed interest was largely the result of the rebirth of monetary policy in Europe under the impact of postwar inflation. The renaissance of monetary policy in the United States occurred somewhat later when the Federal Reserve, under the terms of the Federal-Reserve Treasury Accord of 1951, was relieved of the responsibility for maintaining the prices of government securities.

As has frequently occurred in the history of economic doctrine, academic interest in monetary theory arose out of the challenge of specific policy problems. This attention was greatly stimulated by the Patman Hearings held in 1951[1] and subsequently by two large-scale reports, one by the Radcliffe Committee in the United Kingdom in 1959,[2] the other by the Commission on Money and Credit in the United States in 1961.[3] During the course of these inquiries large numbers of economists and other interested persons were called upon to express their views and interpretations of contemporary monetary problems and many special memoranda and studies were commissioned.

The central theoretical theme of this renaissance has been the integration of monetary theory with value and capital theory. Economists picked up the reins where Keynes and his critics dropped

[1] U.S. Congress, Joint Economic Committee, *Monetary Policy and the Management of the Public Debt*, 2 vols., 82nd Congress, 2nd Session (Washington 1952).

[2] Committee on the Working of the Monetary System (Chairman: The Rt. Hon. Lord Radcliffe), *Report* (London 1959).

[3] Commission on Money and Credit, *Money and Credit: Their Influence on Jobs, Prices, and Growth* (Englewood Cliffs, N.J. 1961).

them at the outset of the war and tried to bridge the dichotomy between "real" economics and "monetary" economics. Money, as Wicksell long ago discovered, is not a veil but a raiment which clothes the economy and forever alters its appearance. Much of the progress that has been made in monetary theory in recent years is a result of the generalization of the Wicksell-Pigou Effect[4] which in essence stated that volume of monetary assets, measured in terms of the general price level, can affect "real" phenomena, such as consumption, investment, and income, not only through the rate of interest but also through its effect on the amount and composition of desired wealth portfolios.

The recognition that consumers' behavior may be influenced by their income and stock of wealth, just as entrepreneurs' investment decisions are influenced by their income and stock of capital, has opened the door to the possibility that both consumption theory and investment theory, which have been developed mostly independently of one another, may be assimilated into a general theory of expenditure. Another important development is the tendency to depart from the broad macroeconomic level to a detailed analysis of how monetary policy affects the spending and saving decisions of various groups and sectors in the economy, thus providing monetary theory with a firmer behavioral basis.

The two most fundamental policy issues that have been raised are whether monetary authorities have sufficient and effective enough policy instruments to achieve the greatly increased number of objectives that the central bank has been asked to consider in conducting monetary policy and whether monetary rules are superior to discretionary monetary policy.

From the following survey of developments of the past fifteen years we may conclude that the re-examination of current doctrine will result in a substantially better integration of monetary theory into the general body of value theory. At present, there is no overall consensus on the major issues that have been raised; however, the intensive empirical testing of new and old ideas gives promise of producing an accepted body of doctrine that will provide a sounder basis for the conduct of monetary policy in the future.

---

[4] Although Pigou is generally credited with introducing what Patinkin has called the "real balance effect" into contemporary monetary discussions, Wicksell gave a classical description of the effect in his *Interest and Prices* (Jena 1898, reprinted by Augustus M. Kelley, New York 1965, trans.), pp. 39–40. Since the term "Pigou Effect" is most commonly used by the authors in this volume, I shall employ the same terminology in place of the more accurate "Wicksell-Pigou Effect."

1 *Monetary Theory and Policy*

Harry G. Johnson *University of Chicago and The London School of Econonics*

In order to isolate a field of study clearly enough demarcated to be usefully surveyed, it is necessary to define monetary theory as comprising theories concerning the influence of the quantity of money in the economic system, and monetary policy as policy employing the central bank's control of the supply of money as an instrument for achieving the objectives of general economic policy. In surveying the field thus narrowly defined fourteen years ago, Henry Villard [124] began by remarking on the relative decline in the significance attached to it as compared with the offshoot fields of business cycle and fiscal (income and employment) theory, a decline related to the experience of the 1930's, the intellectual impact of Keynes' *General Theory* [66], and the inhibiting effects of the wartime expansion of public debt on monetary policy. While this division of labor has continued, and has indeed been accentuated by the emergence of the cross-cutting field of economic growth and development as an area of specialization, the field of money has been increasingly active and has received increasing attention in the past fourteen years.

This recent activity in the money field can be explained in part by the general logic of scientific progress, according to which disputed issues are investigated with the aid of more powerful theoretical tools, and the implications of new approaches are explored in rigorous detail. Thus, in monetary theory, the issues raised by Keynes' attack on "classical" monetary theory have been worked

Reprinted from *American Economic Review*, Vol. 52 (June 1962), 335–84, by permission of the author and the American Economic Association.

over with the apparatus of general equilibrium analysis developed by J. R. Hicks [60] (to the gradual eclipse of the Robertsonian and Swedish period analysis once considered most promising), and Keynes' emphasis on treating money as an asset has been followed by subsequent theorists as a means of bringing money within the general framework of the theory of choice. In larger part, the revival of interest in money is a reflection of external developments —the postwar inflation, the consequent revival of monetary policy, and the persistence of inflation in the face of unemployment— together with recognition of the problems posed for both policy and theory by certain institutional characteristics of the modern economy (notably the widespread holding of liquid assets) and by potential conflicts between the diverse policy objectives now accepted as responsibilities of governmental policy.

The interest of professional economists in these matters has also been directly enlisted in the preparation of testimony and studies for a succession of large-scale enquiries into monetary policy and institutions, most recently the Radcliffe Report in Britain [128] and the Report [129] of the Commission on Money and Credit established by the Committee for Economic Development in the United States.[1] Finally, recent work on both theory and policy has been strongly influenced by the increased postwar emphasis on (and capacity for) econometric model-building and testing, and stimulated by the availability of new data—especially Raymond Goldsmith's data on saving [47] and financial intermediaries [48] in the United States, the Federal Reserve System's flow-of-funds accounts ([127] and subsequent publications), and Milton Friedman and Anna Schwartz' historical series of the United States money supply, forthcoming in [42].

While the impact of Keynes' *General Theory* has been so great that most of recent theory and research on money can be classified either as application and extension of Keynesian ideas or as counter-revolutionary attack on them, it seems preferable in a survey of the field to organize the material according to the main areas of research rather than according to the issues Keynes raised. Readers interested in the present status of Keynes' contributions to economics are referred to anniversary assessments by William Fellner and Dudley Dillard [32], James Schlesinger [103], H. G. Johnson [61], and R. E. Kuenne [71]. This survey deals with four broad topics: the neutrality of money; the theory of demand for money, which becomes the theory of velocity of circulation when the demand for money is related to income; the theory of money supply, monetary control, and monetary dynamics; and monetary policy. In companion articles G. L. S. Shackle has surveyed the theory of interest [106; see also page 419, in this volume], and

Martin Bronfenbrenner and Franklyn Holzman have surveyed the theory of inflation [*American Economic Review*, 53: 593–661 (September 1963)].

The Classical Dichotomy and the Neutrality of Money

From the standpoint of pure theory, the most fundamental issue raised by Keynes in the *General Theory* lay in his attack on the traditional separation of monetary and value theory, the "classical dichotomy" as (following Don Patinkin [95]) it has come to be called, according to which relative prices are determined by the "real" forces of demand and supply and the absolute price level is determined by the quantity of money and its velocity of circulation. Keynes' attack has been followed by a protracted, often confused, and usually intensely mathematical investigation of the "consistency" or "validity" of the classical dichotomy, the requirements of a consistent theory of value in a monetary economy, and the conditions under which money will or will not be "neutral" (in the sense that a change in the quantity of money will not alter the real equilibrium of the system—relative prices and the interest rate). In the course of the controversy at least as much has been learned about the difficulty of extracting theoretical conclusions from systems of equations as has been contributed to usable monetary theory. The argument, it should be noted, has been concerned throughout with a monetary economy characterized by minimal uncertainty, whereas Keynes was concerned with a highly uncertain world in which money provides a major link between present and future (on this point see Shackle [106, p. 211; also pp. 421–22 in this volume]).

THE INTEGRATION OF MONETARY AND VALUE THEORY

The early history of what is often described as "the Patinkin controversy" is not worth recounting in detail; an annotated bibliography of it may be found in Valavanis [123], and Patinkin's own summary in [91; see also page 268 in this volume]. It began with Oskar Lange's argument [72] that Say's Law (which in this context is the principle that people sell goods only for the purpose of buying goods) logically precludes any monetary theory, since in combination with Walras' Law (that the total supply of goods and money to the market must be equal to the total demand for goods and money from the market) it implies that the excess demand for money on the market is identically zero regardless of the absolute price level, which therefore is indeterminate. Patinkin took up this charge, shifting the object of criticism to the classical assumption that the demand and supply functions for commodities are homogeneous of degree zero in commodity prices (that is, a doubling of all commodity prices will leave quantities demanded and supplied unchanged—in other words, quantities demanded depend only on relative prices). This criticism was refined and its mathematical formulation clarified in response to subsequent critical contributions, of which the most important was Karl Brunner's demonstration [17] that a consistent monetary theory could be constructed without assigning utility to money.

In its final form at this stage [91], Patinkin's criticism of the classical dichotomy was that there was a logical contradiction between classical value theory, in which demands and supplies of commodities depended only on relative prices and not on the real value of people's cash balances, and the quantity theory of money, in which the dependence of spending on the real value of money balances provides the mechanism by which the quantity of money determines a stable equilibrium absolute price level, a contradiction which could be removed neither by resort to Say's Law nor by abandonment of the quantity theory in favor of some other monetary theory. But, Patinkin argued, the contradiction could be removed, and classical theory reconstituted, by making the demand and supply functions depend on real cash balances as well as relative prices; while this would eliminate the dichotomy, it would preserve the basic features of classical monetary theory, and particularly the invariance of the real equilibrium of the economy (relative prices and the rate of interest) with respect to changes in the quantity of money.

The integration of monetary and value theory through the explicit introduction of real balances as a determinant of behavior, and the reconstitution of classical monetary theory, is the main theme and contribution of Patinkin's monumentally scholarly work, *Money, Interest, and Prices* [94]. The first part of the book ("Microeconomics") develops the theory of the real balance effect (the effect of a change in the price level on the real value of money balances and hence on expenditure) in terms of a Hicksian exchange economy in which the individual starts each week with an endowment of commodities that must be consumed within the week and a stock of fiat money, and plans to exchange these for commodities to be consumed during the week and cash balances with which to start the next week. The demand for cash balances is a demand for real balances, derived rather artificially from the assumption that though equilibrium prices are fixed at the beginning of the week, cash payments and receipts are randomly distributed over the week and the individual attaches disutility to the prospect of being unable to pay cash on demand. A rise in prices

Real Balance / Wicksell-Pigou Effect

Pigou = Real Bal - (govt debt & money would against priv. debt)

lowers the real value of an individual's initial cash holding and, provided that neither goods nor real balances are "inferior," reduces his demand for both (implying a less than unit-elastic demand curve for money with respect to its purchasing power); but a proportional rise in prices accompanied by an equiproportional increase in the individual's initial money stock does not alter his behavior. Extended to the market as a whole, the first property ensures the stability of the money price level, the second yields the quantity theory result that a doubling of everyone's money stock will double prices but leave the real equilibrium unchanged. When lending and borrowing by means of bonds are introduced, this latter result requires a doubling of everyone's initial bond assets or liabilities as well as his money holdings. Patinkin's chief criticism of the classical economists has now been reduced to their failure to analyze the role of the real balance effect in ensuring price level stability; the charge of definite inconsistency can only be fairly pinned to a few specific writers of later vintage.

Carefully worked out as it is, Patinkin's analysis of the real balance effect is conceptually inadequate and crucially incomplete; both defects are attributable to an unsatisfactory analysis of stock-flow relationships. The conceptual inadequacy is inherent in the lumping together of the stock of cash and the week's income of goods into a total of disposable resources and the application of the conventional concept of inferiority to the possible effects of changes in this hybrid total on the quantities of real balances and goods demanded.[2] The incompleteness is inherent in Patinkin's restriction of his analysis of the effects of a disturbance to the single week in which it occurs. Archibald and Lipsey [2; see also page 297 in this volume] have shown that over succeeding weeks an individual whose real balances differed from their desired level would accumulate or decumulate balances by spending less or more than his income until real balances attained the desired level, at which point expenditure would once again equal income. Thus, they argue, the real balance effect is a transient phenomenon, relevant only to short-run disequilibrium situations. If positions of long-run equilibrium are compared, the effect of a change in the quantity of money does not depend on its initial distribution (since individuals will redistribute it among themselves in adjusting their real balances to the desired level) and the demand for money with respect to its purchasing power has the classical unitary elasticity; finally, real balances can be dropped from the equations determining equilibrium, which can be written as functions of relative prices only.

On the basis of this last result, Archibald and Lipsey attacked the Lange-Patinkin charge of inconsistency in classical theory, and showed that a consistent system could be constructed using demand and supply functions homogeneous of degree zero in prices, supplemented by the quantity equation, though this system would not conform to Walras' Law when out of equilibrium. Earlier, Valavanis [123] had disputed Patinkin's apparent victory in the dichotomy debate, and shown that if the (in my opinion, misnamed) Cambridge equation is interpreted as an independent restraint on behavior rather than as a behavior relationship conflicting with Walras' Law, there is no inconsistency. J. Encarnación has since shown [31] that Lange's mathematical proof of inconsistency is invalid, and Patinkin's rests on a misuse of the term "consistency."

As a subsequent symposium [7] on the Archibald-Lipsey article has helped to show, these demonstrations, while justified perhaps by Patinkin's continued emphasis on the "inconsistency" theme, are really beside the main point. While a formally consistent theory can be constructed by interpreting velocity as an externally imposed restraint on monetary behavior (an interpretation for which there is ample precedent in the literature) this treatment not only leaves velocity itself unexplained on economic grounds, but precludes any analysis of monetary dynamics and the stability of monetary equilibrium by its inability to specify behavior in disequilibrium conditions. As the better classical monetary theorists saw, these problems are most easily handled by assuming that money balances yield services of utility to their holders; and Patinkin's major contribution has been to elaborate a rigorous formal theory of this approach.

THE NEUTRALITY AND NONNEUTRALITY OF MONEY

The second part of Patinkin's book reformulates the argument in terms of a short-run macroeconomic system, Keynesian in structure[3] but based on "classical" behavior assumptions, and arrives at the classical result that relative prices and the rate of interest are independent of the quantity of money. The significance of this demonstration lies mainly in the assumptions required to establish the neutrality of money [94, Ch. 12]: wage and price flexibility, inelastic expectations, absence of "money illusion," absence of "distribution effects," homogeneity of "bonds," and absence of government debt or open-market operations.[4] This rarefied set of assumptions is the main object of attack in J. G. Gurley and E. S. Shaw's *Money in a Theory of Finance* [52], a central purpose of which is to elucidate the conditions under which money will not be neutral.

Mention must first be made of an earlier, and influential, article by L. A. Metzler [84; see also page 324 in this volume], whose analysis underlies the final assumption listed above. Metzler argued that the wealth-saving relationship assumed in the use of the Pigou effect by Keynes' critics to demonstrate that price flexibility would maintain full employment in the Keynesian model[5] implied a theory in which changes in the quantity of money could affect the rate of interest (and consequently the rate of growth). Assuming for simplicity that government obligations are fixed in real terms, and that interest on government holdings of its own debt is returned as income to the community, Metzler showed that the price increase consequent on monetary expansion effected by open-market purchase of government debt would leave the community with a smaller stock of real assets and a greater willingness to save, thus lowering the equilibrium interest rate, though monetary expansion effected through the printing press would not alter the equilibrium interest rate. As Haberler shortly pointed out [54], Metzler's analysis of open-market operations implicitly rests on a distribution effect (the private sector but not the government being assumed to be influenced by a change in the latter's real debt); but subsequent writers, including Patinkin, have accepted this as a legitimate assumption, and Gurley and Shaw's analysis builds on it.

Gurley and Shaw's book is related to their earlier work on financial intermediaries in relation to economic growth and monetary policy; these aspects of their analysis will be taken up in the appropriate context. Their contribution to the neutrality discussion, apart from their insistence that rigidities, money illusion, expectations, and distribution effects may be quite important in actuality, consists in bringing back into the analysis the monetary and financial structure and the differing liquidity characteristics of different assets excluded by assumption in Patinkin's models. They begin by constructing a simple model alternative to Patinkin's, in which money is not itself government debt but is issued by the monetary authority against private debt ("inside" money, as contrasted with "outside" money), and showing that in this model the price level is determinate[6] and money is neutral. They then show that money will not be neutral in a system containing inside and outside money, outside bonds, or a variety of securities against which money can be created. The key to these results is that in these cases an increase in the quantity of money of either variety, accompanied by a proportional increase in the prices of goods and private debts, alters the relative quantities of the various assets to be held by the public; and their significance to the neutrality debate can be reduced to any arbitrarily low level by arguing that they depend on a distribution effect, and that the appropriate test of neutrality is an equiproportional change in inside money, the assets backing it, and outside assets (see Patinkin [92, p. 108]). It may also be remarked that the results depend in no way on the presence of financial intermediaries.

Gurley and Shaw's analysis follows the tradition of Metzler and Patinkin in relating nonneutrality to the existence of government debt; their inside-money analysis merely makes noninterest-bearing as well as interest-bearing government debt a disturber of neutrality. This tradition leaves modern formal monetary theory rather awkwardly dependent on adventitious institutional or historical details; and the question naturally arises whether this is the best that can be done. The source of the difficulty lies in the implicit distribution effect introduced by the recognition that, unlike other debtors, the government does not have to worry about the size of its debts. For this difference there are two reasons: (1) the government can always pay its debts by issuing fresh debts, since it controls the money supply, (2) the government can always command the resources required to pay the interest on its debts, since it possesses the taxing power. The latter is the reason relevant to the level of theoretical generality of the neutrality discussion; and at that level it provides grounds for denying that interest-bearing government debt should be treated as net assets of the public. The existence of government debt implies the levying of taxes to pay the interest on it, and in a world of reasonable certainty these taxes would be capitalized into liabilities equal in magnitude to the government debt; hence, if distribution effects between individuals are ignored, a change in the real amount of government debt will have no wealth-effect.[7] Finally, if this logic applies to interest-bearing government debt, why should it not apply to the limiting case of noninterest-bearing government debt, which is equally a debt of the public to itself, and to commodity moneys, which are the same thing though based on custom rather than law?

This line of reasoning suggests that the more elegant approach to monetary theory lies along inside-money rather than outside-money lines, and that the foundation of the theory of monetary equilibrium and stability should be the substitution effect rather than the (in this case nonexistent) wealth effect of a change in real balances. It also has implications for the dichotomy debate: in the inside-money case the economy can be validly dichotomized into a real and a money sector, since the real-balance effect reduces to a change in the relative quantities of real balances and real debt (see Franco Modigliani [58, pp. 183–84] and Patinkin [92, p. 107]). Finally, it suggests an opportunity for a reassessment of Keynes' theory of employment, which is guiltless of the charges brought against it by

Pigou and elaborated by Patinkin and others if interpreted as applying to an inside-money world.

The Demand for Money and the Velocity of Circulation

As Villard remarked in his earlier survey [124, pp. 316–24], the equation-of-exchange approach to monetary theory was eclipsed by the income-expenditure approach[8] after 1930 largely because of the prevailing tendency to treat velocity as determined in principle by institutional factors governing the rapidity of circulation of the medium of exchange and as in practice a constant— a treatment clearly contradicted by experience in the 1930's. The alternative theory expounded by Keynes emphasized the determinants of expenditure; but it also contained a monetary theory founded on the function of money as a store of value and on the special characteristics of money as a form of holding wealth. This theory has been refined and elaborated by subsequent writers in the Keynesian tradition. In the process, Keynes' most extreme departure from previous analysis of the demand for money—his emphasis on the speculative demand for money at the expense of the precautionary—has been gradually abandoned (as has his awkward separation of the transactions and speculative demand for money), and the speculative motive has been relegated to the short run and reabsorbed into the general theory of asset holding. On the other side, the treatment of velocity as determined by payments institutions, while prominent in some expositions of the quantity theory, was by no means the core of classical monetary theory, which clearly recognized the opportunity cost of holding wealth in monetary form; and modern followers of the classical tradition, building on this foundation, treat velocity explicitly as reflecting a demand for money derived from preferences concerning the disposition of wealth.

In consequence, contemporary monetary theorists, whether avowedly "Keynesian" or "quantity," approach the demand for money in essentially the same way, as an application of the general theory of choice, though the former tend to formulate their analysis in terms of the demand for money as an asset alternative to other assets, and the latter, in terms of the demand for the services of money as a good. Aside from some conceptual perplexities concerning the relation between capital and income in this context, the chief substantive issues outstanding are three: first, what specific collection of assets corresponds most closely to the theoretical concept of money—an issue that arises as soon as the distinguishing characteristic of money ceases to be its function as a medium of exchange; second, what the variables are on which the demand for money so defined depends; and third, whether the demand for money is sufficiently stable to provide, in conjunction with the quantity of money, a better explanation of observed movements of money income and other aggregates than is provided by models built around income-expenditure relationships. These are essentially empirical issues, to which empirical research has as yet produced no conclusive answers; and they clearly have an important practical bearing on monetary policy.

DEVELOPMENTS IN LIQUIDITY PREFERENCE THEORY

To begin with the recent development of Keynesian analysis of the demand for money, subsequent contributions have been concerned with four aspects of Keynes' treatment of this subject: the separation of the demand into a transactions demand dependent on income and a liquidity-preference demand dependent on the rate of interest; the emphasis on the speculative element in liquidity preference; the neglect of wealth as a determinant of liquidity preference; and the aggregation of all assets other than money into bonds implicit in the use of a single (long-term) rate of interest.

The separation of the demand for money into two parts, besides being mathematically inelegant, incorporated the mechanical treatment of transactions demand that Keynes had criticized in the quantity theory. Keynesian writers (for example, Alvin Hansen [56, pp. 66–67]) began to treat transactions demand as reflecting economic behavior and particularly as being interest-elastic, from which it was a short step to making the demand for money as a whole depend on income and the rate of interest. The logic of treating transactions demand as reflecting rational choice was subsequently provided by W. J. Baumol [9; see also page 165 in this volume] and James Tobin [118], the former's analysis being more interesting in that it links the problem to inventory theory. Both authors show that an economic unit starting a period with a transactions balance to be spent evenly over the period, and having the opportunity of investing idle funds at interest and withdrawing them as needed at a cost partly fixed per withdrawal, will disinvest at more frequent intervals (carry a lower average cash balance) the higher the rate of interest. They also show that the average cash balance held by the unit will be higher the higher the amount of the initial transactions balance, but less than proportionately higher.[9]

Keynes' emphasis on the extremely short-run speculative motive as the source of interest-elasticity in the liquidity demand for money was one of the main targets of Keynes' critics. Subsequent Keynesian writing has stressed Keynes' alternative explanation of liquidity preference, which rests this interest-elasticity on uncertainty about the future interest rate rather than on a definite expectation about its level; this explanation is really the precautionary motive in disguise (see Johnson [61, p. 8]). An elegant exposition of both explanations, using the theory of portfolio management, has been provided by Tobin [116; see also page 178 in this volume].

The introduction of the value of wealth, which itself depends on the rate of interest, as an explicit determinant of the demand for money was part of a more general process of freeing Keynes' theory from its short-period equilibrium assumptions. It implied for the theory of liquidity preference, as noticed by Lloyd Metzler [84; see also page 128 in this volume], Ralph Turvey [121] and Frank Brechling [10], that the liquidity-preference curve would be different for a change in the quantity of money brought about by fiscal policy than for a change effected by open-market operations (these two curves, and a third corresponding to constant wealth, are discussed in Turvey [122, Ch. 2]). It also introduces the difficulty, noted earlier by Borje Kragh [69], that the speculative demand curve for money traced out by open-market operations will differ according to the size of the units in which these are conducted, since the effects on wealth will differ. The wealth effects of discontinuity in open-market operations are exploited in Sidney Weintraub's recent contention [125, pp. 156–60] that the speculative demand curve is irreversible, as Richard Davis [30] has subsequently pointed out. At a far more fundamental level, the analysis of the demand for money that emerges from these developments, in which the demand for money depends on the interrelated variables income, the rate of interest, and wealth, raises important conceptual (and econometric) difficulties not always fully appreciated by monetary theorists; these difficulties will be referred to later in connection with Milton Friedman's restatement of the quantity theory.

The fourth development stemming from Keynes' theory of the demand for money has been the disaggregation of assets other than money and the elaboration of liquidity preference theory into a general theory of the relative prices of (rates of return on) assets of different types. The chief contributions in the direct line of Keynes' own thought, by Joan Robinson [99] and Richard Kahn [63], are primarily concerned with reasserting Keynes' view that the long-term rate of interest is determined by expectations about the future long-term rate, against Hicks' dismissal of it as a bootstrap theory and his attempt to explain the long-term rate as an average of expected short-term rates [60, pp. 163–64]. Robinson and Kahn both employ a division of assets into cash, bills, bonds, and equities, and a classification of asset-holders into contrasting types according to whether their asset preferences are dominated by capital-uncertainty or income-uncertainty; but Robinson is concerned to set the argument against the background of a growing economy, while Kahn concentrates on a rather subtle analysis of the interaction of the precautionary and speculative motives.

In contrast, U.S. contributions have been prompted by concern with the problems posed for monetary, fiscal, and debt-management policy by the wartime legacy of a large public debt of short average maturity; two early articles influential in subsequent thinking were those of Roland McKean [81] and Richard Musgrave [88]. The common feature of subsequent work is the treatment of assets as possessing varying degrees of liquidity, and the application of general equilibrium theory to the determination of their relative prices (yields), which are treated as the outcome of the interaction of asset preferences and the relative quantities of the different assets available. This approach (which is also central in the analysis of Robinson and Kahn just mentioned) is exemplified in W. L. Smith's study of debt management for the Joint Economic Committee [111] and Ralph Turvey's book on interest rates and asset prices [122]. The latter is notable for its explicit general equilibrium approach and its careful attention to the requirements of consistent aggregation. The formulation of monetary theory as part of a more general theory of asset holding has been carried farthest by the group working at Yale University under the inspiration of James Tobin; their "portfolio-balance" approach has been strongly influenced by Harry Markowitz's work on rational investor behavior (notably [78]). Unfortunately little of this group's work is yet available in print (see, however, Tobin [114; 116; 117; see also page 205 in this volume]).

The formulation of the general equilibrium approach to the theory of asset prices and yields in the literature just described has some implicit biases which are apt to mislead the unwary, especially in its application to the analysis of the term structure of interest rates.[10] In the first place, there is a tendency to follow too closely Hicks' original sketch of the approach [59] in identifying the typical asset-holder with a bank, borrowing for a shorter term than it lends and therefore preferring the shorter-term assets. In the second place, emphasis on the slippery and ill-defined quality of liquidity as the characteristic differentiating alternative assets tends to divert attention from the linkage of asset markets by speculation, and so to exaggerate the sensitivity of the interest-rate pattern to changes in the relative quantities of assets.[11] In this connection it is appropriate to refer briefly[12] to some recent work on the term structure of interest rates by John Culbertson [29] and Joseph Conard [24, Part III], which on its empirical side contributes to filling the gap noted by Villard [124, pp. 336–37] between the theory and the historical facts of interest-rate behavior. Both authors arrive at essentially the same major result, that short and long rates tend to move together in a rational way, though Culbertson regards his analysis as contradicting the classical "expectations" theory whereas Conard regards his as confirming a modified version of it. The explanation of this difference is ᴜᴀat Culbertson identifies accepted theory with the incorrect Hicks-Lutz formulation of it, according to which the investor is depicted as choosing between holding a bond to maturity and investing in successive short-term loans over the same period, whereas Conard identifies it with the correct formulation, in which the investor compares the expected yields (including interest and changes in capital value) of alternative assets over the period for which he expects or is obliged to remain invested. A more recent study by David Meiselman [82] advances both the theory and explanation of the rate structure (and incidentally refutes one of Culbertson's main arguments against the expectations theory) by interpreting the yield curve as expressing expected future short-term rates and explaining changes in it as the market's reaction to errors of expectation.

RESTATEMENT OF THE QUANTITY THEORY

While Keynes' formulation of the theory of demand for money has been evolving in the directions just described, a fundamentally very similar formulation has been developed by a group of scholars associated with the University of Chicago, inspired by Milton Friedman and claiming allegiance to the quantity theory as handed down in the oral tradition of that institution. The most complete statement of this group's basic theory—which tends usually to be mentioned only briefly in the course of presenting the results of empirical research—is contained in the condensed and rather cryptic restatement of the quantity theory by Friedman that introduces four of their empirical studies [41; see also page 67 in this volume], a restatement that takes the reader at a hard pace from the fundamental theory to the simplifications required for its empirical application. The central points in the restatement are that the quantity theory is a theory of the demand for money, not of output, money income, or prices; and that money is an asset or capital good, so that the demand for it is a problem in capital theory. In formulating the demand for money as a form of capital, however, Friedman differs from the Keynesian theorists in starting from the fundamentals of capital theory. He begins with the broad concept of wealth as comprising all sources of income, including human beings, and relates the demand for money to total wealth and the expected future streams of money income obtainable by holding wealth in alternative forms. Then, by a series of mathematical simplifications, approximations of nonobservable variables (of which the most important is the representation of the influence of human wealth by the ratio of nonhuman to human wealth), simplifying economic assumptions, and rearrangements of variables, he arrives at a demand function for money which depends on the price level, bond and equity yields, the rate of change of the price level, income, the ratio of nonhuman to human wealth, and a taste variable; finally, he makes neat use of the homogeneity assumption to show that the demand for real balances depends only on real variables and that it can be reformulated as a velocity function depending on the same variables.

In its final form, Friedman's demand function for money is hard to distinguish from a modern Keynesian formulation, especially in view of his remark that the nonhuman to human wealth ratio "is closely allied to what is usually defined as the ratio of wealth to income" [41, p. 8]. The apparent similarity is misleading, however, because what comes out as income originally entered as wealth, i.e. capitalized income, the process of capitalizing it being absorbed by Friedman's simplifications into the yield and wealth-ratio arguments of the function; and, as Friedman indicated by various remarks and has since demonstrated by the application of his permanent income concept to the explanation of the behavior of velocity [38; see also page 86 in this volume], the "income" relevant to this equation is not income as measured in the national accounts but income conceived of as the net return on a stock of wealth, or wealth measured by the income it yields. The use of "income" to represent what is really a wealth variable has incidentally contributed to some minor confusions of stock and flow concepts in the writings of Chicago monetary theorists, especially in the alternative formulation of the theory of demand for money as an application of demand theory developed by Richard Selden [105], where money rather than its services is described as the good demanded, the elasticity relating changes in the stock of money demanded to changes in the flow of income is described as an income-elasticity, and money is classed on the basis of the empirical magnitude of this elasticity as a luxury good.

Friedman's application to monetary theory of the basic principle of capital theory—that income is the yield on capital, and capital the present value of income—is probably the most important development in monetary theory since Keynes' *General Theory*.

Its theoretical significance lies in the conceptual integration of wealth and income as influences on behavior: Keynes ignored almost completely the influence of wealth, as was legitimate in short-period analysis; and while subsequent writers in the Keynesian tradition have reintroduced wealth they have generally followed the Cambridge practice of restricting wealth to nonhuman property, a practice which encourages uncritical treatment of wealth and income as entirely independent influences on behavior. In consequence, as mentioned earlier, much of the recent monetary literature contains formulations of the demand for money relating it to income, wealth, and the rate of interest, variables which are in fact interdependent and the use of which in this way involves inelegant redundancy and promotes errors in both theoretical reasoning and empirical applications.

The most important implication of Friedman's analysis, however, concerns not the formulation of monetary theory but the nature of the concept of "income" relevant to monetary analysis, which, as explained above, should correspond to the notion of expected yield on wealth rather than the conventions of national income accounting. This concept Friedman has elaborated under the name of "permanent income," and employed in his theory of the consumption function [35] and subsequent empirical work on the demand for money [38]. The statistical application of it has involved estimating expected income from past income, which means that empirically the theory is very similar to theories employing lagged income as a determinant of behavior.[13] This similarity exemplifies a serious problem in the empirical application and testing of economic theories—the theoretical interpretation of empirical results—which is especially acute in the interpretation of empirical findings on the demand for money because of the interrelationship of income, wealth, and interest.

THE DISTINGUISHING CHARACTERISTICS OF MONEY

While the treatment of money as an asset distinguished from other assets by its superior liquidity is common ground among contemporary theorists, the transition from the conception of money as a medium of exchange to money as a store of value has raised new problems for debate among monetary theorists. These problems result from recognition of the substitutability between money (conventionally defined as medium of exchange) and the wide range of alternative financial assets provided by government debt and the obligations of financial institutions, and between money and the access to credit provided by an elaborate credit system, in a financially advanced economy. They concern the related empirical questions of the definition of an appropriate monetary magnitude, and the specification of the variables on which the demand for the selected magnitude depends, questions that pose little difficulty when money is defined as the medium of exchange and its velocity is assumed to be determined by institutional factors. These questions lead into the fundamental question of the importance of the quantity of money in monetary theory and monetary policy, since unless the demand for money—defined to correspond to some quantity the central bank can influence—can be shown to be a stable function of a few key variables, the quantity of money must be a subordinate and not a strategic element in both the explanation and the control of economic activity. Argument and opinion about these issues have frequently been clouded by confusion between constant velocity and a stable velocity function, and between elasticity and instability of the function. In discussing them, it is convenient to describe first the main schools of thought on these issues,[14] and then the empirical research bearing on them.

At the cost of some arbitrary oversimplification, one can distinguish broadly four main schools of thought. At one extreme are those who continue to find the distinguishing characteristic of money in its function as medium of exchange, and define it as currency plus demand deposits adjusted [73; see also page 118 in this volume]. Next to them are the Chicago quantity theorists, who define the function of money more broadly as a temporary abode of purchasing power,[15] and in their empirical work define money as currency plus total commercial bank deposits adjusted, largely to obtain a consistent long statistical series [105; 38]. Both schools believe that there is a stable demand for money (velocity function), though they define money differently. A third school, at the opposite extreme, consists of those, usually specially interested in monetary policy rather than theory as such, who carry recognition of the similarity between money and other realizable assets or means of financing purchases to the point of rejecting money in favor of some much broader concept, measurable or unmeasurable. A measurable concept is exemplified by the long-established Federal Reserve Board theory that what matters is the total amount of credit outstanding, the quantity of money exercising an influence only because bank credit is a component of total credit (see for example [57, pp. 261–63 and 272–76]). An unmeasurable concept is exemplified by the Radcliffe Committee's concept of the liquidity of the economy [128, Ch. 6], the theory of which was left unexplained in its Report but has since been expounded by Richard Sayers [102]; according to this more extreme theory velocity is a meaningless number, the economy being able to economize on

money by substituting credit for it without limit [128, p. 133].
This school, in both its variants, does not so much advance a theory
as assert a position that implies a highly elastic, complex, or unstable velocity function. The serious controversy of recent years has
been aroused by a fourth school, in between those already mentioned, which has been concerned with the implications for velocity
of the presence of a substantial volume of liquid assets closely
substitutable for money. In the early years after the war, this school
was mainly concerned with the influence of short-term public debt;
since the mid-fifties, the centre of attention has shifted to the
liabilities of nonbank financial intermediaries.

The leading figures in this last development are J. G. Gurley and
E. S. Shaw, who in a series of contributions [50; 51; 53; see also
page 363 in this volume] culminating in a major theoretical work
[52] have developed an analysis of the role of finance and particularly of nonbank financial intermediaries in economic development which has important implications for monetary theory.
Gurley and Shaw start from the fact that real economic development is accompanied by a process of financial development in
which primary securities (those issued to finance expenditure) become differentiated and there emerge financial intermediaries—
of which commercial banks are only one variety—whose function
is to enable asset holders to hold primary securities indirectly in the
more attractive forms of liabilities issued by the intermediaries.
Contrary to the main stream of both classical and Keynesian monetary theory, which treats the financial structure as of secondary importance and relates the demand for money to the long-term rate
of interest or to the rate of return on real capital, Gurley and Shaw
maintain that monetary theory must take account of these details
of financial organization and development, since they affect the
demand for money. In particular, they argue that because nonbank
financial intermediaries generally offer liabilities which are closer
substitutes for money than for primary securities, and hold small
reserves of money themselves, their growth tends to reduce the
demand for money. One implication of this analysis, which comes
out more strongly in their remarks on monetary policy than in their
theory,[16] but to which they do not in fact commit themselves, is
that the "quantity of money" relevant for monetary theory and
policy should include the liabilities of nonbank financial intermediaries.

Gurley and Shaw's work has provoked a number of critical
journal articles, but those most specifically concerned with their
theoretical analysis of the influence of nonbank intermediaries on
the demand for money (by Culbertson [27] and Aschheim [3])
misunderstand both Gurley and Shaw's argument and the theory

of credit creation.[17] The important question Gurley and Shaw raise is the empirical one of whether explanation of the demand for money requires introduction of the amounts of or yields on non-bank intermediary liabilities. This requires an elaborate statistical analysis of the demand for money and other assets which they have not yet produced. In [53] they show only that the facts of financial development in the United States can be rationalized by their theory; and Gurley's independent demonstration [49] that interest rates in the postwar period can be explained on the assumption that an increase in liquid assets reduces the demand for money by half as much—that is, that a correspondingly weighted sum of money and liquid assets can be used to represent the "quantity of money" in applying monetary theory—does not prove that money alone would do less well; indeed Gurley explains in an Appendix why money alone could have been used. The results of recent empirical research on the demand for money and velocity by other economists described below tend to contradict Gurley and Shaw's contention, since the writers concerned find it possible to explain the demand for money without reference to the variety of alternative assets and do not discover the downward trend in demand for money implied by Gurley and Shaw's thesis. This is, however, only an indirect test; and the empirical research in question is itself controversial.

EMPIRICAL RESEARCH ON THE DEMAND FOR MONEY

Prior to the *General Theory*, empirical research on velocity was primarily concerned with the measurement of the institutional determinants of transactions velocity; since then, attention has shifted to econometric explanation of income velocity and its alternative formulation, the demand for money,[18] one of the prime objects being to determine the existence or otherwise of the Keynesian liquidity trap. An influential early contribution by James Tobin [115] followed Keynes' theory in estimating idle balances by subtracting from total deposits an estimate of active balances derived from the maximum recorded velocity of circulation, and found a rough hyperbolic relationship between idle balances and interest rates, implying a liquidity trap. This relationship broke down for the postwar years, one reason being its failure to include the influence of total wealth; and subsequent researchers have generally preferred to avoid its assumption of a separable and proportional transactions demand in favor of analyzing the total demand for money. Tobin's method has, however, been employed in a more sophisticated form in a recent major study by Martin Bronfenbrenner and Thomas Mayer [13], which relates the demand for idle money (total money being defined as currency plus demand deposits adjusted) to the short-term interest rate, wealth, and idle balances of the previous year. They find that the last two variables explain most of the fluctuations in idle balances, and that the demand for idle balances is interest-inelastic with no tendency for the elasticity to increase as the rate falls. They interpret this last result as evidence against the liquidity trap; the validity of this inference depends on whether the liquidity trap is identified with infinite elasticity at some positive interest rate or an unlimited increase in the quantity of money demanded as the interest rate falls.

Estimates of the total demand function for money, besides avoiding arbitrary assumptions about transactions velocity, are easier to relate to income velocity than estimates of the Tobin type, since they usually use income as one of the explanatory variables.[19] Among a number of such estimates the two most important, in terms of length of period covered, simplicity of the demand function fitted, and intrinsic theoretical interest, are those by Henry Latané [73] and Milton Friedman [38]. Latané, adopting what he called a pragmatic approach to the constant-velocity and Keynesian formulations of demand for money, found that a simple linear relationship between the ratio of money (currency plus demand deposits) to income and the reciprocal of high-grade long-term interest rates fitted the historical data closely. Friedman's contribution builds on Selden's earlier finding [105] that the secular decline in velocity could be explained by the hypothesis that the demand for money (currency plus total commercial bank deposits) increases more rapidly than income (money is a "luxury good"), a finding apparently inconsistent with the fact that income and velocity vary together over the cycle. Friedman resolves the paradox by hypothesizing that the demand for real balances is an elastic function of permanent income, and showing that the apparent inconsistency of the cyclical behavior of velocity with this hypothesis disappears when the expected income and expected prices indicated by the theory are used instead of their observed counterparts; moreover, since this empirical analysis explains velocity without introducing interest rates into the demand function for money, it seems to dispose of the liquidity trap.

These two empirical demand functions for money apparently conflict, in that Latané's depends on both income (with a unitary income-elasticity) and the long-term interest rate, whereas Friedman's depends only on income, with an income-elasticity substantially above unity. But there is no necessary conflict, since Friedman's definition of money includes time deposits, and may therefore absorb most of the substitution between demand deposits and currency and interest-bearing assets induced by interest-rate changes. The real issue is which definition of money gives the better empirical results. Latané has since shown [74] that his formulation fits the subsequent data well. He explains the difference between the income-elasticities of the two functions by the facts that over the period covered by Friedman's calculations time deposits (whose inclusion he questions on theoretical grounds) grew more rapidly than demand deposits, and the long-term interest rate declined from 6.4 to 2.9 per cent. (Latané also adduces evidence for the existence of a liquidity trap, though he prefers to explain it by the cost of bond transactions rather than by Keynes' speculative motive.) Friedman's demand function, by contrast, does not fit the subsequent data, since the secular decline in velocity has reversed itself (Latané's analysis would attribute this to the subsequent upward movement of interest rates). Friedman has since been experimenting with an extended permanent income hypothesis that allows for changes in the confidence with which expectations are held [37]. Latané's demand function, incidentally, can be used to illustrate the difficulty of interpretation mentioned earlier: if wealth is assumed to be measured by income capitalized at the long-term interest rate, the quantity of money demanded in Latané's function can be expressed alternatively as a function of interest and wealth or of wealth and income,[20] thus being consistent with a variety of theoretical formulations.

The empirical studies of demand for money just discussed have a bearing on the fundamental issue, the subject of continued controversy in the history of monetary theory: whether monetary theory is more usefully formulated in terms of the demand for and supply of money or of the influence of money on expenditure and income—the equation-of-exchange approach or the income-expenditure approach. This issue, which Keynes' promulgation of the propensity to consume as a behavior relationship more stable than the discredited velocity of circulation seemed to have settled finally in favor of the income-expenditure approach, has become less settled with the postwar failure of the simple consumption function and the increasing complexity of Keynesian models on the one hand, and the increasing sophistication of modern adherents of the velocity approach on the other.

The counterattack on Keynesian income theory first launched by Friedman [36; 41] has been carried further in an article by Friedman and Gary Becker [43], which argues that the proper test of Keynesian theory is not the stability of the consumption function but its ability to predict consumption from investment, and produces some evidence that the investment multiplier is a poorer predictor of consumption than is the trend of consumption. In reply, Lawrence Klein [67] and John Johnston [62] have argued that a proper test should be concerned with the sophisticated and not the naive version of a theory, and should test the predictive power of the complete model and not just one part of it. This preliminary skirmish probably indicates the main lines of the battle that is likely to follow publication of a major study by Friedman and David Meiselman [44], which shows by exhaustive statistical tests on U.S. data since 1897, that except for the 1930's, the quantity of money has been a better predictor of consumption than has autonomous spending.

These results pose an important theoretical problem, since they imply that a change in the quantity of money that has no wealth-effect nevertheless will have an effect on consumption even though it has no effect on interest rates. The difficulty of understanding how this can be prompted the dissatisfaction of Keynes, Wicksell, and other income-expenditure theorists with the quantity theory, and provides the hard core of contemporary resistance to it. Friedman and Meiselman's explanation of their results may therefore initiate a new and possibly fruitful debate on how money influences activity. — *Real*

The Supply of Money, Monetary Control, and Monetary Dynamics

THE SUPPLY OF MONEY

The theory of money supply is virtually a newly discovered area of monetary research. The general practice in monetary theory has been to treat the quantity of money as determined directly by the monetary authority, without reference to the links intervening between reserves provided by the central bank on the one hand, and the total of currency and bank deposits on the other. This treatment has rested on a mechanical analysis of the determination of money supply, very similar to the outmoded treatment of velocity, in which the money supply is related to the reserve base by a multiplier determined by the reserve ratio observed by the banking system, and the ratio between currency and deposits held by the public. In conformity with developments on the side of demand, the trend of recent research on money supply has been towards treating these ratios as behavior relationships reflecting asset choices rather than as exogenous variables, and elaborating the analysis to include the part played by other financial intermediaries than commercial banks, in the process evolving a less mechanical theory of central bank control. In part, recent developments in this area reflect a more general tendency to formulate the dynamics of monetary change in terms of the adjustment of actual to desired stocks rather than in terms of changes in flows.

Though Keynes followed convention in treating the quantity of money as a direct policy variable, other monetary theorists (an early example is Kragh [70]) applied the notion of liquidity preference to the reserve behavior of banks, and the same idea has been incorporated in various Keynesian models (not always consistently) by making the money supply vary with the rate of interest. Theorists concerned with the money supply have, however, tended until recently to stick to the mechanical "money multiplier" approach, extending it to allow for the different reserve requirements against time and demand deposits and the demand for money by financial intermediaries; and empirical research has followed the same line, partitioning changes in the quantity of money among changes in the currency-deposit and reserve-deposit ratios and the reserve base, and changes in the reserve base among changes in reserve bank liabilities and assets. These techniques can be extremely fruitful—notable examples are Donald Shelby's investigation of the monetary implications of the growth of financial intermediaries [108], and Brunner's empirical study of U.S. monetary policy in the middle 1930's [15]—but asset ratios are a crude technique for representing behavior relationships.

Philip Cagan's study of the demand for currency relative to the total money supply [19] has broken new ground in attempting an economic explanation of the ratio of currency to currency plus total deposits. Cagan examines a number of possible determining factors, and finds that expected real income per capita explains most of the decline in the ratio from 1875 to 1919, while changes in the net cost of holding currency instead of deposits explain most of the variation in the ratio from 1919 to 1955, though the rate of personal income tax (taken to represent the possible gain from tax evasion permitted by using currency for transactions) is required to explain the rise in the currency ratio in the Second World War.

Other researchers have concerned themselves with the response of the banking system to changes in reserves, though so far the published results have been theoretical rather than empirical. Recent work on this problem has departed from the "money-multiplier" approach in three respects: first, in basing the analysis on the behavior of the individual bank instead of the banking system; second, in applying economic theory to the explanation of the level of reserves desired by the bank and relating its behavior in expanding or contracting its assets to the difference between its actual and its desired reserves; and third, in treating the loss of reserves consequent on expansion as a stochastic process. These innovations are exemplified in two recent articles, both intended as a basis for empirical research: Brunner's schema for the supply theory of money [16], the central feature of which is a relationship between a bank's surplus reserves and its desired rate of change in its asset portfolio, formulated in terms of a "loss coefficient" measuring the (probable) loss of surplus reserves per dollar of asset expansion; and Daniel Orr and W. J. Mellon's analysis of bank credit expansion [90], which applies inventory theory to the bank's holding of reserves against cash losses (which are assumed to be random and normally distributed). Orr and Mellon show, in contrast to the results of money-multiplier analysis, that the marginal expansion ratio will be lower than the average for a monopoly bank, and lower for a banking system than for a monopoly bank; and that for a banking system the marginal expansion ratio depends on the distribution of the additional reserves among banks.

MONETARY CONTROL: A THEORETICAL ISSUE

The research just mentioned is concerned with introducing into the theory of money supply recognition of the fact that commercial banks are profit-maximizing institutions with economic behavior patterns on which the central bank must operate to control the money supply. The fact that monetary control operates in this way is the source of one group of issues in recent discussions of monetary policy, to be described in the next section; it also poses the interesting theoretical question of what powers the central bank needs to control the price level. This question has been raised and discussed by Gurley and Shaw [52, Ch. 6], who conclude their book by contrasting monetary control in a private commercial banking system with their standard case, in which the government determines the nominal quantity of money and the deposit rate on it. Unfortunately their argument is nonrigorous and inconsistent: having shown [52, pp. 261–62] that control of the nominal quantity of bank reserves and the rate of interest paid on these reserves is sufficient for control of the price level (though they argue that this control is weaker than in their standard case because bank liquidity preferences or deposit rates may change independently of central bank action), they conclude their discussion of the technical apparatus of monetary control with the statement that "of three indirect techniques—fixing nominal reserves, setting the reserve-balance rate, and setting members' own deposit rate—the Central Bank can get along with any two in regulating all nominal variables in the economic system" [52, pp. 274–75].[21] Patinkin [92, pp. 112–16] has shown that this statement is incorrect, and that the central bank needs to control nominal reserves and one of the interest rates.[22]

MONETARY DYNAMICS

As mentioned above, one of the recent innovations in the theory of money supply is the analysis of bank response to changes in reserves in terms of the adjustment of actual to desired reserves. This way of stating the problem reflects a more general tendency towards the formulation of monetary dynamics in terms of adjustment of actual to desired stocks, associated in turn with the formulation of monetary theory in terms of asset choices as described in the previous section. This tendency has developed somewhat apart from, and has been concerned with more fundamental issues than, the controversy over the interrelated issues of stock versus flow analysis and liquidity-preference versus loanable-funds theories that has broken out anew since the war. Much of the relevant literature on the latter subject has been surveyed by Shackle [106]; unfortunately, Shackle's discussion of the issues is vitiated by the erroneous belief that the presence of both a stock of old securities and a flow of new securities implies a conflict of forces—stock demand and supply, and flow demand and supply—operating on the interest rate, and that this conflict poses a dilemma for monetary theory that can only be resolved by the postulation of two rates of interest. It is therefore necessary to describe the controversy briefly, before turning to the more important development in monetary dynamics.

Modern controversy over liquidity-preference versus loanable-funds theories starts from Hicks' demonstration of the formal equivalence of the two [60, pp. 160–62]; Hicks used the fact that Walras' Law permits the elimination of one of the equations in a general equilibrium system to argue that one can omit either the excess-demand-for-money equation, leaving a loanable-funds theory of interest, or the excess-demand-for-securities equation, leaving a liquidity-preference theory of interest. The omitted equations are flow equations; William Fellner and Harold Somers [33] subsequently showed that they could be identified with the desired change in the stock of money or securities over the market period, so that flow analysis and stock analysis of monetary equilibrium were equivalent. Fellner and Somers also argued in favor of the loanable-funds theory and against the liquidity-preference theory that, as the rate of interest is the price of securities, it is more sensible to regard it as determined by the demand for and supply of securities than by the demand for and supply of money. This led to a controversy with L. R. Klein [68], who objected to Fellner and Somers' assumption that the period of analysis starts with equilibrium between actual and desired stocks as begging the question of stock versus flow theory, and declared that the real difference between the liquidity-preference and loanable-funds theories was a dynamic one, liquidity-preference theory maintaining that the rate of interest would change in response to an excess demand for or supply of money, not an excess supply of or demand for securities [68, pp. 236–41].[23]

In commenting on the controversy, Brunner [68, pp. 247–51] pointed out that Fellner and Somers' analysis, while correct, evaded the real issue that Klein was raising—that there is a difference between the dynamic adjustment processes of markets in which the object of demand is primarily a stock to be held, and of those in which the object of demand is primarily a flow to be consumed; but he sided with Fellner and Somers against Klein on the dynamic determinants of interest-rate changes. Earlier, Lerner had produced a much-quoted but untraceable objection to Hicks' original argument: that if the excess demand equation for some commodity (Lerner chose peanuts) is eliminated by Walras' Law, the resulting system includes both a loanable-funds and a money equation, one of which must be used to determine the price of the excluded commodity.

Subsequent contributors to the debate can be classed as those who maintain the identity of the two theories, and those who maintain that the liquidity-preference theory is different from (and superior to) the loanable-funds theory. To clarify the issues, it is convenient to discuss these groups in order. Among the former group, S. C. Tsiang [120], W. L. Smith [112], and Don Patinkin [93] deserve mention—Smith for his compact exposition and explicit recognition of the difference between stock and flow theories of behavior.

Tsiang objects to the Hicks-Fellner and Somers use of Walras' Law to establish the equivalence of the two theories on the Lerner grounds that this law only permits the elimination of one of the general equilibrium equations, and maintains that to establish the equivalence it is necessary to show that the individual can only demand or supply securities by supplying or demanding money. He also objects that the flow demand and supply of money in the Fellner-Somers analysis bears no relation to the stock demand and supply of Keynesian theory. To get around these difficulties (which, as Patinkin [93] shows, are of Tsiang's own creating) Tsiang chooses a period so short that the economic unit cannot plan on using its proceeds from planned sales of commodities to finance planned purchases of them; by this arbitrary device the flow and stock demands for money are equated and the only choice left to the unit is between holding cash (as an idle balance or for spending) and holding securities, so that identity of the two theories (in Tsiang's sense) necessarily follows.

Patinkin's article is àn elegant restatement of the Hicksian position. Patinkin argues that the Lerner objection merely means that it is wrong to classify interest theories by the equation omitted, and that the two theories are simply alternative formulations of one general equilibrium theory of interest. He disposes of Tsiang's objection to the Fellner-Somers analysis by showing that the excess flow-demand for money is identical with the excess stock-demand for money for the period (Patinkin slips in not making explicit that to translate a desired change in a stock over a period into a flow during the period it is necessary to divide the change by the length of the period). Finally, he disposes of Klein's statement of the difference between the two theories by showing that this difference refers to the dynamic behavior of the same market—the securities market—so that the choice of which market to eliminate is not relevant.

Patinkin goes on to argue, with the help of the apparatus of dynamic theory developed in his book, that the Klein hypothesis concerning the dynamics of the interest rate is inherently implausible, since it implies that the interest rate will fall (rise) in the face of excess supply (demand) in the securities market. This argument, appealing as it is, is restricted by its dependence on Patinkin's dynamic apparatus, which permits simultaneous disequilibrium in all markets and relates the direction of movement of individual prices to the excess demand or supply in the corresponding markets. It can be objected both that there is no reason why the movement of price in a market should be dominated by the excess demand or supply in that market (Brunner's argument against Klein recognized this point [68, p. 251]) and that a dynamic analysis of price movements in one market requires specification of how disequilibria in the remaining markets are resolved.[24] Further, in setting up a dynamic analysis—particularly a period analysis—explicitly allowing for the (temporary) resolution of disequilibrium, it is possible and sometimes convenient to define the relationships in such a way that Walras' Law does not hold. This is the procedure that has been adopted (implicitly or explicitly) by recent defenders of the liquidity-preference theory: Joan Robinson's exposition of it [99] employs a period analysis in which retailers confronted with unintended increases in inventories finance themselves by releasing cash or securities, and Hugh Rose's dynamic version of Keynes' theory [101] (which behaves according to Klein's hypothesis) uses the same model with inventories being financed by security issues. In both cases the demand and supply of goods are equated *ex post* by the accommodating behavior of retailers, but this behavior is not included in the *ex ante* description of disturbances to equilibrium. F. H. Hahn's reformulation of the liquidity-preference theory as a theory of the ratios in which cash and securities are held [55] employs a similar but more subtle device—a distinction between the investment-planning period, and a shorter "investment-financing" period during which the loanable-funds but not the liquidity-preference theory applies—to reconcile the two theories dynamically.

Elegant as it is, Patinkin's analysis is confined to the determination of equilibrium in a single period, and ignores the effects of the changes in stocks determined in that period on the equilibrium determined in the next period. Other participants in the controversy have followed him (or rather Keynes) in abstracting from the process of accumulation of real and financial wealth. The discussion has therefore stopped short of the issue raised by Klein, and elaborated on by Brunner, of the dynamics of price in a market characterized by a large stock and small demand-and-supply flows per period. Brunner [68, pp. 247–49] sketched a theory of such a market; in this theory price is determined at every moment by the demand for the existing stock, but at this price there may be a net flow demand or supply which gradually changes the existing stock and therefore the price; and full equilibrium requires a price which both equates the stock demand and supply and induces a zero net flow.[25] A very similar theory has since been elaborated by Robert Clower [22], who uses it to argue that productivity and thrift have only an indirect effect on interest (through the net flow of new securities) unless they affect the stock demand for securities directly by changing expectations. Clower and D. W. Bushaw [23] have produced a general theory of price for an economy that includes commodities appearing only as stocks, commodities appearing only as flows, and commodities appearing as both stocks and flows; in this theory the equilibrium price in the market for a stock-flow commodity must equate both the desired and actual stock and the flow demand and supply, and in the dynamic analysis the rate of change of price depends on both the excess-stock and excess-flow demands.[26]

Neither the Brunner-Clower nor the Clower-Bushaw theory really solves the stock-flow problem: the former subordinates the flow analysis entirely to the stock, the latter simply adds stock and flow analyses together. The defect common to both is the absence of a connection between the price at which a stock will be held and the current rate of change of the stock held, and correspondingly between the price at which a stock will be supplied and the current rate of change of the stock supplied; such connections would yield a simultaneous equilibrium of stock and flow evolving towards full stock equilibrium (zero net flow).[27] The addition of such connections would require treating savings and investment as processes of adding to stock, rather than as flows as they have customarily been treated in the post-Keynesian literature.[28]

This is the approach to monetary dynamics that has been emerging in the past few years, from both "Keynesian" and "quantity" theorists, as an outgrowth of the formulation of monetary theory as part of a general theory of asset holding. The essence of the new approach, elements of which are to be found in recent works of such diverse writers as Cagan [20], Tobin [117], Friedman [40, pp. 461–63] and Brunner [18; see also page 540 in this volume], is to view a monetary disturbance as altering the terms on which assets will be held (by altering either preferences among assets or the relative quantities of them available), and so inducing behavior designed to adjust the available stocks of assets to the changed amounts desired.[29] The new approach has been aptly summarized, from the point of view of monetary policy, by Brunner [18, p. 612]:

> Variations in policy variables induce a reallocation of assets (or liabilities) in the balance sheets of economic units which spills over to current output and thus affect the price level. Injections of base-money (or "high-powered" money) modify the composition of financial assets and total wealth available to banks and other economic units. Absorption of the new base money requires suitable alterations in asset yields or asset prices. The banks and the public are thus induced to reshuffle their balance sheets to adjust desired and actual balance-sheet position.
>
> The interaction between banks and public, which forms the essential core of money-supply theory, generates the peculiar leverage or multiplier effect of injections of base money on bank assets and deposits and, correspondingly, on specific asset and liability items of the public's balance sheet. The readjustment process induces a change in the relative yield (or price) structure of assets crucial for the transmission of monetary policy-action to the rate of economic activity. The relative price of base money and its close substitutes falls, and the relative price of other assets rises.
>
> The stock of real capital dominates these other assets. The increase in the price of capital relative to the price of financial assets simultaneously raises real capital's market value relative to the capital stock's replacement costs and increases the desired stock relative to the actual stock. The relative increase in the desired stock of capital induces an adjustment in the actual stock through new production. In this manner current output and prices of durable goods are affected by the readjustments in the balance sheets and the related price movements set in motion by the injection of base money. The wealth, income, and relative price effects involved in the whole transmission process also tend to raise demand for non-durable goods.

Monetary Policy

There is probably no field of economics in which the writings of economists are so strongly influenced by both current fashions in opinion and current problems of economic policy as the field of monetary policy. In the period immediately after the war, economists writing on monetary policy were generally agreed that monetary expansion was of little use in combating depression. Skepticism about the effectiveness of monetary restraint in combating inflation was less marked, though some took the extreme view that monetary restraint would either prove ineffective or precipitate a collapse. But it was generally thought that the war-time legacy of a large and widely-held public debt was a major obstacle to the application of monetary restraint, both because it was feared that abandonment of the bond-support program adopted to assist war financing would destroy public confidence in government debt, and because the transfer from the government to the private banking system that would result from an increase in the interest payable on the latter's large holdings of public debt was regarded as undesirable. Economists therefore divided into those who advocated schemes for insulating bank-held government debt from general interest-rate movements, as a means of clearing the way for monetary restraint, and those who argued for an extension of selective credit controls.

The inflation that accompanied the Korean War forced the termination of the bond-support program, and thereafter monetary policy became the chief instrument for controlling short-run fluctuations. The nonmaterialization of the disastrous consequences that some had predicted would follow the termination of the bond-support program, together with the development of the availability doctrine (which enlisted liquidity preference on the side of monetary policy and made a widely-held public debt a help rather than a hindrance) strengthened confidence in the power of monetary restraint to control inflation, though the availability doctrine also provided ammunition to advocates of selective controls by depicting monetary policy as achieving its results through irrational and discriminatory mechanisms. Subsequent experience, together with empirical and theoretical research, has fairly conclusively disposed of the availability doctrine's most appealing feature—the proposition that the central bank can produce large reductions in private spending by means of small increases in interest rates—and research has tended to refute the contention that monetary policy operates discriminatorily. Nevertheless, the availability doctrine has left its mark on the field, inasmuch as the majority of monetary economists would probably explain how monetary policy influences the economy by reference to its effects on the availability and cost of credit, with the stress on availability. Trust in the power of monetary restraint to control inflation has been further reduced by the coexistence of rising prices and higher average unemployment in the late 1950's, and the associated revival and elaboration of cost-push theories of inflation. On the other hand, experience of monetary policy in three mild business cycles has revived confidence in the efficacy of monetary expansion in combating recessions and dispelled the belief that monetary restraint in a boom will do either nothing or far too much. In fact, the wheel has come full circle, and prevailing opinion has returned to the characteristic 1920's view that monetary policy is probably more effective in checking deflation than in checking inflation.[30]

Changing fashions in prevailing opinion apart, the revival of monetary policy as a major branch of economic policy has stimulated much controversy, thought, and research on all aspects of monetary policy. In addition, the legacy of war debt and the increased size and frequency of government debt operations that it has entailed, together with the difficulties created for the Treasury by "bills only" and other Federal Reserve and governmental policies, has brought the whole subject of debt management within the purview of monetary economists as a special form of open-market operations. It is neither possible nor worthwhile to attempt to survey all the issues discussed in this voluminous literature: the Report of the Commission on Money and Credit [129] contains a consensus of informed professional opinion on most of them, the usefulness of which is much reduced by the absence of documentation of empirical statements and precise references to conflicting points of view; Friedman's *A Program for Monetary Stability* [34] discusses many of the issues within a consistent theoretical framework; and a 1960 *Review of Economics and Statistics* symposium [57] assembles the views of a variety of monetary specialists. The remainder of this part will instead concentrate on what seem to be the significant developments in three areas: the objectives of economic policy and the instrumental role of monetary policy; the means by which monetary policy influences the economy and their effectiveness; and the adequacy of the tools of monetary policy.

THE OBJECTIVES AND INSTRUMENTAL ROLE OF MONETARY POLICY

In pre-Keynesian days, monetary policy was the single established instrument of aggregate economic policy, and price stability was its established objective. The Keynesian revolution introduced an alternative instrument, fiscal policy, and a second objective, maintenance of full employment (now more commonly described as economic stability), which might conflict with the objective of price stability. Since the war, debt management has been added almost universally to the list of instruments; and since the middle 1950's many economists have added a third item—adequately rapid economic growth—to the list of objectives. In recent years the balance-of-payments problem has been forcing the admission of a fourth objective—international balance—and may eventually establish a fourth instrument—foreign economic policy.

Recognition of several objectives of economic policy introduces the possibility of a conflict of objectives requiring resolution by a compromise. This possibility and its implications have been more clearly recognized elsewhere (for example by the Radcliffe Committee [128, pp. 17–18]), than in the United States, where there has been a tendency to evade the issue by denying the possibility of conflict[31] or by insisting that conflicts be eliminated by some other means than sacrifice of the achievement of any of the objectives.[32] Where a conflict of objectives has been clearly recognized —notably in the criticisms directed at the anti-inflationary emphasis of Federal Reserve policy in 1957–60—the arguments about alternative compromises have been qualitative and nonrigorous; rigorous theoretical exploration and quantitative assessment of the costs and benefits of alternative compromises between conflicting policy objectives remain to be undertaken.

The availability of alternative policy instruments introduces the question of their absolute and comparative effectiveness; research on this range of problems has been undertaken by a number of economists, but has not progressed far towards an accepted body of knowledge. As already mentioned, monetary policy since 1951 has resumed a large part of the responsibility for short-run economic stabilization—a consequence of both the inadaptability of the budgetary process to the requirements of a flexible fiscal policy and the domination of the budget by other objectives of national policy than stabilization. Reliance on monetary policy for this purpose has raised the question of how effectively the task is likely to be performed. The argument for using monetary policy is usually expressed in terms of the "flexibility" of monetary policy, by which is often meant no more than that monetary policy can be changed quickly. But the real issues are whether the monetary authorities are likely to take appropriate action at the right time, and whether the effects of monetary action on the economy occur soon enough and reliably enough to have a significant stabilizing effect.

As to the first question, there is general agreement that the Federal Reserve has committed errors in the timing, extent, and duration of policy changes. Most economists seem inclined to trust the System to improve its performance with experience and the benefit of their criticism. Some, however, are so distrustful of discretionary authority in principle, or so skeptical of the feasibility of effective stabilization by monetary means, as to advocate that the Federal Reserve should not attempt short-run stabilization, but should confine itself (or be confined) to expanding the money supply at a steady rate appropriate to the growth of the economy (for variants of this proposal, see Friedman [34, pp. 84–99], Angell [57, pp. 247–52], and Shaw [107]). The proposal to substitute a monetary rule for the discretion of the monetary authority is not of course new—Henry Simons' classic statement of the case for it [109] appeared in the 1930's—but the definition of the rule in terms of the rate of monetary expansion rather than stability of a price index reflects both the modern concern with growth and a more sophisticated understanding of the stabilization problem.

Whether such a rule would have produced better results than the policy actually followed in the past is a difficult matter to test. Friedman [34, pp. 95–98] discusses the difficulties and describes some abortive tests that tend to favor his (4 per cent annual increase) rule. Martin Bronfenbrenner has devised a more elaborate series of tests of alternative rules, including discretionary policy; his results for annual data 1901–1958 (excluding the Second World War) [11] show that a 3 per cent annual increase rule comes closest to the "ideal pattern" defined by price stability, though his subsequent tests on quarterly data from 1947 on [12] suggest the superiority of a "lag rule" relating changes in the money supply to prior changes in the labor force, productivity, and velocity. These tests are subject to statistical and theoretical objections, but they open up an interesting new line of research. In the absence of a definitely specified standard of comparison, discussions of the appropriateness of the central bank's monetary policy tend to fall back on textual criticism of its explanation of its actions or the exercise of personal judgment about what policy should have been (see, for example, the contributions of Weintraub, Samuelson, and Fellner to [57]).

The question of the extent of the stabilizing effect that monetary action may be expected to achieve was first raised, at the formal theoretical level, by Friedman [39], who argued that policies intended to stabilize the economy might well have destabilizing effects because of the lags involved in their operation. Subsequent work and discussion of this aspect of monetary policy has concentrated on the length and variability of the lag in the effect of monetary policy, and has become enmeshed in intricate arguments about the proper way of measuring the lag. Two alternative approaches to the measurement of the lag have been employed, direct estimate and statistical inference. The outstanding example of the first is Thomas Mayer's study of the inflexibility of monetary policy [80; see also page 594 in this volume]. Mayer estimates the lag in the reaction of investment expenditure and consumer credit outstanding to monetary policy changes, sector by sector, and, taking into account lags in monetary-policy changes and the multiplier process, concludes that monetary policy operates on the economy much too slowly for its effects to be quickly reversed; from a computation of the effect that an optimally-timed monetary policy would have had on the stability of industrial production over six business cycles, he concludes that monetary policy is too inflexible to reduce the fluctuation of industrial production by more than about 5 to 10 per cent on the average [80, p. 374]. W. H. White [126; see also page 628 in this volume] has since argued that Mayer seriously overestimates the average lag, and that the correct estimate would provide almost ideal conditions for effective anti-cyclical policy; White also remarks that Mayer's results do not show the destabilizing effects indicated as possible by Friedman's analysis.

Statistical inference is the basis of Friedman's contention that monetary policy operates with a long and variable lag, a contention which figures largely in his opposition to discretionary monetary policy. Friedman's preliminary references to his results [42; see also page 86 in this volume], made it appear that this contention rested mostly on a comparison of turning points in the rate of change of the money stock with turning points in National Bureau reference cycles (that is, in the level of activity); this comparison automatically yields a lag a quarter of a cycle longer than does a comparison of turning points in the level of the money stock with reference-cycle turning points, the comparison that Friedman's critics regard as the proper one to make. In reply to criticisms by J. M. Culbertson [26], Friedman has produced a lengthy defense of his measure of the lag, together with other supporting evidence [40]. This defense indicates that the measurement of the lag raises much more subtle and fundamental theoretical and methodological issues than appear at first sight; but the majority of monetary economists competent to judge is likely to agree with Culbertson [28] in finding Friedman's arguments unpersuasive.

Statistical inference is also employed in the study of lags in fiscal and monetary policy conducted for the Commission on Money and Credit by Brown, Solow, Ando and Kareken [14]. These authors claim that Friedman's comparison of turning points in the rate of change of the money stock with turning points in the level of activity involves a methodological *non sequitur*, and find from a comparison of turning points in the rates of change of money with the rate of change of aggregate output that the money stock and aggregate output move roughly simultaneously over the cycle. Their own work attempts to estimate the lag between the indication of a need for a change in monetary policy and the effect of the resulting change in policy on output, and finds that a substantial stabilizing effect is achieved within six to nine months. They also find that fiscal policy operating on disposable income is a more powerful stabilizer, achieving as much as half of its effect within six months.

This research on the lag in effect of monetary policy has been orientated towards determining the efficacy of monetary policy as a stabilizer, on the assumption that monetary policy is decided with reference to contemporaneous economic conditions. Little if any research has been devoted to the more ambitious task of designing optimal systems of changing monetary policy in response to movements of relevant economic indicators. A. W. Phillips [96] and more recently W. J. Baumol [8] have shown that what seem like sensible procedures for changing a policy variable in response to changing conditions may well aggravate instability; Phillips has applied the theory and concepts of control systems to the analysis of the effects of alternative operating rules of stabilization policy.

THE EFFECTIVENESS OF MONETARY POLICY

To turn from the instrumental role of monetary policy to the related but broader questions of how monetary action influences the economy, and how effectively, the prevailing tendency has been to approach these questions by analyzing how monetary policy, and particularly open-market operations, affect the spending decisions of particular sectors of the economy. This formulation of the problem is a natural corollary of Keynesian theory, and the evolution of the analysis since the war has closely reflected the evolution of monetary theory, though with a perceptible lag; but the analysis has also been strongly influenced by the availability doctrine. That doctrine, the formulation of which was largely the work of Robert Roosa [100; see also page 559 in this volume], emerged in the later years of the bond-support program as a solution to the conflict between the belief that a large widely-held public debt obliged the central bank to confine interest-rate movements to narrow limits and the belief that large interest-rate changes were necessary to obtain significant effects on spending.

The doctrine comprised two central propositions. The first was that widespread holding of public debt, particularly by financial institutions and corporations, facilitates monetary control by transmitting the influence of interest-rate changes effected by open-market operations throughout the economy. The second was that small interest-rate changes could, by generating or dispelling uncertainty about future rates and by inflicting or eliminating capital losses that institutions were unwilling to realize by actual sales ("the pinning-in effect"), achieve significant effects on spending even if the demands of spenders for credit were interest-inelastic—these effects being achieved by influencing the willingness of lenders to lend or, put another way, by influencing the availability of credit to borrowers by altering the terms of credit and the degree of credit rationing. The second proposition has turned out on subsequent investigation to depend on incorrect empirical assumptions about institutional behavior, particularly with respect to "the pinning-in effect" (see Warren Smith [113]) and on a doubtful asymmetry between the reactions of lender and borrower expectations to interest-rate changes (see Dennis Robertson [98]), as well as to involve some logical inconsistencies (see John Kareken [64], and for a theoretical defense of the availability doctrine, Ira Scott [104; see page 585 in this volume]). Nevertheless, the doctrine and discussion of it have helped to popularize the concept of "availability of credit" as one of the main variables on which monetary policy operates.

"Availability" actually comprises a number of disparate elements—the liquidity of potential lenders' and spenders' assets, the terms on which lenders will extend or borrowers can obtain credit, and the degree to which credit is rationed among eligible borrowers (see Kareken [64]). Emphasis on these factors as influences on spending has provided new arguments for those who favor selective credit controls—specific arguments for controls where the terms of credit rather than the cost of credit seem the effective determinant of spending decisions, as in the case of installment credit, and a general defensive argument based on the discriminatory character of credit rationing. The most powerful attack on the discriminatory character of allegedly general methods of economic control has come from J. K. Galbraith [45], who has maintained that the use of monetary and fiscal policy has favored the monopolistic at the expense of the competitive sectors of the economy to an extent comparable to repeal of the antitrust laws. Others have maintained that monetary restraint discriminates against small business. Empirical studies by Bach and Huizenga [6] and Allen Meltzer [83] show that this is not true of bank credit; Meltzer's study finds that while small firms have greater difficulty in obtaining nonbank credit in tight periods than large firms, this discrimination tends to be offset by extension of trade credit from large firms to small.

The emphasis on the availability of credit as a determinant of expenditure has led to a critical re-examination of the business-attitude survey findings that formerly were used as evidence that business investment is insensitive to monetary policy. In addition, monetary theorists have tended to raise their estimates of the sensitivity of business investment to changes in the cost of credit. These reassessments have been based on the opinion that investors' expected profits are more finely and rationally calculated than used to be thought, rather than on any impressive new empirical evidence of such sensitivity. The most definite new empirical evidence there is confirms the long-time theoretically established sensitivity of residential construction to interest-rate changes, and even this sensitivity has been attributed in part to the influence of ceiling rates on federally-guaranteed mortgages on the willingness of institutional lenders to lend on such mortgages [129, p. 51]. The failure of empirical research to disclose such sensitivity may, as Brunner has suggested [18, p. 613; also p. 546 in this volume], be the consequence of too simple a theoretical approach, the attempt to relate a flow of expenditure on assets to the cost of credit without adequate recognition of the range of alternative assets or the complexities of stock-adjustment processes. The new approach to monetary dynamics described in the previous part suggests that a more sophisticated theory of real investment is necessary for successful empirical work; on the other hand, some of the empirical work described in the first part suggests that better results might be achieved by working with changes in the quantity of money than by attempting to determine the influence of changes in interest rates on particular categories of spending.

The discussion of the effectiveness of monetary policy just described has been concerned with monetary policy operating in a given institutional environment. Since the middle 1950's a new debate has been opened up, concerned with the fact that traditional methods of monetary control are primarily directed at commercial bank credit, and the possibility that institutional change stimulated by monetary restriction may reduce the effectiveness of traditional techniques of monetary control. The main debate has been concerned with Gurley and Shaw's contention [50, pp. 537–38] that the growth of financial intermediaries, prompted in part by the competitive handicaps imposed on commerical banks for purposes of monetary control, progressively provides close substitutes for money the presence of which weakens the grip of monetary policy on the economy; and with their suggestion that the controlling powers of the central bank should be extended beyond the commercial banks to other financial institutions.[33] The debate has ranged over a wide territory, including such matters as whether existing controls over commercial banks are really discriminatory, given that banks enjoy the privilege of creating money (Aschheim [3] and Shelby [108]) and whether imposition of credit controls on financial intermediaries would in fact improve the effectiveness of monetary policy or the competitive position of the banks (David Alhadeff [1]). From the point of view of monetary policy, the central issue is not whether financial development leads to a secular decline in the demand for money—by itself, this would increase the leverage of monetary policy (Shelby [108]) and could readily be assimilated by the monetary authorities ([129, pp. 80–81] and Axilrod [5])—but whether the liabilities of financial intermediaries are such close substitutes for money that monetary restriction is substantially offset through substitution for bank deposits of other financial claims backed by only a small fractional reserve of money —in short, whether financial intermediaries substantially increase the interest-elasticity of demand for money. This is an empirical question; and the empirical evidence so far is that shifts by the public from money into thrift assets in periods of monetary re- straint have not had a significant influence on velocity ([129, pp. 78–80]; see also Smith [111]).

THE ADEQUACY OF THE TOOLS OF MONETARY POLICY

The revival of monetary policy as an instrument of short-run stabilization has provoked a great deal of discussion not only of the use and effectiveness of monetary policy, but also of the use and efficiency of the Federal Reserve's traditional instruments of mone- tary control—open-market operations, rediscount rates, and re- serve requirements. Controversy about open-market operations has centered on the "bills only" policy—the policy of conducting open- market operations in Treasury bills only, adopted by the Federal Reserve in 1953, modified later to "bills usually," and abandoned in 1961. Both the availability doctrine and the assets approach to the theory of interest rates imply that the central bank can obtain differential effects on credit conditions according to the maturity of government debt in which it chooses to conduct open-market operations, and can alter the structure of interest rates by switching between short and long maturities. The bills-only policy therefore appeared to most academic economists as an undesirable re- nunciation by the central bank of an important technique of monetary control, and the reason given for it—the desire to improve the "depth, breadth and resiliency" of the government bond market by eliminating arbitrary central bank intervention in it— as a shallow excuse masking the unwillingness of the Federal Reserve to risk unpopularity with the financial community by overtly subjecting it to capital losses. The surrender of power en- tailed in bills-only was probably greatly exaggerated by many of its opponents: Winfield Riefler [97] has pointed out that the central bank's choice of securities only contributes about one-eighth of the total effect of its open-market operations, the remaining seven-eighths being determined by the asset choices of the banks whose reserves are altered by the operations; and has produced some evidence that substantial changes in the maturity composition of the public debt have had little effect on the rate structure. On the other side of the argument, Dudley Luckett [76] has shown that the empirical evidence fails to indicate any improvement in "depth, breadth and resiliency" since bills-only was adopted.

While much of the discussion of bills-only has been concerned exclusively with Federal Reserve policy, the fundamental issue involved was the division of responsibility for the maturity composition of government debt held by the public between the Federal Reserve and the Treasury. Bills-only assigned this responsibility, and the associated responsibility for smoothing the impact of debt-management operations on the market, to the Treasury. One school of thought, represented for example by A. G. Hart [57, pp. 257–58], has maintained strongly that this is an inappropriate division of responsibility, since the Federal Reserve has both the powers and the continual contact with the market required for the purpose and the Treasury has not. (The limited ability of the Treasury to conduct open-market operations has been demonstrated by Deane Carson's study [21] of debt management after the adoption of bills-only.) Others have seen the source of the trouble in the Treasury's debt-management practices, particularly the practice of issuing debt in large blocks at irregular intervals, at fixed prices and with maturities "tailored" to market requirements. Carson [21] and Friedman [34, Ch. 3] have proposed similar schemes for replacing present practice by a system of auctioning long-term government debt issues; Culbertson [25] and Friedman [34, Ch. 3] have propounded plans for regularizing the timing and composition of debt issues to reduce the market disturbance of government financing. The difficulties the Treasury has experienced with debt management in the postwar period, in consequence not only of bills-only but of other developments adverse to easy Treasury financing,[34] have led many economists to become skeptical of the practicability of a countercyclical debt-management program. Such a program, which would involve issuing long-term debt in booms and short-term debt in depressions, would in any case have a countercyclical influence only insofar as the interest-rate structure is sensitive to change in the composition of the debt, and this sensitivity seems to be too small to yield important stabilizing effects (see Riefler [97] and Meiselman [82]).

Though the growth of the public debt has definitely established open-market operations as the chief instrument of day-to-day monetary control, the revival of monetary policy has been accompanied by a revival of rediscounting and the use of rediscount rates as a control instrument. Controversey over rediscount policy has mainly been concerned with whether rediscount policy is a useful auxiliary instrument of control, or whether the possibility of rediscounting creates an unnecessary and troublesome loophole in the control over member banks afforded by reserve requirements and open-market operations. It can be argued (see Friedman [34, pp. 35–35]) that rediscount rates are a treacherous control instrument, since their restrictiveness depends on their relationship with shifting market rates of interest, and that the growth of bank holdings of public debt and the postwar development of the federal funds market make it unnecessary for the Federal Reserve to continue to perform the function of lender of last resort for its members.[35] There has also been some argument about whether control of the rediscounting privilege gives the Federal Reserve undesirable arbitrary authority over member banks.

Apart from the debate concerning the desirability of rediscounting, a number of writers have criticized the asymmetry of the present reserve-requirement and rediscount-rate system, under which member banks receive no interest on reserves or excess reserves but pay a penalty rate on reserves borrowed to meet deficiencies, and have proposed payment of interest on reserves or excess reserves. Tobin, for example [57, pp. 276–79], has recommended payment of interest at the discount rate on excess reserves, and coupled this with the recommendation to terminate the prohibition of demand-deposit interest and the ceilings on time- and savings-deposit interest, arguing that the justification for intervention in the fixing of deposit rates—to protect depositors by preventing excess competition among banks—has been removed by federal deposit insurance.[36]

The power to change reserve requirements gives the central bank a method of changing the quantity of bank deposits alternative to open-market operations. The chief differences between the two methods[37] are, first, that reserve-requirement changes, being discontinuous, are apt to have disturbing effects on securities markets requiring auxiliary open-market operations; and second, that credit expansion by open-market purchases is less costly for the government and less profitable for the banks than credit expansion by reduction of reserve requirements (and vice versa). The discontinuity and disturbing effects of reserve-requirement changes, dramatically exemplified by their misuse in 1936–37 (see Brunner [15]), have led most economists to believe that they should be used sparingly if at all, especially in restraining credit expansion. The differential effects of the two methods of control on governmental interest costs and bank profits have been the focus of controversy over the policy of lowering reserve requirements followed by the Federal Reserve since 1951. In the course of time the balance of the argument has tilted in favor of reduction of reserve requirements, as the postwar sentiment against high bank profits derived from interest on the public debt has given way to the more recent fear that banks are unduly handicapped by reserve requirements and interest ceilings on deposits in competing with other financial intermediaries.

The controversy has raised the more general issue of how the secular growth of the money supply should be provided for. George Tolley, who first raised this issue [119; see also page 382 in this volume], has shown that the choice between open-market operations and reserve-requirement variation involves some intricate theoretical issues, since in addition to its implications for debt management and the ease of government financing this choice influences the efficiency of allocation of resources to the provision of the supply of deposit money.

Some attention has also been given to the efficiency of the present system of reserve requirements as an instrument of monetary control. Frank Norton and Neil Jacoby [89] have revived the 1930's Federal Reserve proposal to relate required reserve ratios to deposit turnover rates as a means of introducing an automatic offset to changes in the velocity of circulation. The preponderance of professional opinion, however, seems opposed to any system of reserve requirements that discriminates between banks or affects their profits differentially, and in favor of the removal of inequities among banks by the standardization of reserve requirements.

Concluding Remarks

The main impression that emerges from this survey of monetary theory and policy is not only that the field has been extremely active, especially in the past few years, but that it has been on the move towards interesting and important new developments. To summarize what is already a summary is a difficult task, and prediction of the direction of future scientific progress is a risky business; but in the literature surveyed in the preceding sections, two broad trends are evident. One is the trend towards the formulation of monetary theory as a part of capital theory, described on pages 13–25 (and implicitly on pages 7–13). As mentioned on pages 25–44, this trend has only just begun to manifest itself in the formulation of monetary dynamics. More important, almost nothing has yet been done to break monetary theory loose from the mould of short-run equilibrium analysis, conducted in abstraction from the process of growth and accumulation; and to integrate it with the rapidly developing theoretical literature on economic growth (important exceptions are the models of Tobin [114; also page 205 in this volume] and Enthoven [52, App.]). The other trend is that towards econometric testing and measurement of monetary relationships. As is evident on pages 33–44, econometric methods have barely begun to be applied to the study of relationships relevant to the management of monetary policy.

NOTES

1. For a list of Congressional documents bearing on monetary policy, see Friedman [34, pp. 103–40]; to Friedman's list should be added the *Staff Report on Employment, Growth and Price Levels* [130] and the accompanying *Staff Studies*.

2. For example, inferiority of real balances implies that if an individual's initial stock of real balances is reduced, his initial commodity endowment being unchanged, he will reduce his planned consumption in the current week sufficiently to increase his planned real balances. By shortening the week and reducing the individual's weekly endowment of commodities proportionately, a procedure which leaves the rate of flow of the individual's income unchanged, it can be made impossible for the individual to cut his commodity consumption sufficiently to increase his planned balances. "Inferiority" of real balances is therefore not invariant with respect to the time unit of the analysis. Further, inferiority of real balances would imply that any disturbance to an individual's initial equilibrium would be followed by a "cobweb" adjustment of his real balances and consumption in succeeding weeks, a pattern difficult to rationalize. I am indebted to the oral tradition of the University of Chicago Money and Banking Workshop for these points.

3. Goods are produced as well as exchanged; net saving and investment occur but their effects on wealth and productive capacity are abstracted from; for analysis the economy is aggregated into four markets, those for labor services, commodities, bonds, and money. Patinkin uses the dynamic development of this model to investigate Keynes' theory of involuntary unemployment, a subject not considered here; his analytical methods have been adopted by several subsequent writers.

4. Absence of money illusion means that behavior depends on the real and not the money values of income, balances, and bonds; absence of distribution effects, that behavior is unaffected by redistributions of total real income, balances, and bonds among individuals, such as result from price-level changes; homogeneity of bonds, that behavior is affected only by the net creditor position of the private sector, not by the totals and composition of its assets and liabilities; absence of government debt or open-market operations, that the net creditor position of the private sector consists in its holding of fiat money, or that, if government debt

fixed in real terms is introduced (the Metzler case discussed below), its quantity does not alter when the quantity of money changes. The assumption of absence of distribution effects might seem unnecessary, on the Archibald-Lipsey argument, but that argument does not apply to this model, which by construction cannot be in full stationary equilibrium: see Ball and Bodkin's criticism of Archibald and Lipsey, which the latter accept [7, pp. 44–49].

5. The Pigou effect in modern usage is the effect on the demand for goods of a change in private real wealth resulting from the effect of a change in the price level on the real value of net private financial assets, the latter consisting of net government debt outstanding (including fiat money) and the part of the money supply backed by gold; it is the real balance effect corrected for the presence of government debt and money issued against private debt.

6. Their insistence on the determinacy of the price level, in contrast to what they take to be the implication of Patinkin's approach (which they term "net money doctrine") [52, p. 76], rests on an understandable misunderstanding. Patinkin's analysis of price-level stability throws the emphasis on the wealth effect of a change in real balances resulting from a price-level change, an effect which only exists when money is a net asset; but it also provides for a substitution effect. Gurley and Shaw's demonstration that the substitution effect is sufficient to determine the price level therefore does not conflict with Patinkin's analysis (for Patinkin's views, see [92, pp. 100–9]), though it does show that Patinkin's emphasis on the wealth effect is misplaced and misleading. The broader implications of this point are discussed below.

7. In an elegant recent article [87] R. A. Mundell has extended Metzler's analysis by considering explicitly the tax remissions resulting from open-market purchases of government debt. He assumes that corporate taxes are capitalized in the price of equities but that personal income taxes are not capitalized (there being no market for human capital); he allows for the effect of corporate taxation on the incentive to invest; and he demonstrates that Metzler's conclusion is valid if income taxes are remitted, but reversed if corporate taxes are remitted. The non-marketability of human capital seems an inadequate reason for assuming that people do not feel richer when income taxes are reduced; consideration of the incentive effects of tax changes introduces an interesting new aspect of the neutrality problem but one that lies at a somewhat lower level of abstraction.

8. These terms are intended to distinguish the two main (and historically long-established) schools of thought in monetary theory, one of which formulates its analysis in terms of the quantity of money and its velocity of circulation and the other in terms of the determinants of money expenditure, without ensnaring the exposition in the rights and wrongs of Keynes' protracted quarrel with what he understood by "the quantity theory." As this section explains, neither the quantity theory nor the Keynesian theory is now what it was in the 1930's; in particular, the modern quantity theorist is committed to neither full employment nor the constancy of velocity, and his theory is a theory of the relation

between the stock of money and the level of money income, that is, a theory of velocity and not of prices and employment.

9. Ralph Turvey [122, p. 33], following Richard Selden [105, pp. 209–10], argues that the interest-elasticity conclusion does not extend to aggregate behavior because a change in the interest rate will have the opposite effect on the demand for cash of a unit facing a maturing debt and having the alternatives of holding cash in the interim or spending it and borrowing later. This argument involves an elementary confusion between saving behavior and asset management: savings effects of interest-rate changes aside, the unit in question would have the same alternative of investing its idle cash at interest, and react the same way. Turvey also argues [122, pp. 28–30] that an increase in the level of a unit's transactions will raise transactions demand only in a probability sense, since there may be an offsetting change in the timing-structures of the unit's payments and receipts.

10. This phrase has reference to the pattern of rates on loans of successively longer maturity; statistically it is represented by the "yield curve," which charts the yields on government debts against their maturities. In the English literature the problem appears as that of the relation between the long and the short rate of interest (the bill rate and the bond rate), a reflection of the institutional fact that the British government obtains its short-term financing predominantly by three-months bills of exchange, and has a substantial volume of perpetual debt ("consols") outstanding.

11. The sensitivity of the rate pattern to changes in the relative quantities of short-term and long-term debt is the crucial empirical issue in some recent controversies about monetary policy, especially the "bills only" policy.

12. Shackle's survey of interest theory [106], to which the reader has been referred in the introduction, unfortunately makes very little reference to rate-structure theory, presumably because it has not been discussed recently in English journals. The interested reader is referred to Conard's useful book [24].

13. These brief remarks do justice neither to Friedman nor to other consumption theorists, a number of whom have been working towards similar theories (see Johnson [61]).

14. To keep the bibliography within reasonable bounds, the references below are confined as far as possible to authors who have supported their theories with empirical research, or to recent writings.

15. The phrase is Milton Friedman's.

16. Gurley and Shaw believe that present methods of credit control discriminate against banks in their competition with nonbank intermediaries, weakening the effectiveness of monetary policy over the long run, and unlike most of their critics are prepared to contemplate extension of the central bank's regulatory powers.

17. Patinkin's review [92] of the book translates Gurley and Shaw's argument into his own language and interprets the effect of financial intermediation as an increase in the liquidity of bonds which decreases the demand for money and increases its interest-elasticity. Alvin Marty's

review [79] makes the interesting theoretical point that the introduction of a substitute does not necessarily increase the elasticity of demand. Neither reviewer notices that Gurley and Shaw infer increased elasticity only in the special case of an unfunding of government debt, and present a satisfactory reason for it [52, pp. 162–66].

18. For discussion of the earlier literature, see Villard [124] and Selden [105]; a useful survey of the econometric studies preceding their own work is given by Bronfenbrenner and Mayer [13]. The more traditional type of research on transactions velocity has been continued by a number of contemporary economists, notably George Garvey [46].

19. An interesting exception is Harold Lydall's derivation of the demand for money from the hypothesis of a constant ratio of liquidity to wealth [77].

20. In [74] Latané uses a linear relationship between income velocity and the rate of interest, $V = .77r + .38$, where $V = Y/M$, the quantity of money divided into income. This yields the demand function for money, $M = Y/(.77r + .38)$. Using the definition $W = Y/r$, this can be written equivalently as

$$M = \frac{W}{.77 + .38/r} \quad \text{or} \quad M = \frac{W}{.77 + .38W/Y}.$$

21. Gurley and Shaw also state as a prerequisite of monetary control that the authorities take steps to ensure the moneyness of bank deposits; the necessity for this is debatable.

22. Patinkin goes on to argue that price-level determinacy requires fixity of one nominal quantity and one yield, and would be secured by fixity of the nominal quantity of (noninterest-bearing) outside money; and that therefore Gurley and Shaw should have considered the means by which the central bank changes the price level, instead of the powers required to determine it. This argument raises the question discussed earlier, of the usefulness of founding monetary theory on the real-balance effect.

23. An excess demand for money does not necessarily imply an excess supply of securities, since it may be accompanied by an excess supply of goods.

24. Patinkin recognized these difficulties in the discussion of dynamic stability in his book [94, pp. 157–58], and admitted that they made stability a matter of assumption rather than of proof; but he overlooked them in applying his dynamic apparatus to the liquidity-preference loanable-funds controversy.

25. In describing a mathematical model of this theory, Brunner admits two possible situations of partial equilibrium—stock equilibrium and flow disequilibrium and the converse—but nevertheless asserts that the stock relation determines momentary price in both. This inconsistency, which was presumably prompted by his intention to contrast the adjustment processes of markets dominated respectively by stocks and flows, is the source of the dilemma Shackle finds between stock and flow equilibrium as the determinant of price [106, p. 222 (pp. 433–34)].

26. Cliff Lloyd [75] has argued that the presence of two equilibrium equations for a stock-flow commodity may invalidate the Hicksian proof of the equivalence of the loanable-funds and liquidity-preference theories. It may be noted that the Clower-Bushaw theory provides a formal solution to the apparent dilemma created by Brunner's alternative partial equilibria.

27. In one passage [106, p. 223 (pp. 434–35)] Shackle outlines a solution to his dilemma along these lines, but does not pursue it further. The Brunner-Clower theory can (with some difficulty) be interpreted as a special case of the general theory, one in which the price at which a stock is held is independent of the current rate of change in the stock.

28. This observation refers to the literature on the Keynesian general equilibrium system, and not to the specialist work on consumption and investment, where the treatment of saving and investment as processes of adding to stock has become well established since the war.

29. While this approach can be described as new in relation to the time period included in this survey, it can from another point of view be regarded as a development of certain strands in Keynes' thought [65, Vol. 1, pp. 200–9] [66, Ch. 11].

30. This account refers, of course, to developments in the United States (compare Paul Samuelson [57, pp. 263–69]). A parallel evolution of opinion has occurred in other countries, though in Britain prevailing opinion, as reflected notably in the Radcliffe Report [128, Ch. 6], has remained skeptical of the efficacy and usefulness of monetary policy; this difference in prevailing opinion is partly responsible for the generally critical reception of the Report by U.S. commentators. Limitations of space make it necessary to confine this section to developments in the United States.

31. This can always be done by giving priority to one objective and defining the others in terms that implicitly impose consistency with the favored objective; an example is the concept of "sustainable economic growth" promulgated by the Federal Reserve System.

32. One example of this type of evasion is the affirmation that balance-of-payments difficulties should not be allowed to hinder the achievement of domestic policy, an affirmation rarely accompanied by specification of any obviously efficacious solution to these difficulties. Another is the expression of trust that policies designed to increase the competitiveness and efficiency of the economy will eliminate the possibility of conflict between high employment, price stability, and adequate growth. Both are contained in the Report of the Commission on Money and Credit [129, pp. 45, 227].

33. A related but different argument has been advanced by Hyman Minsky [86], to the effect that monetary restriction stimulates financial innovations that progressively reduce the demand for money, increase the velocity of circulation, and threaten to make the money market unstable; Minsky recommends extension of the lender-of-last-resort function to the whole market and not merely the commercial banks. Arguments similar to those of Gurley and Shaw and Minsky may be found in Smith [113].

34. For a comprehensive survey of these developments see Erwin Miller [85].

35. The controversy has aroused some interest in the Canadian innovation of setting the discount rate at a fixed margin above the weekly average tender rate on Treasury bills. In England, where the rediscount rate is the chief instrument of monetary policy, recognition of the loophole in monetary control afforded by rediscounting has led to the promulgation of the theory that the liquidity ratio of the commercial banks and the supply of bills, rather than the cash ratio and the quantity of central bank deposits, determine the amount of commercial bank deposits.

36. The fact that this justification was fallacious to begin with has not prevented the Commission on Money and Credit from endorsing the continuation of control of these rates [129, pp. 167–68].

37. For a fuller analysis, see Aschheim [4, Ch. 2].

REFERENCES

1. Alhadeff, D. A., "Credit Controls and Financial Intermediaries," *American Economic Review*, 50: 655–71 (September 1960).

2. Archibald, G. C., and R. G. Lipsey, "Monetary and Value Theory: A Critique of Lange and Patinkin," *Review of Economic Studies*, 26: 1–22 (October 1958) [reprinted in this volume—Ed.].

3. Aschheim, J., "Commercial Banks and Financial Intermediaries: Fallacies and Policy Implications," *Journal of Political Economy*, 67: 59–71 (February 1959).

4. ———, *Techniques of Monetary Control* (Baltimore, 1961).

5. Axilrod, S. H., "Liquidity and Public Policy," *Federal Reserve Bulletin*, 47: 1161–77 (October 1961).

6. Bach, G. L., and C. J. Huizenga, "The Differential Effects of Tight Money," *American Economic Review*, 51: 52–80 (March 1961).

7. Baumol, W. J., R. W. Clower and M. L. Burstein, F. H. Hahn, R. J. Ball and R. Bodkin, G. C. Archibald and R. G. Lipsey, "A Symposium on Monetary Policy," *Review of Economic Studies*, 28: 29–56 (October 1960).

8. Baumol, W. J., "Pitfalls in Contracyclical Policies: Some Tools and Results," *Review of Economics and Statistics*, 43: 21–26 (February 1961).

9. ———, "The Transactions Demand for Cash: An Inventory Theoretic Approach," *Quarterly Journal of Economics*, 66: 545–56 (November 1952) [reprinted in this volume—Ed.].

10. Brechling, F. P. R., "A Note on Bond-Holding and the Liquidity Preference Theory of Interest," *Review of Economic Studies*, 24: 190–97 (June 1957).

11. Bronfenbrenner, M., "Statistical Tests of Rival Monetary Rules," *Journal of Political Economy*, 69: 1–14 (February 1961).

12. ———, "Statistical Tests of Rival Monetary Rules: Quarterly Data Supplement," *Journal of Political Economy*, 69: 621–25 (December 1961).

13. ———, and T. Mayer, "Liquidity Functions in the American Economy," *Econometrica*, 28: 810–34 (October 1960).

14. Brown, E. C., R. M. Solow, A. Ando and J. H. Kareken, *Lags in Fiscal and Monetary Policy*, Commission on Money and Credit (Englewood Cliffs, N.J., 1963).

15. Brunner, K., "A Case Study of U.S. Monetary Policy: Reserve Requirements and Inflationary Gold Flows in the Middle 30's," *Schweizerische Zeitschrift für Volkswirtschaft und Statistik*, 94: 160–201 (1958).

16. ———, "A Schema for the Supply Theory of Money," *International Economic Review Papers*, 2: 79–109 (January 1961).

17. ———, "Inconsistency and Indeterminacy in Classical Economics," *Econometrica*, 19: 152–73 (April 1951).

18. ———, "The Report of the Commission on Money and Credit," *Journal of Political Economy*, 69: 605–20 (December 1961) [reprinted in this volume—Ed.].

19. Cagan, P., "The Demand for Currency Relative to the Total Money Supply," *Journal of Political Economy*, 66: 303–28 (August 1958).

20. ———, "Why Do We Use Money in Open Market Operations?" *Journal of Political Economy*, 66: 34–46 (February 1958).

21. Carson, D., "Treasury Open Market Operations," *Review of Economics and Statistics*, 41: 438–42 (November 1959).

22. Clower, R. W., "Productivity, Thrift and the Rate of Interest," *Economic Journal*, 64: 107–15 (March 1954).

23. ———, and D. W. Bushaw, "Price Determination in a Stock-Flow Economy," *Econometrica*, 22: 328–43 (July 1954).

24. Conard, J. W., *Introduction to the Theory of Interest* (Berkeley, 1959).

25. Culbertson, J. M., "A Positive Debt Management Program," *Review of Economics and Statistics*, 41: 89–98 (May 1959).

26. ———, "Friedman on the Lag in Effect of Monetary Policy," *Journal of Political Economy*, 68: 617–21 (December 1960).

27. ———, "Intermediaries and Monetary Theory: A Criticism of the Gurley-Shaw Theory," *American Economic Review*, 48: 119–31 (March 1958).

28. ———, "The Lag in Effect of Monetary Policy: Reply," *Journal of Political Economy*, 69: 467–77 (October 1961).

29. ———, "The Term Structure of Interest Rates," *Quarterly Journal of Economics*, 71: 485–517 (November 1957).

30. Davis, R. M., "A Re-examination of the Speculative Demand for Money," *Quarterly Journal of Economics*, 73: 326–32 (May 1959).

31. Encarnación, J., "Consistency between Say's Identity and the Cambridge Equation," *Economic Journal*, 68: 827–30 (December 1958).

32. Fellner, W., and D. Dillard, "Keynesian Economics after Twenty Years," *American Economic Review Proceedings*, 47: 67–87 (May 1957).

33. ———, and H. M. Somers, "Note on 'Stocks' and 'Flows' in Monetary Interest Theory," *Review of Economics and Statistics*, 31: 145–46 (May 1949) [reprinted in this volume—Ed.].

34. Friedman, M., *A Program for Monetary Stability* (New York, 1960).

35. ———, *A Theory of the Consumption Function* (Princeton, 1957).

36. ———, "Price, Income and Monetary Changes in Three Wartime Periods," *American Economic Review Proceedings*, 42: 612–25 (May 1952).

37. ———, "The Demand for Money," *American Philosophical Society Proceedings*, 105: 259–64 (June 1961).

38. ——, "The Demand for Money: Some Theoretical and Empirical Results," *Journal of Political Economy*, 67: 327–51 (August 1959) [reprinted in this volume—Ed.].

39. ——, "The Effects of a Full-Employment Policy on Economic Stability: A Formal Analysis," in *Essays in Positive Economics* (Chicago, 1953), pp. 117–32.

40. ——, "The Lag in Effect of Monetary Policy," *Journal of Political Economy*, 69: 447–66 (October 1961).

41. ——, "The Quantity Theory of Money—A Restatement," in M. Friedman (ed.), *Studies in the Quantity Theory of Money* (Chicago, 1956), pp. 3–21 [reprinted in this volume—Ed.].

42. ——, and A. J. Schwartz, *The Stock of Money in the United States 1867–1960, The Secular and Cyclical Behavior of the Stock of Money in the United States, 1867–1960.* National Bureau of Economic Research and *A Monetary History of the United States, 1870–1960* (Princeton, 1963).

43. ——, and G. S. Becker, "A Statistical Illusion in Judging Keynesian Models," *Journal of Political Economy*, 65: 64–75 (February 1957).

44. ——, and D. Meiselman, *The Relative Stability of Monetary Velocity and the Investment Multiplier in the United States, 1897–1958.* Commission on Money and Credit. *Stabilization Policies* (Englewood Cliffs, N.J., 1963), pp. 165–268.

45. Galbraith, J. K., "Market Structure and Stabilization Policy," *Review of Economics and Statistics*, 39: 124–33 (May 1957).

46. Garvey, G., *Deposit Velocity and its Significance* (New York, 1959).

47. Goldsmith, R. W., *A Study of Saving in the United States* (Princeton, 1955).

48. ——, *Financial Intermediaries in the American Economy Since 1900* (Princeton, 1958).

49. Gurley, J. G., *Liquidity and Financial Institutions in the Postwar Economy*, Study Paper 14, Joint Economic Committee, 86th Congress, 2nd Session (Washington, 1960).

50. ——, and E. S. Shaw, "Financial Aspects of Economic Development," *American Economic Review*, 45: 515–38 (September 1955).

51. —— and ——, "Financial Intermediaries and the Saving-Investment Process," *Journal of Finance*, 11: 257–76 (May 1956) [reprinted in this volume—Ed.].

52. —— and ——, *Money in a Theory of Finance*. With a mathematical appendix by A. C. Enthoven (Washington, 1960).

53. —— and ——, "The Growth of Debt and Money in the United States, 1800–1950: A Suggested Interpretation," *Review of Economics and Statistics*, 39: 250–62 (August 1957).

54. Haberler, G., "The Pigou Effect Once Again," *Journal of Political Economy*, 60: 240–46 (June 1952).

55. Hahn, F. H., "The Rate of Interest and General Equilibrium Analysis," *Economic Journal*, 65: 52–66 (March 1955).

56. Hansen, A. H., *Monetary Theory and Fiscal Policy* (New York, 1949).

57. Harris, S. E., J. W. Angell, W. Fellner, A. H. Hansen, A. G. Hart, H. Neisser, R. V. Roosa, P. A. Samuelson, W. L. Smith, W. Thomas,

J. Tobin, and S. Weintraub, "Controversial Issues in Recent Monetary Policy: A Symposium," *Review of Economics and Statistics*, 42: 245–82 (August 1960).

58. Hazlitt, H. (ed.), *The Critics of Keynesian Economics* (Princeton, 1960).

59. Hicks, J. R., "A Suggestion for Simplifying the Theory of Money," *Economica*, 2: 1–19 (February 1935). Reprinted in F. A. Lutz and L. W. Mints (eds.), *Readings in Monetary Theory* (Homewood, Ill., 1951), pp. 13–32.

60. ———, *Value and Capital* (Oxford, 1939).

61. Johnson, H. G., "The General Theory after Twenty-five Years," *American Economic Review Proceedings*, 51: 1–17 (May 1961). Reprinted in H. G. Johnson, *Money, Trade and Economic Growth* (London, 1962).

62. Johnston, J., "A Statistical Illusion in Judging Keynesian Models: Comment," *Review of Economics and Statistics*, 40: 296–98 (August 1958).

63. Kahn, R. F., "Some Notes on Liquidity Preference," *Manchester School of Economics and Social Studies*, 22: 229–57 (September 1954).

64. Kareken, J. H., "Lenders' Preferences, Credit Rationing, and the Effectiveness of Monetary Policy," *Review of Economics and Statistics*, 39: 292–302 (August 1957).

65. Keynes, J. M., *A Treatise on Money* (London and New York, 1930).

66. ———, *The General Theory of Employment, Interest and Money* (London and New York, 1936).

67. Klein, L. R., "The Friedman-Becker Illusion," *Journal of Political Economy*, 66: 539–45 (December 1958).

68. ———, W. Fellner, H. M. Somers, and K. Brunner, "Stock and Flow Analysis in Economics," *Econometrica*, 18: 236–52 (July 1950).

69. Kragh, B., "The Meaning and Use of Liquidity Curves in Keynesian Interest Theory," *International Economic Papers*, 5: 155–69 (1955).

70. ———, "Two Liquidity Functions and the Rate of Interest: A Simple Dynamic Model," *Review of Economic Studies*, 17: 98–106 (February 1950).

71. Kuenne, R. E., "Keynes's Identity, Ricardian Virtue, and the Partial Dichotomy," *Canadian Journal of Economics and Political Science*, 27: 323–36 (August 1961).

72. Lange, O., "Say's Law: A Restatement and Criticism," in O. Lange, F. McIntyre, and T. O. Yntema (eds.), *Studies in Mathematical Economics and Econometrics* (Chicago, 1942), pp. 49–68.

73. Latané, H. A., "Cash Balances and the Interest Rate—A Pragmatic Approach," *Review of Economics and Statistics*, 36: 456–60 (November 1954) [reprinted in this volume—Ed.].

74. ———, "Income Velocity and Interest Rates: A Pragmatic Approach," *Review of Economics and Statistics*, 42: 445–49 (November 1960).

75. Lloyd, C. L., "The Equivalence of the Liquidity Preference and Loanable Funds Theories and the *New* Stock-Flow Analysis," *Review of Economic Studies*, 27: 206–9 (June 1960).

76. Luckett, D. G., " 'Bills Only': A Critical Appraisal," *Review of Economics and Statistics*, 42: 301–6 (August 1960).

77. Lydall, H. F., "Income, Assets and the Demand for Money," *Review of Economics and Statistics*, 40: 1–14 (February 1958).

78. Markowitz, H. M., *Portfolio Selection: Efficient Diversification of Investments* (New York, 1959).

79. Marty, A. L., "Gurley and Shaw on Money in a Theory of Finance," *Journal of Political Economy*, 69: 56–62 (February 1961).

80. Mayer, T., "The Inflexibility of Monetary Policy," *Review of Economics and Statistics*, 40: 358–74 (November 1958) [reprinted in this volume—Ed.].

81. McKean, R. N., "Liquidity and a National Balance Sheet," *Journal of Political Economy*, 57: 506–22 (December 1949). Reprinted in F. A. Lutz and L. W. Mints (eds.), *Readings in Monetary Theory* (Homewood, Ill., 1951), pp. 63–88.

82. Meiselman, D., *The Term Structure of Interest Rates* (Englewood Cliffs, N.J., 1962).

83. Meltzer, A. H., "Mercantile Credit, Monetary Policy and Size of Firm," *Review of Economics and Statistics*, 42: 429–37 (November 1960).

84. Metzler, L. A., "Wealth, Saving and the Rate of Interest," *Journal of Political Economy*, 59: 93–116 (April 1951) [reprinted in this volume—Ed.].

85. Miller, E., "Monetary Policies in the United States Since 1950: Some Implications of the Retreat to Orthodoxy," *Canadian Journal of Economics and Political Science*, 27: 205–22 (May 1961).

86. Minsky, H. P., "Central Banking and Money Market Changes," *Quarterly Journal of Economics*, 71: 171–87 (May 1957).

87. Mundell, R. A., "The Public Debt, Corporate Income Taxes, and the Rate of Interest," *Journal of Political Economy*, 68: 622–26 (December 1960).

88. Musgrave, R. A., "Money, Liquidity and the Valuation of Assets," in *Money, Trade and Economic Growth*, in honor of John Henry Williams (New York, 1951), pp. 216–42.

89. Norton, F. E., and N. H. Jacoby, *Bank Deposits and Legal Reserve Requirements* (Los Angeles, 1959).

90. Orr, D., and W. J. Mellon, "Stochastic Reserve Losses and Expansion of Bank Credit," *American Economic Review*, 51: 614–23 (September 1961).

91. Patinkin, D., "Dichotomies of the Pricing Process in Economic Theory," *Economica*, 21: 113–28 (May 1954).

92. ———, "Financial Intermediaries and the Logical Structure of Monetary Theory," *American Economic Review*, 51: 95–116 (March 1961).

93. ———, "Liquidity Preference and Loanable Funds: Stock and Flow Analysis," *Economica*, 25: 300–18 (November 1958).

94. ———, *Money, Interest and Prices* (Evanston, Ill., 1956).

95. ———, "The Indeterminacy of Absolute Prices in Classical Economic Theory," *Econometrica*, 17: 1–27 (January 1949).

96. Phillips, A. W., "Stabilization Policy in a Closed Economy," *Economic Journal*, 64: 290–323 (June 1954).

97. Riefler, W., "Open Market Operations in Long-Term Securities," *Federal Reserve Bulletin*, 44: 1260–74 (November 1958).

98. Robertson, D. H., "More Notes on the Rate of Interest," *Review of Economic Studies*, 21: 136–41 (February 1954).

99. Robinson, J., "The Rate of Interest," *Econometrica*, 19: 92–111 (April 1951). Reprinted in J. Robinson, *The Rate of Interest and Other Essays* (London, 1952).

100. Rosa [Roosa], R. V., "Interest Rates and the Central Bank," in *Money, Trade and Economic Growth*, in honor of John Henry Williams (New York, 1951), pp. 270–95 [reprinted in this volume—Ed.].

101. Rose, H., "Liquidity Preference and Loanable Funds," *Review of Economic Studies*, 24: 111–19 (February 1957).

102. Sayers, R. S., "Monetary Thought and Monetary Policy in England," *Economic Journal*, 70: 710–24 (December 1960).

103. Schlesinger, J. R., "After Twenty Years: The General Theory," *Quarterly Journal of Economics*, 70: 581–602 (November 1956).

104. Scott, I. O., "The Availability Doctrine: Theoretical Underpinnings," *Review of Economic Studies*, 25: 41–48 (October 1957) [reprinted in this volume—Ed.].

105. Selden, R. T., "Monetary Velocity in the United States," in M. Friedman (ed.), *Studies in the Quantity Theory of Money* (Chicago, 1956), pp. 179–257.

106. Shackle, G. L. S., "Recent Theories Concerning the Nature and Role of Interest," *Economic Journal*, 71: 209–54 (June 1961) [reprinted in this volume—Ed.].

107. Shaw, E. S., "Money Supply and Stable Economic Growth," in *United States Monetary Policy* (New York, 1958), pp. 49–71.

108. Shelby, D., "Some Implications of the Growth of Financial Intermediaries," *Journal of Finance*, 13: 527–41 (December 1958).

109. Simons, H. C., "Rules versus Authorities in Monetary Policy," *Journal of Political Economy*, 44: 1–30 (February 1936). Reprinted in H. C. Simons, *Economic Policy for a Free Society* (Chicago, 1948), pp. 160–83.

110. Smith, W. L., *Debt Management in the United States*, Study Paper No. 19, Joint Economic Committee, 86th Congress, 2nd Session (Washington, 1960).

111. ———, "Financial Intermediaries and Monetary Controls," *Quarterly Journal of Economics*, 73: 533–53 (November 1959).

112. ———, "Monetary Theories of the Rate of Interest: A Dynamic Analysis," *Review of Economics and Statistics*, 40: 15–21 (February 1958).

113. ———, "On the Effectiveness of Monetary Policy," *American Economic Review*, 46: 588–606 (September 1956).

114. Tobin, J., "A Dynamic Aggregative Model," *Journal of Political Economy*, 63: 103–15 (April 1955) [reprinted in this volume—Ed.].

115. ———, "Liquidity Preference and Monetary Policy," *Review of Economics and Statistics*, 29: 124–31 (May 1947).

116. ———, "Liquidity Preference as Behavior Towards Risk," *Review of Economic Studies*, 25: 65–86 (February 1958) [reprinted in this volume—Ed.].

117. ———, "Money, Capital and Other Stores of Value," *American Economic Review Proceedings*, 51: 26–37 (May 1961).

118. ———, "The Interest-Elasticity of Transactions Demand for Cash," *Review of Economics and Statistics*, 38: 241–47 (August 1956).

119. Tolley, G. S., "Providing for Growth of the Money Supply," *Journal of Political Economy*, 65: 465–85 (December 1957) [reprinted in this volume—Ed.].

120. Tsiang, S. C., "Liquidity Preference and Loanable Funds Theories, Multiplier and Velocity Analysis: A Synthesis," *American Economic Review*, 46: 539–64 (September 1956).

121. Turvey, R., "Consistency and Consolidation in the Theory of Interest," *Economica*, 21: 300–7 (November 1954).

122. ———, *Interest Rates and Asset Prices* (London, 1960).

123. Valavanis, S., "A Denial of Patinkin's Contradiction," *Kyklos*, 4: 351–68 (1955).

124. Villard, H. H., "Monetary Theory," in H. S. Ellis (ed.), *A Survey of Contemporary Economics* (Philadelphia, 1948), pp. 314–51.

125. Weintraub, S., *An Approach to the Theory of Income Distribution* (Philadelphia, 1958).

126. White, W. H., "The Flexibility of Anticyclical Monetary Policy," *Review of Economics and Statistics*, 43: 142–47 (May 1961) [reprinted in this volume—Ed.].

127. "A Flow-of-Funds System of National Accounts: Annual Estimates, 1939–54," *Federal Reserve Bulletin*, 41: 1085–1124 (October 1955).

128. Committee on the Working of the Monetary System (Chairman: The Rt. Hon. The Lord Radcliffe, G.B.E.), *Report* (London, 1959).

129. *Money and Credit: Their Influence on Jobs, Prices and Growth* (Englewood Cliffs, N.J., 1961).

130. U.S. Congress Joint Economic Committee, *Staff Report on Employment, Growth and Price Levels* (Washington, 1959).

Part **II**

The Demand
For Money

The analysis of the demand for money prior to the *General Theory* centered about the quantity theory of money, which has had a venerable reputation, receiving its classical presentation in David Hume's essay *On Money*. The modern discussion of the quantity theory has as its point of departure Irving Fisher's equation-of-exchange which states that the quantity of money, M, times the transaction velocity of money, V', equals the value of transactions, $p'T$, where p' is an index of prices and T is the volume of real transactions measured in base period prices:

$$MV' = p'T$$

An alternative formulation of Fisher's equation, which proved theoretically and empirically more manageable, employed the real value of income measured in base period prices, Y, in place of the volume of real transactions, and employed the income velocity of money, V, in place of transaction velocity, with a suitable redefinition of the price index, p:

$$MV = pY$$

The equation-of-exchange was a truism and was always satisfied by the manner in which the variables were defined. The quantity theory of money was transformed into a theory of demand for money by assuming that velocity was determined largely by institutional factors and that in the short-run it could be treated as a constant. This view was expressed by rewriting the equation-of-exchange in a form that has come to be known as the cash balance or "Cambridge equation":[1]

$$M = kpY$$

where k, the reciprocal of the income velocity of money, can be interpreted as the average length of time money is held between

---

[1] This formulation is often linked with the name of Alfred Marshall even though he stated that the community would hold some proportion of its wealth as well as some proportion of its income in the form of money. Alfred Marshall, *Money, Credit and Commerce* (London 1923), p. 44.

transactions. This interpretation emphasized the role of money as a medium of exchange and implied that money would not be held except to finance transactions.

Keynes' analysis of the demand for money in the *General Theory of Employment, Interest and Money*, emphasized the role of money as a store of value and distinguished a "speculative" demand for money. The speculative demand for money, as introduced by Keynes and subsequently elaborated upon by Tobin, was explained by the logic that in an uncertain world in which interest rates fluctuated, a wealthholder investing in interest-bearing financial assets undertook the risk of a capital loss if the rate of interest rose and if he should at the same time require money to make unforeseen payments (a precautionary motive) or if he wished to take advantage of future investment opportunities (a speculative motive). Thus the risk and the rate of return an individual receives on his stock of wealth is dependent on the rate of interest and on the proportion of his wealth held in the form of interest-yielding assets (securities). If the rate of interest declines, the rate of return on an individual's stock of wealth would no longer offset the risk he undertakes, both because the return is low, and because an "abnormally" low rate of interest may be thought more likely to rise. A wealthholder will reduce his risk by increasing the proportion of wealth he holds in the form of money. It is possible that the rate of interest may be so low that any increases in the stock of money will simply be held by wealthholders as "idle balances."

For analytical convenience Keynes combined the precautionary and transactions motives for holding money since he believed both to be determined largely by the level of income (although as may be seen above, the precautionary motive can just as easily be combined with the speculative demand for money). Keynes' formulation of the demand for money may be written as:

$$M/p = k'Y + L'(i)$$

where $k'Y$ is the transactions demand and $L'(i)$ the speculative demand for money which varies inversely with the rate of interest, i. This manner of expressing the Keynesian demand for money follows Patinkin in that it assumes that both the speculative and transactions demand for money are, for any given income, proportional to the price level. Keynes rejected the idea that for practical purposes velocity in the short-run could be treated as a constant. The main thrust of his speculative demand for money was to demonstrate that there are conditions under which the price mechanism and, specifically, the interest rate mechanism will not work to restore full employment.

Baumol and Tobin subsequently demonstrated that the transactions demand for money was also interest-elastic, so that the demand for money could be written as:

$$M/p = L_1(i, Y) + L_2(i)$$

or more generally as

$$M/p = L(i, Y)$$

Wide agreement has been arrived at by both "quantity" and "Keynesian" monetary theorists in recent years that: (1) money has utility as a store of value in an uncertain world; (2) the demand for money is part of a theory of asset preference; and (3) that the major determinants of the demand for money are wealth, W, income, and the rate of interest (although considerable difference of opinion exists about the relative importance of the variables); and (4) therefore the general form of the demand for money may be written:

$$M/p = L(W, Y, i)$$

The differences that have arisen between the "Keynesian," or what has more recently been called the "portfolio," approach and the "quantity" approach are mainly differences of emphasis. The "portfolio" approach emphasizes the substitution effects of money as an alternative to other financial assets and "dethrones" money from the central position it has occupied, by treating it symmetrically with other assets which yield services. Thus it has tried to treat the theory of money with the apparatus of the theory of rational consumer choice. The "quantity" approach as exemplified by Friedman emphasizes income effects as the principal explanation for the variation in the demand for money, assigning substitution effects a secondary role. This approach has tried to treat the theory of money as a subject within capital theory.

Restatement of the Quantity Theory

The modern restatement of the quantity theory as an asset preference theory, as expounded by Professor Friedman, attempts to integrate monetary theory into value theory via the theory of capital. Friedman following Irving Fisher treats all factor income as emanating from capital. The source of human income is human capital. Friedman makes the demand for money depend on the real rate of interest on financial assets, the rate of return on nominal money which is taken to be the rate of change of price level, $\Delta p/p$, real income, the ratio of non-human capital to human capital, w, and a taste variable, u, so that the demand for money may be written:

$$M/p = L(i, \Delta p/p, Y, w, u)$$

In the empirical application of his theory, Friedman makes clear that he believes that substitution effects are secondary to the role of income effects. He takes the observed decline in velocity to the Second World War as evidence that money is a luxury good and that at higher levels of income proportionally more cash balances are demanded. However, in his study with Anna Schwartz of *The History of Money in the United States* (Princeton 1964), Friedman found a contradiction between the secular and the cyclical behavior of money. Over long periods of time, Friedman and Schwartz found real income and velocity tended to move in opposite directions (i.e., money-holding grew faster than income) while over the business cycle they tended to move in the same direction. The trend and the cycle also differed in the relative importance of the factors, money-holding and velocity with respect to money income. The nominal stock of money statistically tended to dominate the long swings in money income while in the business cycle changes in velocity were of comparable statistical importance in determining changes in money income. To reconcile this contradiction, Friedman introduced the explanation that per capita demand for money, M', was determined by permanent per capita income Y', and the permanent price level, p'', so that the demand for money may be written:

$$M'/p'' = a(Y'/p'')^b$$

where a and b are constants.

The cyclical behavior of velocity was reconciled with the secular behavior by the fact that in the expansionary phase nominal income increases more than permanent income (the level of income which people expect will be sustained), so that *measured* velocity exceeds permanent velocity. Permanent velocity may even be declining while measured velocity is rising. Friedman through a series of statistical manipulations and approximations tested his theory against the data for the United States and found that his computed measured velocity closely approximated observed velocity for most of the period. This explanation was intended to supplant cyclical variations in the interest rate (substitution effect) as the chief determinant of the observed cyclical change in velocity. However, since 1950, observed measured velocity has risen while Friedman's computed measured velocity has fallen.

The Portfolio Approach

The portfolio approach, largely developed by Professor Tobin,[2] like the neo-quantity theory exists largely in the form of an oral tradition, and it is difficult to find a definitive statement of this analysis.[3] It retains the Keynesian two-stage approach to wealth accumulation; saving is largely determined by income but the types of assets in which savings are held is determined by the relative certainty equivalent yields of the different types of wealth assets. If the theory were extended to the stock of human capital, the portfolio approach would not differ much from Friedman's quantity theory. This theory extended still further could embrace consumption theory as well by treating the demand for assets as being determined by their relative yields and existing stocks. Consumption goods would be treated simply as assets of which there were always zero stocks. The present theory has fallen short of this sweeping generalization, however, preferring to retain the dichotomy of consumption and saving. The portfolio approach in its rigorous form has no special place for money except possibly as a policy variable. The denial of any unique qualities to money as an asset does not necessarily deny to money a unique role as a policy instrument. As long as one believes that the composition of wealth assets can affect spending decisions and if one were limited to the possibility of altering the stock of only one type of asset, money would have some special properties to commend it, such as the ease with which its stock may be significantly changed and the pervasiveness of money in wealth portfolios of all sectors of the economy. However, empirical studies by portfolio theorists have tended to discredit money even in this role.

Duesenberry has attempted to analyze empirically the demand for money of corporations and households in the United States from a portfolio approach. He explains the demand for liquid assets of corporations, L_c, in terms of their cash flow (largely profits plus depreciation), F, short-term interest rates, i_s, business confidence, C, and tax rates, T, so the corporate demand for money may be written:

$$L_c = L_c(F, i_s, C, T)$$

Duesenberry found that the stock of corporate liquid assets was strongly influenced by corporations' cash flows and that changes in corporate liquid assets were largely reflected by variations in their holdings of government securities rather than cash; that business confidence was inversely related to the demand for liquid assets and that corporate total holdings of liquid assets respond ". . . fairly strongly to short-run changes in interest rates," but the division of liquid assets between cash balances and other forms of liquid assets was not found responsive to short-run changes in the Treasury Bill rate.

In his analysis of household holdings of demand deposits Duesenberry distinguished between low asset households, which hold almost all their assets in the form of liquid assets, and high asset holders. For low asset holders the level of demand deposits was explained by the rate of interest of financial institutions, i_f, and the difference between gross financial saving and the demand for transaction balances. If the savings function and the transaction demand for money can be considered relatively stable, then the demand of low asset holders for demand deposits may be written:

$$M_l = M_l(i_f, Y_l, C)$$

The demand for high asset holders is, in addition, influenced by the net expected rate of return on marketable securities, i_e, and total financial wealth, W_h. Their demand for demand deposits may be written:

$$M_h = M_h(i_f, i_e, Y_h, W_h, C)$$

Duesenberry's empirical findings were that household liquidity responded to short-run changes in the expected yield of securities. Although a large part of the response resulted in changes in time deposits, demand deposits also were affected. Changes in confidence affected households in much the same way as corporations. The division of liquid assets of households between cash and time deposits responded to changes in the yield on savings deposits and the selling efforts of savings institutions.

The Reconciliation of the Quantity and Portfolio Approaches

We may conclude from this discussion above and the selections that follow that there is wide agreement on the variables that affect the demand for money. The reformulated quantity theory, and the extension of the liquidity preference theory into one of maintaining an optimum portfolio of wealth assets, can in large measure be reconciled. Whether substitution or income effects dominate the demand for money is an empirical question. Duesenberry's study is interesting in the respect that he found substitution effects to be relatively stronger for households than for corporations, which suggests that it is useful to discriminate between their behavior.

From the point of view of policy the important question is, under what circumstances can the demand for some collection of liquid assets, the stock of which may be influenced by monetary authorities, be shown to have a stable functional relationship with income; and, whether the quantitative significance of this relationship is sufficiently great to be useful as a major instrument of economic policy, or, on the other hand, whether policies should be sought that will influence more directly investment and consumption.

A. Quantity Theory

2 The Quantity Theory of Money— A Restatement

Milton Friedman *University of Chicago and National Bureau of Economic Research*

The quantity theory of money is a term evocative of a general approach rather than a label for a well-defined theory. The exact content of the approach varies from a truism defining the term "velocity" to an allegedly rigid and unchanging ratio between the quantity of money—defined in one way or another—and the price level—also defined in one way or another. Whatever its precise meaning, it is clear that the general approach fell into disrepute after the crash of 1929 and the subsequent Great Depression and only recently has been slowly re-emerging into professional respectability.

The present study is partly a symptom of this re-emergence and partly a continuance of an aberrant tradition. Chicago was one of the few academic centers at which the quantity theory continued to be a central and vigorous part of the oral tradition throughout the 1930's and 1940's, where students continued to study monetary theory and to write theses on monetary problems. The quantity theory that retained this role differed sharply from the atrophied and rigid caricature that is so frequently described by the proponents of the new income-expenditure approach—and with some justice, to judge by much of the literature on policy that was spawned by quantity theorists. At Chicago, Henry Simons and

Reprinted from Milton Friedman, ed., *Studies in the Quantity Theory of Money* (Chicago: University of Chicago Press, 1956). Chapter 1, pp. 3–21, by permission of the author and The University of Chicago Press. Copyright 1956 by The University of Chicago Press.

Lloyd Mints directly, Frank Knight and Jacob Viner at one remove, taught and developed a more subtle and relevant version,
one in which the quantity theory was connected and integrated
with general price theory and became a flexible and sensitive tool
for interpreting movements in aggregate economic activity and for
developing relevant policy prescriptions.

To the best of my knowledge, no systematic statement of this
theory as developed at Chicago exists, though much can be read
between the lines of Simons' and Mints's writings. And this is as it
should be, for the Chicago tradition was not a rigid system, an un-
changeable orthodoxy, but a way of looking at things. It was a
theoretical approach that insisted that money does matter—that
any interpretation of short-term movements in economic activity is
likely to be seriously at fault if it neglects monetary changes and
repercussions and if it leaves unexplained why people are willing
to hold the particular nominal quantity of money in existence.

The purpose of this introduction is not to enshrine—or, should
I say, inter—a definitive version of the Chicago tradition. To
suppose that one could do so would be inconsistent with that tradition itself. The purpose is rather to set down a particular "model"
of a quantity theory in an attempt to convey the flavor of the oral
tradition which nurtured the remaining essays in this volume. In
consonance with this purpose, I shall not attempt to be exhaustive
or to give a full justification for every assertion.

1. The quantity theory is in the first instance a theory of the
demand for money. It is not a theory of output, or of money income,
or of the price level. Any statement about these variables requires
combining the quantity theory with some specifications about the
conditions of supply of money and perhaps about other variables
as well.

2. To the ultimate wealth-owning units in the economy, money
is one kind of asset, one way of holding wealth. To the productive
enterprise, money is a capital good, a source of productive services
that are combined with other productive services to yield the products that the enterprise sells. Thus the theory of the demand for
money is a special topic in the theory of capital; as such, it has
the rather unusual feature of combining a piece from each side of
the capital market, the supply of capital (points 3 through 8 that
follow), and the demand for capital (points 9 through 12).

3. The analysis of the demand for money on the part of the
ultimate wealth-owning units in the society can be made formally
identical with that of the demand for a consumption service. As in
the usual theory of consumer choice, the demand for money (or
any other particular asset) depends on three major sets of factors:

(*a*) the total wealth to be held in various forms—the analogue of the budget restraint; (*b*) the price of and return on this form of wealth and alternative forms; and (*c*) the tastes and preferences of the wealth-owning units. The substantive differences from the analysis of the demand for a consumption service are the necessity of taking account of intertemporal rates of substitution in (*b*) and (*c*) and of casting the budget restraint in terms of wealth.

4. From the broadest and most general point of view, total wealth includes all sources of "income" or consumable services. One such source is the productive capacity of human beings, and accordingly this is one form in which wealth can be held. From this point of view, "the" rate of interest expresses the relation between the stock which is wealth and the flow which is income, so if Y be the total flow of income, and r, "the" interest rate, total wealth is

$$W = \frac{Y}{r}. \tag{1}$$

Income in this broadest sense should not be identified with income as it is ordinarily measured. The latter is generally a "gross" stream with respect to human beings, since no deduction is made for the expense of maintaining human productive capacity intact; in addition, it is affected by transitory elements that make it depart more or less widely from the theoretical concept of the stable level of consumption of services that could be maintained indefinitely.

5. Wealth can be held in numerous forms, and the ultimate wealth-owning unit is to be regarded as dividing his wealth among them (point [*a*] of 3), so as to maximize "utility" (point [*c*] of 3), subject to whatever restrictions affect the possibility of converting one form of wealth into another (point [*b*] of 3). As usual, this implies that he will seek an apportionment of his wealth such that the rate at which he *can* substitute one form of wealth for another is equal to the rate at which he is just willing to do so. But this general proposition has some special features in the present instance because of the necessity of considering flows as well as stocks. We can suppose all wealth (except wealth in the form of the productive capacity of human beings) to be expressed in terms of monetary units at the prices of the point of time in question. The rate at which one form can be substituted for another is then simply $1.00 worth for $1.00 worth, regardless of the forms involved. But this is clearly not a complete description, because the holding of one form of wealth instead of another involves a difference in the composition of the income stream, and it is essentially these differences that are fundamental to the "utility" of a particular structure of wealth. In consequence, to describe fully the alternative com-

binations of forms of wealth that are available to an individual, we must take account not only of their market prices—which except for human wealth can be done simply by expressing them in units worth $1.00—but also of the form and size of the income streams they yield.

It will suffice to bring out the major issues that these considerations raise to consider five different forms in which wealth can be held: (i) money (M), interpreted as claims or commodity units that are generally accepted in payment of debts at a fixed nominal value; (ii) bonds (B), interpreted as claims to time streams of payments that are fixed in nominal units; (iii) equities (E), interpreted as claims to stated pro-rata shares of the returns of enterprises; (iv) physical non-human goods (G); and (v) human capital (H). Consider now the yield of each.

(i) Money may yield a return in the form of money, for example, interest on demand deposits. It will simplify matters, however, and entail no essential loss of generality, to suppose that money yields its return solely in kind, in the usual form of convenience, security, etc. The magnitude of this return in "real" terms per nominal unit of money clearly depends on the volume of goods that unit corresponds to, or on the general price level, which we may designate by P. Since we have decided to take $1.00 worth as the unit for each form of wealth, this will be equally true for other forms of wealth as well, so P is a variable affecting the "real" yield of each.

(ii) If we take the "standard" bond to be a claim to a perpetual income stream of constant nominal amount, then the return to a holder of the bond can take two forms: one, the annual sum he receives—the "coupon"; the other, any change in the price of the bond over time, a return which may of course be positive or negative. If the price is expected to remain constant, then $1.00 worth of a bond yields r_b per year, where r_b is simply the "coupon" sum divided by the market price of the bond, so $1/r_b$ is the price of a bond promising to pay $1.00 per year. We shall call r_b the market bond interest rate. If the price is expected to change, then the yield cannot be calculated so simply, since it must take account of the return in the form of expected appreciation or depreciation of the bond, and it cannot, like r_b, be calculated directly from market prices (so long, at least, as the "standard" bond is the only one traded in).

The nominal income stream purchased for $1.00 at time zero then consists of

$$r_b(0) + r_b(0) \, d \frac{\left(\dfrac{1}{r_b(t)}\right)}{dt} = r_b(0) - \frac{r_b(0)}{r_b^2(t)} \cdot \frac{dr_b(t)}{dt}, \qquad (2)$$

where t stands for time. For simplicity, we can approximate this functional by its value at time zero, which is

$$r_b - \frac{1}{r_b}\frac{dr_b}{dt}. \qquad (3)$$

This sum, together with P already introduced, defines the real return from holding \$1.00 of wealth in the form of bonds.

(iii) Analogously to our treatment of bonds, we may take the "standard" unit of equity to be a claim to a perpetual income stream of constant "real" amount; that is, to be a standard bond with a purchasing-power escalator clause, so that it promises a perpetual income stream equal in nominal units to a constant number times a price index, which we may, for convenience, take to be the same price index P introduced in (i).[1] The nominal return to the holder of the equity can then be regarded as taking three forms: the constant nominal amount he would receive per year in the absence of any change in P; the increment or decrement to this nominal amount to adjust for changes in P; and any change in the nominal price of the equity over time, which may of course arise from changes either in interest rates or in price levels. Let r_e be the market interest rate on equities defined analogously to r_b, namely, as the ratio of the "coupon" sum at any time (the first two items above) to the price of the equity, so $1/r_e$ is the price of an equity promising to pay \$1.00 per year if the price level does not change, or to pay

$$\frac{P(t)}{P(0)} \cdot 1$$

if the price level varies according to $P(t)$. If $r_e(t)$ is defined analogously, the price of the bond selling for $1/r_e(0)$ at time 0 will be

$$\frac{P(t)}{P(0)r_e(t)}$$

at time t, where the ratio of prices is required to adjust for any change in the price level. The nominal stream purchased for \$1.00 at time zero then consists of

$$r_e(0) \cdot \frac{P(t)}{P(0)} + \frac{r_e(0)}{P(0)} \cdot d\frac{\left[\frac{P(t)}{r_e(t)}\right]}{dt} = r_e(0) \cdot \frac{P(t)}{P(0)}$$

$$+ \frac{r_e(0)}{r_e(t)} \cdot \frac{1}{P(0)} \cdot \frac{dP(t)}{dt} - \frac{P(t)}{P(0)} \cdot \frac{r_e(0)}{r_e^2(t)} \cdot \frac{dr_e(t)}{dt}. \qquad (4)$$

Once again we can approximate this functional by its value at time zero, which is

$$r_e + \frac{1}{P}\frac{dP}{dt} - \frac{1}{r_e}\frac{dr_e}{dt}. \tag{5}$$

This sum, together with P already introduced, defines the "real" return from holding \$1.00 of wealth in the form of equities.

(iv) Physical goods held by ultimate wealth-owning units are similar to equities except that the annual stream they yield is in kind rather than in money. In terms of nominal units, this return, like that from equities, depends on the behavior of prices. In addition, like equities, physical goods must be regarded as yielding a nominal return in the form of appreciation or depreciation in money value. If we suppose the price level P, introduced earlier, to apply equally to the value of these physical goods, then, at time zero,

$$\frac{1}{P}\frac{dP}{dt} \tag{6}$$

is the size of this nominal return per \$1.00 of physical goods.[2] Together with P, it defines the "real" return from holding \$1.00 in the form of physical goods.

(v) Since there is only a limited market in human capital, at least in modern non-slave societies, we cannot very well define in market prices the terms of substitution of human capital for other forms of capital and so cannot define at any time the physical unit of capital corresponding to \$1.00 of human capital. There are some possibilities of substituting non-human capital for human capital in an individual's wealth holdings, as, for example, when he enters into a contract to render personal services for a specified period in return for a definitely specified number of periodic payments, the number not depending on his being physically capable of rendering the services. But, in the main, shifts between human capital and other forms must take place through direct investment and dis-investment in the human agent, and we may as well treat this as if it were the only way. With respect to this form of capital, there-fore, the restriction or obstacles affecting the alternative com-positions of wealth available to the individual cannot be expressed in terms of market prices or rates of return. At any one point in time there is some division between human and non-human wealth in his portfolio of assets; he may be able to change this over time, but we shall treat it as given at a point in time. Let w be the ratio of non-human to human wealth or, equivalently, of income from non-human wealth to income from human wealth, which means that it is closely allied to what is usually defined as the ratio of wealth to income. This is, then, the variable that needs to be taken into account so far as human wealth is concerned.

6. The tastes and preferences of wealth-owning units for the service streams arising from different forms of wealth must in general simply be taken for granted as determining the form of the demand function. In order to give the theory empirical content, it will generally have to be supposed that tastes are constant over significant stretches of space and time. However, explicit allowance can be made for some changes in tastes in so far as such changes are linked with objective circumstances. For example, it seems reasonable that, other things the same, individuals want to hold a larger fraction of their wealth in the form of money when they are moving around geographically or are subject to unusual uncertainty than otherwise. This is probably one of the major factors explaining a frequent tendency for money holdings to rise relative to income during wartime. But the extent of geographic movement, and perhaps of other kinds of uncertainty, can be represented by objective indexes, such as indexes of migration, miles of railroad travel, and the like. Let u stand for any such variables that can be expected to affect tastes and preferences (for "utility" determining variables).

7. Combining 4, 5, and 6 along the lines suggested by 3 yields the following demand function for money:

$$M = f\left(P, r_b - \frac{1}{r_b}\frac{dr_b}{dt}, r_e + \frac{1}{P}\frac{dP}{dt} - \frac{1}{r_e}\frac{dr_e}{dt}, \frac{1}{P}\frac{dP}{dt}; w; \frac{Y}{r}; u\right). \quad (7)$$

A number of observations are in order about this function.

(i) Even if we suppose prices and rates of interest unchanged, the function contains three rates of interest: two for specific types of assets, r_b and r_e, and one intended to apply to all types of assets, r. This general rate, r, is to be interpreted as something of a weighted average of the two special rates plus the rates applicable to human wealth and to physical goods. Since the latter two cannot be observed directly, it is perhaps best to regard them as varying in some systematic way with r_b and r_e. On this assumption, we can drop r as an additional explicit variable, treating its influence as fully taken into account by the inclusion of r_b and r_e.

(ii) If there were no differences of opinion about price movements and interest-rate movements, and bonds and equities were equivalent except that the former are expressed in nominal units, arbitrage would of course make

$$r_b - \frac{1}{r_b}\frac{dr_b}{dt} = r_e + \frac{1}{P}\frac{dP}{dt} - \frac{1}{r_e}\frac{dr_e}{dt}, \quad (8)$$

or, if we suppose rates of interest either stable or changing at the same percentage rate,

$$r_b = r_e + \frac{1}{P}\frac{dP}{dt},\tag{9}$$

that is, the "money" interest rate equal to the "real" rate plus the percentage rate of change of prices. In application the rate of change of prices must be interpreted as an "expected" rate of change and differences of opinion cannot be neglected, so we cannot suppose (9) to hold; indeed, one of the most consistent features of inflation seems to be that it does not.[3]

(iii) If the range of assets were to be widened to include promises to pay specified sums for a finite number of time units—"short-term" securities as well as "consols"—the rates of change of r_b and r_e would be reflected in the difference between long and short rates of interest. Since at some stage it will doubtless be desirable to introduce securities of different time duration (see point 23 below), we may simplify the present exposition by restricting it to the case in which r_b and r_e are taken to be stable over time. Since the rate of change in prices is required separately in any event, this means that we can replace the cumbrous variables introduced to designate the nominal return on bonds and equities simply by r_b and r_e.

(iv) Y can be interpreted as including the return to all forms of wealth, including money and physical capital goods owned and held directly by ultimate wealth-owning units, and so Y/r can be interpreted as an estimate of total wealth, only if Y is regarded as including some imputed income from the stock of money and directly owned physical capital goods. For monetary analysis the simplest procedure is perhaps to regard Y as referring to the return to all forms of wealth other than the money held directly by ultimate wealth-owning units, and so Y/r as referring to total remaining wealth.

8. A more fundamental point is that, as in all demand analyses resting on maximization of a utility function defined in terms of "real" magnitudes, this demand equation must be considered independent in any essential way of the nominal units used to measure money variables. If the unit in which prices and money income are expressed is changed, the amount of money demanded should change proportionately. More technically, equation (7) must be regarded as homogeneous of the first degree in P and Y, so that

$$f\left(\lambda P, r_b, r_e, \frac{1}{P}\frac{dP}{dt}; w; \lambda Y; u\right)$$
$$= \lambda f\left(P, r_b, r_e, \frac{1}{P}\frac{dP}{dt}; w; Y; u\right)\tag{10}$$

where the variables within the parentheses have been rewritten in simpler form in accordance with comments 7 (i) and 7 (iii).

This characteristic of the function enables us to rewrite it in two alternative and more familiar ways.

(i) Let $\lambda = 1/P$. Equation (7) can then be written

$$\frac{M}{P} = f\left(r_b, r_e, \frac{1}{P}\frac{dP}{dt}; w; \frac{Y}{P}; u\right). \tag{11}$$

In this form the equation expresses the demand for real balances as a function of "real" variables independent of nominal monetary values.

(ii) Let $\lambda = 1/Y$. Equation (7) can then be written

$$\frac{M}{Y} = f\left(r_b, r_e, \frac{1}{P}\frac{dP}{dt}, w, \frac{P}{Y}, u\right)$$

$$= \frac{1}{v\left(r_b, r_e, \frac{1}{P}\frac{dP}{dt}, w, \frac{Y}{P}, u\right)}, \tag{12}$$

or

$$Y = v\left(r_b, r_e, \frac{1}{P}\frac{dP}{dt}, w, \frac{Y}{P}, u\right) \cdot M. \tag{13}$$

In this form the equation is in the usual quantity theory form, where v is income velocity.

9. These equations are, to this point, solely for money held directly by ultimate wealth-owning units. As noted, money is also held by business enterprises as a productive resource. The counterpart to this business asset in the balance sheet of an ultimate wealth-owning unit is a claim other than money. For example, an individual may buy bonds from a corporation, and the corporation use the proceeds to finance the money holdings which it needs for its operations. Of course, the usual difficulties of separating the accounts of the business and its owner arise with unincorporated enterprises.

10. The amount of money that it pays business enterprises to hold depends, as for any other source of productive services, on the cost of the productive services, the cost of substitute productive services, and the value product yielded by the productive service. Per dollar of money held, the cost depends on how the corresponding capital is raised—whether by raising additional capital in the form of bonds or equities, by substituting cash for real capital goods, etc. These ways of financing money holdings are much the same as the alternative forms in which the ultimate wealth-owning

unit can hold its non-human wealth, so that the variables r_b, r_e, P, and $(1/P)(dP/dt)$ introduced into (7) can be taken to represent the cost to the business enterprise of holding money. For some purposes, however, it may be desirable to distinguish between the rate of return received by the lender and the rate paid by the borrower; in which case it would be necessary to introduce an additional set of variables.

Substitutes for money as a productive service are numerous and varied, including all ways of economizing on money holdings by using other resources to synchronize more closely payments and receipts, reduce payment periods, extend use of book credit, establish clearing arrangements, and so on in infinite variety. There seem no particularly close substitutes whose prices deserve to be singled out for inclusion in the business demand for money.

The value product yielded by the productive services of money per unit of output depends on production conditions: the production function. It is likely to be especially dependent on features of production conditions affecting the smoothness and regularity of operations as well as on those determining the size and scope of enterprises, degree of vertical integration, etc. Again there seem no variables that deserve to be singled out on the present level of abstraction for special attention; these factors can be taken into account by interpreting u as including variables affecting not only the tastes of wealth-owners but also the relevant technological conditions of production. Given the amount of money demanded per unit of output, the total amount demanded is proportional to total output, which can be represented by Y.

11. One variable that has traditionally been singled out in considering the demand for money on the part of business enterprises is the volume of transactions, or of transactions per dollar of final products; and, of course, emphasis on transactions has been carried over to the ultimate wealth-owning unit as well as to the business enterprise. The idea that renders this approach attractive is that there is a mechanical link between a dollar of payments per unit time and the average stock of money required to effect it—a fixed technical coefficient of production, as it were. It is clear that this mechanical approach is very different in spirit from the one we have been following. On our approach, the average amount of money held per dollar of transactions is itself to be regarded as a resultant of an economic equilibrating process, not as a physical datum. If, for whatever reason, it becomes more expensive to hold money, then it is worth devoting resources to effecting money transactions in less expensive ways or to reducing the volume of transactions per dollar of final output. In consequence, our ultimate demand function for money in its most general form does not con-

tain as a variable the volume of transactions or of transactions per dollar of final output; it contains rather those more basic technical and cost conditions that affect the costs of conserving money, be it by changing the average amount of money held per dollar of transactions per unit time or by changing the number of dollars of transactions per dollar of final output. This does not, of course, exclude the possibility that, for a particular problem, it may be useful to regard the transactions variables as given and not to dig beneath them and so to include the volume of transactions per dollar of final output as an explicit variable in a special variant of the demand function.

Similar remarks are relevant to various features of payment conditions, frequently described as "institutional conditions," affecting the velocity of circulation of money and taken as somehow mechanically determined—such items as whether workers are paid by the day, or week, or month; the use of book credit; and so on. On our approach these, too, are to be regarded as resultants of an economic equilibrating process, not as physical data. Lengthening the pay period, for example, may save bookkeeping and other costs to the employer, who is therefore willing to pay somewhat more than in proportion for a longer than a shorter pay period; on the other hand, it imposes on employees the cost of holding larger cash balances or providing substitutes for cash, and they therefore want to be paid more than in proportion for a longer pay period. Where these will balance depends on how costs vary with length of pay period. The cost to the employee depends in considerable part on the factors entering into his demand curve for money for a fixed pay period. If he would in any event be holding relatively large average balances, the additional costs imposed by a lengthened pay period tend to be less than if he would be holding relatively small average balances, and so it will take less of an inducement to get him to accept a longer pay period. For given cost savings to the employer, therefore, the pay period can be expected to be longer in the first case than in the second. Surely, the increase in the average cash balance over the past century in this country that has occurred for other reasons has been a factor producing a lengthening of pay periods and not the other way around. Or, again, experience in hyperinflations shows how rapidly payment practices change under the impact of drastic changes in the cost of holding money.

12. The upshot of these considerations is that the demand for money on the part of business enterprises can be regarded as expressed by a function of the same kind as equation (7), with the same variables on the right-hand side. And, like (7), since the analysis is based on informed maximization of returns by enter-

prises, only "real" quantities matter, so it must be homogeneous of the first degree in Y and P. In consequence, we can interpret (7) and its variants (11) and (13) as describing the demand for money on the part of a business enterprise as well as on the part of an ultimate wealth-owning unit, provided only that we broaden our interpretation of u.

13. Strictly speaking, the equations (7), (11), and (13) are for an individual wealth-owning unit or business enterprise. If we aggregate (7) for all wealth-owning units and business enterprises in the society, the result, in principle, depends on the distribution of the units by the several variables. This raises no serious problem about P, r_b, and r_e, for these can be taken as the same for all, or about u, for this is an unspecified portmanteau variable to be filled in as the occasion demands. We have been interpreting $(1/P)(dP/dt)$ as the expected rate of price rise, so there is no reason why this variable should be the same for all, and w and Y clearly differ substantially among units. An approximation is to neglect these difficulties and take (7) and the associated (11) and (13) as applying to the aggregate demand for money, with $(1/P)(dP/dt)$ interpreted as some kind of average expected rate of change of prices, w as the ratio of total income from non-human wealth to income from human wealth, and Y as aggregate income. This is the procedure that has generally been followed, and it seems the right one until serious departures between this linear approximation and experience make it necessary to introduce measures of dispersion with respect to one or more of the variables.

14. It is perhaps worth noting explicitly that the model does not use the distinction between "active balances" and "idle balances" or the closely allied distinction between "transaction balances" and "speculative balances" that is so widely used in the literature. The distinction between money holdings of ultimate wealth-owners and of business enterprises is related to this distinction but only distantly so. Each of these categories of money-holders can be said to demand money partly from "transaction" motives, partly from "speculative" or "asset" motives, but dollars of money are not distinguished according as they are said to be held for one or the other purpose. Rather, each dollar is, as it were, regarded as rendering a variety of services, and the holder of money as altering his money holdings until the value to him of the addition to the total flow of services produced by adding a dollar to his money stock is equal to the reduction in the flow of services produced by subtracting a dollar from each of the other forms in which he holds assets.

15. Nothing has been said above about "banks" or producers of money. This is because their main role is in connection with the

supply of money rather than the demand for it. Their introduction does, however, blur some of the points in the above analysis: the existence of banks enables productive enterprises to acquire money balances without raising capital from ultimate wealth-owners. Instead of selling claims (bonds or equities) to them, it can sell its claims to banks, getting "money" in exchange: in the phrase that was once so common in textbooks on money, the bank coins specific liabilities into generally acceptable liabilities. But this possibility does not alter the preceding analysis in any essential way.

16. Suppose the supply of money in nominal units is regarded as fixed or more generally autonomously determined. Equation (13) then defines the conditions under which this nominal stock of money will be the amount demanded. Even under these conditions, equation (13) alone is not sufficient to determine money income. In order to have a complete model for the determination of money income, it would be necessary to specify the determinants of the structure of interest rates, of real income, and of the path of adjustment in the price level. Even if we suppose interest rates determined independently—by productivity, thrift, and the like—and real income as also given by other forces, equation (13) only determines a unique equilibrium level of money income if we mean by this the level at which prices are stable. More generally, it determines a time path of money income for given initial values of money income.

In order to convert equation (13) into a "complete" model of income determination, therefore, it is necessary to suppose either that the demand for money is highly inelastic with respect to the variables in v or that all these variables are to be taken as rigid and fixed.

17. Even under the most favorable conditions, for example, that the demand for money is quite inelastic with respect to the variables in v, equation (13) gives at most a theory of money income: it then says that changes in money income mirror changes in the nominal quantity of money. But it tells nothing about how much of any change in Y is reflected in real output and how much in prices. To infer this requires bringing in outside information, as, for example, that real output is at its feasible maximum, in which case any increase in money would produce the same or a larger percentage increase in prices; and so on.

18. In light of the preceding exposition, the question arises what it means to say that someone is or is not a "quantity theorist." Almost every economist will accept the general lines of the preceding analysis on a purely formal and abstract level, although each would doubtless choose to express it differently in detail. Yet there clearly are deep and fundamental differences about the im-

portance of this analysis for the understanding of short- and long-term movements in general economic activity. This difference of opinion arises with respect to three different issues: (i) the stability and importance of the demand function for money; (ii) the independence of the factors affecting demand and supply; and (iii) the form of the demand function or related functions.

(i) The quantity theorist accepts the empirical hypothesis that the demand for money is highly stable—more stable than functions such as the consumption function that are offered as alternative key relations. This hypothesis needs to be hedged on both sides. On the one side, the quantity theorist need not, and generally does not, mean that the real quantity of money demanded per unit of output, or the velocity of circulation of money, is to be regarded as numerically constant over time; he does not, for example, regard it as a contradiction to the stability of the demand for money that the velocity of circulation of money rises drastically during hyperinflations. For the stability he expects is in the functional relation between the quantity of money demanded and the variables that determine it, and the sharp rise in the velocity of circulation of money during hyperinflations is entirely consistent with a stable functional relation, as Cagan so clearly demonstrates in his essay.[4] On the other side, the quantity theorist must sharply limit, and be prepared to specify explicitly, the variables that it is empirically important to include in the function. For to expand the number of variables regarded as significant is to empty the hypothesis of its empirical content; there is indeed little if any difference between asserting that the demand for money is highly unstable and asserting that it is a perfectly stable function of an indefinitely large number of variables.

The quantity theorist not only regards the demand function for money as stable; he also regards it as playing a vital role in determining variables that he regards as of great importance for the analysis of the economy as a whole, such as the level of money income or of prices. It is this that leads him to put greater emphasis on the demand for money than on, let us say, the demand for pins, even though the latter might be as stable as the former. It is not easy to state this point precisely, and I cannot pretend to have done so. (See item [iii] below for an example of an argument against the quantity theorist along these lines.)

The reaction against the quantity theory in the 1930's came largely, I believe, under this head. The demand for money, it was asserted, is a will-o'-the-wisp, shifting erratically and unpredictably with every rumor and expectation; one cannot, it was asserted, reliably specify a limited number of variables on which it depends. However, although the reaction came under this head, it was largely rationalized under the two succeeding heads.

(ii) The quantity theorist also holds that there are important factors affecting the supply of money that do not affect the demand for money. Under some circumstances these are technical conditions affecting the supply of specie; under others, political or psychological conditions determining the policies of monetary authorities and the banking system. A stable demand function is useful precisely in order to trace out the effects of changes in supply, which means that it is useful only if supply is affected by at least some factors other than those regarded as affecting demand.

The classical version of the objection under this head to the quantity theory is the so-called real-bills doctrine: that changes in the demand for money call forth corresponding changes in supply and that supply cannot change otherwise, or at least cannot do so under specified institutional arrangements. The forms which this argument takes are legion and are still widespread. Another version is the argument that the "quantity theory" cannot "explain" large price rises, because the price rise produced both the increase in demand for nominal money holdings and the increase in supply of money to meet it; that is, implicitly that the same forces affect both the demand for and the supply of money, and in the same way.

(iii) The attack on the quantity theory associated with the Keynesian underemployment analysis is based primarily on an assertion about the form of (7) or (11). The demand for money, it is said, is infinitely elastic at a "small" positive interest rate. At this interest rate, which can be expected to prevail under underemployment conditions, changes in the real supply of money, whether produced by changes in prices or in the nominal stock of money, have no effect on anything. This is the famous "liquidity trap." A rather more complex version involves the shape of other functions as well: the magnitudes in (7) other than "the" interest rate, it is argued, enter into other relations in the economic system and can be regarded as determined there; the interest rate does not enter into these other functions; it can therefore be regarded as determined by this equation. So the only role of the stock of money and the demand for money is to determine the interest rate.

19. The proof of this pudding is in the eating; and the essays in this book contain much relevant food, of which I may perhaps mention three particularly juicy items.

One cannot read Lerner's description of the effects of monetary reform in the Confederacy in 1864 without recognizing that at least on occasion the supply of money can be a largely autonomous factor and the demand for money highly stable even under extraordinarily unstable circumstances. After three years of war, after widespread destruction and military reverses, in the face of impending defeat, a monetary reform that succeeded in reducing the stock of money halted and reversed for some months a rise in prices that had been going on at the rate of 10 per cent a month most of the war! It would be hard to construct a better controlled experiment to demonstrate the critical importance of the supply of money.

On the other hand, Klein's examination of German experience in World War II is much less favorable to the stability and importance of the demand for money. Though he shows that defects in the figures account for a sizable part of the crude discrepancy between changes in the recorded stock of money and in recorded prices, correction of these defects still leaves a puzzlingly large discrepancy that it does not seem possible to account for in terms of the variables introduced into the above exposition of the theory. Klein examined German experience precisely because it seemed the most deviant on a casual examination. Both it and other wartime experience will clearly repay further examination.

Cagan's examination of hyperinflations is another important piece of evidence on the stability of the demand for money under highly unstable conditions. It is also an interesting example of the difference between a numerically stable velocity and a stable functional relation: the numerical value of the velocity varied enormously during the hyperinflations, but this was a predictable response to the changes in the expected rate of changes of prices.

20. Though the essays in this book contain evidence relevant to the issues discussed in point 18, this is a by-product rather than their main purpose, which is rather to add to our tested knowledge about the characteristics of the demand function for money. In the process of doing so, they also raise some questions about the theoretical formulation and suggest some modifications it might be desirable to introduce. I shall comment on a few of those without attempting to summarize at all fully the essays themselves.

21. Selden's material covers the longest period of time and the most "normal" conditions. This is at once a virtue and a vice—a virtue, because it means that his results may be applicable most directly to ordinary peacetime experience; a vice, because "normality" is likely to spell little variation in the fundamental variables and hence a small base from which to judge their effect. The one variable that covers a rather broad range is real income, thanks to the length of the period. The secular rise in real income has been accompanied by a rise in real cash balances per unit of output—a decline in velocity—from which Selden concludes that the income elasticity of the demand for real balances is greater than unity— cash balances are a "luxury" in the terminology generally adopted. This entirely plausible result seems to be confirmed by evidence for other countries as well.

22. Selden finds that for cyclical periods velocity rises during expansions and falls during contractions, a result that at first glance

seems to contradict the secular result just cited. However, there is an alternative explanation entirely consistent with the secular result. It will be recalled that Y was introduced into equation (7) as an index of wealth. This has important implications for the measure or concept of income that is relevant. What is required by the theoretical analysis is not usual measured income—which in the main corresponds to current receipts corrected for double counting—but a longer term concept, "expected income," or what I have elsewhere called "permanent income."[5] Now suppose that the variables in the v function of (13) are unchanged for a period. The ratio of Y to M would then be unchanged, provided Y is *permanent* income. Velocity as Selden computes it is the ratio of *measured* income to the stock of money and would not be unchanged. When measured income was above permanent income, measured velocity would be relatively high, and conversely. Now measured income is presumably above permanent income at cyclical peaks and below permanent income at cyclical troughs. The observed positive conformity of measured velocity to cyclical changes of income may therefore reflect simply the difference between measured income and the concept relevant to equation (13).

23. Another point that is raised by Selden's work is the appropriate division of wealth into forms of assets. The division suggested above is, of course, only suggestive. Selden finds more useful the distinction between "short-term" and "long-term" bonds; he treats the former as "substitutes for money" and calls the return on the latter "the cost of holding money." He finds both to be significantly related to the quantity of money demanded. It was suggested above that this is also a way to take into account expectations about changes in interest rates.

Similarly, there is no hard-and-fast line between "money" and other assets, and for some purposes it may be desirable to distinguish between different forms of "money" (e.g., between currency and deposits). Some of these forms of money may pay interest or may involve service charges, in which case the positive or negative return will be a relevant variable in determining the division of money holdings among various forms.

24. By concentrating on hyperinflations, Cagan was able to bring into sharp relief a variable whose effect is generally hard to evaluate, namely, the rate of change of prices. The other side of this coin is the necessity of neglecting practically all the remaining variables. His device for estimating expected rates of change of prices from actual rates of change, which works so well for his data, can be carried over to other variables as well and so is likely to be important in fields other than money. I have already used it to estimate "expected income" as a determinant of consumption,[6]

and Gary Becker has experimented with using this "expected income" series in a demand function for money along the lines suggested above (in point 22).

Cagan's results make it clear that changes in the rate of change of prices, or in the return to an alternative form of holding wealth, have the expected effect on the quantity of money demanded: the higher the rate of change of prices, and thus the more attractive the alternative, the less the quantity of money demanded. This result is important not only directly but also because it is indirectly relevant to the effect of changes in the returns to other alternatives, such as rates of interest on various kinds of bonds. Our evidence on these is in some way less satisfactory because they have varied over so much smaller a range; tentative findings that the effect of changes in them is in the expected direction are greatly strengthened by Cagan's results.

One point which is suggested by the inapplicability of Cagan's relations to the final stages of the hyperinflations he studies is that it may at times be undesirable to replace the whole expected pattern of price movements by the rate of change expected at the moment, as Cagan does and as is done in point 5 above. For example, a given rate of price rise, expected to continue, say, for only a day, and to be followed by price stability, will clearly mean a higher (real) demand for money than the same rate of price rise expected to continue indefinitely; it will be worth incurring greater costs to avoid paying the latter than the former price. This is the same complication as occurs in demand analysis for a consumer good when it is necessary to include not only the present price but also past prices or future expected prices. This point may help explain not only Cagan's findings for the terminal stages but also Selden's findings that the inclusion of the rate of change of prices as part of the cost of holding money worsened rather than improved his estimated relations, though it may be that this result arises from a different source, namely, that it takes substantial actual rates of price change to produce firm enough and uniform enough expectations about price behavior for this variable to play a crucial role.

Similar comments are clearly relevant for expected changes in interest rates.

25. One of the chief reproaches directed at economics as an allegedly empirical science is that it can offer so few numerical "constants," that it has isolated so few fundamental regularities. The field of money is the chief example one can offer in rebuttal: there is perhaps no other empirical relation in economics that has been observed to recur so uniformly under so wide a variety of circumstances as the relation between substantial changes over short periods in the stock of money and in prices; the one is in-

variably linked with the other and is in the same direction; this uniformity is, I suspect, of the same order as many of the uniformities that form the basis of the physical sciences. And the uniformity is in more than direction. There is an extraordinary empirical stability and regularity to such magnitudes as income velocity that cannot but impress anyone who works extensively with monetary data. This very stability and regularity contributed to the downfall of the quantity theory, for it was overstated and expressed in unduly simple form; the numerical value of the velocity itself, whether income or transactions, was treated as a natural "constant." Now this it is not; and its failure to be so, first during and after World War I and then, to a lesser extent, after the crash of 1929, helped greatly to foster the reaction against the quantity theory. The studies in this volume are premised on a stability and regularity in monetary relations of a more sophisticated form than a numerically constant velocity. And they make, I believe, an important contribution toward extracting this stability and regularity, toward isolating the numerical "constants" of monetary behavior. It is by this criterion at any rate that I, and I believe also their authors, would wish them to be judged.*

NOTES

1. This is an oversimplification, because it neglects "leverage" and therefore supposes that any monetary liabilities of an enterprise are balanced by monetary assets.

2. In principle, it might be better to let P refer solely to the value of the services of physical goods, which is essentially what it refers to in the preceding cases, and to allow for the fact that the prices of the capital goods themselves must vary also with the rate of capitalization, so that the prices of services and their sources vary at the same rate only if the relevant interest rate is constant. I have neglected this refinement for simplicity; the neglect can perhaps be justified by the rapid depreciation of many of the physical goods held by final wealth-owning units.

3. See Reuben Kessel, "Inflation: Theory of Wealth Distribution and Application in Private Investment Policy" (unpublished doctoral dissertation, University of Chicago).

4. See Phillip Cagan, "The Monetary Dynamics of Hyperinflation," in Milton Friedman (ed.), *Studies in the Quantity Theory of Money* (Chicago: University of Chicago Press, 1956).

5. See Milton Friedman, *A Theory of the Consumption Function*, National Bureau of Economic Research (Princeton, N.J.: Princeton University Press, 1957).

6. See *ibid.*

* A concluding paragraph containing acknowledgments has been omitted. [Editor]

$\eta = 1.8$

3 *The Demand for Money: Some Theoretical and Empirical Results*

Milton Friedman *University of Chicago and National Bureau of Economic Research*

In countries experiencing a secular rise in real income per capita, the stock of money generally rises over long periods at a decidedly higher rate than does money income. Income velocity—the ratio of money income to the stock of money—therefore declines secularly as real income rises. During cycles, to judge from the United States, the only country for which a detailed analysis has been made, the stock of money generally rises during expansions at a lower rate than money income and either continues to rise during contractions or falls at a decidedly lower rate than money income. Income velocity therefore rises during cyclical expansions as real income rises and falls during cyclical contractions as real income falls—precisely the reverse of the secular relation between income and velocity.

These key facts about the secular and cyclical behavior of income velocity have been documented in a number of studies.[1] For the United States, Anna Schwartz and I have been able to document them more fully than has hitherto been possible, thanks

Reprinted from *Journal of Political Economy*, Vol. 67 (August 1959), 327–51, by permission of the author and The University of Chicago Press. Copyright 1959 by The University of Chicago Press.

The article summarizes part of the findings of the author's study with Anna J. Schwartz, *A Monetary History of the United States, 1867–1960* (Princeton, N.J.: Princeton University Press, 1963).

to a new series on the stock of money that we have constructed which gives estimates at annual or semi-annual dates from 1867 to 1907 and monthly thereafter. This fuller documentation does not, however, dispel the apparent contradiction between the secular and the cyclical behavior of income velocity. On the contrary, as the summary of our findings in the following section makes explicit, it reveals an additional contradiction or, rather, another aspect of the central contradiction.

Previous attempts to reconcile the secular and cyclical behavior of the velocity of circulation of money have concentrated on variables other than income, such as the rate of interest or the rate of change of prices. These attempts have been unsuccessful. While such other variables doubtless affect the quantity of money demanded and hence the velocity of circulation of money, most do not have a cyclical pattern that could explain the observed discrepancy. In any event, it seems dubious that their influence on velocity is sufficiently great to explain so large a discrepancy.

An alternative theoretical explanation of the discrepancy is suggested by the work I have done on consumption—a rather striking example of how work in one field can have important implications for work in another that has generally been regarded as only rather distantly related. This theoretical explanation, which concentrates on the meaning attached to "income" and to "prices," is presented in the first two sections below and turns out to be susceptible of quantitative test. The quantitative evidence on pages 98–104 is highly favorable. The result is both a fuller understanding of the observed behavior of velocity and a different emphasis in the theory of the demand for money.

One important feature of monetary behavior not accounted for by this explanation is the consistent tendency for actual cash balances, adjusted for trend, to lead at both peaks and troughs in general business. In the section on Tests of the Explanation, a preliminary attempt is made to explore factors that might account for the discrepancy between desired cash balances as determined by income alone and actual cash balances. Finally, in the last section, some broader implications of the results presented in this paper are explored.

A Summary of the Empirical Evidence for the United States

A full documentation of our findings about the secular and cyclical behavior of the stock of money and its relation to income and prices is given in *A Monetary History of the United States 1867–1910* by Anna J. Schwartz and myself. For present purposes, a brief summary of a few of our findings will suffice.

SECULAR BEHAVIOR

1. Secular changes in the real stock of money per capita are highly correlated with secular changes in real income per capita. In order to study this relation, we have used average values over complete reference cycles as our elementary observations. For twenty cycles measured from trough to trough and covering the period from 1870 to 1954, the simple correlation between the logarithm of the real stock of money per capita and the logarithm of real income per capita is 0.99, and the computed elasticity is 1.8.[2]

A 1 per cent increase in real income per capita has therefore, on the average, been associated with a 1.8 per cent increase in real cash balances per capita and hence with a 0.8 per cent *decrease* in income velocity. If we interpret these results as reflecting movements along a stable demand relation, they imply that money is a "luxury" in the terminology of consumption theory. Because of the strong trend element in the two series correlated, the high correlation alone does not justify much confidence that the statistical regression is a valid estimate of a demand relation rather than the result of an accidental difference in trends. However, additional evidence from other sources leads us to believe that it can be so regarded.

We have investigated the influence of both rates of interest and rates of change of prices. In our experiments, the rate of interest had an effect in the direction to be expected from theoretical considerations but too small to be statistically significant. We have not as yet been able to isolate by correlation techniques any effect of the rate of change of prices, though a historical analysis persuades us that such an effect is present.

2. Over the nine decades that we have studied, there have been a number of long swings in money income. As a matter of arithmetic, these swings in money income can be attributed to movements in the nominal stock of money and in velocity. If this is done, it turns out that the swings in the stock of money are in the opposite direction from those in velocity and so much larger in amplitude that they dominate the movements in money income. As a result, the long swings in prices mirror faithfully the long swings in the stock of money per unit of output. These long swings are much more marked in money income and in the nominal stock of money than in real income and in the real stock of money, which is to say that the long swings are largely price swings.

CYCLICAL BEHAVIOR

1. The real stock of money, like real income, conforms positively to the cycle; that is, it tends to rise during expansions and to fall, or to rise at a less rapid rate, during contractions. However, the amplitude of the movement in the real stock of money is decidedly smaller than in real income. If we allow for secular trends, a 1 per cent change in real income during a cycle is accompanied by a change in the real stock of money in the same direction of about one-fifth of 1 per cent.

It follows that income velocity tends to rise during cyclical expansions when real income is rising and to fall during cyclical contractions when real income is falling—that is, to conform positively. So far as we can tell from data that are mostly annual, velocity reaches both its peak and its trough at roughly the same time as general economic activity does.

2. Cyclical movements in money income, like the long swings, can be attributed to movements in the nominal stock of money and in velocity. If this is done, it turns out that the movements in the stock of money and in velocity are in the same direction and of roughly equal magnitude, so that neither can be said to dominate the movements in money income.

3. Table 1 summarizes the size of the cyclical movements in the variables used in the analysis, where the size of cyclical movement is measured by the excess of the rate of change per month during cyclical expansions over that during cyclical contractions.

THE CONTRAST

These findings are clearly in sharp contrast. Over long periods, *real* income and velocity tend to move in opposite directions; over reference cycles, in the same direction. Over long periods, changes in the nominal stock of money dominate, at least in a statistical sense, the swings in *money* income, and the inverse movements in velocity are of minor quantitative importance; over reference cycles, changes in velocity are in the same direction as changes in the nominal stock of money and are comparable in quantitative importance in accounting for changes in money income. I turn to an attempted reconciliation.

A SUGGESTED EXPLANATION

It is important to note at the outset an essential difference between the determinants of the nominal stock of money, on the one hand, and the real stock of money, on the other. The nominal

TABLE 1*   *Cyclical Movements in Income, Money Stock, Income Velocity, and Prices: Difference in Monthly Rate of Change Between Reference Expansion and Contraction, Annual Analysis, 1870–1954, Excluding War Cycles*

	CHANGE PER MONTH IN REFERENCE-CYCLE RELATIVES DURING REFERENCE		EXCESS OF EXPANSION OVER CONTRACTION
	Expansion (1)	*Contraction* (2)	CONTRACTION (3)
Twelve mild depression cycles:			
Money income	0.64	−0.07	0.71
Money stock	.55	.28	0.27
Income velocity	.08	− .32	0.40
Implicit price deflator	.12	− .02	0.14
Real income	.52	− .05	0.57
Real stock of money	.43	.30	0.13
Six deep depression cycles:			
Money income	.64	− .97	1.61
Money stock	.60	− .28	0.88
Income velocity	.02	− .69	0.71
Implicit price deflator	.16	− .44	0.60
Real income	.46	− .53	0.99
Real stock of money	0.42	0.18	0.24

* The series were analyzed as described in A. F. Burns and W. C. Mitchell, *Measuring Business Cycles* (New York: National Bureau of Economic Research, 1947), pp. 197–202. Because of rounding, col. 3 sometimes disagrees with the difference between cols. 1 and 2. Deep depression cycles are 1870–78, 1891–94, 1904–8, 1919–21, 1927–32, and 1932–38. All others are mild depression cycles except for war cycles 1914–19 and 1938–46, which are excluded. The basis of classification is described in the NBER monograph on the money supply now in preparation. *Money income* is net national product at current prices, preliminary estimates by Simon Kuznets, prepared for use in the NBER study of long-term trends in capital formation and financing in the United States, Variant III (from 1929 based on estimates of commodity flow and services prepared by the Department of Commerce). *Money stock* is averaged to center on June 30 from data in the money monograph just mentioned. *Income velocity* is money income divided annually by money stock. *Implicit price deflator* is money income divided by real income. *Real income* is net national product, 1929 prices, Variant III from the same source as money income. *Real stock of money* is money stock divided by the implicit price deflator.

stock of money is determined in the first instance by the monetary authorities or institutions and cannot be altered by the non-bank holders of money. The real stock of money is determined in the first instance by the holders of money.

This distinction is sharpest and least ambiguous in a hypothetical society in which money consists exclusively of a purely fiduciary currency issued by a single money-creating authority at its discretion. The nominal number of units of money is then whatever amount this authority creates. Holders of money cannot alter this amount directly. But they can make the real amount of money anything that in the aggregate they want to. If they want to hold a relatively small real quantity of money, they will individually seek to reduce their nominal cash balances by increasing expenditures. This will not alter the nominal stock of money to be held—if some individuals succeed in reducing their nominal cash balances, it will only be by transferring them to others. But it will raise the flow of expenditures and hence money income and prices and thereby reduce the real quantity of money to the desired level. Conversely, if they want to hold a relatively large real quantity of money, they will individually seek to increase their nominal cash balances. They cannot, in the aggregate, succeed in doing so. However, in the attempt, they will lower the nominal flow of expenditures, and hence money income and prices, and so raise the real quantity of money. Given the level of real income, the ratio of income to the stock of money, or income velocity, is uniquely determined by the real stock of money. Consequently, these comments apply also to income velocity. It, too, is determined by the holders of money, or, to put it differently, it is a reflection of their decisions about the real quantity of money that they desire to hold. We can therefore speak more or less interchangeably about decisions of holders of money to change their real stock of money or to change the ratio of the flow of income to the stock of money.

The situation is more complicated for the monetary arrangements that actually prevailed over the period which our data cover. During part of the period, when the United States was on an effective gold standard, an attempt by holders of money to reduce their cash balances relative to the flow of income raised domestic prices, thereby discouraging exports and encouraging imports, and so tended to increase the outflow of gold or reduce its inflow. In addition, the rise in domestic prices raised, among other things, the cost of producing gold and hence discouraged gold production. Both effects operated to reduce the nominal supply of money. Conversely, an attempt by holders of money to increase their cash balances relative to the flow of income tended to increase the nominal supply of money through the same channels. These effects still occur but can be and typically are offset by Federal Reserve action.

Throughout the period, more complicated reactions operated on the commercial banking system, sometimes in perverse fashion. For example, an attempt by holders of money to reduce cash balances relative to income tended to raise income and prices, thus promoting an expansionary atmosphere in which banks were generally willing to operate on a slenderer margin of liquidity. The result was an increase rather than a reduction in the nominal supply of money. Similarly, changes in the demand for money had effects on security prices and interest rates that affected the amount of money supplied by the banking system. And there were further effects on the actions of the Federal Reserve System for the period since 1914.

There were also indirect effects running in the opposite direction, from changes in the conditions of supply of money to the nominal quantity of money demanded. If, for whatever reason, money-creating institutions expanded the nominal quantity of money, this could have effects, at least in the first instance, on rates of interest and so on the quantity of money demanded, and perhaps also on money income and real income.

Despite these qualifications, all of which would have to be taken into account in a complete analysis, it seems useful to regard the nominal quantity of money as determined primarily by conditions of supply, and the real quantity of money and the income velocity of money as determined primarily by conditions of demand. This implies that we should examine the demand side for an initial interpretation of the observed behavior of velocity.

Along these lines, the changes in the real stock of money and in the income velocity of circulation reflect either (*a*) shifts along a relatively fixed demand schedule for money produced by changes in the variables entering into that schedule; (*b*) changes in the demand schedule itself; or (*c*) temporary departures from the schedule, that is, frictions that make the actual stock of money depart from the desired stock of money. The rest of this paper is an attempt to see to what extent we can reconcile the secular and cyclical behavior of velocity in terms of *a* alone without bringing in the more complicated phenomena that would be involved in *b* and *c*.

One way to do so would be to regard the cyclical changes in velocity as reflecting the influence of variables other than income. In order for this explanation to be satisfactory, these other variables would have to exert an influence opposite to that of income and also be sufficiently potent to dominate the movement of velocity. Our secular results render this implausible, for we there found that income appeared to be the dominant variable affecting the demand for real cash balances. Moreover, the other variables that come first to mind are interest rates, and these display cyclical patterns that seem most unlikely to account for the sizable, highly consistent, and roughly synchronous cyclical pattern in velocity. Long-term corporate interest rates fairly regularly reached their trough in mid-expansion and their peak in mid-contraction prior to World War I. Since then, the pattern is less regular and is characterized by shorter lags. Rates on short-term commercial paper also tend to lag at peaks and troughs, though by a briefer interval, and the lag has similarly shortened since 1921. Call-money rates come closer to being synchronous with the cycle, and this is true also of yields on long- and short-term government obligations for the six cycles for which they are available. Of the rates we have examined these are the only ones that have anything like the right timing pattern to account for the synchronous pattern in velocity. However, neither call-money rates nor government bond yields have been highly consistent in behavior from cycle to cycle. Even if they had been, it seems dubious that the effects of changes in these particular rates, or other unrecorded rates like them, would be sufficiently more important cyclically then secularly to offset the effects of counter-movements both in other rates and in income. Furthermore, earlier studies that have attempted to explain velocity movements in these terms have had only limited success.[3]

A very different way to reconcile the cyclical and secular behavior of velocity is to regard the statistical magnitude called "real income" as corresponding to a different theoretical construct in the cyclical than in the secular analysis. This possibility was suggested by my work on consumption. In that field, too, it will be recalled, there is an apparent conflict between empirical findings for short periods and long periods: cross-section data for individual years suggest that the average propensity to consume is lower at high-income levels than at low-income levels; yet aggregate time-series data covering a long period reveal no secular decline in the average propensity to consume with a rise in income. It turned out that this conflict could be reconciled by distinguishing between "measured" income, the figure recorded by statisticians, and "permanent" income, a longer-term concept to which individuals are regarded as adjusting their consumption.[4]

According to the permanent income hypothesis, when a consumer unit experiences a transitory increment of income, that is, when its measured income exceeds its permanent income, this transitory component is added to its assets (perhaps in the form of durable consumer goods) or used to reduce its liabilities rather than spent on consumption. Conversely, when it experiences a transitory decrement of income, it nonetheless adjusts consumption to permanent income, financing any excess over measured income by drawing down assets or increasing liabilities.

This theory of consumption behavior is directly applicable to that part of the stock of money held by consumer units rather than by business enterprises. The problem is how to interpret money holding. Much of the theoretical literature on "motives" for holding money suggests interpreting money holdings as one of the balance-sheet items that act as shock absorbers for transitory components of income; as an asset item that is increased temporarily when the transitory component is positive and that is drawn down, if necessary, to finance consumption when the transitory component is negative.

This interpretation may be valid for very short time periods. However, if it were valid for periods as long as a business cycle, it would produce a cyclical behavior of velocity precisely the opposite of the observed behavior. Measured income presumably exceeds permanent income at cyclical peaks and falls short of permanent income at cyclical troughs. Hence cash balances would be drawn down abnormally at troughs and built up abnormally at peaks. In consequence, cash balances would fluctuate more widely over the cycle than income, and velocity would conform inversely to the cycle, falling during expansions and rising during contractions, whereas in fact it conforms positively.

An alternative is to interpret money as a durable consumer good held for the services it renders and yielding a flow of services proportional to the stock, which implies that the shock-absorber function is performed by other items in the balance sheet, such as the stock of durable goods, consumer credit outstanding, personal debt, and perhaps securities held. On this interpretation, the quantity of money demanded, like the quantity of consumption services in general, is adapted not to measured income but to permanent income. This interpretation is consistent with our secular results. The income figure we used in obtaining these is an average value over a cycle, which may be regarded as a closer approximation to permanent income than an annual value. In any case, the long time period covered assures that the movements in money are dominated by the movements in the permanent component of income.[5] For the cyclical analysis, permanent income need not itself be stable over a cycle. It may well rise during expansions and fall during contractions. Presumably, however, it will rise less than measured income during expansions and fall less during contractions. Hence, if money holdings were adapted to permanent income, they might rise and fall more than in proportion to permanent income, as is required by our secular results, yet less than in proportion to measured income, as is required by our cyclical results.

To put the matter differently, suppose that the demand for real cash balances were determined entirely by real permanent income according to the relation estimated in the secular analysis and that actual balances throughout equaled desired balances. Velocity would then fall during expansions and rise (or fall at a smaller rate) during contractions, *provided* that it was computed by dividing *permanent income* by the stock of money. But the numbers we have been calling "velocity" were not computed in this way; they were computed by dividing measured income by the stock of money. Such a *measured* velocity would tend to be lower than what we may call *permanent* velocity at troughs, because measured income is then lower than permanent income and would tend to be higher at peaks, because measured income is then higher than permanent income. Measured velocity might therefore conform positively to the cycle, even though permanent velocity conformed inversely.

These comments apply explicitly only to consumer cash balances. However, they can readily be extended to business cash balances. Businesses hold cash as a productive resource. The question is whether cash is a resource like inventories, in which case it might be expected to fluctuate more over the cycle than current production, or like fixed capital, in which case it might be expected to fluctuate less and to be adapted to the longer-term level of production at which a firm plans to operate. This latter possibility involves a concept analogous to that of permanent income. If the observed positive cyclical conformity of velocity reflects wider movements in income than in both business holdings and consumer holdings, as seems likely in view of the changing importance of these two components and the consistent behavior of velocity, the answer must be that cash balances are analogous to fixed capital rather than to inventories and that some other assets or liabilities serve as shock absorbers for business as for consumers.

The distinction between permanent and measured income can rationalize the observed cyclical behavior of income velocity in terms of a movement along a stable demand curve. It cannot by itself easily rationalize the behavior of real cash balances. Our secular analysis implies that real cash balances should conform positively to the cycle with an amplitude nearly twice that of permanent real income. Observed real cash balances do conform positively, but their amplitude, at any rate for cycles containing mild contractions, is so small that it seems implausible to regard it as larger than that in permanent real income. Put differently, it would take only very moderate changes in the index of prices, well within the margin of error in such indexes, to convert the positive conformity into inverted conformity.

The resolution is straightforward. We have not yet carried our logic far enough. If applied to both money income and real income, the distinction between measured and permanent income implies a corresponding distinction for prices. To put the matter in terms of economics rather than arithmetic, our analysis suggests that holders of cash balances determine the amount to hold in light of their longer-term income position rather than their momentary receipts—this is the justification for distinguishing measured from permanent income. By the same token, they may be expected to determine the amount of cash balances to hold in light of longer-term price movements—permanent prices, as it were—rather than current or measured prices. Suppose, for example, prices were to double permanently or, alternatively, to double for day X only and then return to their initial level and that this behavior was correctly anticipated by holders of money. Holders of money would hardly want to hold the same nominal cash balances on day X in these two cases, even though prices were the same on that day. More generally, whatever the motives for holding cash balances, they are held and are expected to be held for a sizable and indefinite period of time. Holders of money presumably judge the "real" amount of cash balances in terms of the quantity of goods and services to which the balances are equivalent, not at any given moment of time, but over a sizable and indefinite period; that is, they evaluate them in terms of "expected" or "permanent" prices, not in terms of the current price level. This consideration does not, of course, rule out some adjustment to temporary movements in prices. Such movements offer opportunities of profit from shifting wealth from cash to other forms of assets and conversely, and they may affect people's expectations about future price levels. Like "permanent income," the "permanent" price level need not be—and presumably is not—a constant over time; it departs from the current price level in having a smoother and less fluctuating pattern in time but need not go to the extreme of displaying no fluctuations.

On this view, the current price level would presumably fall short of the permanent price level at troughs and exceed it at peaks of cycles; hence measured real cash balances would tend to be larger than permanent real cash balances at troughs and smaller at peaks. It follows that measured real cash balances would show a smaller cyclical movement than permanent real cash balances and, indeed, might conform inversely to the cycle, even though permanent real cash balances conformed positively.

A Symbolic Restatement

The distinction between permanent and measured magnitudes can thus reconcile the qualitative behavior during reference cycles of both measured velocity—its tendency to conform positively—and measured real cash balances—its tendency to show an exceedingly mild cyclical movement—with their behavior over secular periods. The crucial question remains whether it not only can reconcile the qualitative behavior but does in fact rationalize the quantitative behavior of these magnitudes. After all, an interpretation in terms of interest rates can also rationalize the qualitative results; we reject it because it appears likely to be contradicted on a more detailed quantitative level.

It will facilitate such a quantitative test to restate symbolically and more precisely the explanation just presented. Let

Y be measured aggregate income in nominal terms;

P be measured price level;

M be aggregate stock of money in nominal terms, measured and permanent being taken throughout as identical;

N be population, measured and permanent being taken as identical;

Y_p, P_p be permanent nominal aggregate income and permanent price level, respectively;

$y = \dfrac{Y}{P}$ be measured aggregate income in real terms;

$y_p = \dfrac{Y_p}{P_p}$ be permanent aggregate income in real terms;

$m = \dfrac{M}{P}$ be measured aggregate stock of money in real terms;

$m_p = \dfrac{M}{P_p}$ be permanent aggregate stock of money in real terms;

$V = \dfrac{Y}{M} = \dfrac{y}{m}$ be measured velocity;

$V_p = \dfrac{Y_p}{M} = \dfrac{y_p}{m_p}$ be permanent velocity.

In these symbols, the demand equation fitted to the secular data can be written thus:

$$\frac{M}{NP_p} = \gamma \left(\frac{Y_p}{NP_p}\right)^{\delta}, \tag{1}$$

which expresses permanent real balances per capita as a function of permanent real income per capita, or in the equivalent form,

$$m_p = \gamma N \left(\frac{y_p}{N}\right)^{\delta} = \gamma N^{1-\delta} y_p^{\delta}, \tag{2}$$

which expresses aggregate permanent real balances as a function of aggregate permanent real income and population, where γ and δ are parameters and δ was estimated to be approximately 1.8.[6]

By definition,

$$m = \frac{M}{P} = \frac{M}{P_p} \frac{P_p}{P} = \frac{P_p}{P} m_p,$$ (3)

so that still a third form of the demand equation is

$$m = \frac{P_p}{P} \gamma N^{1-\delta} y_p^{\delta},$$ (4)

which expresses aggregate measured real balances as a function of aggregate permanent real income, population, and permanent and measured prices.

This relation can also be expressed in terms of velocity. By definition, $V_p = y_p/m_p$. Divide y_p successively by the two sides of equation (2). This gives

$$V_p = \frac{y_p}{m_p} = \frac{1}{\gamma} N^{\delta-1} y_p^{1-\delta} = \frac{1}{\gamma} \left(\frac{y_p}{N}\right)^{1-\delta}.$$ (5)

By definition,

$$V = \frac{Y}{M} = \frac{Y}{Y_p} \frac{Y_p}{M} = \frac{Y}{Y_p} V_p,$$ (6)

so that

$$V = \frac{Y}{Y_p} \frac{1}{\gamma} \left(\frac{y_p}{N}\right)^{1-\delta}.$$ (7)

In interpreting equations (1), (2), (4), (5), and (7), it should be borne in mind that they will not, of course, be satisfied precisely by observed data. In consequence, at a later stage, I shall want to distinguish between observed values of, for example, measured velocity and the value estimated from, say, equation (7).

Tests of the Explanation

It has so far been sufficient to suppose only that the permanent magnitudes introduced—permanent income and permanent prices—fluctuate less over the cycle than the corresponding measured magnitudes. We can clearly go farther and ask how much less the permanent magnitudes must fluctuate in order to account for the quantitative, as well as the qualitative, average behavior of velocity and real cash balances. The answer may provide some internal evidence on the plausibility of the suggested explanation and will also provide a starting point for bringing external evidence to bear.

Consider the data for the mild depression cycles shown in Table 1 and neglect the mild cyclical movements in population, so that aggregate and per capita values can be regarded as interchangeable. If measured and permanent magnitudes were treated as identical, the income elasticity of 1.8 computed from the secular data would convert the 0.57 cyclical movement in real income into a movement of 1.03 in *real* cash balances demanded. The movement of 0.14 in the implicit price index would, in turn, convert this into a movement of 1.17 in *money* cash balances demanded. The actual movement in cash balances is 0.27, or 23 per cent as large. Hence, to reconcile the secular and cyclical results, the cyclical movements in permanent income and permanent prices would each have to be 23 per cent of those in measured income and measured prices—a result that seems not implausible. For deep depression cycles, the corresponding figure turns out to be 37 per cent, which is equally plausible. Moreover, it seems eminently reasonable that this figure should be larger for deep, than for mild, depression cycles, since the deep depression cycles are longer on the average than the mild depression cycles.[7]

Of course, this test of intuitive plausibility is a weak one. To get a stronger test, we must introduce some independent evidence on the relation of permanent to measured magnitudes. One source of such evidence is the work on consumption that suggested the explanation under test. In deriving a consumption function from aggregate time-series data, I concluded that an *estimate* of permanent income—which I called "expected" income to distinguish it from the theoretical concept—was given by

$$y_p(T) = \beta \int_{-\infty}^{T} e^{(\beta-\alpha)(t-T)} y(t) \, dt. \tag{8}$$

In words, an estimate of expected income at time T is given by a weighted average of past incomes, adjusted for secular growth at the rate of α per cent per year, the weights declining exponentially and being equal to $e^{\beta(t-T)}$, where t is the time of the observation being weighted. The numerical value of β was estimated to be 0.4; of α, 0.02.[8] It is by no means necessary that the concept of permanent income that is relevant in determining total consumption expenditures should also be the one that is relevant in determining cash balances.[9] But it would not be at all surprising if it were. On the assumption that it is, we can get independent estimates of the percentages cited in the previous paragraph by computing estimates of permanent real income and permanent prices from the corresponding observed annual series, using the weighting pattern just described.

The results of these computations are summarized in columns 1, 2, and 3 of Table 2.[10] The agreement between the estimates in column 3 so obtained and the estimates constructed above from internal evidence alone is very good—the two differ by only 15–30

TABLE 2*   *Two Estimates of Cyclical Movements of Permanent Real Income and Prices as Percentages of Those of Measured Real Income and Prices, Reference Cycles 1870–1954, Excluding War Cycles*

	EXCESS OF CHANGE PER MONTH IN REFERENCE-CYCLE RELATIVES DURING REFERENCE EXPANSION OVER THAT DURING REFERENCE CONTRACTION		PERMANENT AS PERCENTAGE OF MEASURED	
	Permanent magnitude (1)	*Measured magnitude* (2)	*Permanent estimated separately* (3)	*Ratio estimated from money equations* (4)
Twelve mild depression cycles:				
Real income	0.11	0.57	19	23
Prices	.02	.14	16	23
Six deep depression cycles:				
Real income	.29	.99	29	37
Prices	0.18	0.60	30	37

* The sources for the columns are as follows (cycles grouped as in Table 1):

1. Permanent real income and permanent prices were estimated as described in the text, using Kuznets' data (see note to Table 1). These data begin in 1869. To obtain an estimate of the permanent magnitude in 1869, measured figures covering the years 1858–69 are required, the weights assigned declining exponentially. Measured figures were therefore extrapolated: for real income by assuming a constant rate of growth of 3.5 per cent per year; for implicit prices by assuming that in each of the years 1858–68 they bore the same relation to the wholesale price index as in 1869.

2. Table 1, col. 3.

3. Column 1 divided by col. 2, the figures in each case being carried to an additional place.

4. Values from Table 1, col. 3, were substituted in the expression $M/(1.82\,\dot{y} + \dot{P})$, where M is money stock, y is real income, P is implicit price deflator, and the dot on top means "excess of change per month in reference-cycle relatives during reference expansion over that during reference contraction."

per cent, even though they are based on independent bodies of data and even though the weights used in estimating the permanent magnitudes directly were derived for another purpose and rest on still other data. Moreover, the discrepancy is consistent; the difference between deep and mild depression cycles is in the same direction and of roughly the same magnitude for both columns.

These results are sufficiently encouraging to justify going beyond this indirect test and seeing how far our interpretation is consistent not only with the size of the cyclical movement in cash balances and measured velocity but also with their entire cyclical patterns and not only on the average but also cycle by cycle.

In order to perform this test on a fully consistent basis, we first recomputed the secular demand equation, using as the independent variable the cycle averages of estimated permanent income rather than measured income. This substitution slightly raised the correlation coefficient, thus giving a minor bit of additional evidence in favor of the permanent income interpretation. It also raised slightly the estimated elasticity of demand, but not by enough to change the numerical value to the number of significant figures given above.

The resulting calculated equation for nominal cash balances is

$$M^* = (0.00323)\left(\frac{y_p}{N}\right)^{1.810} NP_p, \tag{9}$$

and, for measured velocity,

$$V^* = \frac{1}{0.00323}\left(\frac{y_p}{N}\right)^{-0.810}\frac{Y}{Y_p}, \tag{10}$$

where the asterisks are used to indicate values computed from the equation rather than directly observed. These equations, it will be recalled, were estimated from average values over whole reference cycles.[11]

From these equations, one can estimate for each year separately, from the corresponding annual data, desired cash balances and the value of measured velocity that would be observed if actual cash balances equaled desired balances as so estimated. I shall call these "computed cash balances" and "computed measured velocity."[12]

Figure 1. *Observed and Computed Measured Velocity, Annually, 1869–1957*

The estimates of computed measured velocity are plotted in Figure 1, along with observed measured velocity. In judging this figure, it should be borne in mind that the computed velocities were not obtained by trying to fit these observed velocities di-

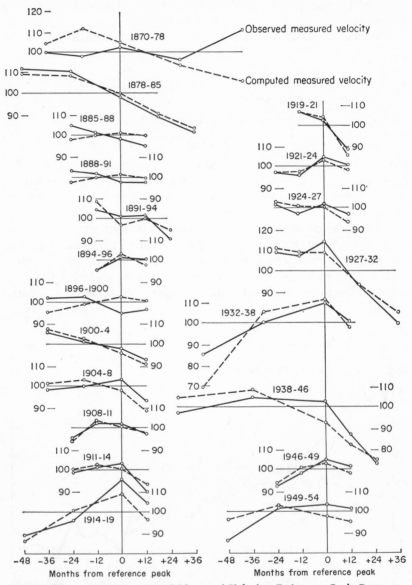

Figure 2. *Observed and Computed Measured Velocity, Reference-Cycle Patterns, 1870–1954*

NOTE: These are reference-cycle relatives computed in the course of the cyclical data shown in Figure 1 (see A. E. Burns and W. C. Mitchell, *Measuring Business Cycles* [New York: National Bureau of Economic Research, 1946], pp. 197–202).

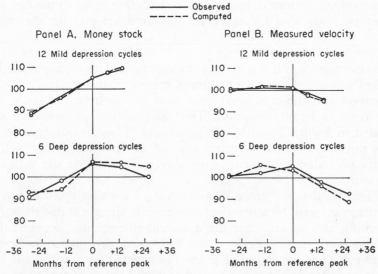

Figure 3. *Observed and Computed Money Stock and Measured Velocity, Average Reference-Cycle Patterns, Mild and Deep Depression Cycles, 1870–1954*

NOTE: Cycles are grouped as in Table 1.

rectly. They were obtained from a correlation for forty-one over-lapping cycle bases—averages of groups of years varying in number from two to seven—plus a formula for estimating permanent income derived from an analysis of the relation of consumption expenditures to income plus a theoretical linkage between these two, summarized in equations (9) and (10). The high correlation between the cycle bases insures a close connection between the longer-term movements in computed and measured velocity; in this respect, Figure 1 is simply a repetition in a different form of the secular finding. What is added by this chart is the relation between year-to-year movements. The secular results in no way insure that these will correspond; still, if anything, the computed velocity series mirrors the year-to-year cycles in observed velocity even more faithfully than it does the longer-term changes.

In order to isolate the cyclical aspect of the analysis, we have computed reference-cycle patterns of computed measured velocity and computed cash balances, thereby eliminating entirely the part of Figure 1 that repeats the secular finding. Figure 2 gives the reference-cycle patterns of computed and observed measured velocity cycle by cycle, and Figure 3 gives average patterns for the mild and deep depression cycles, for both cash balances and measured velocity. It is clear from these that my interpretation accounts for the bulk of the fluctuations in observed measured velocity.

The average pattern of computed measured velocity duplicates almost perfectly that for observed measured velocity for the mild depression cycles and corresponds very closely to that for the deep depression cycles. The cycle-by-cycle patterns demonstrate that this coincidence is not simply in the averages. This closeness might reflect the use of the same values of measured income in both the observed and the computed velocities, in which case it could be regarded as largely spurious. The cash-balance patterns are included in Figure 3 to test this possibility. They demonstrate that this purely statistical interpretation of the findings is not valid. The cash-balance patterns agree about as closely as the velocity patterns.

These results give strong support to the view that cyclical movements in velocity largely reflect movements along a stable demand curve for money and that the apparent discrepancy between the secular and the cyclical results reflects a divergence between measures of income and of prices constructed by statisticians for short periods and the magnitudes to which holders of money adjust their cash balances.

Limitations of the Explanation

Important though this explanation is, it cannot be the whole of the story, since it fails to account for some of the most important of our findings about the behavior of money balances. If the desired real stock of money were determined entirely by permanent real income and if the desired stock were always equal to the actual stock, then the actual real stock (computed in terms of permanent prices) would have a cyclical pattern that duplicated the pattern of permanent real income except for amplitude. Now our evidence suggests that permanent real income conforms positively to the cycle and is either synchronous or lags at the turning points. Hence real cash balances computed at permanent prices would do likewise. Nominal cash balances equal these real cash balances times permanent prices, and our evidence suggests equally that permanent prices conform positively to the cycle either synchronously or with a lag. This train of reasoning therefore implies that, under the supposed conditions, nominal cash balances would conform positively to the cycle and would be either synchronous or lag at the turning points. Yet one of the major findings of the broader study of which the results reported in this paper are a part is that the nominal stock of money, adjusted for trend, tends to lead at both peaks and troughs. Hence there is a residual element in the cyclical behavior of velocity that requires explanation.

A satisfactory analysis of this residual element requires the use of monthly rather than annual data. Annual data are unduly crude for studying timing relationships. For example, the cyclical patterns of the observed money stock in Figure 3, Panel A, reveal no average lead; yet our more detailed analysis of monthly money data establishes such a lead, after adjustment for trend, beyond any reasonable doubt.

It may nevertheless be worth examining the residual element in the annual data as a first step. This residual element is approximated in Figure 4 by the ratio of the observed measured velocity to computed measured velocity. This ratio varies very much less over the cycle than measured velocity itself, and hence the movements it measures tend to be concealed by the movements in velocity arising out of the discrepancy between measured and permanent income. Yet our analysis of the stock of money suggests that this residual element may play a critical cyclical role. Indeed, perhaps the major significance of our analysis of velocity is that it enables us to extract this residual element, to eliminate the largely spurious movements of velocity that have hitherto masked the economically significant movements.

For deep depressions, the residual element has a clearly marked cyclical pattern. During expansion, the residual element at first falls, then rises, reaching a trough in mid-expansion. During contractions, the behavior is harder to determine, because one cycle—the earliest, from 1870 to 1878—has a major influence on the pattern for all cycles and the figures for this cycle are highly dubious.[13] If this cycle is omitted, the pattern for contractions is a mild fall from peak to mid-contraction and a sharper fall thereafter.

The residual element varies much less, on the average, for mild depression cycles than for deep depression cycles. Such cyclical movement as it does show is similar to that for deep depression cycles during expansion and just the reverse of that for deep depression cycles during contraction. This residual element is the cyclical component in cash balances that cannot be explained simply by a movement along a univariate demand curve in response to a cyclical movement in permanent income. It is perhaps not surprising that this component should be so much larger for deep than for mild depression cycles. In the mild depression cycles, there is a relatively small cyclical movement in general, which presumably means that there are only relatively small movements in whatever other variables operate to produce a discrepancy between desired cash balances as judged from income alone and actual cash balances.

What are these other variables? The obvious candidates are measures of the return on other assets that could be held instead

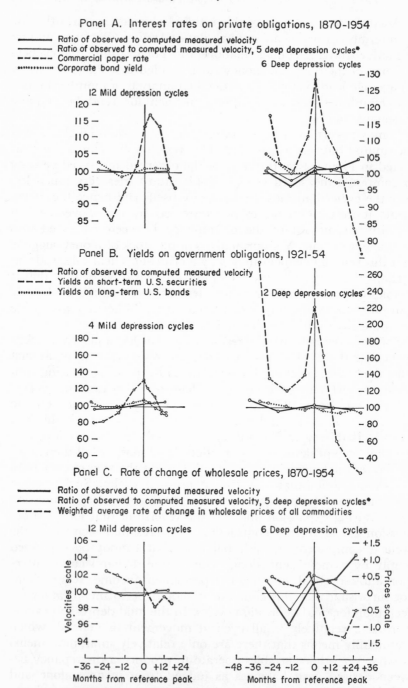

Figure 4. *Ratio of Observed to Computed Measured Velocity, Compared with Other Economic Variables, Average Reference-Cycle Patterns, Mild and Deep Depression Cycles, 1870–1954*

of money. One alternative to holding money is to hold securities; another, to hold physical goods. The return to the first is measured by the rate of return received on the securities. The return to the holding of physical goods is measured by the rate of change of prices minus storage costs; and either of these terms may be positive or negative—prices may rise or fall and storage of goods may yield a convenience return in excess of costs of handling and maintenance. In either case, these returns must be compared with those on money, which may be positive, as when interest is paid on deposits, or negative, as when service charges are incurred.

In our secular analysis, we have found that the yield on corporate bonds is correlated with the real stock of money and velocity in the expected direction: a rise in the bond yield tends to reduce the real stock of money demanded for a given real income—that is, to raise velocity—and conversely. Bond yields, however, play nothing like so important and regularly consistent a role in accounting for changes in velocity as does real income. The short-term interest rate was even less highly correlated with velocity than the yield on corporate bonds.

Figure 4 is designed to provide a rough test whether these secular results carry over to cyclical movements. In addition to the ratio of observed measured velocity to computed measured velocity, which is the residual element we are seeking to explain, Figure 4 also shows the average reference-cycle patterns of corporate bond yields as derived from annual data, of commercial paper rates as derived from monthly data (Panel A),[14] and of the yields on short- and long-term United States securities, as derived from monthly data (Panel B).[15] Panel A covers the whole period 1870–1954, excluding only war cycles; Panel B covers only the six non-war cycles after 1921, since yields on United States securities are not readily available for the earlier cycles.

Short-term rates have, of course, a much larger cyclical amplitude than long-term rates, which in turn have roughly the same amplitude as the residual element in velocity. These differences in amplitude are of no special significance for our purpose except as they reflect the consistency of the cyclical pattern, since the effect of a change in interest rates depends not only on the size of the change but also on the elasticity of the response of cash balances to a change. Volatility of rate can be offset by a small elasticity of response and vice versa. The differences in amplitude do, however,

NOTE: Vertical scales are in reference-cycle relatives, except scale for prices in Panel C, which is in rate of change of reference-cycle relatives per month. The scale of reference-cycle relatives in Panel B is one-fourth that in Panel A, and the scale in Panel C is two and a half times that in Panel A.

* Excluding 1870–78.

make it more difficult to read the chart and tend somewhat to obscure the similarity or divergence in pattern that is of major interest.

The most striking feature of the charts is the high degree of similarity between the pattern of interest rates and that of the residual element of velocity during the expansion phase of deep depression cycles. Long and short rates and rates on private and public obligations all show much the same pattern for this phase, and the pattern of all four is similar to the pattern in the residual element in velocity: interest rates are high at the initial stage of expansion, and so is velocity, which is an appropriate response to a high rate of return on non-cash assets; interest rates then decline to mid-expansion, and so does velocity; interest rates then rise to the peak of the cycle, and so does velocity.

There is no such unanimity of movement for the remaining phase of the deep depression cycles or for the mild depression cycles. For these phases, there is, at best, a family similarity between the movements in rates and those in the residual element in velocity. During the contraction phase of deep depression cycles, short and long rates diverge, short rates declining throughout, long rates leveling off or recovering in mid-contraction. The residual element behaves rather more like short rates, if we abstract from the unusual behavior during the 1870–78 cycle, but the similarity is not close in detail. For mild depression cycles, the cyclical movements in short and long rates are fairly similar, the main differences being a shorter lag in commercial paper rates at peaks and troughs than in the corporate bond yield. For the period as a whole (Panel A), the cyclical movement in the residual element, though fairly clear, is so small that no very precise comparison is justified; for the period since 1921 (Panel B), it is almost nonexistent, the average reference-cycle pattern being dominated by an intra-cycle trend.

A number of empirical studies have demonstrated that the rate of change of prices has an important effect on the quantity of money demanded during periods of considerable instability of prices—as during hyperinflations or major and long-continued inflations.[16] These studies suggest, further, that the expected rate of change of prices, which is the variable that directly influences the demand for money, can be regarded as derived largely from past experience with the actual movement of prices and that it changes more smoothly than actual prices; it is something like the rate of change in what I earlier designated "permanent" prices. These findings imply that any changes in the expected rate of change of prices during periods of relative price stability will be small, perhaps too small to have any appreciable effect. And this is, indeed, the conclusion reached by Richard Selden in his study of the behavior of velocity.[17]

As a further check on this conclusion, we have plotted in Figure 4, Panel C, the rate of change of prices from reference stage to reference stage. This is derived from the nine-stage reference-cycle patterns of the monthly wholesale price index,[18] by dividing the difference between successive average standings by the average time interval between them. The resulting eight rates of change per month are plotted at the mid-points of the corresponding intervals. Since these are the actual rates of change, they presumably vary more than expected rates of change and, in addition, may lead the latter in time. However, one might expect enough similarity between the actual rates of change and the expected rates of change to permit the detection of any moderately close relation between expected rate of change and the residual element in velocity.

Interestingly enough, the results largely duplicate those for interest rates. For the expansion phase of the deep depression cycles, there is the same striking agreement in pattern between the rate of change of prices and the residual element in velocity as there is between interest rates and the residual element. There is only slightly less similarity in pattern for the expansion phase of mild depression cycles. There is no systematic relation for the contraction phase of either group of cycles.

This analysis, based as it is on annual velocity data and on a comparison solely of average reference-cycle patterns, is too crude to be at all decisive. Yet the results are most suggestive. If the cyclical patterns of interest rates and the rate of change in prices are compared with the pattern of measured velocity itself (Figure 3, Panel B), there is no clear relation—as we noted at the outset in explaining why an alternative reconciliation of the secular and cyclical behavior of velocity is required. When the comparison is made instead with the residual element of velocity—that part of the movement in measured velocity that is accounted for neither by the effect of changes in permanent income on desired cash balances nor by the discrepancy between measured and permanent income—there is a striking consistency for one phase of one set of cycles, and at least a family resemblance elsewhere, though, of course, not without considerable irregularity. These results are of the kind that might be expected if the returns on alternative ways of holding assets were the chief factor other than permanent income affecting desired cash balances. Of course, they do not demonstrate that this is so. They might, for example, reflect accidental concurrence of movement in just a few cycles. And they do not provide any estimate of the quantitative strength of the connection. But they certainly justify further research in this direction. The main requirements for such research are the use of monthly data on velocity or indicators of velocity and the examination of cycle-by-cycle relations and not simply relations between average patterns.

Conclusion

The results summarized in this paper have implications for the theory of money, the study of business cycles, and the conduct and possibilities of monetary policy.

In the theory of money, much emphasis has been placed on different "motives" for holding money—the "transactions" motive, the "speculative" motive, and the "assets" or "precautionary" motive being the three commonly distinguished. The transactions motive is often regarded as implying something of a quasi-mechanical relation between cash balances and the flow of payments and is frequently given priority of importance as well as place. Our results cast serious doubt on the acceptability of this emphasis. In the first place, the cyclical results make it clear that changes in cash balances over short periods are adapted to magnitudes less volatile than the volume of transactions. In the second place, the secular decline in income velocity is hard to explain in terms of transactions. It is dubious that there has been any secular increase in the ratio of transactions to income large enough to explain the growth in the ratio of money balances to income that has occurred. Further, improvements in transportation and communication, let alone in financial organization, have almost surely reduced any mechanical requirement for cash balances per unit of transactions—indeed, it was on these grounds that Irving Fisher implied nearly half a century ago that velocity was likely to increase secularly and that others have since expressed similar views.[19]

Our findings equally cast doubt on the importance of the so-called speculative motive. One would expect this motive to be subject to wide cyclical variations and hence, if it dominated the demand for money, to lead to correspondingly wide cyclical variations in desired cash balances, whereas we observe the reverse.

The assets or "precautionary" motive is in a different state. Permanent income can be regarded as a concept closely allied to wealth and indeed as an index of wealth, provided that we count both human and non-human sources of income as components of total wealth. Along these lines, our results can be interpreted in either of two ways. One is that the relevant asset motive is equivalent to a consumption or income motive. As permanent income, which is to say, total wealth, rises, consumer units expand their expenditures on some items disproportionately—we term these items "luxuries." On this interpretation, the services rendered by money can be included among these luxuries. The other interpretation is more nearly an asset motive proper. It is that the holdings of cash are linked not to total wealth but primarily to non-human wealth and that, as permanent income rises, the total value of non-human wealth rises more rapidly than permanent income, either because such a more rapid rise is a necessary condition for a rise in income or because it corresponds to the preferences of individuals as their total wealth rises. Unfortunately, the available evidence on the secular or cyclical behavior of the ratio of non-human wealth to income is inadequate to provide a test of this explanation.[20] On either interpretation, however, our results suggest that motivations and variables linked with assets are the most fruitful category to explore—that the most fruitful approach is to regard money as one of a sequence of assets, on a par with bonds, equities, houses, consumer durable goods, and the like.

Our results have a bearing on another aspect of the so-called precautionary motive, namely, the view that the amount of cash balances held is highly sensitive to "the" or "a" rate of interest, at least for some range of rates of interest. If this were so for rates of interest within the range observed during the period our data cover, it would imply that real cash balances and the ratio of income to money would be highly variable, both secularly and cyclically, since small movements in interest rates would be accompanied by large movements in desired cash balances. The highly stable secular behavior of velocity is evidence against this view. So is our inability to find any close connection between changes in velocity from cycle to cycle and any of a number of interest rates. So also is our finding that most of the cyclical movement in income velocity as ordinarily measured can be accounted for by the use of measured rather than permanent income in the numerator. The remaining movement in velocity, though characterized by a consistent cyclical pattern and though, on the basis of our tentative explorations, it may well be accounted for by movements in interest rates, is much too small to reflect any very sensitive adjustment of cash balances to interest rates.

Some of these comments about the implications of our results for the theory of money have their direct and obvious counterparts for the empirical study of business cycles. The most important additional implications are two that have to do with the interpretation of cyclical movements in velocity. The fact that velocity changes have been about as important as changes in the stock of money in accounting, in an arithmetic sense, for the movements in money income, together with the small amplitude of cyclical movements in the stock of money, has fostered the view that changes in the stock of money cannot be the prime mover, or even of major independent importance, in cyclical change. This view may of course be correct, but it needs re-examination in light of our finding that most of the velocity movement is, from one point of view, "spurious," as well as a possible consequence of this finding, discussed more fully below, that measured income may be highly sensitive to changes in the stock of money. The other important implication for the study of cycles is that the cyclical pattern of velocity changes that needs study and explanation is very different from what it has been supposed to be. Measured velocity has a cyclical pattern roughly synchronous with that in general business, tending to rise relative to its trend from reference trough to reference peak and to fall from reference peak to reference trough. But when this pattern is corrected for the deviation of measured income from permanent income, the residual movement is very different, and it is the residual movement that needs explanation.

The most interesting implication of our analysis for monetary policy is highly speculative and involves taking our findings more seriously in detail than I can fully justify. It may nonetheless be worth recording if only in the hope of stimulating further work. Suppose one accepts fully both the reasonably well-supported finding that money holdings are adapted to permanent magnitudes and also the much more questionable and tentative suggestion that the economic factors derive their estimates of permanent magnitudes from prior measured magnitudes by implicitly constructing some kind of weighted average of them. It will then follow that, given a stable demand function for money, measured income will be highly sensitive in short periods to changes in the nominal stock of money—the short-run money multiplier will be large and decidedly higher than the long-run money multiplier.[21] To illustrate with some figures based on our tentative results: In the long run, if we take real income as given, a $1 increase in the stock of money would imply an annual level of money income higher than otherwise by $1 times the velocity of circulation, or, at current levels of velocity, about $1.50 higher—the long-run money multiplier equals the velocity of circulation. In the short run, however, an increase of $1.50 in measured income would be inadequate, since that much of a rise in measured income would raise permanent money income by decidedly less than $1.50 and hence desired cash balances by less than $1. If we take a year as our unit and accept the numerical weights we have used in estimating permanent income from measured income, measured income would have to rise by roughly $4.50 for estimated permanent income to rise by $1.50, the rise required to raise desired cash balances by $1 for given real income—the short-run money multiplier is thus triple the long-run multiplier.

The story does not, of course, end here. There would be carry-over effects into future years, as estimated permanent income continued to be revised in the light of measured income. These would make the initially assumed rise in money income not sustainable without further rises in the stock of money and hence would give rise to a cyclical reaction in measured income. Further, the assumed change in money income would presumably be associated with changes in output and in prices that would affect the relation of desired cash balances to the change in measured money income. These further complications require much more study than I have given them. They do not, however, affect the main point—the sensitivity of measured income to changes in the stock of money that is implied by our results if they are accepted at face value.

It is interesting that the permanent-income hypothesis should have such contrasting implications for the sensitivity of the economy to changes in the stock of money and to changes in investment—the major other factor regarded as a prime mover in cyclical change. The permanent-income hypothesis implies that the economy is much less sensitive to changes in investment than it would be if consumption were adapted to measured rather than permanent income—the short-run investment multiplier is decidedly smaller than the long-run multiplier.[22] On the other hand, we have just seen that the economy is much more sensitive to changes in the stock of money than it would be if money balances were adapted to measured rather than permanent income.

A corollary for policy is that the effects of monetary policy may be expected to operate rather more than would otherwise be supposed through the direct effects of changes in the stock of money on spending, and rather less through indirect effects on rates of interest, thence on investment, and thence on income. Another corollary is to emphasize the potency of relatively small changes in the stock of money—a potency, needless to say, for good or evil. Relatively small changes in the stock of money, properly timed and correct in magnitude, may be adequate to offset other changes making for instability. On the other hand, relatively small changes in the stock of money, random in timing and size, may equally be an important source of instability. If the reaction mechanism I have described is in any substantial measure valid, the system may not have a large tolerance for mistakes in monetary management.

NOTES

1. See in particular Richard T. Selden, "Monetary Velocity in the United States," in Milton Friedman (ed.), *Studies in the Quantity Theory of Money* (Chicago: University of Chicago Press, 1956), pp. 179–257; and Ernest Doblin, "The Ratio of Income to Money Supply: An International Survey," *Review of Economics and Statistics* (August 1951), p. 201.

2. The corresponding figures for cycles measured from peak to peak are 0.99 and 1.7. In these and later correlations, "money" is defined as including currency held by the public, adjusted demand deposits, and time deposits in commercial banks. This total is available for the period from 1867 on, whereas the total exclusive of time deposits is not available until 1914. For other reasons supporting our definition see our *A Monetary History of the United States 1860–1960*. For income, we have used Simon Kuznets' estimates of net national product adjusted for wartime periods to a concept approximating that underlying the current Department of Commerce estimates, and for prices, the deflator implicit in Kuznets' estimates of net national product in constant prices.

3. E.g., see Selden, *op. cit.*, pp. 195–202.

4. See my *A Theory of the Consumption Function* (a publication of the National Bureau of Economic Research) (Princeton: Princeton University Press, 1957).

5. *Ibid.*, pp. 125–29.

6. The basic analysis holds, of course, whatever the precise form of the demand equation for money. I use this particular form for simplicity and because it gave a satisfactory fit to the available evidence. The whole analysis could, however, be restated in terms of a generalized demand function whose form was unspecified.

7. Let $\dot{M}$ and $\dot{P}$ be the cyclical movements as measured in the final column of Table 1 in the nominal stock of money and in measured prices; let $\dot{m}_p$ and $\dot{P}_p$ be the cyclical movements in permanent real balances and permanent prices. Then, to a first approximation,

$$\dot{M} = \dot{m}_p + \dot{P}_p, \tag{i}$$

since the stock of money is the product of permanent real cash balances and the permanent price level. Using the demand equation (2), we get

$$\dot{m} = 1.8\,\dot{y}_p, \tag{ii}$$

where $\dot{y}_p$ is the cyclical movement in permanent real income (recall that we are neglecting any cyclical movement in population, so $\dot{y}_p$ also equals the movement in permanent real per capita income).

Let

$$\dot{y}_p = k\dot{y}, \tag{iii}$$
$$\dot{P}_p = k'\dot{P}, \tag{iv}$$

where $\dot{y}$ is the cyclical movement in measured real income and k and k' are unspecified constants to be determined. Substituting equations (ii), (iii), and (iv) in equation (i) gives

$$\dot{M} = 1.8k\dot{y} + k'\dot{P}. \qquad \text{(v)}$$

At first glance, it seems possible to derive both k and k' from one set of data by deriving a similar equation starting with an identity like (i) expressing measured velocity in terms of permanent velocity. However, the resulting equation is identical with eq. (v), thanks to the definitional relations connecting velocity, money, and income.

The calculations in the text implicitly assume that $k = k'$ in eq. (v). Separate estimates for k and k' require two sets of data. One possibility is to assume that k and k' differ but that each is the same for mild and for deep depression cycles, an assumption that seems less plausible than the one made in the text that $k = k'$. This calculation yields an estimate of 0.11 for k and 1.15 for k'. The value for k' contradicts the concepts of permanent and measured prices that underlie the analysis.

8. Friedman, *A Theory of the Consumption Function*, pp. 146–47.

9. See *ibid.*, pp. 150–51.

10. These results at first seemed to me relevant also to the choice between the two alternative assumptions used above—the one in the text that $k = k'$ and the one noted in footnote 7, that $k \neq k'$ but that k is the same for mild and deep depression cycles and so is k'. On this issue, the result is unambiguous. The entries in col. 3 clearly speak for the first assumption.

However, James Ford has pointed out to me that this result is largely a consequence of an assumption made in estimating permanent income and prices, namely, the use of the same value of β for both. There is no independent empirical evidence for this assumption, and hence results based on it can give no independent evidence for the essentially equivalent assumption that $k = k'$.

For the special case in which the measured magnitude is given by a sine curve, the relative amplitude of a permanent and a measured magnitude when the permanent is estimated by a weighted average of the measured is determined entirely by the value of β and the duration of the cycle. For $\beta = 0.4$ and a cycle 43 months in length, which is the average length of the mild depression cycles, the relative amplitude for the sine curve is 0.22. For $\beta = 0.4$ and a cycle 47.5 months in length, the average length of the deep depression cycles, the relative amplitude for the sine curve is 0.25. These results are fairly similar to the computed values in Table 2. They differ enough, however, to suggest that the departure from a sine curve affects the results appreciably.

I am indebted to James Ford for these calculations.

11. The numerical values given were computed from combined data for trough-to-trough and peak-to-peak averages. However, separate regressions for each set of averages are almost identical.

12. To make these calculations, estimates of Y, Y_p, y_p, P_p, and N are needed. Measured money income, Y, was taken to be Kuznets' annual net national product in current prices adjusted for wartime periods; Y_p was computed by applying eq. (8) to this same series, except for a minor adjustment in level; y_p, by applying eq. (8) to Kuznets' net national

product in constant prices similarly adjusted, and again with a minor adjustment in level; P_p by applying eq. (8) to the price index implicit in computing net national product in constant prices; and N was taken as the mid-year population of the United States as estimated by the Census.

Equation (8) with $\beta = 0.40$ and $\alpha = 0.02$ implies that expected income is 1.05 times the weighted average of actual income, where the weights are the declining exponential weights inside the integral of eq. (8), adjusted to sum to unity. When permanent net national product per capita in constant prices was computed in this way, it turned out that the geometric mean of the ratios of the cycle bases of real measured net national product per capita to the cycle bases of permanent net national product in constant prices so computed was 1.057. This factor of 1.057 was used to adjust the level of the latter series rather than the 1.05 strictly called for by eq. (8) and was used also for permanent net national product in current prices. The logical implication of employing the same multiple for net national product in constant and current prices is that α was treated as zero for prices alone. None of these adjustments is of any moment for the present analysis, since they affect only the level of the series and hence all cancel out when cycle relatives are computed.

13. The problem is in the income estimates for the early period. These are characterized by an extraordinarily rapid rate of increase from 1869 to 1879. Other evidence suggests that this is at least partly a statistical artifact, reflecting the extreme paucity of reliable data for estimating income for this period.

14. The corporate bond yield data through 1900 are railroad bond yields from F. R. Macaulay, *Some Theoretical Problems Suggested by the Movements of Interest Rates, Bond Yields and Stock Prices in the United States since 1856*, a publication of the National Bureau of Economic Research (New York 1938), pp. A145–A152, col. 5, with 0.114 per cent arithmetic addition to raise them to the level of the following segment. After 1900 the data are "Basic Yields of Corporate Bonds to 50 Years Maturity," from *Historical Statistics of the United States, 1789–1945* (Bureau of the Census), p. 279; *Continuation to 1952 of Historical Statistics*, p. 36; *Statistical Abstract of the United States*, annually from 1953. Commercial paper rates in New York City, monthly, through January, 1937, are from Macaulay, *op. cit.*, pp. A145–A161; thereafter, monthly averages of weekly figures from *Bank and Quotation Record of the Commercial and Financial Chronicle*. This series was seasonally adjusted through December, 1933. No seasonal adjustment has been necessary since.

15. Yields on short-term United States securities are from *Banking and Monetary Statistics*, p. 460, and *Federal Reserve Bulletin*, monthly issues, May, 1945, to May, 1948, and September, 1950, to December, 1954. This series was seasonally adjusted, 1920–30, 1951–54. Yields on long-term United States securities are from the same sources and are unadjusted.

16. See Phillip Cagan, "The Monetary Dynamics of Hyperinflation," in Milton Friedman (ed.), *Studies in the Quantity Theory of Money*, pp. 25–117. The same relation has been documented for other countries and episodes in a number of unpublished studies done in the Workshop on Money and Banking of the University of Chicago.

17. Selden, *op. cit.*, p. 202.

18. *Historical Statistics of the United States, 1789–1945* (Warren-Pearson series, 1870–89; B.L.S. series, 1890–1945 [Bureau of the Census]), p. 344; *Continuation to 1952 of Historical Statistics*, p. 47; thereafter, U.S. Department of Labor, Bureau of Labor Statistics, *Wholesale (Primary Market) Price Index*, monthly issues.

19. Irving Fisher, *The Purchasing Power of Money*, rev. ed. (New York 1913), pp. 79–88.

20. Raymond Goldsmith's estimates in *A Study of Saving* (Princeton, N.J. 1955) suggest that, if anything, the ratio of non-human wealth to income has declined secularly rather than risen.

21. This point was first suggested to me by Gary S. Becker.

22. See *A Theory of the Consumption Function*, p. 238.

4 Cash Balances and the Interest Rate—A Pragmatic Approach

Henry A. Latané *University of North Carolina*

This paper is concerned with the interrelations of cash balances, that is, demand deposits adjusted plus currency in circulation (M), national income in current dollars (Y), and long-term interest rates on high-grade obligations. In it we attempt first to set up hypothetical aggregative equations involving the two variables, cash balances as proportion of income (M/Y) and the interest rate (r); second, to select appropriate statistical series to measure the variables; and third, to test the equations. Quantitative relationships which have been statistically significant in the past are developed in this manner. Policy implications are discussed.

Aggregative Equations

We will test four equations:

1. The crude Cambridge version of the quantity theory of money may be expressed by the following equation:

$$M/Y = k. \tag{1.1}$$

Reprinted from *Review of Economics and Statistics*, Vol. 36 (Cambridge, Mass.: Harvard University Press, November 1954), 456–60, by permission of the author and publisher. Copyright, 1954, by the President and Fellows of Harvard College.

Latané published a sequel to this article, "Income Velocity and Interest Rates: A Pragmatic Approach," *Review of Economics and Statistics*, Vol. 42 (November 1960), 443–49, in which he fitted the function, $\log M/Y = a \log r + b$, to data for the period 1909–58. He concluded his results were "consistent with the hypothesis that there has been a rather constant interest elasticity of demand for cash balances of approximately .85 over this period." He did not find any secular trend in the income velocity of money.

This assumes that cash balances tend to be a fixed proportion of income whatever the interest rate. Equation (1.1) forms the basis for our first test.

2. Keynesian theory emphasizes the separation of money into its two functions as a store of value and as a medium of exchange. Following Modigliani in his "Liquidity Preference and the Theory of Interest and Money,"[1] we may use the following as a first approximation:

$$M = D_a(r) + D_T(Y) \qquad (2.1)$$

where D_a is the demand for money as an asset and D_T is demand for money to spend. It is assumed as a first approximation that the demand for money as an asset is a function of the interest rate and the demand for money as a medium of exchange is a function of income. This assumption is open to question even as a first approximation because it ignores the effect of the interest rate on the opportunity cost of holding money for transactions,[2] and it also ignores the effect of the income level on the desire to hold money as an asset.

Equation (2.1) can be made operative by assuming linearity in Y and the reciprocal of r. We then have:

$$M = a/r + bY + c \qquad (2.2)$$

which is based on the assumption that the demand for money as an asset varies inversely with the interest rate, and the demand for money as a medium of exchange varies directly with income.[3] We will test this form.

3. A modified quantity theory equation may be stated in the form:

$$M/Y = f_1(r). \qquad (3.1)$$

This states that the proportion of income which is held in cash balances is a function of the interest rate. There are several reasons for thinking that this form of the equation of exchange may be a reasonably satisfactory tool for exploring the interrelations of the three variables. It bypasses the major problem of separation of money by use. This seems fully justified as both types of monetary uses, that is, as a store of value and as a medium of exchange, clearly are influenced by both the interest rate and the level of income. As both types of monetary demand are affected in the same direction by the two forces under consideration, there seems to be no major reason to separate the two types in our equation.

Equation (3.1) can be made operative by changing to:

$$M/Y = c/r + d. \qquad (3.2)$$

We will test it in this form.[4]

4. In equation (3.1) we have assumed that the interest rate was the independent, and the proportionate cash balances, M/Y, the dependent variable. That is, the direction of causation was assumed to flow from the interest rate to the size of the cash balances in proportion to the income. If it is assumed that the cash balances relative to income determine the interest rate, equation (3.1) becomes:

$$r = f_2(M/Y) \tag{4.1}$$

which can be converted to:

$$1/r = g(M/Y) + h \tag{4.2}$$

where g is a constant coefficient. This form also can be tested.

STATISTICAL DATA

We are dealing with aggregates and broad economic classes. Differing quantitative results will flow from differing selections of representative indexes. We know that there are many different types of monies and near-monies which are held for many different reasons. Likewise, there is not one interest rate but a whole range of rates and yields. The income of one segment of the economy may have a far different effect on the demand for money and on interest rates than the income of another group. If we attempt to allow for all of these factors, we become lost in the web of interrelations. In spite of these qualifications, we believe that there are now available statistical data sufficiently accurate to permit broad tests of our equations. We use the following definitions and sources of data:

M: demand deposits adjusted plus currency in circulation on the mid-year call date (Federal Reserve Board data). We have limited money to this definition to avoid all the complexities of the near-monies, none of which is a final means of payment.

Y: Gross National Product—Department of Commerce series from 1929 to date; 1919–28 Federal Reserve Board estimates on the same basis (National Industrial Conference Board, *Economic Almanac*, 1952, p. 201); 1889–1919 from Kuznets, *National Product Since 1869*, p. 119, increased by 9.5% which is the average difference in the two series during the overlap from 1919–38.

r: interest rate on high-grade long-term corporate obligations. The U. S. Treasury series giving the yields on corporate high-grade bonds as reported in the *Federal Reserve Bulletin* is used from 1936 to date. Before 1936 we use annual averages of Macaulay's high-grade railroad bond yields given in column 5, Table 10, of his *Bond Yields, Interest Rates, Stock Prices*.

M/Y: the ratio of cash balances to income, as defined above, is used both as the independent and the dependent variable in our tests. We make no attempt to solve the problem of whether money is an exogenous or an endogenous variable in the system. In other words, we examine the stability and attempt to explain changes in the ratio M/Y, but do not attempt to determine whether this stability is brought about by adjustments in Y to a given level of M or whether M itself is determined by the level of income.

$1/r$: the reciprocal of the interest rate is also used either as the independent or the dependent variable. The reciprocal is used because theory calls for the demand for money to vary inversely with the interest rate and therefore directly with the reciprocal of the interest rate. The use of the reciprocal has another important justification in that the loss or gain in capital value to the holder of a perpetual obligation due to a change in interest rates, measured in time, is closely related to the change in $1/r$. For example, a .09 change in the interest rate from 3.00% to 3.09% would reduce $1/r$ by .9709 and would cost the holder of a perpetual bond a full year's interest through a decline in capitalized value. Similarly, a change in the interest rate from 6.00% to 6.36% would cost the holder of a perpetual obligation a loss in capitalized value equivalent to one year's interest, and $1/r$ would decline .9434.

We have reasonably satisfactory annual data on the indicated series extending back to 1919. The period 1919–52 is used to make the basic tests of the models.

Tests of Equations

1. $M/Y = k$ (1.1)

It is apparent from the data for the past 33 years, shown in Figure 1, that M/Y is much more stable than either M or Y, but that, even so, it is subject to wide variations. Little is to be gained from assuming it a constant as is done in equation (1.1). The fit over various periods can be improved if time is introduced as a variable. For example, Lawrence Klein in *Economic Fluctuations in the United States 1921–1941* (Cowles Commission, 1950), p. 109, develops the equation

$$M = 8.45 + .24Y_1 + .03Y_1(t-1931) - 1.43(t-1931) + u \qquad (1.2)$$

to fit the period 1921–41; Y_1 is the Net National Product in current dollars, t is time, and u is the error term. This equation fits the period for which it was designed, but cannot be extended and does not seem to have any justification in logic. If carried back to

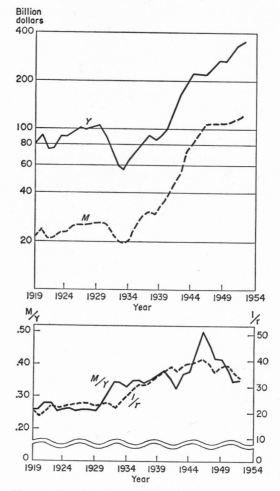

Figure 1. *Data for Test of* M/Y=k *(Equation 1.1),*
Annual Data

the 1904–13 decade, it gives an estimated value for M which is three times the actual. Likewise, if the estimate is carried through to 1952 it would give an estimate of M about three times larger than the actual. There seems to be no logic in the assumption, implicit in equation (1.2), that the demand for money as a percentage of the national income—$.03Y_1(t-1931)$—increases with time and the absolute demand for money—$1.43(t-1931)$—decreases.

2. $M = a/r + bY + c$ 　　　　　　　　　　　　　(2.2)

This equation (2.2) can be converted to the form

$$M/Y = a/rY + b + c/Y.$$ 　　　　　　　　(2.3)

In this form it is clearly faulty. The fractions a/rY and c/Y will get smaller as Y increases if r remains relatively constant. In other words the cash balance as proportion of income would get smaller as income increases if the rate of interest remains relatively steady. This assumption does not fit the data. For example, in the period 1938–52, Y quadrupled, yet M/Y and r were about the same at the end as at the beginning.

In *Economic Fluctuations in the United States 1921–1941*, p. 110, Klein tested for the effects of the interest rate on the demand for money, using an equation of the same general form as our (2.2). On the basis of this test, he concluded that the desire to hold demand deposits was not significantly affected by the interest rate in the period 1921–41. The test may have failed because (a) the type of equation is unsatisfactory in itself, as is indicated above, or (b) Klein assumed a linear relationship between demand for money and r rather than its reciprocal in making his calculations.

3. $M/Y = c/r + d$ \hfill (3.2)

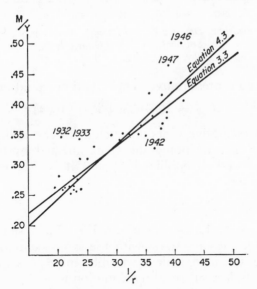

Figure 2. *Data for Test of M/Y=c/r+d*
(Equation 3.2), Annual Data, 1919–52

The scatter diagram shown in Figure 2 was prepared to test equation (3.2). The regression line equation

$$M/Y = .0074328/r + .10874 \qquad (3.3)$$

was derived by the least-squares method, excluding the data for the years 1932, 1933, 1942, 1946, and 1947 because they were

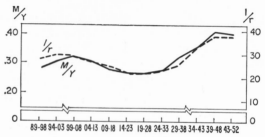

Figure 3a. *Data for Test of* $1/r = g\,(M/Y) + h$,
Ten-Year Averages, 1889–1952

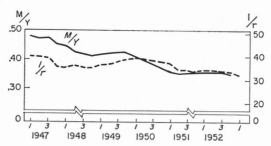

Figure 3b. *Data for Test of* $1/r = g\,(M/Y) + h$,
*Seasonally Adjusted Quarterly Data
at Annual Rates*

not considered representative. The equation would be

$$M/Y = .00795304/r + .100418 \qquad (3.4)$$

if the unrepresentative years are included. The coefficient of correlation is .87173 including the years affected by bank failures, mobilization, and demobilization; and it is .911 excluding the years so affected.

4. $1/r = g(M/Y) + h$ \qquad\qquad\qquad (4.2)

Equation (4.3) $1/r = 111.775M/Y - 7.233$ shows the least-squares fit for the same data with the same exclusions, assuming that M/Y is the independent variable and $1/r$ is the dependent variable. Including all years the equation is

$$1/r = 95.4M/Y - 2.44. \qquad (4.4)$$

From the data available, it is impossible to tell which is the independent and which the dependent variable. Consequently, it is impossible to choose between equation (3.3) and (4.3) on the basis of this test. Whatever the direction of causation, the correlation is high considering the number of observations, the few degrees of freedom sacrificed by the form of the equation, and the number of changes in trend involved.

If the relations derived from data in one period explain events in other periods their claim for recognition is increased. As is apparent from Figure 2 equations (3.3) and (4.3) do not differ substantially in the area of past experience. The formula

$$M/Y = .008/r + .09 \qquad (3.5)$$

or

$$1/r = 125M/Y - 11.25 \qquad (4.5)$$

falls between the two lines and is taken as a satisfactory approximation to a joint estimating equation. This formula was used in setting the scales for M/Y and $1/r$ in Figure 1. Similar comparisons are shown in Figures 3 showing (3a) ten-year averages going back to 1889 and (3b) quarterly data since 1947. The fit seems to indicate that the structural relations established from the 1919–52 data had some significance both over the longer period and currently.

Implications of Formula

Based on the above, equation (3.5) seems to be a reasonable joint estimating equation for the relationship between cash balances as a proportion of income and the long-term interest rate. This relationship is linear between M/Y and $1/r$. In the past thirty years each 1.0% change in $1/r$ has tended to be associated with a change of .8% in gross national product held as currency and demand deposits.

The relationship between M/Y and r (rather than $1/r$) is shown in Figure 4. As is apparent from this chart, changes in interest

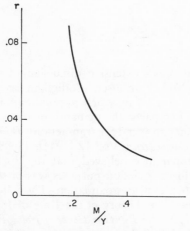

Figure 4. *Data for Relationship of M/Y and r*

rates have relatively little absolute effect on the size of cash balances associated with given levels of income as long as the interest rate is relatively high, say above 5%. When rates are 3% or under, on the other hand, changes in interest rates have a substantial absolute effect on M/Y. When interest rates drop from 8% to 7% there is an increase in the associated M/Y of only 1.4 points from 19% to 20.4%. When rates drop from 3% to 2%, however, M/Y tends to rise from 35.7% to 49%.

On a proportionate basis the effects of a change in the interest rate are much more stable over the range of experience. When the interest rate drops by 10%, from 8% to 7.2%, we would expect the proportionate cash balances (M/Y) to increase 5.8%, from 19% to 20.1% based on past experience. Likewise, when the interest rate drops 10%, from 3% to 2.7%, M/Y should increase 8.2%, from 35.7% to 38.6%.

Conclusion

The policy implications of changes in long-term interest rates are especially important at this time of debt-funding. It is clear that a higher rate tends to be associated with a speed-up in the turnover of money. Conversely, a decline in rates has been associated with an increased demand for cash balances at a given level of income. Based on past experience an increase in the yield on long-term high-grade corporate bonds from 3.00% to, say, 3.30% would tend to be associated with a 7.5% expansion in income if cash balances remained constant. Whether this will prove true in the future, the effect is important enough to deserve careful consideration when formulating monetary and fiscal policy.

NOTES

1. At the conclusion of an extensive discussion of the demand for money for transactions and as an asset, Modigliani says, "On the basis of these considerations we may, in a first approximation, split the total demand for money into two parts: the demand for money to hold, $D\ (r)$, and the demand for money to spend for transactions, $D\ (Y)$; and write . . . [our equation (2.1)]" (*Econometrica*, Vol. 12 [1944], 45–88).

2. Keynes himself apparently believed that the opportunity cost of holding cash balances for transaction purposes was of some importance but could be ignored as a first approximation. The following quotation is taken from his article "The Theory of the Rate of Interest" included in *Lessons of Monetary Experience: Essays in Honor of Irving Fisher* (New York 1937), pp. 145–52: "So far as the active circulation is concerned, it is

sufficiently correct as a first approximation to regard the demand for money as proportionate to the effective demand, i.e., to the level of money income; which amounts to saying that the velocity of the active circulation is independent of the quantity of money. This is, I say, only a first approximation because the demand for money in the active circulation is also to some extent a function of the rate of interest, since a higher rate of interest may lead to a more economical use of active balances, though this only means that the active balances are under the same influence as the inactive balances."

3. Lawrence Klein on page 194 of the technical appendix of his book *The Keynesian Revolution* (New York 1947) derives a somewhat similar formula to express the usual Keynesian liquidity preference function. It is his equation (20a) $M/p = f8 + f9r + f10Y/p$. It is to be noted, however, that he assumes a linear relation between M/p and r rather than $1/r$.

4. James Tobin in the *Review of Economics and Statistics*, Vol. 30 (November 1948), 315, in a rejoinder to Clark Warburton on "Monetary Velocity and Monetary Policy," shows a scatter diagram comparing Warburton's Circuit Velocity and the yield on U.S. bonds for the period 1919–45. In this comparison he is using different series measuring the reciprocals of the variables used in equation (3.2). In spite of the inclusion of time deposits in calculating velocity and the effects of income taxes on government bond yields, the scatter appears significant for the period covered. Tobin also shows a comparison of "idle balances" expressed in current dollars and the yields on government bonds. This relationship clearly is open to the criticism outlined in the test of equation (2.2) which follows. A small change in interest rates from 1941 through 1945 is associated with a tripling of "idle balances."

5 The Demand for Money: The Evidence from the Time Series

Allan H. Meltzer *Carnegie Institute of Technology*

The arguments or variables that enter the demand function for money, and the definition of the quantity of money appropriate for the demand function, have received substantial attention in both the recent and more distant past. For present purposes, it is useful to distinguish three separate disputes about these variables. First, there is the question of the constraint that is imposed on money balances—whether the appropriate constraint is a measure of wealth, income, or some combination of the two. A second dispute has centered on the importance of interest rates and price changes as arguments in the demand function. Third, the question of the definition of money balances has often been raised. Is a more stable demand function obtained if money is defined inclusive or exclusive of time and/or savings deposits, and perhaps other assets that have value fixed in money terms?

In his recent survey of monetary theory, Harry Johnson has suggested that the above issues—the definition of money to be used in the money demand function, the variables on which the demand for money depends, and the stability of the demand function—are the chief substantive issues outstanding in monetary theory.[1] This paper deals with each of them and attempts to evaluate empirically the results obtained from some alternative money demand functions and some alternative definitions of

Reprinted from *Journal of Political Economy,* Vol. 71 (June 1963), 219–46, by permission of the author and The University of Chicago Press. Copyright 1963 by The University of Chicago Press.

money. These results are used to appraise some propositions that have been advanced in monetary theory.

With respect to one of these issues, the constraint on money balances, the well-known work of Hicks and the more recent studies of Friedman and Tobin suggest that monetary theorists are now agreed that the demand function for money is to be treated as a problem in balance sheet equilibrium or asset choice.[2] However, there are important differences among those who view monetary theory as a part of capital theory. Two of these differences are noted here. One concerns the importance of money for macroeconomic theory; the other is the question of the definition of wealth.

One approach to the demand for assets, the "modern quantity theory," views the demand for and supply of money as the most stable macrorelation and the one most significant for an analysis of economic behavior.[3] For the quantity theorist, adjustments of the economy to policy variables or changes in desired asset composition operate principally, but not exclusively, by creating discrepancies between desired and actual money holdings. These in turn lead to adjustments of other assets in the portfolios of ultimate wealth holders. The non-quantity theorist views money as but one of a number of financial assets.[4] Neither the long-term bond rate nor the quantity of money is an adequate measure of the "strategic variable—the ultimate gauge of expansion or deflation, of monetary tightness or ease."[5] For Tobin, the strategic variable is the yield required to absorb the existing capital stock into the balance sheets of the public.

Thus within the general framework of a capital theoretic view of the demand for money, there is an important difference. One view emphasizes the importance of the supply-and-demand functions for money; the other group chooses the demand for and supply of real capital as the crucial equations of a general equilibrium model.

Moreover, there is disagreement about the procedures to be applied in measuring the constraint imposed by the balance sheets. In particular, if income is defined as the flow corresponding to a stock of human and non-human wealth, as Friedman has emphasized, there is substantial difficulty in separating wealth, interest, and income variables empirically. Despite the apparent general consensus that the demand for money should be treated as a part of the theory of asset choice, both the studies referred to and Johnson's survey article suggest that precise specification of the variable that acts as a constraint on money balances remains an open question.

Differences in the specification of the variables in the money demand function have produced important differences in implications or results. For example, Tobin and Baumol separately considered the demand for transactions balances as a problem in capital theory and each obtained a demand function for cash balances which depends on costs and yields. Both Baumol and Tobin deduce from their models that there are economies of scale in holding transaction balances.[6] An income or wealth elasticity less than unity would confirm this implication.

Friedman's empirical findings suggest that money is a "luxury" and that the relevant elasticity is in the neighborhood of 1.8.[7] Economists would be likely to accept Friedman's empirical result in preference to the untested deductions of Baumol and Tobin were it not for some problems in the specification of the variables in his money demand function. Specifically, Friedman's use of per capita permanent income combines wealth, interest rates, population, and lagged income in a single variable and thus combines their separate effects. The inclusion of time deposits at commercial banks, in the definition of money that Friedman used, leaves open the question of whether his results reject the Baumol-Tobin implication when money is defined exclusive of time deposits.

Most of the work in monetary theory to which I have referred has been at the level of hypothesis building. Much less attention has been given in the literature to the appraisal of the proposed demand functions by empirical tests, although Friedman's work is a notable exception. As yet no attempt has been made to compare theoretical results by testing alternative equations.

The absence of detailed empirical studies has important bearing on several issues; among them one of the more important is the role of interest rates in a demand function for money that uses wealth as a constraint. Tobin gives rates of return on financial and non-financial assets an important role in his theory of asset choice.[8] Friedman's essay on the quantity theory stresses a view of the quantity theory as a theory of the demand for money. He uses bond and equity yields as direct arguments in the demand function. But his empirical findings suggest the importance of per capita permanent income and exclude interest rates as direct arguments of the function or assign them a role of second order of importance.[9] Bronfenbrenner and Mayer estimated the separate effects of wealth and interest rates along with income and lagged money balances.[10] Their results show that interest rate, income, and lagged money balances are statistically significant by the usual tests, but the wealth variable is non-significant.[11] Empirical studies that support the role of interest rates in the long-term demand function for money, notably Latané's, are based on the use of income, not wealth, as a constraint on money balances.[12] Thus the role of interest rates in a demand function for money that takes wealth as a constraint, like the measurement procedure for wealth itself, remains an open empirical question.

Furthermore, the definition of money is itself an open question. Gurley and Shaw suggest that monetary theory should be concerned with a concept broader than the liabilities of commercial banks.[13] Friedman's empirical work is based on a concept of money that includes the time deposit liabilities of commercial banks while Latané, Bronfenbrenner and Mayer and others have been chiefly concerned with money defined as the sum of demand deposits and currency.

An important issue in the dispute about the appropriate definition of money for monetary analysis is the stability of the demand function for money. The problem is one of defining money so that a stable demand function can be shown to have existed under differing institutional arrangements, changes in the social and political environment, and changes in economic conditions, or to explain the effects of such changes on the function. Very little effort has as yet been made to compare the performance of particular money demand functions for the same time periods to obtain insight into this question. Since the variables specified in alternative forms of the demand function for money are often highly correlated during short periods of time, a comparison of relative performance over long periods of time is one important means of resolving disputes about the definitions and measurement procedures for the variables that enter as arguments in the function.

This paper starts from the apparent consensus on the broad principle that the demand function for money is subject to a wealth constraint. Section I develops and tests a particular form of the function using both nominal and real balances and alternative definitions of money. Section II tests for differences in the results when some alternative definitions of wealth are used. Sections III and IV compare the model based on a wealth constraint to models that use measured or permanent income as a constraint. The velocity relation is discussed in Section V. A brief section on policy and a conclusion that suggests some implications of the results complete the paper.

I. *The Demand for Money*

In this section the quantity theory of money is expressed as an aggregate demand function for money containing variables that reflect wealth and substitution effects on the amount of real cash balances that the private economy desires to hold at any point in time. The general approach follows the procedures developed by Friedman; money is an asset held for the services which it provides.[14] These services and the low transactions cost associated with exchanges of money for other assets explain the existence of a positive demand for money.[15]

Here I assume that such a function exists and that the arguments of the function are the variables r^*, the yield on financial assets, ρ, the yield on physical assets, d^*, the yield on human wealth, and W_n, non-human wealth. Let M represent the quantity of money demanded (nominal value). Then $M = f(r^*, \rho, d^*, W_n)$ is a general demand function for money that contains the principal variables consistent with recent theoretical and empirical work discussed in the introduction.

W_n represents the constraint which wealth imposes on the demand for money. r^*, ρ and d^* measure the yields of assets other than money that compete for a place in the balance sheet of households and business. The derivative of M with respect to each of these yields is, of course, negative. Assuming that no additional variables, for example, measures of dispersion, need to be introduced when this general function is aggregated over all money holders, I will use the general equation as an aggregate demand function for money.

If the demand function is homogeneous of first degree in the money value of W_n,[16]

$$M = f^*(r^*, \rho, d^*, 1)W_n.$$

Let $d^* = Y_h/W_h$, the ratio of human income to human wealth. Multiply d^* by $Y_h^*/Y_h^*\ (= 1)$ where Y_h^* is the stream of income expected from a stock of human wealth.

$$M = f^*\left(r^*, \rho, \frac{Y_h}{Y_h^*} \cdot \frac{Y_h^*}{W_h}, 1\right)W_n.$$

The yield on human wealth is now viewed as the product of two components. The first term measures short-run deviations of actual from expected human income; it is an index of the transitory component of human income. Let this index be denoted by β. In the short-run, wealth holders may adjust the composition of their portfolios in response to changes in β, but β will equal one in the long-run. This paper is primarily concerned with the long-run demand function for money, and β is assumed to be constant. The second term in d^*, Y_h^*/W_h, is the ratio of expected human income to its capitalized value. This ratio is denoted by d and will also be taken as a constant. Finally, I will assume that r^* and ρ may be combined in r.

The extent to which the rates r^* and ρ may be measured by a single number—*the* rate of interest, r—depends on the covariance of the rates. The question has often been prejudged in the absence of empirical evidence. However, over long periods of time, it would be surprising if asset adjustments did not lead to high covariance between rates like r^* and ρ. Here I have assumed that at least one of the interest rates quoted in financial markets is an adequate measure of both r^* and ρ. This question will be reopened in a later section after we have seen the evidence which can be brought to bear.[17]

With these assumptions introduced and the subscript n dropped from W the equation becomes $M = g(r; d, \beta)W$, which will be shortened to

$$M = g(r)W. \tag{1}$$

Note that as a result of the assumption that the equation is homogeneous in W_n, the non-human wealth variable appears as a multiplicative factor in the function with a coefficient of 1. Additional assumptions about the form of the g function and the coefficient of r, the definition $Y = rW$, and the assumed constancy of β permit equation (1) to be rewritten as the familiar quantity theory of money in Cambridge form.

In its present form, equation (1) reflects the wealth constraint and substitution effect on the demand for money. That is, the equation reflects the general view that the demand function for money is a part of the general theory of portfolio composition or asset choice to which reference was made in the introduction. However, to complete the construction of a testable hypothesis, operational definitions of the variables must be specified. To examine the stability of equation (1) for various definitions of money, I define the monetary assets of the public in three ways—(1) as the sum of currency plus demand deposits, M_1, (2) M_1 + time deposits at commercial banks, M_2, and (3) M_2 + savings deposits, M_3. For the interest rate, I have used Durand's basic yield on twenty-year corporate bonds. Wealth poses a more difficult problem. As noted earlier, we wish to choose the appropriate measure of wealth to act as a budget restraint in the demand function for money in a manner analogous to the role of income in household utility maximization.

Once we drop the arbitrary distinction between "transactions" and "asset" balances and regard money as an asset that, like the other stocks, is held for the services it provides, a variety of alternative definitions of wealth can be suggested. In particular, three questions are raised. First, should human wealth be treated along with non-human wealth as a constraint in the determination of asset equilibrium? This is the approach that Friedman, in particular, has used, but it differs from the approach used here because I have assumed that the ratio d can be treated as a constant.

Second, should non-human wealth be consolidated or combined? That is, do we consider each economic entity (individual or firm) to be constrained by its gross wealth and the aggregate constrained by the unconsolidated sum? Such an approach involves substantial double counting but may nonetheless more closely approximate the behavior of economic units. Third, how do we treat the assets and liabilities of the government? A substantial literature has grown up around the Pigou or Patinkin effect that suggests that we should include the net liabilities of the government sector to the public but should exclude the assets held by government. But Goldsmith's measure of the consolidated wealth of the economy includes net government assets and excludes government debt and non-metallic money.[18]

At heart the issue is empirical. The relevant definition is the one that includes those balance sheet items which when aggregated act as a constraint on the demand for money by households and business. In this section, W is defined as total wealth from Goldsmith's Table W-1 plus monetary and non-monetary government debt minus government assets.[19] In the following section some alternative measures of wealth will be used. The three questions raised in the preceding paragraph with respect to the operational definition of the wealth constraint will then be reopened.

Let $g(r) = r^b$. Equation (1), $[M = g(r)W]$, may then be rewritten in log form as $\ln M = a + b \ln r + c \ln W$, where M, r, W are as defined and b and c are the interest rate and wealth elasticities, respectively. Again noting that W appears in (1) as a multiplicative factor with an implied coefficient $c = 1$, we test the hypothesis that $c = 1$. The regression estimate for the period 1900–1958 is shown in equation (2).

$$\ln M_1 = -1.65 \quad -.781 \ln r + 1.01 \ln W + u_1\bar{R} = .994. \quad (2)$$

t values   (13.5)   (66.8)

Partial correlations $-.88$ $+.99$

$$\ln \frac{M_1}{p} = -1.48 \quad -.949 \ln r + 1.11 \ln \frac{W}{P} + u_2\bar{R} = .992. \quad (3)$$

t values   (21.8)   (42.0)

Partial correlations $-.93$ $+.98$

$$\ln \frac{M_2}{p} = -1.98 \quad -.50 \ln r \quad + 1.32 \ln \frac{W}{P} + u_3\bar{R} = .994. \quad (3')$$

t values   (10.8)   (53.2)

Partial correlations $-.82$ $+.99$

Note that M and W are measured in nominal terms and that the t values and partial correlations are given below the variables.

A regression using deflated values of M and W for the same period is shown in (3).

Note that p is the implicit price deflator for net national product while P is the price level for assets obtained by computing the implicit price deflator from Goldsmith's nominal and real wealth estimates. To obtain (3) again let $g(r) = r^b$ in (1), divide both sides by p, and multiply the right side by

$$\frac{P^c}{P^c} \, (= 1)$$

to give

$$\frac{M}{p} = ar^b \frac{W^c}{P^c} \frac{P^c}{p}.$$

The wealth elasticity c, in (2), is approximately $= 1$ as the hypothesis implies. We may treat the ratio of asset to output prices $P^c/p = P/p$, as an index of interest rates. For the regression estimates in (3) P/p has been combined with r. As might be expected, this results in a somewhat higher estimate for the coefficient of $\ln r$ in (3) than in (2).

Similar results are obtained if M_2 (including time deposits at commercial banks) is substituted for M_1. For the log of real balances, the regression result is shown in (3').

Three statistical details about these results merit comment. First, the two arguments of the demand function, interest rates and wealth, explain almost all of the observed variance in money balances whether money is defined inclusive or exclusive of time deposits at commercial banks. Second, the partial correlation coefficients suggest that both variables are of approximately equal importance in the long-run demand functions. Third, the interest rate and wealth elasticities differ substantially depending on the definition of money balances used.

These findings—and others using a third definition of nominal and real balances—bear on long-standing issues in monetary theory. They suggest that a stable demand function for money is consistent with more than a single definition of money balances. But they also suggest that the definition of money is important for a proper appraisal of issues in monetary theory. For if money is defined as M_2/p or M_3/p, the effects of general and relative changes in interest rates are combined in the estimated interest elasticity.[20] A general rise in market interest rates raises all quoted interest rates in proportion and sets off substitution effects between currency plus demand deposits, M_1, and other assets. When money is defined inclusive of time or savings deposits, part of these substitution effects are hidden by changes within the composition of money itself. Thus the interest elasticity of an equation like (3′) makes it difficult to distinguish between two quite different changes: (1) the results of a general rise in interest rates and (2) the substitution between time deposits and other assets stemming from an increase (say) in the Federal Reserve Board's Regulation Q or higher posted rates at commercial banks, other interest rates remaining unchanged.

The estimated elasticities also bear on two issues raised by Gurley and Shaw.[21] First, Gurley and Shaw suggest that the definition of money should include more than the sum of currency plus demand deposits, M_1. This follows from their argument that the creation of liabilities by financial intermediaries is analogous to the creation of money by commercial banks. Substitution between the liabilities of financial intermediaries and M_1 is regarded as closer than substitution between M_1 and other assets. Second, the Gurley-Shaw analysis presupposes that the demand for M_1 has declined relative to other assets.

The results of (3) and (3′) suggest a different interpretation: that the growth of financial intermediaries was a wealth effect and not primarily a substitution effect. For the wealth elasticity of (3′) is substantially above the wealth elasticity shown in (3). These elasticities indicate that, for a given percentage increase in real wealth, the community has chosen to increase its time deposits by a greater percentage than its demand deposits and currency. In short, the public has chosen to hold a larger proportion of its wealth in the form of income-yielding assets.

However, the wealth elasticity of (3) denies that real M_1 balances have declined relative to real wealth. If we extrapolate from this result to consider the relation between savings deposits at non-commercial banks and real wealth, we should expect to find that including the liabilities of financial intermediaries—for example, savings and loan associations and mutual savings banks—in the definition of money balances also raises the wealth elasticity of money thus defined above the elasticity shown in (3). The evidence from the time series estimates for the M_3 function supports this extrapolation. The relevant elasticity is 1.34. Thus the data are consistent with the view that the relative growth of financial intermediaries, exhibited by the Goldsmith data, reflects the allocation of an increased stock of wealth rather than substitution between the liabilities of competing financial institutions as in Gurley and Shaw.

Moreover, the stability of the long-run demand function for money defined as M_1 or M_1/p denies the necessity for incorporating

the liabilities issued (or the rates of return paid) by financial intermediaries as a part of the definition of money or as arguments in
the long-run demand function. And the greater interest elasticity
of real money balances M_1/p suggests that a given change in
interest rates over the business cycle changes M_2 and M_3 balances
by a much smaller percentage than it changes M_1. We should
expect from the interest elasticities that the principal liabilities of
financial intermediaries other than commercial banks are much
more stable than the demand liabilities of commercial banks when
the Federal Reserve alters the determinants of the money supply.
This in turn leads us to believe that changes in the liabilities of
financial intermediaries may be a much smaller source of short-run
instability than has been supposed. But direct empirical evidence
on this point is required for a precise answer to this question.

Much of the theory of money and macroeconomics has been
formulated on the explicit assumption that the money demand
function is homogeneous of degree one in prices *and* financial assets.
To my knowledge none of the empirical studies of the demand for
money has explicitly considered this assumption. Either homogeneity of degree one in prices and financial assets has been assumed or the question has not been considered. The similarity of
the parameters of equations (2) and (3) for nominal and real
balances suggests that the assumption holds for the demand function developed here. A doubling of prices and the value of financial
assets doubles the demand for nominal balances but leaves the
demand for real balances unaffected.

Further, we should note that the results presented above are
consistent with those which have been obtained in the 126 cross-
section studies of the demand for money by business firms referred
to earlier. Specifically, the existence of a positive wealth elasticity
in the neighborhood of 1.0 and a negative interest elasticity are
suggested by the cross-section estimates. While there may be some
bias in the parameter estimates and some errors in the observations,
the consistency of the two sets of results again implies the existence
of a stable demand curve for money with properties similar to
those I have suggested. Moreover, one difficulty that commonly
affects the estimates from economic time series appears to be largely
absent. For the fifty-nine years covered by our data, there is little
significant correlation between interest rates and wealth, $r_{W,r} =
-0.44$ and $r_{W/p,r} = -0.47$.

The demand function for money developed here (eq. [1]) and
the evidence that supports it contribute to an understanding of the
issues in monetary theory that I set out to discuss. First, the long-
run data strongly suggest that the demand function for money has
been quite stable despite major institutional, social, and political

changes. Second, the theory and the evidence support the view that the long-run demand function is consistent with the quantity theory of money and contains two principal arguments of almost equal explanatory power: interest rates and non-human wealth. Third, with respect to the definition of money, the results strongly indicate that the demand to hold currency plus demand deposits is at least as stable as other alternative demand functions. The evidence does not suggest any compelling reason for broadening the definition of money to include time deposits at commercial banks (Friedman), or liabilities of financial intermediaries (Gurley-Shaw). Fourth, the data support the assumption of homogeneity of first degree in prices and financial assets. Finally, the results suggest that the measurement of yields on a variety of alternative assets by a single financial rate provides a reasonable approximation for the long-run function.

I shall discuss the more general implications of these findings in the concluding section. Before doing so it is useful, first, to evaluate the measurement procedures used here by introducing alternative specifications of the variables in the function and, second, to compare the results obtained, and the theory that lies behind them, to some alternative theories of the demand for money.

II. *Some Alternative Formulations*

To obtain equations (2) and (3), several assumptions were made about the measurement of variables, wealth in particular, that enter into the demand function for money. Alternative specifications of the wealth variable permit a direct test of the extent to which the measurement of W_n used in Section I is critical for the results. Indirect evidence has also been obtained on the assumption that ρ and r^* may be approximated by r. In this section we consider problems of measurement only. The following two sections assess some alternative hypotheses involving income rather than wealth as a constraint.

Previously wealth was defined as the consolidated net non-human wealth of the public. One alternative definition of wealth is the unconsolidated total assets of households, business, and government. If the money balances of households in the aggregate are constrained by their asset holdings and the money balances of business are constrained by the unconsolidated value of business assets, the aggregate demand for money may be related to the unconsolidated sum of assets held by the economy as a whole. Similarly, if the proper constraint for households and business is the net worth of the sector, aggregate net worth may be the constraint that enters the aggregate money demand function. Alternatively, the relevant constraint may be the consolidated wealth of households, business, government, and the rest of the world. The latter measure is the one that Goldsmith has computed on an annual basis.[22]

Table 1 shows estimates based on alternative definitions of wealth and money balances. The estimated elasticities in equations (4), (5), and (6) for the period 1900–1949 vary from those presented earlier, and, in general, the more inclusive the definition of money, the lower the interest elasticity. This result is not surprising since the more inclusive the definition of money, the more likely that there will be both positive and negative responses to a relative rise in interest rates. The conclusions reached in the previous section are altered little by these results. M_1 again approaches unit elasticity with respect to interest rates and the wealth measures, A, A/P, and N.

TABLE 1   *Regression Estimates,* t *Values and Correlation for Alternative Money Demand Functions**

EQUATION	DEFINITION OF M	VARIABLE AND COEFFICIENT	t VALUE	VARIABLE AND COEFFICIENT	t VALUE	MULTIPLE CORRELATION
			Period: 1900–49			
(4)	$\ln M_1$	$-0.80 \ln r$	9.1	$.997 \ln A$	34.8	.99
(5)	$\ln M_1/p$	$-0.90 \ln r$	10.7	$1.15 \ln A/P$	20.5	.97
(4″)	$\ln M_3$	$-0.40 \ln r$	8.2	$1.07 \ln A$	71.2	.99
(5″)	$\ln M_3/p$	$-0.45 \ln r$	8.5	$1.37 \ln A/P$	38.2	.99
(6)	$\ln M_1$	$-1.00 \ln r$	11.1	$1.08 \ln N$	32.9	.98
(6″)	$\ln M_3$	$-0.65 \ln r$	11.5	$1.17 \ln N$	56.0	.99
(7)	$\ln M_1$	$-0.50 \ln r$	5.6	$-0.02 \ln G$	0.65	.64
			Period: 1900–58			
(4)	$\ln M_1$	$-0.80 \ln r$	10.1	$1.00 \ln A$	47.9	.99
(5)	$\ln M_1/p$	$-1.04 \ln r$	11.6	$1.02 \ln A/P$	22.2	.98
(5′)	$\ln M_2/p$	$-0.59 \ln r$	8.4	$1.24 \ln A/P$	34.9	.98
			Period: 1900–29			
(2)	$\ln M_1$	$-0.15 \ln r$	1.1	$0.90 \ln W$	27.1	.99
(3)	$\ln M_1/p$	$-0.32 \ln r$	3.0	$1.84 \ln W/P$	16.1	.98
(3′)	$\ln M_2/p$	$-0.42 \ln r$	3.9	$1.41 \ln W/P$	27.2	.99

* Definitions of symbols:
  M_i = nominal money balances subscripts as before
  M_i/p = real money balances
  r = interest rate
  A = gross (unconsolidated) value of total assets
  A/P = gross (unconsolidated) value of real assets
  N = aggregate (unconsolidated) net worth
  G = nominal (consolidated) wealth, Goldsmith, Table W-1, estimate
  W/P = real wealth as before
  W = nominal wealth
  For further description see n. 10.

Moreover, equations (4), (5), and (6) have some implications for the measurement of *the* interest rate. For the empirical work we have used the same measured interest rate in all cases, the yield on twenty-year corporate bonds. But the rate that theoretically enters (4) and (5) is a weighted average of the yield on all non-human assets—tangible and intangible, financial, and physical. In (6) *r* is theoretically a weighted average over both assets and liabilities. The similarity of the interest elasticities at least suggests that *over long periods of time* these two average rates move in direct proportion to the yield on long-term corporate bonds or financial assets. The result of this indirect test is not inconsistent with the assumption that the interest rate used to measure the return on assets may be roughly proportional to other asset rates in the long run. Furthermore, there appears to be little difference between the elasticity of money balances with respect to those assets that have been included in net worth and those assets that have been included in total assets but not in net worth.

The largest group of assets excluded from net worth but included in total assets is, of course, financial assets—bonds, mortgages, insurance, pensions, and money itself. The computed elasticities may be taken as weighted averages of the elasticity of the demand for money with respect to the components of the various wealth measures. Thus the data suggest that, on the average, money is as much a substitute for real assets as for other financial assets. Moreover, the inclusion or exclusion of money itself from the measure of wealth does not alter the elasticities substantially.

We can pursue this point further by considering an additional measure of wealth—the net wealth estimates which Goldsmith obtained by consolidating the balance sheets for all sectors. For this definition of wealth, we get (eq. [7], Table 1) a result that is much less satisfactory than those obtained when total assets and net worth were used as the measure of wealth or when government assets were subtracted and government liabilities added as in equations (2) and (3) earlier.

There appears to be no effect of Goldsmith wealth, *G*, on the demand for money; this contrasts with the very strong effects exhibited when wealth is measured by net worth, total assets, or as in Section I above. Moreover the results for the three other measures of wealth are homogeneous of first degree in prices and financial assets, while the demand function does not have this property when wealth is measured as *G*. The principal cause of this difference appears to be that *G* includes government assets (buildings, inventories, and public lands) but excludes government liabilities. Some government liabilities are included in the three other wealth measures used here as a part of the assets or net worth of the public. Including such liabilities as a part of the assets of the public appears to be important for the proper specification of the wealth variable.[23]

The lower part of Table 1 presents some estimates of the elasticities for both shorter and longer time periods. It appears that the parameters of the demand function are more stable when money is defined to include time deposits at commercial banks, M_2. This result is tentatively confirmed by the estimates that have been computed for a variety of time periods and a number of different demand functions. I will return to this point in a following section where some subperiod estimates are presented.

In summary, the alternative formulations that have been used here tend to support the conclusions reached at the end of Section I, most notably the importance of variables representing substiution and wealth effects as arguments in the demand function for money and the stability of the function. For several definitions of money and non-human wealth, we have seen (1) that a stable demand function can be isolated using interest rates and real wealth as arguments and (2) that the demand for money is approximately unit elastic with respect to wealth when money is defined as the sum of currency plus demand deposits. In addition, the results of this section provide some evidence about the relative substitutability of particular assets for money and suggest that increases in aggregate wealth have roughly the same effect on the demand for money when non-human wealth is measured by any one of a number of aggregate values that include government debt as assets of the public.

III. *Comparisons with Some Hypotheses Incorporating Income*

Traditionally theories of the demand function for money have used income as an argument in the function.[24] The model used here like many of the models used in recent work in monetary theory has been developed in terms of a wealth constraint. The effects of human income and human wealth have been dropped from demand equation (1) above by assuming that $d\beta$ remains constant or nearly so. This formulation has been shown to yield a stable demand function for money. Nevertheless, in this section we consider some alternative hypotheses where income is taken as the constraint or incorporated as a variable. The evidence seems to suggest that the money demand relation is more stable when equation (1) above is retained.

The use of income as a constraint in the demand function for money often has been associated with the notion that money is a commodity used principally to effect a given transactions volume. This is explicitly stated in the formulation of the Keynesian demand function $M = kY + L(r)$ and in the so-called Cambridge equation $M = kY$ (M and r are as defined earlier, Y is aggregate money income). In contrast to the view taken here, the Keynesian approach views a large part of money balances as a separable, fixed, linear function of income or transactions that is not dependent on interest rates. Much of the empirical evidence for this approach to the Keynesian demand function rests heavily on rather tenuous evidence from the interwar period and particularly on the prolonged fall in interest rates associated with the depression and war periods.

Even when it is not assumed that money balances can be divided into separable "transaction" and "speculative" balances, there are important differences between the income and wealth approaches. The use of current income as a constraint has generally been rationalized in terms of the desire to use money to carry out some transactions volume. The quantity theory of money in its Cambridge form posits a direct link between money and money income. As Friedman has noted, the link, k, in the Cambridge equation, is written as if the average cash balance, M/Y, can be treated as a technologically fixed constant.[25] Of course quantity theorists did not regard it in that way, but they emphasized long-run institutional factors, habits of payment, etc., rather than costs and yields associated with asset exchanges and portfolios as determinants of k.

The wealth constraint emphasizes the role of money as a productive asset and focuses attention on the equilibrium of the balance sheet, the allocation of assets, and the services that money provides. Effecting a volume of transactions is but one of these services. Empirical evidence is required to separate the income and wealth models of the demand for money and to evaluate the importance of the difference in constraints.

For it may be argued that if income is treated as the yield on wealth, the distinction between an income and wealth constraint is arbitrary. If $Y = rW$ is treated as a definition of income, the point is tautological, that is, there exists a definition of income for which the income and wealth constraints give precisely the same results. But the open question is: Do measures of permanent or current income, that have been used as arguments in the demand function for money, correspond to the theoretical definition of income as the yield on wealth? Since the measure of wealth used here excludes human income, the empirical question is worth investigation.

Equation (8) (Table 2) shows the regression estimates of interest and real income elasticities of the demand for money for three time periods in this century. It is clear from these data that the

TABLE 2   Estimates Using Income as an Argument*

EQUATION	DEFINITION OF M	VARIABLE AND COEFFICIENT	t VALUE	VARIABLE AND COEFFICIENT	t VALUE	VARIABLE AND COEFFICIENT	t VALUE	MULTIPLE CORRELATION
				Period: 1900–58				
(8)	$\ln M_1/p$	$-0.79 \ln r$	9.5	$1.05 \ln Y/p$	25.6			.98
(9)	$\ln M_1/p$	$-0.92 \ln r$	17.2	$0.13 \ln Y/p$	1.4	$0.97 \ln W/P$	9.5	.99
(10)	$\ln M_2/p$	$-0.48 \ln r$	9.5	$0.13 \ln Y/p$	1.4	$1.18 \ln W/P$	12.4	.99
(11)	$\ln M_1/p$	$-1.77 \ln r$	22.1	$0.93 \ln Z/p$	19.3	(1900–1949 only)		.97
				Period: 1900–29				
(8)	$\ln M_1/p$	$-0.05 \ln r$	0.53	$0.70 \ln Y/p$	15.6			.98
(9)	$\ln M_1/p$	$-0.22 \ln r$	1.8	$0.31 \ln Y/p$	1.6	$0.48 \ln W/P$	2.0	.98
(10)	$\ln M_2/p$	$-0.30 \ln r$	2.5	$0.35 \ln Y/p$	1.8	$1.00 \ln W/P$	4.4	.99
(11)	$\ln M_1/p$	$-0.70 \ln r$	5.4	$0.66 \ln Z/p$	15.6			.98
				Period: 1930–58				
(8)	$\ln M_1/p$	$-0.69 \ln r$	4.3	$0.94 \ln Y/p$	10.0	$1.35 \ln W/P$	8.7	.95
(9)	$\ln M_1/p$	$-1.15 \ln r$	11.8	$-0.10 \ln Y/p$	0.8	$1.10 \ln W/P$	7.3	.99
(10)	$\ln M_2/p$	$-0.70 \ln r$	7.4	$0.03 \ln Y/p$	0.2			.98

* Definitions of symbols:
M_i/p = real money balances
r = interest rate
Y/p = net national product
W/P = real wealth
Z/p = $(A/P)r$ + real wage and salary payments

statistical significance of the interest elasticity for the entire period is largely derived from the inverse movements in real money balances and interest rates during recent decades, if real income, Y/p, is used as a constraint. Estimates presented earlier, and others that appear in the following section, show that the interest rate remains significant when real non-human wealth is used as the constraint. Thus those who argue that the demand for money depends on real income must deny the importance of the interest rate during much of the time period we have considered. In short, the results are different and imply that the underlying models are different when Y is defined as measured net national product.

The assumption that income should not appear along with wealth in equation (1) is examined in equations (9) and (10) of Table 2. Real income has no significant effect on the demand for real money balances when real non-human wealth appears in the equation. Interpretation of these findings is difficult owing to substantial multicollinearity due to the high correlation between real income and real wealth. However, we note that the interest rate and real wealth coefficients are generally quite similar to those estimated earlier while those for the real income coefficients are quite different.[26] From this it appears that the addition of real income to the money demand equation adds little additional information.

There remains the problem of human wealth. Specifically, does the exclusion of human wealth from the right side of equations (2), (3), (4), (5), and (6) alter the estimated wealth elasticities? Statistical problems rather than questions of economic interpretation prevent a completely satisfactory answer to these questions. Nevertheless the evidence seems to suggest that the omission of human wealth (or the income received as wages and salaries) does not introduce a substantial bias. Compare the long-run income elasticity of equation (8) with the long-run wealth elasticity of equation (3) earlier. Note that they are of the same order of magnitude. This suggests that the elasticity of the demand for money with respect to human wealth or wage and salary income is approximately the same as the elasticity with respect to non-human wealth or non-property income. Similar evidence is given in equation (11), which attempts a crude estimate of the elasticity of the demand for money with respect to wage and salary income. While Z/p ($= r \cdot A/p$ + real wage and salary payments, that is, a measure of human plus non-human income) and r are highly correlated, it again appears that real money balances, M_1/p, are approximately unit elastic with respect to Z/p.[27] A variety of other tests that I have attempted point to the same general conclusion.

The findings of this section suggest, first, that the demand function for money is more stable when the function is formulated in terms of a wealth constraint rather than an income constraint. This conclusion is supported by numerous additional estimates, some of which are presented in the following section; it suggests that it is more fruitful to view the demand for money as influenced by cost and yield considerations rather than primarily as a means of effecting a volume of "transactions" and subject to an income constraint. Second, the results here support the assumptions made earlier that eliminated the direct effects of human income from the money demand relation. Third, the findings suggest that little bias results from the exclusion of human wealth from the measure of wealth used to test the hypothesis. While this third finding is subject to some qualification owing to problems of estimation, I have failed to uncover evidence which strongly suggests that a large bias has been introduced or which does not suggest that the bias is small.

Finally, one income hypothesis remains to be considered. This is the permanent income model suggested by Friedman. The following section compares the two formulations, attempts to reconcile them, and provides some additional evidence on the assumption of homogeneity of the money demand function.

IV. *The Permanent Income Hypothesis*

Among recent studies of the demand function for money, none is closer to the present study than Friedman's. But two of his conclusions differ substantially from those presented here. First, he is unable "to find any close connection between changes in velocity from cycle to cycle and any of a number of interest rates."[28] However, from his secular results, he notes that the "yield on corporate bonds is correlated with the real stock of money and velocity in the expected direction. . . . Bond yields, however, play nothing like so important and regularly consistent a role in accounting for changes in velocity as does real income."[29] Second, he concludes that the demand for real money balances is highly elastic with respect to permanent real income. A 100 per cent increase in real permanent income leads individuals to increase their real money balances by 180 per cent on the average, that is, money is a "luxury."

In the two earlier sections, I have presented a variety of estimates which suggest the conclusions that interest rates do play a consistent and significant role in the long-run demand for money and that the wealth elasticity of the demand for real money balances, M_1/p, does not support the view that money is a "luxury." In this section I show the relation between Friedman's demand function for money and the one presented here and argue that the two demand functions are conceptually similar. Most of the empirical differences between the two can be accounted for by differences in specification of the variables rather than by inherently conflicting implications. Some evidence is then presented for a number of different time periods. It suggests that the money demand function presented here is more stable and somewhat more consistent with the evidence than the alternative proposed by Friedman.

Following Friedman, let $Y_p = rW$ be the definition of permanent income as the income flow resulting from a stock of wealth.[30] In equation (1), $M = g(r)W$. If we define W as human plus non-human wealth and r as the yield applicable to total wealth, we may substitute Y_p/r for W to get

$$M = \frac{g(r)\, Y_p}{r}. \tag{12}$$

If $g(r)/r$ is approximately constant, equation (12) becomes

$$M = k\, Y_p. \tag{12'}$$

To compare Friedman's empirical evidence with my earlier results, we divide equations (1) and (12') by population, N', and prices, p (or permanent prices P_p), define money as M_2, take logs and get

$$\ln \frac{M_2}{N'p} = \alpha - \beta \ln r + \gamma \ln \frac{W}{N'P} \tag{13}$$

and

$$\ln \frac{M_2}{N'P_p} = a + b \ln \frac{y_p}{N'}. \tag{13'}$$

It should be clear from the preceding discussion that (13) and (13') are not mutually exclusive in the sense that evidence which confirms one must fail to confirm the other. Rather they are alternative forms of the same hypothesis since the definition of permanent income and the results of the preceding section suggest that krW can be substituted for ky_p. They differ only in that the parameter estimates of (1) or (13) will explicitly reflect the separate effects of interest rates and wealth while those of (12') or (13') will not.

This point is of some relevance. Theoretical considerations used to obtain equation (1), Friedman's essay on the quantity theory, and a variety of empirical results stemming from short- and long-period estimates of the interest elasticity suggest that both velocity and the demand for money are significantly dependent on interest rates. Friedman's finding that permanent real income dominates is an empirical result. The evidence he presents in support of this conclusion is based on an analysis of the within cycle residuals from an equation like (13'). The evidence presented here comes from the explicit use of interest rates as an argument in the demand function for money. Friedman's conclusion that interest rates play a small role in the demand function for money seems to stem from the measurement procedure he employs. As we shall see, a similar argument holds for velocity.

Though the two hypotheses are theoretically consistent, the empirical evidence distinguishes between them. Table 3 compares the estimated elasticities of equations (13), (13'), and (3') for a number of different time periods.[31] Note that the parameter estimates for equation (3') are a much more stable proportion of their 1900–1958 values than those for equation (13) and slightly more stable than those of equation (13').[32] Note also that the assumption of homogeneity in population generally raises the wealth elasticity for the longer periods (but not for the shorter periods) and generally does not affect the longer period interest elasticities or their significance. Finally, note that the proportion of the variance explained by equation (3') is usually greater than that explained by the permanent income hypothesis. The one striking exception to this last conclusion occurs when permanent per capita money balances are *negatively* related to permanent per capita income for the nine years 1950–58.

It would appear therefore that interest rates do enter significantly into the demand function for money. Indeed the results are so pervasive for widely different time periods and alternative definitions of money and wealth that the issue seems beyond dispute. Friedman's contrary findings are not supported by the evidence from one variant of the permanent income hypothesis itself. For equation (13'') shows that when interest rates are used along with per capita permanent income, interest rates enter significantly into the money demand relation. For 1900–1958[33] the regression estimates are shown in equation (13'').

A second major difference between the findings in this paper and those presented earlier by Friedman relates to the value of the wealth or permanent income elasticity. As noted above, Friedman concludes that money is a luxury. This conclusion is largely a result of the definition of money that he employs and the process of deflating by population which raises the wealth and permanent income elasticities when money is defined as M_2. Equation (14) affirms that, when the parameters for permanent prices, population, and real per capita wealth (in permanent prices) are left free, regression estimates of the interest rate and wealth elasticity con-

TABLE 3   Regression and Correlation Coefficients for Three Equations*

PERIOD	(13) $\ln M_2/N'p = \alpha + \beta \ln r + \gamma \ln W/N'P + V_1$			(13') $\ln M_2/N'P_p = a + b \ln y_p/N' + V_2$		(3') $\ln M_2/p = A + B \ln r + C \ln W/P + V_3$		
	β and t value	γ and t value	$\bar{R}^2$	b and t value	$\bar{R}^2$	B and t value	C and t value	R^2
1900–58	− 0.52 / 10.5	1.62 / 31.0	.97	1.59 / 33.7	.95	− 0.50 / 10.8	1.32 / 53.2	.99
1900–29	− 0.32 / 2.8	1.75 / 15.4	.94	1.37 / 27.1	.96	− 0.42 / 3.9	1.41 / 27.2	.98
1930–58	− 0.71 / 10.6	1.24 / 14.1	.94	1.39 / 14.4	.88	− 0.72 / 10.3	1.12 / 20.6	.96
By Decades								
1900–09	− 0.42 / 7.4	2.19 / 3.6	.81	1.38 / 12.3	.94	− 1.09 / 2.3	2.24 / 7.1	.96
1910–19	− 0.61 / 1.6	1.42 / 2.5	.56	1.66 / 3.9	.61	− 0.72 / 2.9	1.36 / 6.4	.90
1920–29	− 0.84 / 2.6	0.95 / 2.2	.93	1.25 / 12.0	.94	− 0.72 / 2.0	1.08 / 3.9	.96
1930–39	− 0.73 / 7.6	1.92 / 4.8	.89	1.03 / 2.0	.24	− 0.64 / 8.4	1.97 / 4.2	.91
1940–49	− 2.06 / 4.2	1.37 / 7.3	.90	1.49 / 12.2	.94	− 2.05 / 4.2	1.30 / 8.9	.93
1950–58	− 0.03 / 0.16	− 2.78 / 0.71	.44	− 0.51 / 7.7	.88	− 0.65 / 4.0	0.54 / 2.1	.75

*Definition of symbols:

$M_2/N'p$ = real per capita money balances
$M_2/N'P_p$ = real per capita permanent money balances
M_2/p = real aggregate money balances

r = interest rate
y_pN' = real per capita permanent income
$W/N'P$ = real per capita wealth
W/P = real aggregate wealth

sistent with those presented earlier are obtained if money is measured as the sum of currency plus demand deposits.[34]

$$\ln \frac{M_2}{N'P_p} = -2.8 - .37 \ln r + 1.41 \ln \frac{y_p}{N'} + v_4. \quad (13'')$$

t values	(7.3)	(34.1)
Partial correlations	$-.72$	.98

$\ln M_1 =$

$$-.39 - .79 \ln r + 1.11 \ln \frac{W}{NP_p} + .74 \ln N' + 1.08 \ln P_p.$$

t values	(7.0)	(7.0)	(4.2)	(7.1)	(14)

Friedman has provided no compelling reason for selecting the population variable for consideration from the many others that might affect the demand for money. A plausible case can be made for a number of variables such as the age composition of the population, the number or distribution of commercial and savings banks, or the distribution of population between urban and rural areas. Including the latter variable might suggest that the money demand function is not homogeneous of first degree in population alone. A shift toward greater urban concentration accompanied by an increase in population might easily lead to an elasticity of the demand for money, M_1 or M_2, with respect to population, that is less than one. The costs and yields of holding money balances are not unaffected by the location of savings banks in shopping centers, the development of "bank by mail," and a host of other devices that have accompanied the increase in population and increasing urbanization.

In the absence of theory which specifies that the demand function for money is homogeneous in population, we are left to decide on the evidence and its possible rationale. Equation (14) is at least consistent with the view that increased urbanization or changes in age composition of the population (life-cycle) make the demand function for money less than unit elastic in population. While it is most likely that there is multicollinearity in the estimates of equation (14), as I noted above, all of the other variables—per capita non-human wealth, interest rates, and permanent prices—have coefficients that are consistent with the theory of Section I and the empirical estimates of equation (3) above. Moreover, a comparison of equations (3') and (13) of Table 3 seems to suggest that the parameters of the wealth model are more stable and the proportion of the variance explained is always higher when homogeneity of the first degree in population is not assumed (equation [3']) than when it is (equation [13]). I therefore reject the assumption that the demand function for money is homogeneous of the first degree in the stock of population.[35]

When we compare the wealth elasticities in Tables 1 and 3 with those in Section I, we find that the wealth elasticity generally exceeds unity only when money is defined to include assets other than demand deposits and currency. Thus the conclusion that money is a luxury relates to the particular definition of money that Friedman has used. The data in this paper strongly imply that it is time deposits at commercial banks and other forms of savings accounts that are "luxuries."

Thus it appears that Friedman's contrary findings reflect the assumption of homogeneity in population and the definition of money that he chose. Differences in theoretical structure between my model based on interest rates and non-human wealth and his use of permanent income do not appear to be the major source of differences in findings. Rather, Friedman's conclusions appear to result from his measurement procedures. His conclusion that interest rates do not significantly affect the demand for money is not reflected by annual data, and his conclusion that money is a "luxury" is purely definitional. Moreover, at the opposite pole, the Baumol-Tobin conclusion that "transactions" money balances are subject to economies of scale is not supported by the aggregate data for any reasonable definition of money balances.

V. *Velocity*

The literature of economics contains numerous suggestions about the velocity relation. These range from the assumption of constant velocity, that has been imputed to some authors, to the low-level liquidity trap of Keynes' *General Theory* and the upper bound suggested by Ritter.[36] Of particular relevance to our discussion is the work of Latané. His two studies suggest a stable relationship between velocity and interest rates over long periods which is linear in the logarithms.[37] His evidence is based on the period 1909–58 and is obtained when income velocity measured as the ratio of GNP to M_1 is related to the yield on long-term corporate bonds.

Attention is drawn to the latter point because specification of the measurement procedure for velocity is as critical for an understanding of this problem as the specification of the wealth constraint is for the demand function for money. Latané's high correlations suggest that the log of velocity, measured as the ratio GNP/M_1, is directly related to the log of interest rates. However, we may formulate his model as a demand function for money subject to an income constraint $M = L(r, Y)$, as in Section III of this paper. Assuming homogeneity in prices and real income gives $M/Y = L^*(r)$, the velocity equation that Latané used. Since the real income elasticity of equation (8) (Table 2) is approximately unity, Latané's implicit assumption about real income elasticity seems reasonable.

However the tests in Table 2 also show that the interest elasticity of equation (8) does not differ significantly from zero in the period 1900–1929. Thus Latané's result is spurious since it combines the significant results of the later period with the non-significant results of the first two or three decades.[38]

With respect to the definition of M, the results presented above strongly suggest that the effect of a rise in interest rates on the percentage change in the quantity of money demanded is much greater when time deposits are excluded from M than when they are included in it. It would not be surprising therefore to find that measures of income velocity that include a large proportion of money substitutes in the denominator are less sensitive to interest changes than those that are based on currency and demand deposits alone. The problem is one of disentangling relative and general changes in asset prices just as in the demand for money itself.

The velocity function or its inverse, money per unit of income, which is used here, is derived from equation (1) by dividing by income measured as rW to get

$$\frac{M_i}{rW} = \frac{1}{V_i} = v_i(r, W) \qquad i = 1, 2, 3.$$

If interest rate and asset parameters of the money demand functions are denoted b and c respectively, simple algebra makes clear that the parameters of the velocity functions should equal $b - 1$ and $c - 1$. This is the case for the interest rate and the asset parameters shown in equations (15) and (15'). No changes were introduced on the right-hand side of the equation. These equations appear to be quite consistent with their money demand functions, a further check on earlier results and an indication of the absence of major bias from deflating.[39]

For 1900–1958, the results are shown in (15) and (15').

$$\ln \frac{1}{V_1} = 2.21 - 1.78 \ln r + .02 \ln \frac{W}{P} + w_1 \bar{R} = .98 \qquad (15)$$

t values   (30.4)   (.61)

$$\ln \frac{1}{V_2} = 1.37 - 1.34 \ln r + .23 \ln \frac{W}{P} + w_2 \bar{R} = .96 \qquad (15')$$

t values   (19.5)   (6.4)

Note that V_1 depends only on interest rates while V_2 depends on both interest rates and wealth as the hypothesis (and the arithmetic) implies. The results for V_1 are quite consistent with those obtained by Latané, except that the interest elasticity is much higher (in absolute value) as a consequence of the measurement procedure used here.

Evidence of the time trend in velocity is given by the asset elasticities. This question has often been discussed by economists, and Selden in particular has noted that much of the difference in findings has been due to differences in definition.[40] However, Selden chooses to include time deposits in his measure of velocity and concludes that there was a marked decline in V from 1839–1939 or from 1909–46, and little net change from 1929–51. A similar result, obtained by Warburton earlier, is also due to the inclusion of time deposits in the definition of money.[41]

The results here clearly indicate that for 1900–1958 the secular trend in velocity holds only for V_2. V_1 is dependent solely on the interest rate—a trend-free variable. But V_2 depends on real assets, which increased approximately 275 per cent during the first half of the century. Hence during that period V_2 fell by approximately 40 per cent according to the estimate of equation (15′). This fall, however, is largely a result of measurement procedures representing as it does the increase in time deposits relative to other components of the money stock. Moreover, the denial of a time trend in V_1 does not depend on the choice of rW as the denominator in equation (15). Similar results with respect to secular trend are obtained for the V_i if velocity is defined as the ratio of net national product to money stock.

Those who have argued that there has been a secular decline in velocity have often pointed to the latter part of the nineteenth century, particularly the last two decades, in support of their position. Indeed the fall in measured velocity during that period is most striking. My results do not directly bear on this point. However, a "prediction" of the results for earlier years has been obtained by extrapolating beyond the sample period.

From 1859–99, Selden's series V-39 fell by 70 per cent.[42] Macaulay's Railroad Bond Yields fell approximately 50 per cent during the same period. Since Selden's V-39 includes time deposits, we multiply the percentage fall in bond yields by the estimated elasticity from equation (15′) (1.34). The predicted fall in velocity for the forty-year period is therefore 67 per cent—that is, within 3 per cent of the actual fall in velocity.

Friedman's measure shows that velocity (again including time deposits) peaked about 1880. In 1879, his graph shows V as approximately 4.75. By 1899 it had fallen to 2.5, a drop of roughly 48 per cent in twenty years.[43] Macaulay's Bond Yields declined by 34 per cent during the same period. Again multiplying by the interest elasticity from equation (15'), the predicted fall in velocity is 46 per cent, or 2 per cent less than the actual fall.

Thus it appears that the demand function for money has been stable for almost a century. But these results are too good, for as noted, there has been a secular fall in V_2 in this century resulting from the inclusion of time deposits in this measure. Applying the asset elasticity would indicate a further fall in velocity and an over-estimate of the decline in the nineteenth century. Nevertheless, the "predictions" do suggest that the much discussed fall in velocity at the end of the last century can be interpreted as a response to the decline in interest rates when the elasticity is estimated for M/rW rather than M/Y. If we interpret the secular trend in V_2 as a reflection of the growth of time deposits relative to other components of the money stock, the "prediction" suggests that the growth of financial intermediaries and thus the non-zero asset elasticity of equation (15') are phenomena associated with the twentieth rather than the late nineteenth century.

The successful prediction of the fall in velocity at the end of the nineteenth century as an interest rate phenomenon is of course critically dependent on the value of parameters. These in turn are the result of a particular specification for the velocity variable— that is, the use of $r \cdot W$ as the numerator in place of the more commonly used measure of income. A good prediction is not obtained when measured net national product (or for Latané, measured gross national product) is used as the numerator of velocity. Therefore this result lends strong support to the wealth hypothesis developed here and to the use of permanent velocity, M/rW, in the explanation of economic behavior over time.[44]

Ritter's notion that there is an upper bound to velocity seems to be denied by the data. For interest rates that have ranged from 2.35 to 5.31 per cent there is little evidence of a velocity ceiling. If such a ceiling exists, evidence for it should take the form of large positive values for w_1 in equation (15) during periods of high interest rates; that is, the measured value of $1/V_1$ should exceed the predicted value by a large amount. In fact, the measured value did exceed the predicted value when interest rates were above 5 per cent, but the size of the residual is not substantial. This suggests that the velocity relation has not reached an upper bound for any of the interest rates observed in this century.

The results of this section, like those for the money demand function in earlier sections, support the conclusions reached at the end of Section I. They strongly suggest that the demand function for money constructed here, based on a theory of asset preference, is stable. The theory and the empirical tests have required only two arguments—interest rates and real non-human wealth—to approximate the recorded behavior of real money balances for almost sixty years and for a number of shorter sub-periods. Of the two arguments, one (real wealth) appears to be unnecessary for the velocity relation when money is defined as currency plus demand deposits. Both arguments appear to be relevant when time deposits are included in the definition of money. This suggests that the much discussed issue of a trend in velocity is analogous to the problem of whether or not money is a luxury. Both depend on the use of a definition of money which is broader than M_1.

The velocity estimates provide additional evidence on the stability of the demand function for they suggest that the prolonged fall in velocity at the end of the nineteenth century can be explained in terms of the hypothesis developed here. We now turn briefly to discuss some additional evidence of the stability of the money demand function and some policy considerations before indicating some implications of the results for monetary theory.

VI. *Policy Considerations*

Policy actions are designed primarily for their short-run effects and are a response principally to short-run changes. The results here are based on longer periods of time and refer more to the secular than to the cyclical performance of the economy. Two methods of relating short- and long-run functions are (1) comparison of the estimates obtained for sub-periods, for example, cycles or decades, with those for the entire period, and (2) comparison of related cross-section studies. A considerable body of evidence of both types has now been accumulated. Some of the major findings are reported here before I briefly consider some policy implications.

The most impressive finding from the decade estimates is the relative stability of the money demand or velocity function. The major exceptions (see Table 4) include observations drawn from the forties, particularly from the postwar, pre-Accord period. Interest rate ceilings were effectively maintained on financial assets during this period, but it is likely that such ceilings were largely irrelevant with respect to reducing the rising yields on non-financial assets.

The earlier discussion of the measure of assets which is relevant for money-holding decisions suggested that over time the yields on most aggregate measures of wealth move in roughly parallel fashion. Suppose velocity (or money demand) adjusts to the relative yield on real wealth (or the spread between yields on financial and real assets). Then for the period up to World War II, the choice between broadly based measures of asset yields is largely a

TABLE 4   Elasticity of V_1 with Respect to Interest Rates

PERIOD	INTEREST ELASTICITY
1900–58	1.78
1900–09	2.37
1910–19	1.10
1920–29	1.21
1930–39	1.66
1940–49	2.14
1950–58	1.02

matter of convenience. But once price control is instituted for financial assets, this is no longer true. In short, my study of the interest elasticity for various cycles suggests that the interest rate to which velocity adjusted during the forties was considerably higher than the quoted corporate bond yield, the measure that works well for earlier and later periods.

Of course there is an alternative interpretation. The result might suggest that the velocity function, hence the demand for money, was unstable in the war and immediate postwar years. I reject this explanation. In a regime of price controls, it would be surprising to find the price ratios equal to the marginal rates of substitution between commodities. The effect of price controls is to distort observed economic relationships. Similar results undoubtedly hold for bond price controls or pegged interest rates.

The decade of the thirties would require little comment were it not for the many attempts to find evidence in support of the low-level liquidity trap. The data deny that the interest elasticity of the demand for money or velocity became exceptionally large during that decade. Indeed, the interest elasticity of V_1 (1.66) was slightly *below* the average for the fifty-nine years (1.78). Substantially similar conclusions are reached if we consider the data for individual cycles. Moreover, interest rates on long-term corporate bonds continued to adjust downward during the decade from the high of 4.70 reached in 1932. Annual rates fell to 2.90 in 1937, rose very slightly in the recovery of 1938, and fell again to 2.50 in 1941. Like the evidence on velocity that I have examined, the almost continual fall in interest rates denies the existence of the low-level liquidity trap.

None of the foregoing implies that a given change in the interest rate is equally effective with respect to absolute money holdings in deep and mild depression. The money demand function is a curve of relatively constant elasticity—not constant marginal propensity to hold money. Taking derivatives of (say) equation (3) shows that the marginal propensity to hold money with respect to interest rates is negative and dependent on the ratio M/r as well as the parameters of the equation. At low interest rates the slope of the function becomes quite large in absolute value. Relatively large increases in the money supply would therefore be required to restore equilibrium once a deep depression has occurred.

The cross-section studies give results that are quite consistent with those presented here.[45] In particular, they suggest strongly that the demand for money is approximately unit elastic with respect to wealth. However, they imply that some additional variables must be considered in discussions of the reaction of the economy to cyclical and policy changes.

For one important implication of the cross-section studies is that changes in the distribution of output between industries result in quite different totals for the aggregate demand for cash balances. Similar effects appear to operate if the composition of output changes such that large firms within an industry increase their sales relative to small firms or vice versa. In short, during cycles the demand for money appears to depend on the composition of output.

It follows then that both the flow of aggregate income (or its rate of change) and the money supply (or its rate of change) may be the same at corresponding points in any two cycles while the excess demand for money is different in one than the other. The variables that serve as guides to policy, for example, excess or free reserves and the rate of change of prices, need not be the same in the two cases. Under these circumstances policy-makers can easily be misled into making excessive, insufficient, or ill-timed changes.

If additional studies confirm the above results, the policy-maker must be equipped with more, or at least different, information than he now collects. In particular, the existence of a stable demand function for money suggests that the quantity of money demanded would be a most useful addition to the list of variables that the policy-maker studies. Certainly the quantity demanded would be helpful in deciding whether money is "tight" or "loose" in the aggregate. But if distribution effects are important, as the cross-section studies seem to suggest, knowledge of the aggregate quantity of money demanded and supplied will be useful but insufficient for policy purposes.

VII. *Conclusion*

Three issues in contemporary monetary theory—(1) the variables or arguments on which the demand for money depends, (2) the stability of the demand function, and (3) the definition of money to be used in monetary analysis—are noted in the introduction. Other issues, such as the assumption of homogeneity of the demand function with respect to prices and financial assets or the conclusion that money is a "luxury," were introduced at other points in the paper. It seems useful to summarize the empirical findings with respect to these questions before considering some more general implications of the results.

First, with respect to the arguments of the function, we have found that, during the first six decades of this century, non-human wealth and interest rates have been of almost equal importance in explaining the demand for real cash balances. Interest rates have played the predominant role in determining the level of velocity.

Second, a comparison of estimates for various measures of wealth and various definitions of money strongly suggest that the demand function developed here is stable for several alternative definitions of money. These results seem to hold for both nominal and real cash balances and for a number of short and long periods. When the wealth model was compared to other hypotheses, based on measured or permanent income, the results supported the present hypothesis. The parameters of the wealth model appear to be more stable over time than those obtained from the estimates of the income and permanent income equations.

Third, with respect to the definition of money, the evidence from the time series does not support the view that monetary theory must be concerned with a concept more inclusive than currency plus demand deposits to obtain a stable demand relation. The demand functions for money defined inclusive of time or time plus savings deposits are no more stable in the long run than the demand function for money defined exclusive of these financial assets. Moreover, the time series evidence suggests that the use of more inclusive definitions of money mixes the effects of general and relative changes in interest rates on desired money holdings. The evidence further suggests that the observed growth of financial intermediaries relative to commercial banks reflects the effect of increased wealth on the desired allocation of wealth rather than a substitution effect as Gurley and Shaw have suggested.

Taken together the evidence bears on some additional issues. It supports the interpretation that the demand function developed here is homogeneous of first degree in prices and financial assets, a result that has been assumed in much aggregate theory. It denies that money is a "luxury." Examination of the evidence shows that the "luxury" proposition holds only when money is defined to include time or savings deposits. And the data deny the existence of a low-level liquidity trap, a proposition that has received attention in discussions of the ineffectiveness of monetary policy.

A more general issue in monetary and macroeconomic theory is involved in the disputes about the variables that enter the demand function for money and the stability of the function. Once monetary theory is formulated in terms of the demand to hold an asset subject to cost and yield considerations, rather than as a direct relation among money, income, and prices, attention is shifted to the determinants of the desired asset composition of households and business.

The importance of the stability of asset demand functions to this approach is obvious. The definition of money balances is also important. If stability of the demand function for money requires that a number of financial assets be included in the definition of money, the problem of finding stable relations is shifted to the supply function for money. The exogenous stock of base money, the part directly controlled by central banks and governments, is but a small part of demand deposits plus currency. To predict the effect of policy changes on the excess supply of or demand for money, a theory of money supply is required. At a minimum, such a theory must be able to specify the desired allocation of assets into cash and portfolio assets by banks and the desired allocation of money between currency and demand deposits by the public. Broader definitions of money that include liabilities of financial intermediaries as part of the money supply require the specification of additional behavior relations including the interaction between banks and financial intermediaries, the desired asset allocation of intermediaries, etc.[46] In short, broader definitions of money require more useful knowledge about both the precise behavior relations on the supply side and the stability of such relations.

For the monetary theorist, the joint interaction of the demand for and supply of money are central to the problem of monetary policy and the stabilization of the economy. Monetary policy, debt management, and other policy changes operate through the money supply mechanism and thereby change interest rates and other determinants of the supply of money. If the elasticities of the variables in the demand-and-supply functions for money are such that the quantity of money demanded is always equal to the quantity supplied, the economy is in a low-level liquidity trap. The addition of the yield on real capital and the value of expected human income to the model of the demand for money developed here, the substitution of wealth for income as the principal constraint on money holdings, and/or the specification of a supply function for money in place of an exogenously determined quantity of money do not *then* alter the conclusion that changing the exogenous determinants of the money supply will not change the level of income.

The model and the evidence presented here together with recent developments in money supply theory (see n. 46) suggest that changes in the policy variables that are exogenous determinants of the supply of money give rise to desired money holdings that differ from actual money holdings. The relevant elasticities suggest that exogenous changes in base money initiated at the discretion of the central bank lead to changes in the actual supply of money. Denial of the liquidity trap suggests that desired money balances neither rise nor fall as much as actual money balances in the initial response to increases or decreases in the policy variables. Thus the exogenous change in base money leads to a reallocation of assets in the portfolios of households and business by altering relative yields on financial assets or other determinants of the demand for money. Attempts by the public to readjust its portfolios, to find new balance sheet equilibriums, give rise to further changes in asset composition, to changes in the flow variables income, consumption, and investment, and to attendant changes in total wealth.

One alternative view of economic behavior, the income-expenditure approach, concentrates directly on the determinants of the flow variables and ignores portfolio adjustments or considers only the adjustment between money and bonds.[47] A third macroeconomic model looks at the economy in terms of the allocation of assets in portfolios but, as noted in the introduction, considers the demand-and-supply equations for physical capital as the relations of central theoretic and practical interest. In this model, money is but one of a number of financial assets.[48]

The problem for the economist is to decide between these three broad approaches and the many variants of each approach. Central to such a decision is the ability to find more stable functional relations in one approach than in the others, to be able to predict more accurately with one than with the others. The evidence from the time series suggests that the monetary approach presented here is promising.

NOTES

1. H. G. Johnson, "Monetary Theory and Policy," *American Economic Review* (June 1962), pp. 344–45 (pp. 13–14).

2. J. R. Hicks, "A Suggestion for Simplifying the Theory of Money," *Economica* (1935), reprinted in F. Lutz and L. Mints (eds.), *Readings in Monetary Theory* (New York: Blakiston, 1951); M. Friedman, "The Quantity Theory of Money—A Restatement," in M. Friedman (ed.), *Studies in the Quantity Theory of Money* (Chicago 1956) [reprinted in this volume—Ed.], J. Tobin, "Liquidity Preference as Behavior Towards Risk," *Review of Economic Studies* (1958) [reprinted in this volume—Ed.], and "Money, Capital and Other Stores of Value," *American Economic Review* (May 1961). See also R. Turvey, *Interest Rates and Asset Prices* (New York: The Macmillan Co., 1961). For a more extensive discussion and bibliography see Johnson, *op. cit.*

3. Friedman, *op. cit.*

4. See articles by Tobin cited in note 2 above, and J. Gurley and E. Shaw, *Money in a Theory of Finance* (Washington: Brookings Institution, 1960).

5. Tobin, "Money, Capital and Other Stores of Value," *op. cit.*, p. 35.

6. Tobin, "The Interest Elasticity of the Transactions Demand for Cash," *Review of Economics and Statistics* (1956), and W. J. Baumol, "The Transactions Demand for Cash: An Inventory Theoretic Approach," *Quarterly Journal of Economics* (November 1952) [reprinted in this volume— Ed.]. It should be noted that neither author has provided evidence in support of this conclusion. My direct test of the model produces generally negative results (see my paper, "The Demand for Money: A Cross-Section Study of Business Firms," *Quarterly Journal of Economics* (August 1963).

7. M. Friedman, "The Demand for Money: Some Theoretical and Empirical Results," *Journal of Political Economy* (August 1959) [reprinted in this volume—Ed.].

8. Cf. Tobin's "Money, Capital and Other Stores of Value," *op. cit.*, for example.

9. Freidman, "The Demand for Money . . . ," *op. cit.* On page 349 he refers to his "inability to find any close connection between changes in velocity from cycle to cycle and any of a number of interest rates." See also his discussion of the residuals from the velocity equation and his argument that a "highly sensitive" response to interest rates would imply that real cash balances would be highly variable both secularly and cyclically and his citation of the evidence on secular stability of cash balances.

10. M. Bronfenbrenner and T. Mayer, "Liquidity Functions in the American Economy," *Econometrica* (1960).

11. In "Rejoinder to Professor Eisner," *Econometrica* (July 1963), Bronfenbrenner and Mayer now note that the definition of wealth that they used was inappropriate for a proper test of the wealth model.

12. H. A. Latané, "Cash Balances and the Interest Rate: A Pragmatic Approach," *Review of Economics and Statistics* (November 1954), and "Income Velocity and Interest Rates: A Pragmatic Approach," *ibid.* (November 1960) [reprinted in this volume—Ed.].

13. The view is expressed most clearly in J. Gurley, "Liquidity and Financial Institutions in the Postwar Economy," *Study of Employment, Growth and Price Levels* (Joint Economic Committee [Washington 1960]). It is implicit in the argument of Gurley and Shaw, *op. cit.*

14. Friedman, "The Quantity Theory . . . ," *op. cit.*

15. The latter point has been stressed by Karl Brunner in "The Report of the Commission on Money and Credit," *Journal of Political Economy* (December 1961) [reprinted in this volume—Ed]. See also P. Cagan, "Why Do We Use Money in Open Market Operations?" *Journal of Political Economy* (February 1958).

16. Some alternative assumptions and the inclusion of some additional variables have been suggested. For example, Friedman assumes that the function is homogeneous in population. This question and the question of homogeneity in prices and financial assets are discussed below.

17. The question and some evidence on the short-run behavior of the function are considered also in a paper by the present author and Karl Brunner, "Predicting Velocity: Implications for Theory and Policy," *Journal of Finance* (May 1963).

18. R. W. Goldsmith, *A Study of Saving in the United States* (Princeton, N.J.: Princeton University Press, 1956), Vol. 3, Table W–1. I return to a discussion of the measurement of wealth below. See especially note 22 and the section to which it relates.

19. The series on money M_1 was taken from the U.S. Bureau of the Census, *Historical Statistics of the United States* (Washington 1960), Series X 267. Series X 266, denoted M_3 in the text, which includes time deposits at commercial banks, mutual savings banks, and the postal savings system, was also used. M_2 includes time deposits of commercial banks but not at other savings institutions. It was courteously supplied by Anna J. Schwartz. Interest rates are from Series X 346 as published in *Historical Statistics* . . . . The data on wealth are from Goldsmith, *op. cit.*, Table W–1, with adjustments to exclude government structures, inventories, public land, and the monetary gold and silver stock and to include the monetary and non-monetary (interest bearing and non-interest bearing) debt of state, local, and federal governments. The exclusions were based upon Goldsmith's estimates; I am indebted to Phillip Cagan for supplying a series of unpublished estimates of interest bearing and non-interest bearing federal debt. I am also indebted to Goldsmith and Lipsey for providing balance sheets for the postwar years that appear in their *Studies in the National Balance Sheet of the United States*, 2 vols., National Bureau of Economic Research (Princeton, N.J.: Princeton University Press, 1963).

20. The interest elasticity of $M_3/p = -.54$ for 1900–1958.

21. Gurley and Shaw, *op. cit.*

22. Goldsmith, *op. cit.*, Vol. 3, Table W-1. The Goldsmith definition of wealth is approximately equal to the sum of tangible assets shown on the balance sheets in Tables W-9 through W-16. (The difference arises because of the inclusion in wealth, but not on the balance sheets, of net foreign assets and the inclusion on the balance sheets, but not in wealth, of the Treasury's net holdings of silver certificates minus minor coins.) Goldsmith's wealth exceeds tangible assets when net foreign assets are positive and vice versa. Goldsmith's total assets exceed wealth by the sum of intangible assets plus or minus the above differences. His measure of net worth is always larger than his measure of wealth. The difference is equal to (tangible assets minus wealth) plus (intangible assets minus liabilities). The latter difference is, of course, always positive and equals Δ currency plus Δ deposits in other financial institutions plus receivables from business and households minus payables to financial intermediaries, other business, and households plus securities and equities minus bond and note liabilities plus other intangible assets minus other liabilities (Δ = the difference between the corresponding asset and liability items). The principal difference between the two is the ownership of equity assets. If this item is excluded, the remaining difference is never more than 1.5 per cent of total intangible assets. Total assets (A) were taken from

Goldsmith, *op. cit.*, Tables W-9 through W-16, and were available for eight benchmark dates from 1900–1949. The series used in the estimates for 1900–1945 was obtained by taking the ratio of total assets, A, to wealth, G (from Table W-1). Denote this ratio for any base year as b_o. Let b_n = the next base year ratio, and let $i = 0, 1, \ldots, n$ be an index of the years between base year dates inclusive of the end points. Then

$$A_i = \left[\frac{(n - i)}{n} b_o + \frac{i}{n} b_n \right] G_i.$$

A similar procedure was used to construct the net worth series, denoted N.

As noted, these measures of wealth, A and N, involve double counting. Of particular importance is the inclusion of equities as a part of the assets of households while at the same time plant and equipment are included among the assets of business. I am indebted to Goldsmith and Lipsey for supplying preliminary estimates of their data for the years 1945–58. These have been used to extend the estimates based on total assets through 1958 as shown in Table 1.

23. In passing it should be noted that this result is quite similar to the one obtained by Bronfenbrenner and Mayer ("Liquidity Functions . . . ," *op. cit.*) in their estimate 3, which used total money balances as the dependent variable. This suggests that their failure to find a positive coefficient for wealth results, in part at least, from an incorrect specification of the wealth variable.

24. As is well known, Marshall introduced wealth into the money demand function in *Money, Credit and Commerce* (London: Macmillan & Co., 1923), Chapter 4, when he described the function but dropped wealth in the rest of his discussion.

25. Friedman, "The Quantity Theory . . . ," *op. cit.*, p. 12 (p. 76).

26. Note that the interest elasticities in (9) and (10) are always lower than those shown earlier in (3) and (3'). It was pointed out above that combining P/p, an index of interest rates, with the measured interest rate would raise the interest elasticity. The results here suggest that the change is small but in the appropriate direction.

27. The relatively high interest elasticity of eq. (11) (-1.77) has an interesting implication. Let Z/p be an approximation of permanent income from human and non-human wealth, that is, $Z/p = rW/p$. If $\ln Z/p - \ln r = \ln W/p$ is substituted in (3) above, we obtain $\ln M_1/p = k - .95 \ln r + 1.11 (\ln Z/p - \ln r) = k - 2.06 \ln r + 1.11 \ln Z/p$ as the parameters of (11) which would be consistent with (3). In fact, the parameters of (11) are slightly lower owing most likely to errors of measurement.

28. Friedman, "The Demand for Money . . . ," *op.cit.*, p. 349 (pp. 111–12).

29. *Ibid.*, p. 345 (p. 106).

30. It should be noted that the precise meaning of Y_p needs clarification. Friedman defines it as the yield on wealth, refers to it as expected income, and measures it as an exponentially weighted average of past incomes. Clearly, it could be all three in principle although the extent to which they are equal is an open (and difficult) empirical question.

From the fact that Friedman at times refers to Y_p as wealth, we may infer that he may mean that "permanent" interest rates rather than current rates equate some permanent measure of wealth to permanent income. Permanent interest rates would most likely have lower cyclical amplitude than market rates. Permanent income would then reflect changes in permanent wealth principally. I have taken the equation as a definition of permanent income.

31. I am indebted to Anna J. Schwartz for making available to me the data that she and Milton Friedman used in their books and that served as the basis for Friedman's estimates.

32. A notable exception is the interest elasticity for 1940–49. We will return to this point in the discussion of velocity.

33. The interest elasticity is not altered greatly by the fact that Friedman deflates by population, though the permanent income elasticity is raised by this procedure. When (14) is not deflated by population, the interest elasticity $= -.39$ and the income elasticity $= 1.23$. These coefficients are quite similar to those obtained when the function is stated in terms of interest rates and real wealth.

34. Note that despite the problem of multicollinearity, eq. (14) again suggests that the function is homogeneous of first degree in prices and financial assets.

35. See also note 39 below and the paragraph to which it relates.

36. L. Ritter, "Income Velocity and Anti-Inflationary Monetary Policy," *American Economic Review* (March 1959). A rather complete ancient history of the discussion may be found in A. W. Marget, *The Theory of Prices* (New York: Prentice-Hall, Inc., 1938), and in H. Hegeland, *The Quantity Theory of Money* (Göteborg 1951). A more recent bibliography and a stimulating discussion are provided by R. Selden in his "Monetary Velocity in the United States," M. Friedman (ed.) in *Studies in the Quantity Theory of Money*, (Chicago: University of Chicago Press, 1956).

37. Latané, "Cash Balances and the Interest Rate . . . ," *op. cit.*, and "Income Velocity and Interest Rates . . . ," *op. cit.*

38. Problems of specification are also involved in the choice of the ratio of debits to demand deposits as a measure of velocity. There is little a priori reason to suggest that this ratio should behave in a manner similar to that of income velocity. Assume, for example, that changes in expectations of future yields cause readjustment of asset portfolios such that the quantity of money demanded remains the same. Specifically, at the existing asset prices, assume that there is an excess demand for land and an excess supply of equities. Portfolio adjustments will change the relative prices until asset equilibrium is restored. Income velocity, the ratio of income to money stock, need not change, since neither the flow of income nor the stock of money necessarily changes in the process of adjustment. But debits to demand deposits have risen and this measure of velocity is higher. Other explanations of the differences in these ratios have been suggested elsewhere and need not be elaborated here (see Selden, *op. cit.*, pp. 215–17).

39. Note two points: first, the definition of V_i differs from the usual definition since rW is a measure of the "permanent" income from non-

human assets; second, eq. (15) and (15') provide a further check on the question of homogeneity of first degree in population. If the absence of population, N', as an argument in the development of eq. (1) introduces bias, the empirical estimates of (15) and (15') would not be consistent with the estimates for (3) and (3'). Since $M_i/rW = M_iN'/rWN'$, the consistency of the two sets of estimates is another test of whether the population variable should be included in a proper specification of the demand function for money. Of course we cannot be certain about the results of this test since other (unnamed) variables may be operating to make the money demand and velocity estimates consistent. Nevertheless, the consistency of the M_i and V_i parameter estimates does increase confidence in the demand function for money developed here.

40. Selden, *op. cit.*, pp. 187–90.

41. C. Warburton, "The Secular Trend in Monetary Velocity," *Quarterly Journal of Economics* (1949).

42. Selden, *op. cit.*, p. 220, Table 9.

43. Friedman, "The Demand for Money . . . ," *op. cit.*, p. 340, Chart 1. (Figure 1, p. 101).

44. Scatter diagrams plotting the relation between $1/V_1$ and r confirm the velocity function's stability in the first 59 years of this century.

45. Meltzer, *op. cit.*

46. For some developments in supply theory, see Karl Brunner, "A Schema for the Supply Theory of Money," *International Economic Review* (January 1961), and "The Structure of the Monetary System and the Supply Function for Money"; Cagan, "The Demand for Currency Relative to the Total Money Supply," *Journal of Political Economy* (August 1958); Allan H. Meltzer, "The Behavior of the French Money Supply, 1938–1954," *Journal of Political Economy* (June 1959); and a paper by Karl Brunner and Allan H. Meltzer, "The Place of Financial Intermediaries in the Transmission of Monetary Policy," *American Economic Review* (May 1963).

47. The term "income-expenditure approach" refers to a class of models rather than to a specific set of hypotheses. In its simplest form, the income-expenditure approach is perhaps best represented by the familiar textbook "models of income determination." Cf. G. L. Bach, *Economics*, or P. A. Samuelson, *Economics: An Introductory Analysis*, for examples. Numerous more sophisticated versions of the general approach exist. Perhaps the most familiar version is the Klein-Goldberger model. Cf. L. R. Klein and A. S. Goldberger, *An Econometric Model of the United States, 1929–1952* (Amsterdam: North Holland Publishing Co., 1955).

48. Cf. Tobin, "Money, Capital and Other Stores of Value," *op. cit.*

B. Asset Preference Theory

6 The Transactions Demand for Cash: An Inventory Theoretic Approach

William J. Baumol *Princeton University*

A stock of cash is its holder's inventory of the medium of exchange, and like an inventory of a commodity, cash is held because it can be given up at the appropriate moment, serving then as its possessor's part of the bargain in an exchange. We might consequently expect that inventory theory and monetary theory can learn from one another. This note attempts to apply one well-known result in inventory control analysis to the theory of money.[1]

A Simple Model

We are now interested in analyzing the transactions demand for cash dictated by rational behavior, which for our purposes means the holding of those cash balances that can do the job at minimum cost. To abstract from precautionary and speculative demands let us consider a state in which transactions are perfectly foreseen and occur *in a steady stream*.

Suppose that in the course of a given period an individual will pay out T dollars in a steady stream. He obtains cash either by

Reprinted from *Quarterly Journal of Economics*, Vol. 66 (Cambridge, Mass.: Harvard University Press, November 1952), 545–56, by permission of the author and publisher. Copyright, 1952, by the President and Fellows of Harvard College.

borrowing it, or by withdrawing it from an investment, and in either case his interest cost (or interest opportunity cost) is i dollars per dollar per period. Suppose finally that he withdraws cash in lots of C dollars spaced evenly throughout the year, and that each time he makes such a withdrawal he must pay a fixed "broker's fee" of b dollars.[2] Here T, the value of transactions, is predetermined, and i and b are assumed to be constant.

In this situation any value of C less than or equal to T will enable him to meet his payments equally well provided he withdraws the money often enough. For example, if T is \$100, he can meet his payments by withdrawing \$50 every six months or \$25 quarterly, etc.[3] Thus he will make $\frac{T}{C}$ withdrawals over the course of the year, at a total cost in "brokers' fees" given by $\frac{bT}{C}$.

In this case, since each time he withdraws C dollars he spends it in a steady stream and draws out a similar amount the moment it is gone, his average cash holding will be $\frac{C}{2}$ dollars. His annual interest cost of holding cash will then be $\frac{iC}{2}$.

The total amount the individual in question must pay for the use of the cash needed to meet his transaction when he borrows C dollars at intervals evenly spaced throughout the year will then be the sum of interest cost and "brokers' fees" and so will be given by

$$\frac{bT}{C} + \frac{iC}{2}. \tag{1}$$

Since the manner in which he meets his payments is indifferent to him, his purpose only being to pay for his transactions, rationality requires that he do so at minimum cost, i.e., that he choose the most economical value of C. Setting the derivative of (1) with respect to C equal to zero we obtain[4]

$$-\frac{bT}{C^2} + \frac{i}{2} = 0,$$

i.e.,

$$C = \sqrt{\frac{2bT}{i}}. \tag{2}$$

Thus, in the simple situation here considered, the rational individual will, given the price level,[5] demand cash in proportion to the square root of the value of his transactions.

Before examining the implications of this crude model we may note that, as it stands, it applies to two sorts of cases: that of the individual (or firm) obtaining cash from his invested capital and that of the individual (or firm) spending out of borrowing in anticipation of future receipts. Since our problem depends on non-coincidence of cash receipts and disbursements, and we have assumed that cash disbursements occur in a steady stream, one other case seems possible, that where receipts precede expenditures. This differs from the first case just mentioned (living off one's capital) in that the individual now has the option of withholding some or all of his receipts from investment and simply keeping the cash until it is needed. Once this withheld cash is used up the third case merges into the first: the individual must obtain cash from his invested capital until his next cash receipt occurs.

We can deal with this third case as follows. First, note that any receipts exceeding anticipated disbursements will be invested, since, eventually, interest earnings must exceed ("brokerage") cost of investment. Hence we need only deal with that part of the cash influx which is to be used in making payments during the period between receipts. Let this amount, as before, be T dollars. Of this let I dollars be invested, and the remainder, R dollars, be withheld, where either of these sums may be zero. Again let i be the interest rate, and let the "broker's fee" for withdrawing cash be given by the linear expression $b_w + k_w C$, where C is the amount withdrawn. Finally, let there be a "broker's fee" for investing (depositing) cash given by $b_d + k_d I$ where the b's and the k's are constants.

Since the disbursements are continuous, the $R = T - I$ dollars withheld from investment will serve to meet payments for a fraction of the period between consecutive receipts given by $\dfrac{T - I}{T}$. Moreover, since the average cash holding for that time will be $\dfrac{T - I}{2}$, the interest cost of withholding that money will be $\dfrac{T - I}{T} i \dfrac{T - I}{2}$. Thus the total cost of withholding the R dollars and investing the I dollars will be

$$\frac{T - I}{2} i \frac{T - I}{T} + b_d + k_d I.$$

Analogously, the total cost of obtaining cash for the remainder of the period will be

$$\frac{C}{2} i \frac{I}{T} + (b_w + k_w C) \frac{I}{C}.$$

Thus the total cost of cash operations for the period will be given by the sum of the last two expressions, which when differentiated partially with respect to C and set equal to zero once again yields our square root formula, (2), with $b = b_w$.

Thus, in this case, the optimum cash balance after the initial cash holding is used up will again vary with the square root of the volume of transactions, as is to be expected by analogy with the "living off one's capital" case.

There remains the task of investigating $R/2$, the (optimum) average cash balance before drawing on invested receipts begins. We again differentiate our total cost of holding cash, this time partially with respect to I, and set it equal to zero, obtaining

$$ -\frac{T - I}{T} i + k_d + \frac{Ci}{2T} + \frac{b_w}{C} + k_w = 0, $$

i.e.,

$$ R = T - I = \frac{C}{2} + \frac{b_w T}{Ci} + \frac{T(k_d + k_w)}{i}, $$

or since from the preceding result, $C^2 = 2Tb_w/i$, so that the second term on the right-hand side equals $C^2/2C$,

$$ R = C + T\left(\frac{k_w + k_d}{i}\right). $$

The first term in this result is to be expected, since if *everything* were deposited at once, C dollars would have to be withdrawn at that same moment to meet current expenses. On this amount two sets of "brokers' fees" would have to be paid and no interest would be earned—a most unprofitable operation.[6]

Since C varies as the square root of T and the other term varies in proportion with T, R will increase less than in proportion with T, though more nearly in proportion than does C. The general nature of our results is thus unaffected.[7]

Note finally that the entire analysis applies at once to the case of continuous receipts and discontinuous payments, taking the period to be that between two payments, where the relevant decision is the frequency of investment rather than the frequency of withdrawal. Similarly, it applies to continuous receipts and payments where the two are not equal.

Some Consequences of the Analysis

I shall not labor the obvious implications for financial budgeting by the firm. Rather I shall discuss several arguments which have been presented by monetary theorists, to which our result is relevant.

The first is the view put forth by several economists,[8] that in a stationary state there will be no demand for cash balances since it will then be profitable to invest all earnings in assets with a positive yield in such a way that the required amount will be realized at the moment any payment is to be made. According to this view no one will want any cash in such a stationary world, and the value of money must fall to zero so that there can really be no such thing as a truly static monetary economy. Clearly this argument neglects the transactions costs involved in making and collecting such loans (the "broker's fee").[9] Our model is clearly compatible with a static world and (2) shows that it will generally pay to keep some cash. The analysis of a stationary monetary economy in which there is a meaningful (finite) price level does make sense.

Another view which can be reëxamined in light of our analysis is that the transactions demand for cash will vary approximately in proportion with the money value of transactions.[10] This may perhaps even be considered the tenor of quantity theory though there is no necessary connection, as Fisher's position indicates. If such a demand for cash balances is considered to result from rational behavior, then (2) suggests that the conclusion cannot have general validity. On the contrary, the square root formula implies that demand for cash rises less than in proportion with the volume of transactions, so that there are, in effect, economies of large scale in the use of cash.

The magnitude of this difference should not be exaggerated, however. The phrase "varying as the square" may suggest larger effects than are actually involved. Equation (2) requires that the average transactions velocity of circulation vary exactly in proportion with the quantity of cash, so that, for example, a doubling of the stock of cash will *ceteris paribus*, just double velocity.[11]

A third consequence of the square root formula is closely connected with the second. The effect on real income of an injection of cash into the system may have been underestimated. For suppose that (2) is a valid expression for the general demand for cash, that there is widespread unemployment, and that for this or other reasons prices do not rise with an injection of cash. Suppose, moreover, that the rate of interest is unaffected, i.e., that none of the new cash is used to buy securities. Then so long as transactions do not rise so as to maintain the same proportion with the square of the quantity of money, people will want to get rid of cash. They will use it to demand more goods and services, thereby forcing the volume of transactions to rise still further. For let ΔC be the quantity of cash injected. If a proportionality (constant velocity) assumption involves transactions rising by $k\Delta C$, it is easily shown that (2) involves transactions rising by more than twice as much, the magnitude of the excess increasing with the ratio of the injection to the initial stock of cash. More precisely, the rise in transactions would then be given by[12]

$$2k\Delta C + \frac{k}{C}\,\Delta C^2.$$

Of course, the rate of interest would really tend to fall in such circumstances, and this would to some extent offset the effect of the influx of cash, as is readily seen when we rewrite (2) as

$$T = C^2 i / 2b. \tag{3}$$

Moreover, prices will rise to some extent,[13] and, of course, (3) at best is only an approximation. Nevertheless, it remains true that the effect of an injection of cash on, say, the level of employment, may often have been underestimated.[14] For whatever may be working to counteract it, the force making for increased employment is greater than if transactions tend, *ceteris paribus*, toward their original proportion to the quantity of cash.

Finally the square root formula lends support to the argument that wage cuts can help increase employment, since it follows that the Pigou effect and the related effects are stronger than they would be with a constant transactions velocity. Briefly the phenomenon which has come to be called the Pigou effect[15] may be summarized thus: General unemployment will result in reduction in the price level which must increase the purchasing power of the stock of cash provided the latter does not itself fall more than in proportion with prices.[16] This increased purchasing power will augment demand for commodities[17] or investment goods (either directly, or because it is used to buy securities and so forces down the rate of interest). In any case, this works for a reduction in unemployment.

Now the increase in the purchasing power of the stock of cash which results from fallen prices is equivalent to an injection of cash with constant prices. There is therefore exactly the same reason for suspecting the magnitude of the effect of the former on the volume of transactions has been underestimated, as in the case of the latter. Perhaps this can be of some little help in explaining why there has not been more chronic unemployment or runaway inflation in our economy.

The Simple Model and Reality

It is appropriate to comment on the validity of the jump from equation (2) to conclusions about the operation of the economy. At best, (2) is only a suggestive oversimplification, if for no other reason, because of the rationality assumption employed in its derivation. In addition the model is static. It takes the distribution of the firm's disbursements over time to be fixed, though it is to a large extent in the hands of the entrepreneur how he will time his expenditures. It assumes that there is one constant relevant rate of interest and that the "broker's fee" is constant or varies linearly with the magnitude of the sum involved. It posits a steady stream of payments and the absence of cash receipts during the relevant period. It deals only with the cash demand of a single economic unit and neglects interactions of the various demands for cash in the economy.[18] It neglects the precautionary and speculative demands for cash.

These are serious lacunae, and without a thorough investigation we have no assurance that our results amount to much more than an analytical curiosum. Nevertheless I offer only a few comments in lieu of analysis, and hope that others will find the subject worth further examination.

1. It is no doubt true that a majority of the public will find it impractical and perhaps pointless to effect every possible economy in the use of cash. Indeed the possibility may never occur to most people. Nevertheless, we may employ the standard argument that the largest cash users may more plausibly be expected to learn when it is profitable to reduce cash balances relative to transactions. The demand for cash by the community as a whole may then be affected similarly and by a significant amount. Moreover, it is possible that even small cash holders will sometimes institute some cash economies instinctively or by a process of trial and error not explicitly planned or analyzed.

2. With variable b and i the validity of our two basic results—the non-zero rational transactions demand for cash, and the less than proportionate rise in the rational demand for cash with the real volume of transactions, clearly depends on the nature of the responsiveness of the "brokerage fee" and the interest rate to the quantity of cash involved. The first conclusion will hold generally provided the "broker's fee" never falls below some preassigned level, e.g., it never falls below one mill per transaction, and provided the interest rate, its rate of change with C and the rate of change of the "broker's fee" all (similarly) have some upper bound, however large, at least when C is small.

The second conclusion will not be violated persistently unless the "brokerage fee" tends to vary almost exactly in proportion with C (and it pays to hold zero cash balances) except for what may roughly be described as a limited range of values of C. Of course, it is always possible that this "exceptional range" will be the one relevant in practice. Variations in the interest rate will tend to strengthen our conclusion provided the interest rate never decreases with the quantity of cash borrowed or invested.[19]

It would perhaps not be surprising if these sufficient conditions for the more general validity of our results were usually satisfied in practice.

3. If payments are lumpy but foreseen, cash may perhaps be employed even more economically. For then it may well pay to obtain cash just before large payments fall due with little or no added cost in "brokers' fees" and considerable savings in interest payments. The extreme case would be that of a single payment during the year which would call for a zero cash balance provided the cash could be loaned out profitably at all. Cash receipts during the relevant period may have similar effects, since they can be used to make payments which happen to be due at the moment the receipts arrive. Here the extreme case involves receipts and payments always coinciding in time and amounts in which case, again, zero cash balances would be called for. Thus lumpy payments and receipts of cash, with sufficient foresight, can make for economies in the use of cash, i.e., higher velocity. This may not affect the rate of increase in transactions velocity with the level of transactions, but may nevertheless serve further to increase the effect of an injection of cash and of a cut in wages and prices. With imperfect foresight, however, the expectation that payments may be lumpy may increase the precautionary demand for cash. Moreover, the existence of a "broker's fee" which must be paid on lending or investing cash received during the period is an added inducement to keep receipts until payments fall due rather than investing, and so may further increase the demand for cash.

4. The economy in a single person's use of cash resulting from an increase in the volume of his transactions may or may not have its analogue for the economy as a whole. "External economies" may well be present if one businessman learns cash-economizing techniques from the experiences of another when both increase their transactions. On the diseconomies side it is barely conceivable that an infectious liquidity fetishism will permit a few individuals reluctant to take advantage of cash saving opportunities to block these savings for the bulk of the community. Nevertheless, at least two such possible offsets come to mind: (a) The rise in the demand for brokerage services resulting from a general increase in transactions may bring about a rise in the "brokerage fee" and thus work for an increase in average cash balances (a decreased number of visits to brokers). If cash supplies are sticky this will tend to be offset by rises in the rate of interest resulting from a rising total demand for cash, which serve to make cash more expensive to hold. (b) Widespread cash economizing might require an increase in

precautionary cash holdings because in an emergency one could rely less on the ability of friends to help or creditors to be patient. This could weaken but not offset the relative reduction in cash holdings entirely, since the increase in precautionary demand is contingent on there being some relative decrease in cash holdings.

5. A priori analysis of the precautionary and the speculative demands for cash is more difficult. In particular, there seems to be little we can say about the latter, important though it may be, except that it seems unlikely that it will work consistently in any special direction. In dealing with the precautionary demand, assumptions about probability distributions and expectations must be made.[20] It seems plausible offhand, that an increase in the volume of transactions will make for economies in the use of cash for precautionary as well as transactions purposes by permitting increased recourse to insurance principles.

Indeed, here we have a rather old argument in banking theory which does not seem to be widely known. Edgeworth,[21] and Wicksell[22] following him, suggested that a bank's precautionary cash requirements might also grow as the square root of the volume of its transactions (!). They maintained that cash demands on a bank tend to be normally distributed.[23] In this event, if it is desired to maintain a fixed probability of not running out of funds, precautionary cash requirements will be met by keeping on hand a constant multiple of the standard deviation (above the mean). But then the precautionary cash requirement of ten identical banks (with independent demands) together will be the same as that for any one of them multiplied by the square root of ten. For it is a well-known result that the standard deviation of a random sample from an infinite population increases as the square root of the size of the sample.

NOTES

1. T. M. Whitin informs me that the result in question goes back to the middle of the 1920's when it seems to have been arrived at independently by some half dozen writers. See, e.g., George F. Mellen, "Practical Lot Quantity Formula," *Management and Administration*, Vol. 10 (September 1925). Its significant implications for the economic theory of inventory, particularly for business cycle theory, seems to have gone unrecognized until recently when Dr. Whitin analyzed them in *The Theory of Inventory Management* (Princeton, N.J.: Princeton University Press, 1963) which, incidentally, first suggested the subject of this note to me. See also, Dr. Whitin's "Inventory Control in Theory and Practice" (*Quarterly Journal of Economics* [November 1952], p. 502), and Kenneth J. Arrow, Theodore Harris, and Jacob Marschak, "Optimal Inventory Policy," *Econometrica*, Vol. 19 (July 1951), especially pp. 252–55.

2. The term "broker's fee" is not meant to be taken literally. It covers all non-interest costs of borrowing or making a cash withdrawal. These include opportunity losses which result from having to dispose of assets just at the moment the cash is needed, losses involved in the poor resale price which results from an asset becoming "second-hand" when purchased by a non-professional dealer, administrative costs, and psychic costs (the trouble involved in making a withdrawal) as well as payment to a middleman. So conceived it seems likely that the "broker's fee" will, in fact, vary considerably with the magnitude of the funds involved, contrary to assumption. However, *some* parts of this cost will not vary with the amount involved—e.g., postage cost, bookkeeping expense, and, possibly, the withdrawer's effort. It seems plausible that the "broker's fee" will be better approximated by a function like $b + kC$ (where b and k are constants), which indicates that there is a part of the "broker's fee" increasing in proportion with the amount withdrawn. As shown in a subsequent footnote, however, our formal result is completely unaffected by this amendment.

We must also extend the meaning of the interest rate to include the value of protection against loss by fire, theft, etc., which we obtain when someone borrows our cash. On the other hand, a premium for the risk of default on repayment must be deducted. This protection obtained by lending seems to be mentioned less frequently by theorists than the risk, yet how can we explain the existence of interest-free demand deposits without the former?

3. In particular, if cash were perfectly divisible and no elapse of time were required from withdrawal through payment he could make his withdrawals in a steady stream. In this case he would never require any cash balances to meet his payments and C could be zero. However, as may be surmised, this would be prohibitive with any b greater than zero.

4. This result is unchanged if there is a part of the "broker's fee" which varies in proportion with the quantity of cash handled. For in this case the "broker's fee" for each loan is given by $b + kC$. Total cost in "brokers' fees" will then be

$$\frac{T}{C}(b + kC) = \frac{T}{C}b + kT.$$

Thus (1) will have the constant term, kT, added to it, which drops out in differentiation.

5. A doubling of *all* prices (including the "broker's fee") is like a change in the monetary unit, and may be expected to double the demand for cash balances.

6. Here the assumption of constant "brokerage fees" with $k_d = k_w = 0$ gets us into trouble. The amount withheld from investment then is never greater than C dollars only because a strictly constant "broker's fee" with no provision for a discontinuity at zero implies the payment of the fee even if nothing is withdrawn or deposited. In this case it becomes an overhead and it pays to invest for any interest earning greater than zero.

For a firm, *part* of the "broker's fee" may, in fact, be an overhead in this way. For example, failure to make an anticipated deposit will sometimes involve little or no reduction in the bookkeeping costs incurred in keeping track of such operations.

7. If we replace the linear functions representing the "brokers' fees" with more general functions $f_w(C)$ and $f_d(I)$ which are only required to be differentiable, the expression obtained for R is changed merely by replacement of k_w, and k_d by the corresponding derivatives $f_{w'}(C)$ and $f_{d'}(I)$.

8. See, e.g., Frank H. Knight, *Risk, Uncertainty and Profit* (Preface to the Re-issue), No. 16 in the series of Reprints of Scarce Tracts in Economic and Political Science (London: The London School of Economics and Political Science, 1933), p. xxii; F. Divisia, *Économique Rationelle* (Paris: G. Doin, 1927), Chapter 19 and the Appendix; and Don Patinkin, "Relative Prices, Say's Law and the Demand for Money," *Econometrica*, Vol. 16 (April 1948), 140–45. See also, P. N. Rosenstein-Rodan, "The Coordination of the General Theories of Money and Price," *Economica*, N. S., Vol. 3 (August 1936), Part 2.

9. It also neglects the fact that the transfer of cash takes time so that in reality we would have to hold cash at least for the short period between receiving it and passing it on again.

It is conceivable, it is true, that with perfect foresight the difference between money and securities might disappear since a perfectly safe loan could become universally acceptable. There would, however, remain the distinction between "real assets" and the "money-securities." Moreover, there would be a finite price for, and non-zero yield on the former, the yield arising because they (as opposed to certificates of their ownership) are not generally acceptable, and hence not perfectly liquid, since there is trouble and expense involved in carrying them.

10. Marshall's rather vague statements may perhaps be interpreted to support this view. See, e.g., Book 1, Chapter 4 in *Money, Credit and Commerce* (London 1923). Keynes clearly accepts this position. See *The General Theory of Employment, Interest and Money* (New York 1936), p. 201. It is also accepted by Pigou: "As real income becomes larger, there is, prima facie, reason for thinking that, just as, up to a point, people like to invest a larger proportion of their real income, so also they like to hold real balances in the form of money equivalent to a larger proportion of it. On the other hand, as Professor Robertson has pointed out to me, the richer people are, the cleverer they are likely to become in finding a way to *economize* in real balances. On the whole then we may, I think, safely disregard this consideration . . . for a close approximation . . . " (*Employment and Equilibrium*, 1st ed. [London 1941], pp. 59–60). Fisher, however, argues: "It seems to be a fact that, at a given price level, the greater a man's expenditures the more rapid his turnover; that is, the rich have a higher rate of turnover than the poor. They spend money faster, not only absolutely but relatively to the money they keep on hand. . . . We may therefore infer that, if a nation grows richer per capita, the velocity of circulation of money will increase. This proposition of course, has no reference to *nominal* increase of expenditure" (*The Purchasing Power of Money* [New York 1922], p. 167).

11. Since velocity equals $\dfrac{T}{C} = \dfrac{i}{2b}\, C$ by (2).

12. This is obtained by setting $k = Ci/2b$ in (3), below, and computing ΔT by substituting $C + \Delta C$ for C.

13. Even if (2) holds, the demand for cash may rise only in proportion with the money value of transactions when all prices rise exactly in proportion, the rate of interest and transactions remaining unchanged. For then a doubling of all prices and cash balances leaves the situation unchanged, and the received argument holds. The point is that b is then one of the prices which has risen.

14. But see the discussions of Potter and Law as summarized by Jacob Viner, *Studies in the Theory of International Trade* (New York 1937), pp. 37–39.

15. See A. C. Pigou, "The Classical Stationary State," *Economic Journal*, Vol. 53 (December 1943).

16. Presumably the "broker's fee" will be one of the prices which falls, driven down by the existence of unemployed brokers. There is no analogous reason for the rate of interest to fall, though it will tend to respond thus to the increase in the "real stock of cash."

17. The term "Pigou effect" is usually confined to the effects on consumption demand while the effect on investment demand, and (in particular) on the rate of interest is ordinarily ascribed to Keynes. However, the entire argument appears to antedate Pigou's discussion (which, after all, was meant to be a reformulation of the classical position) and is closely related to what Mr. Becker and I have called the Say's Equation form of the Say's Law argument. See our article "The Classical Monetary Theory: The Outcome of the Discussion," *Economica* (November 1952).

18. I refer here particularly to considerations analogous to those emphasized by Duesenberry in his discussion of the relation between the consumption functions of the individual and the economy as a whole in his *Income, Saving and the Theory of Consumer Behavior* (Cambridge, Mass. 1950).

19. For people to want to hold a positive amount of cash, the cost of cash holding must be decreasing after $C = 0$. Let b in (1) be a differentiable function of C for $C > 0$ (it will generally be discontinuous and equal to zero at $C = 0$). Then we require that the limit of the derivative of (1) be negative as C approaches zero from above, where this derivative is given by

$$-b\,\frac{T}{C^2} + \frac{T}{C}\,b' + \frac{i + i'C}{2}. \tag{i}$$

Clearly this will become negative as C approaches zero provided b is bounded from below and b', i, and i' are all bounded from above.

The second conclusion, the less than proportionate rise in minimum cost cash holdings with the volume of transactions, can be shown, with only b not constant, to hold if and only if $b - b'C + b''C^2$ is positive. This result is obtained by solving the first order minimum condition (obtained by setting (i), with the i' term omitted, equal to zero) for $\dfrac{T}{C}$

and noting that our conclusion is equivalent to the derivative of this ratio with respect to C being positive.

Now successive differentiation of (i) with the i' term omitted yields as our second order minimum condition $2(b - b'C) + b''C^2 > 0$ (note the resemblance to the preceding condition). Thus if our result is to be violated we must have

$$b - Cb' \leqq - b''C^2 < 2(b - Cb'), \tag{ii}$$

which at once yields $b'' \leqq 0$. Thus if b' is not to become negative (a decreasing *total* payment as the size of the withdrawal increases!) b'' must usually lie within a small neighborhood of zero, i.e., b must be approximately linear. However we know that in this case the square root formula will be (approximately) valid except in the case $b = kC$ when it will always [by (i)] pay to hold zero cash balances. Note incidentally that (ii) also yields $b - Cb' \geqq 0$ which means that our result must hold if ever the "brokerage fee" increases more than in proportion with C.

Note, finally, that if i varies with C the first order condition becomes a cubic and, provided $\infty > i' > 0$, our conclusion is strengthened, since T now tends to increase as C^2.

20. See Arrow, Harris, and Marschak, *op. cit.* for a good example of what has been done along these lines in inventory control analysis.

21. F. Y. Edgeworth, "The Mathematical Theory of Banking," *Journal of the Royal Statistical Society*, Vol. 51 (1888), especially pp. 123–27. Fisher (*op. cit.*) points out the relevance of this result for the analysis of the cash needs of the public as a whole. The result was independently rediscovered by Dr. Whitin (*op. cit.*) who seems to have been the first to combine it and (2) in inventory analysis.

22. K. Wicksell, *Interest and Prices* (London 1936), p. 67.

23. The distribution would generally be approximately normal if its depositors were large in number, their cash demands independent and not very dissimilarly distributed. The independence assumption, of course, rules out runs on banks.

M is one fun ass.
strategic variable is yield

7 *Liquidity Preference as Behavior Towards Risk*

James Tobin *Yale University*

One of the basic functional relationships in the Keynesian model of the economy is the liquidity preference schedule, an inverse relationship between the demand for cash balances and the rate of interest. This aggregative function must be derived from some assumptions regarding the behavior of the decision-making units of the economy, and those assumptions are the concern of this paper. Nearly two decades of drawing downward-sloping liquidity preference curves in textbooks and on classroom blackboards should not blind us to the basic implausibility of the behavior they describe. Why should anyone hold the non-interest bearing obligations of the government instead of its interest bearing obligations? The apparent irrationality of holding cash is the same, moreover, whether the interest rate is 6%, 3% or $\frac{1}{2}$ of 1%. What needs to be explained is not only the existence of a demand for cash when its yield is less than the yield on alternative assets but an inverse relationship between the aggregate demand for cash and the size of this differential in yields.[1]

1. *Transactions balances and investment balances.*

Two kinds of reasons for holding cash are usually distinguished: transactions reasons and investment reasons.

1.1 *Transactions balances: size and composition.* No economic unit—firm or household or government—enjoys perfect synchronization

Reprinted from *Review of Economic Studies*, Vol. 25 (February 1958), 65–86, by permission of the author and publisher.

between the seasonal patterns of its flow of receipts and its flow of expenditures. The discrepancies give rise to balances which accumulate temporarily, and are used up later in the year when expenditures catch up. Or, to put the same phenomenon the other way, the discrepancies give rise to the need for balances to meet seasonal excesses of expenditures over receipts. These balances are *transactions balances*. The aggregate requirement of the economy for such balances depends on the institutional arrangements that determine the degree of synchronization between individual receipts and expenditures. Given these institutions, the need for transactions balances is roughly proportionate to the aggregate volume of transactions.

The obvious importance of these institutional determinants of the demand for transactions balances has led to the general opinion that other possible determinants, including interest rates, are negligible.[2] This may be true of the size of transactions balances, but the composition of transactions balances is another matter. Cash is by no means the only asset in which transactions balances may be held. Many transactors have large enough balances so that holding part of them in earning assets, rather than in cash, is a relevant possibility. Even though these holdings are always for short periods, the interest earnings may be worth the cost and inconvenience of the financial transactions involved. Elsewhere[3] I have shown that, for such transactors, the proportion of cash in transactions balances varies inversely with the rate of interest; consequently this source of interest-elasticity in the demand for cash will not be further discussed here.

1.2 *Investment balances and portfolio decisions.* In contrast to transactions balances, the investment balances of an economic unit are those that will survive all the expected seasonal excesses of cumulative expenditures over cumulative receipts during the year ahead. They are balances which will not have to be turned into cash within the year. Consequently the cost of financial transactions—converting other assets into cash and vice versa—does not operate to encourage the holding of investment balances in cash.[4] If cash is to have any part in the composition of investment balances, it must be because of expectations or fears of loss on other assets. It is here, in what Keynes called the speculative motives of investors, that the explanation of liquidity preference and of the interest-elasticity of the demand for cash has been sought.

The alternatives to cash considered, both in this paper and in prior discussions of the subject, in examining the speculative motive for holding cash are assets that differ from cash only in having a variable market yield. They are obligations to pay stated cash amounts at future dates, with no risk of default. They are, like cash, subject to changes in real value due to fluctuations in the price level. In a broader perspective, all these assets, including cash, are merely minor variants of the same species, a species we may call monetary assets—marketable, fixed in money value, free of default risk. The differences of members of this species from each other are negligible compared to their differences from the vast variety of other assets in which wealth may be invested: corporate stocks, real estate, unincorporated business and professional practice, etc. The theory of liquidity preference does not concern the choices investors make between the whole species of monetary assets, on the one hand, and other broad classes of assets, on the other.[5] Those choices are the concern of other branches of economic theory, in particular theories of investment and of consumption. Liquidity preference theory takes as given the choices determining how much wealth is to be invested in monetary assets and concerns itself with the allocation of these amounts among cash and alternative monetary assets.

Why should any investment balances be held in cash, in preference to other monetary assets? We shall distinguish two possible sources of liquidity preference, while recognizing that they are not mutually exclusive. The first is inelasticity of expectations of future interest rates. The second is uncertainty about the future of interest rates. These two sources of liquidity preference will be examined in turn.

2. Inelasticity of interest rate expectations.

2.1 *Some simplifying assumptions.* To simplify the problem, assume that there is only one monetary asset other than cash, namely consols. The current yield of consols is r per "year." $1 invested in consols today will purchase an income of $\$r$ per "year" in perpetuity. The yield of cash is assumed to be zero; however, this is not essential, as it is the current and expected differentials of consols over cash that matter. An investor with a given total balance must decide what proportion of this balance to hold in cash, A_1, and what proportions in consols, A_2. This decision is assumed to fix the portfolio for a full "year."[6]

2.2 *Fixed expectations of future rate.* At the end of the year, the investor expects the rate on consols to be r_e. This expectation is assumed, for the present, to be held with certainty and to be independent of the current rate r. The investor may therefore expect with certainty that every dollar invested in consols today will earn over the year ahead not only the interest $\$r$, but also a capital gain or loss g:

$$g = \frac{r}{r_e} - 1 \tag{2.1}$$

For this investor, the division of his balance into proportions A_1 of cash and A_2 of consols is a simple all-or-nothing choice. If the current rate is such that $r + g$ is greater than zero, then he will put everything in consols. But if $r + g$ is less than zero, he will put everything in cash. These conditions can be expressed in terms of a critical level of the current rate r_c, where:

$$r_c = \frac{r_e}{1 + r_e} \qquad (2.2)$$

At current rates above r_c, everything goes into consols; but for r less than r_c, everything goes into cash.

· 2.3 *Sticky and certain interest rate expectations.* So far the investor's expected interest-rate r_e has been assumed to be completely independent of the current rate r. This assumption can be modified so long as some independence of the expected rate from the current

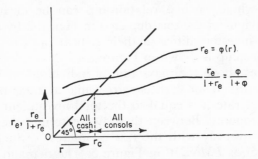

Figure 1. *Stickiness in the Relation between Expected and Current Interest Rate*

rate is maintained. In Figure 1, for example, r_e is shown as a function of r, namely $\varphi(r)$. Correspondingly $\dfrac{r_e}{1 + r_e}$ is a function of r.

As shown in the figure, this function $\dfrac{\varphi}{1 + \varphi}$ has only one intersection with the 45° line, and at this intersection its slope $\dfrac{\varphi'}{(1 + \varphi)^2}$ is less than one. If these conditions are met, the intersection determines a critical rate r_c such that if r exceeds r_c the investor holds no cash, while if r is less than r_c he holds no consols.

2.4 *Differences of opinion and the aggregate demand for cash.* According to this model, the relationship of the individual's investment demand for cash to the current rate of interest would be the discontinuous step function shown by the heavy vertical lines *LMNW* in Figure 2. How then do we get the familiar Keynesian liquidity preference function, a smooth, continuous inverse relationship

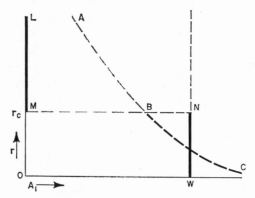

Figure 2. *Individual Demand for Cash Assuming Certain but Inelastic Interest Rate Expectations*

between the demand for cash and the rate of interest? For the economy as a whole, such a relationship can be derived from individual behaviour of the sort depicted in Figure 2 by assuming that individual investors differ in their critical rates r_c. Such an aggregate relationship is shown in Figure 3.

At actual rates above the maximum of individual critical rates the aggregate demand for cash is zero, while at rates below the minimum critical rate it is equal to the total investment balances for the whole economy. Between these two extremes the demand for cash varies inversely with the rate of interest r. Such a relationship is shown as $LMN\Sigma W$ in Figure 3. The demand for cash at r is the total of investment balances controlled by investors whose critical rates r_c exceed r. Strictly speaking, the curve is a step function; but, if the number of investors is large, it can be approximated by a smooth curve. Its shape depends on the distribution of dollars of investment balances by the critical rate of the investor controlling them; the shape of the curve in Figure 3 follows from a unimodal distribution.

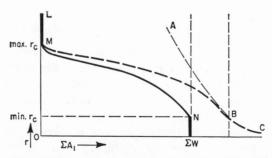

Figure 3. *Aggregate Demand for Cash Assuming Differences Among Individuals in Interest Rate Expectations*

2.5 *Capital gains or losses and open market operations.* In the foregoing analysis the size of investment balances has been taken as independent of the current rate on consols r. This is not the case if there are already consols outstanding. Their value will depend inversely on the current rate of interest. Depending on the relation of the current rate to the previously fixed coupon on consols, owners of consols will receive capital gains or losses. Thus the investment balances of an individual owner of consols would not be constant at W but would depend on r in a manner illustrated by the curve ABC in Figure 2.[7] Similarly, the investment balances for the whole economy would follow a curve like ABC in Figure 3, instead of being constant at ΣW. The demand for cash would then be described by $LMBC$ in both figures. Correspondingly the demand for consols at any interest rate would be described by the horizontal distance between $LMBC$ and ABC. The value of consols goes to infinity as the rate of interest approaches zero; for this reason, the curve BC may never reach the horizontal axis. The size of investment balances would be bounded if the monetary assets other than cash consisted of bonds with definite maturities rather than consols.

According to this theory, a curve like $LMBC$ depicts the terms on which a central bank can engage in open-market operations, given the claims for future payments outstanding in the form of bonds or consols. The curve tells what the quantity of cash must be in order for the central bank to establish a particular interest rate. However, the curve will be shifted by open-market operations themselves, since they will change the volume of outstanding bonds or consols. For example, to establish the rate at or below $min\,r_c$, the central bank would have to buy all outstanding bonds or consols. The size of the community's investment balances would then be independent of the rate of interest; it would be represented by a vertical line through, or to the right of, B, rather than the curve ABC. Thus the new relation between cash and interest would be a curve lying above LMB, of the same general contour as $LMN\Sigma W$.

2.6 *Keynesian theory and its critics.* I believe the theory of liquidity preference I have just presented is essentially the original Keynesian explanation. The *General Theory* suggests a number of possible theoretical explanations, supported and enriched by the experience and insight of the author. But the explanation to which Keynes gave the greatest emphasis is the notion of a "normal" long-term rate, to which investors expect the rate of interest to return. When he refers to uncertainty in the market, he appears to mean disagreement among investors concerning the future of the rate rather than subjective doubt in the mind of an individual investor.[8] Thus Kaldor's correction of Keynes is more verbal than substantive when he says, "It is . . . not so much the *uncertainty* concerning future interest rates as the *inelasticity* of interest expectations which is responsible for Mr. Keynes' 'liquidity preference function,' . . ."[9]

Keynes' use of this explanation of liquidity preference as a part of his theory of underemployment equilibrium was the target of important criticism by Leontief and Fellner. Leontief argued that liquidity preference must necessarily be zero *in equilibrium*, regardless of the rate of interest. Divergence between the current and expected interest rate is bound to vanish as investors learn from experience; no matter how low an interest rate may be, it can be accepted as "normal" if it persists long enough. This criticism was a part of Leontief's general methodological criticism of Keynes, that unemployment was not a feature of equilibrium, subject to analysis by tools of static theory, but a phenomenon of disequilibrium requiring analysis by dynamic theory.[10] Fellner makes a similar criticism of the logical appropriateness of Keynes' explanation of liquidity preference for the purposes of his theory of underemployment equilibrium. Why, he asks, are interest rates the only variables to which inelastic expectations attach? Why don't wealth owners and others regard pre-depression price levels as "normal" levels to which prices will return? If they did, consumption and investment demand would respond to reductions in money wages and prices, no matter how strong and how elastic the liquidity preference of investors.[11]

These criticisms raise the question whether it is possible to dispense with the assumption of stickiness in interest rate expectations without losing the implication that Keynesian theory drew from it. Can the inverse relationship of demand for cash to the rate of interest be based on a different set of assumptions about the behaviour of individual investors? This question is the subject of the next part of the paper.

3. *Uncertainty, risk aversion, and liquidity preference.*

3.1 *The locus of opportunity for risk and expected return.* Suppose that an investor is not certain of the future rate of interest on consols; investment in consols then involves a risk of capital gain or loss. The higher the proportion of his investment balance that he holds in consols, the more risk the investor assumes. At the same time, increasing the proportion in consols also increases his expected return. In the upper half of Figure 4, the vertical axis represents expected return and the horizontal axis risk. A line such as OC_1 pictures the fact that the investor can expect more return if he assumes more risk. In the lower half of Figure 4, the left-hand

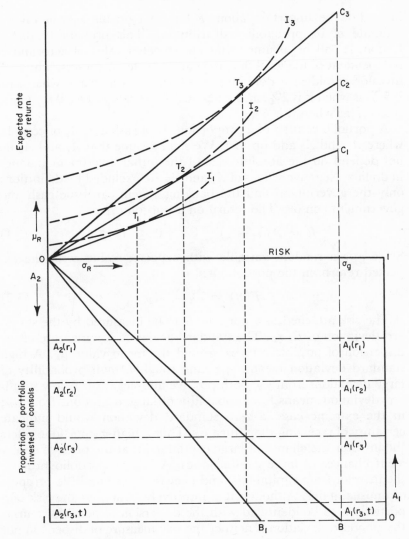

Figure 4. *Portfolio Selection at Various Interest Rates and Before and After Taxation*

vertical axis measures the proportion invested in consols. A line like OB shows risk as proportional to the share of the total balance held in consols.

The concepts of expected return and risk must be given more precision.

The individual investor of the previous section was assumed to have, for any current rate of interest, a definite expectation of the capital gain or loss g [defined in expression (2.1) above] he would obtain by investing one dollar in consols. Now he will be assumed instead to be uncertain about g but to base his actions on his estimate of its probability distribution. This probability distribution, it will be assumed, has an expected value of zero and is independent of the level of r, the current rate on consols. Thus the investor considers a doubling of the rate just as likely when rate is 5% as when it is 2%, and a halving of the rate just as likely when it is 1% as when it is 6%.

A portfolio consists of a proportion A_1 of cash and A_2 of consols, where A_1 and A_2 add up to 1. We shall assume that A_1 and A_2 do not depend on the absolute size of the initial investment balance in dollars. Negative values of A_1 and A_2 are excluded by definition; only the government and the banking system can issue cash and government consols. The return on a portfolio R is:

$$R = A_2(r + g) \qquad\qquad 0 \leq A_2 \leq 1 \qquad (3.1)$$

Since g is a random variable with expected value zero, the expected return on the portfolio is:

$$E(R) = \mu_R = A_2 r \qquad\qquad (3.2)$$

The risk attached to a portfolio is to be measured by the standard deviation of R, σ_R. The standard deviation is a measure of the dispersion of possible returns around the mean value μ_R. A high standard deviation means, speaking roughly, high probability of large deviations from μ_R, both positive and negative. A low standard deviation means low probability of large deviations from μ_R; in the extreme case, a zero standard deviation would indicate certainty of receiving the return μ_R. Thus a high-σ_R portfolio offers the investor the chance of large capital gains at the price of equivalent chances of large capital losses. A low-σ_R portfolio protects the investor from capital loss, and likewise gives him little prospect of unusual gains. Although it is intuitively clear that the risk of a portfolio is to be identified with the dispersion of possible returns, the standard deviation is neither the sole measure of dispersion nor the obviously most relevant measure. The case for the standard deviation will be further discussed in section 3.3 below.

The standard deviation of R depends on the standard deviation of g, σ_g, and on the amount invested in consols:

$$\sigma_R = A_2 \sigma_g \qquad\qquad 0 \leq A_2 \leq 1 \qquad (3.3)$$

Thus the proportion the investor holds in consols A_2 determines both his expected return μ_R and his risk σ_R. The terms on which the investor can obtain greater expected return at the expense of assuming more risk can be derived from (3.2) and (3.3):

$$\mu_R = \frac{r}{\sigma_g} \sigma_R \qquad\qquad 0 \leq \sigma_R \leq \sigma_g \qquad (3.4)$$

Such an *opportunity locus* is shown as line OC_1 (for $r = r_1$) in Figure 3.1. The slope of the line is $\dfrac{r_1}{\sigma_g}$. For a higher interest rate r_2, the opportunity locus would be OC_2; and for r_3, a still higher rate, it would be OC_3. The relationship (3.3) between risk and investment in consols is shown as line OB in the lower half of the figure. Cash holding $A_1(= 1 - A_2)$ can also be read off the diagram on the right-hand vertical axis.

3.2 *Loci indifference between combinations of risk and expected return.* The investor is assumed to have preferences between expected return μ_R and risk σ_R that can be represented by a field of in-difference curves. The investor is indifferent between all pairs (μ_R, σ_R) that lie on a curve such as I_1 in Figure 4. Points on I_2 are preferred to those on I_1; for given risk, an investor always prefers a greater to a smaller expectation of return. Conceivably, for some investors, *risk-lovers*, these indifference curves have nega-tive slopes. Such individuals are willing to accept lower expected return in order to have the chance of unusually high capital gains afforded by high values of σ_R. *Risk-averters*, on the other hand, will not be satisfied to accept more risk unless they can also expect greater expected return. Their indifference curves will be posi-tively sloped. Two kinds of risk-averters need to be distinguished. The first type, who may be called *diversifiers* for reasons that will become clear below, have indifference curves that are concave up-ward, like those in Figure 4. The second type, who may be called *plungers*, have indifference curves that are upward sloping, but either linear or convex upward.

3.3 *Indifference curves as loci of constant expected utility of wealth.* The reader who is willing to accept the indifference fields that have just been introduced into the analysis may skip to section 3.4 without losing the main thread of the argument. But these in-difference curves need some explanation and defence. Indifference curves between μ_R and σ_R do not necessarily exist. It is a simpli-fication to assume that the investor chooses among the alternative probability distributions of R available to him on the basis of only two parameters of those distributions. Even if this simplification is accepted, the mean and standard deviation may not be the pair of parameters that concern the investor.

3.3.1 One justification for the use of indifference curves be-tween μ_R and σ_R would be that the investor evaluates the future of consols only in terms of some two-parameter family of prob-ability distributions of g. For example, the investor might think in terms of a range of equally likely gains or losses, centered on zero. Or he might think in terms that can be approximated by a normal distribution. Whatever two-parameter family is assumed—uniform, normal, or some other—the whole probability distribution is determined as soon as the mean and standard deviation are specified. Hence the investor's choice among probability distributions can be analyzed by μ_R-σ_R indifference curves; any other pair of independent parameters could serve equally well.

If the investor's probability distributions are assumed to belong to some two-parameter family, the shape of his indifference curves can be inferred from the general characteristics of his utility-of-return function. This function will be assumed to relate utility to R, the percentage growth in the investment balance by the end of the period. This way of formulating the utility function makes the investor's indifference map, and therefore his choices of proportions of cash and consols, independent of the absolute amount of his initial balance.

On certain postulates, it can be shown that an individual's choice among probability distributions can be described as the maximization of the expected value of a utility function.[12] The ranking of probability distributions with respect to the expected value of utility will not be changed if the scale on which utility is measured is altered either by the addition of a constant or by multiplication by a positive constant. Consequently we are free to choose arbitrarily the zero and unit of measurement of the utility function $U(R)$ as follows: $U(0) = 0$; $U(-1) = -1$.

Suppose that the probability distribution of R can be described by a two-parameter density function $f(R; \mu_R, \sigma_R)$. Then the expected value of utility is:

$$E[U(R)] = \int_{-\infty}^{\infty} U(R) f(R;\ \mu_R, \sigma_R)\ dR \qquad (3.5)$$

Let
$$z = \frac{R - \mu_R}{\sigma_R}$$

$$E[U(R)] = E(\mu_R, \sigma_R) = \int_{-\infty}^{\infty} U(\mu_R + \sigma_R z) f(z;\ 0, 1)\ dz. \qquad (3.6)$$

An indifference curve is a locus of points (μ_R, σ_R) along which expected utility is constant. We may find the slope of such a locus by differentiating (3.6) with respect to σ_R:

$$0 = \int_{-\infty}^{\infty} U'(\mu_R + \sigma_R z) \left[\frac{d\mu_R}{d\sigma_R} + z \right] f(z;\ 0, 1)\ dz$$

$$\frac{d\mu_R}{d\sigma_R} = - \frac{\displaystyle\int_{-\infty}^{\infty} z U'(R) f(z;\ 0, 1)\ dz}{\displaystyle\int_{-\infty}^{\infty} U'(R) f(z;\ 0, 1)\ dz} \qquad (3.7)$$

$U'(R)$, the marginal utility of return, is assumed to be everywhere non-negative. If it is also a decreasing function of R, then the slope of the indifference locus must be positive; an investor with such a utility function is a risk-averter. If it is an increasing function of R, the slope will be negative; this kind of utility function characterizes a risk-lover.

Similarly, the curvature of the indifference loci is related to the shape of the utility function. Suppose that (μ_R, σ_R) and (μ'_R, σ'_R) are on the same indifference locus, so that $E(\mu_R, \sigma_R) = E(\mu_R, \sigma_R)$. Is $\left(\dfrac{\mu_R + \mu'_R}{2}, \dfrac{\sigma_R + \sigma'_R}{2}\right)$ on the same locus, or on a higher or a lower one? In the case of declining marginal utility we know that for every z:

$$\tfrac{1}{2}U(\mu_R + \sigma_R z) + \tfrac{1}{2}U(\mu'_R + \sigma'_R z)$$

$$< U\left(\frac{\mu_R + \mu'_R}{2} + \frac{\sigma_R + \sigma'_R}{2} z\right)$$

Consequently $E\left(\dfrac{\mu_R + \mu'_R}{2}, \dfrac{\sigma_R + \sigma'_R}{2}\right)$ is greater than $E(\mu_R, \sigma_R)$ or $E(\mu'_R, \sigma'_R)$, and $\left(\dfrac{\mu_R + \mu'_R}{2}, \dfrac{\sigma_R + \sigma'_R}{2}\right)$, which lies on a line between (μ_R, σ_R) and (μ'_R, σ'_R), is on a higher locus than those points. Thus it is shown that a risk-averter's indifference curve is necessarily concave upwards, provided it is derived in this manner from a two-parameter family of probability distributions and declining marginal utility of return. All risk-averters are diversifiers; plungers do not exist. The same kind of argument shows that a risk-lover's indifference curve is concave downwards.

3.3.2 In the absence of restrictions on the subjective probability distributions of the investor, the parameters of the distribution relevant to his choice can be sought in parametric restrictions on his utility-of-return function. Two parameters of the utility function are determined by the choice of the utility scale. If specification of the utility function requires no additional parameters, one parameter of the probability distribution summarizes all the information relevant for the investor's choice. For example, if the utility function is linear $[U(R) = R]$, then the expected value of utility is simply the expected value of R, and maximizing expected utility leads to the same behaviour as maximizing return in a world of certainty. If, however, one additional parameter is needed to specify the utility function, then two parameters of the probability distribution will be relevant to the choice; and so on. Which parameters of the distribution are relevant depends on the form of the utility function.

Focus on the mean and standard deviation of return can be justified on the assumption that the utility function is quadratic. Following our conventions as to utility scale, the quadratic function would be:

$$U(R) = (1 + b)R + bR^2 \qquad (3.8)$$

Here $0 < b < 1$ for a risk-lover, and $-1 < b < 0$ for a risk-averter. However (3.8) cannot describe the utility function for the whole range of R, because marginal utility cannot be negative. The function given in (3.8) can apply only for:

$$(1 + b) + 2bR \geq 0;$$

that is, for:

$$R \geq -\left(\frac{1 + b}{2b}\right) (b > 0) \qquad \text{(Risk-lover)}$$

$$R \leq -\left(\frac{1 + b}{2b}\right) (b < 0) \qquad \text{(Risk-averter)} \qquad (3.9)$$

In order to use (3.8), therefore, we must exclude from the range of possibility values of R outside the limits (3.9). At the maximum investment in consols ($A_2 = 1$), $R = r + g$. A risk-averter must be assumed therefore, to restrict the range of capital gains g to which he attaches non-zero probability so that, for the highest rate of interest r to be considered:

$$r + g \leq -\left(\frac{1 + b}{2b}\right) \qquad (3.10)$$

The corresponding limitation for a risk-lover is that, for the lowest interest rate r to be considered:

$$r + g \geq -\left(\frac{1 + b}{2b}\right) \qquad (3.11)$$

Given the utility function (3.8), we can investigate the slope and curvature of the indifference curves it implies. The probability density function for $R, f(R)$, is restricted by the limit (3.10) or (3.11); but otherwise no restriction on its shape is assumed.

$$E[U(R)] = \int_{-\infty}^{\infty} U(R)f(R)\, dR = (1 + b)\mu_R + b(\sigma_R^2 + \mu^2{}_R) \qquad (3.12)$$

Holding $E[U(R)]$ constant and differentiating with respect to σ_R to obtain the slope of an indifference curve, we have:

$$\frac{d\mu_R}{d\sigma_R} = \frac{\sigma_R}{-\dfrac{1 + b}{2b} - \mu_R} \qquad (3.13)$$

For a risk-averter, $-\dfrac{1+b}{2b}$ is positive and is the upper limit for R, according to (3.9); $-\dfrac{1+b}{2b}$ is necessarily larger than μ_R. Therefore the slope of an indifference locus is positive. For a risk-lover, on the other hand, the corresponding argument shows that the slope is negative.

Differentiating (3.13) leads to the same conclusions regarding curvature as the alternative approach of section 3.3.1, namely that a risk-averter is necessarily a diversifier.

$$\frac{d^2\mu_R}{d\sigma^2{}_R} = \frac{1 + \left(\dfrac{d\mu_R}{d\sigma_R}\right)^2}{-\dfrac{1+b}{2b} - \mu_R} \tag{3.14}$$

For a risk-averter, the second derivative is positive and the indifference locus is concave upwards; for a risk-lover, it is concave downwards.

3.4 *Effects of changes in the rate of interest.* In section 3.3 two alternative rationalizations of the indifference curves introduced in section 3.2 have been presented. Both rationalizations assume that the investor (1) estimates subjective probability distributions of capital gain or loss in holding consols, (2) evaluates his prospective increase in wealth in terms of a cardinal utility function, (3) ranks alternative prospects according to the expected value of utility. The rationalization of section 3.3.1 derives the indifference curves by restricting the subjective probability distributions to a two-parameter family. The rationalization of section 3.3.2 derives the indifference curves by assuming the utility function to be quadratic within the relevant range. On either rationalization, a risk-averter's indifference curves must be concave upwards, characteristic of the diversifiers of section 3.2, and those of a risk-lover concave downwards. If the category defined as *plungers* in 3.2 exists at all, their indifference curves must be determined by some process other than those described in 3.3.

The opportunity locus for the investor is described in Figure 4 and summarized in equation (3.4). The investor decides the amount to invest in consols so as to reach the highest indifference curve permitted by his opportunity locus. This maximization may be one of three kinds:

I. Tangency between an indifference curve and the opportunity locus, as illustrated by points T_1, T_2, and T_3 in Figure 4. A regular maximum of this kind can occur only for a risk-averter, and will lead to diversification. Both A_1, cash holding, and A_2, consol holding, will be positive. They too are shown in Figure 4, in the bottom half of the diagram, where, for example, $A_1(r_1)$ and $A_2(r_1)$ depict the cash and consol holdings corresponding to point T_1.

II. A corner maximum at the point $\mu_R = r$, $\sigma_R = \sigma_g$, as illustrated in Figure 5. In Figure 5 the opportunity locus is the ray OC, and point C represents the highest expected return and risk obtainable by the investor, i.e. the expected return and risk from holding his entire balance in consols. A utility maximum at C can occur either for a risk-averter or for a risk-lover. I_1 and I_2 represent indifference curves of a diversifier; I_2 passes through C and has a lower slope, both at C and everywhere to the left of C, than the opportunity locus. I_1' and I_2' represent the indifference curves of a risk-lover, for whom it is clear that C is always the optimum position. Similarly, a plunger may, if his indifference curves stand with respect to his opportunity locus as in Figure 6 (OC_2) plunge his entire balance in consols.

III. A corner maximum at the origin, where the entire balance is held in cash. For a plunger, this case is illustrated in Figure 6 (OC_1). Conceivably it could also occur for a diversifier, if the slope of his indifference curve at the origin exceeded the slope of the opportunity locus. However, case III is entirely excluded for investors whose indifference curves represent the constant-expected-utility loci of section 3.3. Such investors, we have already noted, cannot be plungers. Furthermore, the slope of all constant-expected-utility loci at $\sigma_R = 0$ must be zero, as can be seen from (3.7) and (3.13).

We can now examine the consequences of a change in the interest rate r, holding constant the investor's estimate of the risk of capital gain or loss. An increase in the interest rate will rotate

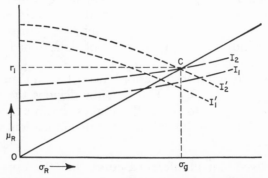

Figure 5. *"Risk-lovers" and "Diversifiers": Optimum Portfolio at Maximum Risk and Expected Return*

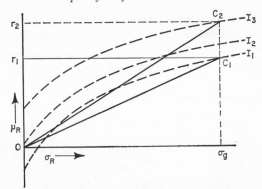

Figure 6. *"Plungers"—Optimum Portfolio at Minimum or Maximum Risk and Expected Return*

the opportunity locus OC to the left. How will this affect the investor's holdings of cash and consols? We must consider separately the three cases.

I. In Figure 4, OC_1, OC_2, and OC_3 represent opportunity loci for successively higher rates of interest. The indifference curves I_1, I_2, and I_3 are drawn so that the points of tangency T_1, T_2, and T_3, correspond to successively higher holdings of consols A_2. In this diagram, the investor's demand for cash depends inversely on the interest rate.

This relationship is, of course, in the direction liquidity preference theory has taught us to expect, but it is not the only possible direction of relationship. It is quite possible to draw indifference curves so that the point of tangency moves left as the opportunity locus is rotated counter-clockwise. The ambiguity is a familiar one in the theory of choice, and reflects the ubiquitous conflict between income and substitution effects. An increase in the rate of interest is an incentive to take more risk; so far as the substitution effect is concerned, it means a shift from security to yield. But an increase in the rate of interest also has an income effect, for it gives the opportunity to enjoy more security along with more yield. The ambiguity is analogous to the doubt concerning the effect of a change in the interest rate on saving; the substitution effect argues for a positive relationship, the income effect for an inverse relationship.

However, if the indifference curves are regarded as loci of constant expected utility, as derived in section 3.3, part of this ambiguity can be resolved. We have already observed that these loci all have zero slopes at $\sigma_R = 0$. As the interest rate r rises from zero, so also will consol holding A_2. At higher interest rates, however, the inverse relationship may occur.

This reversal of direction can, however, virtually be excluded in the case of the quadratic utility function (section 3.3.2). The condition for a maximum is that the slope of an indifference locus as given by (3.13) equal the slope of the opportunity locus (3.4).

$$\frac{r}{\sigma_g} = \frac{A_2 \sigma_g}{-\dfrac{1+b}{2b} - A_2 r} \; ; \; A_2 = \frac{r}{r^2 + \sigma_g^2}\left(-\frac{1+b}{2b}\right) \tag{3.15}$$

Equation (3.15) expresses A_2 as a function of r, and differentiating gives:

$$\frac{dA_2}{dr} = \frac{\sigma_g^2 - r^2}{(\sigma_g^2 + r^2)^2}\left(-\frac{1+b}{2b}\right); \; \frac{r}{A_2}\frac{dA_2}{dr} = \frac{\sigma_g^2 - r^2}{\sigma_g^2 + r^2} \tag{3.16}$$

Thus the share of consols in the portfolio increases with the interest rate for r less than σ_g. Moreover, if r exceeds σ_g, a tangency maximum cannot occur unless r also exceeds g_{max}, the largest capital gain the investor conceives possible (see 3.10).[13] The demand for consols is less elastic at high interest rates than at low, but the elasticity is not likely to become negative.

II and III. A change in the interest rate cannot cause a risk-lover to alter his position, which is already the point of maximum risk and expected yield. Conceivably a "diversifier" might move from a corner maximum to a regular interior maximum in response either to a rise in the interest rate or to a fall. A "plunger" might find his position altered by an increase in the interest rate, as from r_1 to r_2 in Figure 6; this would lead him to shift his entire balance from cash to consols.

3.5 *Effects of changes in risk.* Investor's estimates σ_g of the risk of holding monetary assets other than cash, "consols," are subjective. But they are undoubtedly affected by market experience, and they are also subject to influence by measures of monetary and fiscal policy. By actions and words, the central bank can influence investors' estimates of the variability of interest rates; its influence on these estimates of risk may be as important in accomplishing or preventing changes in the rate as open-market operations and other direct interventions in the market. Tax rates, and differences in tax treatment of capital gains, losses, and interest earnings, affect in calculable ways the investor's risks and expected returns. For these reasons it is worth while to examine the effects of a change in an investor's estimate of risk on his allocation between cash and consols.

In Figure 7, T_1 and $A_2(r_1, \sigma_g)$ represent the initial position of an investor, at interest rate r_1 and risk σ_g. OC_1 is the opportunity locus (3.4), and OB_1 is the risk-consols relationship (3.3). If the

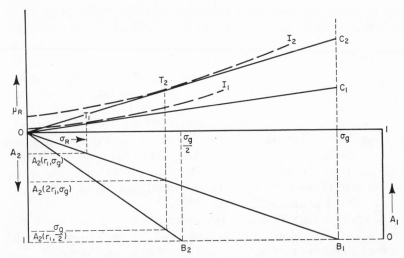

Figure 7. *Comparison of Effects of Changes in Interest Rate* (r) *and in "Risk"* (σ_g) *on Holding of Consols*

investor now cuts his estimate of risk in half, to $\dfrac{\sigma_g}{2}$, the opportunity locus will double in slope, from OC_1 to OC_2, and the investor will shift to point T_2. The risk-consols relationship will have also doubled in slope, from OB_1 to OB_2. Consequently point T_2 corresponds to an investment in consols of $A_2\left(r_1, \dfrac{\sigma_g}{2}\right)$. This same point T_2 would have been reached if the interest rate had doubled while the investor's risk estimate σ_g remained unchanged. But in that case, since the risk-consols relationship would remain at OB_1, the corresponding investment in consols would have been only half as large, i.e., $A_2(2r_1, \sigma_g)$. In general, the following relationship exists between the elasticity of the demand for consols with respect to risk and its elasticity with respect to the interest rate:

$$\frac{\sigma_g}{A_2}\frac{dA_2}{d\sigma_g} = -\frac{r}{A_2}\frac{dA_2}{dr} - 1 \qquad (3.17)$$

The implications of this relationship for analysis of effects of taxation may be noted in passing, with the help of Figure 7. Suppose that the initial position of the investor is T_2 and $A_2(2r_1, \sigma_g)$. A tax of 50% is now levied on interest income and capital gains alike, with complete loss offset provisions. The result of the tax is to reduce the expected net return per dollar of consols from $2r_1$ to r_1 and to reduce the risk to the investor per dollar of consols from σ_g to $\sigma_g/2$. The opportunity locus will remain at OC_2, and the investor will still wish to obtain the combination of risk and ex-

pected return depicted by T_2. To obtain this combination, however, he must now double his holding of consols, to $A_2(r_1, \sigma_g/2)$;
the tax shifts the risk-consols line from OB_1 to OB_2. A tax of this
kind, therefore, would reduce the demand for cash at any market
rate of interest, shifting the investor's liquidity preference schedule
in the manner shown in Figure 8. A tax on interest income only,
with no tax on capital gains and no offset privileges for capital
losses, would have quite different effects. If the Treasury began to
split the interest income of the investor in Figure 7 but not to share
the risk, the investor would move from his initial position, T_2 and
$A_2(2r_1, \sigma_g)$; to T_1 and $A_2(r_1, \sigma_g)$. His demand for cash at a given
market rate of interest would be increased and his liquidity preference curve shifted to the right.

3.6 *Multiple alternatives to cash.* So far it has been assumed that
there is only one alternative to cash, and A_2 has represented the
share of the investor's balance held in that asset, "consols." The
argument is not essentially changed, however, if A_2 is taken to be
the aggregate share invested in a variety of non-cash assets, e.g.,
bonds and other debt instruments differing in maturity, debtor,
and other features. The return R and the risk σ_g on "consols" will
then represent the average return and risk on a composite of these
assets.

Suppose that there are m assets other than cash, and let $x_i(i = 1, 2, \ldots, m)$ be the amount invested in the ith of these assets. All
x_i are non-negative, and $\sum_{i=1}^{m} x_i = A_2 \leqq 1$. Let r_i be the ex-

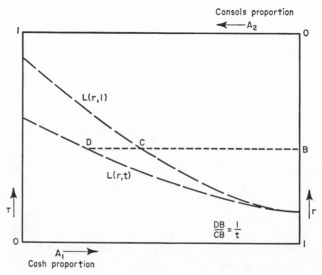

Figure 8. *Effect of Tax (at Rate 1-t) on Liquidity Preference Function*

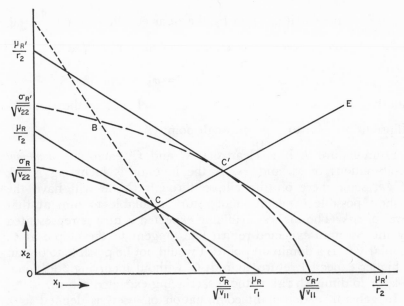

Figure 9. *Dominant Combinations of Two Assets*

pected yield, and let g_i be the capital gain or loss, per dollar invested in the ith asset. We assume $E(g_i) = 0$ for all i. Let v_{ij} be the variance or covariance of g_i and g_j as estimated by the investor.

$$v_{ij} = E(g_i g_j) \quad (i, j, = 1, 2, \ldots, m) \tag{3.18}$$

The over-all expected return is:

$$\mu_R = A_2 r = \sum_{i=1}^{m} x_i r_i \tag{3.19}$$

The over-all variance of return is:

$$\sigma_R^2 = A_2^2 \sigma_g^2 = \sum_{i=1}^{m} \sum_{j=1}^{m} x_i x_j v_{ij}. \tag{3.20}$$

A set of points x_i for which $\sum_{i=1}^{m} x_i r_i$ is constant may be defined as a *constant-return locus*. A constant-return locus is linear in the x_i. For two assets x_1 and x_2, two loci are illustrated in Figure 9. One locus of combinations of x_1 and x_2 that give the same expected return μ_R is the line from $\dfrac{\mu_R}{r_2}$ to $\dfrac{\mu_R}{r_1}$, through C; another locus, for a higher constant, μ_R', is the parallel line from $\dfrac{\mu_R'}{r_2}$ to $\dfrac{\mu_R'}{r_1}$, through C'.

A set of points x_i for which σ_R^2 is constant may be defined as a *constant-risk locus*. These loci are ellipsoidal. For two assets x_1 and

x_2, such a locus is illustrated by the quarter-ellipse from $\dfrac{\sigma_R}{\sqrt{v_{22}}}$ to $\dfrac{\sigma_R}{\sqrt{v_{11}}}$, through point C. The equation of such an ellipse is:

$$x_1^2 v_{11} + 2x_1 x_2 v_{12} + x_2^2 v_{22} = \sigma_R^2 = \text{constant}$$

Another such locus, for a higher risk level, σ_R', is the quarter-ellipse from $\dfrac{\sigma_R'}{\sqrt{v_{22}}}$ to $\dfrac{\sigma_R'}{\sqrt{v_{11}}}$ through point C'.

From Figure 9, it is clear that C and C' exemplify *dominant* combinations of x_1 and x_2. If the investor is incurring a risk of σ_R, somewhere on the ellipse through C, he will have the highest possible expectation of return available to him at that level of risk. The highest available expected return is represented by the constant-expected-return line tangent to the ellipse at C. Similarly C' is a dominant point: it would not be possible to obtain a higher expected return than at C' without incurring additional risk, or to diminish risk without sacrificing expected return.

In general, a dominant combination of assets is defined as a set x_i which minimizes σ_R^2 for μ_R constant:

$$\sum_i \left(\sum_j v_{ij} x_j \right) x_i - \lambda \left(\sum_i r_i x_i - \mu_R \right) = \text{min} \qquad (3.21)$$

where λ is a Lagrange multiplier. The conditions for the minimum are that the x_i satisfy the constraint (3.19) and the following set of m simultaneous linear equations, written in matrix notation:

$$[v_{ij}][x_i] = [\lambda r_i] \qquad (3.22)$$

All dominant sets lie on a ray from the origin. That is, if $[x_i^{(0)}]$ and $[x_i^{(1)}]$ are dominant sets, then there is some non-negative scalar κ such that $[x_i^{(1)}] = [\kappa x_i^{(0)}]$. By definition of a dominant set, there is some $\lambda^{(0)}$ such that:

$$[v_{ij}][x_i^{(0)}] = [\lambda^{(0)} r_i]$$

and some $\lambda^{(1)}$ such that:

$$[v_{ij}][x_i^{(1)}] = [\lambda^{(1)} r_i]$$

Take $\kappa = \dfrac{\lambda^{(1)}}{\lambda^{(0)}}$. Then:

$$[v_{ij}][\kappa x_i^{(0)}] = [\kappa \lambda^{(0)} r_i] = [\lambda^{(1)} r_i] = [v_{ij}][x_i^{(1)}]$$

At the same time, $\sum_i r_i x_i^{(0)} = \mu_R^{(0)}$ and $\sum_i r_i x_i^{(1)} = \mu_R^{(1)}$.

Hence, $\mu_R^{(1)} = \kappa \mu_R^{(0)}$. Conversely, every set on this ray is a dominant set. If $[x_i^{(0)}]$ is a dominant set, then so is $[\kappa x_i^{(0)}]$ for any non-negative constant κ. This is easily proved. If $[x_i^{(0)}]$ satisfies (3.19) and (3.22) for $\mu_R^{(0)}$ and $\lambda^{(0)}$, then $[\kappa x_i^{(0)}]$ satisfies (3.19) and (3.22) for $\lambda^{(\kappa)} = \kappa \lambda^{(0)}$ and $\mu_R^{(\kappa)} = \kappa \mu_R^{(0)}$. In the two-dimensional case pictured in Figure 9, the dominant pairs lie along the ray $OCC'E$.

There will be some point on the ray (say E in Figure 9) at which the investor's holdings of non-cash assets will exhaust his investment balance ($\sum_i x_i = 1$) and leave nothing for cash holding. Short of that point the balance will be divided among cash and non-cash assets in proportion to the distances along the ray; in Figure 9 at point C for example, $\dfrac{OC}{OE}$ of the balance would be non-cash, and $\dfrac{CE}{OE}$ cash. But the convenient fact that has just been proved is that the proportionate composition of the non-cash assets is independent of their aggregate share of the investment balance. This fact makes it possible to describe the investor's decisions as if there were a single non-cash asset, a composite formed by combining the multitude of actual non-cash assets in fixed proportions.

Corresponding to every point on the ray of dominant sets is an expected return μ_R and risk σ_R; these pairs (μ_R, σ_R) are the opportunity locus of sections 3.1 and 3.4. By means of (3.22), the opportunity locus can be expressed in terms of the expected return and variances and covariances of the non-cash assets: Let:

$$[V_{ij}] = [V_{ij}]^{-1}$$

Then:

$$\mu_R = \lambda \sum_i \sum_j r_i r_j V_{ij} \tag{3.23}$$

$$\sigma_R^2 = \lambda^2 \sum_i \sum_j r_i r_j V_{ij}. \tag{3.24}$$

Thus the opportunity locus is the line:

$$\mu_R = \sigma_R \sqrt{\sum_i \sum_j r_i r_j V_{ij}} = \sigma_R \frac{r}{\sigma_g}. \tag{3.25}$$

This analysis is applicable only so long as cash is assumed to be a riskless asset. In the absence of a residual riskless asset, the investor has no reason to confine his choices to the ray of dominant sets. This may be easily verified in the two-asset case. Using Figure 9 for a different purpose now, suppose that the entire investment balance must be divided between x_1 and x_2. The point (x_1, x_2) must fall on the line $x_1 + x_2 = 1$, represented by the line through BC in the diagram. The investor will not necessarily choose point

C. At point B, for example, he would obtain a higher expected yield as well as a higher risk; he may prefer B to C. His opportunity locus represents the pairs (μ_R, σ_R) along the line through $BC(x_1 + x_2 = 1)$ rather than along the ray OC, and is a hyperbola rather than a line. It is still possible to analyze portfolio choices by the apparatus of (μ_R, σ_R) indifference and opportunity loci, but such analysis is beyond the scope of the present paper.[14]

It is for this reason that the present analysis has been deliberately limited, as stated in section 1.2, to choices among monetary assets. Among these assets cash is relatively riskless, even though in the wider context of portfolio selection, the risk of changes in purchasing power, which all monetary assets share, may be relevant to many investors. Breaking down the portfolio selection problem into stages at different levels of aggregation—allocation first among, and then within, asset categories—seems to be a permissible and perhaps even indispensable simplification both for the theorist and for the investor himself.

4. *Implications of the analysis for liquidity preference theory.*

The theory of risk-avoiding behaviour has been shown to provide a basis for liquidity preference and for an inverse relationship between the demand for cash and the rate of interest. This theory does not depend on inelasticity of expectations of future interest rates, but can proceed from the assumption that the expected value of capital gain or loss from holding interest-bearing assets is always zero. In this respect, it is a logically more satisfactory foundation for liquidity preference than the Keynesian theory described in section 2. Moreover, it has the empirical advantage of explaining diversification—the same individual holds both cash and "consols"—while the Keynesian theory implies that each investor will hold only one asset.

The risk aversion theory of liquidity preference mitigates the major logical objection to which, according to the argument of section 2.6, the Keynesian theory is vulnerable. But it cannot completely meet Leontief's position that in a strict stationary equilibrium liquidity preference must be zero unless cash and consols bear equal rates. By their very nature consols and, to a lesser degree, all time obligations contain a potential for capital gain or loss that cash and other demand obligations lack. Presumably, however, there is some length of experience of constancy in the interest rate that would teach the most stubbornly timid investor to ignore that potential. In a pure stationary state, it could be argued, the interest rate on consols would have been the same for so long that investors would unanimously estimate σ_g to be zero. So stationary a state is of very little interest. Fortunately the usefulness of comparative statics does not appear to be confined to comparisons of states each of which would take a generation or more to achieve. As compared to the Keynesian theory of liquidity preference, the risk aversion theory widens the applicability of comparative statics in aggregative analysis; this is all that need be claimed for it.

The theory, however, is somewhat ambiguous concerning the direction of relationship between the rate of interest and the demand for cash. For low interest rates, the theory implies a negative elasticity of demand for cash with respect to the interest rate, an elasticity that becomes larger and larger in absolute value as the rate approaches zero. This implication, of course, is in accord with the usual assumptions about liquidity preference. But for high interest rates, and especially for individuals whose estimates σ_g of the risk of capital gain or loss on "consols" are low, the demand for cash may be an increasing, rather than a decreasing, function of the interest rate. However, the force of this reversal of direction is diluted by recognition, as in section 2.5, that the size of investment balances is not independent of the current rate of interest r. In section 3.4 we have considered the proportionate allocation between cash and "consols" on the assumption that it is independent of the size of the balance. An increase in the rate of interest may lead an investor to desire to shift towards cash. But to the extent that the increase in interest also reduces the value of the investor's consol holdings, it automatically gratifies this desire, at least in part.

The assumption that investors expect on balance no change in the rate of interest has been adopted for the theoretical reasons explained in section 2.6 rather than for reasons of realism. Clearly investors do form expectations of changes in interest rates and differ from each other in their expectations. For the purposes of dynamic theory and of analysis of specific market situations, the theories of sections 2 and 3 are complementary rather than competitive. The formal apparatus of section 3 will serve just as well for a non-zero expected capital gain or loss as for a zero expected value of g. Stickiness of interest rate expectations would mean that the expected value of g is a function of the rate of interest r, going down when r goes down and rising when r goes up. In addition to the rotation of the opportunity locus due to a change in r itself, there would be a further rotation in the same direction due to the accompanying change in the expected capital gain or loss. At low interest rates expectation of capital loss may push the opportunity locus into the negative quadrant, so that the optimal position is clearly no consols, all cash. At the other extreme, expectation of capital gain at high interest rates would increase sharply the slope of the opportunity locus and the frequency of no cash, all consols positions, like that of Figure 6. The stickier the investor's expectations, the more sensitive his demand for cash will be to changes in the rate of interest.

NOTES

1. "... in a world involving no transaction friction and no uncertainty, there would be no reason for a spread between the yield on any two assets, and hence there would be no difference in the yield on money and on securities ... in such a world securities themselves would circulate as money and be acceptable in transactions; demand bank deposits would bear interest, just as they often did in this country in the period of the twenties." (Paul A. Samuelson, *Foundations of Economic Analysis* [Cambridge: Harvard University Press, 1947], p. 123). The section, pp. 122–24, from which the passage is quoted makes it clear that liquidity preference must be regarded as an explanation of the existence and level not of the interest rate but of the differential between the yield on money and the yields on other assets.

2. The traditional theory of the velocity of money has, however, probably exaggerated the invariance of the institutions determining the extent of lack of synchronization between individual receipts and expenditures. It is no doubt true that such institutions as the degree of vertical integration of production and the periodicity of wage, salary, dividend, and tax payments are slow to change. But other relevant arrangements can be adjusted in response to money rates. For example, there is a good deal of flexibility in the promptness and regularity with which bills are rendered and settled.

3. "The Interest Elasticity of the Transactions Demand for Cash," *Review of Economics and Statistics*, Vol. 38 (August 1956), 241–47.

4. Costs of financial transactions have the effect of deterring changes from the existing portfolio, whatever its composition; they may thus operate against the holding of cash as easily as for it. Because of these costs, the *status quo* may be optimal even when a different composition of assets would be preferred if the investor were starting over again.

5. The author attempts to apply to this wider choice some of the same theoretical tools here used to analyze choices among the narrow class of monetary assets, in "A Dynamic Aggregative Model," *Journal of Political Economy*, Vol. 63 (April 1955), 103–15 [reprinted here—Ed.].

6. As noted above, it is the costs of financial transactions that impart inertia to portfolio composition. Every reconsideration of the portfolio involves the investor in expenditure of time and effort as well as of money. The frequency with which it is worth while to review the portfolio will obviously vary with the investor and will depend on the size of his portfolio and on his situation with respect to costs of obtaining information and engaging in financial transactions. Thus the relevant "year" ahead for which portfolio decisions are made is not the same for all

investors. Moreover, even if a decision is made with a view to fixing a portfolio for a given period of time, a portfolio is never so irrevocably frozen that there are no conceivable events during the period which would induce the investor to reconsider. The fact that this possibility is always open must influence the investor's decision. The fiction of a fixed investment period used in this paper is, therefore, not a wholly satisfactory way of taking account of the inertia in portfolio composition due to the costs of transactions and of decision making.

7. The size of their investment balances, held in cash and consols, may not vary by the full amount of these changes in wealth; some part of the changes may be reflected in holdings of assets other than monetary assets. But presumably the size of investment balances will reflect at least in part these capital gains and losses.

8. J. M. Keynes, *The General Theory of Employment, Interest and Money* (New York: Harcourt Brace & Co., 1936), Chapters 13 and 15, especially pp. 168–72 and 201–3. One quotation from page 172 will illustrate the point: "It is interesting that the stability of the system and its sensitiveness to changes in the quantity of money should be so dependent on the existence of a *variety* of opinion about what is uncertain. Best of all that we should know the future. But if not, then, if we are to control the activity of the economic system by changing the quantity of money, it is important that opinions should differ."

9. N. Kaldor, "Speculation and Economic Stability," *Review of Economic Studies*, Vol. 7 (October 1939), 15.

10. W. Leontief, "Postulates: Keynes' *General Theory* and the Classicists," Chapter 19 in S. E. Harris (ed.), *The New Economics* (New York: Knopf, 1947), pp. 232–42. Section 6, pp. 238–39, contains the specific criticism of Keynes' liquidity preference theory.

11. W. Fellner, *Monetary Policies and Full Employment* (Berkeley: University of California Press, 1946), p. 149.

12. See J. Von Neumann and O. Morgenstern, *Theory of Games and Economic Behavior*, 3rd ed. (Princeton: Princeton University Press, 1953), pp. 15–30, 617–32; I. N. Herstein and J. Milnor, "An Axiomatic Approach to Measurable Utility," *Econometrica*, Vol. 23 (April 1953), 291–97; J. Marschak, "Rational Behavior, Uncertain Prospects, and Measurable Utility," *Econometrica*, Vol. 18 (April 1950), 111–41; M. Friedman and L. J. Savage, "The Utility Analysis of Choices Involving Risk," *Journal of Political Economy*, Vol. 56 (August 1948), 279–304; and "The Expected Utility Hypothesis and the Measurability of Utility," *Journal of Political Economy*, Vol. 60 (December 1952), 463–74. For a treatment which also provides an axiomatic basis for the subjective probability estimates here assumed, see L. J. Savage, *The Foundations of Statistics* (New York: Wiley, 1954).

13. For this statement and its proof, I am greatly indebted to my colleague Arthur Okun. The proof is as follows:
If $r^2 \geq \sigma_g^2$, then by (3.15) and (3.10):

$$1 \geq A_2 \geq \frac{r}{2r^2}\left(-\frac{1+b}{2b}\right) \geq \frac{1}{2r}(r + g_{max})$$

From the two extremes of this series of inequalities it follows that $2r \geq r + g_{max}$ or $r \geq g_{max}$. Professor Okun also points out that this condition is incompatible with a tangency maximum if the distribution of g is symmetrical. For then $r \geq g_{max}$ would imply $r + g_{min} \geq 0$. There would be no possibility of net loss on consols and thus no reason to hold any cash.

14. Harry Markowitz's *Techniques of Portfolio Selection* (New York 1959), treats the general problem of finding dominant sets and computing the corresponding opportunity locus, for sets of securities all of which involve risk. Markowitz's main interest is prescription of rules of rational behaviour for investors; the main concern of this paper is the implications for economic theory, mainly comparative statics, that can be derived from assuming that investors do in fact follow such rules. For the general nature of Markowitz's approach, see his article, "Portfolio Selection," *Journal of Finance*, Vol. 7 (March 1952), 77–91.

8 *A Dynamic Aggregative Model*

James Tobin *Yale University*

Contemporary theoretical models of the business cycle and of economic growth typically possess two related characteristics: (1) they assume production functions that allow for no substitution between factors, and (2) the variables are all real magnitudes; monetary and price phenomena have no significance. Because of these characteristics, these models present a rigid and angular picture of the economic process: straight and narrow paths from which the slightest deviation spells disaster, abrupt and sharp reversals, intractable ceilings and floors. The models are highly suggestive, but their representation of the economy arouses the suspicion that they have left out some essential mechanisms of adjustment.

The purpose of this paper is to present a simple aggregative model that allows both for substitution possibilities and for monetary effects. The growth mechanism in the model is not radically different from the accelerator mechanism that plays the key role in other growth models. But it is unlike the accelerator mechanism in that there is not just one tenable rate of growth. As in accelerator models, growth is limited by the availability of factors other than capital. But here these limitations do not operate so abruptly, and they can be tempered by monetary and price adjustments that the accelerator models ignore.

The cyclical behavior of the model is similar to the nonlinear cyclical processes of Kaldor, Goodwin, and Hicks.[1] But the cycle

Reprinted from *Journal of Political Economy*, Vol. 63 (April 1955), 103–15, by permission of the author and The University of Chicago Press. Copyright 1955 by The University of Chicago Press.

in the present model depends in an essential way on the inflexibility of prices, money wages, or the supply of monetary assets.

Furthermore, the model to be described here does not restrict the economic process to two possibilities, steady growth or cycles. An alternative line of development is continuing underemployment—"stagnation" during which positive investment increases the capital stock and possibly the level of real income. This outcome, like the cycle, depends on some kind of price or monetary inflexibility.

In Part I the structure of the model will be described, and in Part II some of its implications will be examined.

I

The building blocks from which this model is constructed are four in number: (1) the saving function; (2) the production function; (3) asset preferences; and (4) labor-supply conditions.

THE SAVING FUNCTION

At any moment of time output is being produced at a rate Y, consumption is occurring at a rate C, and the capital stock, K, is growing at the rate $\dot{K}$, equal to $Y - C$. The saving function tells how output is divided between consumption and net investment:

$$\dot{K} = S(Y). \tag{1}$$

This relationship is assumed to hold instantaneously. That is, consumption is adjusted without lag to the simultaneous level of output; any output not consumed is an addition to the capital stock. Whether or not it is a welcome addition is another matter, which depends on the asset preferences of the community, discussed below.

Of the saving function, it is assumed that $S'(Y)$ is positive and that $S(Y)$ is zero for some positive Y. Otherwise the shape of the saving function is not crucial to the argument. Variables other than Y—for example, W, total real wealth—could be assumed to affect the propensity to save without involving more than inessential complications.

THE PRODUCTION FUNCTION

The rate of output, Y, depends jointly on the stock of capital in existence, K, and the rate of input of labor services, N:

$$Y = P(K, N). \tag{2}$$

The production function is assumed to be linear homogeneous. It follows that the marginal products are homogeneous functions of degree zero of the two factors; in other words, the marginal products depend only on the proportions in which the two inputs are being used. The real wage of labor, w, is equated by competition to the marginal product of labor; and the rent, r, per unit of time earned by ownership of any unit of capital is equated to the marginal product of capital:

$$w = P_N(K, N), \tag{3}$$
$$r = P_K(K, N). \tag{4}$$

If labor and capital expand over time in proportion, then output will expand in the same proportion, and both the real wage and the rent of capital will remain constant. If capital expands at a faster rate than labor, its rent must fall, and the real wage must rise.

A production function with constant returns to scale, both at any moment of time and over time, is a convenient beginning assumption. In judging the appropriateness of this kind of production function to the model, it should be remembered that, if it ignores technical improvement, on the one hand, it ignores limitations of other factors of production, "land," on the other. In the course of the argument the consequences of technological progress will be briefly discussed.

ASSET PREFERENCES

Only two stores of value, physical capital and currency, are available to owners of wealth in this economy. The own rate of return on capital is its rent, r, equal to its marginal product. Currency is wholly the issue of the state and bears an own rate of interest legally and permanently established. This rate will be assumed to be zero. The stock of currency, M, is exogenously determined and can be varied only by budget deficits or surpluses. The counterpart of this "currency" in the more complex asset structure of an actual economy is not money by the usual definition, which includes bank deposits corresponding to private debts. It is, for the United States, currency in circulation plus government debt plus the gold stock.[2]

If p is the price of goods in terms of currency, the community's total real wealth at any moment of time is

$$W = K + \frac{M}{p}. \tag{5}$$

Given K, M, and p, the community may be satisfied to split its wealth so that it holds as capital an amount equal to the available stock, K, and as currency an amount equal to the existing real supply, M/p. Such a situation will be referred to as "portfolio balance."

Portfolio balance is assumed to be the necessary and sufficient condition for price stability ($\dot{p} = 0$). If, instead, owners of wealth desire to hold more goods and less currency, they attempt to buy goods with currency. Prices are bid up ($\dot{p} > 0$). If they desire to shift in the other direction, they attempt to sell goods for currency ($\dot{p} < 0$). These price changes may, in turn, be associated with changes in output and employment; but that depends on other parts of the model, in particular on the conditions of labor supply.

What, then, determines whether an existing combination of K and M/p represents a situation of portfolio balance or imbalance? Portfolio balance is assumed in this model to be defined by the following functional relationship:

$$\frac{M}{p} = L(K, r, Y), \qquad L_K \gtreqless 0, \qquad L_r < 0, \qquad L_Y > 0. \qquad (6)$$

Requirements for transactions balances of currency are assumed, as is customary, to depend on income; this is the reason for the appearance of Y in the function. Given their real wealth, W, owners of wealth will wish to hold a larger amount of capital, and a smaller amount of currency, the higher the rent on capital, r. Given the rent on capital, owners of wealth will desire to put some part of any increment of their wealth into capital and some part into currency. It is possible that there are levels of r (e.g., negative rates) so low that portfolio balance requires all wealth to be in the form of currency and that there is some level of r above which wealth owners would wish to hold no currency. But the main argument to follow in part II concerns ranges of r between those extremes.

The assumption about portfolio balance has now been stated, and the reader who is more interested in learning its consequences than its derivation can proceed to the next section. But since this is the one of the four building blocks of the model that introduces possibly unconventional and unfamiliar material into the structure, it requires some discussion and defense.

The theory of portfolio balance implicit in most conventional aggregative economic theories of investment implies that rates of return on all assets must be equal. Applied to the two assets of the mythical economy of this paper, this theory would go as follows: Owners of wealth have a firm, certain, and unanimous expectation of the rate of price change, $\dot{p}_e$. This may or may not be the same as the actual rate of price change $\dot{p}$ at the same moment of time.[3] The rate at which a unit of wealth is expected to grow if it is held in the form of currency is, therefore, $-\dot{p}_e/p$.

Similarly, owners of wealth have a firm and unanimous view of the rate at which wealth will grow if it is held as physical capital. This rate is r_e, the expected market rent, which may or may not be the same as r. Owners of wealth will choose that portfolio which makes their wealth grow at the fastest rate. If $-\dot{p}_e/p$ were to exceed r_e, they would desire to hold all currency and no capital; if r_e were greater than $-\dot{p}_e/p$, they would desire to hold all capital and no currency. Only if the two rates are equal will they be satisfied to hold positive amounts of both assets; and, indeed, in that case, they will not care what the mix of assets is in their portfolios. On this theory of asset preferences the relative supplies of the assets do not matter. Whatever the supplies, portfolio balance requires that the real expected rates of return on the assets be equal. In particular, if $r_e = r$ and $\dot{p}_e = 0$, equilibrium requires that $r = 0$.

Keynes departed from this theory in his liquidity-preference explanation of the choice between cash balances and interest-bearing monetary assets. He was able to show that, given uncertainty or lack of unanimity in the expectations of wealth owners, the rate of interest that preserves portfolio balance between cash and "bonds" is not independent of the supplies of the two kinds of assets. But he did not apply the same reasoning to the much more important choice between physical goods or capital, on the one hand, and monetary assets, on the other. His theory of investment was orthodox in requiring equality between the marginal efficiency of capital and the rate of interest.

The assumptions behind the portfolio-balance equation in the present model, equation (6), may be briefly stated. Each owner of wealth entertains as possibilities numerous values of both r_e and $-\dot{p}_e/p$, and to each possible pair of values he attaches a probability. The expected value of r_e, that is, the mean of its marginal probability distribution, is assumed to be r. The expected value of $-\dot{p}_e/p$ is assumed to be zero. In other and less precise words, the owner of wealth expects *on balance* neither the rent of capital nor the price level to change. But he is not sure. The dispersions of possible rents and price changes above and below their expected values constitute the risks of the two assets.

Owners of wealth, it is further assumed, dislike risk. Of two portfolios with the same expected value of rate of return, an investor will prefer the one with the lower dispersion of rate of return.[4] The principle of "not putting all your eggs in one basket" explains why a risk-avoiding investor may well hold a diversified portfolio even when the expected returns of all the assets in it are not identical. For the present purpose it explains why an owner of wealth will hold currency in excess of transactions requirements, even when its expected return is zero and the expected return on capital is positive. It also explains why, given the risks associated with the two assets, an investor may desire to have more of his wealth in capital the larger is r. The higher the prospective yield of a portfolio, the greater is the inducement to accept the additional risks of heavier concentration on the more remunerative asset.[5]

LABOR SUPPLY

The behavior of the model depends in a crucial way on assumptions regarding the relations of the supply of labor to the real wage, to the money wage, and to time. It will be convenient, therefore, to introduce alternative assumptions in the course of the argument of part II.

II

STATIONARY EQUILIBRIUM

The model would be of little interest if its position of stationary equilibrium were inevitably and rapidly attained, but, for the sake of completeness, this position will be described first. There are any number of combinations of labor and capital that can produce the zero-saving level of output. To each combination corresponds a marginal productivity of labor, to which the real wage must be equal; this marginal productivity is higher the more capital-intensive the combination. Suppose there is a unique relation between the supply of labor and the real wage. An equilibrium labor-capital combination is one that demands labor in an amount equal to the supply forthcoming at the real wage corresponding to that combination. The equilibrium absolute price level is then determined by the portfolio-balance equation. Given the rent and amount of capital in the equilibrium combination and the supply of currency, portfolio balance must be obtained by a price level that provides the appropriate amount of real wealth in liquid form.

BALANCED GROWTH

Proportional growth of capital, income, and employment implies, according to the assumed production function, constancy of capital rent, r, and the real wage, w. Maintenance of portfolio balance requires, therefore, an increase in M/p. Given the supply of currency, the price level must fall continuously over time. Balanced growth requires an expanding labor supply, available at the same real wage and at an ever decreasing money wage.

GROWTH WITH CAPITAL DEEPENING

In this model, unlike those of Harrod, Hicks, and others, failure of the labor supply to grow at the rate necessary for balanced growth does not mean that growth at a slower rate is impossible. If the real wage must rise in order to induce additional labor supply, the rent of capital must, it is true, fall as capital grows. Portfolio balance requires, therefore, that a given increment of capital be accompanied by a greater price decline than in the case of balanced growth. But there is some rate of price decline that will preserve portfolio balance, even in the extreme case of completely inelastic labor supply. Although the rate of price decline per increment of capital is greater the less elastic the supply of labor with respect to the real wage and with respect to time, the time rate of price decline is not necessarily faster. The growth of income, saving, and capital is slower when labor is less elastic, and it takes longer to achieve the same increment of capital.

TECHNOLOGICAL PROGRESS AND PRICE DEFLATION

The preceding argument has assumed an unchanging production function with constant returns to scale. In comparison with that case, technological progress is deflationary to the extent that a more rapid growth of income augments transactions requirements for currency. But technological progress has offsetting inflationary effects to the extent that it raises the marginal productivity of capital corresponding to given inputs of capital and labor. Conceivably technical improvement can keep the rent on capital rising even though its amount relative to the supply of labor is increasing. This rise might even be sufficient to keep the demand for real currency balances from rising, in spite of the growth of the capital stock and of transactions requirements. At the other extreme, it is possible to imagine technological progress that fails to raise or even lowers the marginal productivity of capital corresponding to given inputs of the two factors. Progress of this kind contains nothing to counteract the deflationary pressures of a growing capital stock, declining capital rent, and increasing transactions needs.

MONETARY EXPANSION AS AN ALTERNATIVE
TO PRICE DEFLATION

Growth with continuous price deflation strains the assumption that wealth owners expect, on balance, the price level to remain constant. The process itself would teach them that the expected value of the real return on currency is positive, and it would perhaps also reduce their estimates of the dispersion of possible returns on currency. This lesson would increase the relative attractiveness of currency as a store of value and thus force an ever faster rate of price decline.

An alternative to price deflation is expansion of the supply of currency. As noted above, monetary expansion cannot, in this model, be accomplished by monetary policy in the conventional sense but must be the result of deficit financing.[6] Assume that the government deficit $\dot{M}$ takes the form of transfer payments. Then equation (1) must be changed to read:

$$\dot{K} + \frac{\dot{M}}{p} = s\left(Y + \frac{\dot{M}}{p}\right). \tag{7}$$

The normal result is that consumption will be a larger and investment a smaller share of a given level of real income. Thus, the greater is $\dot{M}$, the slower will be the rate of capital expansion. At the same time the growth of the currency supply meets growing transactions requirements and satisfies the desire of wealth owners to balance increased holdings of capital, possibly yielding lower rents, with enlarged holdings of liquid wealth.

That there is a time path of M compatible with price stability may be seen by considering the inflationary consequences of large values of $\dot{M}$. There is presumably a value of $\dot{M}$ large enough so that the desire of the community to save at the disposable income level $Y + \dot{M}/p$ would be satisfied by saving at the rate $\dot{M}/p$. Then the capital stock would remain constant, its marginal product would stay constant, and transactions requirements would remain unchanged. Portfolio balance could then be maintained only by inflation at the same rate as $\dot{M}/M$. Somewhere between this value of $\dot{M}$ and zero there is a rate of growth of the currency supply compatible with price stability.

WAGE INFLEXIBILITY AS AN OBSTACLE TO GROWTH

If the currency supply grows too slowly, the necessity that price deflation—probably an ever faster price deflation—accompany growth casts considerable doubt on the viability of the growth processes described above. This doubt arises from the institutional limits on downward flexibility of prices, in particular money wage rates, characteristic of actual economies. The purpose of this and the two following sections is to analyze the behavior of the system when money wage rates are inflexible.

For this analysis it is convenient to work with two relationships between the price level, p, and employment of labor, N. Both relationships assume a constant capital stock, K. The first, called the "labor market balance" (*LMB*) relation, gives for any level of employment, N, the price level, p, that equates the marginal productivity of labor to the real wage. Given the money wage, this p is higher for larger values of N, because the marginal product of labor declines with employment with a given capital stock. This relation is shown in Figures 1a and 1b as curve *LMB*. The level of employment N_f is the maximum labor supply that can be induced at the given money wage. At that level of employment the money wage becomes flexible upward. If the money wage is raised or lowered, the *LMB* curve will shift up or down proportionately. If the capital stock is expanded, the *LMB* curve will shift downward, because an addition to capital will raise the marginal product of labor at any level of employment.

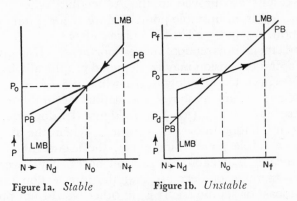

Figure 1a. *Stable*   **Figure 1b.** *Unstable*

The second relation between the same two variables, p and N, is the "portfolio balance" relation *PB*, also shown in Figures 1a and 1b. As the name indicates, it shows for any level of employment the price level required for portfolio balance between the given stock of capital K and the given supply of currency M. Its slope may be either positive or negative. The marginal productivity of the given stock of capital, and hence the rent of capital, is greater the higher the volume of employment. Currency is thus a relatively less attractive asset at higher levels of employment; so far as this effect is concerned, the price level must be higher at higher levels of employment in order to reduce the real supply of currency. The transactions relation of demand for currency to the level of real income works, however, in the opposite direction. Whatever its slope, the *PB* curve will, for obvious reasons, shift upward if currency supply M is expanded, and downward if capital expands.

It is not possible to establish a priori which curve, *LMB* or *PB*, has the greater slope. The two possibilities are shown in Figures 1a and 1b. In Figure 1a the *LMB* curve has the greater slope; both curves are drawn with positive slopes, but the *PB* curve could equally well have a negative slope. In Figure 1b the *PB* curve has the greater slope. As indicated by the arrows, the intersection (p_0, N_0) is a stable short-run equilibrium in Figure 1a but an unstable one in Figure 1b. This follows from the assumption that $\dot{p}$ will be positive, zero, or negative, depending on whether wealth owners regard their currency holdings as too large, just right, or too small.[7] In Figure 1b (p_f, N_f) is a stable short-run equilibrium. And there may be another stable intersection (p_d, N_d). Here N_d would be a level of employment so low and, correspondingly, a real wage so high that the rigidity of the money wage breaks down.

Capital expansion shifts both the *LMB* and the *PB* curve downward. How does capital expansion affect the point (p_0, N_0)? The following results are proved in the Appendix: When the intersection (p_0, N_0) is an unstable point (Figure 1b), capital expansion increases both N_0 and p_0. The *PB* curve shifts more than the *LMB* curve, and their intersection moves northeast. The qualitative effect of capital expansion may be depicted graphically by imagining the *PB* curve to shift downward while the *LMB* curve stays put. The same argument shows that capital accumulation moves a point like (p_f, N_f) or (p_d, N_d) in Figure 1b downward, while capital decumulation moves it upward. When the intersection (p_0, N_0) is a stable point (Figure 1a), the argument of the Appendix indicates that capital expansion necessarily lowers p_0 but may either increase or decrease N_0; the intersection may move either southeast or southwest. It is, in other words, not possible to say which curve shifts more as a consequence of a given change in the capital stock.

These results permit consideration of the question whether growth with full employment of labor is compatible with a floor on the money-wage rate. Except in the case where labor supply grows as rapidly as capital or more rapidly, the growth process brings about an increase of the real wage. A certain amount of price deflation is therefore compatible with rigidity of the money wage. But, according to the results reported in the previous paragraph, certainly in the unstable case and possibly in the stable case, too, the amount of price deflation needed to maintain portfolio balance is too much to enable employment to be maintained at a rigid money wage. Capital growth shifts the *PB* curve down more than the *LMB* curve. However, it is also possible in the stable case that the *LMB* curve shifts more than the *PB* curve, so that employment could be maintained and even increased while the money wage remains rigid and prices fall. But even this possibility depends on the assumption that wealth owners balance their portfolios on the expectation that the price level will remain the same.

As noted above, it is only realistic to expect that a process of deflation would itself teach owners of wealth to expect price deflation rather than price stability. Such expectations would inevitably so enhance the relative attractiveness of currency as an asset that the process could not continue without a reduction of the money-wage rate.

WAGE INFLEXIBILITY AND CYCLICAL FLUCTUATIONS

It is the situation depicted in Figure 1b that gives rise to the possibility of a cycle formally similar to those of Kaldor, Goodwin, and Hicks. Suppose the economy is at point (p_f, N_f). Capital expansion will sooner or later cause this point to coincide with (p_0, N_0) at a point like R in Figure 2. This day will be hastened by any inflation in the money-wage floor fostered by full employment; it may be that, once having enjoyed the money wage corresponding to (p_f, N_f) in Figure 1b, labor will not accept any lower money wage. Once R is reached, any further capital expansion will require a price decline that will push the real wage of labor, given that the money wage cannot fall, above its marginal productivity. Employers will therefore contract employment. But this does not obviate the necessity of price deflation. Indeed, it aggravates it, because the reduction of employment lowers the marginal productivity of capital. Balance cannot be restored both in the labor market and in wealth holdings until a level of employment is reached at which the wage rate becomes flexible downward (N_d in Figure 2).

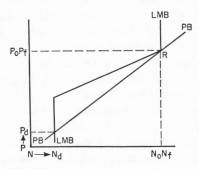

Figure 2.

The permanence of this "floor" equilibrium depends upon the saving function. If positive saving occurs at the levels of income produced by labor supply N_d, capital expansion will continue; and so also will price and wage deflation. Increase of employment then depends on the willingness of labor to accept additional employment at the low level to which severe unemployment has driven the money wage. Willingness to accept additional employment at this money wage may be encouraged by the increase in the real wage due to continued capital accumulation. A sufficient lowering of the money-wage rate demanded for increased employment would result in a situation like that represented by point S in Figure 3, and full employment could be restored.

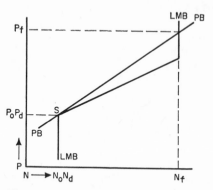

Figure 3.

Alternatively, the "floor" may correspond to a level of income at which there is negative saving. The gradual attrition of the capital stock will then move the PB curve up relative to the LMB curve. As capital becomes scarcer, its marginal product rises; and for both reasons its attractiveness relative to that of currency increases. Whatever happens to the money-wage terms on which labor will accept additional employment, the decumulation of capital will eventually lead to a position like S in Figure 3.

Once S is reached, any further reduction in the money wage, or any further decumulation of capital, will lead to an expansion of employment. But increasing employment only enhances the relative attractiveness of the existing stock of capital, causing the price level to rise and employment to be still further increased. As Figure 3 shows, the only stopping point is (p_f, N_f). Once N_f is reached, the money wage becomes flexible upward and follows the price level upward until portfolio balance is restored at the price level p_f. The cycle then repeats itself.

The floor in this model is provided by a level of employment so low, and a real wage correspondingly so high, that money-wage rates become flexible downward. The breakdown of money-wage rigidity may also be interpreted as a function of time; as Leontief has suggested, money-wage rigidity may not reflect any persistent "money illusion" on the part of workers and their organizations but only a lag in their perception of the price level to use in reckoning their real wage.[8] Trouble occurs at full employment, even when real wages are increasing, because the time rate of price deflation becomes too fast in relation to this lag. Likewise, contraction of employment can be stopped and even reversed when money-wage demands have had time to catch up with what has been happening to the price level.

In this discussion of the floor it has been assumed that the rate of capital decumulation is controlled by the saving function. An interesting question arises when the saving function indicates dissaving at a rate higher than that at which the capital stock can physically decumulate. In the models of Goodwin and Hicks, in fact, the floor is the level of income at which dissaving equals the maximum possible rate of capital decumulation.

A physical limit on the rate of capital decumulation cannot really be handled within the framework of an aggregative model that takes account of only one industry, one commodity, and one price level. Such a model assumes that the output of the economy is essentially homogeneous and can equally well be consumed or accumulated in productive stocks, from which it can be withdrawn at will. If capital goods and consumers' goods are regarded as less than perfect substitutes, it is necessary to imagine that they have different price levels. Encountering a Goodwin-Hicks floor would then mean that the two price levels diverge. At any lower level of income the community would be unable to consume capital at the rate at which it wished to dissave. Consequently, the community would dissave from its holdings of currency. This would stop the fall in the price level of consumption goods and make the Goodwin-Hicks floor an equilibrium level of employment and income. The price of capital goods would continue to fall as owners of wealth attempted to convert capital into either currency or consumption. This fall in the value of capital goods would restore portfolio balance—even though consumers' goods prices ceased to fall and money-wage rates remained rigid—by making capital a smaller proportion of the community's wealth.

With the model thus amended, the physical limit on capital decumulation provides a floor that will stop and eventually reverse a contraction even if the money-wage rate is intractable. But the contraction need not proceed to this extreme, if the wage-flexibility floor described above occurs at a higher level of employment and output.

WAGE INFLEXIBILITY AND STAGNATION

The cycle just described arises from the situation depicted in Figure 1b. But the situation of Figure 1a, where the LMB curve has an algebraically greater slope than the PB curve and the intersection (p_0, N_0) is a stable equilibrium, also is a possibility. In this case the intersection may move to the left as the capital stock increases. Growth of capital is accompanied by reduction of employment, so long as the money-wage rate is maintained. This process may end in a stationary equilibrium position if it entails such a reduction in output (or, if wealth is relevant to the saving function, such an increase in wealth) as to reduce saving to zero. But it is also possible that a process with positive saving, growth of capital, and increasing unemployment will continue indefinitely.

SUMMARY

The simple aggregative model that has been presented here differs from others used in discussions of growth and cycles in two main respects. The production function allows for substitution between capital and labor. The willingness of the community to hold physical capital depends on its rate of return and on the value of the liquid wealth held by the community. These two assumptions provide a link, generally absent in other models, between the world of real magnitudes and the world of money and prices. This link provides the model with some adjustment mechanisms ignored in other growth and cycle models. The following conclusions result:

1. Growth is possible at a great variety of rates and is not necessarily precluded when the labor supply grows slowly or remains constant.

2. The course of the price level as capital grows depends on (*a*) the accompanying rate of expansion of the labor force, (*b*) the rate at which the supply of currency is augmented by government deficits, and (*c*) the rate of technological progress. The first two factors are both inflationary. Technological progress has mixed effects. In the absence of monetary expansion and technological progress, price deflation is a necessary concomitant of growth even when the labor supply is increasing just as rapidly as capital. In these circumstances, therefore, growth with stable or increasing employment cannot continue if the money-range rate is inflexible downward.

3. Given wage inflexibility, the system may alternate between high and low levels of employment and, concurrently, between periods of price inflation and deflation. The ceiling to this cyclical process is provided by inelasticity of the labor supply. The floor may be provided either by the breakdown of the rigid money wage or by physical limits on the rate of consumption of capital. Alternatively, the system may "stagnate" at less than full employment, quite conceivably with capital growth and reduction of employment occurring at the same time. Whether the system behaves in this manner or with cyclical fluctuations depends on the relation between the conditions of portfolio balance and the rate of return

on capital. The greater the shift in portfolios that owners of wealth wish to make when the rate of return on capital changes, the more likely it is that the system will have a cyclical solution.

Appendix

The equation of the labor-market-balance curve, for given K, is

$$pP_N(K, N) = w_0, \tag{1}$$

where w_0 is the rigid money-wage rate. The slope of this curve is

$$\left(\frac{dp}{dN}\right)_{LMB} = \frac{-p^2 P_{NN}}{w_0}. \tag{2}$$

Since $P_{NN} < 0$, this slope is positive.

The equation of the portfolio-balance curve, for given K and M, is

$$
\begin{aligned}
M &= pL(K, r, Y) \\
&= pL(K, P_K[K, N], P[K, N]). \tag{3}
\end{aligned}
$$

The slope of this curve is

$$\left(\frac{dp}{dN}\right)_{PB} = \frac{-p^2}{M}(L_r P_{KN} + L_Y P_N). \tag{4}$$

Since $L_r < 0$, $P_{KN} > 0$, and $L_Y > 0$, this slope may be either positive or negative.

The point (p_0, N_0) is determined by the intersection of (1) and (3). The problem is to find the changes in p_0 and N_0 associated with an increase in K.

Differentiating (1) and (3) with respect to K gives

$$\frac{\partial p_0}{\partial K}\left(\frac{w_0}{p_0}\right) + \frac{\partial N_0}{\partial K}(p_0 P_{NN}) = -p_0 P_{NK}, \tag{5}$$

$$
\begin{aligned}
\frac{\partial p_0}{\partial K}\left(\frac{M}{p_0}\right) &+ \frac{\partial N_0}{\partial K}(p_0 L_r P_{KN} + p_0 L_Y P_N) \\
&= -p_0 L_K - p_0 L_r P_{KK} - p_0 L_Y P_K. \tag{6}
\end{aligned}
$$

Equations (5) and (6) give the following solutions:

$$
\begin{aligned}
\frac{\partial p_0}{\partial K} &= -\frac{p^2}{D}(P_{NK}^2 L_r - P_{NN} P_{KK} L_r \\
&\quad - L_K P_{NN} + P_{NK} P_N L_Y - P_{NN} P_K L_Y), \tag{7}
\end{aligned}
$$

$$\frac{\partial N_0}{\partial K} = -\frac{1}{D}(w_0 L_K + w_0 L_r P_{KK} - MP_{NK} + w_0 L_Y P_K), \tag{8}$$

where

$$D = w_0 L_r P_{KN} - MP_{NN} + w_0 L_Y P_N. \tag{9}$$

From (2), (4), and (9), it can be concluded that D will be positive, zero, or negative according as the slope of the LMB curve is greater than, equal to, or less than the slope of the PB curve. In the stable case (Figure 1a), D is positive. In the unstable case (Figure 1b), D is negative.

The production function is assumed to be homogeneous of degree one. Consequently,

$$P_N N + P_K K = P.$$

Differentiating this with respect to N and K gives

$$P_{NN} N + P_{KN} K = 0, \tag{10}$$

$$P_{NK} N + P_{KK} K = 0. \tag{11}$$

Using (10) and (11) in (7) gives

$$\frac{\partial p_0}{\partial K} = \frac{-p_0^2}{D} (P_{NN} L_K + P_{NK} P_N L_Y - P_{NN} L_K L_Y). \tag{12}$$

Since P_{NN} is negative, this derivative has the opposite sign of D. Consequently, in the stable case it is negative, and in the unstable case it is positive.

Using (9), (10), and (11) in (8) gives

$$\frac{\partial N_0}{\partial K} = \frac{1}{D} \left(\frac{N}{K} D - w_0 L_K - w_0 L_Y \frac{Y}{K} \right), \tag{13}$$

where L_K and L_Y are positive. Consequently, if D is negative—the unstable case—$\partial N_0 / \partial K$ must be positive. But if D is positive—the stable case—the derivative may have either sign.

A point like (p_f, N_f) represents the intersection of the portfolio-balance curve (3) with a vertical labor-market-balance curve. To find out whether employment can be maintained at N_f when K is increased, it is necessary only to find $\partial w_0 / \partial K$ for fixed N_f from (1) and (3). If this $\partial w_0 / \partial K$ is negative, then maintenance of employment is not consistent with maintenance of portfolio balance unless the money-wage floor w_0 is lowered. If the derivative is zero or positive, then employment can be maintained or indeed increased even though the money-wage rate remains fixed or rises. Differentiating (1) and (3) with respect to K, for fixed N, gives:

$$\frac{\partial w_0}{\partial K} - \frac{\partial p_f}{\partial K} \left(\frac{w_0}{p_f} \right) = p_f P_{NK}, \tag{14}$$

$$\frac{\partial p_f}{\partial K} \left(\frac{M}{p_f} \right) = -p_f L_K - p_f L_r P_{KK} - p_f L_Y P_K. \tag{15}$$

Therefore:

$$\frac{\partial w_0}{\partial K} = \frac{-w_0 L_K - w_0 L_r P_{KK} - w_0 L_Y P_K + M P_{NK}}{M / p_f}. \tag{16}$$

Comparing (8) and (16),

$$\left(\frac{\partial w_0}{\partial K}\right)_{N\text{const.}} = \frac{D}{M/p_f}\left(\frac{\partial N_0}{\partial K}\right)_{w_0\text{const.}} \tag{17}$$

From the conclusions previously reached with the aid of (13), it follows that, when D is negative (unstable case), $\partial w_0/\partial K$ is negative. But when D is positive (stable case), $\partial w_0/\partial K$ may have either sign.

NOTES

1. N. Kaldor, "A Model of the Trade Cycle," *Economic Journal*, Vol. 50 (March 1940), 78–92; R. Goodwin, "The Nonlinear Accelerator and the Persistence of Business Cycles," *Econometrica*, Vol. 19 (January 1951), 1–17, and "Econometrics in Business Cycle Analysis," in A. H. Hansen, *Business Cycles and National Income* (New York: W. W. Norton & Co., 1951), Chapter 22; J. R. Hicks, *A Contribution to the Theory of the Trade Cycle* (Oxford: Oxford University Press, 1950).

2. This is the same concept developed in connection with discussions of the "Pigou effect"; see Herbert Stein, "Price Flexibility and Full Employment: Comment," *American Economic Review*, Vol. 39 (June 1949), 725–26; and Don Patinkin, "Price Flexibility and Full Employment: Reply," *American Economic Review*, Vol. 39 (June 1949), 726–28.

3. An individual may be assumed to know the historical course of prices $p(t)$ up to the present (for $t \lessgtr t_0$) and to expect a future course of prices $p_e(t)$ (for $\gtrless t_0$). Presumably the expected course starts at the same price at which the historical course ends ($p[t_0] = p_e[t_0]$). But there is no reason that one should start with the same slope with which the other ends: $p'(t_0)$, referred to in the text as $\dot{p}$, is not necessarily the same as $p'_e(t_0)$, referred to in the test as $\dot{p}_e$.

4. Risk aversion in this sense may be deduced from the assumption of generally declining marginal utility of income. Here, however, it is not necessary to go into the question of the usefulness of the concept of cardinal utility in explaining behavior under uncertainty.

5. There is an "income effect" working in the opposite direction. The portfolio-balance function, equation (6), assumes the substitution effect to be dominant.

6. The implications of the approach of this paper concerning the effects of conventional monetary policy are left for discussion elsewhere. Clearly such a discussion requires the introduction of additional types of assets, including bank deposits and private debts.

7. Employment has been assumed always to be at the point where the marginal product of labor equals the real wage. But the conclusions on the stability of (p_0, N_0) in Figures 1a and 1b would not be altered if it were assumed instead that $\dot{N}$ is positive, zero, or negative depending on whether the marginal product of labor exceeds, equals, or is less than the real wage.

8. W. Leontief, "Postulates: Keynes' *General Theory* and the Classicists," in S. E. Harris (ed.), *The New Economics* (New York: Knopf, 1947), Chapter 19.

9 The Portfolio Approach to the Demand for Money and Other Assets

James S. Duesenberry *Harvard University*

The theory of the demand for financial assets has come in for a good deal of discussion in the last few years. Undoubtedly the discussion has been fruitful and has given us many new insights into the nature of financial processes. But it cannot be said that there is any generally agreed upon view as to the way in which those processes work. It would be appropriate at a conference of this kind to review the different hypotheses and give a systematic summary of the present state of knowledge. Unfortunately, though I have read the literature assiduously I have found it rather indigestible. I do not feel prepared to give a fair summary of other people's views. I must fall back therefore on giving my own.

In this paper I shall deal with the demand for liquid assets and money by households and corporations. Those two groups hold over two-thirds of all liquid assets, and the same general approach though not the details can probably be applied to the demands of unincorporated businesses, farmers, state and local governments. In dealing with the demand for liquid assets we must at least implicitly deal with the demand for other types of assets, but I shall

Reprinted from *Review of Economics and Statistics*, Vol. 45 (Cambridge, Mass.: Harvard University Press, February 1963), 9–24, by permission of the author and publisher. Copyright, 1963, by the President and Fellows of Harvard College.

not, except incidentally, say anything in detail about the demand for stocks, bonds, or physical assets. I shall confine myself to the demand for currency, demand deposits, commercial bank time deposits, mutual savings bank deposits, savings and loan shares, savings bonds, and short-term federal securities. There are, of course, other liquid assets, but I shall have little to say about them.

I have occasionally used the term money in the sense of demand deposits and currency but have usually referred to those assets specifically to avoid any confusion with other definitions of money. But though I am happy to try to avoid the semantic confusion involved in arguments about whether any particular asset should be included under the heading money, I do cling to the view that commercial bank time deposits are significantly different from demand deposits. For that matter, so is currency, and so perhaps we ought to dispense with the term money in theoretical discussions and say clearly what we mean.

In the first section of the paper I have discussed very briefly the conditions under which liquid assets are supplied. There follow in section two a discussion of corporate motives for holding liquid assets and money and a review of some empirical evidence on the relative importance of various factors influencing corporate decisions. In section three, this theory of household demand for liquid assets and money is discussed together with some empirical evidence.

The Supply of Liquid Assets

The major liquid assets today are cash, short-term government securities, savings bonds, and time deposits at commercial banks, mutual savings banks, and savings and loan associations. Various other assets, e.g., commercial paper, supply some liquidity and, under other circumstances, could supply more, but we shall confine ourselves here to short governments, savings bonds, and time deposits.

Savings bonds are, of course, on tap at fixed yields and may be regarded as exogenously determined.

The total volume of short-term Treasury securities is determined by the Treasury (assuming that it may affect conversions if it wishes). For theoretical purposes, we may regard the composition of the federal debt as an exogenous policy variable. The fact remains, however, that there is some tendency for the proportion of short-term issues outstanding to rise in tight money periods and fall in easy money periods.

If we are concerned with the determinants of nonbank liquid asset holdings, then the willingness of banks to switch maturities becomes important. In general, banks appear to have been willing to switch out of very short maturities into somewhat longer ones in response to changes in the yield curve. As a result, the supply of under-one-year maturities to nonbank holders has considerable elasticity in terms of yield spreads, though the supply curve is certainly not flat.

The supply of savings deposits is a very different matter from the supply of Treasury bills and commercial paper. In the short run, the supply of savings deposits is elastic at the announced rates. In the long run (except when the regulatory authorities interfere) the rate offered by savings institutions is related to market rates and operating costs. For savings and loan associations, the relevant rates are mainly those on conventional mortgages in the areas where they operate. For mutual savings banks, yields on mortgages in their own areas, on guaranteed mortgages in other areas, and on bonds which they are eligible to buy are relevant. If legal restrictions on rates did not interfere, commercial bank time deposit rates would presumably tend to reflect yields on mortgages and municipal securities.

In the long run the differentials between savings deposit rates and those available on credit market instruments depend not only on cost factors in bank operations but also on the relative supplies of debt instruments of different types. A large supply of mortgages tends to raise savings institution yields relative to others because those institutions have a comparative advantage in handling mortgages.

If we are content with a partial analysis, the above comments are perhaps sufficient. There are, however, some additional considerations affecting the availability of liquid assets. Let us suppose that for some reason the public's tastes change so that households collectively wish to switch out of other assets into savings deposits. Since savings institutions appear to be willing to take all the deposits they can get at the going rate, there appears to be no reason why the public should not make the switch. But, of course, that is not true. If the yield spreads existing when tastes change are to persist, the savings institutions must not only be willing to take deposits but they must also be willing to buy the assets from which the public wants to switch (if we rule out asset expansion by banks). If the public wished to sell a set of assets having the same relative composition as the existing portfolios of savings institutions, there is no reason why the switch should not take place. But suppose the public wished to sell stocks and take savings deposits. They cannot sell the stocks to savings institutions. In the end the stocks must remain in the hands of holders other than savings institutions. If the initial holders come to like stocks less, their prices must fall until the original or some other holders other than savings institutions are willing to hold them. That change in yields may set up repercussions which will result in some increase in savings deposits (and the shifting of some assets to savings institutions). But even when the yields offered by savings institutions are a fixed function of yield on credit market instruments, the public cannot trade freely between savings deposits and other assets at fixed yields.[1]

We cannot properly analyze the forces influencing the volume of savings deposits in partial equilibrium supply and demand terms. Those forces work themselves out through the whole system of interrelated supplies and demands for different kinds of assets.

Corporate Holdings of Money and Other Liquid Assets

In this section we shall consider the factors influencing the total amount of liquid assets held by corporations and the division of those assets between cash and interest-bearing forms of liquidity. We start from the assumption that the decision-making process involves first a decision about the amount of liquid assets to be held and then a decision about the proportion to be held in cash.

We begin with a brief outline of the rationale for holding liquid assets and then consider in equally general terms the rationale of the choice between cash and other liquid assets. We then turn to the empirical problem of explaining observed movements of liquid assets. We first review some work which seems to explain the short-term cyclical movements of liquidity positions during the postwar period, and then consider the trend of liquidity positions in the postwar period. Finally there are some rather sketchy comments on liquidity movements in the twenties and thirties.

We then turn to the problem of explaining observed movements in the division of liquidity between cash and other forms of liquidity. Once again, we begin with the postwar period and then proceed to comment briefly on the events of earlier periods.

BUSINESS DEMAND FOR LIQUIDITY

Corporate treasurers wish to have liquid assets on hand for a variety of reasons. First, some minimum of liquid assets is required to cover the day-to-day variations in receipts and expenditures without continually borrowing and repaying bank loans. Second, many corporations have wide seasonal variations in their cash inflows and outflows. Some choose to borrow from banks during seasons when cash outflows exceed inflows and repay when the balance of the flows turns the other way. Others, however, raise enough from long-term sources to cover all or part of their seasonal cash outflows, and therefore have surplus liquidity during the seasons of net cash inflow. In doing that they make an interest sacrifice which depends on the relations between the cost of long-term funds, the cost of bank borrowing, and the yield on liquid assets.[2]

Third, most, though not all, business firms seem to feel that it is desirable to fund all or a very large part of their tax liability. A sophisticated treasurer may feel that he need only be prepared to meet the net reduction in tax liability which will occur when profits decline, but most of them do not appear to take that view.

Fourth, most firms wish to have liquidity to meet the problems arising from a decline in cash flow from current operations during a depression. In a depression a firm must be able to draw down liquid assets or borrow to meet the cumulative difference between net cash flow from operations and the sum of (1) debt service (2) dividends (3) a minimum level of investment. It should be noted that net cash flow from operations can become negative because, in order to maintain its market share, a firm is willing to continue production when average variable cost exceeds price.

It is not, of course, strictly necessary to maintain dividends in periods of adversity, but it is clear that many firms are willing to bear some cost in order to do so.

Investment will, of course, decline to a low level during a depression but, even when there is a great deal of excess capacity, certain investments can be avoided only at great cost. Those investments include replacements necessary to maintain production, and investments required to adapt to changing market conditions. In addition, technical developments or the possibility of buying out financially weak competitors may present investment opportunities promising very high returns.

A firm always has the possibility of financing those cash requirements by borrowing, but in a depression lenders may not be disposed to gamble on the firm's prospects. If they are willing to lend they may require some measure of control or impose restrictions on the borrower's action.

To avoid or reduce borrowing under adverse conditions, a firm can raise more long-term capital than it needs for current outlays, during periods when it can do so advantageously, and build up a stock of liquidity against adversity. It then pays the difference between the cost of long-term funds and return on liquid assets (less the cost of borrowing avoided during periods of adversity).

The cost may be somewhat reduced because the improvement in its current ratio will reduce the cost of its long-term borrowing.

In all the cases so far mentioned, the firm gains in convenience and reduction of risk by paying more in interest charges than would otherwise be necessary, and the amount of liquidity maintained will be determined at the point where the marginal gains are balanced by the costs of obtaining additional liquidity. That implies, of course, that the amount of liquidity held by the firm will (other things equal) tend to increase as long-term capital costs fall relative to the yields on Treasury bills or other short-term investments.

We should, of course, expect business liquidity at a given phase of the business cycle to be roughly scaled to the volume of sales or total receipts and payments—with the proportionality factor varying with interest rate differentials. Since risk is involved, we should expect firms to hold less liquidity as they become more confident of the stability of the economy and to increase liquidity ratios with a deterioration of confidence. Finally, the level of corporate income tax rates and the length of the collection lag should influence the volume of liquid assets held.

Before going on to review some empirical evidence on these propositions, it is necessary to introduce some other considerations.

The variation in corporate liquidity over the cycle reflects some "mechanical" aspects of cash inflows and cash outflows. Firms that do not rely heavily on bank financing will tend to have certain passive inflows and outflows of cash (which may be shifted into other forms of liquid assets). To put it another way, firms may have certain target levels of liquid assets but they do not always eliminate discrepancies between actual and target levels very rapidly.

During recovery years, like 1955 and 1959, corporations tend to gain liquidity because profits rise rapidly while tax payments lag. Fixed investment appropriations rise rapidly but actual outlays rise more slowly. Inventories and receivables also rise but a considerable part of the increase is bank financed. The result is a large net cash inflow. Firms gaining liquidity in this way could pay off long-term debt, but have little incentive to do so since they are committed to higher investment outlays in the near future and will also have larger tax payments to make.

In the later years of the cycle, retained earnings and depreciation level off, tax payments catch up, and the rate of investment outlays catches up with new appropriations for investment. Some of the liquidity gained earlier is then disgorged.

The record in slump years is mixed. Corporations lost liquidity in 1954 and 1960 but gained in 1958. The difference appears to be due in part to (1) differences in the relative changes in profits and tax payments arising from changes in the tax law, (2) differences in the magnitude of inventory reduction, (3) differences in the magnitude of the change in plant and equipment investment.

CORPORATE DEMAND FOR DEMAND DEPOSITS

Corporate demand for demand balances has to be explained in terms of the rationale of the choice between demand balances and other types of liquid assets which earn interest—in this case, mainly Treasury bills.

As in the case of households, a substantial part of corporate liquidity is held to cover fairly near-term net cash outflows arising from the uneven rates of receipts and expenditures. The gross return to be obtained from holding Treasury bills depends on the amounts involved, the interest rate, and the length of the holding period. The gross return is offset by the transactions cost of going into and out of bills—dealer spread and any other direct costs. However, dealer spreads on bills are very low so that the direct cost of transactions in bills can be earned by holding bills for very short periods even at low interest rates.

However, the direct costs of transactions are only part of the cost of holding Treasury bills. If bills are held only for a few definite, large out-payments—e.g., tax payments—the only additional cost is a little thought on the part of the treasurer. But as soon as a firm embarks on a program of trying to earn interest by predicting cash inflows and outflows, and investing temporary excess funds, it has to bear some overhead costs to keep track of its cash position.

In entering on a program of investing short-term surpluses of funds and in deciding how far to carry it, a firm must balance the expected average return from its bill holdings (or an increment in them) against the overhead cost of controlling its cash position. The expected return will vary with the average rate of interest on bills expected over a period of years. The cost will vary with the tightness of the cash management. As we pass from simple operations such as funding tax liabilities to the very close cash management practiced by a few large companies, the cost of increasing the average amount invested (for a firm on a given scale) by closer management will rise. The cost per dollar invested will rise as the scale of the firm becomes smaller. We should expect, therefore, that at low interest rates only large firms will use Treasury bills for any purpose other than funding tax liabilities, and even the large firms may not find very close cash management worthwhile. A rise in interest rates should push out both the extensive (size of firm) and intensive (closeness of cash management) margins and cause a shift from cash to bills. However, since the costs of cash management are mainly overhead costs, we do not expect much shifting between cash and bills in response to short-run fluctuations in bill rate. Instead, we expect shifts in response to changes in the average rate expected for a period of years—probably best measured by a fairly long moving average of past rates. Moreover, some of the costs are costs of getting started and learning the tricks of cash management, so that a rise in bill rates may result in a shift from cash to bills. A later fall (even on a long-term basis) may not bring the cash-bill ratio back to its initial position.

Shifting from cash to interest-bearing liquid assets is not the only way to reduce cash balances in relation to activity. Close attention to cash management may enable a firm to reduce its operating cash without any investment. For example, measures to speed up processing and collection of checks may reduce the float of unavailable cash. There are many examples of this sort. It is not clear whether developments of this sort represent a response to changing interest rates or whether they are simply improvements in managerial techniques which, like other changes in techniques, occur even when no factor price has changed. One would expect, however, that enthusiasm for measures to reduce the need for cash would increase with rising interest rates. It should be noted that increased efficiency in the use of operating cash is likely to reduce total liquidity and to affect cash directly so that the share of cash in total liquidity will fall.

Corporate managements also appear to have achieved some reduction in their cash balances in relation to activity by sharper negotiation with banks. It is customary for corporations holding payroll, dividend, or other accounts involving a large volume of check processing to maintain an average balance on which the bank can earn a return (in lieu of a service charge), which covers the costs of servicing the account. In recent years, a good many corporations which do not depend on bank loan finance have tried systematically to hold these balances down to a minimum. But, so long as the custom of remunerating banks by holding balances rather than by explicit service charges continues, a substantial amount of corporate funds will be tied up in this way.

SHORT-RUN MOVEMENTS IN TOTAL LIQUIDITY

In discussions of the demand for money and liquid assets, attention is usually centered on the elasticity of demand for liquid assets with respect to interest rates. In fact, however, the variation in corporate liquid asset holdings over the business cycle is principally due to variations in the cash flows from operations. Cash flows are generated by retained earnings, plant and equipment outlays, increases or decreases in inventory and variables, tax accounts and tax payments. The net balance of those flows—each of which has a large cyclical variation—is first reflected in corporate liquid asset holdings. Managements then have to decide whether the resulting liquidity position is too high or too low with respect to some target. If the liquidity position is out of line with this target position, firms must then raise funds from outside sources or repay debt.

Interest rates may enter this picture in two ways. On the one hand, target levels of liquidity may be influenced by the cost of holding liquidity, as indicated above. On the other hand, even if target levels are not affected by interest costs, the timing of borrowing may be influenced by cyclical movements in the interest rate.

Following this reasoning, we may treat liquid asset holdings as an inventory and explain movements in liquidity in terms of a stock adjustment process of the same type used in explaining physical inventories.

This has been done by Locke Anderson in a paper presented to the Econometric Society. Briefly, his results can be interpreted as follows.

1. Target levels of liquid asset holdings appear to depend on sales and tax liability, with the desired holdings of liquidity equal to about 15 per cent of annual sales and 60 per cent of tax liability.

2. The amount of outside funds raised in a quarter (for a given position in terms of other variables mentioned below) increases by about 25¢ for every dollar of increase in the difference between actual and target liquid asset holdings at the start of the quarter. That is, firms act as though they tried to close the gap between actual and target holdings in about a year.

3. Borrowing in a given quarter also responds to changes in cash flows from retained earnings and depreciation, plant and equipment expenditures, and inventories and receivables. Short-term borrowing declines by about 75 per cent of any increase in retained earnings, but the response of borrowing to cash flows of the other types is much weaker. As a result, an increase in the rate of inventory investment will reduce liquid assets, and vice versa.

4. The rate of borrowing is also significantly influenced by the debt position of corporations.

5. Finally the rate of long-term borrowing is significantly influenced by the corporate bond yield. A one percentage point increase in the bond yield appears to reduce corporate borrowing by $700 million per quarter. If all other flow variables remained constant while the bond yield rose, the result would be a decline

in borrowing followed by a gradual rise as the liquidity stock was reduced. A one-time rise in the interest rate would result in a one-time reduction in the liquidity stock. However, there are some indications that the relevant interest rate variable is not the absolute rate but some indicator of the cyclical position of the rate. That view is supported by the fact that the bill rate did not appear to have any significant influence on borrowing. Since the cost of liquidity is the difference between bill and bond yield, it seems probable that the interest rate coefficient represents a timing variable rather than a variable affecting the long-term level of liquidity.

Anderson's results are supported not only by aggregate regressions for all manufacturing but also by separate analysis of a number of manufacturing industries. They seem to show, first, that the bulk of the variation in corporate liquidity is explained by variations in operating cash flows. Second, they do show that the interest rate can have a very substantial short-run effect on corporate borrowing but leave it uncertain whether the upward trend in interest rates plays a significant role in determining the trend of corporate liquidity.

POSTWAR TREND IN TOTAL LIQUIDITY

We need not give any account of movements of corporate liquidity in the years immediately after the war. It seems reasonable to take the view that most corporations had made their basic adjustment to postwar conditions by about 1952. Since that time there has been a downward trend in the ratio of corporate liquid asset holdings to GNP and to corporate sales.

Part of the decline is probably due to the decline in the ratio of tax liabilities to corporate sales as a result of the decline in profit margins and the shortening of the lag between accrual and payment. The ratio of liquid assets, less tax liabilities, to sales shows almost no decline. However, it is going too far to offset tax liabilities against liquidity, one for one. We know that some corporations borrow at tax dates so they cannot have fully funded their tax liability. Some corporations have less total liquidity than their tax liability, so it is obvious that they cannot have done so. Anderson's research suggests about 60 per cent funding as a norm. If that figure or one somewhere near it is used, then the ratio of corporate liquidity to GNP (adjusted for the tax factor) fell from about .11 in 1952, to .09 in 1960 and 1961. The downward drift in the relative holdings of cash, governments, and time deposits may have been offset by an increase in holdings of various other liquid assets not included in our figures, but those other assets cannot have increased enough to offset the downward trend in relative holdings of the ones included.

To what should we attribute the decline? Even if we took Anderson's results with respect to the interest rate at face value, we would expect to get a decline in liquidity of less than 1 per cent of GNP from the 1952–61 rise in BAA bond yields. Moreover, the net cost of holding liquidity has increased very little because the average spread between bill and bond yields has changed relatively little. Rising interest rates may have had some effect on the trend of liquidity ratios, but it seems doubtful that it has been very large.

Three other factors have probably played a role: (1) improved cash management, partly as a result of higher interest rates but also simply as a part of the general and continuing effort to reduce costs; (2) improved confidence in the stability of the economy may have induced some firms to reduce holdings of liquidity for protective purposes; (3) some firms still had "excessive" liquidity in 1952 and have worked it off since.

I know of no way to measure the influence of these factors but it seems unlikely that more than a fraction of the decline in liquidity ratios is due to changes in interest costs.

LIQUIDITY IN THE TWENTIES COMPARED WITH POSTWAR LIQUIDITY

The ratio of corporate liquidity to GNP during the 1920's stood at about .14 until 1928, when it rose sharply to .17, returning to about .15 at the end of 1929. The ruling ratio during the twenties was higher than that ruling in 1952 (after adjustment for tax liability). Moreover liquidity ratios showed no downward trend during the twenties. The rise at the end of the twenties is probably due to the large volume of stock issues in 1928 and 1929, and the rise would be even larger if corporate holdings of call loans were included in the ratio.

The net cost of holding liquidity has probably not increased significantly between the twenties and the fifties. Indeed (leaving call loans aside) it has probably decreased because of income tax and the availability of Treasury bills. It does not seem reasonable to argue that people have become more confident about income stability now than they were in the twenties. We can conclude, it seems to me, that the difference in liquidity ratios between the two periods is due to factors other than confidence or the cost of liquidity. It is hardly surprising that changes in the composition of output, in methods of financing, in the concentration of industry, should have produced some substantial changes in liquidity ratios.

It seems unlikely that, interest costs aside, practices with respect to liquidity should follow simple and immutable laws over long periods.

LIQUIDITY MOVEMENTS IN THE GREAT DEPRESSION

Corporate liquidity rose relative to GNP from the already high level in 1929 to 1932 and 1933. Thereafter liquidity ratios fell slowly, but even at the beginning of World War II the ratio of corporate liquid asset holdings to GNP was .16. With some allowance for corporate tax liability, the corporate liquidity ratio in 1941 was near the level of the 1920's.

It seems probable that most of the swing in liquidity during the thirties was attributable to the confidence factor. Firms preferred to hold on to liquid assets in the early thirties rather than pay back debt, because the chance that economic conditions would deteriorate was taken very seriously. With recovery, firms permitted liquidity ratios to decline gradually. The movements of liquidity ratios conform much more closely to one's guess about the state of business confidence than to the variations in the net interest cost of holding liquidity.

CASH VERSUS OTHER FORMS OF LIQUID ASSETS IN THE POSTWAR PERIOD

In the years since 1952, corporate cash holdings have increased slowly and steadily, while holdings of governments have shown little trend and have varied from year to year in a range of about $3 billion. Another set of regression studies by Anderson suggests that most of the short-term variations in liquidity positions are reflected in holdings of government securities, while cash positions respond much more weakly to those factors. It is easy to understand that, if a firm has an improvement in its liquidity position as a result of a cyclical swing in earnings and finds it inconvenient to repay debt, it will invest the surplus. When the cash flow picture reverses, it will not have any surplus cash because of its previous action and will have to sell bills if it does not borrow. In spite of a number of efforts to do so, I believe no one has found a statistically significant relationship between short-term variations in bill yields and the distribution of corporate liquidity between cash and governments. That is to be expected in view of the considerations with respect to overhead costs given above.

It does not follow that the trend in the ratio of cash to other forms of liquidity has not been influenced by interest rates. The share of liquidity in the form of time deposits (though still small) has risen since 1952, and that can probably be attributed to interest rates (though the willingness of banks to take corporate time deposits is also a factor).

The ratio of government security holdings to cash holdings has fallen since 1952 but, if we make allowance for the large proportion of governments held against tax liability, the ratio of cash to total liquidity has fallen from 75 to 72 per cent. That is a relatively small decline and does not constitute very impressive evidence of a large-scale switch from cash to bills.

The proportion of liquid assets held in the form of cash is of course influenced by other factors. An increase in efficiency in the use of operating cash works to reduce the ratio of cash to liquid assets. On the other hand, a reduction in protective liquidity resulting from a gain in confidence should tend to reduce bills relatively more than cash.

There is room, therefore, for some switch from cash to Treasury securities and time deposits, but there is no evidence that rising interest rates have produced a strong swing to interest-bearing forms of liquidity or that rising interest rates have accounted for a large part of the reduction in the ratio of corporate cash to sales and GNP.

CASH VERSUS OTHER FORMS OF LIQUIDITY
IN THE PREWAR PERIOD

The ratio of corporate cash to total liquid assets rose slightly in the early years of the depression and then after 1933 rose to nearly 80 per cent of total liquidity. The shift must, I think, be put down to the very low levels of interest rates on time deposits and short-term government securities ruling in the late thirties.

The ratio of corporate cash to total liquidity in the 1920's was higher than in the postwar period but, after adjustment of postwar data for tax liabilities, the cash liquidity ratio in the twenties was slightly higher than the one ruling in the postwar period.

The differences are not great enough to call for extended comment except to note that the development of Treasury bills does not seem to have had a great effect on the distribution of corporate liquidity.

Household Demand for Liquid Assets and Money

DEMAND FOR LIQUID ASSETS

Personal motives for holding liquid assets—transactions and precautionary motives, liquidity preferences, risk avoidance—are all so familiar that it is not necessary to discuss them in any detail. Just as in the corporate case, an individual who holds liquid assets takes a reduction in expected yield on his portfolio in return for a reduction in risk and inconvenience. The loss in expected yield depends on the price difference between the expected yields of variable assets—real estate, stocks, long-term bonds—and the yields on liquid assets. Just as in the corporate case, we expect that, other things equal, the amount of liquid assets an individual will wish to hold will decline as the cost of holding them increases. We also expect that increased confidence in the future stability of income will reduce the demand for liquid assets, and vice versa. An increase in the variance of the expected performance of variable price assets will increase the demand for liquid assets, while a decrease will reduce it.

Some of the reasons for holding liquid assets are related to uncertainties or unevenness in the flow of receipts and expenditures. On that account we might expect the demand for liquid assets to increase, other things equal, with the level of permanent income. But liquid assets are also required in an optimum portfolio even when there is no problem of income or expenditure variation. Other things equal, then, we should expect the demand for liquid assets to grow with both the level of income and the level of assets.

In individual portfolio management the size of the portfolio has an important influence on the proportion of assets held in liquid form. That is so for two reasons. Since borrowing is costly and inconvenient, most people wish to hold enough liquid assets to provide for short-term variations in income and expenditure. Persons whose total financial assets are small in relation to their incomes will find it advantageous to hold all their assets in liquid form. Second, asset management is an activity with decreasing costs to scale. The cost in terms of cash and effort of choosing assets subject to risk is much smaller per dollar invested for a large portfolio than for a small one. The net gain to be obtained from buying variable price securities as opposed to savings deposits of one type or another is not likely to be worth the trouble for the holder of a relatively small portfolio.

It seems probable that a substantial volume of liquid assets is held in connection with asset transfers. Individuals who sell marketable securities or real estate may hold funds pending reinvestment for periods ranging from a few days to several months. In some cases they may go liquid because they are bearish on variable price assets generally. But it is very common for people to sell a particular asset because they consider its net yield prospects unsatisfactory without having chosen another asset. They will hold liquid assets until they find a satisfactory alternative investment. We have no idea what volume of assets is tied up in this way but it may be very substantial.

Finally, there appears to be an interchange between strictly fixed-price assets—demand deposits, currency, savings deposits, and savings bonds—and assets with low credit risk and price variability, particularly high grade bonds. Individuals who have sufficient liquid assets to take care of short-term variations in income and expenditure may wish to have additional low-risk assets in their portfolio which they expect to hold for a fairly long time. The fact that savings deposits of various types can be converted to cash at any time with no transactions cost is of relatively little significance if one plans to hold an asset for a long time. Price variability is of some significance but those who plan to hold to maturity, anyway, need not give it a very heavy weight. Savings deposits of various types are therefore close substitutes for high quality bonds, particularly those with only moderately long maturities.

On that basis we should expect that, during periods when market yields on bonds are low relative to time deposit rates, the flow of household funds into bonds would be relatively low and the flow into time deposits relatively high. Conversely, when bond yields rise relative to time deposit yields, we should expect household bond purchases to rise relative to household takings of time deposits.

Of course the competitive relationship between time deposits and bonds is not just a cyclical phenomenon. The relative levels of time deposit yields and bond yields over the whole cycle will influence the division of individual portfolios. But because time deposit yields move slowly relative to market yields over the cycle (though linked in the long run to market yields), the cyclical influence of bond-time deposit substitution is much more apparent than any long-run substitution.

Liquid assets and expenditure. A number of writers have expressed the view that variations in household holdings of liquid assets have a strong influence on the rate of consumer expenditure. The rationale of that view has never been entirely clear to me.

It seems reasonable to expect that an increase in the real net worth of the household sector might tend to reduce saving and increase consumption. If people are saving in order to accumulate assets for some particular purpose, the desire to save may wane as they approach their goal. Of course, they may discover or recognize new goals for accumulation as they satisfy old ones, so it remains an empirical question whether an increase in net worth or in the ratio of net worth to income actually depresses saving.

But why should the possession of liquid assets, as distinguished from other assets, have a special effect on saving? One does not come any closer to any goal for accumulation by holding a deposit in a savings institution than by holding an equivalent amount of stocks and bonds.

The only difference seems to be that one can convert liquid assets into cash more easily and quickly than other kinds of assets. Consequently, one can give in to impulses to spend more easily if one holds liquid assets than if one holds other kinds of assets. There is some plausibility in that argument, but it obviously only applies to a limited part of the variation in liquid assets. The impulse consideration does not apply to persons who save regularly a substantial proportion of income or to persons who always have a substantial liquid position. For reasons which I will indicate below it seems likely that—except for the war and early postwar periods—most of the variation in liquid asset holdings is in the holdings of high income, high asset holders. In that case it is unlikely that cyclical variations in liquid asset holdings have much to do with variations in saving.

DEMAND FOR MONEY

In the last section we discussed the demand for liquid assets as a group without any distinction between money and other liquid assets. We must now turn to the question why people hold part of their liquid assets in noninterest-bearing demand deposits and currency. It should be noted at the outset that, in the literature, the reasons given in the last section for holding liquid assets are often given as reasons for holding demand deposits and currency. That may have been appropriate in periods when other forms of virtually riskless, readily marketable assets were not generally available. But it is not a satisfactory answer nowadays. The demand for currency and demand deposits must be analyzed, first, in terms of choices between liquid and nonliquid assets and, second, in terms of choices between currency and demand deposits and other forms of liquid assets.

Demand for currency. The total amount of currency outstanding since the war has varied between $25 and $30 billion. Estimates made by the Federal Reserve Board of Governors suggest that about one-third of this amount is in business hands and the rest either in the hands of households, lost, destroyed, or gone abroad. It is fairly obvious that the bulk of the currency in nonbusiness hands is not being used for pocket money or being carried around by people who do not have bank accounts. The amount of currency not in business hands represents nearly a month's wages for the entire labor force. Over half of American families have checking accounts and some of the remainder deposit pay checks in savings accounts and withdraw currency and registered checks as needed. Moreover, the bulk of the families who do not use bank accounts receive wages weekly. A full week's wages for one part of the families and an average of a couple of hundred dollars for the rest—which seems a generous estimate even after allowing for travelers—will not account for as much as $10 billion of currency.

Some of the remainder is, no doubt, lost, destroyed, or gone abroad. The rest must be in hoards for some special reason. These would include currency used in illegal transactions or held by small businessmen and professionals who receive currency and hold part of it to evade taxes, and hoarded savings of farmers who saved during the war and distrusted banks.

The amount of currency outstanding nearly doubled during the depression and rose by a factor of about four during the war. After the war it fell slightly until 1950 and has risen slowly since then by nearly $5 billion. It should be noted that the amount of currency outstanding showed little trend in years from 1900 to 1914, rose sharply during World War I, and then remained more or less stationary during the twenties.

If currency were used only for transaction purposes, we should expect the amount outstanding to rise with income but at a slower rate because of the increasing use of checking accounts, registered checks, the spread of check-cashing facilities, and the increased use of credit cards. We might also expect that currency held for tax evasion and illegal activities would grow with the scale of the economy—if the incentives for tax evasion do not change much.

On the other hand, it is likely that special factors connected with war resulted in the generation of abnormally high levels of hoarding relative to income and tax rate levels. The gradual liquidation of some of those wartime hoards may be offsetting the other factors tending to make the currency outstanding to grow. That position gains some support from the fact that the currency grew rapidly during World War I and then leveled off during the twenties, even though income grew. The rate of liquidation of currency hoards other than those connected with tax evasion or illegal activities may have been speeded up by the rise in interest rates, but we have no real information on that point.

Household demand for demand deposits. We can approach the analysis of the demand for demand deposits by asking why a man, given that he has some liquid assets, should hold them in a form which yields no interest. Certainly a major part of the answer lies in the fact that checking accounts are more convenient than other liquid assets and that funds left with savings institutions for short periods yield no return or a very small one.

Persons who hold liquid assets against a certain or fairly probable excess of payments over receipts in the near future will not find the return from savings deposits or savings bonds worth the trouble of converting from cash to earning assets and back again unless the amounts involved are very large. The income transactions demand for money will certainly account for some substantial amount of personal demand deposits. As the savings deposit interest rate rises, the proportion of "transient" liquid assets held in the form of demand deposits should decline.

The full theory of an optimum demand deposit inventory policy is just as complex as any other kind of inventory policy, but a simple example suffices to make the point in question. Suppose we consider only the disposition of liquid assets held against known lump-sum out-payments to be made at known dates and which cannot be financed out of expected net cash inflows in the intervening period. A sum of p dollars held for m months yields the holder $p \times \dfrac{m}{12} \times r$ dollars (when r is the yield on savings deposits neglecting compounding). If an individual requires a given dollar return to make worthwhile one round trip from cash to savings deposit and back to cash, the size of the payment p and the length of the interval m required to earn that amount of dollars obviously becomes shorter as r rises. When interest rates are low, savings deposits will be held only against large distant payments. As interest rates rise, people will hold savings deposits against smaller near-term payments which will produce a shift from demand balances to savings accounts.

It is unlikely, however, that the bulk of personal demand deposits are held for income transactions purposes. On January 31 (which is about the low point of the year for individual deposits), banks' records show that 85 per cent of personal demand deposit accounts had less than $1,000, but those accounts had only about 30 per cent of the total amount of personal demand deposits. Since the larger holders have more than one account, it is probable that the remaining 14 per cent of the accounts were held by no more than 10 per cent of the persons holding demand deposit accounts. And since nearly half of families have no demand deposit account it must be concluded that about 5 per cent of families own 70 per cent of personal demand deposits. Moreover, half the personal demand deposits are in accounts of over $5,000.

No doubt some part of the relatively large deposits is required for income transactions. But it seems probable that a large proportion of the larger personal demand deposit accounts is held in connection with financial transactions.

At a rough guess, individual purchases and sales of stocks, bonds, real estate, and other assets amount to something like $100 billion per year. An average holding period—between sale of one asset and purchase of another—of about four months would tie up over $30 billion. If half that sum were in demand deposits, $15 billion would be accounted for. I have no way of testing what amounts are tied up in asset float, but it seems probable that they are a significant part of personal demand deposits.

Now any individual who sells an asset and plans to reinvest in nonliquid assets, at a time some distance in the future or at an unspecified time, has the option of keeping his funds in a demand deposit or obtaining interest from a time deposit. Persons who plan to hold for periods less than a month cannot get interest from time deposits generally, and people in high tax brackets, who are interested only in capital gains, may not bother to try to get it. At low interest rates the proportion of people who will take the trouble to get time deposit interest in the circumstances under discussion is low. As rates rise, the proportion willing to take the trouble will rise and this will tend to shift funds (in relative terms) from demand deposits to time deposits.

A summary and a model. My conclusions on the relation of liquid assets to income, interest rate, and interest rate differentials may be summarized in the following way.

1. Composition of portfolios. Persons whose total financial assets are relatively small will tend to hold them all in liquid form because the differential return from other forms of financial assets is too small to make the additional effort required worthwhile, and because the probability of occurrence of a situation requiring conversion of a large proportion of financial assets to cash is high.

Persons with larger portfolios of financial assets will divide them between liquid and nonliquid assets. The proportion held in liquid form will tend to increase if confidence in the stability of income deteriorates, if the differential between the expected net yield on nonliquid assets and that on liquid assets decreases, if the variance of the expected yield on nonliquid assets increases, if the ratio of total assets to income decreases. In particular, an improvement in confidence will tend to raise the value of stocks in relation to income and reduce the need for protective liquidity, thus tending to reduce the ratio of liquid assets to total financial assets. A change in the differential between mortgage and high-grade bond yields will—if it persists long enough to be reflected in savings institution yields—tend to cause a redistribution between holdings of savings deposits and near-liquid assets like high-grade bonds.

Since savings deposit yields move slowly, the differential between savings deposit yields and bond yields will reflect short-term movements of bond yields. A cyclical increase in bond yields tends to draw funds from liquid assets to bonds, and vice versa.

2. Liquid assets in relation to income. For a given state of confidence, relation of total financial assets to income, and given interest rate differentials, we should expect the liquid asset holdings of persons with relatively large financial assets to grow from cycle to cycle in rough proportion to income.

For persons with relatively small total financial assets, our expectation about the liquid asset-income ratio is less clear. If changes in the liquid asset-income ratio do not influence the savings ratio then, over a decade in which the growth rate of income is above average, the ratio of liquid assets to income for small asset holders should tend to fall. But, because the gross financial savings ratio varies not only with the total savings ratio but also with the amount of net investment in housing equity and the net flow of consumer credit, we cannot reach any very clear conclusion on the probable movements of the ratio of liquid assets to income for persons with small portfolios. We cannot, therefore, attach any great significance to observed movements in the ratio of liquid assets to income.

3. Money holdings versus liquid asset holdings. In general, we expect that as the yields on savings deposits rise, the proportion of liquid assets held in the form of demand deposits will decline. However, the relationship between interest rates and the distribution of liquid assets between demand and savings deposits will differ, as between different classes of people and as between assets held for different purposes. Finally, it should be noted that the yield on savings deposits should be interpreted to represent not only the rate of interest or dividend paid, but also the whole complex of advertising and selling efforts which may induce people to shift from demand to time deposits.

The whole position may be summarized in terms of a few very simple equations. Let us first divide households into high-asset and low-asset households. Low-asset households hold all financial assets in liquid form. One part of their liquid assets is held for purposes directly related to income and these "transactions" holdings are proportional to income; the remainder is a residual. The proportion of transactions assets held in the form of demand deposits is a decreasing function of a moving average of savings deposit interest rates (strictly speaking, separate rates for different types of institutions and different locations should be used—a single rate is used only as a shorthand device). The proportion of the residual liquid assets held in demand deposit form is also a decreasing function of savings deposit rates. In general, since the residual balances are by definition not needed for near-term outlays, a smaller proportion of those balances will be held in demand deposit form than the proportion of transactions balances. Thus

$$DD^L = D^L(\bar{r}^s)Ay^L + D_2^L(\bar{r}^s)(L^L - Ay^L), \text{ where}$$

DD^L = demand deposits of low-asset holders

$\bar{r}^s$ = a moving average of savings deposit yields

y^L = the income of the low-asset group.[3]

The change in liquid assets of the low-asset group over any time period equals the gross financial saving of the group during the period $L^L = GFS^L$.

For the high-asset group, the same considerations govern the division of liquid assets between demand deposits and others, except that we should add a factor to allow for the asset transactions demand for liquid assets and eliminate the residual element.

$$DD^H = D_2^H(\bar{r}^s)Ay^H + D_1^H(\bar{r}^s)$$
$$\times D_3(r^M - r^s)W^{HF} + \phi(r^s) \sum_{i=1}^{M} F(r_{ti}^M - \bar{r}^s{}_t)GFS_{t-i}^H$$

when

DD^H = demand balances of high-asset holders

y^H = income of high-asset holders

W^{FH} = total financial wealth of high-asset holders

r^M = net expected yield on marketable securities.

The final term is really another kind of asset float which arises from the fact that persons who normally make little use of savings deposits will take some time to shift from demand deposits to savings deposits, if they should accumulate liquid funds as a result of a decline in the attractiveness of securities.

The variable W^{FH} will vary in proportion to income if the share of property income, valuation factors, and the concentration of income remain constant.

Gross financial saving for the higher-income groups should not be much influenced by variations in consumer credit or net investment in residential property but may show some tendency to rise when income rises rapidly. However, it would take us too far afield to discuss that point here.

MOVEMENTS OF HOUSEHOLD HOLDINGS OF LIQUID ASSETS AND MONEY IN THE POSTWAR PERIOD

It is clear that if (1) the ratio of wealth to income, (2) yields on nonliquid assets and on savings deposits and (3) the size distribution of wealth are all constant, the ratio of demand deposits to income will tend to be constant except for minor fluctuations resulting from variations in the ratio of gross financial savings to income.

If the other conditions are satisfied while savings deposit yields have an upward trend, there will be a downward trend in the ratio of demand deposits to income.

Now suppose that there are short-run variations in interest rates as a result of changes in monetary policy and changes in economic activity. A fall in investment activity will be accompanied by a decline in corporate retained earnings and a rise in government deficit. In mild depressions such as we have had in the postwar period, there is little decline in gross financial saving. Changes in required reserve ratios make it possible for banks to bid for securities and drive down interest rates to induce households to reduce their purchases of securities and increase holdings of both demand and time deposits. When disposable income remains constant, the residual liquid assets of those with small portfolios will also rise and some part of this will take the form of demand deposits.

Of course, households, who withdraw from or are pushed out of marketable securities, shift their funds into savings deposits as well as into demand deposits (indeed, in the postwar period the increase in the flow into time deposits in recession years has been considerably greater than the increase in the flow of household funds into demand deposits). Since savings institutions hold little cash (unless we count reserve absorption by commercial-bank time deposits as the equivalent of cash), these funds come right back into the market and draw securities away from households.[4] However, after a time, savings institutions begin taking mortgages on new houses and the increase in economic activity increases the transactions demand for cash.

Households go into cash and time deposits when interest rates fall, partly because bond yields are low relative to savings deposits yields, and partly because they expect a recovery and higher yields in the future. Some households, of course, speculate for a capital gain from a continued fall in interest rates, hoping to get out before the recovery. They, however, are usually bank financed and therefore merely supplement the demand for bonds generated by the expansion of bank reserves.

The process described above for the downswing works in reverse on the upswing, though not in an entirely symmetrical way. Rising levels of income will increase transactions balance requirements for liquidity, but a continued upward trend in the moving average of savings deposit rates works to lower the proportion of such balances held in demand deposit form. The same considerations apply to the effects of increasing total wealth. Thus, in the absence of a change in the level of yields on marketable securities, demand deposit holdings of households are likely to grow at a slower rate than income. A rise in household purchases of securities, associated with a rise in yields on marketable securities, may reduce both time and demand balances held as part of the asset float.

It seems to me that the analysis given above does conform fairly well to the actual experience of the postwar period. The ratio of total liquidity to personal income has shown no trend since 1952. Total liquidity (as defined here) has risen relative to income in recession years and fallen in booms. There has been a fairly obvious trade-off between time deposits and high-grade bonds—e.g., the "magic fives." The proportion of household liquidity in the form of currency and demand deposits has fallen steadily since 1952.

MOVEMENTS OF HOUSEHOLD LIQUIDITY AND DEMAND
FOR MONEY IN THE PREWAR PERIOD

Total household liquidity remained a fairly constant proportion of personal income from 1922 to 1927 but fell rapidly during 1928 and 1929. The decline may be attributed to the large volume of new security issues floated and the general belief in the prospect of high net yields from investment in common stocks.

The level of liquidity in relation to personal income was lower (varying about a ratio of .6) than in the years since 1952 when the ratio of household liquid asset holdings to personal income has varied about a figure of .7. Some of the difference may be merely definitional since the treatment of high-grade bonds as an element in household liquidity is somewhat ambiguous. In addition, changes in income distribution have probably increased the share of financial saving by low-income groups who tend (for reasons given above) to hold all their financial assets in liquid form.

The most interesting and puzzling thing about the twenties is the steady reduction in the share of liquid assets held in the form of demand deposits and currency. In 1922, 38 per cent of household liquid asset holdings took the form of currency and demand deposits. By 1927 the proportion held in those forms had fallen to 30 per cent and by 1929 a further fall to 25 per cent had taken place. The sharp decline in household holdings of cash from 1927 to 1928 may be attributed to the rapid flow of household funds into common stocks. The furious pace of stock market activity resulted in a sharp reduction of the "asset float."

The decline in relative cash holdings in the earlier years is more difficult to explain. It was not due to rising yields on savings deposits because those yields were not rising. There is, however, some reason to believe that at least part of the shift resulted from changes in the competitive position of national banks with respect to time deposits. The establishment of differential reserve ratios for time deposits in 1914 and the widening of national bank mortgage lending powers, together with the strength of the demand for mortgages in the early 1920's, made time-deposit business attractive to commercial banks. It was generally believed during the 1920's that commercial banks encouraged customers to switch from demand to time deposits and even permitted checking against time deposits. It seems perfectly possible that increased nonprice competition for time deposits resulted in some redistribution of liquid assets between demand and time deposits. It is also possible that there was some shift from Liberty bonds to time deposits as a result of the decline in bond prices in 1920. Since we did not include those bonds in liquid assets, a switch from bonds to time deposits would reduce the ratio of demand deposits to the liquid assets included in the ratios quoted above.

Those explanations appear a little ad hoc and the possibility of other explanations cannot be ruled out.

During the decade of the thirties the ratio of household liquid assets to personal income reached the high figure of 74 per cent in 1932. The ratio then fell almost continuously until, by 1941, it had reached the 60 per cent level which ruled during the middle 1920's. It seems reasonable to attribute the variation to changes in confidence particularly in the early part of the period.

The share of liquid assets held in the form of demand deposits and currency rose throughout the 1930's, reaching 40 per cent by 1941. Since the yields offered for savings deposits declined throughout the period, there seems to be no special difficulty in explaining the rising share of demand deposits and currency in total liquidity.

CONCLUSIONS

The household demand for liquid assets and money is a complex matter which does not seem to have a simple explanation. Without repeating what has been said above we may conclude that, putting aside short cycle movements, the distribution of income and the extent of confidence in income stability are the major factors determining the demand for liquid assets in general. The distribution of liquid assets between demand and time deposits is significantly influenced by the efforts of savings institutions— through rate competition and other selling efforts—to obtain time deposits.

In the shorter cyclical movements, the volume of narrowly defined liquid assets held by households varies considerably with the variation in the difference between rate of return on time deposits and expected yield on marketable securities. Demand deposits holdings are also significantly affected by variations in expected yields on marketable securities.

Although demand and time deposits are competitive with one another, their short-run cyclical movements often tend to be positively correlated.

Conclusions

In this paper I have tried to do two things: (1) to review the major factors which seem likely to influence the amount and composition of liquid assets held by households and corporations; and (2) to examine the data over the last forty years to see whether they can be explained in terms of the factors discussed under (1).

The major conclusions for corporations are as follows:

(1) Short-run movements of corporate liquidity are strongly influenced by variations in cash flow from operations—most of these variations are reflected in holdings of government securities rather than in holdings of cash.

(2) The movement of total corporate liquidity during the 1930's suggests a fairly strong connection between business confidence and ratio of liquid asset holdings to activity.

(3) The decline in the ratio of corporate liquidity to sales in the years since 1952 is partly attributable to the decline in tax liabilities but also to improved cash management, and confidence in income stability.

(4) Corporate holdings of liquid assets respond fairly strongly to short-run changes in interest rates.

(5) There is no indication that the division of liquid assets between cash and other liquid assets responds to short-run changes in bill rates.

(6) After allowance for the effect of changing tax liabilities, there has been only a slight downward trend in the proportion of liquid assets held in cash. The rise in interest rates since 1952 therefore appears to have had little effect. However, it may be that improvements in cash management have been due to rising interest rates, while reduction in liquidity in other forms was due to improved confidence. In that case, changing interest rates may have had some influence on the distribution of liquid assets.

(7) During the depression of the thirties the proportion of liquid assets held in cash did rise as interest rates fell. It therefore appears that the elasticity of cash holdings to interest rates is greater at low interest-rate levels than at high ones.

The conclusions with regard to households can be summarized as follows:

Short-run movements of household liquidity show considerable response to short-run changes in net expected yields in marketable securities. A large part of this response is reflected in time-deposit holdings but demand deposits also respond.

Total liquid asset holdings responded to changes in confidence during the 1930's in the same way that corporate holdings did.

The division of liquid asset holdings between cash and time deposits appears to have responded to changes in yields on savings deposits and to changes in the advertising and selling efforts of savings institutions.

NOTES

1. Of course, the public's holdings of stocks will in the long run be affected by a change in tastes because changes in the yields of stocks relative to other assets will influence the composition of corporate security issues and the composition of investment.

2. In return for that cost they reduce the risk of being burdened with short-term debt during a business decline and reduce the cost of long-term borrowing by improving the current ratio.

3. The question of permanent income arises here. When an individual's income declines and he remains a positive saver, he may keep his working cash balance unchanged, out of force of habit. If he becomes a negative saver (in cash-flow terms) he must draw down liquid assets and I should be inclined to think he would draw down his cash balance because he holds it to absorb fluctuations in expenditures relative to income. If aggregate income falls, we shall have three groups of people: (1) those whose incomes are unchanged and who, other things equal, keep cash balances unchanged; (2) those whose incomes fall but who remain positive cash savers—if their cash balances do not fall, the ratio of cash balances to current income rises—the permanent income factor; (3) those whose incomes fall and who become negative savers, draw down cash balances absolutely and relatively to income. The buffer stock factors 2 and 3 affect the ratio of cash balances to income in opposite directions. For simplicity I have written the equation as though the two effects cancel out.

4. Secondary market purchases of mortgages from F.N.M.A. reduce federal issues of securities and, therefore, reduce the amount available for households.

Part **III**

The Integration of
Monetary and
Value Theory

Keynes in the *General Theory* attacked what he called the traditional separation of monetary and value theory, what Patinkin was later to call the "classical dichotomy." Keynes' answer to the classical dichotomy was his asset preference theory embodied in his concept of "liquidity preference." He employed a two-stage theory of wealth accumulation; first, individuals decided how much they wished to save of their income after which they decided how their savings should be divided between monetary and non-monetary assets. In Keynes' theory of liquidity preference, the rate of interest determined the distribution of individuals' assets between money and income-earning assets, given their level of wealth. Thus the four basic functions in the Keynesian system are the supply of money, the liquidity preference schedule, the marginal propensity to consume, and the marginal efficiency of capital which together with a given wage unit determines the level of output and employment.

Hicks attempted to demonstrate that the principal novelty of Keynes was his liquidity preference theory and that with the exception of this, the economic system of Keynes was compatible with the classical model and might even be regarded as an extention of it. Furthermore, Hicks demonstrated that at full employment the Keynesian model was identical with the classical model. This reconciliation was not accepted by Lange, who claimed there was a fundamental "inconsistency" in the classical economic system which, furthermore, was not removed by the Keynesian analysis. Lange maintained that Say's Law (which he interpreted as meaning that people only produce goods in order to buy other goods) in combination with Walras' Law (that at some set of *relative* prices there would be no excess demand for goods or money) precluded any monetary theory since the excess demand for money in the market is equal to zero at some set of relative prices regardless of the absolute price level. Patinkin restated Lange's criticism by saying these two laws were inconsistent with the quantity theory of money. He pointed out that if the demand for commodities was not affected by changes in the absolute price level at full employment, it was difficult to understand the concern with the effects of inflation generated by an increase in the supply of money as postulated by the quantity theory. Patinkin challenged a "classical" system which said that the demand for commodities was determined by relative prices only, and the function of money was only to determine the absolute price level (although it may have been more the proponents of the classical system rather than the classical economists themselves who were guilty of this type of statement). In particular, Patinkin challenged the classical assumption that the doubling of all commodity prices would leave supply and demand for goods unchanged (i.e., the supply and demand functions of commodities were homogeneous of zero order in commodity prices).

This latter point of Patinkin's argument may be illustrated by rewriting the cash balance equation[1] of the demand for money as an excess (or deficit) demand equation:

$$kpY - \hat{M} = X_m \tag{1}$$

where kpY, the demand for nominal cash balances, less the money supply determined by the monetary authorities, $\hat{M}$, defines the excess (or deficit) demand for money, X_m. If the price level and the supply of money are increased in the same proportion, the excess demand for money will be increased by the same proportion:

$$kp(1 + \alpha)Y - M(1 + \alpha) = X_m(1 + \alpha) \tag{2}$$

If, however, the money supply is increased exogenously by the monetary authority, then the excess demand for money will not increase proportionately to the increase in the supply of money:

$$kpY - M(1 + \alpha) = X_m - \alpha M \tag{3}$$

However, assuming individuals possess no "money illusion," and find that at the existing price level they are holding more "real" balances, M/p, than they wish, they would then plan an increase in expenditures for goods and services which would lead to a rise in prices proportional to the increase in money supply, thus restoring the relationship in equation (2). A similar result would be obtained from an exogenous rise in the price level. The "real balance effect" is the change in the purchase of commodities and services required to restore the "real value" of cash balances upset by an initial rise in the price level, or change in the money supply. The spelling out of this "real balance" or "Pigou" effect, Patinkin argues, is necessary in order to establish a valid classical model where money is "neutral," which means that changes in the money supply affect only absolute prices and not relative prices or the rate of interest. The real balance effect provides an explicit bridge

[1] See page 59.

between the world of "real" economics and that of "monetary" economics. Patinkin's formal solution is that if money, defined as real balances, is introduced like another commodity into the Walrasian demand and supply functions along with some additional assumptions (more of this in Part IV) then the dichotomy between real and monetary markets is removed and the classical economic system is consistent. Patinkin explains the failure of the classical economists to introduce explicitly the real balance effect, which they recognized, as due to the fact that in the quantity equation they regarded the level of output as fixed by the size of the labor force and independent of the price level.

Patinkin, in part, created some of his own problems by the manner in which he introduced changes in the supply of money. Money is created like "manna" from heaven outside the economic system which he is analyzing. In two of the important methods by which the money supply is normally increased, that is by an expansion of assets of the banking system, or by government deficits financed at the central bank, an excess demand _precedes_ an increase in the money supply rather than the reverse. In the case where money supply is increased through open market operations the interest rate mechanism operates to increase the demand for goods since, as Patinkin has pointed out, the Keynesian "liquidity trap" is an institutional, not a theoretical, restraint. If the monetary authority wished to become the sole holder of debt in the economy, it could force the interest rate down to any level it wished through further increases in the money supply, but the consequence of this would be the destruction of the financial system.[2] None of these methods excludes the operation of the "Pigou Effect" but each minimizes the central importance Patinkin attaches to it.

Archibald and Lipsey in replying to Patinkin argued that if one regards classical theory as employing the method of comparing one equilibrium position with another (comparative statics), then the classical theory is consistent and the general price level is determinate without reference to Patinkin's "real balance" effect. This is illustrated by equation (3). If the initial excess demand for money, X_m, is zero, then the excess demand for money will change proportionally with changes in the money supply. The importance of the "real balance" effect, they claim, is in explaining how the system behaves in disequilibrium, that is, when Walras' Law does not apply.

The ultimate contribution of the "dichotomy" controversy appears to be the rigorous demonstration by Patinkin that it is

---

[2] See the interesting exchange between Hicks and Patinkin where they apparently are in agreement on this point: J. R. Hicks, "A Rehabilitation of 'Classical' Economics?" *Economic Journal*, Vol. 67 (June 1957), 278–89, and D. Patinkin's "Rejoinder," *Economic Journal*, Vol. 69 (September 1959), 582–87.

not possible to divide the pricing process between a real market where relative prices are determined and a monetary market where absolute prices are determined. The equilibrium value of relative and absolute prices and the rate of interest are determined simultaneously by the interaction of both markets, a result also arrived at by Hicks, although without specifying the behavioral link provided by the "real balance effect."[3]

Lange and Patinkin concentrated their attack on the "neutrality" of money principally on the classical idea that a change in the money supply would leave relative prices unchanged. Metzler questioned whether the interest rate at full employment would remain unchanged (homogeneous in degree zero) in the face of changes in the supply of money. Neoclassical economists such as Wicksell believed that at full employment there existed a unique "natural" rate of interest. Keynes' analysis also implied that the rate of interest was uniquely determined at full employment.

Metzler's position was that whether or not the classical view was correct depended on how the money supply was changed. He demonstrated, by applying the "Pigou Effect," that if the money supply at full employment is changed by the monetary authorities through a purchase of securities which changes the stock of private financial assets, the results will differ from those when the money supply is varied without changing the stock of private financial assets (for example, by government deficit financing through the central bank). The latter method of changing the money supply yields results in conformity with the classical model while the former method does not, if one accepts the Pigouvian idea that consumption is not only a function of income but also of wealth.

In the case of an open market purchase of securities by the monetary authorities, the rate of interest will initially decline, increasing investment so that total demand exceeds full employment output, causing prices to rise. Metzler demonstrated that this increase in prices would leave the community with a smaller stock of *real* assets and a consequently greater desire to save so that the new equilibrium rate of interest would not return it to former level. Metzler's wealth effect is the complement of Keynes' liquidity preference; just as changes in one form of wealth, the stock of money, may change the rate of interest, so can changes in the stock of other forms of wealth, securities, for example, change the rate of interest. Metzler's conclusion has implications for growth theory since if it is possible for the monetary authority to effect changes in the rate of saving and interest at full employment, it opens the door to the possibility that the full employment rate of growth may be influenced by monetary policy.

[3] See below p. 414.

10 Mr. Keynes and the "Classics": A Suggested Interpretation

John R. Hicks *Cambridge University*

I

It will be admitted by the least charitable reader that the entertainment value of Mr. Keynes' *General Theory of Employment* is considerably enhanced by its satiric aspect. But it is also clear that many readers have been left very bewildered by this Dunciad. Even if they are convinced by Mr. Keynes' arguments and humbly acknowledge themselves to have been "classical economists" in the past, they find it hard to remember that they believed in their unregenerate days the things Mr. Keynes says they believed. And there are no doubt others who find their historic doubts a stumbling block, which prevents them from getting as much illumination from the positive theory as they might otherwise have got.

One of the main reasons for this situation is undoubtedly to be found in the fact that Mr. Keynes takes as typical of "Classical economics" the later writings of Professor Pigou, particularly *The Theory of Unemployment*. Now *The Theory of Unemployment* is a fairly new book, and an exceedingly difficult book; so that it is safe to say that it has not yet made much impression on the ordinary

Reprinted from *Econometrica*, New Series, Vol. 5 (April 1937), 147–59, by permission of the author and publisher.

Professor Hicks discussed this subject again in his book *A Contribution to the Theory of the Trade Cycle* (Oxford 1950), Chapters 11 and 12, and in a later article, "A Rehabilitation of 'Classical' Economics?" *Economic Journal*, Vol. 67 (June 1957), 278–89.

teaching of economics. To most people its doctrines seem quite as strange and novel as the doctrines of Mr. Keynes himself; so that to be told that he has believed these things himself leaves the ordinary economist quite bewildered.

For example, Professor Pigou's theory runs, to a quite amazing extent, in real terms. Not only is his theory a theory of real wages and unemployment; but numbers of problems which anyone else would have preferred to investigate in money terms are investigated by Professor Pigou in terms of "wage-goods." The ordinary classical economist has no part in this *tour de force*.

But if, on behalf of the ordinary classical economist, we declare that he would have preferred to investigate many of those problems in money terms, Mr. Keynes will reply that there is no classical theory of money wages and employment. It is quite true that such a theory cannot easily be found in the textbooks. But this is only because most of the textbooks were written at a time when general changes in money wages in a closed system did not present an important problem. There can be little doubt that most economists have thought that they had a pretty fair idea of what the relation between money wages and employment actually was.

In these circumstances, it seems worth while to try to construct a typical "classical" theory, built on an earlier and cruder model than Professor Pigou's. If we can construct such a theory, and show that it does give results which have in fact been commonly taken for granted, but which do not agree with Mr. Keynes' conclusions, then we shall at last have a satisfactory basis of comparison. We may hope to be able to isolate Mr. Keynes' innovations, and so to discover what are the real issues in dispute.

Since our purpose is comparison, I shall try to set out my typical classical theory in a form similar to that in which Mr. Keynes sets out his own theory; and I shall leave out of account all secondary complications which do not bear closely upon this special question in hand. Thus I assume that I am dealing with a short period in which the quantity of physical equipment of all kinds available can be taken as fixed. I assume homogeneous labour. I assume further that depreciation can be neglected, so that the output of investment goods corresponds to new investment. This is a dangerous simplification, but the important issues raised by Mr. Keynes in his chapter on user cost are irrelevant for our purposes.

Let us begin by assuming that w, the rate of money wages per head, can be taken as given.

Let x, y, be the outputs of investment goods and consumption goods respectively, and N_x, N_y, be the numbers of men employed in producing them. Since the amount of physical equipment specialised to each industry is given, $x = f_x(N_x)$ and $y = f_y(N_y)$, where f_x, f_y, are *given* functions.

Let M be the *given* quantity of money.

It is desired to determine N_x and N_y.

First, the price-level of investment goods = their marginal cost = $w(dN_x/dx)$. And the price-level of consumption goods = their marginal cost = $w(dN_y/dy)$. perfect competition?

Income earned in investment trades (value of investment, or simply Investment) = $wx(dN_x/dx)$. Call this I_x.

Income earned in consumption trades = $wy(dN_y/dy)$.

Total Income = $wx(dN_x/dx) + wy(dN_y/dy)$. Call this I.

I_x is therefore a given function of N_x, I of N_x and N_y. Once I and I_x are determined, N_x and N_y can be determined.

Now let us assume the "Cambridge Quantity Equation"—that there is some definite relation between Income and the demand for money. Then, approximately, and apart from the fact that the demand for money may depend not only upon total Income, but also upon its distribution between people with relatively large and relatively small demands for balances, we can write

$$M = kI.$$

As soon as k is given, total Income is therefore determined.

In order to determine I_x, we need two equations. One tells us that the amount of investment (looked at as demand for capital) depends upon the rate of interest:

$$I_x = C(i).$$

This is what becomes the marginal-efficiency-of-capital schedule in Mr. Keynes' work.

Further, Investment = Saving. And saving depends upon the rate of interest and, if you like, Income. $\therefore I_x = S(i, I)$. (Since, however, Income is already determined, we do not need to bother about inserting Income here unless we choose.)

Taking them as a system, however, we have three fundamental equations,

$$M = kI, \quad I_x = C(i), \quad I_x = S(i, I),$$

to determine three unknowns, I, I_x, i. As we have found earlier, N_x and N_y can be determined from I and I_x. Total employment, $N_x + N_y$, is therefore determined.

Let us consider some properties of this system. It follows directly from the first equation that as soon as k and M are given, I is completely determined; that is to say, total income depends directly upon the quantity of money. Total employment, however, is not necessarily determined at once from income, since it will usually depend to some extent upon the proportion of income saved, and thus upon the way production is divided between investment and consumption-goods trades. (If it so happened that the elasticities of supply were the same in each of these trades, then a shifting of demand between them would produce compensating movements in N_x and N_y, and consequently no change in total employment.)

An increase in the inducement to invest (i.e., a rightward movement of the schedule of the marginal efficiency of capital, which we have written as $C(i)$) will tend to raise the rate of interest, and so to affect saving. If the amount of saving rises, the amount of investment will rise too; labour will be employed more in the investment trades, less in the consumption trades; this will increase total employment if the elasticity of supply in the investment trades is greater than that in the consumption-goods trades—diminish it if *vice versa*.

An increase in the supply of money will necessarily raise total income, for people will increase their spending and lending until incomes have risen sufficiently to restore k to its former level. The rise in income will tend to increase employment, both in making consumption goods and in making investment goods. The total effect on employment depends upon the ratio between the expansions of these industries; and that depends upon the proportion of their increased incomes which people desire to save, which also governs the rate of interest.

So far we have assumed the rate of money wages to be given; but so long as we assume that k is independent of the level of wages, there is no difficulty about this problem either. A rise in the rate of money wages will necessarily diminish employment and raise real wages. For an unchanged money income cannot continue to buy an unchanged quantity of goods at a higher price-level; and, unless the price-level rises, the prices of goods will not cover their marginal costs. There must therefore be a fall in employment; as employment falls, marginal costs in terms of labour will diminish and therefore real wages rise. (Since a change in money wages is always accompanied by a change in real wages in the same direction, if not in the same proportion, no harm will be done, and some advantage will perhaps be secured, if one prefers to work in terms of real wages. Naturally most "classical economists" have taken this line.)

I think it will be agreed that we have here a quite reasonably consistent theory, and a theory which is also consistent with the pronouncements of a recognizable group of economists. Admittedly it follows from this theory that you may be able to increase employment by direct inflation; but whether or not you decide to favour that policy still depends upon your judgment about the probable reaction on wages, and also—in a national area—upon your views about the international standard.

Historically, this theory descends from Ricardo, though it is not actually Ricardian; it is probably more or less the theory that was held by Marshall. But with Marshall it was already beginning to be qualified in important ways; his successors have qualified it still further. What Mr. Keynes has done is to lay enormous emphasis on the qualifications, so that they almost blot out the original theory. Let us follow out this process of development.

II

When a theory like the "classical" theory we have just described is applied to the analysis of industrial fluctuations, it gets into difficulties in several ways. It is evident that total money income experiences great variations in the course of a trade cycle, and the classical theory can only explain these by variations in M or in k, or, as a third and last alternative, by changes in distribution.

(1) Variation in M is simplest and most obvious, and has been relied on to a large extent. But the variations in M that are traceable during a trade cycle are variations that take place through the banks—they are variations in bank loans; if we are to rely on them it is urgently necessary for us to explain the connection between the supply of bank money and the rate of interest. This can be done roughly by thinking of banks as persons who are strongly inclined to pass on money by lending rather than spending it. Their action therefore tends at first to lower interest rates, and only afterwards, when the money passes into the hands of spenders, to raise prices and incomes. "The new currency, or the increase of currency, goes, not to private persons, but to the banking centers; and therefore, it increases the willingness of lenders to lend in the first instance, and lowers the rate of discount. But it afterwards raises prices; and therefore it tends to increase discount."[1] This is superficially satisfactory; but if we endeavoured to give a more precise account of this process we should soon get into difficulties. What determines the amount of money needed to produce a given fall in the rate of interest? What determines the length of time for which the low rate will last? These are not easy questions to answer.

(2) In so far as we rely upon changes in k, we can also do well enough up to a point. Changes in k can be related to changes in confidence, and it is realistic to hold that the rising prices of a boom occur because optimism encourages a reduction in balances; the falling prices of a slump because pessimism and uncertainty dictate an increase. But as soon as we take this step it becomes natural to ask whether k has not abdicated its status as an independent variable, and has not become liable to be influenced by others among the variables in our fundamental equations.

(3) This last consideration is powerfully supported by another, of more purely theoretical character. On grounds of pure value theory, it is evident that the direct sacrifice made by a person who holds a stock of money is a sacrifice of interest; and it is hard to believe that the marginal principle does not operate at all in this field. As Lavington put it: "The quantity of resources which (an individual) holds in the form of money will be such that the unit of money which is just and only just worth while holding in this form yields him a return of convenience and security equal to the yield of satisfaction derived from the marginal unit spent on consumables, and equal also to the net rate of interest."[2] The demand for money depends upon the rate of interest! The stage is set for Mr. Keynes.

As against the three equations of the classical theory,

$$M = kI, \quad I_x = C(i), \quad I_x = S(i, I),$$

Mr. Keynes begins with three equations,

$$M = L(i), \quad I_x = C(i), \quad I_x = S(I).$$

These differ from the classical equations in two ways. On the one hand, the demand for money is conceived as depending upon the rate of interest (Liquidity Preference). On the other hand, any possible influence of the rate of interest on the amount saved out of a given income is neglected. Although it means that the third equation becomes the multiplier equation, which performs such queer tricks, nevertheless this second amendment is a mere simplification, and ultimately insignificant.[3] It is the liquidity preference doctrine which is vital.

For it is now the rate of interest, not income, which is determined by the quantity of money. The rate of interest set against the schedule of the marginal efficiency of capital determines the value of investment; that determines income by the multiplier. Then the volume of employment (at given wage-rates) is determined by the value of investment and of income which is not saved but spent upon consumption goods.

It is this system of equations which yields the startling conclusion, that an increase in the inducement to invest, or in the propensity to consume, will not tend to raise the rate of interest, but only to increase employment. In spite of this, however, and in spite of the fact that quite a large part of the argument runs in terms of this system, and this system alone, *it is not the General Theory*. We may call it, if we like, Mr. Keynes' *special theory*. The General Theory is something appreciably more orthodox.

Like Lavington and Professor Pigou, Mr. Keynes does not in the end believe that the demand for money can be determined by one variable alone—not even the rate of interest. He lays more stress on it than they did, but neither for him nor for them can it be the only variable to be considered. The dependence of the demand for money on interest does not, in the end, do more than qualify the old dependence on income. However much stress we lay upon the "speculative motive," the "transactions" motive must always come in as well.

Consequently we have for the General Theory

$$M = L(I, i), \quad I_x = C(i), \quad I_x = S(I).$$

With this revision, Mr. Keynes takes a big step back to Marshallian orthodoxy, and his theory becomes hard to distinguish from the revised and qualified Marshallian theories, which, as we have seen, are not new. Is there really any difference between them, or is the whole thing a sham fight? Let us have recourse to a diagram (Figure 1).

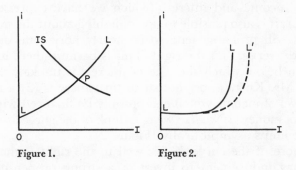

Figure 1.   Figure 2.

Against a given quantity of money, the first equation, $M = L(I, i)$, gives us a relation between Income (I) and the rate of interest (i). This can be drawn out as a curve (LL) which will slope upwards, since an increase in income tends to raise the demand for money, and an increase in the rate of interest tends to lower it. Further, the second two equations taken together give us another relation between Income and interest. (The marginal-efficiency-of-capital schedule determines the value of investment at any given rate of interest, and the multiplier tells us what level of income will be necessary to make savings equal to that value of investment.) The curve IS can therefore be drawn showing the relation between Income and interest which must be maintained in order to make saving equal to investment.

Income and the rate of interest are now determined together at P, the point of intersection of the curves LL and IS. They are determined together; just as price and output are determined together in the modern theory of demand and supply. Indeed, Mr. Keynes' innovation is closely parallel, in this respect, to the innovation of the marginalists. The quantity theory tries to determine income without interest, just as the labour theory of value tried to determine price without output; each has to give place to a theory recognising a higher degree of interdependence.

III

But if this is the real "General Theory," how does Mr. Keynes come to make his remarks about an increase in the inducement to invest not raising the rate of interest? It would appear from our diagram that a rise in the marginal-efficiency-of-capital schedule must raise the curve *IS*; and, therefore, although it will raise Income and employment, it will also raise the rate of interest.

This brings us to what, from many points of view, is the most important thing in Mr. Keynes' book. It is not only possible to show that a given supply of money determines a certain relation between Income and interest (which we have expressed by the curve *LL*); it is also possible to say something about the shape of the curve. It will probably tend to be nearly horizontal on the left, and nearly vertical on the right. This is because there is (1) some minimum below which the rate of interest is unlikely to go, and (though Mr. Keynes does not stress this) there is (2) a maximum to the level of income which can possibly be financed with a given amount of money. If we like we can think of the curve as approaching these limits asymptotically (Figure 2).

Therefore, if the curve *IS* lies well to the right (either because of a strong inducement to invest or a strong propensity to consume), *P* will lie upon that part of the curve which is decidedly upward sloping, and the classical theory will be a good approximation, needing no more than the qualification which it has in fact received at the hands of the later Marshallians. An increase in the inducement to invest will raise the rate of interest, as in the classical theory, but it will also have some subsidiary effect in raising income, and therefore employment as well. (Mr. Keynes in 1936 is not the first Cambridge economist to have a temperate faith in Public Works.) But if the point *P* lies to the left of the *LL* curve, then the *special* form of Mr. Keynes' theory becomes valid. A rise in the schedule of the marginal efficiency of capital only increases employment, and does not raise the rate of interest at all. We are completely out of touch with the classical world.

The demonstration of this minimum is thus of central importance. It is so important that I shall venture to paraphrase the proof, setting it out in a rather different way from that adopted by Mr. Keynes.[4]

If the costs of holding money can be neglected, it will always be profitable to hold money rather than lend it out, if the rate of interest is not greater than zero. Consequently the rate of interest must always be positive. In an extreme case, the shortest short-term rate may perhaps be nearly zero. But if so, the long-term rate must lie above it, for the long rate has to allow for the risk that the short rate may rise during the currency of the loan, and it should be observed that the short rate can only rise, it cannot fall.[5] This does not only mean that the long rate must be a sort of average of the probable short rates over its duration, and that this average must lie above the current short rate. There is also the more important risk to be considered, that the lender on long term may desire to have cash before the agreed date of repayment, and then, if the short rate has risen meanwhile, he may be involved in a substantial capital loss. It is this last risk which provides Mr. Keynes' "speculative motive" and which ensures that the rate for loans of indefinite duration (which he always has in mind as *the* rate of interest) cannot fall very near zero.[6]

It should be observed that this minimum to the rate of interest applies not only to one curve *LL* (drawn to correspond to a particular quantity of money) but to any such curve. If the supply of money is increased, the curve *LL* moves to the right (as the dotted curve in Figure 2), but the horizontal parts of the curve are almost the same. Therefore, again, it is this doldrum to the left of the diagram which upsets the classical theory. If *IS* lies to the right, then we can indeed increase employment by increasing the quantity of money; but if *IS* lies to the left, we cannot do so; merely monetary means will not force down the rate of interest any further.

So the General Theory of Employment is the Economics of Depression.

IV

In order to elucidate the relation between Mr. Keynes and the "Classics," we have invented a little apparatus. It does not appear that we have exhausted the uses of that apparatus, so let us conclude by giving it a little run on its own.

With that apparatus at our disposal, we are no longer obliged to make certain simplifications which Mr. Keynes makes in his exposition. We can reinsert the missing i in the third equation, and allow for any possible effect of the rate of interest upon saving; and, what is much more important, we can call in question the sole dependence of investment upon the rate of interest, which looks rather suspicious in the second equation. Mathematical elegance would suggest that we ought to have I and i in all three equations, if the theory is to be really General. Why not have them there like this:

$$M = L(I, i), \quad I_x = C(I, i), \quad I_x = S(I, i)$$

Once we raise the question of Income in the second equation, it is clear that it has a very good claim to be inserted. Mr. Keynes is in fact only enabled to leave it out at all plausibly by his device of measuring everything in "wage-units," which means that he allows for changes in the marginal-efficiency-of-capital schedule when there is a change in the level of money wages, but that other changes in Income are deemed not to affect the curve, or at least not in the same immediate manner. But why draw this distinction? Surely there is every reason to suppose that an increase in the demand for consumers' goods, arising from an increase in employment, will often directly stimulate an increase in investment, at least as soon as an expectation develops that the increased demand will continue. If this is so, we ought to include I in the second equation, though it must be confessed that the effect of I on the marginal efficiency of capital will be fitful and irregular.

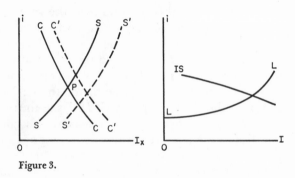

Figure 3.

The Generalized General Theory can then be set out in this way. Assume first of all a given total money Income. Draw a curve CC showing the marginal efficiency of capital (in money terms) at that given Income; a curve SS showing the supply curve of saving at that *given* Income (Figure 3). Their intersection will determine the rate of interest which makes savings equal to investment at that level of income. This we may call the "investment rate."

If Income rises, the curve SS will move to the right; probably CC will move to the right too. If SS moves more than CC, the investment rate of interest will fall; if CC more than SS, it will rise. (How much it rises and falls, however, depends upon the elasticities of the CC and SS curves.)

The IS curve (drawn on a separate diagram) now shows the relation between Income and the corresponding investment rate of interest. It has to be confronted (as in our earlier constructions) with an LL curve showing the relation between Income and the "money" rate of interest; only we can now generalize our LL curve a little. Instead of assuming, as before, that the supply of money is given, we can assume that there is a given monetary system—that up to a point, but only up to a point, monetary authorities will prefer to create new money rather than allow interest rates to rise. Such a generalized *LL* curve will then slope upwards only gradually—the elasticity of the curve depending on the elasticity of the monetary system (in the ordinary monetary sense).

As before, Income and interest are determined where the *IS* and *LL* curves intersect—where the investment rate of interest equals the money rate. Any change in the inducement to invest or the propensity to consume will shift the *IS* curve; any change in liquidity preference or monetary policy will shift the *LL* curve. If, as the result of such a change, the investment rate is raised above the money rate, Income will tend to rise; in the opposite case, Income will tend to fall; the extent to which Income rises or falls depends on the elasticities of the curves.[7]

When generalized in this way, Mr. Keynes' theory begins to look very like Wicksell's; this is of course hardly surprising.[8] There is indeed one special case where it fits Wicksell's construction absolutely. If there is "full employment" in the sense that any rise in Income immediately calls forth a rise in money wage rates, then it is *possible* that the *CC* and *SS* curves may be moved to the right to exactly the same extent, so that *IS* is horizontal. (I say possible, because it is not unlikely, in fact, that the rise in the wage level may create a presumption that wages will rise again later on; if so, *CC* will probably be shifted more than *SS*, so that *IS* will be upward sloping.) However that may be, if *IS* is horizontal, we do have a perfectly Wicksellian construction;[9] the investment rate becomes Wicksell's *natural rate*, for in this case it may be thought of as determined by real causes; if there is a perfectly elastic monetary system, and the money rate is fixed below the natural rate, there is cumulative inflation; cumulative deflation if it is fixed above.

This, however, is now seen to be only one special case; we can use our construction to harbour much wider possibilities. If there is a great deal of unemployment, it is very likely that $\partial C/\partial I$ will be quite small; in that case *IS* can be relied upon to slope downwards. This is the sort of Slump Economics with which Mr. Keynes is largely concerned. But one cannot escape the impression that there may be other conditions when expectations are tinder, when a slight inflationary tendency lights them up very easily. Then $\partial C/\partial I$ may be large and an increase in Income tend to *raise* the investment rate of interest. In these circumstances, the situation is unstable at *any* given money rate; it is only an imperfectly elastic monetary system—a rising *LL* curve—that can prevent the situation getting out of hand altogether.

These, then, are a few of the things we can get out of our skeleton apparatus. But even if it may claim to be a slight extension of Mr. Keynes' similar skeleton, it remains a terribly rough and ready sort of affair. In particular, the concept of "Income" is worked monstrously hard; most of our curves are not really determinate unless something is said about the distribution of Income as well as its magnitude. Indeed, what they express is something like a relation between the price-system and the system of interest rates; and you cannot get that into a curve. Further, all sorts of questions about depreciation have been neglected; and all sorts of questions about the timing of the processes under consideration.

The *General Theory of Employment* is a useful book; but it is neither the beginning nor the end of Dynamic Economics.

NOTES

1. Marshall, *Money, Credit and Commerce* (London 1923), p. 257.
2. Lavington, *English Capital Market* (London 1921), p. 30. See also Pigou, "The Exchange-value of Legal-tender Money," in *Essays in Applied Economics* (London 1922), pp. 179–81.
3. This can be readily seen if we consider the equations

$$M = kI, \quad I_x = C(i), \quad I_x = S(I),$$

which embody Mr. Keynes' second amendment without his first. The third equation is already the multiplier equation, but the multiplier is shorn of its wings. For since I still depends only on M, I_x now depends only on M, and it is impossible to increase investment without increasing the willingness to save or the quantity of money. The system thus generated is therefore identical with that which, a few years ago, used to be called the "Treasury View." But Liquidity Preference transports us from the "Treasury View" to the "General Theory of Employment."
4. Keynes, *General Theory* (New York 1936), pp. 201–2.
5. It is just conceivable that people might become so used to the idea of very low short rates that they would not be much impressed by this risk; but it is very unlikely. For the short rate may rise, either because trade improves, and income expands; or because trade gets worse, and the desire for liquidity increases. I doubt whether a monetary system so elastic as to rule out both of these possibilities is really thinkable.
6. Nevertheless something more than the "speculative motive" is needed to account for the system of interest rates. The shortest of all short rates must equal the relative valuation, at the margin, of money and such a bill; and the bill stands at a discount mainly because of the "convenience and security" of holding money—the inconvenience which may possibly be caused by not having cash immediately available. It is the chance that you may want to discount the bill which matters, not the chance that you will then have to discount it on unfavourable terms. The "precaution-

ary motive," not the "speculative motive," is here dominant. But the prospective terms of rediscounting are vital, when it comes to the *difference* between short and long rates.

7. Since $C(I, i) = S(I, i)$,

$$\frac{dI}{di} = - \frac{\partial S/\partial i - \partial C/\partial i}{\partial S/\partial I - \partial C/\partial I}.$$

The savings investment market will not be stable unless $\partial S/\partial i + (-\partial C/\partial i)$ is positive. I think we may assume that this condition is fulfilled.

If $\partial S/\partial i$ is positive, $\partial C/\partial i$ negative, $\partial S/\partial I$ and $\partial C/\partial I$ positive (the most probable state of affairs), we can say that the *IS* curve will be more elastic, the greater the elasticities of the *CC* and *SS* curves, and the larger is $\partial C/\partial I$ relatively to $\partial S/\partial I$. When $\partial C/\partial I > \partial S/\partial I$, the *IS* curve is upward sloping.

8. Cf. Keynes, *General Theory*, p. 242.

9. Cf. Myrdal, "Gleichgewichtsbegriff," in Hayek (ed.) *Beiträge zur Geldtheorie* (Vienna 1933).

11 *A Critique of Neoclassical Monetary Theory*

Don Patinkin *Hebrew University, Jerusalem*

Introduction. The Deficiencies of the Traditional Transactions and Cash-Balance Approaches in Analyzing the Effects of a Change in M. *The Failure to Test the Stability of the Equilibrium Absolute Price Level and the Significance Thereof*

Terminological disputes are rather sterile. Hence it is best to preclude them by making clear at the outset that "neoclassical" is being used here as a shorthand designation for the once widely accepted body of thought which organized monetary theory around a transactions or cash-balance type of equation, and which then used these equations to validate the classical quantity theory of money. Subsidiary—though, as we shall see, persistently recurring—components of this body of thought were a certain description of the demand function for money and a certain conception of the role of monetary theory *vis-à-vis* value theory.

Reprinted from *Money, Interest, and Prices*, second edition, by Don Patinkin, by permission of the author and Harper & Row, Publishers. Copyright © 1965 by Don Patinkin.

The footnotes that make reference to the series of historical notes included at the end of the original work have been deleted along with several cross references to other parts of the book. The Notes provide documentation from the literature in support of the interpretation presented in the text.

In its cash-balance version—associated primarily with the names of Walras, Marshall, Wicksell, and Pigou—neoclassical theory assumed that, for their convenience, individuals wish to hold a certain proportion, K, of the real volume of their planned transactions, T, in the form of real money balances. The demand for these balances thus equals KT. Correspondingly, the demand for nominal money balances is KPT, where P is the price level of the commodities transacted. The equating of this demand to the supply of money, M, then produced the famous Cambridge equation, $M = KPT$. In the transactions version—associated primarily with the names of Newcomb and Fisher—the velocity of circulation, V, replaced its reciprocal, K, to produce the equally famous equation of exchange, $MV = PT$. These equations were the parade-grounds on which neoclassical economists then put the classical quantity theory of money through its paces.[1]

The most persuasive formulations of this theory were develop-ments of the following tripartite thesis: an increase in the quantity of money disturbs the optimum relation between the level of money balances and the individual's expenditures; this disturbance generates an increase in the planned volume of these expenditures (the real-balance effect); and this increase creates pressures on the price level which push it upwards until it has risen in the same proportion as the quantity of money. Among the writers mentioned above, only Wicksell[2] and Fisher[3] provided complete, systematic statements of this thesis. Nevertheless, the other writers made sufficient—if unintegrated—use of its individual components to justify our identifying these components with the general analytic background of neoclassical monetary theory.

Indeed, the basic fact underlined by the foregoing thesis—that the causal relationship between money and prices is not at all a mechanical one, but is instead the economic consequence of the prior effect of changes in the quantity of money on the demand for commodities—was already a commonplace of the classical quantity-theory tradition of Cantillon, Thornton, Ricardo, and Mill,[4] and was particularly vivid in the expositions of those writers who emphasized that the effects of an increase in the quantity of money on prices could not in general be said to be equiproportionate, but depended instead on whose money holdings, and hence whose demands, were increased.[5] This, after all, was the consideration which brought both classical and neoclassical economists to the recognition that a change in the quantity of money could generate "forced savings" and need not therefore always be neutral in its effects.

On the other hand, it must be emphasized that, in contrast to the neoclassical ones, none of these earlier expositions of the quantity theory should be regarded as having recognized the real-balance effect in the fullest sense of the term; for none of them brought out the crucial intermediary stage of the foregoing thesis in which people increase their *flow* of expenditures because they feel that their *stock* of money is too large for their needs. Instead, in a Keynesian-like fashion, these expositions more or less directly connected the increased *outflow* of money expenditures with the increased *inflow* of money receipts: people spend more money because they receive more money, not because their real cash balances as such have been augmented beyond the amount "which their convenience had taught them to keep on hand."[6] But it is precisely this augmentation—and the real-balance effect which it engenders—which helps explain why demand, and hence prices, remain at a higher level even in periods subsequent to the one in which the injection of new money into the economy takes place.

* * *

. . . [T]he neoclassical equations suffer from the obvious disability that they assign no explicit role to the rate of interest and hence cannot deal with that whole body of theory which analyzes this rate. In particular, they cannot serve to validate the classical proposition that a change in the quantity of money leaves the rate of interest unaffected. Indeed, not only can they not help, they hinder. For the omission of the rate of interest from the cash-balance equation creates the misleading impression that the classical invariance of this rate holds only in the special case where it does not affect the demand for money. No such restriction is necessary. This is not to deny that in other contexts neoclassical economists did recognize the influence of the rate of interest on the demand for money, and did make other significant extensions of classical interest theory. But it is to stress that these contributions found no place in those fundamental equations which, more than anything else, are the hallmarks of neoclassical monetary theory.

Again, our approach does not depend on the use of the cumbersome and frequently criticized aggregates K, V, P, T, but instead builds only on individual demands for individual commodities with their individual prices. And even when presented in an aggregative form—as it will be on pp. 273–84—it does not needlessly cripple the quantity theory by implying—as does the MV of the transactions equation—that the validity of this theory holds only in the obviously unrealistic case where the aggregate demand for commodities is directly proportionate to the quantity of money. The preceding approach insists only that the demand functions be free of money illusion; otherwise it leaves them free to reflect the full range and variety of individual reactions to changes in the level of initial money balances.

The cash-balance equation frequently replaced these unnecessary and vitiating restrictions on the commodity functions with equally unnecessary—and possibly invalid—restrictions on the money function. Since the details of these restrictions will be described on pp. 273–84, there is no need to discuss them further here. Aside from this substantive criticism, the neoclassical cash-balance approach is subject to the more general, pragmatic criticism that has already been voiced in the Introduction. In its neat description of the factors which lead individuals to hold money balances, this approach certainly accomplished its proclaimed objective of bringing these holdings "into relation with volition."[7] But all too often this "humanizing" of the demand for money led to an undue concentration on the money market, a corresponding neglect of the commodity markets, and a resulting "dehumanizing" of the analysis of the effects of monetary changes.

What we are saying is that despite the already emphasized fact that adherents of the cash-balance approach recognized the real-balance effect, . . . they frequently failed to provide a systematic dynamic analysis of the way in which the monetary increase generated real-balance effects in the commodity markets which propelled the economy from its original equilibrium position to its new one. Now, as the incisive counterexample of Wicksell proves, such an omission is *not* a necessary consequence of this approach. Nevertheless, it cannot be mere coincidence that it is precisely this dynamic analysis which was *not* integrated into the Cambridge cash-balance tradition of Marshall, Pigou, Keynes, and Robertson, with its deliberate emphasis on the money market. It thus appears that, in its analysis of the inflationary impact of a monetary increase, the Cambridge theory was actually less illumed by the spark of "volition" and individual behavior than the Fisherine transactions theory whose "mechanicalism" it was designed to correct![8]

As emphasized sufficiently above, it is one of the specific objectives of the alternative approach developed in this book to avoid this pitfall by taking the analysis directly into the commodity markets. A corollary advantage of this approach is that it enables a precise economic explanation of why, say, a doubling of the quantity of money causes a doubling—and just a doubling, neither more nor less—of the price level. It shows the essence of the quantity theory to lie in the automatic, corrective market forces which continue to operate through the real-balance effect until this doubled price level is attained. Once again, there is no logical reason why these forces could not have been developed as a standard component of neoclassical monetary theory. Nevertheless, the stubborn fact seems to be that only Wicksell bestirred himself to ask what would happen if prices deviated from the equilibrium level called for by the quantity of money, and to describe how the dynamic forces thereby generated would return them to this level.

The essence of the three preceding paragraphs can be summed up in one sentence: There is a basic chapter missing in practically all neoclassical monetary theory—the chapter which presents a precise dynamic analysis of the determination of the equilibrium absolute level of money prices through the workings of the real-balance effect. This is said, not for that aspect of dynamic analysis which describes the forces propelling the economy toward its new equilibrium position after an initial monetary increase—a problem adequately discussed by many neoclassical economists[9]—but for that aspect which describes the forces stabilizing the economy at this new position once it is reached—a problem separated by just a nuance from the preceding one, but nevertheless discussed only by Wicksell.

It would be a serious error to underestimate the significance of this nuance. The easiest way of convincing the reader of this is to bring him up sharply against the following facts: Walras was a man who never tired of establishing the stability of his system by elaborating on the corrective forces of excess supply that would be called into play should the price lie above its equilibrium value, and the forces of excess demand that would be called into play should it lie below. He did it when he explained how the market determines the equilibrium prices of commodities; he did it again when he explained how the market determines the equilibrium prices of productive services; and he did it a third time when he explained how the market determines the equilibrium prices of capital goods. But he did not do it when he attempted to explain how the market determines the equilibrium "price" of paper money. And Walras is the rule, not the exception. Precisely the same asymmetry recurs among writers of the Cambridge tradition—with their standard supply-and-demand exercise of testing the stability of the equilibrium price in value theory and their standard omission of a corresponding exercise for testing the equilibrium absolute price level in monetary theory![10]

Thus in back of this nuance is the persistent failure of these economists to carry over to their monetary theory a simple, familiar technique of their value theory—and this despite their declared intention of integrating these two theories. We shall return to the significance of this fact on pp. 284–91.

The Cash-Balance Equation and the "Uniform Unitary Elasticity of Demand for Money"

Another familiar proposition of the neoclassical cash-balance approach—one already alluded to in the preceding section—is that the demand for paper money has "uniform unitary elasticity" and is accordingly represented by a rectangular hyperbola. This theme recurs specifically in the writings of Walras, Marshall, and Pigou. In the case of the latter it is clear that it was considered to be a necessary condition for the validity of the quantity theory of money. In Pigou's words, "an increase in the supply of legal tender ought always, since the elasticity of demand [for legal tender] is equal to unity, to raise prices in the proportion in which the supply has increased." And there is the strong impression that this was also the intended context in which this proposition was advanced by other writers as well. Indeed, it is probably this assumed causal relationship which explains the importance that was attached to it.[11]

This makes it all the more essential to recall that not only is this proposition not necessary for the quantity theory, it is not even generally true. [T]he real-balance effect makes it generally impossible for the demand for money to be of uniform unitary elasticity, but that nevertheless an increase in the quantity of money causes a proportionate increase in prices. It should, however, be clear that the neoclassical contention about unitary elasticity is not inherent in the Cambridge function as such. Thus, if KPT is the demand for money and M its supply, the excess demand for money, $KPT - M$, correctly reflects the by-now familiar property that an equiproportionate change in P *and* in M causes a proportionate change in the excess amount of money demanded. On the other hand, a change in P alone generates a real-balance effect, hence a change in the planned volume of transactions, T, and hence a *non*proportionate change in the amount of money demanded, KPT. Thus, if properly interpreted, the Cambridge function does *not* imply uniform unitary elasticity.

There are two possible explanations for the failure of neoclassical economists to see this. First, they apparently never realized the need to pin down the meaning of T. Only occasionally did they give it the volitional connotation on which the argument of the preceding paragraph depends. At other times they treated it as something beyond the will of individuals—as the fixed "total resources . . . enjoyed by the community." And at still other times they shifted unawares from one connotation to the next. Second, even when they used T in its volitional sense—which is, of course, the only one that is consonant with the *raison d'être* of the cash-balance approach—they never realized that the real-balance effect precludes T from remaining constant in the face of a change in P. Indeed, a standard lemma of the neoclassical proof of the quantity theory of money was that P and T were independent!

The force of the foregoing criticism is, however, highly attenuated by two considerations. First, if the Marshallian demand curve of value theory is interpreted as one from which the income effect has been eliminated; and if this interpretation is also extended to the Marshallian demand curve of monetary theory[12]— then the appropriate form of this curve is indeed the rectangular hyperbola, generated by confronting individuals with an equiproportionate change in both P and M. Second, even if this interpretation is not accepted, it should in all fairness be said that some exponents of the cash-balance approach merely used "unitary elasticity of demand" as a complicated way of stating that an increase in the quantity of money causes a proportionate increase in prices. In other words, they had in mind the elasticity of the market-equilibrium curve, not that of the demand curve, so that they were not really referring to what Marshall denoted by "elasticity of demand." This, however, should not be taken as implying that these writers indicated any awareness of the existence of two conceptually distinct curves. Indeed, they shifted uninhibitedly from one meaning of elasticity to the other—sometimes even within the same sentence. This points up the general fuzziness from which neoclassical monetary theory suffered as a result of its failure to draw the fundamental distinction between individual-experiments, on the one hand, and market-experiments, on the other.[13]

Valid and Invalid Dichotomies of the Pricing Process.
The Proper Relation Between Monetary Theory and
Value Theory

Let us return to the analysis of the effects of a change in the quantity of money. Instead of carrying out this analysis in terms of the absolute level of money prices—which is, of course, the usual approach—we can do it equivalently in terms of the *real* quantity of money; for once the nominal quantity of money is fixed, its real value varies in inverse proportion to the absolute level of money prices—or, in short, to the absolute price level. Such an approach can then proceed as follows: In the initial equilibrium position of our economy, the real quantity of money is just at that level which satisfies its transactions and precautionary needs. An exogenous increase in the nominal quantity of money then pushes the real quantity above this equilibrium value and thereby creates inflationary pressures in the various markets. The resulting price rise then reduces this real quantity and thereby lessens the disequilibrating inflationary pressures themselves. Now, by assumption, the initial monetary increase has not affected the economy's "taste" for real balances—that is, its desire to hold such balances in order to avoid the inconveniences, costs, and/or embarrassment of default. Hence the economy cannot achieve a new equilibrium position until the absolute price level has risen sufficiently to reduce the real quantity of money to its initial level once again.[14]

Let us now separate into two categories the given conditions (independent variables) which determine the nature of our exchange economy's equilibrium position. First, there are those which describe the economy's "real framework": namely, tastes (including those for *real* money balances) and initial holdings of commodities. Second, there are the conditions which describe its "monetary framework": namely, initial nominal holdings of money. Correspondingly, let us also separate the dependent variables of the analysis into two categories: "real variables," namely, the equilibrium values of relative prices, the rate of interest, and the real quantity of money; and the "monetary variable," namely, the equilibrium value of the absolute price level.[15]

Consider now the classical proposition that a change in the quantity of money merely causes an equiproportionate change in equilibrium money prices. The opening paragraph of this section enables us to replace this proposition by the equivalent one that such a change has no effect on the equilibrium values of relative prices, the rate of interest, and the real quantity of money. Now, to say that these values are independent of the nominal quantity of money is to say that they can be determined even without knowing this quantity. This permits us to conceive of the pricing process of our exchange economy as being divided into two successive stages: In the first one, specification of the real framework determines the equilibrium values of the real variables of the system. In the second, specification of the monetary framework then determines the equilibrium value of the monetary variable—for this value is simply the ratio between the specified nominal quantity of money and the equilibrium real quantity.

It should be clear that this arbitrary and mechanical act of specifying the nominal quantity of money has nothing whatsoever to do with monetary theory. For, as we shall argue below, this theory is concerned, at the individual level, with the relation between commodity demands and real balances and, at the market level, with the causes of changes in the equilibrium value of these balances. And both of these problems are fully analyzed in the first stage of the foregoing dichotomy. Thus this stage is coterminous with economic analysis: it comprises both value theory and monetary theory. Correspondingly, the second stage of this dichotomy is beyond the pale of economic analysis: it deals with a completely adventitious act.

It should also be clear that the foregoing dichotomy is purely a conceptual one. The real and monetary frameworks of the actual market place are obviously "specified" simultaneously. Similarly, there are only money prices in this market, and these are simultaneously determined. In brief, our dichotomy has no operational significance other than that of the basic quantity-theory proposition from which it is derived.

This dichotomy between relative and money prices must be sharply distinguished from that between money and accounting prices. First of all, there is the obvious difference in the nature of the prices involved. Parallel to this difference is the one between the data respectively specified at the second stages of these dichotomies. In the latter dichotomy this consists of the accounting price of one of the goods; in the present one it consists of the nominal quantity of money. Correspondingly, a change in the value of the supplementary datum in the present dichotomy affects money prices, whereas between money and accounting prices it does not. Finally, the dichotomy between money and accounting prices can have direct operational significance: there can be actual economics in which first money prices and then accounting prices are determined. Clearly, this additional set of prices is of no economic significance; but, in the present context, this is irrelevant.

Both of these dichotomies must be even more sharply distinguished from yet a third one which, though it has neoclassical roots in the works of Walras, Fisher, Pigou, and Cassel, did not achieve its most explicit form until the later expositions of Divisia, Lange, Modigliani, Schneider, and others. In this form it became undisputedly accepted as a statement of the proper relation between monetary theory, on the one hand, and value theory, on the other.

The point of departure of this familiar dichotomy (in practically every case in which it appears in the literature) is a pure outside-money economy consisting of commodities and money, but not bonds. The dichotomy then begins by dividing the economy into two sectors: a real sector, described by the excess-demand functions for commodities, and a monetary sector, described by the excess-demand function for money. The former functions are assumed to depend only on relative prices; the latter, on these variables and the absolute price level as well. This assumed insensitivity of the demand functions of the real sector to changes in the absolute level of money prices is referred to as the "homogeneity postulate"[16] and is said to denote absence of "money illusion."[17]

In a corresponding way, the market excess-demand equations corresponding to these functions are also separated into two groups. The equations of the real sector taken by themselves are then able to determine the equilibrium values of the only variables which appear in them—relative prices. These equations and the variables they determine thus constitute the domain of value theory. The equation of the monetary sector then determines the equilibrium value of the remaining variable—the absolute price level. And this equation and the variable it determines thus constitute the domain of monetary theory.

As with the "unitary elasticity of demand," much of the attractiveness of this dichotomy lay in the belief that it was a necessary condition for the validity of the quantity theory of money.[18] It was felt that unless the demand functions were independent of the absolute price level, monetary increases—which necessarily affect this level—could not preserve their classical neutrality with respect to the real phenomena of the economy. But once again the truth of the matter is that not only is this dichotomy not necessary, not only is it not valid, but its basic assumption is even a denial of the quantity theory itself! For to say that the demand functions of the real sector are not affected by changes in the absolute price level—that is, to assert that they satisfy the "homogeneity postulate"—is to imply that they are not affected by changes in the real value of cash balances. But it is precisely on this real-balance effect that the quantity theory in our present model depends for the inflationary impact of a monetary increase! On the other hand, this dependence in no way violates the *final* neutrality of, say, a doubling of the quantity of money. For in the new equilibrium position the individual is confronted not only with a doubled price level, but also with a doubled initial holding of money. Hence—as compared with the initial equilibrium position—there is no real-balance effect; hence there is no change in behavior; and hence the classical neutrality of money is reaffirmed.

More generally, if the function of monetary theory is to explain the determination of the absolute price level, then the "homogeneity postulate"—or, equivalently, absence of "money illusion" in the sense of the foregoing dichotomy—is the antithesis of all monetary theory within the simple model considered by the foregoing writers. For let the assumptions of the dichotomy obtain. Assume now that an initial position of equilibrium is disturbed in such a way as to cause an equiproportionate change in all money prices. Since this does not change relative prices, the "homogeneity postulate" implies that none of the demand functions in the real sector are thereby affected. Hence, since the commodity markets of this sector were initially in equilibrium, they must continue to be so. By Walras' Law, so must the money market. Thus the equiproportionate departure of money prices from any given equilibrium level creates no market forces—that is, creates no amounts of excess demand anywhere in the system—which might cause money prices to return to their initial level. Hence if any set of money prices is an equilibrium set, any multiple of this set must also be an equilibrium set. The absolute price level is indeterminate.

It follows that the foregoing dichotomy is involved in a basic internal contradiction. For if the demand functions of the real sector have the property it attributes to them, there cannot possibly be a "second stage" in which the absolute price level is determined.

Since the foregoing argument has on occasion been misunderstood, it may be worth while elaborating upon it. The first thing that should be noted is that the contradiction with which it is concerned has nothing to do with the possible inconsistency of a system of static excess-demand equations in the sense that such a system may not have a formal mathematical solution;[19] indeed, as has been emphasized, this type of question lies outside the interests of this book. Instead the notion of inconsistency with which the foregoing argument is concerned is the standard (and general) one of formal logic that a set of propositions is inconsistent if it simultaneously implies a proposition and its negative.[20]

The details of the foregoing argument can now be spelled out as follows: We start with the following three fairly reasonable assumptions: (1) Market forces will be generated to increase (decrease) the price of any given commodity if, and only if, there exists an excess demand (supply) for that commodity. (2) Market forces will be generated to increase (decrease) the absolute price level if, and only if, there exists an excess supply (demand) for money. (3) The absolute price level can change only if at least one commodity price changes.

Let the assumptions of the foregoing dichotomy now hold. For simplicity—and in accordance with the usual presentation of the dichotomy—assume also that the money equation is of the Cambridge form

$$KPT - M = 0.$$

Assume finally that the system is in an initial state of equilibrium which is disturbed in such a way as to cause a chance equiproportionate departure of commodity prices (and hence the absolute price level) from their equilibrium levels. As we have already seen, this does not generate any excess demands in any of the commodity markets. Hence by assumptions (1) and (3) above, there *will not* be generated market forces to cause a corrective change in the absolute price level; that is, this level is indeterminate.

Consider now the foregoing Cambridge equation—under the usual assumption that K, T, and M are kept constant during the discussion. Assume that the initial equiproportionate disturbance in commodity prices causes P to rise. It is then clear from the foregoing equation and assumption (3) that an excess demand for money is generated which *will* cause a corrective downward movement in the absolute price level; that is, this level is determinate. Hence a contradiction.

This contradiction can be expressed alternatively—and equivalently—in terms of an inconsistent system of *dynamic* market-adjustment equations. Graphically, the argument is as follows: Consider first the assumptions of the traditional dichotomy. These imply that the demand function for commodities is independent of real balances and hence the price level, and should therefore be represented by a vertical line. Now, if this vertical line does not coincide with the vertical supply curve, the *static* system of equations would be inconsistent: that is, it would have no equilibrium solution for a price level greater than zero. This, however, is *not* the inconsistency described in the three preceding paragraphs: for this continues to obtain even if the vertical commodity demand curve should coincide with the commodity supply curve as in Figure 1a, so that the *static* system of equilibrium equations would have a (indeed, an infinite number of) positive solution(s).[21] In particular, the foregoing argument states that even in this case there would remain the inconsistency that Figure 1a would show us that the system is in a state of *neutral* or *unstable* equilibrium, whereas Figure 1b (which depicts the Cambridge equation, and which must logically

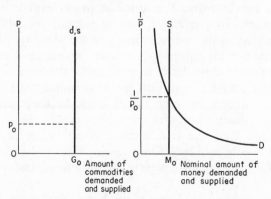

Figure 1a.   **Figure 1b.**

represent the obverse side of Figure 1a) would show us that it is in a state of *stable* equilibrium.

Yet another expression of this contradiction is the following: Start once again from a position of equilibrium, and assume that the quantity of money is doubled. Since the commodity equations of the foregoing dichotomy are assumed to be independent of real balances, this does not disturb the initial equilibrium in these markets. Hence—by assumptions (1) and (3)—no market forces are generated by this monetary increase to push the price level upwards. From the Cambridge equation and assumption (2), on the other hand, we see that such market forces are created. Hence a contradiction.

Actually, a much simpler way of dealing with this dichotomy is to note that it provides an operationally significant hypothesis—one capable of being tested by the facts of the real world. In particular, its basic "homogeneity postulate" implies that the behavior of consumers in commodity markets can never be affected by the real value of their money balances. But . . . there is considerable empirical evidence that this behavior has been so affected. Hence this evidence alone suffices to refute this dichotomy. In brief, reality shows that there cannot be a money economy without a "money illusion."[22]

This empirical approach enables us to dispose of a certain variation of the foregoing dichotomy which—though it has never been advanced as such in the literature—can pass the test of internal consistency. Specifically, though continuing to consider an outside-money economy, we now assume the existence of bonds as well as commodities and money. We assume further that though the commodity equations continue to be independent of real balances, the bond equation is not. In such a Keynesian system, relative prices and the rate of interest can be determined in the commodity markets and the absolute price level in the bond or money market. In particular, the argument by which we previously established the indeterminacy of the absolute price level no longer holds. For an equiproportionate departure of money prices from their equilibrium level now disturbs the equilibrium of the bond market, and the resulting excess demand then acts through the rate of interest to force prices back to their original level. Nevertheless, this variation of the dichotomy is also unacceptable. For it implies that the real-balance effect never manifests itself in the commodity markets. Once again, this implication is refuted by the aforementioned empirical studies of the consumption function.[23]

It should also be noted that if the bond market, too, is assumed to be independent of real balances, then the resulting model is not even internally consistent. In particular, it is involved in exactly the same type of indeterminacy already shown to hold for the invalid dichotomy. For once again an equiproportionate departure of money prices from an initial equilibrium position, the rate of interest being held constant, does not create any excess demands anywhere in the system. Hence no force is generated to bring prices back to their initial position.

The conclusion to be drawn from the foregoing discussion is that, once the real and monetary data of an economy with outside money are specified, the equilibrium values of relative prices, the rate of interest, and the absolute price level are simultaneously determined by all the markets of the economy. It is generally impossible to isolate a subset of markets which can determine the equilibrium values of a subset of prices. In the true spirit of general-equilibrium economics, "everything depends on everything else."

In particular, as we have seen, it is fatal to succumb to the temptation to say that relative prices are determined in the commodity markets and absolute prices in the money market. This does not mean that value theory cannot be distinguished from monetary theory. Obviously, there is a distinction; but it is based on a dichotomization of *effects*, not on a dichotomization of *markets*. More specifically, both monetary theory and value theory consider *all* markets of the economy simultaneously. But, in each of these markets, value theory analyzes individual-experiments which measure the substitution effect and that part of the wealth effect which does not stem from changes in real balances; and monetary theory, individual-experiments which measure the real-balance effect. Correspondingly, value theory analyzes market-experiments which do not (significantly) affect the absolute price level and hence do not generate real-balance effects; and monetary theory, market-experiments which do not (significantly) affect relative prices and hence do not generate substitution and non-monetary wealth effects. Thus shifts in tastes, changes in technology, and the like are in the domain of value theory. Changes in the quantity of money and—as we shall see—shifts in liquidity preference are in the domain of monetary theory.

If we now examine this classificatory scheme, we will discover the grain of truth in the intuitive feeling that in some sense value theory is connected with the determination of relative prices and monetary theory with the determination of absolute prices. In particular, assume that by a *tâtonnement* involving all prices and all markets the equilibrium values of money prices have been reached. We can now make use of this information to take a step backwards and approach the equilibrium position once again—but this time by a restricted *tâtonnement*. For example, holding the absolute price level constant at its already determined *equilibrium* value, we can arbitrarily shift relative prices from theirs, and then study the nature of the dynamic forces that—working simultaneously in *all* markets—return the economy to its original equilibrium position. By the very definition of this procedure, such a return can be accomplished without any change in the absolute price level. Hence the restricted *tâtonnement* by which equilibrium relative prices are thus redetermined need involve only these prices, need accordingly generate only substitution and nonmonetary wealth effects, and can therefore be studied entirely within the confines of value theory.

Similarly, we can define a restricted *tâtonnement* which—starting from a knowledge of the *equilibrium* values of relative prices and interest—works simultaneously through *all* the markets of the economy to redetermine the equilibrium value of the absolute price level. Such a *tâtonnement* can clearly succeed without requiring any changes in relative prices and interest; that is, it need generate only real-balance effects. Hence it can be studied entirely within the confines of monetary theory.

This decomposition of the overall *tâtonnement* into two components is a convenient expository device. It can be used safely provided we are clear in our own minds that it separates out effects and not markets. In particular, we must guard against the apparent tendency to slip over from this valid device into the invalid proposition of the false dichotomy that, starting with an absolute price level held constant at an *arbitrary* level, a *tâtonnement* on relative prices in the *commodity markets alone* can determine these prices; that, holding these relative prices constant at the values so determined, a *tâtonnement* on the absolute price level in the *money market alone* can then determine this level; and that the absolute price level so determined, together with the relative prices determined by the first *tâtonnement* in the commodity markets, must *necessarily* preserve the equilibrium initially achieved in these markets. Clearly, this last statement will generally *not* be true unless the excess-demand equations of the commodity markets are actually independent of the absolute price level.

This is the crucial point. The dynamic groping of the absolute price level towards its equilibrium value will—through the real-balance effect—react back on the commodity markets and hence on relative prices. And it is precisely the constant failure to find this point explicitly recognized—and, indeed, the constant sensation of being just on the verge of having it explicitly contradicted—that is the basis of our original contention that the roots of the invalid dichotomy are to be found in the neoclassical analyses of Walras, Fisher, Pigou, and Cassel.[24]

The preceding discussion not only analyzes the invalid dichotomy, but also brings out the many deceptive similarities between it and the valid ones. That these similarities have played a significant role in the etiology and persistence of the dichotomy is suggested by several instances in the literature. Thus there is at least one explicit example of the way in which the valid insensitivity of demand to equiproportionate changes in *accounting* prices shifts undetected into the invalid insensitivity to equiproportionate changes in *money* prices. That is, the valid dependence of demand solely on the ratios of accounting prices is confused with the invalid dependence solely on the ratios of money prices. Indeed, this example considers this dependence to be a direct consequence of the "postulate . . . that the consumer's behavior is independent of the units in which prices are expressed. . . ." But here again the same confusion is at work. For after a change in the monetary unit has worked itself out, the individual is confronted with an equiproportionate change in money prices *and* in his money holdings. Thus if the dollar is replaced by the half dollar as the unit of measure, all money prices will eventually double; but—as the very first result of this conversion itself—so will halve the initial money holdings of each and every individual. Hence the proper analog of a change in the monetary unit is an equiproportionate change in *accounting* prices (which leaves the real value of initial money balances intact), not an equiproportionate change in *money* prices (which does not).[25]

Similarly, there are instances in which the valid dichotomy between accounting and money prices is confused with the invalid dichotomy between money and relative prices. Thus, in order to prove that *money* prices cannot be determined unless a special equation is added, it is argued that: "There are always just one *too few equations* to determine the unknown quantities involved. The equation of exchange [$MV = PT$] is needed in each case to supplement the equations of supply and demand"—and the first sentence is supported by an explicit reference to a mathematical development by the same author which, in order to determine *accounting* prices, adds an equation arbitrarily setting the accounting price of one of the goods equal to unity![26]

Examples in the literature of an alleged connection between the invalid dichotomy and the quantity theory of money have already been noted above.[27] As will be recalled, these allegations were based on a misunderstanding of the nature of the neutrality of money. It remains now to suggest that in its more sophisticated form this may have expressed itself as a confusion between the invalid dichotomy and the first dichotomy described above (p. 276)—the one which is essentially a restatement of the quantity theory and which shows the valid sense in which relative and absolute prices are independently determined. In particular, we can find an example which states that "the proposition that the material set-up of our economic system determines only the *relative* and not the absolute prices of all commodities is so familiar that it hardly deserves further discussion"—and then justifies this statement with an implicit reference to the "homogeneity postulate" that demand remains unaffected by an equiproportionate change in money prices. Here we can almost see the exact point at which the line of reasoning slips off the correct path: Relative prices are determined independently of the absolute price level by the "material set-up of our economic system"—the valid dichotomy; "material set-up" means the conditions of demand in the commodity markets—the invalid dichotomy; but if these conditions alone determine relative prices, they can depend only on these prices—the "homogeneity postulate."[28]

Finally, we can find an example which—though not as clear as the preceding ones—seems to show how the valid intuitive feeling that different forces determine absolute and relative prices slips imperceptibly into the invalid identification of these forces with separate equations. How else can we interpret the train of thought revealed by the following passage: "... it is important to distinguish between the influences determining the general price level and the influences determining an individual price. The price level is determined by a comparatively simple mechanism, that of the equation of exchange. It is the result of the quantity of money and deposits, the velocities of their circulation, and the volume of trade. The general price level then helps to fix individual prices, although not interfering with relative variations among them...."[29]

This is admittedly a small number of examples. Nevertheless, the stature of the economists who provide them, the definitive aura of received doctrine that they all gave to the reasoning by which they justified their statements, and the fact that this reasoning was never challenged—all this endows these few examples with a weight far out of proportion to their number. All this permits us to suggest that the explicit reasoning of these examples is representative of the general intellectual process that gave rise to the invalid dichotomy.

Conclusion: The Failure of Neoclassical Monetary Theory to Fully Understand the Real-Balance Effect

In view of the continued discussion of the foregoing issues in the recent literature, it is worthwhile—even at the cost of some repetition—to summarize the argument of this chapter until this point. We must first of all emphasize that we are dealing with an *empirical* question: namely, the role of the real-balance effect in neoclassical monetary theory. Correspondingly, the universe from which our observations must be, and have been, drawn is the relevant body of neoclassical literature.

The specific empirical findings that have emerged from our study can be set out as follows:

1. In their discussion of value theory, neoclassical economists generally included an analysis of the stability of equilibrium. By this is meant nothing more complicated than the usual simple graphical exposition by which neoclassical economists showed that if the price of any given commodity were above (below) the intersection of the demand and supply curves, then there would exist an excess supply (demand) to drive it down (up) again.

2. Neoclassical economists consistently proclaimed their objective of integrating their monetary theory with their value theory; that is, of analyzing the former in the same manner as they had analyzed the latter.

3. Nevertheless, with one or two exceptions, neoclassical economists did not include a stability analysis in their monetary theory. That is, they did not explain the nature of the corrective market forces that would be brought into play should the absolute price level deviate from its equilibrium value.

4. Therefore, the omission of this analysis cannot be explained away as being the result of either a chance oversight, on the one hand, or a conscious lack of interest in monetary stability analysis, on the other.

5. An alternative hypothesis to explain this phenomenon is that though the neoclassical economists did recognize the real-balance effect, they did not achieve a full understanding of it and therefore did not carry out the monetary stability analysis which is so vitally dependent upon it.

6. Like any other empirical hypothesis, this one too achieves additional credibility from the fact that it explains some additional phenomena: namely, the fact that neoclassical economists supported both the rectangular-hyperbola demand curve for money and—in all probability—the invalid dichotomy.

a. The evidence from the form of the demand curve is the weakest link in the chain. For it is not absolutely clear if neoclassical economists assumed the demand curve to have the form of a rectangular hyperbola because they failed to take into account the real-balance effect—or whether they did so because they assumed this effect to be eliminated as a result of compensating variations in initial money balances, or, alternatively, because they did not have in mind a demand curve at all, but instead a market-equilibrium curve. It is also possible that they had in mind [a] long-run rectangular hyperbola.

b. On the other hand, to the extent that we find indications of the invalid dichotomy in the neoclassical literature, the implications are straightforward. For this dichotomy reflects a failure to realize the direct contradiction between the real-balance effect, on the one hand, and the "homogeneity postulate" on the other; or, from an alternative viewpoint, a failure to realize the complete inappropriateness of denoting sensitivity of the individual to a change in the absolute price level by the term "money illusion," when in fact it is precisely this sensitivity which demonstrates the existence of a rational concern on the part of the individual with the surely nonillusory impact of such a change on the real value of his money holdings.

7. The foregoing hypothesis is on even stronger grounds with reference to the later literature, and this for two reasons. First, this literature explicitly accepts the invalid dichotomy as the undisputed statement of the relationship between monetary and value theory in an economy with outside money;[30] indeed, this view has persisted in some of the most recent writings. Second, this literature provides yet another phenomenon which accords with our hypothesis: namely, the failure to see the equilibrating role that the real-balance effect can play in eliminating an inflationary gap.

8. With reference to this later literature we might also note that the approach of Keynesian economics, with its emphasis on analyzing the demand for commodities as a function of the flow of income instead of the stock of assets, was hardly conducive to breaking down a mental block whose essence was the failure to see the significance of the effect of a change in the absolute price level on the real value of the *stock* of money.

In concluding this critique of neoclassical monetary theory, I would like to emphasize once again[31] that not only does it not require the abandonment of any significant aspect of this theory, but it actually rigorizes and completes it. Correspondingly, to the extent that it is meaningful to speculate about such matters, I have no doubt that neoclassical economists would have readily accepted the criticisms involved; would have declared the explicit introduction of the real-balance effect into the commodity demand functions to be a more precise reflection of their thinking on this matter all along and, indeed, a modification that could only strengthen their quantity-theory conclusions; and would accordingly have rejected the implication of some of their recent would-be defenders that they (neoclassical economists) had a vested intellectual interest in the "homogeneity postulate" and its related dichotomy.[32]

The Effects of a Change in K

Let us now leave doctrinal history and return to analytical questions proper. Until now, this chapter has essentially been concerned with the relation between the quantity of money and the level of prices—that is, with the relation between M and P in the Cambridge equation $M = KPT$. But neoclassical monetary theory also used this equation to analyze the relation between K and P, on the one hand, and T and P, on the other. Since, unlike changes in M, the exact translation of changes in K and T into terms of our model is difficult to determine, the exact bearing of the following argument on the neoclassical one must also remain slightly unclear. Nevertheless, as the reader will see, the economic forces that appear in this argument have a distinctly neoclassical character.

We begin with the effects of a change in K. (Obviously, whatever will be said for these effects holds in the inverse for those of a change in the V of $MV = PT$.) Consider, in particular, an economy whose equilibrium is disturbed by a sudden increase in K. This is represented in our model by an increased desire for liquidity resulting from an increase in the probability of running out of cash, or an increase in the inconvenience or penalty costs of so doing. More specifically, this "change in tastes" reflects itself as an increase in the amount of money individuals demand at a given set of prices, interest, and initial endowments. By the budget restraint, this upward shift in the demand for money implies a simultaneous downward shift in the demand for commodities and real bond holdings. That is, because of their given incomes, individuals cannot demand more of one good unless they give up something of another. As a result of this latter shift, equilibrium prices will fall. The interesting question which now confronts us is whether the equilibrium rate of interest must also change.

There is a simple, intuitive answer that can be given at this point. To say that there has been an increase in the individuals' liquidity preferences is analytically equivalent to saying that the liquidity convenience of one dollar of cash balances is now less than it was before. And this, in turn, is equivalent to saying that the "subjective quantity" of money in the hands of individuals has decreased. Hence it seems only natural to argue that the conditions under which the rate of interest remains constant after an increase in liquidity preference are precisely those under which it remains constant after a decrease in the quantity of money.

Let us state this somewhat more exactly. As in the case of a decrease in the quantity of money, we abstract from distribution effects. We also assume the increase in liquidity preferences to be "uniformly distributed"; that is, the liquidity preference of each and every individual is assumed to change with the same "intensity." As explained above, this increase causes downward shifts in the demands of all markets and hence replaces their original state of equilibrium by one of excess supply. Consider now any one market. Clearly, the excess supply in this market can now be removed by an equiproportionate decline in prices, while the rate of interest remains constant. Specifically, this decline will continue until the real value of cash balances has increased sufficiently to satisfy the individuals' increased liquidity preferences and hence restore their demand in this market to its original level. Thus, in some subjective sense, the real quantity of money that influences this market is the same as it originally was. Now, by assumption, the initial shift in liquidity preferences is a "neutral" one: it changes only the relative desirability of money *vis-à-vis* all other goods, not the relative desirabilities of these other goods amongst themselves. Hence if this subjective quantity of money is "the same" with respect to the market for one of these goods, it must be "the same" with respect to that for any other. That is, the equiproportionate price decline needed to equilibrate one market must be equal to that needed to equilibrate any other. Hence equilibrium can be restored to the economy as a whole at a lowered price level and an unchanged rate of interest.

Thus under these assumptions we obtain a reaffirmation of the classical position: An increase in K causes a decrease in P but leaves T and the rate of interest unaffected. By resorting to the device of carrying out the analysis in terms of changes in the real quantity of money instead of changes in P,[33] we can bring out the deeper connotation that neoclassical economists ascribed to this proposition: An increase in K creates automatic market forces which themselves generate the increased equilibrium quantity of real balances desired by the community. The wonders of the "invisible hand" never cease.

The Effects of a Change in T

Consider now an economy whose equilibrium is disturbed by a sudden increase in T. Let this be represented in our model by an exogenous doubling, say, of the individuals' initial commodity endowments. Such a change creates two opposing forces. On the one hand, there is, of course, an increase in the fixed supply of every commodity. On the other hand, there is an increase in wealth and a consequent increase in demand. If it should so happen that the increased demand for each and every commodity exactly offsets its increased supply, no further changes will occur, and the economy will remain in equilibrium at its original set of prices and interest rate. Clearly, this latter case implies a unitary marginal propensity to spend on commodities out of wealth. In general, however, this propensity can be assumed to be less than unity, for part of the increased wealth will be devoted to increasing the demand for money balances. Hence it can be expected that the increases in the amounts of commodities demanded will be less than in the respective amounts supplied, thus generating a downward pressure on prices.

Let us now see if an equiproportionate decline in prices can return the economy as a whole to a position of equilibrium. Consider first the market for one particular commodity. Clearly, it is possible to conceive of the price decline continuing until the resulting positive real-balance effect together with the original positive wealth effect suffice to increase the amount demanded to the same extent that the amount supplied was originally increased. That is, it is possible that by an equiproportionate decline in prices, the rate of interest being held constant, the market for *any one* particular commodity can be brought back into equilibrium.

But the economy consists of many commodity markets, and each of them has been disturbed by the original increase in endowments. In general, the resulting wealth effect will not be the same in all markets. Hence, in contrast with the preceding section, there is no reason why the equiproportionate decline in prices needed to bring one of these markets into equilibrium should be the same as that needed for any other one. That is, there is no reason why a given equiproportionate decline in prices should succeed in equilibrating all markets simultaneously. Hence, in order for such an over-all equilibrium to be restored, relative prices and interest will, in general, also have to change.

Assume now that the exceptional occurs and that an equiproportionate decline in prices—interest constant—does succeed in restoring the economy as a whole to equilibrium. Clearly, even in this case there is no reason why this decline should be in inverse proportion to the original increase in commodity endowments. For the necessary magnitude of this decline depends on the strength of the wealth effect, as well as on the size of the increase in endowments.

Thus we can confirm the neoclassical position that an increase in T decreases P. Furthermore, we also confirm the neoclassical contention that (even when there is no change in the rate of interest) this decrease will, in general, *not* be an inversely proportionate one. In terms of the Cambridge equation, this contention rests on the assumption that K and T are *not* independent; that a change in the latter will affect the former. In particular, it assumes that an increase in the volume of transactions creates the possibility of economies in the relative magnitude of money balances necessary for a given level of security against insolvency. That is, it implies that an increase in T decreases K. Hence, $M = KPT$ can continue to be satisfied even though P does not change in inverse proportion to T.[34]

The Implications of Say's Identity

We conclude this chapter with a discussion of Say's Identity. My own sympathies are with those who deny that this identity is a basic component of the classical and neoclassical position. Nevertheless, there are certain passages which can be cited in support of the opposite contention. Furthermore, whatever the proper interpretation, the attention that has been given to the identity since Keynes makes it desirable to analyze it in detail—particularly since some of its logical implications have not been correctly understood.[35]

Following Lange, we define Say's Identity as stating that—regardless of the prices and interest with which they are confronted—individuals always plan to use all of their proceeds from the sale of commodities and bonds for the purpose of purchasing other commodities and bonds. In other words, they never plan to change the amount of money they hold: its amount of excess demand is identically zero. In still other words—and as a direct consequence of the budget restraint—the aggregate value of the amounts of excess *supply* of commodities must always equal the value of the amount of *demand* for bonds: people divert any reduced expenditures on commodities to the purchase of bonds, never to the building up of money balances.[36]

It can readily be seen that this assumption implies that equilibrium money prices are indeterminate. For consider an economy with n goods: $n-2$ commodities, bonds, and money. Assume that this economy is in equilibrium at a certain set of values for the rate of interest and for the $n-2$ money prices. Let us now arbitrarily change one of these prices. Consider first the $n-2$ commodity markets. In general, it will be possible to find another set of $n-2$ values for the rate of interest and for the remaining $n-3$ money prices which will again equilibrate these $n-2$ markets. But, by Say's Identity, any set of prices and interest which equilibrates these markets must also equilibrate the bond market, for, under this assumption, if the excess supplies of commodities are zero, so is the demand for bonds.[37] Finally, since the excess demand for money is identically zero, this market too is obviously in equilibrium. Thus the economy as a whole can be in equilibrium at an infinite number of sets of money prices. In mathematical terms, Say's Identity reduces the number of independent market excess-demand equations to $n-2$, and these do not suffice to determine the equilibrium values of the $n-1$ price and interest variables.[38]

Thus Say's Identity is inconsistent with the existence of a money economy with determinate prices. But this is the only type of money economy that has any economic meaning. Hence we can say that the existence of Say's Identity implies the existence of a barter economy. Conversely, the existence of a barter economy implies the existence of Say's Identity. For in such an economy it is physically impossible to "sell" one commodity or bond without "buying" another; thus Say's Identity in this economy is nothing but a statement of the budget restraint. In other words, people never plan to change their level of money balances in a barter economy, because, by definition, such balances are always zero.

Let us now return for a moment to the "homogeneity postulate." As was demonstrated above,[39] this postulate implies the absence of a real-balance effect and the consequent indeterminacy of money prices. By the same argument as in the preceding paragraph, we can then say that the existence of the "homogeneity postulate" implies the existence of a barter economy. Conversely, the existence of a barter economy implies the existence of the "homogeneity postulate." For in such an economy there are no money holdings, the "absolute price level" has no meaning, and hence there can be no real-balance effect.

Thus, contrary to the accepted opinion, Say's Identity and the "homogeneity postulate" are logically equivalent properties: both are necessarily present in a barter economy; both are necessarily absent from a money economy. Thus the existence of the one implies the coexistence of the other.[40]

With this we have also said all that need be said for our purpose about a barter economy. Such an economy is the home—the necessary and only home—of the "homogeneity postulate" and Say's Identity. Prices in this economy can be measured either in terms of one of the commodities or—as in a Wicksellian "pure credit economy"—in terms of an abstract unit of account. Thus, at most, only relative and accounting prices are defined. The former are determined by the workings of market forces, the latter—as always—by arbitrary decree. Money prices not even being defined, their determinacy or indeterminacy cannot be meaningfully discussed.[41]

NOTES

1. The reader will observe that $M = KPT$ and $MV = PT$ are treated here as *equations*, and not as *identities*. It will also be observed that these two equations have been treated as analytically equivalent. Without committing ourselves on the attempts that have sometimes been made to distinguish substantively between them, we merely note that for our present purposes any such distinction can be disregarded. Cf. J. M. Keynes, *Treatise on Money* (London 1930), Vol. 1, pp. 237–39; Marget, *Theory of Prices*, Vol. 1 (New York 1938), pp. 424–33.

For good recent accounts of the two neoclassical equations and their respectively associated theories, see L. V. Chandler, *The Economics of Money and Banking*, rev. ed. (New York 1953), Chapters XXIII–XXV; A. G. Hart, *Money, Debt, and Economic Activity*, rev. ed. (New York 1953), Chapters 10 and 12.

2. K. Wicksell, *Interest and Prices*, trans. R. F. Kahn (London 1936), pp. 39–41.

3. I. Fisher, *Purchasing Power of Money* (New York 1911), pp. 153–54.

4. This is one of the central themes of Marget's study; see, in particular, *Theory of Prices*, Vol. 1, pp. 307, 345 ff., and 500 ff. It also seems to me that a good part of H. Hegeland's monograph on the *Quantity Theory of Money* (Göteborg 1951) suffers from the failure to recognize this fact; see *ibid.*, especially pp. 38–9, 57, 87–92.

5. Cf., e.g., R. Cantillon, *Essay on the Nature of Trade* (1755), trans. and ed. H. Higgs (London 1931), p. 179; Mill, *Principles*, pp. 491–92. Marget (*Theory of Prices*, Vol. 1, p. 502) cites similar passages from Lubbock and Cairnes.

For this emphasis in later writers, see Walras, *Eléments d'économie politique pure*, first ed. (Lausanne 1874), p. 181, who essentially repeats Mill; see also the definitive ed. of the *Eléments*, ed. Jaffé (London 1954), p. 328. See also Wicksell, *Interest and Prices*, p. 40; Schumpeter, "Money and the Social Product," *op. cit.*, pp. 191–92, 204–6; and Mises, *op. cit.*, pp. 139–40. But Mises carries himself away to an invalid extreme when he attempts to prove that even in the case of an equiproportionate increase in initial individual money balances, prices will not rise equiproportionately (*ibid.*, pp. 141–42).

6. Fisher, *Purchasing Power of Money*, p. 153, with "his" changed to "their," and "him" to "them."

7. Pigou, "The Value of Money," *Quarterly Journal of Economics* (November 1917); reprinted in *Readings in Monetary Theory*, eds. F. A. Lutz and L. W. Mints (Philadelphia 1951), p. 174.

8. It is for this reason that the foregoing Cambridge economists are not listed together with Wicksell and Fisher on p. 269 as having presented a full statement of the tripartite quantity-theory thesis. In order to evaluate the validity of this criticism, the reader must himself compare the expositions of the Cambridge school with those of Wicksell and Fisher. It is similarly instructive to contrast the Cambridge expositions with those of such cash-balance theorists as Mises (*op. cit.*, pp. 132–35, 138–40, 147–49) and R. G. Hawtrey [*Currency and Credit*, 3rd ed. (London

1927), Chapters 3–4, especially pp. 35, 59–60; as can be seen from p. 35, Hawtrey's "unspent margin" is identical with what is usually referred to as a cash balance].

9. Cf. the references to Fisher, Wicksell, Mises, and Hawtrey in note 8 above.

10. That the asymmetry just described has persisted down to the present can be seen by examining the more recent literature from the same viewpoint that has just been used for the neoclassical. On the other hand, there is not much point in trying to trace this inconsistency back to the classical literature: its value-theory discussions are of too different a nature.

11. Pigou, *Essays in Applied Economics* (London 1923), p. 195.

12. The foregoing interpretation is, of course, that of Milton Friedman, who argues that Marshall assumed movements along his demand curve to be accompanied by compensating variations which keep real income constant ["The Marshallian Demand Curve," *Journal of Political Economy*, Vol. 57 (1949), as reprinted in *Essays in Positive Economics* (Chicago 1953), pp. 50–53]. While not accepting the specifics of this argument, I do agree that Marshall's demand curve does not reflect the income effect; see my "Demand Curves and Consumer's Surplus," in Carl Christ, *et al.*, *Measurement in Economics: Studies in Mathematical Economics and Econometrics in Memory of Yehuda Grunfeld* (Stanford 1963), pp. 104–8.

13. Once again Wicksell is an exception. For he makes it clear that the rectangular hyperbola he draws in his monetary theory is a market-equilibrium curve.

14. Compare this with the change in the equilibrium real quantity of money that characterizes a shift in liquidity preference; see below, pp. 287–88.

15. Throughout the following analysis we abstract from distribution effects. This enables us to consider the total of initial nominal—and hence real—bond holdings as identically zero. Accordingly, neither one of these holdings appears in the preceding classificatory scheme.

16. This term was first used by W. Leontief, "The Fundamental Assumption of Mr. Keynes' Monetary Theory of Unemployment," *Quarterly Journal of Economics*, Vol. 51 (1936–37), p. 193. It originates in the fact that, in mathematical terms, demand functions which are not affected by an equiproportionate change in money prices are said to be "homogeneous of degree zero" in these prices.

17. It should be clear to the reader that this does *not* correspond to our use of this term, which defines absence of money illusion as insensitivity to changes in the absolute level of *accounting*—and not *money*—prices.

In order to avoid any possible confusion, we might repeat that throughout this discussion "absolute price level" is a shorthand expression for "absolute level of *money* prices."

18. This was explicitly claimed by, for example, Leontief, "The Fundamental Assumption of Mr. Keynes," *op. cit.*, p. 193, and Modigliani, "Liquidity Preference," *op. cit.*, p. 217.

19. A fact that has been duly noted by various commentators on the dichotomy discussion; thus see Assar Lindbeck, "Den Klassiska 'Dichoto-

mien,' " *Ekonomisk Tidskrift*, Vol. 63 (1961), pp. 32, 35, and 39; and H. G. Bieri, "Der Streit um die 'klassische Dichotomie,' " *Schweizerische Zeitschrift für Volkswirtschaft und Statistik*, Vol. 2 (1963), pp. 177–78.

On the other hand as has already been indicated in a symposium participated in by Baumol ("Monetary and Value Theory," *Review of Economic Studies* [October 1960], section I and p. 31, final paragraph), Hahn (*op. cit.*, p. 42), and Ball and Bodkin (*op. cit.*, p. 49, footnote 4), recent criticism of the foregoing argument by Archibald and Lipsey (*Review of Economic Studies* [October 1958], pp. 9–17) stems from failure to see this fact and is therefore beside the point (see pp. 306–20 in this volume).

Though relying on this symposium for his summing-up of the dichotomy discussion, Harry Johnson's recent survey also incorrectly implies that the foregoing argument deals with the inconsistency of a system of static equations ("Monetary Theory and Policy," *op. cit.*, p. 340, lines 13–20) [reprinted in this volume, p. 10—Ed.].

20. Cf., e.g., M. R. Cohen and E. Nagel, *An Introduction to Logic and the Scientific Method* (New York 1934), p. 144; Patrick Suppes, *Introduction to Logic* (Princeton 1957), pp. 36–7.

21. It is this coincidence of the demand and supply curves which is assured by the assumption of Say's Identity (cf. pp. 290–91 above) made by Hickman, Archibald and Lipsey, and the other writers.

22. Once again, the reader is warned that this is *not* being used here in our sense of the term.

23. For a more precise statement of the argument see my "Indeterminacy of Absolute Prices in Classical Economic Theory," *Econometrica*, Vol. 17 (1949), p. 22.

24. It should be clear that the criticism of these paragraphs is *not* directed against the frequent neoclassical practice of taking the absolute price level as given in the partial-equilibrium analysis of value theory. The same methodological considerations which permit this analysis to hold constant certain relative prices also permit it to do the same for the absolute price level. The purpose of this assumption is simply to enable the money price of a commodity to serve as a perfect index of its relative price. Cf. Marshall, *Principles*, eighth ed., p. 62. This practice goes back at least to Mill, *Principles*, p. 439; cf. Marget, *Theory of Prices*, Vol. 2, (New York 1942), p. 281, footnote 128.

25. The example referred to here is that of Samuelson; the quotation is also his.

The line of reasoning in the second half of this paragraph is one that I have frequently heard—though I have not succeeded in finding any additional example of it in the literature. Cf., however, Boulding, *Economic Analysis*, p. 320.

26. Cf. above, pp. 276 f.

The passage cited is from Fisher, italics in original. Precisely the same confusion can be found in Cassel.

27. See the references to Leontief and Modigliani above, p. 293, note 18.

28. The example referred to is that of Leontief, italics in original.

29. The example is that of Fisher.

30. On an outside-money economy, see note 23 above.

31. Cf. my "Indeterminacy of Absolute Prices in Classical Monetary Theory," *Econometrica*, XVII (1949), pp. 23–7. Cf. also pp. 271–72 and 277–78 above.

32. On these speculations, see again the reference cited in note 31.

It should also be clear from all this that there is no logical connection between the dichotomy issue and the classical-Keynesian controversy.

It might also be noted that the explicit use of the real-balance effect helps tie together other loose ends of the traditional theory. Thus see Amotz Morag's use of the real-balance effect in public finance theory to prove the long-debated equivalence of an income tax and a uniform sales tax ["Deflationary Effects of Outlay and Income Taxes," *Journal of Political Economy*, Vol. 67 (1959), pp. 266–74]. See also Michael Michaely's use of the real-balance effect in international trade theory to resolve the apparent contradiction between the "relative-price" and "absorption" approaches to the analysis of devaluation ["Relative-Prices and Income-Absorption Approaches to Devaluation: A Partial Reconciliation," *American Economic Review*, Vol. 50 (1960), pp. 144–47].

33. See above, pp. 271–72.

34. On these economies, cf. the reference to Fisher, *Purchasing Power of Money*, pp. 153–54.

35. "Say's Identity" is the useful term suggested by G. S. Becker and W. J. Baumol in order to emphasize that it may not really represent "Say's Law" in its classical and neoclassical meaning. But Becker and Baumol's attempt to give a classical connotation to the concept they call "Say's Equality" can only mislead.

36. The budget restraint is

the amount of market excess demand for current money holdings
   = the aggregate value of the amounts of market excess supplies of current commodities
   — the (discounted) value of the amount of market demand for current bond holdings.

By Say's Identity, the left-hand side of this equation is identically zero, so that this yields the conclusion just stated in the text.

37. The demand and *excess* demand for bonds are identical, so that equilibrium exists in this market when either is zero.

38. For a graphical analysis of the indeterminacy generated by Say's Identity in the case of an economy consisting only of commodities, see Figure 1a and its related discussion on pp. 270–72 above.

39. Page 280 f. Note that the extension of the present argument to an economy with bonds has caused us to make a corresponding extension of the "homogeneity postulate" to include the bond market. However, the reader who prefers to retain the original sense of this term as applying only to the commodity markets can simply ignore all references here to the bond market and the rate of interest and follow the analysis as if it applied to an economy with only commodities and money. This does not change the argument in any significant way. At the same time, this modification brings us back to the framework actually considered by Lange and Modigliani.

40. Note that the proof of this proposition rests on the basic assumption that—from the viewpoint of meaningful economic analysis—the class of monetary economies with indeterminate price levels is an empty one. This fact has been overlooked in Archibald and Lipsey's recent criticism [*op. cit.*, p. 14, footnote 2 (p. 311)].

41. As the reader has undoubtedly realized, here is another (cf. pp. 282 ff. above) deceptive similarity which may have helped give rise to the invalid dichotomy: the "homogeneity postulate" *is* a correct description of rational behavior in a barter economy—but not in a money economy.

12 Monetary and Value Theory: A Critique of Lange and Patinkin

G. C. Archibald
and Richard G. Lipsey *University of Essex*

A change in the price level which causes a departure of desired from actual real balances may lead to a change in individuals' spending. The object of this paper is to enquire into the operation and significance of this real-balance effect in classical value and monetary theory, about which there has for some time been controversy. Lange argued that the classical dichotomy between the real and monetary sectors of the economy is invalid, and that an integration of value and monetary theory is required. Patinkin has attempted this integration in his book *Money, Interest, and Prices*, arguing that the real-balance effect provides the necessary link between the two parts of the system. In this paper we argue that the classical dichotomy is valid, and that the integration undertaken by Patinkin is therefore unnecessary. In part one we enquire into the operation of the real-balance effect in a classical exchange model. This is necessary because Patinkin's analysis is incomplete and leaves many important points obscure. We find that, while the price level is of course determined by the desire to hold balances together with the stock of money, the role of the real-balance effect is only to provide an explanation of how the system behaves in disequilibrium. Thus the real-balance effect is irrelevant to those

Reprinted from *Review of Economic Studies*, Vol. 26 (October 1958), 1–22, by permission of the authors and publisher.

famous propositions of the quantity theory which are the result of comparative static analysis. In part two we enquire into the formal consistency of the classical model, a question which is given great importance by the fact that nearly all modern value theory presupposes the validity of the classical dichotomy. We find that the model has a consistent solution which does not depend in any way on the presence in the model of the real-balance effect. We find, however, that the model offers no explanation of behaviour out of equilibrium, and that the role of the real-balance effect is again to provide an explanation of disequilibrium behaviour. We see that it is the absence of such an explanation from the formal classical model that has led to the persistent and erroneous view that the system is inconsistent. We also see in what way Lange's original argument was mistaken.

In part three we investigate the role of the real-balance effect in a classical model with production and saving as well as exchange. We find once again that the role of this effect is to explain how this system behaves out of equilibrium, but that the equilibrium level of employment is independent of its operation in the model. We argue that Patinkin's claim, that his analysis "invalidates" the Keynesian theory of employment, is completely unfounded.

The Real Balance Effect in a Classical Exchange Model

We start by considering the exchange model of the first part of Patinkin's book. In this model, in which time is divided into discrete contracting periods called weeks, it is important to distinguish between equilibrium at a point of time and equilibrium over time. As Hicks has put it, a stationary economy ". . . is in full equilibrium, not merely when demands equal supplies at the currently established prices, but also when the same prices continue to rule at all dates . . ."[1] Patinkin apparently overlooks this distinction; his analysis never goes beyond the conditions for equilibrium in one week. It is, as we shall see in (7) below, for this reason that he is forced to make some unusual assumptions to obtain the classical results. Our investigation of the properties of the model in full, as well as in weekly, equilibrium is necessary in order to understand how Patinkin arrives at his results, how the classical results may in fact be obtained directly from the comparative static analysis of the model in full equilibrium, and what role is played by the real-balance effect in the many cases that may be studied.

The individual is assumed to have a given real income paid in goods,[2] and a given initial stock of money. We assume for the moment that relative prices do not vary so that goods may be treated as a single composite (G) with a single price (p). The individual's stock of money divided by p is his real balance H. We assume an indifference system between *holding* real balances for the week and *consuming* goods. The demand for balances is assumed to be purely a transactions demand.[3] The market opens every Monday, and a process of *tâtonnement* and recontract continues until equilibrium prices are reached. The market then closes, all contracts become binding, and trade takes place. The *tâtonnement*, in which equilibrium prices are found, is quite distinct from the actual trading, which takes place afterwards. The conditions for *weekly* equilibrium are, for the individual, that he has achieved the preferred division of his total resources between consumption and holding balances for the week, and, for the market, that supplies of and demands for goods are equal. It is consistent with these conditions, however, that the individual shall have added to or subtracted from his balances. If this is the case, he will begin the following week with a different total of resources, and his behaviour will be different. *Full* equilibrium obtains when market prices are unchanged from week to week. This requires that each individual's behaviour be unchanged from week to week, that is, that his consumption be constant. Since in this model an individual must divide the whole of his resources between consumption and balances it follows that, when his consumption is constant, so also are his balances (i.e., he consumes a bundle of goods equal in value to the bundle with which he was endowed at the beginning of the week). Thus the full equilibrium level of consumption is necessarily equal to total income, and independent of the desire to hold balances, the stock of money, and the equilibrium level of prices.

In order to understand how this model works, it is necessary to analyse:

(1) the individual's weekly equilibrium;

(2) how he reaches full equilibrium;

(3) how this full equilibrium is altered by a changed desire for balances;

(4) how it is altered by a change in the price level;

(5) how the market reaches full equilibrium;

(6) how full equilibrium in the market is altered by a change in the money stock;

(7) how weekly market equilibrium is altered by a change in the money stock which takes place when full equilibrium does not obtain;

(8) the effects on the market of a non-proportional change in individuals' stocks of money;

(9) the bearing of the above on the demand for money; and

(10) the part played in the above by the real-balance effect. Since Patinkin neglects the conditions for full equilibrium, his analysis is devoted mainly to (1), (7), (8) and (9).

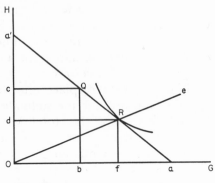

Figure 1.

(1) The individual's behaviour in this model may now be analysed with the aid of Patinkin's diagram. In Figure 1, units of the composite good are measured along the G axis and of *real* balances along the H axis. The budget line relating real goods to real balances must have an invariant slope of 135°; in Patinkin's words, "The unitary negative slope of this line reflects the fact that, by definition, one unit of liquid command over commodities-in-general [real balances] can always be exchanged for one unit of actual commodities-in-general" (*op. cit. ibid.*, p. 69). At the beginning of any week the individual's total resources consist of his income for that week *plus* his stock of real balances (money balances held over from the previous week divided by the price level which, for the moment, we assume to remain constant). If this total equals Oa in goods, it is necessarily also Oa' in balances, where $Oa = Oa'$, and the budget line is aa'. The individual is in equilibrium for the week when he is at a point of tangency between his budget line and an indifference curve. The locus of such points of tangency defines an expansion path Oe.

(2) We now come to the essential part of the argument that Patinkin overlooked. Intersection of the budget line and the expansion path only provides an equilibrium for the week in question. Suppose that the individual, in the diagram just considered, starts the week in the position Q. This means that he has received income equal to Ob, and has retained balances equal to Oc ($= ba$). To attain his preferred position, R, he spends cd ($= bf$ of goods) from his balances, in addition to spending his whole income. Thus his balances carried over to next week will be only Od. Hence, even if he receives the same income next week, he starts the period

with a different (smaller) total of resources. The budget line the following Monday will be closer to the origin by the distance $bf = cd$, and the individual's market behaviour will therefore be changed. Full (stock) equilibrium, which is only attained when his behaviour is repeated each week, requires that the division of his resources between goods and balances with which he starts the week is the preferred division for that total of resources. We now amend Patinkin's diagram to make explicit the distinction between expenditure out of income and expenditure out of balances. Consider Figure 2. The individual has a constant real income OY. Erect a perpendicular YY' which intersects the expansion path Oe at i. If his initial real balances are Ya, his budget line is aa', his initial position S_1, at the intersection of aa' with YY', and his preferred position P_1. In the first week he therefore consumes Og goods, running down his balances by Yg. It follows that next period his budget line will be $jj'(ja = Yg)$, and his initial position S_2. The preferred position is now P_2, obtained by spending S_3P_2 from balances; and the starting point for the next period is in turn S_3. It is clear that this process continues, with ever smaller adjustments, as the individual approaches ever closer to i (which cannot be attained in a finite number of periods). Only when the individual is at i is he in full stock equilibrium; that is to say, at i he spends the whole of his income OY, while maintaining his stock of balances unchanged. (This analysis can obviously be repeated

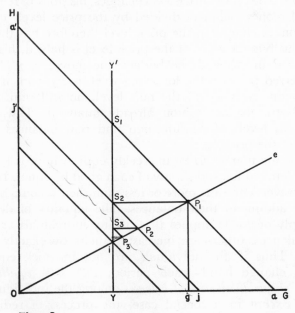

Figure 2.

for the case in which the individual starts with too low a level of real balances.)

(3) Suppose that a change in tastes were to alter the expansion path in Figure 3 from Oe to Oe', indicating an increase in the desire to hold balances. The position of stock equilibrium is given by the intersection of YY' with the new expansion path at k. The equilibrium level of real balances is increased by ik; the equilibrium level of consumption is unchanged at OY, i.e., is independent of the desired level of balances, although, in the weeks in which balances are being built up, consumption is less than income.

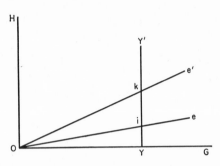

Figure 3.

(4) Suppose that the individual is in a position of full equilibrium, i in Figure 2, where with income OY his balances are constant at Yi. Now, if the price level changes, his stock of real balances (nominal money balances divided by the price level) changes in proportion. A change in the price level therefore has the effect of moving his budget line.[4] If the price level is halved, his real balances are doubled, and the budget line moves to $jj'(Yi = iS_2)$. His preferred position the following week is P_2, and, if the price level remains constant at the new level, he will return to i, by weekly steps, in the fashion already analysed. Thus the full-equilibrium levels of consumption and real balances are independent of the price level.

(5) For the market to be in weekly equilibrium, it is necessary that the demand for and supply of each good be equal. Individuals may, however, consume more or less than their income by running down or adding to their balances. The equality of demand for and supply of goods implies that, if any individuals are running down balances, others are increasing theirs by exactly the same amount. Thus if all individuals are not in stock equilibrium, balances change hands each period. *Full stock equilibrium thus requires a unique distribution of balances* among the individuals in the market. Except in a special case, the process of redistributing balances by trade will cause the price level to vary from week to

week.[5] Apart from this special case, a constant price level requires full equilibrium for each consumer.

Let us take a simple example, illustrated in Figure 4, in which there are only two individuals with identical incomes of OY, identical non-linear expansion paths Oe, but different initial balances. Individual I has balances Yc and budget line cc'; individual II has balances Yf and budget line ff'. I now wishes to add Yv to his balances, and is therefore an excess supplier of goods by the same amount. II wishes to spend Yd out of his balances, and is therefore an excess demander of goods by the same amount. Equilibrium in the market this week requires that $Yv = Yd$. Assume that this is the case, and that the *tâtonnement* is therefore concluded and trade takes place. Next week I's budget line, which has moved out by $Yv = Yd$, passes through Z; and II's, which has moved in by $Yd = Yv$, passes through W. I wishes to move to L, and II to M. Given the shape of Oe, the horizontal distance of L from YY' exceeds that of M from YY'. Hence I's excess supply of goods exceeds II's excess demand, and trade cannot take place at last week's price level. Prices are therefore bid down. This, however, increases the real balances of both individuals, and therefore moves both budget lines to the right. As the budget lines move to the right, I's excess supply of goods diminishes, and II's excess demand increases. When the two have been brought into equality the *tâtonnement* ends, and the market is in equilibrium this week.

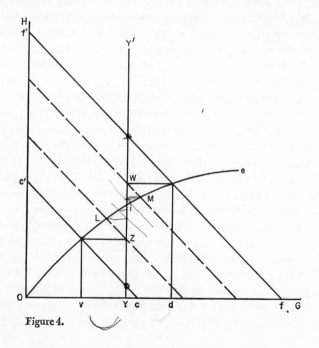

Figure 4.

The process of adjustment is therefore as follows:[6] trade each week moves the two budget lines closer together; the price reduction required to equilibrate the market the following week moves them both to the right; the week's trade then again brings them closer together. Ultimately the two budget lines coincide, passing through i, the position of full equilibrium for each individual. Only then will the price level cease to vary. (This analysis can obviously be repeated for the case in which the price level increases from week to week.)

(6) Now suppose that each individual in the market is in a position of full equilibrium, such as point i in Figure 2, when the stock of money is doubled. In order to avoid distribution effects we shall assume for the present that each individual simply wakes up on Monday morning to find his nominal money balances doubled. At the prevailing price level each individual's budget line therefore moves out, e.g., to jj' in Figure 2. Now *each* individual wishes to spend out of balances. When the market opens there is therefore an excess demand for goods (equal to S_3P_2 for the individual in Figure 2). This excess demand causes a rise in the price level, which continues, through the process of *tâtonnement*, until supply of and demand for goods are restored to equality. The rising price level *during* the *tâtonnement* reduces each individual's real balances, and therefore moves his budget line inwards *without trade taking place*. The *tâtonnement* must continue, with the price level rising, until the excess demand for goods has been removed. This requires that individuals cease to attempt to alter their balances. This in turn requires that the price level rise until balances are restored to their original real worth, i.e., that the price level is doubled. In terms of Figure 2, the individual endeavouring to spend S_3P_2 of his newly increased balances finds that the efforts of others to do likewise are increasing the price level. The increase moves his budget line closer to the origin, and continues until the budget line is restored to its original position. Thus a doubling of each individual's stock of cash leads to a doubling of the price level on the first occasion that the market opens. When the whole market starts from full equilibrium, full equilibrium is restored by the *tâtonnement alone*, there being no actual expenditure out of balances and no week-by-week adjustment.

(7) In (6) above we saw that a change in the stock of money leads to a proportionate change in the full equilibrium price level. Patinkin, however, does not analyse the model in full equilibrium: he considers a change in the stock of money which takes place during a process of adjustment such as that analysed in (5) above. We may now see how he obtains his results. Suppose that the *tâtonnement* has just ended, *but that no goods have yet changed hands*.

The price level is therefore such as would clear the market this week, i.e., the excess supply of goods offered by some individuals is equal to the excess demanded by the others (the price level is not, however, one which will necessarily be repeated the following week, nor the same as that which prevailed in the preceding week). Now we follow Patinkin in doubling the stock of money by doubling the balances of each individual. We cancel all the contracts of the previous *tâtonnement*, and start a new *tâtonnement*. Those individuals who had contracted to reduce their balances will now wish to make a larger reduction, and will therefore increase their excess demand for goods; those who had contracted to add to their balances will now wish to make a smaller addition, and will therefore decrease their excess supply of goods. Thus the price level must rise, and must continue to rise until excess supplies and demands for goods are again equal. This requires that the budget lines be restored to the position they occupied at the close of the previous *tâtonnement*, i.e., that the price level double. The price level that is doubled is not, however, that of the previous week: it is the price level at which trade *would* have taken place this week had the stock of money not doubled. If, in the absence of a change in the stock of money, this week's price level would not have been equal to last week's, a doubling of the stock of money which doubles this week's price level does not cause it to be double last week's. Thus Patinkin obtains conclusions which appear to agree with those of the quantity theory only by comparing prices at which trade takes place (after the second of the week's two *tâtonnements*) with prices at which it would have taken place (after the first).[7] To obtain the result that doubling the quantity of money doubles actual market prices, we must compare positions of full equilibrium as in (6) above.

(8) The analysis has so far been conducted on Patinkin's assumption that, when the stock of money is increased, there are no distribution effects. Patinkin argues that the absence of distribution effects is a necessary condition for the result that doubling the money stock doubles the price level.[8] If the doubling is conducted in the fashion analysed in (7) above, this is true. In the usual case, in which positions of full equilibrium are compared, it is not true. Let us now consider the consequences of an increase in the stock of money which is not distributed in such a fashion as to cause an equi-proportionate increase in the money balances of all individuals. Since each individual's final equilibrium is fully defined by his expansion path and his real income, any given increase in the stock of money has the same effect on the position of final equilibrium as that of any other equal increase however it may be initially distributed. In the case of a non-proportionate distribution

the equilibrium cannot, of course, be reached *merely* by a change in the price level, but will require a redistribution of balances by the process of adjustment through trade already analysed. The path of adjustment, but not, of course, the final equilibrium, depends on the actual distribution of the increase in the money stock. We must notice that the conclusion obtained in (7) above, that a doubling of the money stock causes the price level at which trade next takes place to be double what it otherwise would have been, depends on the absence of distribution effects. The conclusion that doubling the stock of money doubles the full equilibrium price level does not depend on this assumption.

(9) The equilibrium level of real balances is uniquely determined by tastes and incomes, and invariant to the money stock. Hence the total market demand for nominal money with respect to the reciprocal of the price level is the rectangular hyperbola of the classical writers. Consider, however, the case of an individual who is in full equilibrium when the price level is halved. Since, by assumption, he does not spend the whole increase in his real balances in the first week, his nominal balances are not at once halved. Hence his immediate demand curve for money is of less than unit elasticity. Each week, however, he reduces his balances until, when full equilibrium is restored, his nominal balances are half their original amount. The inelastic individual demand curve discussed by Patinkin[9] therefore belongs solely to weeks in which full equilibrium has not been attained. The individual's curve relating the full equilibrium demand for money to the price level is, of course, always, like the market curve, a rectangular hyperbola.

(10) Patinkin defines the real-balance effect as "... the influence on demand of a change in real balances, other things being held constant" (*ibid.*, p. 21). Since in full equilibrium consumption is equal to income, a change in real balances can only change real consumption during a process of adjustment. Thus the real-balance effect is a transitory phenomenon, which is operative only in some disequilibrium situations.[10] Its role is to provide a possible *dynamic* explanation of how the economy moves from one position of static equilibrium to another. Thus, if we are interested in those well-known propositions of the quantity theory which are propositions in comparative statics, the real-balance effect is irrelevant.[11]

The Consistency of the Classical Exchange Model

In the traditional classical system it was assumed that the demand and supply functions for goods were homogeneous of degree zero in absolute prices; relative prices and equilibrium quantities were uniquely determined in the "real" sector of the economy, and the absolute price level by a demand function for money to hold of the Cambridge type and a given stock of money. Lange opened the modern controversy by arguing that this model is necessarily inconsistent.[12] Patinkin then took up and elaborated Lange's argument. Patinkin's position has been criticised,[13] but the authors of the main summaries of the controversy have found substantially in his favour.[14] The opinion that the classical system is inconsistent has led Patinkin to the view, already expressed by Lange, that relative and absolute prices cannot be separately determined, and hence to the attempt to combine their determination with the aid of the real-balance effect. This question of the consistency of the classical system is of considerable importance. In the first place, it is fundamental to real static theory. Patinkin writes that ". . . once the real and monetary data of the economy are specified, the equilibrium values of relative prices, the rate of interest, and the absolute price level are simultaneously determined by all the markets of economy. It is generally impossible to isolate a subset of markets which can determine the equilibrium values of a subset of prices."[15] If this is correct, then most existing real static theory, e.g., of international trade, must be radically at fault. In the second place, if we are to understand the proper role of the real-balance effect in economics, we must know whether it is required to restore consistency to the otherwise inconsistent classical model, or has some other function. In this section, therefore, we shall enquire into the question of consistency (which has been much confused by the fact that different authors appear to have used the term in different senses).

(1) The view that the classical system is inconsistent appears to rest mainly on the argument that it contains two excess demand functions for money. One excess demand function is obtained from the supply and demand functions for goods. The excess demand for money is equal to the total amount of money demanded in exchange for goods *minus* the total amount supplied in exchange for goods. Since the physical volume of transactions is independent of the absolute price level in this model, the money value of transactions varies in proportion to the price level. Thus this excess demand function for money is homogeneous of degree one in absolute prices. The second excess demand function is for money to hold. It is obtained from the Cambridge equation where the demand for money (K times the money value of transactions) is homogeneous of degree one in absolute prices, and the stock supply of money is an institutionally determined constant (i.e., homogeneous of degree zero in the prices). The excess demand function,

which is the difference between the demand (homogeneous of degree one) and the supply (homogeneous of degree zero) is therefore non-homogeneous. It is alleged that the existence of these two functions makes the model inconsistent.[16] The usual demonstration runs as follows: assume that the system is in equilibrium; double all money prices; since relative prices are unaffected, the goods markets are still in equilibrium; hence, by Walras' Law, the money market is in equilibrium; thus either the system leaves money prices undetermined, in the absence of a stock demand for money, or, if there is a stock demand, there are two inconsistent excess demand functions.[17]

The existence of these two excess demand functions raises two separate questions which have been much confused during the controversy. These are:

1. Has the model, in general, a solution, i.e., is it formally consistent?
2. Does it make economic sense?

It has been demonstrated, by both Hickman and Valavanis, that the model is not, in general, formally inconsistent. We shall present Hickman's example of a classical model here and, for convenience, provide a numerical example. The fact that this example has a consistent solution answers the first question. The second question is more difficult. If non-equilibrium values of some of the variables are substituted into the model, the results appear to be, in some sense, "self-contradictory." That is to say, if the price level is arbitrarily doubled, there is an excess demand for money to hold but no excess supply of goods. The answer to the question is that the model has no economic interpretation when it is out of equilibrium. Some writers have apparently inferred from this that the answer to the first question is also no. This is not a valid inference.[18] The fact that the model has no interpretation out of equilibrium, however, presents problems which we must consider. Before doing so, we shall show that, although Hickman's example is formally consistent, it does not conform to *all* the requirements of a static economic model. We shall accordingly modify it and present a second numerical example. We shall then show what significance is to be attached to the difficulties which occur out of equilibrium. Finally, we shall consider what modifications are made to the model by the inclusion of a real-balance term.

(2) Now let us consider the example of the classical model set out by Hickman, in which there are only two goods and money (d_1, d_2, s_1, and s_2 are the parameters). The monetary equation is linearly dependent on the goods equations; when X_1 and X_2 equal zero, X_3 must equal zero and is, therefore, redundant as an equilibrium condition. We have two commodity equations, but only

TABLE 1

	DEMAND	SUPPLY	EXCESS DEMAND
Good I	$D_1 \equiv d_1 \dfrac{p_2}{p_1}$	$S_1 \equiv s_1 \dfrac{p_1}{p_2}$	$X_1 \equiv d_1 \dfrac{p_2}{p_1} - s_1 \dfrac{p_1}{p_2} = 0$
Good II	$D_2 \equiv d_2 \dfrac{p_1}{p_2}$	$S_2 \equiv s_2 \dfrac{p_2}{p_1}$	$X_2 \equiv d_2 \dfrac{p_1}{p_2} - s_2 \dfrac{p_2}{p_1} = 0$
Money	$D_3 \equiv p_1 S_1 + p_2 S_2$	$S_3 \equiv p_1 D_1 + p_2 D_2$	$X_3 \equiv -p_1 X_1 - p_2 X_2 = 0$

one relative price. If the two equations were independent they would in general solve for different relative prices, hence consistency in the model requires that the commodity equations be dependent. "A necessary and sufficient condition [for dependence] is that . . . the determinant of the matrix of the coefficients of X_1 and X_2 vanishes, i.e., that $s_2 = d_1(d_2/s_1)$."[19] If this condition is satisfied, then by solving either of the commodity equations we obtain the relative price which may be substituted into the supply or demand functions to obtain equilibrium quantities. We may now complete the system by adding a Cambridge equation

$$K(p_1 D_1 + p_2 D_2) = M_0$$

where K and M_0 are constants. The values of D_1, D_2, and p_1/p_2 are already known $\left(\dfrac{p_1}{p_2} = \sqrt{(d_1/s_1)} = \sqrt{(s_2/d_2)} \right)$, and the money prices can now be obtained.

Let us now take a numerical example by giving specific values to the parameters of the system, and show that it has a solution. If we put $d_1 = 4$ and $s_1 = 16$ into the excess demand equation for Good I, we obtain $\dfrac{p_1}{p_2} = \tfrac{1}{2}$ and $D_1 = S_1 = 8$. Consistency requires that $\dfrac{d_1}{s_1} = \dfrac{s_2}{d_2}$; hence, if we arbitrarily put $d_2 = 4$, we must have $s_2 = 1$. Putting these values into the second commodity equation, we have

$$4 \frac{p_1}{p_2} - \frac{p_2}{p_1} = 0$$

which gives $\dfrac{p_1}{p_2} = \tfrac{1}{2}$, the value which satisfied the first equation. We also have $D_2 = S_2 = 2$. Now, having determined relative prices and equilibrium quantities, we may determine money prices. If we take $K = \tfrac{1}{3}$ and the supply of money as \$10, we have

$$\tfrac{1}{3}(8p_1 + 2p_2) = \$10.$$

With $\dfrac{p_1}{p_2} = \frac{1}{2}$, this yields $p_1 = \$2.50$ and $p_2 = \$5.00$.

This example is a sufficient refutation of the charge that the system of homogeneous goods equations, together with the Cambridge equation, can have no solution, i.e., is formally inconsistent.

(3) There remains the question of the economic interpretation which is to be put on this model when it is not in equilibrium. Before we can discuss this, however, there is a problem about the equilibrium properties of the model which we must take up, and which will necessitate some modifications. Let us again consider the numerical example. Its solution was

$$D_1 = S_1 = 8 \qquad\qquad p_1 = \$2.50$$
$$D_2 = S_2 = 2 \qquad\qquad p_2 = \$5.00.$$

If we substitute these values into the money equations (third row of the table above) we obtain

$$D_3 = S_3 = 8 \times \$2.50 + 2 \times \$5.00 = \$30,$$

the money value of transactions. The money value of trade in Good I is $20.00, and in Good II $10.00. Since, however, one good can only be purchased by selling the other good or by running down balances, it follows that, in the aggregate, purchasers of Good I are running down their balances, while suppliers of that good are adding to theirs; and that purchasers of Good II are adding to their balances while suppliers are reducing theirs. Hence this model, while mathematically consistent, does not yield a full static equilibrium solution. In the solution obtained there is a continuous flow of balances from one set of individuals to another. One of the conditions of full equilibrium described in part one was that each individual be satisfied with his balances, i.e., a unique distribution of balances is one of the conditions of full equilibrium. This condition is simply not to be found in the model just examined. There is no equilibrium distribution of balances, and cannot be unless behaviour is altered. The alteration of behaviour, however, requires that we alter the supply and demand functions.

We must now modify the model to allow for an equilibrium distribution of balances. We must therefore select forms of the supply and demand functions which are not merely consistent but which also conform to this condition. We now require that in equilibrium the money value of the goods supplied by each individual equal the money value of the goods demanded by him. Now any individual can, in general, reach balance equilibrium at any set of relative prices with which he is faced. Hence we have, for any set of relative prices, a set of demands and supplies for each individual which describes his desired sales and purchases if he is in balance equilibrium at that set of prices. This is the set which must be described by the functions used for full-equilibrium static analysis. Thus the supply and demand functions we now require will have the property that the flow demand will equal the flow supply of goods for each individual at each set of relative prices, i.e., will give supply and demand when balances are in equilibrium. If this is not the case, then either (*a*), as in the example above, we never reach balance equilibrium, or (*b*), the analysis must include the process of adjustment described in part one. If we want balance equilibrium, and propose to consider only positions of full equilibrium (if, that is, the analysis is static, and omits the process of adjustment), then the supply and demand functions must be appropriately written. The selection of the set of functions appropriate to comparative statics, however, has the effect of writing Say's Identity into the model—if the functions give balance equilibrium at every set of relative prices for all individuals, then the aggregate excess demand for goods in general is zero at every set of relative prices, which is Say's Identity.[20] This is necessary if the solution is to be consistent with balance equilibrium.[21] In the models considered here, in which we are concerned only with trade in two goods, Say's Identity requires that the value of trade in the two goods be identical.[22] In a multi-good exchange model in which Say's Identity held for each individual, and so for the goods market as a whole, we should not, of course, have this simple relationship between pairs of goods.

The example may now be modified to conform with this requirement. First, we notice that the two excess demand functions were, to meet the requirements of consistency, made linearly dependent. That is, we had

$$X_1 \equiv 4\frac{p_2}{p_1} - 16\frac{p_1}{p_2} = 0,$$

and

$$X_2 \equiv 4\frac{p_1}{p_2} - 1\frac{p_2}{p_1} = 0.$$

The second is obtained when the first is multiplied by $-\frac{1}{4}$. The two are, of course, consistent whenever one can be obtained by multiplying the other by any constant λ. Our new requirement, however, is that money receipts from the sale of the first good equal money expenditure on the purchase of the second.[23] Hence

$D_1 p_1$ must equal $S_2 p_2$, i.e., S_2 must equal $\frac{p_1}{p_2} D_1$. Similarly D_2 must

equal $S_1 \frac{p_1}{p_2}$. Hence the second equation is obtained from the first by multiplying by $-\dfrac{p_1}{p_2}$. Say's Identity is therefore equivalent in the two-good model to restricting the choice of the constant λ to the particular value $-\dfrac{p_1}{p_2}$.

Let us now alter our numerical example to illustrate these requirements. We had

$$D_1 \equiv 4\frac{p_2}{p_1}, \quad S_1 \equiv 16\frac{p_1}{p_2}, \quad \text{and} \quad X_1 \equiv 4\frac{p_2}{p_1} - 16\frac{p_1}{p_2} = 0,$$

which gave $\dfrac{p_1}{p_2} = \tfrac{1}{2}$ and $D_1 = S_1 = 8$.

Now taking as our constant $\lambda = -\dfrac{p_1}{p_2} = -\tfrac{1}{2}$, we obtain

$$X_2 \equiv 8\frac{p_1}{p_2} - 2\frac{p_2}{p_1} = 0,$$

that is,

$$D_2 \equiv 8\frac{p_1}{p_2} \quad \text{and} \quad S_2 \equiv 2\frac{p_2}{p_1},$$

which gives $D_2 = S_2 = 4$ and $\dfrac{p_1}{p_2} = \tfrac{1}{2}$.

Taking $K = \tfrac{1}{3}$ and $M_0 = \$10.00$ as before, we have

$$\tfrac{1}{3}(8p_1 + 4p_2) = \$10.00$$

which, with $\dfrac{p_1}{p_2} = \tfrac{1}{2}$, gives $p_1 = \$1.875$ and $p_2 = \$3.75$. Since, by construction, $p_1D_1 = p_2S_2$ and $p_2D_2 = p_1S_1$, we obviously have $D_3 \equiv S_3$.[24] The value of trade in Good I is $8 \times \$1.875 = \$15.00$, and in Good II is $4 \times \$3.75 = \$15.00$.

(4) We have now seen, following Hickman, that the classical system is not necessarily inconsistent. We have also demonstrated that we must have Say's Identity to obtain full static equilibrium, but that this does not prevent us from solving the Cambridge equation to obtain money prices. We must now return to the second of our two original questions: what happens to this model in disequilibrium? Suppose that, in the numerical example above, we double money prices. As we leave relative prices unaltered, equilibrium in the goods markets is undisturbed, and the physical volume of transactions is unchanged although its money value has doubled, i.e., the value of trade in each good has increased from $\$15.00$ to $\$30.00$, so that $D_3 \equiv S_3$ now equal $\$60.00$. Substituting these values into the Cambridge equation, however, we find an excess demand for money equal to K times the value of

trade *minus* the stock of money, here ($\frac{1}{3} \times 60$) $-$ 10, which gives an excess demand of $10.00. Now the problem is to reconcile this with the identity $D_3 \equiv S_3$.

There are three points to consider here.

(i) Whatever interpretation may be put on the fact that $D_3 \equiv S_3$ while the Cambridge equation shows an excess demand, it is invalid to conclude from this that the model is formally inconsistent. The fact that the model has an equilibrium solution from which we can depart in the first place is sufficient to rule out this argument.

(ii) The example above, in which we doubled prices, is in denial of Walras' Law. Although there is an excess demand for money to hold, there is no excess supply of goods. In fact, Walras' Law does not hold in this model at all. This raises a problem of interpretation which we shall consider in (iii) below. The absence of Walras' Law, however, follows directly from the division of the system into two subsections, the real and the monetary, which can be solved separately. If we assume that the quantities of goods traded depend *only* on relative prices, and that the money price level can be determined independently, then we cannot expect to find the Walrasian relation between the goods equations and the Cambridge money equation. *Thus the classical dichotomy consists in building a model in which Walras' Law does not hold.* Now we can understand the error in Lange's original argument. He wrote (*op. cit.*, p. 52)

$$D_n - S_n \equiv \Delta M,$$

that is, the excess of the flow demand for money over the flow supply is identical with the desired change in money balances (Walras' Law). In our example this would be

$$D_3 - S_3 \equiv K(p_1 D_1 + p_2 D_2) - M_0,$$

which is not true. He then argued that if $D_n \equiv S_n$ (Say's Identity) there could be no monetary theory, because ΔM would be identical with zero. The error lies simply in identifying $D_n - S_n$ with ΔM in the classical model.[25] The dichotomy precludes this relationship between the two parts of the system—Walras' Law does not hold. If Lange's identification were valid, then the rest of his argument would follow. Thus Lange's criticism of the classical model depends on his assuming that Walras' Law holds whereas, as we have seen, the classical dichotomy precludes Walras' Law.

(iii) Now we have the problem of interpretation. Walras' Law says that goods can only be demanded if goods or money are offered in exchange. It is therefore a relationship which must obtain if a model is to make economic sense. When the classical model is in equilibrium the relation does obtain, i.e., the excess demands for both goods and money to hold are zero. Hence the equilibrium solution to the system makes sense. The relationship does not, however, hold out of equilibrium, i.e., is not an identity in this model. Hence, out of equilibrium, the system does not make economic sense. It does not describe a possible form of disequilibrium behaviour. Formally, what this means is that, in the classical model, the Cambridge equation is an independent *constraint*.[26] The model, although it has a determinate static solution, does not display any *market* mechanism that we can look to to correct a disequilibrium. If we want the system to do this, we may abandon the homogeneity assumption, and insert the real-balance terms into the supply and demand functions. Now, if there is an excess supply of, or demand for, money to hold, we shall find a corresponding excess demand for or supply of goods which will explain the revision of the price level. Thus Walras' Law will hold, and Say's Identity will not. The real-balance effect provides an *explanation* of the price level adjustment by which equilibrium is achieved which is not to be found in the classical model. It is not, however, required to obtain consistency in the model.

(5) Suppose, then, that we do insert the real-balance term into the demand and supply functions for goods. As we have repeatedly emphasized, expenditure out of balances must be zero in full equilibrium. Hence, in comparative statics, the real-balance term may immediately be removed from the functions without making any difference whatever to the *solution* of the system. It follows that the functions into which it is inserted must be such that, in its absence, they would not only be consistent but would also be free of the problem of the distribution of real balances. To obtain full static equilibrium without the real-balance effect, we require Say's Identity. To obtain full static equilibrium with the real-balance effect, we require a form of the functions such that, when the real-balance term is removed, Say's Identity holds.[27]

Thus if, for example, we attempt to insert the real-balance term into the functions of our first numerical example, in (2) above, we are at once involved in a genuine contradiction. It will be remembered that the solution of the example involved an endless redistribution of balances. To obtain a stable distribution of balances, it would be necessary to insert the real-balance terms into the functions in such a fashion that desired and actual balances were *never* equal. Indeed, it would be necessary to provide for a permanent discrepancy between desired and actual balances which exactly counterbalanced, in each case, the changes in balances which would otherwise be made. We should thus be attributing to the individuals the following behaviour: the equilibrium level of relative prices would always induce them to spend more (less) than they received, but the non-equilibrium level of their real balances would always exactly prevent them. Thus a system which does not have a full static equilibrium solution cannot be given one by the insertion of the real-balance term.

We may conclude, therefore, that the real-balance effect can usefully be inserted to provide an explanation, absent from the formal classical model, of the market process which leads to monetary equilibrium. If, however, we are concerned only with the full static equilibrium solution of the model, then we do not require the real-balance term.[28]

The Real-Balance Effect in a Classical Production Model[29]

(1) We shall now investigate the model of Part II of Patinkin's book in which there is production as well as exchange. We have already shown, in part one of this paper, how equilibrium in the goods market, the equilibrium level of real balances, and the price level are determined. So far, however, real income has been taken as given. It is now determined in accordance with purely classical assumptions. Patinkin assumes an upward sloping curve of labour as a function of *real* wages, and a downward sloping demand curve for labour, also as a function of *real* wages. As the stock of capital is fixed,[30] and perfect competition is assumed, the demand curve is the real marginal product curve of labour. The equilibrium levels of employment and real income are *uniquely* determined by the intersection of these two curves. A bond market is now added to the model. Individuals may now divide their resources between spending on consumption (a flow), buying bonds (a flow), and holding real balances (a stock). The bonds are supplied by firms which are also assumed to have a transactions demand for balances. The proceeds of the sale of bonds may be used either to increase balances or to finance new investment. The rate of interest equates the demand for with the supply of bonds.

We now come to a source of considerable confusion. In full equilibrium, as before, individuals must be neither adding to, nor subtracting from, their balances. In full equilibrium, therefore, income is divided only between consumption and purchases of new bonds, i.e., the whole of current saving is necessarily devoted to the purchase of bonds.[31] Similarly, if the balances of firms are in equilibrium, the whole proceeds of the sale of bonds must be devoted to investment. It follows that, if balance equilibrium obtains, i.e., if the price level is in equilibrium, equality of saving and investment, and equality of supply of and demand for bonds, are alternative statements of the same equilibrium condition. Patinkin, however, writes (*Money, Interest, and Prices*, p. 188):

> It must finally be emphasized that the savings-investment condition is *not* an alternative statement of the equilibrium condition in the bond market. In particular, an act of saving is not necessarily an act of demanding bonds; for the funds withdrawn from consumption might be added instead to cash balances. Conversely, the demand for bonds might be at the expense of cash balances, instead of at the expense of consumption. Similarly, an act of investment is not necessarily an act of supplying bonds; for the funds for the investment program might be forthcoming instead from cash balances. Conversely, the supply of bonds might be for the purpose of adding to cash balances and not for financing investment.

It seems that Patinkin is again thinking only in terms of a weekly equilibrium.

The main characteristics of the model are now apparent: since, in full equilibrium, income is divided between consumption and the purchase of bonds, and since expenditure on bonds flows entirely into investment, equilibrium expenditure cannot diverge from the full-employment level of income determined in the labour market. Consider what happens in this model if people wish to reduce their present level of consumption. They may either buy more bonds or endeavour to add to their real balances. In the first case, the increased supply of saving flows into investment, and there cannot be any change in equilibrium total real expenditure. In the second case, the reduced demand for goods simply reduces the price level until the real value of the nominal balances is raised to the desired level. There is no change in real consumption or saving: again the equilibrium level of total real expenditure is unchanged. Thus the crucial assumptions in Patinkin's model are that the levels of income and employment are uniquely determined by the real forces in the labour market, and that the rate of interest is free to equate saving and investment at any level of income so determined. If a unique equilibrium condition is specified for the labour market, and if the equilibrium level of employment is defined as full employment, it follows tautologically[32] that equilibrium in the model requires full employment.

Let us consider how the full equilibrium conditions of Patinkin's model may be illustrated in a 45° diagram. In Figure 5 the C curve relating households' consumption to their income is drawn on the assumption that their balances are fully adjusted to each level of income. The vertical distance between the C curve and the 45° line then measures their desired bond purchases. When real balances held by firms are in full equilibrium, equilibrium in the bond market requires that firms spend on investment exactly the amount

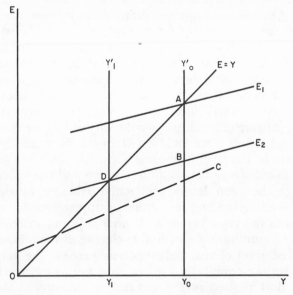

Figure 5.

saved by households. It follows that, when balances are fully adjusted and the bond market is in equilibrium, the addition of the firms' demand curve for investment goods to the households' demand curve yields an aggregate demand curve which coincides throughout with the 45° line. The equilibrium level of income is determined in the labour market; and *any* level of income determined in the labour market (such as OY_0) yields an equilibrium here (where the perpendicular to $Y°$ intersects the 45° line). This construction is used by Patinkin (*ibid.*, p. 249) to illustrate a classical model in which ". . . regardless of the rate of interest and level of prices, the total demand of households and firms for commodities is always equal to the total income of the economy" (Say's Identity). He then argues that, if account is taken of the real-balance effect and the "aggregate supply curve," the classical position is seen to depend ". . . *not* on any special form of the aggregate demand function, but on the assumption that this function—whatever its form—is sufficiently sensitive to price and interest variations . . ." to ensure full employment (pp. 249–50, our italics). He accordingly draws an aggregate demand function, Keynesian in appearance, of less than unit slope.[33] Since this differs from the presentation of the model which we gave above, we must see how it is in fact obtained.

Suppose that we start from a position of full equilibrium, such as A in Figure 5, and that the level of income is then varied. Then the curve E_1 traces desired aggregate expenditure when the rate of interest and the price level, and therefore real balances, are held constant. On the assumptions that, when income rises, neither household consumption nor bond purchases rise to the equilibrium level appropriate to the new level of income until balances have been adjusted, and that firms' investment does not rise to the new equilibrium level until their balances have been adjusted, the E_1 curve has a slope of less than unity. There is, of course, an E curve through every point on the 45° line. Each curve shows how desired aggregate expenditure would vary if income varied while interest and prices were held constant at the equilibrium level appropriate to the level of income at which the E curve cuts the 45° line. The distance between the E curve and the 45° line measures the gap between desired and actual balances *plus* the gap between desired saving and investment. Suppose that we start from a position of full equilibrium at D on $Y_1 Y_1'$, and increase income to OY_0 by assuming, e.g., a suitable change in the labour market. The desired level of real balances now exceeds the actual level, hence to restore equilibrium prices must fall as income rises, and *vice versa*. Both desired saving and desired investment also rise, so that the gap between the two may be positive or negative, and the change in the rate of interest required to restore equilibrium may be in either direction.[34] The distance AB measures the amount by which desired expenditure falls short of the new level of income. The disequilibrium is corrected *not* by moving along the "aggregate demand curve" with changing income until the 45° line is reached, but by moving along the income line $Y_0 Y_0'$ by changing the price level and the rate of interest until the position A is reached.

(2) Patinkin attempts many comparisons with, and criticisms of, Keynesian analysis. It will be apparent that his model cannot be used to "validate" or "invalidate" the Keynesian model, which is simply different. Patinkin, however, argues that his analysis

> . . . forces upon Keynesian economics the abandonment of the once-revolutionary "diagonal-cross" diagram [the familiar 45° diagram] with which it swept its way into the textbooks. It compels it to realize that this diagram takes account neither of the supply side of the commodity market nor of the real-balance effect which its excess over the demand side generates. It therefore compels it to concede that . . . the intersection of the aggregate demand curve . . . with the 45° diagonal . . . does not imply that there exist no automatic market forces to push real income up from the unemployment level . . . Indeed, it compels it to accept the classical contention that such forces not only exist, but even succeed eventually in raising income to the full-employment level . . . [35]

So far as we know, a model can be usefully criticised on only two grounds, its consistency and its empirical relevance. A model can of course be constructed that includes features omitted from the Keynesian model. Which model is to be used, and for what problems, is then a matter for empirical investigation: no conclusion can be reached *a priori* that one model is "better" than another or "forces the abandonment" of another.

Patinkin actually appears to rest this conclusion on three particular arguments.[36]

(i) The effect on "the" aggregate demand function of the real-balance effect. This has been extensively explored. What has not been explored is the result of inserting the real-balance effect into a (Keynesian) model from which unemployment equilibrium was not *already* excluded by the assumptions about the labour market.

(ii) An argument about the Keynesian labour market which we must now consider. Patinkin argues that, since unemployment in his model can occur if the equilibrium conditions in the labour market are not satisfied, unemployment could occur in a Keynesian model for the same reason (pp. 237–39). Hence, he argues, the Keynesian labour supply function (perfectly elastic over a range at the ruling money wage rate) can be replaced by the classical labour supply function (upward sloping against real wages). If this is done it follows, as is well known, that equilibrium involved full employment.[37] The argument that this shows that the Keynesian analysis (for the case of fixed money wages) should be *abandoned* is a *non sequitur*.

(iii) That ". . . Keynesian economics is the economics of unemployment *dis*equilibrium" (p. 235, italics in original). Let us see what this might mean.

(*a*) That the Keynesian model has been misunderstood, and that unemployment equilibrium cannot in fact be obtained in it. This does not appear to be Patinkin's case.

(*b*) That, since unemployment can occur only in disequilibrium in the classical model, it can occur only in disequilibrium in any model. This is a *non sequitur*.

(*c*) That, in Patinkin's opinion, unemployment could not be permanent in the real world. This, whether or not it is true, can establish nothing about either the consistency of a short-run static model or its usefulness in explaining unemployment when unemployment does occur.

(*d*) That a dynamic model might be constructed in which unemployment was not permanent. Again, this establishes nothing about the consistency or relevance of a static model.

The claim that Keynesian economics is the economics of "unemployment *dis*equilibrium" cannot be established on any of these interpretations. "Equilibrium" is, in any case, nothing but the short-hand for the set of values of the variables that satisfies the equations of the given model.

There are many strands to Patinkin's argument,[38] some of which have doubtless eluded us. It is certain, however, that one model cannot be used to invalidate another. A consistent model may be constructed in which equilibrium can obtain with fixed money wages and unemployment. Another consistent model may be constructed in which fixed money wages lead to disequilibrium and unemployment. The question of which model is to be preferred, and in what circumstances, is one for empirical rather than *a priori* investigation.

NOTES

1. J. R. Hicks, *Value and Capital*, 2nd ed. (London 1939), p. 132.
2. Each individual is assumed throughout the analysis to receive the same bundle of goods at the beginning of each week. The total income of the community is consumed each week, i.e., no stocks of goods are carried forward from week to week.
3. It is always necessary, but not always easy, to provide a motive for the stock demand for money without which its marginal utility and hence its price would be zero. Patinkin endeavours to solve this problem by constructing an elaborate system of random payments in which a balance is required to provide security against the risk of default caused by the lack of synchronization between payments and receipts. There are some awkward problems involved: it is difficult to make the transition from a demand for security in Patinkin's model, in which the security provided by balances of given size depends non-linearly upon the volume of the individual's transactions, to a unique relationship between total resources and desired balances. These problems were the subject of a paper circulated to the members of Professor Robbins' seminar by G. C. Archibald in January 1957. In the present paper we merely assume that the individual's tastes are such that the allocation of his total resources between consumption and balances depends uniquely on the amount of his total resources. This means that the demand for balances depends on income *and* existing balances. It is one of the purposes of this section to show that a model based on this assumption produces, in full equilibrium, results identical with those which follow from the more usual assumption that the demand for balances is a function of income only.
4. It will be noticed that, if real income is constant, the budget line can move only if real balances change, while real balances change either if consumption is not equal to income or if the price level changes.
5. If all individuals have identical linear expansion paths, then balances can be redistributed until full stock equilibrium is reached without variation in the price level.

6. We cannot assume that relative prices are constant in this process. We are therefore involved in an index number problem in measuring *G* and *H*. The argument of the text, however, does not depend on the assumption of constant relative prices, although, strictly speaking, the graphical illustration does.

7. Don Patinkin, *Money, Interest, and Prices: An Integration of Monetary and Value Theory*, 1st ed. (Illinois 1956), Chapter 3, section 4.

8. Cf. *ibid.*, p. 41.

9. See particularly *ibid.*, Chapter 3, sections 5 and 6.

10. If the individual is not in full equilibrium, he changes his consumption from week to week as his balances change. Similarly if the market is not in full equilibrium, balances and expenditure change from week to week. If, however, real balances are changed by a change in the money stock without distribution effects when the market is in full equilibrium, equilibrium is restored by the *tâtonnement alone*. Thus correction of a disequilibrium in balances only requires a change in individuals' real consumption when it is necessary to redistribute balances among the individuals in the market. When the disequilibrium can be corrected by a change in the price level alone, then no one in fact alters consumption.

11. Thus we cannot accept Patinkin's claim that the real-balance effect ". . . is the *sine qua non* of monetary theory" (*op. cit.*, p. 22).

12. O. Lange, "Say's Law: A Restatement and a Criticism," in *Studies in Mathematical Economics and Econometrics* (Chicago 1942), pp. 49–68.

13. Patinkin, "The Indeterminacy of Absolute Prices in Classical Economic Theory," *Econometrica*, Vol. 17 (January 1949), and "The Invalidity of Classical Monetary Theory," *Econometrica*, Vol. 19 (April 1951). For criticism see W. Braddock Hickman, "The Determinacy of Absolute Prices in Classical Economic Theory," Wassily Leontief, "The Consistency of the Classical Theory of Money and Prices," and Cecil G. Phipps, "A Note on Patinkin's 'Relative Prices,' " all in *Econometrica*, Vol. 18 (January 1950). See also the later article by S. Valavanis, "A Denial of Patinkin's Contradiction," *Kyklos*, Fasc. 4 (1955).

14. Karl Brunner, "Inconsistency and Indeterminacy in Classical Economics," *Econometrica*, Vol. 19 (April 1951), and G. S. Becker and W. J. Baumol, "The Classical Monetary Theory: The Outcome of the Discussion," *Economica*, Vol. 19 (November 1952). For a full bibliography of the controversy see Patinkin, *Money, Interest, and Prices*, 1st ed., pp. 454–59 note 1; and for a critical bibliography see Valavanis, *op. cit.*

15. Patinkin, *Money, Interest, and Prices*, 1st ed., p. 110.

16. Cf. Patinkin, Mathematical Appendix 7a to *Money, Interest, and Prices*, 1st ed., pp. 333–35, and "The Invalidity of Classical Monetary Theory," p. 138.

17. Cf. Patinkin, *Money, Interest, and Prices*, 1st ed., pp. 108–9. These arguments for inconsistency are accepted by Becker and Baumol, *op. cit.*, sections II and III.

18. See Becker and Baumol, *op. cit.*, note 1, p. 360, where, after repeating the argument for inconsistency outlined above, they merely assert that "Hickman's system . . . must be in error."

19. Hickman, *op. cit.*, p. 14.

20. We follow Lange, *op. cit.*, in our use of the terms Walras' Law and Say's Law. Consider an economy with $n - 1$ goods and money. Walras' Law is the identity $\sum_{i=1}^{n-1} p_i S_i + p_n S_n \equiv \sum_{i=1}^{n-1} p_i D_i + p_n D_n$, i.e., total supply of goods and money is identical with total demand for goods and money. Say's Law is the identity $\sum_{i=1}^{n-1} p_i S_i \equiv \sum_{i=1}^{n-1} p_i D_i$, i.e., total supply of goods is identical with total demand for goods. In the text we call this relation Say's Identity.

21. Patinkin, *Money, Interest, and Prices*, 1st ed., p. 121, writes that ". . . Say's Identity and the 'homogeneity postulate' are logically equivalent properties . . . " From the fact that, in the example discussed above, we had the latter without the former, it can be seen that this is mistaken.

22. This follows from the Say's Identity requirement that the value of Good I demanded by each individual equal the value of Good II supplied by him.

23. We may interpret this graphically as follows: consistency only requires that the two pairs of supply and demand curves intersect at the same relative price; thus if the curves D_1 and S_1 intersect at the price z, any pair D_2 and S_2 which intersect at the same price are consistent whatever the quantity traded at this price. By our new requirement, given the curves D_1 and S_1, we are restricted to the single pair D_2 and S_2, which not only intersect at the same price, but also satisfy the condition that the values of the quantities traded in each market be identical.

24.
$$X_1 \equiv d_1 \frac{p_2}{p_1} - s_1 \frac{p_1}{p_2} = 0;$$

$$X_2 \equiv s_1 \frac{p_1^2}{p_2} - d_1 = 0;$$

and

$$X_3 \equiv p_1 X_1 + p_2 X_2 \equiv d_1 p_2 - s_1 \frac{p_1^2}{p_2} + s_1 \frac{p_1^2}{p_2} - d_1 p_2 \equiv 0.$$

25. This point has been clearly argued by Valavanis, *op. cit.*

26. This point is made by both Hickman and Valavanis. To ask how the system *behaves* out of monetary equilibrium is to ask how a system behaves when a constraint is violated.

27. The real-balance term Patinkin inserts into his functions is $\dfrac{M_0}{p}$, where M_0 is the given stock of money and p the price level. Since, as we have shown, behaviour in equilibrium does not depend upon the level of $\dfrac{M_0}{p}$ in this model, this may be misleading. We should write the demands for goods

$$D_i \equiv f_i \left[p_1, \ldots, p_{n-1}, \left(\frac{M_0}{p} - B \right) \right],$$

and the supplies

$$S_i \equiv g_i \left[p_1, \ldots, p_{n-1}, \left(B - \frac{M_0}{p} \right) \right], \qquad (i = 1, \ldots, n - 1),$$

where B is the desired level of real balances and $\dfrac{M_0}{p}$ the actual level.

We now add the equilibrium condition $\dfrac{M_0}{p} - B = 0$. Hence, if we only require the static solution to the system, we may immediately remove the real-balance term from these functions. Thus any properties required in the static solution must be contained in the system when it is written without the real-balance term.

28. Thus we cannot accept Patinkin's claim that the analysis of the real-balance effect provides ". . . the ultimate rigorous validation of the classical theory of money itself" (*Money, Interest, and Prices*, 1st ed., p. 99).

29. Our analysis of the full equilibrium properties of the model described in this section was subsequently shown to contain certain inadequacies. None of these, however, affect the substance of our basic criticism of Patinkin. See R. J. Ball and R. Bodkin, "The Real Balance Effect and Orthodox Demand Theory: A Critique of Archibald and Lipsey," *Review of Economic Studies*, Vol. 28 (October 1960), 44–49, and our own comments in the same issue.

30. This is a short-run model in the sense that net investment has no discernible effect on the stock of capital nor, therefore, on the demand curve for labour.

31. We should notice that, just as there is a unique distribution of the stock of money in full equilibrium, so also is there a unique distribution of the stock of old bonds. Trading in this stock would involve a redistribution of balances among individuals incompatible with full equilibrium.

32. See Patinkin, *Money, Interest, and Prices*, 1st ed., pp. 213–14.

33. *Ibid.*, pp. 131–32 and Figure 11.

34. Patinkin, *ibid.*, p. 130, puts the level of income into the investment function. If it is omitted, then the rate of interest must fall as income rises unless a zero increase in saving is assumed.

35. *Ibid.*, p. 237. Words omitted refer only to a diagram in Patinkin's book.

36. The first is the subject of extensive discussion; the second directly follows this conclusion in Patinkin's text; and the third immediately precedes it.

37. If we alter an otherwise Keynesian model by specifying an upward-sloping supply curve of labour plotted against the real wage rate, we make underemployment equilibrium impossible. This is one of the models considered by F. Modigliani, "Liquidity Preference and the Theory of Interest and Money," *Econometrica* (1944), reprinted in *Readings in Monetary Theory* (American Economic Association, 1952).

38. See the whole of Patinkin's Chapters 13 and 14, *Money, Interest, and Prices*.

13 *Wealth, Saving, and the Rate of Interest*

Lloyd A. Metzler *University of Chicago*

I

The fundamental thesis of classical economics, that a free-market economy has an automatic tendency to approach a state of full employment, has been a subject of heated controversy in recent decades. Indeed, after the publication of Keynes's *General Theory* there were many economists who rejected the classical thesis completely on the ground that it contained internal inconsistencies. Today, however, we are witnessing a renaissance of the classical doctrines. In part, the renaissance is attributable to world-wide economic developments since the end of the war, which have been characterized by a high level of demand and by full employment in almost all industrial countries. But the rebirth of classical theory is also attributable, in part, to attempts to reconstruct the classical doctrines along lines which make them immune to the Keynesian criticisms.

The principal architect of the reconstruction is Pigou,[1] but the basic idea of the remodeled classical theory can be found in the works of other economists as well, particularly in the works of Scitovszky[2] and Haberler.[3] The innovation which these economists introduced was a reconsideration, or perhaps I should say an

Reprinted from *Journal of Political Economy*, Vol. 59 (April 1951), 93–116, by permission of the author and The University of Chicago Press. Copyright 1951 by The University of Chicago Press.

elaboration, of the forces determining the quantity of real saving. In the classical theory the amounts of saving and investment out of a full-employment level of income were regarded as functions of the interest rate alone, and the latter was thus the primary governing force of the economic system as a whole. Equilibrium was attained, according to the classical theory, only when the interest rate was such that the quantity of real saving out of a full-employment income was equal to the quantity of real investment.[4] Scitovszky, Pigou, and Haberler retained this basic concept of equilibrium but argued that saving depends upon the real value of privately held wealth as well as upon the interest rate. Other things remaining the same, they said, real saving tends to be smaller and real expenditure for consumption tends to be larger, the larger is the real value of private wealth. For convenience, I shall hereafter use the expression "saving-wealth relation" to designate such a functional connection between current saving and private wealth.

The saving-wealth relation was employed by Pigou and Haberler to defend the classical theory against the criticism of Keynesian economics. In particular, the relation was employed to show that a flexible-wage economy has an automatic tendency to approach a state of full employment, as postulated in the classical theory. On account of the special purpose which it originally served, the saving-wealth relation is now widely considered to be a modification, but not a fundamental change, in the classical theory. Indeed, Haberler even suggests that some sort of functional connection between saving and wealth is implicit in works on economics which preceded the explicit recognition of the saving-wealth relation.[5]

I do not share these views. In my opinion the saving-wealth relation is more nonclassical in its implications than any of the contributions to the subject would lead one to believe. Although the Scitovszky-Pigou-Haberler system resembles the classical system in its tendency toward a state of full employment, it is quite unlike the classical system in other respects, and these other respects have generally been overlooked. The most striking difference between the new system and the classical concerns the interest rate, and this is the subject which I wish to explore in the present paper.

The distinguishing feature of the classical theory of the interest rate is its emphasis upon so-called "real" conditions of demand and supply and its denial of the influence of monetary policy or banking policy. The classical economists believed that there exists a unique interest rate, or a unique pattern of long-term and short-term rates, at which the economic system is in equilibrium and that this unique interest rate cannot be influenced by changes in the quantity of money. The following quotation from Ricardo is representative of the classical opinion:

> Interest for money . . . is not regulated by the rate at which the bank will lend, whether it be 5, 4, or 3 per cent, but by the rate of profits which can be made by the employment of capital, and which is totally independent of the quantity or of the value of money. Whether a bank lent one million, ten million, or a hundred million, they would not permanently alter the market rate of interest; they would alter only the value of money which they thus issued. In one case, ten or twenty times more money might be required to carry on the same business than what might be required in the other.[6]

In contrast to the classical doctrine, the theory of the interest rate implicit in the Scitovszky-Pigou-Haberler system is at least partly a monetary theory, as I shall demonstrate below. In this system there is no single interest rate and no single pattern of rates at which the economy is in equilibrium. Rather, there are an infinite number of different rates capable of performing the equilibrating function, and the particular rate that prevails at any given time depends to a considerable extent upon the policy of the banking authorities. Thus, in salvaging one feature of classical economics—the automatic tendency of the system to approach a state of full employment—Pigou and Haberler have destroyed another feature, namely, the real theory of the interest rate. In this respect Pigou, the archdefender of classical economics, has deserted Mill and Marshall and joined Schumpeter and Keynes![7] Although remnants of the classical, real theory of the interest rate remain, these are over-shadowed, I believe, by the monetary feature which has been added. Moreover, the added feature which transforms the interest rate into a monetary rate is not liquidity preference, as in Keynesian economics, but the saving-wealth relation.

The subsequent analysis will be more understandable, I believe, if I digress from my principal theme long enough to indicate briefly the way in which the saving-wealth relation became prominent in economic theory. For this purpose consider an economic system in which the demand for investment is so low and the supply of saving so high that potential full-employment saving exceeds potential full-employment investment at all positive interest rates. In this event, there is no achievable interest rate which fulfils the classical condition of equilibrium. Whatever the interest rate may be, the demand for goods and services as a whole falls short of productive capacity. This is the Keynesian system in its simplest form. And the outcome of this situation, as envisaged by Keynes, is a cumulative reduction in output and employment, the reduction continuing until potential saving is reduced to the level of potential investment through a reduction in real income.

Suppose, however, that wages and other factor costs tend to fall when unemployment develops. To what extent will the reduction in costs stimulate output and move the system back toward full employment? Keynes argued that a general wage reduction affects output primarily through its influence on the interest rate. Any decline in wages and other costs is likely to result, he asserted, in a corresponding decline in other prices. In real terms, then, the only significant effect of the reduction in wages and other costs is an increase in the real value of money balances which tends, through liquidity preference, to reduce the interest rate. If full-employment saving exceeds full-employment investment at all possible interest rates, however, the reduction in the interest rate cannot conceivably eliminate all the deflationary gap and restore output to the full-employment level. Keynes's theory thus leads to the conclusion that wage-and-cost reductions are not an effective remedy for deficient demand.[8]

Pigou attempted to refute this Keynesian view concerning wage-and-cost reductions, and in doing so he introduced the saving-wealth relation. He suggested that, as wages and prices decline, the resulting increase in the real value of money balances will stimulate demand in a way which is independent of the change in the interest rate. Money balances constitute a part of private wealth, and the increase in the former accordingly implies an increase in the latter. As the real value of private wealth increases, the amount of saving out of a full-employment level of real income tends to decline. In this manner the excess of potential saving over potential investment which accounted for the initial unemployment is eventually eliminated. In the absence of barriers to price-and-cost reductions, the system thus has an automatic tendency to approach a state of full employment, as envisaged in the classical theory. Saving is brought into line with investment not primarily through a reduction of the interest rate but rather through a general deflation and a corresponding increase in the real value of the money supply.

I do not wish to discuss the relevance of the saving-wealth relation to the arguments frequently heard for a policy of over-all flexibility of wages and prices. Other economists have pointed out that the portion of cash balances whose real value is increased by a general deflation normally constitutes a relatively small part of total assets and that an enormous reduction of prices would therefore be required to increase the real value of a country's total wealth by any substantial amount. They have argued, further, that the general increases or decreases in prices and costs required for the successful operation of such a system might easily lead to expectations of additional price increases or decreases which would upset the stability of the whole system.[9] Such questions of economic policy, however, are not the immediate concern of this paper. I mention them here only to avoid a possible misunderstanding of what I shall say later. In what follows, I shall make the most favorable assumptions possible as to the effects of price movements upon the demand for goods and services; I shall ignore the adverse influence of fluctuating prices upon expectations and assume that there is a substantial tendency for saving to decline when the real value of private wealth rises. Given these favorable assumptions, I shall then ask how an economic system containing the saving-wealth relation is related to classical theory.

II

Before describing the theory of interest implicit in the Scitovszky-Pigou-Haberler system, I wish to say something about the meaning of a "monetary" theory of interest rates. A theory is usually regarded as a monetary theory if the economic system envisaged is one in which the equilibrium interest rate, or the equilibrium pattern of rates, can be altered by a change in the quantity of money. Although this definition is satisfactory for most purposes, it is not sufficiently accurate to characterize an economic system containing the saving-wealth relation. It is inadequate, in particular, because it does not indicate the manner in which the quantity of money is altered. As I shall demonstrate below, the influence of a change in the quantity of money in the Scitovszky-Pigou-Haberler system depends not only upon the magnitude of the change but also upon the way in which it is brought about. Some changes in the quantity of money will alter the equilibrium interest rate while others will not.

We may distinguish, I believe, between two fundamentally different types of increase or decrease in the quantity of money. The first type is a change which takes place through open-market transactions of the central bank. The significant feature of this type of change is that it consists of an exchange of one form of asset for another. When money holdings are increased through central-bank purchase of securities, for example, holdings of securities outside the central bank are reduced by a corresponding amount. The second type of change consists of a direct increase or decrease in the money supply without any offsetting changes in private holdings of other assets. The supply of money may be reduced, for example, by a currency reform in which one unit of new money is exchanged for two units of old. Or the supply of money may be reduced by means of a governmental budgetary

surplus, provided that the excess monetary receipts are impounded. In both these examples the supply of money is altered
without altering private holdings of other assets, and it is this
characteristic which distinguishes the second type of monetary
change from the first.

I intend to show in subsequent parts of this paper that the theory
of interest implicit in the Scitovszky-Pigou-Haberler system is a
monetary theory if the change in the quantity of money is of the
first type and a real theory if the change is of the second type.
This means that open-market transactions of the central bank will
have a *permanent* influence on the interest rate at which the system
is in equilibrium, even after the bank has stopped its purchases or
sales of securities. If the change in the quantity of money does not
affect the private holdings of other assets, however, it will have
no lasting influence on the interest rate. With respect to the rate
of interest, the Scitovszky-Pigou-Haberler theory thus occupies an
intermediate position between the classical theory and the Keynesian. The classical theory is a real theory of the interest rate from
the point of view of both types of monetary change. According to
the classical doctrine, neither a central-bank purchase or sale of
securities nor an arbitrary increase or decrease in the quantity of
money can have any effect upon the interest rate at which the
economic system returns to equilibrium. As I have indicated above,
the equilibrium interest rate of the classical theory is the rate at
which full-employment potential saving is equal to full-employment potential investment, and this equilibrium rate is independent of both the quantity of money and the policy of the
central bank. The classical theory, then, is a nonmonetary or real
theory of the interest rate, regardless of whether the monetary
disturbance is of the first type or the second type.

At the other extreme is Keynes's theory, which is a purely monetary theory from the point of view of either type of monetary disturbance. According to Keynes, the rate of interest is governed
largely by the decisions of asset-holders concerning the proportions
in which they wish to hold money and securities; that is, in Keynes's
terminology, the rate is determined by liquidity preference.[10]
Other things remaining unchanged, the desired ratio between
money and securities tends to rise with a fall in the interest rate,
and the equilibrium interest rate is the one at which the desired
ratio of money to securities corresponds to the actual ratio. From
this it follows that any monetary or banking policy which increases
the actual quantity of money relative to the actual quantity of
securities will reduce the interest rate at which the system is in
equilibrium. Thus, both an arbitrary increase in the quantity of
money (a disturbance of the second type) and an increase in the

quantity of money through a limited and temporary purchase of securities by the central bank (a disturbance of the first type) will reduce the equilibrium interest rate in Keynes's system.

This brief and somewhat elliptical summary of the Keynesian and classical theories of the interest rate is intended to emphasize the polar positions which the two theories occupy, relative to the theory implicit in the Scitovszky-Pigou-Haberler system. The equilibrium interest rate in the classical theory is independent of monetary disturbances, regardless of whether such disturbances are of the first type or the second type. The equilibrium interest rate in Keynes's theory, on the other hand, can be permanently altered by a monetary disturbance of either type. In short, the classical theory is a real theory from the point of view of either type of disturbance, while the Keynesian theory is a monetary theory from the point of view of either type. The polar positions of the two theories explain, I believe, why no distinction has been made in the past between the two types of monetary disturbance. As I shall demonstrate below, however, the theory of the interest rate implicit in the Scitovszky-Pigou-Haberler system is intermediate between the classical theory and the Keynesian theory. It is a monetary theory from the point of view of the first type of monetary disturbance and a real theory from the point of view of the second type. But all this will, I hope, become clear as we proceed.

III

The economic system which will be investigated below is one in which the capital market is subject to three main influences: (1) the influence of current saving and investment, as in the classical or neoclassical theory; (2) the influence of decisions concerning the holding of cash or securities, as in Keynes's doctrine of liquidity preference; and (3) the influence of wealth on current saving, as in the Scitovszky-Pigou-Haberler reconstruction of the classical theory. I assume that the equilibrium rate of interest, or the equilibrium pattern of rates, is determined by the interplay of these three influences.

At the outset I wish to make a number of simplifying assumptions. Although these assumptions are somewhat unrealistic, few of them are absolutely essential, and most of them could be substantially modified without altering any of my principal results. I assume, in the first place, that the economy with which we are dealing is a closed economy with a fixed amount of labor. Second, I assume that the wage rate tends to rise whenever the demand for labor is greater than the fixed supply and to fall whenever the demand is smaller than the fixed supply. Third, I assume that all agents of production except labor are produced means of production and that all production is carried on at constant returns to scale. Under these conditions the relative prices of all commodities and services are determinate and independent of the commodity composition of the national income. We can therefore speak unambiguously of a rate of total output, or of a level of national income, at which the economy's resources are fully employed. Fourth, I assume that owners of private wealth hold such wealth in only two forms, money (including demand deposits) and common stock, and that all common stock involves approximately the same degree of risk.[11] Fifth, I assume that the central bank is legally authorized to buy and sell the common stock held by the owners of private wealth and that this common stock constitutes the only non-monetary asset of the banking system.

Given these assumptions, one can readily construct a simple geometric interpretation of the forces governing the interest rate. These forces will operate in two different markets: a market for goods and services as a whole and a market for securities. Consider, first, the market for goods and services. Stability of the general price level in the goods-and-services market obviously requires that the total demand arising from a full-employment level of real income shall be equal to the economy's productive capacity; and this is equivalent to the requirement that potential saving out of a full-employment level of income shall be equal to potential investment. If potential investment at full employment exceeds potential saving, the demand for goods and services as a whole exceeds full-employment output; prices and costs accordingly tend to rise. If potential full-employment investment falls short of potential full-employment saving, on the other hand, this implies that the demand for goods and services as a whole falls short of full-employment output. Hence prices and costs tend to fall.

In the classical theory real saving and real investment were functions of a single variable—the interest rate—and the economy was assumed to be in equilibrium at only one rate. In the theory now being investigated, however, the amount of real saving at full employment is regarded as a function of two variables—the interest rate and the real value of wealth in the hands of the savers. As soon as the second variable is introduced, the concept of a single interest rate at which the goods-and-services market is in equilibrium loses its meaning. In place of the equilibrium rate of classical theory, we now have a schedule of rates, or a functional relation between the interest rate and the real value of private wealth.

In order to see how such a schedule can be derived, suppose that on a certain date the total of all privately held wealth—money and securities combined—has a certain real value. If the value of private wealth is fixed, saving may be regarded as a function of the rate of interest alone, and I shall assume that with this given saving schedule a rate of interest can be found at which full-employment saving is equal to full-employment investment. Consider, now, what would happen if the interest rate were arbitrarily increased above its equilibrium level. At the higher interest rate potential saving out of a full-employment income would exceed potential investment, which means that, other things remaining the same, the community's demand for goods and services would fall short of its capacity to produce. In other words, the increase in the rate of interest, taken by itself, would bring about a deflationary gap. But if the community's combined holdings of money and securities were increased in some manner at the same time that the rate of interest were raised, then the deflationary gap might be avoided. The increase in asset holdings would tend to reduce the amount of saving corresponding to any given rate of interest, thereby off-setting, or perhaps more than offsetting, the tendency toward excessive saving attributable to the rise in the rate of interest. The rise in the rate of interest would reduce investment, but the in-crease in the value of private wealth would reduce saving; and it is thus conceivable that full-employment potential saving might equal potential investment at the higher interest rate as well as at the lower rate.

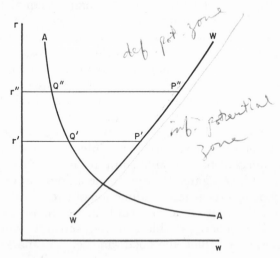

Figure 1.

Many other combinations of the interest rate and the real value of private wealth will fulfil the condition that full-employment saving equals full-employment investment, and we may accord-ingly conceive of a schedule or a functional relation indicating what the real value of private wealth would have to be, for many different interest rates, in order to make the community's demand for goods and services as a whole equal its capacity to produce. The real value of private wealth which fulfils this condition will be an increasing function of the rate of interest. Such a function is plotted as the line *WW* in Figure 1. For convenience, *WW* will be called the "wealth-requirements schedule." At any point on this line potential saving out of full-employment income is equal to potential investment. But, as we move upward and to the right along the line, both saving and investment decline. Investment declines because of the rise in the interest rate, while saving declines because of the increase in the real value of private wealth. Any point below *WW* in Figure 1 represents a point of inflationary potential. At such a point the rate of interest is too low, given the value of private wealth, to bring about an equality between full-employment saving and investment. The demand for goods and services thus exceeds capacity, and prices tend to rise. In the same way one can show that any point *above* *WW* represents a point of *de*flationary potential. It follows that the demand for goods and services is equal to the economy's productive capacity only for combinations of the interest rate and the value of private wealth lying on *WW*.

The wealth-requirements schedule has been developed, above, in terms of the real value of private wealth as a whole and no distinction has been made between private holdings of money and private holdings of securities. Such a distinction has thus far been unnecessary because saving was assumed to be a function of *total* asset holdings and not of the *composition* of these assets. When we later discuss the securities market, however, we shall find that the division of total assets between money and securities is the decisive factor in this market. Our later task will accordingly be simplified if the wealth-requirements schedule can be broken down into its two component parts, namely, money and common stock.

If the community holds a given amount of common stock, the real value of these stock holdings will obviously depend upon the interest rate. Indeed, the interest rate itself is nothing more than the yield of the stock, and this yield, in turn, is the ratio of the income earned by the stock to its market price. In the short run the income earned by the common stock is a given amount, determined by the fixed supplies of the various agents of production; and this means that the yield, or the rate of interest, varies inversely with the real value of the stock. To put the matter the other way round, we may say that the real value of the given common stock is inversely related to the prevailing rate of interest. The higher the rate of interest, the lower the real value of common-stock holdings and conversely. In Figure 1 the value of the community's security holdings is expressed as such a function of the interest rate by the line AA.

I wish to show, now, how the wealth-requirements schedule, WW, can be expressed in terms of money and interest rates rather than in terms of total wealth and interest rates. For this purpose, suppose that the interest rate is temporarily set at r'' in Figure 1. The wealth-requirements schedule tells us that, in order to prevent an excess or deficiency of demand from developing in the goods-and-services market at this interest rate, the community's holdings of money and securities combined will have to be $r''P''$. But the value of securities alone, at an interest rate of r'', is the distance $r''Q''$ in Figure 1. If the community is to have a sufficient amount of total assets to maintain a balance between demand and supply in the goods-and-services market, its holdings of money will therefore have to equal the difference between $r''P''$ and $r''Q''$, or $Q''P''$. This difference is plotted in Figure 2 as the line $r''T''$. A similar construction for a rate of interest r' carries over the distance $Q'P'$ of Figure 1 to $r'T'$ of Figure 2. The line MM of Figure 2 is the locus of all such points as T' and T''. Given the community's private holdings of securities, MM indicates the amount of money which will have to be held, at any particular interest rate, in order to keep the amount of saving out of full-employment income equal to the amount of investment. For brevity, MM will be called the "money-requirements schedule." The money-requirements schedule is thus the horizontal difference between the wealth-requirements schedule, WW, and the schedule of the real value of securities, AA.

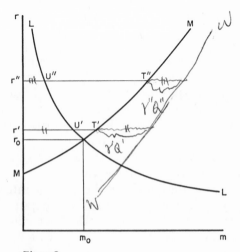

Figure 2.

IV

The line MM of Figure 2, like WW of Figure 1, indicates the conditions needed to maintain a balance between supply and demand in the market for currently produced goods and services. In addition to this goods-and-services market, the market for securities must also be taken into account. The entire economic system cannot be in equilibrium unless the latter market, as well as the former, has reached a balanced position. The market for *new* securities has already been allowed for, by implication, in the preceding discussion of saving and investment; in the absence of hoarding, equality between saving and investment implies equality between the supply of and the demand for new securities. But this new-securities market is usually a relatively small part of the total securities market; in many countries, indeed, the value of new securities offered on the market in a given year is an exceedingly small fraction of the value of previously issued, or old, securities. This means that decisions of asset-holders to augment or reduce their stocks of old securities will frequently exert a much greater influence on the rate of interest than will discrepancies between current saving and current investment. The old-securities market must therefore be taken into account, along with the market for goods and services as a whole, in order to complete the description of interest rates given by Figures 1 and 2.

The existing stock of securities will influence security prices and the rate of interest only if asset-holders, on balance, decide to increase or decrease their holdings of securities, that is, only if the typical asset-holder wishes to substitute additional money for part of his security holdings or additional securities for part of his money holdings. Decisions of this sort depend largely upon the *composition* rather than the size of asset portfolios. Thus, in deciding whether to buy or sell securities, the typical asset-holder compares the existing ratio between his money holdings and his security holdings with the ratio which he regards as satisfactory under the given economic conditions. The degree of his actual liquidity, compared with a sort of optimum liquidity, governs his actions in the securities market.

I shall follow Keynes in assuming that, other things remaining the same, the typical asset-holder wishes to increase his liquidity as the rate of interest falls. Unless the banking authorities intervene, however, private asset-holders cannot, on balance, increase or decrease their holdings of old securities; as of a given moment of time, both the number of shares of stock and the quantity of money in private hands are fixed quantities. This means that, if the prevailing money-securities ratio differs from the desired ratio, security prices and the rate of interest must continue to change until the desired ratio is brought into line with the prevailing ratio; in short, the demand must be adjusted to the existing supply through appropriate movements in the rate of interest.

The influence of liquidity preference may be examined from another direction, and for present purposes this alternative point of view is more convenient. Instead of starting with a fixed amount of securities and a fixed quantity of money and asking how the rate of interest will be adjusted so that demand will equal supply, we may start with a fixed amount of securities and a fixed interest rate and ask what the total money holdings would have to be in order to satisfy the typical asset-holder with his money-securities ratio. By assuming a number of different interest rates and making similar calculations for each, a liquidity-preference schedule, or a demand-for-money schedule, can thus be built up. Suppose, for example, that, at an interest rate of r'' (Figure 1), the typical asset-holder wishes to hold money in an amount equal to two-thirds the value of his security holdings. At this interest rate the security holdings of the community as a whole have a real value of $r''Q''$, as shown in Figure 1. It follows that asset-holders as a group will attempt to alter their security holdings and hence alter the rate of interest, unless the real value of money holdings amounts to two-thirds of $r''Q''$. Let the point U'' in Figure 2 be chosen so as to make $r''U''$ equal to two-thirds of $r''Q''$. Suppose, now, that, when the interest rate falls to r', the typical asset-holder wishes to hold money equal to the full value of his securities. The value of total securities at an interest rate of r' is $r'Q'$ (Figure 1), and the condition of equilibrium in the old-securities market requires that money holdings shall equal this same amount. We may therefore select a point, U', in Figure 2 such that $r'U'$ is equal to $r'Q'$. The liquidity-preference schedule, LL, in Figure 2 is the locus of all such points as U'' and U'; it shows what the community's holdings of money would have to be, at any given interest rate, in order to create a proper balance between cash and securities.

From the construction of the diagram it is apparent that there are two reasons why the demand for money, LL (Figure 2), tends to rise as the rate of interest falls. First, the typical asset-holder usually wants to hold a larger ratio of cash to securities at low interest rates than at high rates. And, second, the real value of securities, the denominator of the cash-securities ratio, is increased by a fall in the interest rate. In most discussions of liquidity preference only the first of these reasons is taken into account, but the second may be equally important.[12]

V

I have now discussed two different functional relations between the rate of interest and the real quantity of money; the first of these I called a money-requirements schedule, while the second is the usual liquidity-preference schedule. The money-requirements schedule represents all combinations of money balances and the rate of interest for which the community's demand for goods and services as a whole is exactly equal to its capacity to produce. At any point not on this schedule there is either an excess or a deficiency of demand and consequently a tendency for prices and costs to rise or fall. The money-requirements schedule, MM, thus indicates the possible combinations of the interest rate and the quantity of real cash balances which will maintain over-all price equilibrium in the goods-and-services market. The liquidity-preference schedule, on the other hand, describes the conditions of price equilibrium in the *securities* market. If the actual quantity of real cash balances lies on LL, there will be no tendency for asset-holders as a whole to attempt to shift from securities to cash or from cash to securities and, accordingly, no tendency for the price of securities or the rate of interest to change. At any point *not* on LL, however, the price of securities will either rise or fall, depending upon whether the demand for cash at the prevailing interest rate is smaller or greater than the actual amount.

From Figure 2 it is now apparent that only one combination of the interest rate and the real value of money balances will satisfy the conditions of equilibrium in both the goods-and-services market and the securities market. I have denoted this combination by the two letters r_0 and m_0. If all prices, including wages and the costs of other agents of production, tend to rise when demand exceeds supply and to fall when supply exceeds demand, the combination r_0 and m_0 is the one toward which the economic system will gravitate. The nature of this market mechanism will be clarified, I believe, if we consider what happens to the system when the interest rate and the real value of money balances differ from the equilibrium combination r_0 and m_0.

This is done in Figure 3, where I have reproduced the essential features of Figure 2. The points B, C, D, and E in Figure 3 represent four points which do not lie on either the liquidity-preference schedule or the money-requirements schedule. Suppose, first, that the actual situation with regard to the rate of interest and the real value of cash balances at a given moment of time can be represented by the point B. What happens, in this event, to the variables of our system? The liquidity-preference schedule shows that, at the rate of interest represented by B, the community's demand for real money balances falls short of actual money holdings. Asset-holders accordingly attempt to substitute securities for their excess cash holdings, thereby forcing up security prices and reducing the rate of interest. Moreover, in the situation B the goods-and-services market as well as the securities market is out of balance. The

diagram shows that, at the prevailing interest rate, money holdings are too large to bring about an equality between full-employment saving and full-employment investment. Saving is below the
equilibrium level because of the excessive cash holdings, and the
demand for goods and services thus exceeds the economy's capacity
to produce. As a result, prices tend to rise, and the real value of
money balances is reduced. The movements in the rate of interest
and in the real value of money balances are indicated by the short
arrows emanating from point *B*.

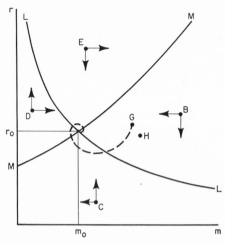

Figure 3.

By similar reasoning one can demonstrate that, at point *C*,
security prices tend to fall, and the interest rate is correspondingly
increased, while the prices of goods and services rise and the real
value of cash balances is reduced. Likewise, at *D*, security prices
fall, the rate of interest is increased, commodity prices and wages
fall, and the real value of cash balances tends to rise. Finally, if the
actual position of the variables is at *E*, security prices rise, the interest rate is reduced, commodity prices fall, and the real value
of cash balances is thus increased. Movements of the variables in
the neighborhood of the points *C*, *D*, and *E* have again been indicated by arrows.

Figure 3 demonstrates that when the economic system is out of
balance at least one force is always operating to bring the variables
of the system closer to the equilibrium point, r_0, m_0. The other
force, indicated by the second of the two arrows at each of the
points *B*, *C*, *D*, and *E*, operates in such a way as to impart a circular
or cyclical movement to the variables. This suggests that, if the rate
of interest and the quantity of real cash balances were initially at
some nonequilibrium point such as *G*, the approach to equilibrium

might be a spiral or damped cycle like the one depicted in Figure 3. Although such a damped cycle is possible, it is not inevitable, as I shall demonstrate in the Appendix. In any event, I believe it is highly unlikely that the cyclical movement implied by Figure 3 bears any close resemblance to the typical observed business cycle. Most observed cycles are cycles of output and employment, whereas the cycle depicted in Figure 3 is largely a cycle of prices and interest rates.[13] I have presented the dynamic problem concerning the movements of prices and interest rates merely to show the tendency of the system to approach an equilibrium position and not as a contribution to the theory of business cycles.

VI

I have now shown that the market for goods and services and the market for securities can be in equilibrium simultaneously only at the point r_0, m_0 and that the economic system has an automatic tendency to approach this equilibrium. Superficially, this suggests a close analogy between the rate of interest, r_0, and the classical concept of the equilibrium rate. Like the equilibrium rate of classical theory, the rate r_0 is the only one compatible, under the assumed conditions, with equilibrium of the economic system as a whole; that is, r_0 is the only rate which satisfies both the liquidity-preference requirement and the requirement that full-employment saving shall be equal to full-employment investment. Why, then, does r_0 not have as much claim to be regarded as a real rate as does the classical concept of the real rate of interest?

Whether the rate r_0 is a real rate or a monetary rate depends, as I have indicated earlier, upon the nature of the monetary disturbance. If the disturbance is of the first type—that is, if it is a change in the quantity of money associated with the purchase or sale of securities by the central bank—it will alter some of the functional relations of Figures 1 and 2 and will accordingly change the equilibrium interest rate. The rate r_0 must therefore be regarded as a monetary rate from the point of view of monetary disturbances of this sort. On the other hand, if the monetary disturbance is of the second type, which consists of an increase or decrease in the quantity of money without any offsetting changes in other assets, then it will not alter the functional relations of Figures 1, 2, and 3 and will not permanently change the interest rate. The rate r_0 is thus a real rate from the point of view of monetary disturbances of the second type. Because it is simple to describe, I shall first consider a monetary disturbance of the second type.

Suppose that the economic system is initially in equilibrium at a rate of interest r_0 and a quantity of real cash balances m_0. And suppose that, while other things initially remain unchanged, the quantity of money is arbitrarily doubled by giving to each holder of money an additional quantity equal to the amount he already holds. Temporarily, the variables of the system will then be at point H of Figure 3; except for the increase in the quantity of money, nothing in the system will have changed. As I have shown above, however, there will be an automatic tendency for the variables of the system to return eventually to the former equilibrium position, r_0 and m_0. At point H both the securities market and the goods-and-services market will be out of balance, and changes will therefore occur in the interest rate and in the level of prices. The changes in prices, in turn, will affect the real value of cash balances.

Consider, first, the securities market. After the initial monetary disturbance, the quantity of money held by the typical asset-holder is larger than he would like to hold at the prevailing interest rate, r_0. Asset-holders as a group therefore attempt to convert some of their excess cash into securities. As a result, security prices rise, which means that the interest rate falls. The fall in the interest rate increases investment, while the initial increase in the real value of cash balances reduces saving. The demand for goods and services as a whole thus exceeds productive capacity, so that commodity prices and costs begin to rise. The rise in prices tends to reduce the real value of cash balances and thereby initiates a movement of the variables back toward the original equilibrium position. The details of this dynamic process need not concern us here. Suffice it to say that the system as a whole will not be restored to equilibrium until the real value of cash balances is reduced to m_0 and the rate of interest is restored to its former level, r_0.

If the central bank does not acquire or dispose of any assets during the period of adjustment, the real value of money balances can be reduced only by an increase in the price level. Since the real value of cash balances is ultimately restored to its former level, m_0, we know that the increase in prices, in the final position of equilibrium, must be as large as the original increase in the quantity of money. In other words, doubling the nominal quantity of money must result eventually in doubling all money prices and costs, including the money prices of securities as well as the money prices of goods and services. The real variables of the system all return to their former equilibrium levels. The rate of interest, the real value of saving and investment, and the real value of securities, as well as the real value of cash balances, are all the same in the new equilibrium as before the monetary disturbance occurred. The only permanent effect of increasing the quantity of money is a proportionate increase in the general level of prices and costs.[14]

With respect to monetary disturbances of the second type, such as the one I have just described, the economic system embodying both a saving-wealth relation and a liquidity-preference schedule is evidently quite similar to the classical system. In both the classical system and the system depicted in Figure 3 the values of all real variables are independent of the quantity of money. But this is true of the system in Figure 3 only if the monetary disturbances are of the second type, whereas it is true of the classical system for both types of monetary disturbance. If the disturbance is of the first type, which consists of open-market transactions by the central bank, then the equilibrium interest rate will be altered, as I have suggested above. With respect to monetary disturbances of the first type, the equilibrium interest rate of Figure 3 is therefore a monetary rate, and in this regard it resembles the Keynesian interest rate more closely than it does the classical. In other words, by purchasing or selling securities, the banking authorities can alter not only the temporary interest rate which prevails while the open-market transactions are taking place but also the rate at which the system will return to equilibrium after the bank's transactions in securities have ceased.

The power of the banking authorities to alter the equilibrium interest rate is attributable not to their influence upon the nominal quantity of money but to their influence upon the quantity and value of privately held securities. A central-bank purchase of securities, for example, reduces the quantity of privately held securities. This means that the AA schedule of Figure 1 is shifted to the left. And since the liquidity-preference schedule, LL, and the money-requirements schedule, MM, were both derived, in part, from the AA schedule, a shift in the latter causes the former schedules to shift as well. The system as a whole therefore comes into balance, after the securities purchases have been made, at a different rate of interest.

The effect of open-market transactions upon the equilibrium of the system can be described in terms of a ratio indicating the proportion of the total supply of securities held in private hands. Let this ratio be represented by the letter λ. Consider, first, the situation in which λ has a value of 1.0. This means that the total available supply of securities is held by private asset-holders, so that the central bank's assets consist exclusively of currency. Given the holdings of securities by private asset-holders, the rate of interest at which the system is in equilibrium can be determined, as in our earlier illustration, by the intersection of a liquidity-preference schedule, LL, and a money-requirements schedule, MM. Assuming that the value of private asset holdings when $\lambda = 1.0$ is given in Figure 4 by the solid line AA and that the

wealth-requirements schedule is WW, the liquidity-preference
schedule and the money-requirements schedule can be derived as
in my earlier illustration. These derived schedules, for $\lambda = 1.0$,
are represented in Figure 5 by the solid lines LL and MM,
respectively. Under the assumed conditions with respect to
security holdings, the equilibrium rate of interest is r_0, and the
equilibrium value of real cash balances is m_0, as shown in Figure 5.

Suppose that this equilibrium is disturbed by a substantial
purchase of securities on the part of the central bank. The dynamic
process by which the economy adapts itself to such open-market
transactions will probably be highly complicated. The securities
will be purchased at many different prices from the various asset-
holders, and this means that we cannot predict exactly how the
open-market transactions will affect the cash balances of all asset-
holders together. In any event, the real value of cash balances
will be influenced by price movements as well as by the central
bank's dealings in securities, and it is the combined effect of both
influences which ultimately governs the equilibrium value of the
real money supply. In view of our interest in the equilibrium of the
system, we may pass over the dynamic problems and investigate,
instead, the influence of the central bank's security purchases upon
the schedules in Figures 4 and 5 which determine the ultimate
resting places of our variables.

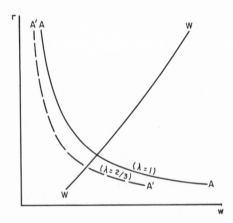

Figure 4.

Suppose that the central bank continues to purchase securities
until it has acquired one-third of the common stock available to
the economy as a whole and that all transactions between asset-
holders and the central bank cease at this point. When the securities
market and the goods-and-services market are once again in
equilibrium, how will the rate of interest compare with the rate

that prevailed before the open-market transactions began? According to the classical theory, the rate of interest should return to its former level as soon as the bank's security purchases have ceased. According to the system depicted in Figures 4 and 5, however, the security purchases by the central bank will permanently *lower* the equilibrium rate of interest.

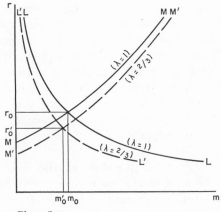

Figure 5.

If the bank acquires one-third of all available securities, the security holdings of private asset-holders will of course be only two-thirds as large as they formerly were, so that λ will have a value of $\frac{2}{3}$. This means that at any given interest rate the real value of private security holdings will be two-thirds of its former value. The broken line $A'A'$ of Figure 4 is drawn at two-thirds of the horizontal distance of the solid line AA from the vertical axis, and $A'A'$ thus represents the real value of private security holdings, expressed again as a function of the rate of interest, after the central bank has acquired its securities. The wealth-requirements schedule, WW, depends upon preferences and upon the savings and investment schedules and presumably will be unaffected by the open-market transactions. Since the money-requirements schedule, MM, depends upon the value of private security holdings as well as upon WW, however, the MM schedule will be shifted. At any given rate of interest, the total assets—money and securities combined—needed to maintain equality between full-employment saving and full-employment investment will be the same as before. But the value of private security holdings has been reduced by the central bank's purchases, and this means that total assets cannot be maintained at the level needed for full employment unless private money holdings are increased by a corresponding amount. In short, the money-requirements schedule, MM, is moved to the right by the same amount that the securities schedule, AA, is moved to the left.[15] The new money-requirements schedule corresponding to $\lambda = \frac{2}{3}$ is shown in Figure 5 as the broken line $M'M'$.

The liquidity-preference schedule, as well as the money-requirements schedule, is affected by the central bank's purchase of securities. At any given interest rate, the proportions in which the typical asset-holder wishes to hold money and securities are presumably the same as in the old equilibrium. The value of private security holdings, however, is now only two-thirds of the former value at the same interest rate. The desired ratio between money holdings and security holdings will thus not be maintained unless the real value of money balances is reduced to two-thirds of its former value. In other words, the LL schedule in Figure 5 is shifted to the left, the relative amount of the shift being the same as the leftward shift of the securities schedule, AA. The new liquidity-preference schedule, for $\lambda = \frac{2}{3}$, is represented in Figure 5 by the line $L'L'$.

The combined effect of the shift in the liquidity-preference schedule and of the shift in the money-requirements schedule is a reduction in the equilibrium rate of interest from r_0 to r'_0, as indicated in Figure 5. Thus, the banking authorities by means of a limited purchase of securities have *permanently* reduced the interest rate at which the economic system is in equilibrium. The dynamic process of adjustment by which the equilibrium interest rate moves from r_0 to r'_0 will probably be highly complex, as I have indicated earlier. Nevertheless, I believe that the influence of the central bank upon the equilibrium interest rate will stand out more clearly if we consider a greatly simplified dynamic sequence.

When the central bank begins to purchase securities, the first effect is a rise in security prices and a corresponding decline in the rate of interest. The actual security transactions themselves do not alter the total value of private asset holdings but merely change the form in which assets are held. The initial result of the bank's purchases, therefore, is a rise in the value of private asset holdings (capital gains) together with a reduction in the rate of interest and a shift on the part of asset-holders from securities to money. One may presume that at the new, lower rate of interest the asset-holders have exchanged securities for cash in such a way as to satisfy their demands for liquidity; for, if this were not true, the prices of securities would continue to rise, and the interest rate to fall, until the asset-holders were willing to part with the amount of securities that the central bank wanted to buy. Although the point representing the new quantity of private money holdings and the new, temporary rate of interest will thus lie somewhere on the liquidity-preference schedule $L'L'$, it cannot at the same time lie on the money-requirements schedule, $M'M'$, or the wealth-requirements schedule, WW. The fall in the interest rate, taken by itself, would normally lead to an excess of full-employment investment over full-employment saving and thus create an excess demand for goods and services. The inflationary pressure is further increased, however, by the capital gains, which increase the value of total private wealth holdings and thereby reduce current saving. As a result, prices and costs tend to rise, and the real value of the money supply is correspondingly reduced. The rise in prices and the reduction in the real value of private money holdings must continue until the real value of security-and-cash holdings combined is low enough to encourage a sufficient amount of saving to make full-employment saving once more equal to full-employment investment. The new equilibrium is finally achieved, as Figures 4 and 5 demonstrate, at a permanently lower rate of interest.

Now, since the new equilibrium must lie on the wealth-requirements schedule, WW, as well as on the money-requirements schedule, $M'M'$, it is obvious that, when prices have finally stopped rising and the rate of interest has reached its new and lower equilibrium, the value of total private wealth must be smaller than in the old equilibrium. In short, the final result of the open-market security purchases by the central bank is a reduction in the real value of the total wealth in private hands. This reduction has occurred in two stages: the liquidity of the typical asset-holder has first been increased through the central-bank purchase of securities; and the real value of the larger liquid balances has subsequently been reduced through inflation. Thus, under a regime of flexible prices, central-bank purchase of securities is an indirect means of reducing the real value of the total assets—cash and securities combined—in private hands. The reduction in the value of privately held wealth tends, in turn, to increase saving and thereby reduces the rate of interest at which full-employment saving is equal to full-employment investment. To summarize briefly, then, we may say that the central bank is able to alter the equilibrium rate of interest through its power to alter the real value of private wealth.

VII

Assuming that saving depends upon the real value of private wealth as well as upon the interest rate, I have now demonstrated that the equilibrium interest rate is partly a real rate, as in the classical theory, and partly a monetary rate, as in Keynes's theory. Monetary disturbances of one type affect the equilibrium interest rate of the system, while disturbances of another type do not. In general, any monetary disturbance which alters the amount of securities held by the typical asset-holder tends also to affect the interest rate at which the economic system as a whole is in equilibrium. On the other hand, any monetary disturbance which does not affect private security holdings will leave the equilibrium interest rate unchanged.

The distinction which I have made between the two types of monetary disturbance suggests that the true cause of a change in the interest rate is not a change in the quantity of money per se but a change in the amount of other assets held by the typical asset-holder. This conjecture is, indeed, correct. Open-market transactions of the central bank alter the equilibrium interest rate not because they affect the quantity of money but because they affect the quantity of privately held securities. Consider again, for example, the open-market transactions which I have described in Figures 4 and 5. In those illustrations the central bank is assumed to purchase one-third of all privately held securities. As a consequence, the level of prices is increased, the real value of private wealth declines, the propensity to save increases, and real saving finally comes into balance with real investment at a permanently lower interest rate.

Suppose, now, that the amount of privately held securities were reduced without any offsetting change in the quantity of money. Such a reduction could be brought about by a capital levy of one-third on all securities, payable only in kind. In other words, the government could require that one-third of all privately held securities be turned over to it. In what respects would the effects of such a policy differ from the effects of the open-market transactions described in Figures 4 and 5? Examination of the figures reveals that the interest rate, the volume of real investment, the real value of cash balances, and the other real variables of the system are affected in exactly the same way by a one-third levy in kind upon all securities as by a central-bank purchase of the same amount of securities. The nominal quantity of money is of course larger when the securities are acquired by purchase than when they are acquired by taxation. But the real value of bank balances is exactly the same, in the new position of equilibrium, in both cases. Thus, the only difference between the effects of the two means of acquiring the securities is a difference in the level of prices and costs. The price level is higher when the securities are acquired by purchase than when they are acquired by taxation. In all other respects the two situations are identical as far as the final results are concerned.

The foregoing example reveals the close analogy between central-bank security purchases and a capital levy on securities. In the system investigated above, a purchase of securities by the central bank is a means of reducing the real value of privately held wealth and operates just as effectively in this direction as a corresponding capital levy payable in kind. Indeed, the central bank's power to alter the equilibrium interest rate arises exclusively from its influence on the real value of privately held securities.

Through its power to change the interest rate, the central bank can also affect the rate of growth of the economy as a whole. At each different equilibrium interest rate full-employment saving is of course equal to full-employment investment, but the amount of real saving and investment varies with variations in the equilibrium interest rate. When the equilibrium rate is increased, the economic system comes into balance at a lower real value of investment and saving; and, when the equilibrium rate is reduced, the real value of saving and investment tends to increase. By purchasing securities, the central bank can reduce the real value of private wealth, thereby increasing the propensity to save and causing the system to attain a new equilibrium at a permanently lower interest rate and a permanently higher rate of capital accumulation. In a similar manner, the bank, through sales of securities, can increase the real value of private wealth, lower the propensity to save, raise the equilibrium rate of interest, and reduce the rate of capital accumulation.

Whether the bank has a substantial influence or only a negligible influence upon the rate of growth of the system depends upon its authority to buy and sell securities and upon the magnitude of the saving-wealth relation. If the saving-wealth relation is large, so that the propensity to save increases or decreases appreciably as the real value of private wealth falls or rises, and if the bank is authorized to buy and sell securities in large quantities, then the rate of growth may be affected to a considerable extent by central-bank policy. In practice, however, there will usually be an institutional barrier to the amount of securities the bank can sell; it cannot sell more securities than its owns. And this means that, when the bank has divested itself of all its securities, it has no further power to raise the equilibrium interest rate and lower the rate of growth. There may be a similar barrier to the amount of securities the bank can purchase, since only certain types of assets are eligible for the bank's portfolio. If the bank has acquired all the assets it is authorized to purchase, no further reduction of private wealth, and no further increase in private saving, can be accomplished by central-bank activity in the securities market.

In terms of the theory set out above, we may say that the central
bank's power over the equilibrium interest rate and the equilibrium rate of growth will usually be determined by institutional
arrangements which prevent it from purchasing more than a small
fraction of private wealth or from selling more assets than it
possesses. This might mean, for example, that the institutional arrangements were such that the value of λ would have to lie between 0.9 and 1.0. In most countries these institutional limits may
well be so narrow that the actual power of the central bank to influence the equilibrium of the system is negligible. Nevertheless,
if saving depends upon the real value of private wealth as described
in the saving-wealth relation, the rate of interest must be regarded
as partly a monetary rate. For, if the institutional limits to central-
bank action were removed or reduced, the possible variation in
the equilibrium interest rate which could be brought about by the
central bank would be correspondingly increased.

Appendix

The geometrical methods employed in the text of this paper
were not sufficiently powerful to deal with some of the more
difficult problems encountered, particularly the dynamic problems. I am therefore adding an analytical appendix. The symbols
used in this appendix have the following meanings:

r represents the rate of interest, or the yield on common stock
m represents the real value of private money holdings
a represents the real value of all common stock, whether held by
    private owners or by the central bank
λ represents the proportion of the total supply of common stock
    held by private owners
w represents the real value of all privately held wealth, including
    both money and common stock
S represents the real value of current saving
I represents the real value of current investment

The amount of real saving out of a full-employment income is
assumed to depend upon the real value of private wealth as well
as upon the rate of interest, and we may accordingly write $S = S(r, w)$. Investment, under conditions of full employment, is assumed to depend only upon the rate of interest, and the investment
function may therefore be written as follows: $I = I(r)$. If real
national income under conditions of full employment is y_0, and if
a proportion, c, of this consists of business profits, the real value

of all common stock will be the capitalized value of these profits, thus: $a = cy_0/r$. The only remaining functional relation to be defined is the liquidity-preference function. Let $L(r)$ be such a function, indicating the proportion in which asset-holders as a group wish to hold money and common stock. With the aid of these definitions we may now write down the following system of equations:

$$\left.\begin{aligned} S(r,\, w) &= I(r), \\ L(r) &= \frac{m}{\lambda a}, \\ w &= \lambda a + m, \\ a &= \frac{cy_0}{r}. \end{aligned}\right\} \tag{1}$$

The first of equations (1) expresses the condition that, in equilibrium, full-employment saving must equal full-employment investment. The second equation says that the rate of interest must be such that the desired proportion between money holdings and security holdings on the part of the owners of private wealth is equal to the actual proportion. The third equation is an identity, defining the real value of private wealth as the sum of private money holdings and private security holdings. Finally, the fourth of equations (1) says that the real value of all common stock is the capitalized value of business profits, where the capitalization is done at the prevailing rate of interest, r.

If the value of λ is given, equations (1) are sufficient to determine the equilibrium values of the four variables, r, w, m, and a; i.e., the equations determine the rate of interest, the total real value of privately held wealth, the real value of money balances, and the real value of all common stock. The price level does not enter explicitly in equations (1), since all variables are in real terms. Nevertheless, price movements are implicitly taken into account through movements of m, the real value of the money supply. In the absence of open-market transactions, indeed, m can change only by means of general inflation or deflation.

Security purchases or sales by the central bank are indicated in equations (1) by changes in the value of λ. An increase in λ, for example, indicates a larger proportion of total securities in private hands and hence signifies security sales by the central bank. Changes in λ will obviously alter the equilibrium values of all our variables. In order to see how a central-bank sale of securities affects these equilibrium values, we may differentiate (1) with respect to λ, as follows:

$$(S_r - I_r)\frac{dr}{d\lambda} + S_w\frac{dw}{d\lambda} = 0,$$

$$-\frac{1}{\lambda a}\frac{dm}{d\lambda} + L_r\frac{dr}{d\lambda} + \frac{m}{\lambda a^2}\frac{da}{d\lambda} = -\frac{m}{\lambda^2 a},$$

$$\frac{dm}{d\lambda} - \frac{dw}{d\lambda} + \lambda\frac{da}{d\lambda} = -a$$

$$-\frac{a}{r}\frac{dr}{d\lambda} - \frac{da}{d\lambda} = 0$$

(2)

Solving equations (2) for

$$\frac{dr}{d\lambda}, \quad \frac{dm}{d\lambda}, \quad \frac{dw}{d\lambda}, \quad \text{and} \quad \frac{da}{d\lambda},$$

we find

$$\frac{dr}{d\lambda} = -\frac{S_w}{\Delta}\left(\frac{1}{\lambda} + \frac{m}{\lambda^2 a}\right),$$

$$\frac{dm}{d\lambda} = \frac{1}{\Delta}\left\{(S_r - I_r)\frac{m}{\lambda^2 a} - aS_wL_r\right\},$$

$$\frac{dw}{d\lambda} = \frac{1}{\Delta}(S_r - I_r)\left(\frac{1}{\lambda} + \frac{m}{\lambda^2 a}\right),$$

$$\frac{da}{d\lambda} = \frac{1}{\Delta}\frac{aS_w}{r}\left(\frac{1}{\lambda} + \frac{m}{\lambda^2 a}\right).$$

(3)

The symbol Δ in equations (3) represents the basic determinant of the system, i.e.,

$$\Delta \equiv \begin{vmatrix} 0 & S_r - I_r & S_w & 0 \\ -\dfrac{1}{\lambda a} & L_r & 0 & \dfrac{m}{\lambda a^2} \\ 1 & 0 & -1 & \lambda \\ 0 & -\dfrac{a}{r} & 0 & -1 \end{vmatrix},$$

$$\equiv (S_r - I_r)\frac{1}{\lambda a} + S_wL_r - \frac{S_w}{r} - \frac{mS_w}{\lambda ar}.$$

(4)

The subscripts in equations (3) and (4) indicate differentiation of the *S, I,* and *L* functions with respect to the variable appearing in the subscript. I assume the system is stable in the classic sense that an increase in the rate of interest creates an excess of potential saving over potential investment; this implies that $S_r - I_r$ is positive. The saving-wealth relation is represented in (3) and (4) by S_w, which is negative, indicating that an increase in the real value of private wealth reduces real saving. The slope L_r of the liquidity-preference schedule is assumed to be negative, which implies that an increase in the rate of interest reduces the desired ratio between money and securities.

With the given signs of S_r, I_r, etc., one can see from (4) that Δ is a positive determinant. Moreover, the direction of change of most of the variables of the system can be readily determined. Thus, (3) shows that $dr/d\lambda$ is positive, $dw/d\lambda$ is positive, and $da/d\lambda$ is negative. This means that open-market sales of securities have increased the rate of interest, increased the real value of private wealth (cash and securities combined), and reduced the real value of the total supply of common stock. The only change whose sign is indeterminate is $dm/d\lambda$, the change in the real value of private money holdings. The reason for this indeterminacy is not far to seek: the central-bank sales of securities have reduced private money balances, but the real value of the remaining private balances have subsequently been increased through a general deflation. The final position of real money balances thus depends upon the relative strength of these opposing forces. But whatever happens to the real value of privately held money, equations (3) show that privately held wealth as a whole has been increased by the central bank's sales of securities. The increase in the real value of private wealth has reduced the rate of saving, and it is this reduction of saving which accounts for the permanent rise in the equilibrium rate of interest.

Thus far I have investigated the stationary or equilibrium values of the system without saying anything about the dynamic process of adjustment. I shall conclude this appendix with a few remarks concerning the behavior of the variables through time, during intervals when the system is not in equilibrium.

Consider, first, the behavior of prices when total demand is different from productive capacity. The difference between demand and productive capacity is measured, of course, by the difference between potential full-employment saving and potential full-employment investment. If the former exceeds the latter, demand for goods and services falls short of productive capacity, and prices and costs accordingly tend to decline. Conversely, if full-employment investment exceeds full-employment saving, total demand exceeds capacity, and both prices and costs rise. In the absence of new borrowing or lending by the banking system, however, an increase in prices is equivalent to a fall in the real value of money balances, and the time movement of the general price level may therefore be described in terms of movements in the value of money. As a first dynamic postulate, then, I write:

$$\frac{dm}{dt} = k_1[S(r, w) - I(r)]. \tag{5}$$

Equation (5) says that the price level tends to fall, and the real value of money balances tends to rise, whenever potential saving exceeds potential investment. Likewise, prices rise, and the real value of money balances falls, when potential saving falls short of potential investment. The speed of the price movement, in both cases, is assumed in (5) to be proportional to the size of the inflationary or deflationary gap, and the constant, k_1, represents this speed of adjustment.

So much for the general price level in the commodity-and-service market. Consider next the movement of prices in the securities market. I assume, as I indicated in the text, that the securities market is dominated by transactions in old securities rather than by supply-and-demand conditions in the new-securities market. Specifically, I assume that security prices tend to rise whenever asset-holders on balance attempt to shift from money to securities and that security prices fall when asset-holders attempt a shift in the opposite direction. The attempted shift, in turn, depends upon whether the actual ratio of cash to securities is higher or lower than the desired ratio, as indicated by the liquidity-preference function. Since a rise in security prices is equivalent to a fall in the rate of interest, our second dynamic postulate may be written

$$\frac{dr}{dt} = k_2\left[L(r) - \frac{m}{\lambda a}\right]. \tag{6}$$

In words, equation (6) says that the rate of interest rises, which means that security prices fall, when the desired ratio of money to securities exceeds the actual ratio. And, conversely, the rate of interest falls when the desired ratio is less than the actual ratio.

Equations (5) and (6) are the only equations of adjustment that we shall need. These two equations are the dynamic counterpart of the first two of equations (1). They do not form a complete system, however, since we have only two equations in four unknowns. Before we can solve our dynamic equations, we must have two more equations. The two missing equations are the third and fourth equations of our static system (1). These are merely definitional equations and are assumed to be satisfied at any moment of time, without lag. The third equation defines private wealth at a given moment as the sum of private security holdings and private money holdings, while the fourth equation defines the rate of interest as the yield on securities. The complete dynamic system is as follows:

$$
\left.
\begin{aligned}
\frac{dm}{dt} &= k_1[S(r, w) - I(r)], \\[2mm]
\frac{dr}{dt} &= k_2\left[L(r) - \frac{m}{\lambda a}\right], \\[2mm]
w &= \lambda a + m \\[2mm]
a &= \frac{cy_0}{r}.
\end{aligned}
\right\}
\tag{7}
$$

Equations (7) cannot be explicitly solved, since we do not know the exact form of the functions S, I, and L. I shall therefore make a linear approximation of (7), which will be valid only for small deviations from the equilibrium values of the variables. If r_0, w_0, m_0, and a_0 represent the equilibrium values, we may write, as such a linear approximation,

$$
\left.
\begin{aligned}
\frac{dm}{dt} &= k_1(S_r - I_r)(r - r_0) + k_1 S_w(w - w_0), \\[2mm]
\frac{dr}{dt} &= - k_2 \frac{1}{\lambda a}(m - m_0) + k_2 L_r(r - r_0) + k_2 \frac{m}{\lambda a^2}(a - a_0), \\[2mm]
0 &= (m - m_0) - (w - w_0) + \lambda(a - a_0), \\[2mm]
0 &= - \frac{a}{r}(r - r_0) - (a - a_0).
\end{aligned}
\right\}
\tag{8}
$$

The solution of (8) takes the form

$$
m = m_0 + A_1 e^{\rho_1 t} + A_2 e^{\rho_2 t_1},
\tag{9}
$$

with similar results for r, a, and w, where A_1 and A_2 depend upon the initial values of the variables, and where ρ_1 and ρ_2 are the roots of the following equation:

$$
\begin{vmatrix}
-\rho & k_1(S_r - I_r) & k_1 S_w & 0 \\[2mm]
-\dfrac{k_2}{\lambda a} & k_2 L_r - \rho & 0 & \dfrac{k_2 m}{\lambda a^2} \\[2mm]
1 & 0 & -1 & \lambda \\[2mm]
0 & -\dfrac{a}{r} & 0 & -1
\end{vmatrix}
= 0.
\tag{10}
$$

Equation (10) may be expended in powers of ρ as follows:

$$\rho^2 + \left(\frac{k_2 m}{\lambda a r} - k_2 L_r - k_1 S_w\right)\rho + k_1 k_2 \Delta = 0, \qquad (11)$$

where Δ is the basic determinant of the static system, (1).

The coefficients of the powers of ρ in equation (11) are positive, which means that the real parts of the roots of equation (11) are all negative. Thus the dynamic system is stable, for small deviations from equilibrium, regardless of the numerical values of L_r, S_w, etc. In other words, if the liquidity-preference function, the saving function, and the investment function do not alter their form or position as prices rise or fall, the dynamic system will eventually reach a stationary or static position. This does not mean, of course, that an economic system in which the saving-wealth relation is operative will always be a stable system in reality; for equations (7) and (8) have made no allowance for expectations, and such expectations may exert a strongly destabilizing influence on the system. If prices of commodities are rising, for example, consumers and producers may anticipate further price increases; if so, saving will probably decline and investment will increase, thereby widening the inflationary gap and accelerating the price rise. Likewise, if security prices are rising, asset-holders may revise downward their estimate of what constitutes a normal ratio between money and securities; and, if they do, the resulting attempt to shift from money to securities will cause a further rise in securities prices. These possibilities suggest that equations (7) and (8) are stable only in a narrow sense.

Assuming that the system is stable, we may inquire, in conclusion, about the nature of the approach toward equilibrium. Is the solution of equation (8) cyclical or noncyclical? The answer to this question depends upon the roots of equation (10) or (11). The dynamic system will not be cyclical unless these roots are complex numbers. This means that $b^2 - 4c$ is negative, where b is the coefficient of ρ in (11) and c is the constant term. I leave it to the reader to prove the following propositions: (1) the roots of equation (11) may be either real or complex, which means that the dynamic system may or may not have a cyclical solution. (2) If k_1 and k_2, the speeds of adjustment in the commodity market and the securities market, respectively, are decidedly different in magnitude, the roots are likely to be real and the dynamic system is thus likely to be a noncyclical system. (3) If $S_r - I_r$ is large, so that a small rise in the rate of interest creates a substantial deflationary gap, the system will probably be cyclical.

NOTES

1. A. C. Pigou, *Employment and Equilibrium* (London 1941), Chapter 7; "The Classical Stationary State," *Economic Journal*, Vol. 53 (December 1943), 342–52.

2. T. Scitovszky, "Capital Accumulation, Employment and Price Rigidity," *Review of Economic Studies*, Vol. 8 (1940–41), 69–88.

3. G. Haberler, *Prosperity and Depression*, 3d ed. (Geneva 1941), pp. 491–503.

4. Consider, for example, the following remark of J. S. Mill: "There must be, as in other cases of value, some rate [of interest] which . . . may be called the natural rate; some rate about which the market rate oscillates, and to which it always tends to return. This rate partly depends on the amount of accumulation going on in the hands of persons who cannot themselves attend to the employment of their savings, and partly on the comparative taste existing in the community for the active pursuits of industry, or for the leisure, ease, and independence of an annuitant" (*Principles* [5th ed.], Book 3, Chapter 23, § 1). Although Mill does not specify in this passage that the saving and investment which govern the interest rate are full-employment saving and full-employment investment, the tenor of his work strongly suggests that this is what he had in mind (see, e.g., *ibid.*, Book 3, Chapter 14).

5. Haberler, *op. cit.*, p. 499, note 2.

6. David Ricardo, *Principles of Political Economy* (London 1948), p. 246.

7. Although Pigou is usually considered to be a defender of classical or neoclassical economic theory, his ideas concerning the interest rate were somewhat nonclassical even before the publication of his *Employment and Equilibrium*. He believed, in particular, that the banking system has a limited influence upon the equilibrium interest rate as well as upon the market rate. If the banks establish a market rate below the equilibrium rate, for example, prices and costs tend to rise, and the real expenditures of fixed-income groups are reduced. The resources thus freed are available for capital development, and the increased supply of capital reduces the equilibrium interest rate. Apart from this reservation, Pigou's earlier conception of the interest rate seems to be largely classical in its implications (see A. C. Pigou, *Industrial Fluctuations*, 2d ed. [London 1929], *passim*, but esp. p. 277).

8. J. M. Keynes, *General Theory of Employment, Interest and Money* (New York 1936), Chapter 19. On p. 267 of this chapter, Keynes says: "There is, therefore, no ground for the belief that a flexible wage policy is capable of maintaining a state of continuous full employment; . . . The economic system cannot be made self-adjusting along these lines."

9. M. Kalecki, "Professor Pigou on 'The Classical Stationary State,' a Comment," *Economic Journal*, Vol. 54 (April 1944), 131–32; D. Patinkin, "Price Flexibility and Full Employment," *American Economic Review*, Vol. 38 (September 1948), 543–64.

10. Keynes, *op. cit.*, Chapters 13, 15, and 18.

11. Common stock has been selected as the typical security in order to avoid the difficulties associated with bonds during periods of inflation

or deflation. Throughout the paper I assume that, in the absence of movements in interest rates, common-stock prices rise or fall to the same extent that other prices rise or fall, so that a general inflation or deflation does not affect the real value of securities. This means that the real value of a given quantity of securities is a function of the rate of interest alone. (See below.) Although the theory is simplified in this respect by regarding common stock as the typical security, two new problems are thereby introduced, and these must not be overlooked. Perhaps most important, when all investment is financed by issuing common stock, the idea of a functional relation between the rate of interest and the real volume of investment becomes somewhat vague. Under these circumstances business-men do not commit themselves, as they do when they issue bonds, to the payment of fixed capital charges. Saying that investment depends upon the rate of interest when all securities are common stocks is equivalent to saying that businessmen undertake more investment when stock prices are high than when they are low.

Apart from the problem of defining an investment function, the use of common stock in our argument presents the further problem of separating risk payments from interest payments per se. I have attempted to avoid this second problem by assuming that the degree or risk is about the same for one stock as for another. I realize, however, that such an assumption does not meet the basic difficulty and that, in a more ex-tended treatment of the subject, allowance should be made for differences in risk.

12. The best account I have found of the second reason for the negative slope of the liquidity-preference schedule is by E. Solomon in "Money, Liquidity, and the Long-Term Rate of Interest: An Empirical Study, 1909–38" (University of Chicago dissertation, 1950).

13. Superficially, the cycle of interest rates and prices described above seems to be somewhat like the monetary part of Hicks's business-cycle theory. In reality, however, the two cyclical processes are quite different. The process envisaged by Hicks involves movements of output and em-ployment rather than movements of prices and costs; and savings in Hicks's theory depend upon the rate of interest and real income, whereas savings in the present paper depend upon the rate of interest and the real value of private wealth (J. R. Hicks, *A Contribution to the Theory of Business Cycles* [London: Oxford University Press, 1949], Chapters 11 and 12).

14. Using a model more complex than the one I have been considering, D. Patinkin previously demonstrated that if both the saving-wealth rela-tion and liquidity preference are active forces, monetary disturbances of the second type will not affect the equilibrium interest rate (see "The Indeterminacy of Absolute Prices in Classical Economic Theory," *Econometrica*, Vol. 17 [January 1949], 23–27). Patinkin did not examine the effects of monetary disturbances of the first type and accordingly concluded that the model he had constructed was closer to the classical model than to the Keynesian.

15. In describing the consequences of open-market transactions, I assume that the securities schedule, *AA*, is the only schedule of Figure 4 which is *directly* influenced by the central bank's purchase or sale o

securities; the other schedules (i.e., the wealth-requirements schedule, the money-requirements schedule, and the liquidity-preference schedule) are assumed to be affected only in so far as they are related to, or derived from, the securities schedule, AA. This implies that the income available to the typical asset-holder is not altered by the central bank's dealings in securities. If disposable income tended to fall or to rise with an increase or decrease in the central bank's holdings of securities, the saving and investment schedules would also be affected, and the wealth-requirements schedule, which is derived from the saving and investment schedules, would tend to shift.

Taken by themselves, however, open-market transactions may well have a slight influence on disposable income. If the central bank buys securities, for example, the income on these securities is transferred from the former owners to the bank. In the absence of offsetting transactions, the security purchases thus reduce the disposable income of private asset-holders and increase the profits of the central bank by a corresponding amount. I do not wish to discuss the complications introduced by this connection between open-market transactions and disposable income. I therefore assume throughout that any additional profits which the central bank earns by reason of its acquisition of securities are ultimately passed on to private hands in the form of reduced taxes. Under these circumstances, the security purchases by the bank will redistribute income between former asset owners and taxpayers but will not influence the total of disposable income.

Part IV

The Supply of Money

Patinkin in his attempt to reformulate Keynesian theory on the basis of classical assumptions demonstrated that money would be "neutral" if one postulated wage and price flexibility, inelastic $\varepsilon = 1$ expectations, and the absence of money illusion, distribution effects and government debt operations. Many economists felt that the heart of several economic problems had been assumed away, and therefore sought to elaborate the conditions under which money might not be "neutral."

It has been pointed out that the development of the financial structure of a country might have significant effects on the supply of money and money substitutes. The net debtor position of a closed economy must be zero since for every debtor there must be a creditor. However, it has long been accepted that the behavior of the government as a debtor is not analogous to that of private debtors and that analytically it is not desirable to net out government debt which includes part of the money supply. The generalization of this idea that there might be differences in the behavior between various debtors and creditors in the private sector and that the financial structure might have some influence on the type of debt issued and held by various groups in the economy led to several attempts to develop monetary theory under more general assumptions. One well-known attempt was that of Gurley and Shaw in their book *Money in a Theory of Finance* (Washington 1960), where they examined situations where money was not "neutral."

Money is unique in that it provides both a medium of exchange and a store of value. In its former function it has few close substitutes but in its latter capacity, there are many assets which provide similar services. Financial intermediaries, in particular supply assets which provide a substitute store of value. To the extent that there are other substitute stores of value, the amount of money needed to maintain a certain level of income and prices may be economized upon by increasing the supply of substitute financial assets. Thus Gurley and Shaw examined the conditions under which these non-bank financial intermediaries supply substitute assets.

Gurley and Shaw stated that the rate of interest from the supply side may not be determined only by the rate of growth of the money supply, as Keynes maintained, but also to a large extent by the rate of growth of non-bank financial intermediaries. The rate of growth of non-bank financial intermediaries may be an important factor in explaining the secular trend in the velocity of money. From the point of view of counter-cyclical policy the central concern is whether the rate of growth of financial intermediaries will be such as to produce destabilizing changes in velocity counter to the direction of government policy.[1] The answer to this question in turn depends on the short-run determinants of the rate of growth of non-bank financial intermediaries which issue money substitutes.

The traditional way of looking at the money supply was to consider it the result of government debt operations and the average reserve ratio of commercial banks. Tolley pointed out that the reserve ratio may also be treated as a behavioral variable, determined jointly by the government—when it changes legal reserve requirements; the public—when it changes its division of assets between currency and deposits; and by banks—by their willingness to maintain excess reserves. It has been shown that changes in the supply of money by open market operations or by changes in legal reserve requirements will have different repercussions on the cost and size of the government debt and on resource allocation. The result of these developments has been to evolve a supply theory of money to complement the highly developed demand theory for money.[2]

[1] See Richard S. Thorn, "Non-Bank Financial Intermediaries, Credit Expansion and Monetary Policy," *IMF Staff Papers*, Vol. 6 (November 1958), 375–78.

[2] One interesting attempt of this type is Karl Brunner's "A Scheme for the Supply Theory of Money," *International Economic Review* (January 1961), pp. 79–109.

14 Financial Intermediaries and the Saving-Investment Process

John G. Gurley
and Edward S. Shaw *Stanford University*

It is fashionable these days to speak of the growing institutionalization of saving and investment. Rapid advances in recent years by pension funds, open-end investment companies, credit unions, and savings and loan associations, among others, have caught our eye. But the advance has been going on at least since the Civil War, and, as Raymond Goldsmith has recently shown, it was quite pronounced during the first three decades of this century. It is with these three decades that our paper is primarily concerned. Our method of analyzing financial data, however, requires explanation since it is based on unconventional theory. Accordingly, the first portions of the paper are largely theoretical. After that, we get down to brass tacks.

Deficits, Security Issues, and GNP

It is easy to imagine a world in which there is a high level of saving and investment, but in which there is an unfavorable climate for financial intermediaries. At the extreme, each of the economy's spending units—whether of the household, business, or government

Reprinted from *Journal of Finance*, Vol. 11 (March 1956), 257–76, by permission of the authors and publisher.

variety—would have a balanced budget on income and product account. For each spending unit, current income would equal the sum of current and capital expenditures. There could still be saving and investment, but each spending unit's saving would be precisely matched by its investment in tangible assets. In a world of balanced budgets, security issues by spending units would be zero, or very close to zero.[1] The same would be true of the accumulation of financial assets. Consequently, this world would be a highly uncongenial one for financial intermediaries; the saving-investment process would grind away without them.

Financial intermediaries are likely to thrive best in a world of deficits and surpluses, in a world in which there is a significant division of labor between savers and investors. In the ideal world for financial intermediaries, all current and capital expenditures would be made by spending units that received no current income, and all current income would be received by spending units that spent nothing. One group of spending units would have a deficit equal to its expenditures, and the other group would have a surplus equal to its income. And, of course, the *ex post* deficit would necessarily be equal to the *ex post* surplus. In this setting, the deficit group would tend to issue securities equal to its deficit, and the other group would tend to accumulate financial assets equal to its surplus. Security issues and financial-asset accumulations, therefore, would tend to approximate GNP or the aggregate of expenditures. No more congenial world than this could exist for financial intermediaries.

Unfortunately for these intermediaries, our own economy has been much closer to the first than to the second world. With some exceptions during the past half-century, the annual security issues of spending units over complete cycles have averaged somewhat below 10 per cent of GNP in current prices. These issues include government securities, corporate and foreign bonds, common and preferred stock, farm and non-farm mortgages, and consumer and other short-term debt. We shall call these primary security issues. Thus, at the turn of the century when GNP was around $20 billion, primary security issues ran a bit less than $2 billion per annum. In the late 1940's, with a GNP of approximately $250 billion, primary issues hovered around $20 billion per annum. Dividing the half-century into thirteen complete cycles, we find that the average annual ratio of primary issues to GNP was between 7 and 10 per cent in nine of the cycles. The exceptional cases include World War I, when the ratio reached 20 per cent, the 1930's, when the ratio fell to 3 or 4 per cent, and World War II, when it climbed to 25 per cent. However, if we consider longer phases, 1897–1914, 1915–32, and 1933–49, the ratio was between 9 and 10 per cent in each phase. There is sufficient strength, then, in the link between borrowing and GNP to make the relationship useful for financial analysis. And while the ratio lies closer to zero than to 100 per cent, still it is high enough to permit financial intermediation to be a substantial business.

The Role of Financial Intermediaries

What is the business of financial intermediaries? They lend at one stratum of interest rates and borrow at a lower stratum. They relieve the market of some primary securities and substitute others—indirect securities or financial assets—whose qualities command a higher price. This margin between yields on primary and indirect securities is the intermediaries' compensation for the special services they supply.

The financial institutions that fit these specifications are savings and loan associations, insurance companies, mutual savings banks, Postal Savings banks, investment companies, common trust funds, pension funds, government lending agencies, and others. In addition, we count the monetary system, including commercial banks, as one among many intermediaries. It is a vitally important intermediary, in view of its functions and its size. But its elevated rank among intermediaries does not alter the principle that the monetary system, like other intermediaries, transmits loanable funds by issues of indirect financial assets to surplus units and purchases of primary securities from deficit units. The indirect financial assets, deposits and currency that it issues or creates, are, like the indirect financial assets issued or created by other intermediaries, substitutes for primary securities in the portfolios of spending units. We shall return to this point in a few moments.

Internal and External Finance of Expenditures

In a world of balanced budgets, each spending unit's current and capital expenditures would be financed entirely from its current income. Thus, aggregate expenditures in the economy would be self-financed or internally financed. Internal finance would be equal to GNP.

In a world of deficits and surpluses, some expenditures would be financed externally. The extent of such financing is measured by the sum of the deficits (or surpluses) run by spending units. If at a GNP of $400 billion, the sum of all spending units' deficits is $40 billion, then 10 per cent of GNP is financed externally and 90 per cent is financed internally.

External finance may take two forms: direct finance and indirect finance. The distinction is based on the changes that occur in the financial accounts of surplus units' balance sheets. The finance is indirect if the surplus units acquire claims on financial intermediaries.[2] It is direct if surplus units acquire claims on debtors that are not financial intermediaries.[3]

While the proportion of GNP that is externally financed has not changed much over the past half-century, the proportion that is indirectly financed has risen and, of course, the proportion that is directly financed has fallen. In short, a growing share of primary issues has been sold to financial intermediaries.[4] But the relative gainers have been the non-monetary intermediaries and the relative loser has been the monetary system. Now, if we look at these trends from the standpoint of surplus spenders, we have the following picture: the surplus units have accumulated financial assets in annual amounts that, over long periods, have been a fairly steady percentage of GNP. However, these accumulations have been relatively more and more in the form of indirect financial assets, and relatively less and less in the form of primary securities. Moreover, the accumulations of indirect financial assets have swung toward the non-monetary types and away from bank deposits and currency. Commercial banks and the monetary system have retrogressed relative to financial intermediaries generally.

A Reconsideration of Banking Theory

A traditional view of the monetary system is that it determines the supply of money: it determines its own size in terms of monetary debt and of the assets that are counterparts of this debt on the system's balance sheet. Other financial intermediaries transfer to investors any part of this money supply that may be deposited with them by savers. Their size is determined by the public's choice of saving media.

As we see it, on the contrary, the monetary system is in some significant degree competitive with other financial intermediaries. The growth of these intermediaries in terms of indirect debt and of primary security portfolios is alternative to monetary growth and inhibits it. Their issues of indirect debt displace money, and the primary securities that they hold are in some large degree a loss of assets to the banks.

Bank deposits and currency are unique in one respect: they are means of payment, and holders of money balances have immediate access to the payments mechanism of the banking system. If money were in demand only for immediate spending or for holding in transactions balances, and if no other financial asset could be substituted as a means of payment or displace money in transactions balances, the monetary system would be a monopolistic supplier exempt from competition by other financial intermediaries.

But money is not in demand exclusively as a means of payment. It is in demand as a financial asset to hold. As a component of balances, money does encounter competition. Other financial assets can be accumulated preparatory to money payments, as a precaution against contingencies, or as an alternative to primary securities. For any level of money payments, various levels of money balances will do and, hence, various sizes of money supply and monetary system.

The more adequate the non-monetary financial assets are as substitutes for money in transactions, precautionary, speculative, and—as we shall see—diversification balances, the smaller may be the money supply for any designated level of national income. For any level of income, the money supply is indeterminate until one knows the degree of substitutability between money created by banks and financial assets created by other intermediaries. How big the monetary system is depends in part on the intensity of competition from savings banks, life insurance companies, pension funds, and other intermediaries.

Financial competition may inhibit the growth of the monetary system in a number of ways. Given the level of national income, a gain in attractiveness of, say, savings and loan shares vis-à-vis money balances must result in an excess supply of money. The monetary authority may choose to remove this excess. Then bank reserves, earning assets, money issues, and profits are contracted. This implies that, at any level of income, the competition of non-monetary intermediaries may displace money balances, shift primary securities from banks to their competitors, and reduce the monetary system's requirement for reserves. In a trend context, bank reserves cannot be permitted to grow as rapidly as otherwise they might, if non-monetary intermediaries become more attractive channels for transmission of loanable funds.

Suppose that excess money balances, resulting from a shift in spending units' demand away from money balances to alternative forms of indirect financial assets, are not destroyed by central bank action. They may be used to repay bank loans or to buy other securities from banks, the result being excess bank reserves. At the prevailing level of security prices, spending units have rejected money balances. But cannot banks force these balances out again, resuming control of the money supply? They can do so by accepting a reduced margin between the yield of primary securities they buy and the cost to them of deposits and currency they create. But this option is not peculiar to banks: other intermediaries can stimulate demand for their debt if they stand ready to accept a reduced markup on the securities they create and sell relative to the securities they buy. The banks can restore the money supply, but the cost is both a decline in their status relative to other financial intermediaries and a reduction in earnings.

The banks may choose to live with excess reserves rather than pay higher prices on primary securities or higher yields on their own debt issues. In this case, as in the previous two, a lower volume of reserves is needed to sustain a given level of national income. With their competitive situation improved, non-monetary intermediaries have stolen away from the banking system a share of responsibility for sustaining the flow of money payments. They hold a larger share of outstanding primary securities; they owe a larger share of indirect financial assets. They have reduced the size of the banking system at the given income level, both absolutely and relatively to their own size, and their gain is at the expense of bank profits.[5]

A Reconsideration of Interest Theory

It is clear from the foregoing remarks that this way of looking at financial intermediaries leads to a reconsideration of interest theory. Yields on primary securities, the terms of borrowing available to deficit spenders, are influenced not only by the amount of primary securities in the monetary system—that is, by the supply of money—but also by the amount of these securities in non-monetary intermediaries—that is, by the supply of indirect financial assets created by these intermediaries. Suppose that savings and loan shares become more attractive relative to bank deposits, resulting in an excess supply of money. Now, if we suppose that the monetary system chooses and manages to keep the money supply constant under these circumstances, the excess supply of money will cause yields on primary securities to fall. The activities of non-monetary financial intermediaries, then, can affect primary yields. The same money supply and national income are compatible with various interest rate levels, depending upon the size of non-monetary intermediaries and upon the degree to which their issues are competitive with money.[6]

The analysis is only a bit more complicated when we allow for issues of primary securities and the growth of income. Let us take these one at a time. At any income level, some spending units will have deficits and others surpluses. During the income period, the deficit spenders will tend to issue primary securities in an amount equal to their aggregate deficits. Now, if the surplus spenders are willing to absorb all of the issues at current yields on these securities, there will be no tightening effect on security markets. Surplus spenders will accumulate financial assets, all in the form of primary securities, and financial intermediaries will purchase none of the issues.

But this is an unlikely outcome. Ordinarily, surplus spenders can be expected to reject some portion of the primary securities emerging at any level of income and demand indirect financial assets instead, unless their preference for the latter is suppressed by a fall in prices of primary securities and a corresponding rise in interest rates charged to deficit spenders. This incremental demand for indirect financial assets is in part a demand for portfolio diversification. The diversification demand exists because there is generally no feasible mixture of primary securities that provides adequately such distinctive qualities of indirect securities as stability of price and yield or divisibility. The incremental demand for indirect assets, however, reflects not only a negative response, a partial rejection of primary securities, but also a positive response, an attraction to the many services attached to indirect assets, such as insurance and pension services and convenience of accumulation. Part of the demand is linked to the flow of primary security issues, but another part is linked more closely to the level of income.

For these reasons, then, ordinarily some portion of the primary issues must be sold to financial intermediaries if present yields on these securities are to be defended. Assuming for the moment that the monetary system is the only financial intermediary, the increase in the money supply must be equal to the portion of primary issues that spending units choose not to accumulate at current yields. If the monetary system purchases less than this, spending units will accumulate the residual supply at rising interest rates to deficit spenders. The emergence of security issues and a diversification demand for money based on these issues means that the money supply must rise at a given income level to maintain current yields on primary securities.

Still retaining the assumption that the monetary system is the only financial intermediary, we now permit income to grow. As money income gains, spending units demand additions to their active or transactions balances of means of payment. An upward trend in money payments calls for an upward trend in balances too. The income effect also applies to contingency or precautionary balances. If spending units are increasingly prosperous in the present, they feel able to afford stronger defenses against the hazards of the future.[7]

The combination of the income and diversification effects simply means that, when income is rising, a larger share of the issues must be purchased by the monetary system to prevent a rise in primary yields. The system must supply money for both diversification and transactions, including contingency, balances.

We may now introduce non-monetary intermediaries. The growth of these intermediaries will ordinarily, to some extent, reduce the required growth of the monetary system. We have already presented the reasons for this, so it suffices to say that primary yields may be held steady under growth conditions even with a monetary system that is barely growing, provided other intermediaries take up the slack.

In summary, primary security issues depend on aggregate deficits, and the latter in turn are related to the income level. At any income level, the diversification effect of these issues means that financial intermediaries must grow to hold primary yields steady. If income is rising, too, there is an incremental demand for money and perhaps for other indirect assets for transactions and contingency balances, requiring additional intermediary growth. To the extent that the issues of non-monetary intermediaries are competitive with money balances of whatever type, the required growth of the monetary system is reduced by the expansion of other intermediaries.

Financial Aspects of Output Growth, 1898–1930

We turn now to the task of attaching empirical content to this theoretical structure.[8] Our period runs from about 1898 through 1930. It starts with an upturn in economic activity, following the depression of the 1890's. It then traces the especially high rate of growth in real output through 1906, the Panic of 1907 and the ensuing depression, and the continuance of output growth, at a reduced pace, from 1909 to World War I. It covers the accelerated activity of the war and postwar years and the sharp downturn in 1920–21. Finally, the homestretch of the period is characterized by fairly steady output growth, with minor setbacks in 1924 and 1927. Over the entire period, GNP in current prices rose by more than 500 per cent, while GNP in 1929 prices grew by almost 200 per cent, at an average annual rate of about 3.5 per cent.

PRIMARY SECURITY ISSUES

From 1898 to 1930, the annual ratio of primary security issues to GNP in current prices averaged just a bit more than 10 per cent.[9] However, the range of fluctuation in the annual ratios was large, from about 2 to 20 per cent. During years of rapid acceleration in GNP, the ratio was relatively high, and this was especially true during the war years. During years of retarded growth, the ratio dipped below its average value, but there was no year when primary security issues were negative.

A steadier picture, then, is obtained when the years are grouped into complete cycles, as Table 1 shows. Each of these subperiods, of which there are nine, commences with a recovery year and ends with either a recession or a depression year. These subperiods are: 1898–1900, 1901–4, 1905–8, 1909–11, 1912–14, 1915–21, 1922–24, 1925–27, and 1928–30. In this way, nine ratios are obtained, each of which is equal to the cumulated primary issues divided by cumulated GNP during a subperiod. Leaving aside the exceptional years from 1915 to 1921, the ratios fall within the range of 7.1 per cent and 10.0 per cent, with six of them between 8.8 per cent and 10.0 per cent. The "exceptional" ratio was 14.1 per cent. All in all, the series shows remarkable stability, with no evidence of an upward or downward trend.[10]

TABLE 1   *Primary Security Issues and GNP 1898–1930, by Subperiods*

(In Millions of Dollars; Percentages)

PERIOD	TOTAL NET ISSUES*	GNP	RATIO OF NET ISSUES TO GNP	ALTERNATIVE RATIO†
1898–1900	4,731	50,812	9.3	9.3
1901–04	8,603	86,174	10.0	10.0
1905–08	10,117	110,141	9.2	9.2
1909–11	9,126	98,081	9.3	9.3
1912–14	9,557	109,170	8.8	8.8
1915–21	67,595	479,394	14.1	14.1
1922–24	17,197	244,207	7.0	7.1
1925–27	26,497	282,652	9.4	9.5
1928–30	23,196	291,878	7.9	8.2

* Unadjusted for mortgage write-downs and foreclosures.
† Net issues adjusted for mortgage write-downs and foreclosures.

DIRECT AND INDIRECT FINANCE

The primary security issues were directly financed through spending units or indirectly financed through financial intermediaries. In terms of the nine cycles, the indirect finance ratio—the ratio of primary securities purchased by intermediaries to total primary issues—commenced at 56 per cent and then fell slowly and steadily, with a single interruption, until it reached 36 per cent in 1915–21. In the next phase, 1922–24, the ratio leaped to almost

80 per cent, and then fell to 65 per cent in 1925–27, and finally to 50 per cent in 1928–30. There were two downward sweeps in the series. The first covered the initial two decades of the period. The second, starting from a fantastically high level, covered most of the third decade. Because of this high starting-point, the indirect finance ratio was unusually high, on the average, during most of the 1920's. From 1922 to 1929, for example, the ratio averaged about 65 per cent. This compares to 47 per cent from 1898 to 1914, and 36 per cent from 1915 to 1921.

The direct finance ratio—the proportion of total issues purchased by non-financial spending units—naturally behaved in the opposite fashion. In 1898–1900 it began a long upward sweep, which carried to the subperiod 1915–21. In the following cycle, it fell to an extremely low level, and then rose during the remainder of the period. Table 2 records these trends.

The significant finding here is the steady retrogression of financial intermediation during the first two decades and its resurgence during the 1920's. The counterpart of the retrogression was the growing share of primary issues absorbed by spending units, and the counterpart of the resurgence was the relatively low share of issues absorbed by spending units.

TABLE 2   Direct and Indirect Finance Ratios 1898–1930, by Subperiods

(In Percentages)

	DIRECT FINANCE RATIOS			INDIRECT FINANCE RATIOS		
	I*	II†	III‡	I*	II†	III‡
1898–1900	43.7	43.7	45.2	56.3	56.3	54.8
1901–04	46.0	46.0	45.9	54.0	54.0	54.1
1905–08	56.7	56.7	55.0	43.3	43.3	45.0
1909–11	53.5	53.5	49.7	46.5	46.5	50.3
1912–14	58.5	58.5	58.3	41.5	41.5	41.7
1915–21	63.5	63.5	64.5	36.5	36.5	35.5
1922–24	20.7	21.2	18.8	79.3	78.8	81.2
1925–27	35.1	35.3	34.5	64.9	64.7	65.5
1928–30	49.7	49.4	47.5	50.3	50.6	52.5

* Unadjusted for mortgage write-downs and foreclosures.
† Adjusted for mortgage write-downs and foreclosures.
‡ Above adjustment plus adjustment for foreign purchases of primary securities.

INDIRECT FINANCE AND FINANCIAL INTERMEDIARIES

The principal intermediary during the period was the monetary system, including Federal Reserve Banks after 1914. Up to World War I, life insurance companies, mutual savings banks, and savings and loan associations dominated the non-monetary intermediary group. After the war, land banks, management investment companies, and federal agencies and trust funds became important.

The main responsibility for the retrogression of financial intermediation during the first two decades, or at least up to 1915, must be laid at the door of the monetary system, that is, commercial banks. In 1898–1900, the system absorbed over 40 per cent of the primary issues. By 1912–14, it was purchasing less than 25 per cent of the issues. This relatively low share was not raised during the subperiod 1915–21, even with the addition of the Federal Reserve Banks to the monetary system. However, this perhaps is not surprising in view of the abnormally heavy issues of securities during these years. But the performance of the system did not improve from 1922 to 1930, on the average, when security issues were normal relative to GNP. In fact, during these years, the average annual share of issues taken by the system fell to 21 per cent.[11]

The group of non-monetary intermediaries purchased 15 per cent of total issues in 1898–1900. The share rose very slowly to 17 per cent just before the war, and then fell to 11 per cent in the face of the heavy issues of the war period. After that, the activity of these intermediaries was phenomenal. During 1922–24, their share jumped to 40 per cent, remained at about this level in the following sub period, and then hit 50 per cent during the final three years of the period. The high indirect finance ratio during most of the 1920's, therefore, was due principally to the growth of non-monetary intermediation. These and the monetary trends are shown in Table 3.

In short, the monetary system retrogressed up to World War I and it participated very little in the resurgence of intermediation after that date.

TABLE 3   *Indirect Finance Ratios of Selected Intermediaries, 1898–1930, by Subperiods*

(In Percentages)

	MONETARY SYSTEM*	LIFE INSURANCE COMPANIES	MUTUAL SAVINGS BANKS	SAVINGS AND LOAN ASSN'S	MNGM'T INVEST. CO'S	ALL OTHERS
1898–1900	41.3	6.7	7.7	−0.8		1.4
1901–04	38.3	8.1	5.3	0.5		1.8
1905–08	25.6	9.7	4.2	1.6		2.2
1909–11	28.0	8.0	5.5	2.2		2.8
1912–14	24.4	8.2	4.0	2.7		2.2
1915–21	24.5	4.3	2.7	1.9	0.1	3.0
1922–24	39.3	12.8	7.8	8.0	0.1	11.3
1925–27	26.3	13.6	6.2	7.7	1.8	9.3
1928–30	0.2	17.2	5.0	4.7	17.1	6.1

* Includes Federal Reserve Banks after 1914.

DIRECT FINANCE RATIOS AND LONG-TERM YIELDS

Our theoretical framework suggests that there should be a positive relationship between the direct finance ratio and changes in interest rates on primary securities. We should expect interest rates to rise whenever a large share of primary issues is absorbed by spending units; in the opposite case, when intermediation is heavy, we should expect falling rates.

The direct finance ratio may be a crude indicator of changes in primary yields. This may be most easily seen in terms of a simple financial growth model. Assuming that non-monetary indirect assets are competitive only with money, spending units' incremental demand for primary securities is: $e(abY - tdY)$. [The term] abY is primary security issues, where a is the ratio of issues to aggregate deficits of spending units, b is the ratio of deficits to GNP in current prices, and Y is GNP in current prices. tdY expresses spending units' incremental demand for transactions and contingency balances. At given interest rates, spending units will desire to purchase the proportion, e, of the residual supply of primary securities. The remainder of the issues, $1 - e$, they will want sold to financial intermediaries so that an equivalent amount of indirect assets for diversification balances may be accumulated. Thus, $e(abY - tdY)$ is the desired incremental demand of spending units for primary securities. Interest rates will remain steady if the incremental realized supply of the securities to spending units is equal to this demand.

Now, dividing through by abY, we have:

$$\begin{pmatrix} \text{Realized Direct} \\ \text{Finance Ratio} \end{pmatrix} = \begin{pmatrix} \text{Desired Direct} \\ \text{Finance Ratio} \end{pmatrix} = e - g \, (et/ab),$$

where g is the annual growth rate of GNP. When the realized exceeds the desired ratio, interest rates will rise. When the desired ratio is the larger, interest rates will fall. If we assume that the desired ratio moves within relatively narrow limits, a high realized ratio will generally indicate upward pressure on yields, and a low realized ratio will generally mean downward pressure on yields. With this assumption, then, we can compare the realized ratio to changes in interest rates.

Before doing this, though, we should take a moment to comment on the last assumption. Is it likely that the desired ratio will move within narrow limits? The answer is almost certainly "no" when we are dealing with annual data. To begin with, as we have seen, ab fluctuated between 2 per cent and 20 per cent during the period. Second, the annual growth rate of GNP was highly unstable.[12] Third, speculative demand, reflected in e, was undoubtedly quite high in some years and quite low in others. Finally, even annual t may have been unstable. Consequently, a high realized ratio, for example, may not indicate upward pressure on interest rates because the desired ratio may be just as high or higher.

But, in some large degree, these problems disappear when we work with annual averages during complete cycles. We have previously observed that, in these terms, *ab* was remarkably stable. In addition, fluctuations in speculative demand are likely to be smoothed out when annual data are averaged over a cycle. Moreover, the growth rate of GNP is less unstable when it is expressed as an average annual rate during a cycle, and the same is probably true of *t*. The assumption, then, that the desired ratio fluctuates within relatively narrow limits would appear to be reasonable, provided that annual averages for our subperiods are used. Nevertheless, there is nothing to prevent the desired ratio from showing an upward or downward drift over long periods of time. Our results should be checked against this possibility.

There is one more problem to straighten out. The interest rate used in this paper is the long-term yield on high-grade corporate bonds. This series, extending from 1900 to 1950, was recently compiled by W. Braddock Hickman.[13] For our period, it is probably the best series available. However, we have experimented with other long-term yields and with unweighted averages of several, and the results are substantially the same in every case. On the other hand, our results are much less satisfactory when short-term rates are used. There are some obvious reasons for this, and probably others not so obvious, but there is no time to explore them here.

We may now return to the heart of the matter. We have seen that the (realized) direct finance ratio,[14] starting at 44 per cent, rose almost without interruption through the sixth subperiod, 1915–21, at which time it was 64 per cent. It then fell sharply to 20 per cent, moved up to the still relatively low level of 35 per cent, and ended the period a little below 50 per cent. On the basis of these movements, we should expect growing upward (or diminishing downward) pressures on the long rate lasting through the phase 1915–21. We should then expect the rate to fall sharply in 1922–24, fall again but less sharply in 1925–27, and perhaps rise a little (or fall a little) in 1928–30.

In a way it is embarrassing to find that the actual world is almost identical to this mental image of it. The average yearly changes in the long rate during the eight subperiods were as shown in Table 4. The sole interruption to the rise in the direct finance ratio during

TABLE 4

1901–04	+0.017	1915–21	+0.189
1905–08	+0.068	1922–24	−0.313
1909–11	−0.037	1925–27	−0.143
1912–14	+0.073	1928–30	+0.040

the first two decades came in the phase 1909–11. Over the same period, the only interruption to the upward trend of interest rates also came in this phase. With this exception, each increase in rates up to the 1920's was larger than the preceding one. This conforms exactly to movements in the direct finance ratio. The sharpest fall in rates came in 1922–24, and the next sharpest in the following subperiod. Again, this is in conformity with the ratio. Finally, there was a small upward movement in yields, as we would expect, during the final years of the period.

Using the direct finance ratio as the independent variable and the average annual change in bond yield as the dependent one, the coefficient of correlation is 97.5 per cent, with a standard error of about one-tenth of 1 per cent. A direct finance ratio of 48 per cent was sufficient to hold the yield almost constant. Anything higher raised it, and anything lower reduced it. A change in the ratio of 5 percentage points changed the yield by 0.05[15] (see Figure 1).

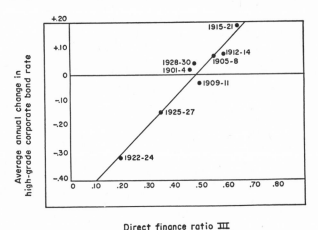

Direct finance ratio **III**

Figure 1.

SOME ALTERNATIVE MODELS

An alternative model frequently used is that which relates the income velocity of the money supply to interest rates. Aside from some basic difficulties with this model, which we have discussed elsewhere, it is not likely to be useful under growth conditions, especially when non-monetary intermediation is important. For one thing, under ordinary circumstances, the money supply has to grow relative to national income to keep interest rates stable. This is because primary security issues tend to force rates up unless a portion of the issues is sold to the monetary system. Moreover, the money supply growth required to stabilize interest rates depends on the growth of other indirect assets that are competitive with money. If non-monetary intermediaries are growing rapidly, it is perfectly possible for money supply growth to lag behind income growth without any adverse effects on security markets.

There is a good example of this in our period from 1922 to 1929 or 1930. In the subperiod, 1922–24, income velocity averaged 3.63. It was 3.67 in the next phase, and 3.74 from 1928 to 1930. Over these years, income velocity was higher than it was during any other phase of the full period with the exception of the war years. And yet these high and rising velocities were compatible with downward trends in interest rates over most of this decade. The reason is simply that non-monetary intermediaries grew so rapidly that the required growth of the monetary system was sharply reduced. Financial analysis cannot stop with the money supply when other indirect assets are of growing importance.

Nevertheless, as other investigators have discovered, there was a fairly good relationship between income velocity and interest rates during the period 1900 to 1930, in spite of the negative correlation between the two variables during most of the 1920's. But the relationship is much less impressive than the one presented above, especially when one views the 1920's as the crucial decade, the decade of rapid growth in non-monetary intermediation (see Figure 2).

The link between velocity and yields is weakened, moreover, when time deposits are included in the money supply. In fact, in this case, a negative correlation for most of the period is evident (see Figure 3). Finally, the relationship between marginal velocity and the change in yields is not very close, whether time deposits are included in or excluded from the money supply (see Figures 4 and 5).

Briefly, then, we have obtained the best results when account is taken of primary security issues and the growth of all intermediaries, including the monetary system. The two familiar variables, the money supply and national income, form only a part of the total picture.

NOTES

1. Securities might be issued by spending units to build up their financial assets or their holdings of existing real assets. However, in a world of balanced budgets, no spending unit would have a *net* accumulation of these assets, positive or negative.

2. In our empirical work, we exclude from indirect finance some kinds of claims on intermediaries, such as accrued expenses or even stockholder equities, that are essentially like debt issues of non-financial spending units.

3. It may help to illustrate these financing arrangements. Suppose that at a GNP of $400 billion the sum of all spending units' deficits is $40 billion. Suppose further that $40 billion of primary securities, such

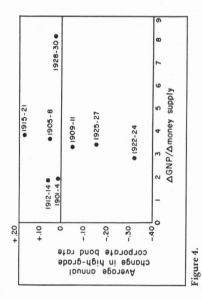

Figure 2.

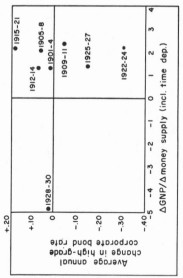

Figure 4.

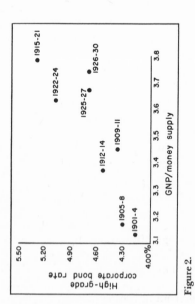

Figure 3.

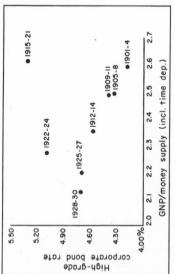

Figure 5.

as corporate bonds and mortgages, are issued to cover the deficits. The primary securities may be sold directly to surplus spending units whose aggregate surplus will also be equal to $40 billion, looking at it *ex post*. In this case direct finance will take place, with surplus spenders acquiring various types of primary securities. Alternatively, if the primary securities are sold to financial intermediaries, surplus spenders will accumulate claims on these intermediaries, indirect financial assets instead of primary securities. In this event we say that the expenditures represented by the primary securities have been indirectly financed. If indirect finance occurs through commercial banks, surplus spenders accumulate bank deposits; if through savings and loan associations, they acquire savings and loan shares; if through life insurance companies, policyholder equities; and so on.

4. This growth has not been steady. Indeed, it is shown later that there was retrogression in intermediation from 1898 to 1921. The share of issues going to intermediaries rose in the 1920's, rose further in the 1930's, and remained high in the 1940's.

5. We may mention a few additional issues in banking theory. As intermediaries, banks buy primary securities and issue, in payment for them, deposits and currency. As the payments mechanism, banks transfer title to means of payment on demand by customers. It has been pointed out before, especially by Henry Simons, that these two banking functions are at least incompatible. As managers of the payments mechanism, the banks cannot afford a shadow of insolvency. As intermediaries in a growing economy, the banks may rightly be tempted to wildcat. They must be solvent or the community will suffer; they must dare insolvency or the community will fail to realize its potentialities for growth.

All too often in American history energetic intermediation by banks has culminated in collapse of the payments mechanism. During some periods, especially cautious regard for solvency has resulted in collapse of bank intermediation. Each occasion that has demonstrated the incompatibility of the two principal banking functions has touched off a flood of financial reform. These reforms on balance have tended to emphasize bank solvency and the viability of the payments mechanism at the expense of bank participation in financial growth. They have by no means gone to the extreme that Simons proposed, of divorcing the two functions altogether, but they have tended in that direction rather than toward indorsement of wildcat banking. This bias in financial reform has improved the opportunities for non-monetary intermediaries. The relative retrogression in American banking seems to have resulted in part from regulatory suppression of the intermediary function.

Turning to another matter, it has seemed to be a distinctive, even magic, characteristic of the monetary system that it can create money, erecting a "multiple expansion" of debt in the form of deposits and currency on a limited base of reserves. Other financial institutions, conventional doctrine tells us, are denied this creative or multiplicative faculty. They are merely middlemen or brokers, not manufacturers of credit. Our own view is different. There is no denying, of course, that the monetary system creates debt in the special form of money: the monetary system can borrow by issue of instruments that are means of payment.

There is no denying, either, that non-monetary intermediaries cannot create this same form of debt. They would be monetary institutions if they could do so. It is granted, too, that non-monetary intermediaries receive money and pay it out, precisely as all of us do: they use the payments mechanism.

However, each kind of non-monetary intermediary can borrow, go into debt, issue its own characteristic obligations—in short, it can create credit, though not in monetary form. Moreover, the non-monetary intermediaries are less inhibited in their own style of credit creation than are the banks in creating money. Credit creation by non-monetary intermediaries is restricted by various qualitative rules. Aside from these, the main factor that limits credit creation is the profit calculus. Credit creation by banks also is subject to the profit condition. But the monetary system is subject not only to this restraint and to a complex of qualitative rules. It is committed to a policy restraint, of avoiding excessive expansion or contraction of credit for the community's welfare, that is not imposed explicitly on non-monetary intermediaries. It is also held in check by a system of reserve requirements. The legal reserve requirement on commercial banks is a "sharing ratio"; it apportions assets within the monetary system. The share of assets allocated to the commercial banks varies inversely with the reserve requirement. The proportion of the commercial banks' share to the share of the central bank and Treasury is the "multiple of expansion" for the commercial banking system. The "multiple of expansion" is a remarkable phenomenon not because of its inflationary implications, but because it means that bank expansion is anchored, as other financial expansion is not, to a regulated base. If credit creation by banks is miraculous, creation of credit by other financial institutions is still more a cause for exclamation.

6. We can reach the same conclusion by looking at the supply of and the demand for primary securities. The shift in demand to savings and loan shares reduces spending units' demand for bank deposits by, say, an equivalent amount. Consequently, the demand by spending units for primary securities is unchanged at current yields. Also, there is no change in this demand by the monetary system, since we have assumed the money supply constant. However, there is an increase in demand for primary securities by savings and loan associations. So, for the economy as a whole, there is an excess demand for primary securities at current yields, which is the counterpart of the excess supply of money.

Downward pressure on primary yields is exerted as long as the indirect debt of non-monetary intermediaries is to some degree competitive with money and as long as the additional demand for primary securities by these intermediaries is roughly equivalent to their creation of indirect debt.

7. For periods longer than the Keynesian short run, it is hardly safe to assume that transactions and contingency demands for additional money balances are proportional to increments in the level of money income. They may be elastic to interest rates on such primary securities as Treasury bills and brokers' loans. For any increment in money income, they may rise with real income. As a larger share of national income involves market transactions, as population moves from farms to cities, as a dollar of income is generated with more or fewer dollars of inter-

mediate payments, as credit practices change, as checks are collected more efficiently or as deposits cease to bear interest and bear service charges instead, one expects the marginal ratio of active balances to income to vary. And incremental demand for contingency balances must be sensitive not only to income, and perhaps to interest rates, but to the evolution of emergency credit facilities, to job security and social security, to an array of circumstances that is largely irrelevant in short-period analysis.

8. Our empirical work was made possible by Raymond W. Goldsmith's significant contributions, especially his *A Study of Saving in the United States* (Princeton, N.J.: Princeton University Press, 1955).

9. The flow of securities is measured in issue prices. The issues are net of retirements. The average for the full period is the cumulated flow of securities divided by cumulated GNP. For the entire period, this flow was about $180 billion. In 1898, the current value of outstanding primary securities was between $35 and $40 billion.

10. This is somewhat surprising in view of the large changes during the period in the proportion of total issues represented by each of the several types of issue. For example, at the turn of the century, mortgage issues were about 10 per cent of total issues, but the proportion grew rapidly to 25 per cent a decade later, and then to 35 per cent at the end of the period. On the other hand, consumer and other debt, mainly short-term consumer and business borrowing, moved in exactly the opposite way, from 35 per cent to about 10 per cent. United States government securities fluctuated widely as a percentage of total issues. Except for the first subperiod, the ratio was negligible to 1914. It was 33 per cent from 1915 to 1921, and then averaged over minus 10 per cent for the remainder of the period. Common and preferred stock issues, with two exceptions, were either a bit below or above 20 per cent of total issues during each subperiod. In the 1915–21 phase, the proportion was about 12 per cent, and it was 44 per cent from 1928 to 1930. State and local government securities gained relative to the others during the period while corporate and foreign bonds, if anything, lost some ground.

11. The share was a great deal higher than this though from 1922 to 1924 and somewhat higher from 1925 to 1927. The system purchased only 0.2 per cent of the issues from 1928 to 1930. However, excluding the "bad" years of 1929 and 1930, the system purchased only 29 per cent of the issues (from 1922 through 1928), which is much lower than its share from 1898 to 1904.

12. The first two factors may partly cancel. When g is high, ab tends to be high, too, and the reverse is also true.

13. W. Braddock Hickman, *Trends and Cycles in Corporate Bond Financing*, (Occasional Paper No. 37 [New York: National Bureau of Economic Research, 1952]), pp. 34–35. The use of the series carries a disadvantage, since our initial subperiod, 1898–1900, cannot be used in the correlation analysis.

14. The ratio used here is corrected for net foreign purchases of primary securities (see Table 2, ratio III).

15. The estimating equation is: average annual change in bond yield = $-0.50 + 1.04049$ (direct finance ratio).

15 *Providing for Growth of the Money Supply*

George S. Tolley *North Carolina State College*

One often sees the observation that economic growth necessitates a continuing increase in the money supply. Some writers view the provision of this increase as the most important consideration of monetary policy. Others have taken account of it in formulating specific stabilization schemes for the economy, and still others feel that it offers a convenient way of helping to reduce the national debt. In spite of these views, there has been little explicit consideration of the alternative ways in which a given growth in the quantity of money might be achieved and even less consideration of the effects on policy goals of the various alternatives.

Decisions concerning the growth of the quantity of money may both affect and be affected by broader choices concerning the level of taxes and government expenditures and the management of the national debt. Moreover, the way in which increases in the quantity of money come about is closely related to the functioning of the banking system. This article considers the relevance of growth of the money supply for these matters.

Part one of the article identifies the reserve base of the money supply and the average reserve ratio for the money supply. The determinants of these two variables are discussed, and suggestions

Reprinted from *Journal of Political Economy*, Vol. 65 (December 1957), 465–85, by permission of the author and The University of Chicago Press. Copyright 1957 by The University of Chicago Press.

from previous literature as to their appropriate values are noted. Part two deals with the relation of choices of the reserve base and the average reserve ratio to the national debt. It makes explicit the sense in which growth of the money supply implies debt retirement and examines factors that have affected historical debt retirement associated with the money supply. Suggestions are made for predicting this debt retirement. The problem of how to relate choices of the reserve base and the average reserve ratio to debt policy is then discussed. Part three deals with the implications for resource allocation of the choice of the reserve base and the average reserve ratio. From this analysis emerges an estimate of the tax on deposits that is implied by the fact that no interest is paid on the reserve base. Finally, two specific programs are considered that are within the spirit of the present institutional framework and would take account of resource-allocation objectives in the choice of the reserve base and the average reserve ratio.

Framework for Analyzing Decisions Concerning the Money Supply

In the familiar consolidated statement published by the Federal Reserve Board called "Member-Bank Reserves, Reserve Bank Credit, and Related Items," the two terms "money in circulation" and "member bank reserve balances" are directly relevant to the money supply. I shall refer to the sum of the two terms as the "reserve base of the money supply." If we were interested only in the part of the money supply that is in the form of bank deposits, the reserve base would include member-bank reserves but not money in circulation. The latter is included because hand-to-hand currency forms part of the money supply.[1]

The reserve base, R, equals the money supply, M, multiplied by the average reserve ratio, ρ:

$$\rho M = R.$$

The average reserve ratio is jointly determined by government, banks, and the non-bank public. An important way in which the public may affect ρ is by changing the desired ratio of currency holdings to deposits. For example, a shift toward deposits away from currency decreases ρ, since every dollar of deposits requires only ten or fifteen cents of reserve base on the average, whereas a dollar of currency requires a full dollar of reserve base. One of several ways in which banks can influence ρ is through changes in excess reserves. In this paper we are particularly interested in government's influence on ρ. Government influences ρ via changes in required reserve ratios for deposits.[2]

From the equation in the preceding paragraph it is evident that there is a variety of reserves and reserve ratios that will result in a given stock of money. If we suppose that there will be a unique stock of money in some future year consistent with employment and price-level objectives, any change in the average reserve ratio implies a corresponding and proportionate change in the reserve base. For this reason, the reserve ratio affects the amount of debt retirement occurring as the quantity of money increases secularly. Moreover, the reserve ratio is an important variable in its own right, since it affects the functioning of the banking system. One part of monetary-fiscal management is thus the choice of a desirable combination of reserve ratios and reserves.

Aside from calling attention to this particular policy problem of the choice each year of one pair among the many possible pairs of values of ρ and R, the formulation that has been given helps to clarify the effects on government operations of growth in the money supply. The formulation might also be useful, even though no government action to influence ρ was contemplated in a particular year, in suggesting how to predict the debt retirement that would accompany growth of the money supply. One of the major purposes of this study is to clarify such effects so that they may be better predicted and planned for in monetary-fiscal management.

The main suggestions for an appropriate solution of the problem posed here come from writers who have not been directly concerned with growth of the money supply. We may distinguish four main types of suggested solutions. The solution that has perhaps received most attention is the 100 per cent reserve proposal. That is, in the terms used here, the reserve ratio would be (roughly) 1, and the amount of reserves would be equal to the quantity of money.[3] A second suggested solution has been that the creation of new money be backed by 100 per cent reserves. This implies (again, roughly) raising ρ gradually through time in such a way that R would increase by the same amount as the money supply.[4] A third solution does not lend itself readily to the present formulation, but it is so closely related to the others that it clearly deserves mention here. This solution is embodied in the various bond-reserve proposals for banks. These proposals differ from the others in having a somewhat more direct bearing on problems of debt management and bank earnings.[5] A fourth solution, namely, simply to maintain present arrangements, is implicit in most writings. Required reserve ratios would be maintained at present levels (or perhaps varied in connection with countercyclical actions), with ρ and R determined by the public and the banks given these required reserve ratios.

In expressed opinion we find no consensus as to whether ρ or R should largely guide our choice. Some of the proposals have been motivated by one and some by the other.[6] The tendency for debt rather than banking considerations to be more important in recent thinking is undoubtedly due in part to growth of the debt and in part to a loss of faith in the efficacy of monetary reform such as is embodied in the 100 per cent reserve plan.

National Debt Considerations

The statement was made earlier that increases in the money supply are a source of debt retirement. If this statement is true, where do we look in the government accounts to find this debt retirement? Debt retirement attributable to the money supply cannot be seen clearly in the budget surplus or deficit as usually defined, and a reinterpretation of government accounts is therefore desirable. One of the main manifestations of growth in the money supply is the increase at the Federal Reserve banks in member-bank reserve balances and in the item "currency in circulation," both of which tend to expand with growth of the money supply. These are liabilities, and their growth makes for a corresponding increase in assets. If we momentarily neglect changes in the gold stock, we see that the Federal Reserve banks in the normal course of their operations—open-market operations and the like—must find themselves accumulating earning assets, mainly government bonds.

Increases in earning assets of the Federal Reserve banks are a major part of the debt retirement associated with growth of the money supply. The view advanced here is that the holdings of securities of the Federal Reserve banks should be subtracted from the nominal national debt if we are to get a meaningful picture of the debt. Most of the earning assets of the Federal Reserve banks are, in any case, government bonds. The Federal Reserve banks might be viewed as repositories for fictitious federal debt. The fictitious nature of this debt is evidenced by the fact that, although interest is paid by the Treasury on this debt, a large portion of Federal Reserve bank earnings are transferred to the Treasury.

Like growth of the money supply, acquisitions or losses of gold do not appear in the budget as usually defined. In much the same way that the growth of the money supply represents debt retirement, an outflow of gold represents debt retirement. A normal effect of a gold outflow would be to deplete member-bank reserves, but Federal Reserve policy rightly aims at not allowing gold movements to affect the money supply. The ultimate effect of a gold outflow tends to be that the gold assets lost are replaced

TABLE 1   Yearly Changes Derived from "Member-Bank Reserves, Reserve Bank Credit, and Related Items"

(Millions of Dollars)[a]

	SOURCES OF DEBT RETIREMENT		DISPOSITION OF DEBT RETIREMENT		
Year[b]	Increase in reserve base, R[c]	Decrease in gold stock	Increase in net Treasury currency[d]	Increase in reserve bank credit	Decrease in Federal Reserve liability items[e]
1921	− 775	− 410	99	−1247	− 39
1922	− 232	− 510	90	− 894	63
1923	392	− 265	124	0	3
1924	118	− 438	34	− 371	16
1925	190	128	− 7	313	12
1926	131	− 87	− 8	50	2
1927	− 14	− 140	7	− 112	− 48
1928	22	478	14	503	− 17
1929	− 20	− 215	9	− 185	− 60
1930	− 191	− 209	0	− 382	− 20
1931	292	− 421	− 17	− 75	− 37
1932	474	1037	41	1367	104
1933	336	− 399	183	− 90	− 156
1934	1487	−3825	−2607	252	18
1935	1334	−1260	225	8	− 159
1936	1327	−1492	361	− 7	− 521
1937	1473	−1710	− 896	89	571
1938	1138	− 645	1305	34	− 846
1939	2580	−3147	− 92	− 17	− 457
1940	4564	−3853	509	− 48	248
1941	1034	−2661	47	− 264	−1408
1942	2025	− 113	252	508	1152
1943	4818	349	683	4801	− 317
1944	5864	1215	− 1	7696	− 618
1945	6296	960	58	7032	167
1946	2702	− 57	422	2152	73
1947	41	− 996	950	−2286	378
1948	883	−2266	9	− 270	−1113
1949	68	− 934	52	−2204	1287
1950	−2270	235	19	− 993	−1060
1951	3739	2475	65	5340	808
1952	1578	−1590	97	− 492	382
1953	1279	883	124	1863	176
1954	− 753	536	553	228	− 999
1955	− 638	249	42	−1041	611
1956	863	− 121	74	618	50

[a] Sources: *Banking and Monetary Statistics* (Washington: Board of Governors of the Federal Reserve System, 1943), pp. 373–77, with more recent figures from *Federal Reserve Bulletin.*

by earning assets—probably government bonds—leaving member-bank reserves unaffected. The acquisition of earning assets by the Federal Reserve banks in response to the gold outflow is debt retirement in the same sense that acquisition of earning assets associated with growth of the money supply is debt retirement. Naturally, by the same line of reasoning, contractions in the money supply and inflows of gold can be considered to be debt-increasing.

It will be apparent that, in interpreting the government accounts, the Federal Reserve banks are being viewed in the present analysis as part of the government sector of the economy. This way of viewing them seems reasonable, since Federal Reserve banks are inseparably involved with the Treasury in buying and selling gold and in issuing money or the right to create money. The main determinant of Federal Reserve earnings is the extent of these transactions, and a large part of these earnings are transferred to the Treasury.

All this is made more explicit in Tables 1 and 2. In Table 1, yearly changes from the consolidated account "Member-Bank Reserves, Reserve Bank Credit, and Related Items" have been arranged to show how debt-retirement items have impinged on the government accounts. Debt retirement stems from increases in the reserve base, R, and decreases in the gold stock, which are shown in the first two columns. The sum of these two columns equals the sum of the remaining columns. Most of the debt retirement is reflected in increases in reserve bank credit, as suggested in the preceding discussion. However, because of institutional happenstance, which will not be considered here, the debt retirement may also be reflected in net Treasury currency and other Federal Reserve accounts.

"Member-Bank Reserves, Reserve Bank Credit, and Related Items" is a capital account or balance sheet. The interpretation just advanced can be extended to the current accounts by considering the earnings and expense statement of the Federal Reserve banks as summarized in Table 2. Since the bulk of the banks' earning assets are government securities, the banks receive few payments from the public. Treasury payments on these securities are "fictitious" government expenditures. That is, the government budget records them as expenditures, whereas in the present interpretation they are like an interagency transfer. Federal Reserve bank earnings other than on government securities are unrecorded

---

[b] End of June.

[c] Money in circulation plus member-bank reserve balances.

[d] Treasury currency outstanding minus Treasury cash holdings.

[e] Deposits other than member-bank reserve balances with Federal Reserve banks and other Federal Reserve accounts.

TABLE 2   Receipts and Disposition of Receipts of Federal Reserve
Banks

(Millions of Dollars)*

| | RECEIPTS | | DISPOSITION OF RECEIPTS | | |
| | From government securities | Other† | Paid to public‡ | Paid to Treasury | Transferred to surplus |
Year					
1920	7	174	38	61	83
1921	6	117	47	60	16
1922	17	34	40	11	— 1
1923	7	43	45	4	3
1924	15	24	41		— 3
1925	13	29	39		2
1926	13	35	38	1	8
1927	14	29	38		5
1928	11	53	40	3	21
1929	8	63	44	4	23
1930	17	19	39		— 2
1931	12	17	37		— 7
1932	27	23	37	2	11
1933	38	12	50		— 1
1934	46	3	42		6
1935	40	3	42		1
1936	35	3	37		
1937	39	2	38		3
1938	34	2	35		1
1939	37	2	34		4
1940	42	1	26		18
1941	40	1	41		1
1942	51	1	49		4
1943	68	1	29		40
1944	103	2	55		49
1945	140	3	60		82
1946	147	3	69		81
1947	156	3	75	75	8
1948	299	5	119	167	19
1949	312	4	102	193	21
1950	273	3	57	197	22
1951	389	6	111	255	28
1952	442	14	118	292	46
1953	497	16	130	343	40
1954	435	4	126	276	36
1955	399	14	128	252	33
1956	572	24	140	402	54

* Sources: *Banking and Monetary Statistics* (Washington: Board of Governors of the Federal Reserve System, 1943), p. 356, with more recent figures from *Federal Reserve Bulletin*.

† Total current earnings minus earnings from government securities.

‡ Total current earnings minus net current earnings before payments to the Treasury plus dividends paid.

government receipts. Federal Reserve receipts are offset in part by expenses of the Federal Reserve banks and by payments to the Treasury. The offset is not exact, however; the difference is equal to transfers to surplus. In consolidating the Federal Reserve banks into the government sector, these transfers to surplus should be added to the receipts of the government to arrive at the budget surplus or deficit.

Tables 1 and 2 have shown how, in the accounts, the effect of the money supply on the debt is obscured by the handling of gold under present arrangements and by the issuance of Treasury currency. Were it not for these two items, the effects of the money supply on debt could be directly related to holdings of securities by the Federal Reserve banks. These items have reduced the amount of debt accumulated by the Federal Reserve in connection with growth of the money supply. There has nevertheless been a substantial increase in Federal Reserve earnings because of increased holdings of government securities. The government budget surplus or deficit, as usually measured, has not been greatly affected by these intra-government payments because (1) the Federal Reserve has, in turn, made payments to the public and (2) it has made offsetting intra-government payments by transferring a large part of its unspent earnings to the Treasury.

Having considered how the money supply is a source of debt retirement, let us now consider factors that affect the extent of this debt retirement.

Because—as we saw on pages 83–85—the reserve base, R, is equal to the average reserve ratio, ρ, times the money supply, M, debt retirement may stem from increases both in the average reserve ratio and in the money supply. Moreover, the money supply can be related to variables that have considerable interest both analytically and from a policy point of view. Consider the Cambridge-type equation of exchange,

$$M = KPY,$$

where P is the price level, Y is real national income, and K is the reciprocal of the income velocity of money. If we substitute this in the fundamental relation from Part I (namely, $R = \rho M$), we have

$$R = \rho KPY.$$

Two different interpretations of this identity may be considered. First, it may be viewed as a way of predicting the effects of increases in the reserve base, R, which might be brought about through Federal Reserve open-market purchases. Viewed in this way, the identity delineates the possible effects of the increase. At one extreme, there might be a compensating increase in the average reserve ratio, ρ, perhaps due simply to an increase in excess reserves. In this event the money supply and hence the remaining variables, K, P, and Y, might not change. As we shall see shortly, however, the determinants of ρ are ordinarily rather stable, so that a compensating increase in ρ is unlikely.[7] Another possibility is that there would be a compensating decline in velocity (increase in K), in which case P and Y still might not be affected. If we could predict the extent of the change in velocity, then, depending on the state of full employment or unemployment in the economy, we could go about predicting the effect of the increase in the reserve base, R, on the price level, P, and real income, Y.

A second interpretation of the identity is of more interest for this discussion than the one just considered. This second interpretation is suggested by the observation that policy objectives pertaining to the price level and income are obviously of overriding importance in comparison with debt retirement. The identity allows one to see what the implications of price level and income changes are for debt retirement. A given set of values of the variables on the right-hand side is consistent with one and only one value for the reserve base R. Hence the identity enables us to see how debt retirement attributable to the money supply has been associated with the joint outcome of changes in the average reserve ratio, velocity, the price level, and real income.

With this second interpretation of the identity in mind, let us look at the historical data. Table 3 is derived by multiplying the percentage changes in ρ, K, P, and Y by the value of R in the previous year. Estimates are thus obtained of an amount of debt retirement associated with these variables each year. The sum of these changes is not exactly equal to the change in R, and the interaction effect of the variables is also presented.[8]

The figures in Table 3 suggest that all the factors shown have at times been significant. As we might expect, the growth of real income appears to be the most consistent factor making for debt retirement. The price-level column suggests very literally and dramatically how much debt was monetized through inflation in the 1940's. Changes associated with velocity have at times been substantial in both directions. The effects of the much-discussed secular decline in velocity, however, do not show through in these figures. Even in the relatively stable period of the 1920's, changes associated with velocity seem to be positive about as often as negative. Apparently, then, it is principally because of growth in real income and of inflation that increases in M have been a highly consistent and substantial source of debt retirement.

For ρ, the pattern is one of decreases in the 1920's, increases in the 1930's, and decreases in the 1940's and 1950's. For some years, such as 1922 and 1950, the decreases were big enough to outweigh

TABLE 3   Analysis of Yearly Changes in the Reserve Base, R

(Millions of Dollars)*

		ASSOCIATION OF CHANGE IN *R* WITH OTHER VARIABLES				
Year†	Change in R	ρ	K	P	Y	Interaction of ρ, K, P, Y
1921	− 775	− 409	1839	−1322	− 538	−344
1922	− 232	− 458	− 178	− 221	674	− 49
1923	392	− 149	− 319	170	732	− 42
1924	118	− 161	387	− 52	− 42	− 14
1925	190	− 341	− 150	202	506	− 28
1926	131	− 168	87	− 159	388	− 16
1927	− 14	− 232	357	− 139	12	− 12
1928	22	− 280	144	62	106	− 10
1929	− 20	− 68	− 346	− 39	458	− 25
1930	− 191	− 102	872	− 259	− 619	− 83
1931	292	506	1061	− 644	− 492	−140
1932	474	1697	805	− 711	− 995	−322
1933	336	1125	− 373	− 274	− 48	− 93
1934	1487	779	− 532	409	804	27
1935	1334	293	− 25	212	814	39
1936	1327	261	− 407	65	1427	− 19
1937	1473	1306	− 877	532	566	− 54
1938	1138	782	1226	− 234	− 592	− 44
1939	2580	1392	− 48	− 129	1259	106
1940	4564	2611	− 178	256	1626	249
1941	1034	−1213	−2362	1705	3352	−449
1942	2025	− 48	−3260	3125	2786	−579
1943	4818	−1535	1466	1744	3046	98
1944	5864	1452	1144	619	2268	381
1945	6296	− 247	6301	1065	− 789	− 33
1946	2702	−2757	6757	3653	−4074	−877
1947	41	−1668	−2592	4652	64	−416
1948	883	453	−4450	2403	2132	345
1949	68	86	127	303	− 448	0
1950	−2270	−3642	−3733	599	3974	532
1951	3739	2340	−5128	3042	2771	714
1952	1578	−1123	159	810	1662	70
1953	1279	− 707	− 286	445	2086	−259
1954	− 753	−2325	2022	94	− 994	450
1955	− 638	−2951	−1297	601	2809	200
1956	863	− 416	−1251	1474	1183	−127

* Sources: *Banking and Monetary Statistics* (Washington: Board of Governors of the Federal Reserve System, 1943), pp. 34–35, 373–77, with more recent figures from *Federal Reserve Bulletin;* U.S. Department of Commerce, *National Income and Product of the United States* (Washington: Government Printing Office, 1951), pp. 146 and 150, with more recent figures from *Survey of Current Business.*

† R and ρ, end of June.

the effects of increases in the money supply. The years 1931–33 are particularly interesting. Here the money supply was contracting. This was more than offset, however, by increases in ρ, so that the net effect was one of debt retirement. All the changes associated with ρ are sizable. Changes in this variable significantly increased debt retirement in the 1930's and decreased it in the rest of the period.

Table 4 shows the relative importance of the various determinants of ρ and suggests why it has changed.[9] Declines in the proportion of the money supply in the form of currency have been the chief source of changes in ρ in recent years. Over the longer run, increases in the average required reserve ratio for deposits have also been important.

Tables 3 and 4 suggest how the identity we have been considering might be used by policy-makers to predict future debt retirement associated with the growth of the money supply. The identity might be used in the following way. Trends for the variables on the right-hand side would be studied. Given that full employment is desirable and may ordinarily be achieved, a growth in real income, Y, of something like 3 per cent per year may be expected. Policy-makers may wish to plan for a stable level of prices, or, perhaps more realistically, for slightly rising prices. In a secular context, velocity as determined by behavior in the private sector appears to be rather stable—perhaps subject to slight decline over time. Aside from required reserve ratios, ρ is also largely determined in the private sector and appears to be subject to a rather smooth secular decrease. All these trends would be put into the identity so as to predict and plan for the debt retirement associated with the growth of the money supply. The effect of planned changes in ρ resulting from changes in required reserve ratios could obviously also be included in the scheme.[10]

Thus far we have been largely concerned with the mechanics of the debt retirement and its prediction. Let us now consider the central question of what light the debt effects of the money supply throw on choosing optimal values of ρ and R. In doing this, it may be well to emphasize that large sums are involved and that therefore the question appears to be important. The figures that have been presented indicate that, under present circumstances, with ρ in the neighborhood of 0.20 to 0.25, the growth of the money supply accounts for about one and a half billion dollars of debt retirement yearly.

The possibilities for debt retirement through changes in ρ are also great. As indicated in Table 3, the effects of changes in ρ have often been of the same order of magnitude as the effects of real income. Many of the changes in ρ have, of course, been the

TABLE 4   Analysis of the Average Reserve Ratio, ρ*

| Year† | ρ | NON-BANK PUBLIC | | BANKS | | | |
		Currency $\rho_C \times M_C/M$	Deposits‡ $\rho_M \times D/M \times M_M/D$	Excess reserves‡ R_E/M	Currency $\rho_C \times M'_C/M$	Deposits‡ $\rho_M \times M'_M/M$	Government deposits‡ $\rho_M \times M'_M/M$
1920	0.177	1 × 0.104	× 0.896 × 0.609		1 × 0.027	× 0.087	× 0.009
1921	.167	1 × .098	× .902 × .600		1 × .026	× .072	× .012
1922	.154	1 × .086	× .914 × .626		1 × .021	× .080	× .005
1923	.151	1 × .088	× .912 × .609		1 × .019	× .075	× .008
1924	.147	1 × .082	× .918 × .626		1 × .021	× .086	× .006
1925	.139	1 × .074	× .926 × .633		1 × .020	× .083	× .006
1926	.137	1 × .072	× .928 × .631		1 × .020	× .078	× .006
1927	.131	1 × .068	× .932 × .640		1 × .019	× .078	× .006
1928	.126	1 × .067	× .933 × .627		1 × .016	× .071	× .007
1929	.124	1 × .066	0.065 × .934 × .620	0.004	1 × .015	0.065 × .067	0.065 × .008
1930	.123	1 × .062	× .938 × .651		1 × .016	× .086	× .008
1931	.132	1 × .070	× .930 × .628		1 × .017	× .091	× .013
1932	.164	1 × .103	.065 × .897 × .587		1 × .018	.065 × .069	.065 × .022
1933	.189	1 × .117	.068 × .883 × .601	.012	1 × .016	.068 × .081	.068 × .039
1934	.208	1 × .105	.068 × .895 × .617	.039	1 × .016	.068 × .098	.068 × .051
1935	.215	1 × .097	.073 × .903 × .643	.049	1 × .016	.073 × .110	.073 × .022
1936	.220	1 × .097	.072 × .903 × .676	.050	1 × .019	.072 × .123	.072 × .022
1937	.244	1 × .101	.145 × .900 × .707	.016	1 × .018	.145 × .111	.145 × .013
1938	.259	1 × .097	.125 × .903 × .675	.051	1 × .019	.125 × .117	.125 × .011
1939	.284	1 × .100	.128 × .900 × .688	.069	1 × .017	.128 × .130	.128 × .013

(Continued)

TABLE 4 (Continued)

		NON-BANK PUBLIC		BANKS			
Year†	ρ	Currency $\rho_C \times M_C/M$	Deposits‡ $\rho_M \times D/M \times M_M/D$	Excess reserves‡ R_E/M	Currency $\rho_C \times M_C/M$	Deposits‡ $\rho_M \times M_M/M$	Government deposits‡ $\rho_M \times M'_M/M$
1940	.327	1 × .101	.134 × .899 × .694	.104	1 × .017	.134 × .147	.134 × .012
1941	.309	1 × .112	.134 × .888 × .727	.071	1 × .019	.134 × .142	.134 × .009
1942	.308	1 × .136	.151 × .863 × .747	.034	1 × .018	.151 × .124	.151 × .022
1943	.289	1 × .155	.126 × .845 × .767	.014	1 × .016	.126 × .103	.126 × .072
1944	.303	1 × .179	.113 × .821 × .758	.012	1 × .014	.113 × .093	.113 × .152
1945	.301	1 × .181	.113 × .819 × .742	.011	1 × .012	.113 × .088	.113 × .159
1946	.281	1 × .168	.123 × .832 × .751	.007	1 × .011	.123 × .075	.123 × .077
1947	.271	1 × .160	.133 × .840 × .749	.004	1 × .012	.133 × .067	.133 × .007
1948	.273	1 × .155	.142 × .846 × .747	.004	1 × .014	.142 × .065	.142 × .012
1949	.274	1 × .153	.145 × .847 × .744	.006	1 × .013	.145 × .063	.145 × .013
1950	.254	1 × .148	.126 × .852 × .748	.003	1 × .012	.126 × .064	.126 × .021
1951	.268	1 × .148	.143 × .852 × .755	.002	1 × .012	.143 × .065	.143 × .034
1952	.262	1 × .143	.141 × .857 × .759	.001	1 × .014	.141 × .069	.141 × .031
1953	.258	1 × .142	.138 × .858 × .752	.001	1 × .014	.138 × .067	.138 × .019
1954	.246	1 × .136	.124 × .863 × .749	0.003	1 × .014	.124 × .074	.124 × .028
1955	.232	1 × .132	.117 × .868 × .750		1 × .014	.117 × .069	.117 × .024
1956	0.230	1 × 0.132	0.116 × 0.868 × 0.750		1 × 0.011	0.116 × 0.068	0.116 × 0.022

* Sources: *Banking and Monetary Statistics* (Washington: Board of Governors of the Federal Reserve System, 1943), pp. 34–35, 72–75, and 373–77, with more recent figures from *Federal Reserve Bulletin*.
† End of June.
‡ Excess reserves not available for 1920–31; calculation of ρ_M for those years is prevented.

effect of private rather than government behavior. Many of the changes have been associated with shifts in the form in which the public holds money. For instance, a shift away from low-reserve-using money, such as time deposits, toward high-reserve-using money, such as demand deposits and currency, implies a rise in ρ. However, there have also been changes in required reserve ratios.

Two effects of a change in ρ on debt retirement may be noted. First, if there is a rise in ρ, the reserve base—for a given money supply—must increase proportionally. Second, in subsequent periods changes in the money supply will have a magnified influence on the reserve base.

As an example of possibilities at an extreme, suppose 100 per cent reserve requirements were introduced. Then ρ would be somewhat greater than 1.[11] The increase in the reserve base R would be something like $175 billion, given the present money supply. We may suppose that most of the assets acquired by the Federal Reserve banks would be government bonds. As noted previously, this may be considered to be debt retirement, since the interest on bonds held by the Federal Reserve tends not to be paid to the public but to revert to the Treasury or to some extent to be transferred to the surplus account of the Federal Reserve banks. With 100 per cent reserves, then, the federal debt held outside the Federal Reserve would be reduced to a small fraction of its present value.

A second result of 100 per cent reserves would be a magnified effect of future increases in the money supply. If we conservatively suppose that the money supply will grow at a rate of 3 per cent per year, the asset acquisitions of the Federal Reserve—if member banks were required to carry 100 per cent reserves—would be over $6 billion per year in view of the fact that the money supply is well over $200 billion. This would quadruple the debt retirement that is taking place under present arrangements.

The literature is not completely lacking in proposals motivated by the debt effects of the money supply. It has been suggested that we plan a yearly deficit equal to the debt retirement arising from increases in the money supply.[12] This would seem to imply that the present size of the debt, whatever it may happen to be, is optimal. It has also been suggested that, by maintaining a balanced budget, we allow the growth of the money supply gradually to retire the debt.[13] This would seem to imply that the optimal debt is zero and that the optimal rate of retirement is arbitrarily dictated by the growth of the money supply.

To relate the choice of ρ and R explicitly to debt policy might be more desirable than the two procedures just noted. We may conjecture that, even in the absence of any transition problems, the optimal size of the debt is greater than zero and, further, that it increases secularly, perhaps being some multiple of income.[14] If we make these suppositions and abstract from transition problems, the optimal values of ρ and the debt, together with the increasing money supply, determine the optimal government deficit in any year. This proposal, unlike the proposals mentioned above, involves a deficit somewhat greater than the debt retirement associated with the growth of the money supply, in order to increase the debt secularly.

The idea that it would be desirable to have a secularly increasing debt arises from visualizing a moving equilibrium in which the portfolio items of the banks and the non-bank public all grow according to some secular pattern. Suppose, for instance, that the optimal situation is one in which the quantities of all assets are increasing at the same rate—say at 3 per cent per year. Then, in order that the quantity of government securities may increase by 3 per cent, the required government deficit is 0.03 (public debt $+$ ρ_M). This is because the injection of new securities must allow for the debt retirement that will be associated with growth.[15]

Since the present values of ρ and the debt are probably non-optimal, both the optimal values and the rate of transition would need to be determined. There is probably universal agreement that we should not attempt very large changes in the debt in any one year, and there is probably nearly as complete agreement that the present debt is too large. These considerations suggest that, for the years in the immediate future, declines in the quantity of government securities are desirable.[16]

Resource-Allocation Considerations

Changes in ρ may affect bank service charges. This is because such changes affect a main source of bank earnings, namely, holdings of earning financial assets. This raises the suspicion that we are involved in a resource-allocation problem. Variations in service charges may be expected to influence the volume of deposits that people wish to hold, and thus we find that we are concerned with the question: What is the optimum volume of bank deposits?[17]

The optimum quantity of commodity X, so the usual analysis runs, is that which would prevail under perfect competition. Applied to bank deposits, a *first* supposition might be that bank charges corresponding to 100 per cent reserves would induce the optimum volume of deposits. This would be supported by the notion that the cost of producing money is the cost of mining gold, to which should be added the service costs associated with deposit procedures. However, the notion that the cost of producing money is the cost of mining gold is not tenable, as is perhaps most convincingly shown by the existence of fractional reserve banking. Put more strongly, the absurdity of foregoing the resources needed to mine an amount of gold equivalent to the entire money supply is apparent. Yet such a view is inherent in this first supposition. A *second* supposition might be at the opposite extreme that, in holding deposits, depositors should forego only service costs, since resources other than those used for servicing are not required to produce deposits. (The difference between the interest on securities and interest on deposits would just equal service costs.) Banking procedures indicate that this supposition is also wrong, at least if applied to a gold standard. As a practical matter, banks cannot function without some reserves. A *third* supposition is, then, that under a gold standard, with competition in banking, we might expect an optimal situation in which depositors' costs included both service charges and the cost of mining the fractional amount of gold behind each dollar. This supposition seems tenable, except that nations do not operate on a gold standard nowadays. Our final position is that without a gold standard, since reserves then cost nothing to produce, we revert to the second solution, in which depositors forego only service costs.

If this final position is valid—as I believe it to be—what are the indications for policy? Disregarding policy aims other than optimum resource allocation, ρ should be determined by competition in the banking system, which would almost certainly result in a lower ρ than now prevails. Alternatively, interest might be paid by the Federal Reserve banks on member-bank reserves. In this way banks would be enabled to pass on to depositors the savings from having fiat instead of gold reserves.

The preceding argument suggests that the acquisition of assets by the Federal Reserve in connection with the growth of deposit money constitutes the proceeds from a tax on deposits. Let us try to examine the way in which the tax manifests itself. To do this, assume that banking is a competitive industry, one of whose functions is to provide bank-account services. With fractional reserve banking, deposit creation enables banks to earn income other than from service charges. Competition keeps service charges below the cost of providing bank-account services by the amount of income associated with the asset holdings made possible by deposit creation. Service charges may then possibly be negative, taking the form of interest paid on deposits.

The following expression estimates the average rate of return on non-cash assets:

$$\frac{\text{Gross bank earnings minus service-charge income}}{\text{Total assets minus cash assets}}.$$

The numerator of this expression is of particular interest. It is intended to approximate bank income associated with holdings of assets. Suppose that a part of this income can be attributed to deposit creation, as follows: (Average rate of return on non-cash assets) × (total deposits minus cash assets). The idea is that for all deposits in excess of reserves of cash assets there are corresponding holdings of earning assets yielding the average rate of return.[18] Our estimate of the cost per deposit dollar of providing bank-account service, then, is: (Average rate of return on non-cash assets) × (1 minus the ratio of cash assets to deposits) + (service-charge income per deposit dollar). This estimate is obtained by adding service-charge income to the component of asset earnings attributed to deposits and dividing the resulting expression by total deposits. The procedure arises from the assumption made in the preceding paragraph that competition will make the sum of these two kinds of income equal to the cost to banks of providing bank-account services.

For member banks, the 1951–54 average estimated cost of providing bank-account services is 2.44 per cent. The estimate results from multiplying the average rate of return on non-cash assets, 3.44 per cent, by the fraction of deposits not backed by cash, 0.748, and adding service charges of −0.13 per cent. The net negative service charge results from interest paid on time deposits, which is about twice as great as receipts of service charges on deposits.[19]

Let us pause to note that the preceding calculations permit us to conjecture what changes might take place with changes in required reserves for deposits. Perhaps the simplest way to state the conclusion is that, as cash assets are raised toward 100 per cent of deposits, service charges must approach about $2\frac{1}{2}$ per cent if bank earnings are not to change and if the composition of banks' remaining earning assets is not altered. Since required reserves are only part of cash assets, required ratios could actually be raised to a point at which service charges somewhat exceeded my estimate. The opinion may be ventured that the estimated maximum service charge is not so large as to cause great concern, given time for adjustments to take place; that is, no disaster seems to be implied by the adjustments in service charges that the alternative choices would involve.

We are now in a position to obtain a crude measure of the tax on deposits. Let us assume for a minute that cash assets are zero. Then, corresponding to every dollar of deposit liability, we could visualize a full dollar's worth of earning assets. This would contrast with the situation in 1951–54, when, because of cash assets, we find only $0.748 of non-cash assets for a dollar of deposit liability. Hence the estimate of the rate of return on non-cash assets is 3.44 per cent, we can visualize an increase in bank earnings for every deposit dollar of $(1 - 0.748) \times 3.44$ per cent, or 0.87 per cent. To estimate the tax, we need to consider required reserves and not simply total cash assets. During the period, required reserves were almost exactly half of total cash assets.[20] Applying this figure to total cash assets gives the estimate that earnings per deposit dollar would be increased 0.43 per cent if required reserves were zero.

This result may be incorporated into the previous analysis. Since banks' earning assets yield 3.44 per cent and banks pay (net) 0.13 per cent on deposits, we can call 3.31 per cent the charge for money. The latter is the return foregone in holding money, assuming that money-holders could choose the same average asset composition as banks if they substituted earning assets for money. It is supposed here that, of this charge, 2.44 per cent is paid to the productive factors (labor and capital) that provide bank-account services.[21] An additional cost is the return foregone by banks in holding non-reserve cash assets, amounting to 0.43 per cent, as derived in the preceding paragraph. If this reduction in asset earnings is added to the cost of bank-account services, the estimated total cost of providing a deposit dollar is 2.87 per cent. The remaining 0.43 per cent as we total to the 3.31 per cent charge for money is the return foregone in holding required reserves.[22] The 0.43 per cent is the estimate of the tax. Put in ad valorem terms, the estimate of the tax is about 15 per cent[23] of the cost of providing deposit money.[24]

Suppose one wished to alleviate the tax on deposits. This would require that service charges be reduced on deposits where these are now levied, and it would require that interest rates be increased on deposits that draw interest. Existing legal restrictions over banks in these matters might therefore need to be lifted or altered. As required reserves were lowered or—alternatively—as interest began to be paid on reserves, it would be desirable to watch banks' behavior to check on whether the increased earnings tended to be kept by banks or whether through competition they were passed along to depositors. If they were not passed along, the establishment of maximum service charges and minimum interest rates might be contemplated.

In the manner just described, the return foregone in holding deposits would be reduced. That is, the price of deposits would decline, and one would expect the demand for them to increase, with deposits being substituted for other assets. This conjecture stems from a belief that the demand for money—in real or deflated terms—depends on the return foregone in holding money. We would be moving along the demand schedule for (real) money and for this reason would expect the real quantity of money to increase. Other things being equal, this implies a decline in the velocity of circulation of money. Would there be undesirable disorganization in the financial markets because of the asset substitutions just referred to? My feeling is that the substitutions would not be large enough to cause disorganization. As a precautionary measure, however, the tax on deposits might be reduced only gradually. This would help to prevent disorganization that might be caused by sudden change, and it would enable one to see through experience the magnitude of the effects of reducing the tax on deposits.

Thus far, we have discussed taxation only on deposit money. What about the other part of the money supply—hand-to-hand currency? The tax on hand-to-hand currency consists of the earnings that holders of currency forego over and above the small costs of creating the currency. The revenue from the tax is the increased holding of earning assets by the Federal Reserve, made possible by the fact that currency is provided to the public at a price greater than its cost of production. The tax is much higher on currency than on deposits, since the Federal Reserve accumulates several fold more earnings assets for each dollar's growth in currency than for an equal growth in deposits.[25]

The tax on currency could be alleviated by paying interest on currency. This would be more novel than the previous proposal to pay interest on reserves, but it is suggested by the same logic.[26]

Resource-allocation considerations thus give us a very definite answer to the choice of ρ and R. It is important to note that this choice, if taken, would make unnecessary much of the analysis in the earlier parts of this paper. There would be no debt retirement associated with growth of the money supply, since earnings on securities deposited as reserves would not be retained by the government.

Are there policy desiderata that militate against the choice that is indicated by resource-allocation considerations? One argument against the choice might be that the contribution to *aggregate cyclical stability* of maintaining higher reserves than would prevail under banking competition is worth the cost in resource allocation. However, this argument seems weak for two reasons. First, other equally good (better?) counter cyclicaldevices are available. Second, regardless of the level of required reserves, interest could be paid on reserves so as to alleviate the tax on deposits.[27]

A second possible argument against the choice indicated by resource-allocation considerations might be that continued *purchases of gold are a cost of providing money*. It can be argued that, were it not for monetary arrangements, these purchases would be unnecessary and that they can be offset, roughly, by debt retirement associated with the growth in reserves. From our earlier consideration of the government accounts, it can be seen that debt retirement from reserves would exactly offset gold purchases under a gold standard. This argument condones the practice of having the government accumulate gold. The costs of this practice are hardly negligible, and it does not seem to be desirable to obscure these costs by pretending that there is a relation between the money supply and the stock of gold.[28]

A third argument might be that the *tax on deposits is a legitimate excise*. Obviously, however, the tax came about by historical accident. It is difficult to think of reasons for regarding it as a good tax in its own right.

A final argument might be that the *assumption of competition in banking is invalid*. This argument fails not because of any proof that competition is effective in banking but because forcing banks to forego interest on required reserves does not seem a sensible way to combat lapses from competition.

Aside from the policy desiderata that have been considered, are there serious practical problems of implementation that stand in the way of the resource-allocation choice? One problem in implementing the choice would be to specify the rate of interest to be paid by the Federal Reserve. Conceptually, we can visualize a rate such that the central bank pays out exactly the earnings on assets acquired in money creation. These assets may not be completely identifiable in practice, partly because the Federal Reserve acquires some assets not connected with money creation and partly because some non-Federal Reserve accounts (for example, Treasury currency) are connected with money creation. It is even more challenging to specify what form the Federal Reserve ought to give to the assets it holds, since this obviously affects the extent of its earnings. This article has not attempted to throw any light on the question of what is optimum portfolio composition for the central bank.

Other problems of implementation center around gold. We may accurately say that in the past the acquisition of the gold stock has been financed by the tax on money. As we saw in discussing national debt considerations, the *decrease* in earning assets that is implied by gold acquisition is the government payment for the gold. The *increase* in government earning assets implied by additions to member-bank reserves and to currency in circulation is the revenue from the tax on money. A principal reason for the historical net acquisition of earning assets by the Federal Reserve is that the revenue from the tax has been greater than the value of gold purchases.

Under the policy in question, that of eliminating the tax, there would be no increase in earnings from future additions to the money supply. The Federal Reserve would not have the means it has had in the past of offsetting its gold acquisitions and could thus look forward to a continuous decrease in earnings as assets were exchanged for gold. Other sources of revenue would become necessary to carry out this program.

Perhaps the worst difficulty of all is that the Federal Reserve might find itself insolvent immediately. Not only must additions to the gold stock be financed, but the existing stocks of gold and money must be considered. Because of past gold acquisitions, the offsetting asset to a large amount of member-bank reserves and currency in circulation is gold rather than earning assets. Consequently, the Federal Reserve does not have enough earnings to make the tax on the present money stock zero. To alleviate the tax on money completely, that is, to be able to pay interest on liabilities by having an amount of earning assets equal to them, it would be necessary not only to make provision for paying for continuing additions to the gold stock but also—in effect—to purchase the existing stock of gold. The purchase could be accomplished by issuing government securities to the Federal Reserve in an amount equal to the gold stock. This would obviously represent a sizable increase in the national debt and in concomitant payments of interest on the debt. These additional receipts of interest on the government bonds by the Federal Reserve are precisely what would enable it to pay the interest on its own liabilities.

Do these problems that would be encountered rule out any practical application of the conclusions reached in our earlier analysis? A negative answer to this question is indicated by two more restricted applications of the analysis that will be discussed in closing.

Most of the difficulties just mentioned could be circumvented by paying interest on member-bank reserves at the same rate as on government bonds. In fact, reserves might simply take the form of government bonds. Since government bonds are the type of security that has usually been acquired by the Federal Reserve, no drastic change from present portfolio behavior would be required of the Federal Reserve.

If interest were paid on member-bank reserves only, perhaps both the chief strength and the chief weakness would arise in refraining from paying interest on hand-to-hand currency. It would not then be necessary to make adjustments connected with the existing stock of gold because currency in circulation somewhat exceeds the gold stock. The Federal Reserve has enough earning assets to pay interest on bank reserves if it does not attempt to pay interest on currency. Future increases in the amount of hand-to-hand currency would provide some offset to possible future additions to the gold stock. However, it might still be necessary to find supplemental sources of revenue in order to finance gold acquisitions completely.[29]

While the pricing of deposits vis-à-vis non-money should be improved by paying interest on member-bank reserves, perhaps the main weakness of the scheme would be worse pricing of deposits vis-à-vis currency. The scheme aims at eliminating the tax on deposits but would not reduce the present high tax on currency that is implied in failure to pay interest on currency.

Now consider a second possible application of our conclusions. Though this proposal does not go so far as the scheme just considered, it might nonetheless represent a substantial improvement over present procedures. An explicit policy might be followed of making the proceeds of the tax on money equal to the value of additions to the gold stock. Central-bank operations, *including* gold acquisition, would then yield zero profit. From the point of view of welfare, we would have a situation resembling the gold standard.

This policy assumes that we should try to do at least as well as a gold standard in achieving welfare goals while providing the money supply. The historical net acquisition of earning assets by the Federal Reserve suggests that we may not now be meeting that norm. Under a gold standard, the charge for money tends to be just enough to cover costs of acquiring the gold that is concomitant to the money, while, under present arrangements, the charge for money more than covers gold costs.

The important difference between this policy and a gold standard as usually visualized is that the stock of money would not vary in response to changes in the gold stock. Rather, the average reserve ratio, ρ, would vary. The stock of money would be varied according to price level and employment objectives, as is clearly in line with present policy intent. That is, countercyclical action could continue to be taken independently of the gold stock, as it is at present, which is not possible under a gold standard as traditionally visualized. The contrast with present policy is that, at present, the earning assets of the Federal Reserve rather than ρ tend to vary with changes in the gold stock.

Under present procedure, when gold is acquired, the Federal Reserve loses earning assets. Depending on the rate of gold accumulation as compared with increases in the money supply, the Federal Reserve may have either a net gain or a net loss of earning assets over time.[30] Historically, as we have seen, it has had a net gain. Under the policy being considered, required reserve ratios would be varied in response to differing relative rates of gold accumulation and increases in the money supply, so that in the future there might be little or no net change in earning assets. Ideally, the policy would be started from a position of substantially no earning assets—a zero profit level—that would be unaltered as the policy operated through time. However, the policy would not necessarily have to be initiated at such a position. If initiated from the present level, the implication would be that the Federal Reserve would keep present earning assets but would look forward to acquiring—or losing—no more in the future.

Typically, under the suggested policy, there would be two responses to an inflow of gold. First, there would be sales of securities, in an amount equal to the gold inflow. In this way potential reserve funds would be kept from rising. Second—and this is the novel part of the policy—required reserve ratios would be raised so that reserve funds required for the existing quantity of money would rise by the amount of the gold inflow. The earning assets acquired as member banks increased their reserves would then just equal the amount lost through the open-market sale.

On the other hand, increases in the quantity of money would result in lower required reserve ratios. With no change in required reserve ratios, earning assets of the Federal Reserve normally tend to rise as the quantity of money increases. As this happened, the Federal Reserve would simply reduce required reserve ratios, so as to restore its original volume of earning assets.

Perhaps the most significant difference between present practice and the policy suggested here is that under the latter more frequent changes would be made in required reserve ratios. The Federal Reserve could thus begin following the policy immediately in its day-to-day operations if it so desired.[31] Unlike the possible policy discussed earlier, this policy does not involve any drastic change, such as paying interest on reserves or currency. It seems entirely consistent with the spirit of present arrangements. This is particularly true because present institutional arrangements obviously still have a strong gold-standard orientation. The policy may be viewed as an attempt to follow a gold standard as nearly as is feasible, given that internal monetary policies are to be pursued independently of the gold stock.

The possibility we have been discussing may also be viewed as providing a criterion for setting required reserve ratios. There has been a notable lack of criteria for desirable levels of reserve ratios. Although reserve ratios are often adjusted countercyclically, on an *ad hoc* basis, there appears to be no consensus that they provide a good countercyclical weapon. Meanwhile, the amount of earning assets of the Federal Reserve has tended to be a meaningless residual of effects of gold movements and changes connected with the money supply. The possibility we have discussed would eliminate these imprecisions. It would aim at a situation in which users of money bear neither more nor less than the cost of the gold stock, in place of a situation in which money is taxed capriciously.

Conclusion

The reserve base, R, of the money supply has been defined here to comprise currency in circulation plus member-bank reserves, and the average reserve ratio, ρ, has been defined as the ratio of the reserve base to the money supply. Determinants of the reserve base and the average reserve ratio are often considered as independent variables, whose net effect is to determine the money supply. For instance, under present arrangements, a shift of the public's desired ratio of currency to deposits would change the money supply—if there were no compensating change in the reserve base. That is, such a shift would change the average reserve ratio and, with a given reserve base, would change the money supply.

In the present analysis, however, compensating changes in the reserve base and the average reserve ratio have been realistically supposed to take place. The assumption has been that the Federal Reserve authorities will insure that adjustments between the reserve base and the average reserve ratio will result in a given money supply, dictated by price level and income objectives largely independent of the reserve base and the average reserve ratio.

An advantage of the framework used in this paper is that it permits a simple summary of the factors relating the money supply to government. Such a summary has been presented in Tables 1–4.

Two major conclusions about optimal values of the reserve base and the average reserve ratio have been reached: (1) interrelationships of variables influenced by government suggest that the choice of the reserve base and the average reserve ratio be related explicitly to debt policy; and (2) resource-allocation considerations suggest having lower required reserves or interest-bearing reserves or both. The same type of reasoning suggests paying interest on hand-to-hand currency. Guided by the second conclusion, the last part of the paper suggests two specific programs within the spirit of the present institutional framework that would take account of resource-allocation objectives in choosing values of the reserve base and the average reserve ratio.

There remains the question of how debt and resource-allocation objectives might be taken into account simultaneously. This question has not been dealt with in this article. Most of the debt could be eliminated by imposing high reserve requirements for commercial banks. This would imply a large, but hardly disastrous, tax. In order to maintain bank earnings, service charges on deposits would have to rise. At the other extreme—as was emphasized in part three—the tax on money could be completely eliminated, in which case there would be no debt retirement associated with the growth of the money supply.

The opinion may be ventured that, in the absence of some attempted balancing between the two types of objectives, even to pursue one to the complete exclusion of the other would represent an improvement over present practices. Until now decisions concerning the reserve base and the average reserve ratio do not seem to have been mobilized toward the accomplishment of any particular aim. Yet this paper has indicated that these decisions can make a significant contribution either to achieving an optimal size of the national debt or to achieving optimal arrangements from the standpoint of resource allocation in the use of money.

NOTES

1. Lloyd W. Mints has stated this point of view succinctly in observing that banks operate with a "mixture of 100 per cent and fractional reserve requirements. They may not issue notes to be used as hand-to-hand currency, which is equivalent to a right of note issue with a requirement of 100 per cent reserves; but against their deposits they are required to hold only fractional reserves" (*Monetary Policy for a Competitive Society* [New York: McGraw-Hill Book Co., Inc., 1950], p. 6).

2. I ignore some details concerning government deposits, whose influence is usually negligible. The various influences on ρ are reflected in this expression:

$$\rho = \rho_C \left[\frac{M_C}{M}\right] + \rho_M \left[\frac{D}{M}\right]\left[\frac{M_M}{D}\right] + \frac{R_E}{M}$$
$$+ \rho_C \left[\frac{M'_C}{M}\right] + \rho_M \left[\frac{M'_M}{M}\right] + \rho_M \left[\frac{M''_M}{M}\right].$$

The first term is the reserve ratio for currency multiplied by the proportion of the total stock of money which the public holds in the form of currency. Thus ρ_C is the required reserve ratio for currency, equal to 1 under present arrangements, and M_C is the amount of currency held outside banks. The second term is the required reserve ratio for deposits ρ_M, times the proportion of the total stock of money which the public holds in the form of deposits times the proportion of these deposits held in member banks. The ratio ρ_M is itself a weighted reserve ratio; that is, it is the average of required ratios for different kinds of deposits, weighted by the proportions of the kinds of deposits. The third term is excess reserves, R_E, divided by the stock of money. The remaining terms are the same as the first or second terms, except that they pertain to the banks and the government instead of the public. Thus, in the fourth term, M'_C is the amount of currency held by the banks; and, in the fifth term, M'_M is the amount of interbank deposits held in member banks. In the last term, M''_M is the amount of government deposits held in member banks.

The preceding expression is derived by considering the reserve base as equal to the sum of reserve-using magnitudes and dividing the resultant equality by the money supply. Table 4 presents values of ρ and reveals the importance of each of the components in this expression.

3. Among recent writers, Milton Friedman has advocated this proposal. See his "A Monetary and Fiscal Framework for Economic Stability," *American Economic Review*, Vol. 38 (June 1948), 245–64; and "Commodity Reserve Currency," *Journal of Political Economy*, Vol. 59 (June 1951), 203–32. Earlier literature includes Laughlin Currie, *Supply and Control of Money in the United States* (Cambridge: Harvard University Press, 1934); Irving Fisher, *100% Money* (New York: Adelphi Co., 1935); Albert G. Hart, "The Chicago Plan of Banking Reform," *Review of Economic Studies*, Vol. 2 (May 1935), 104–16; and Henry C. Simons, *A Positive Program for Laissez-faire: Some Proposals for a Liberal Economic Policy* (Chicago: University of Chicago Press, 1934).

4. See Mints, *op. cit.*, pp. 191–96.

5. Apparently, this type of proposal was originally made in L. H. Seltzer, "The Problem of Our Excessive Banking Reserves," *Journal of the American Statistical Association*, Vol. 35 (March 1940), 24–36.

6. All except the fourth, of course, might be taken to imply little conflict between ρ and R, since these proposals would result in higher values for both variables. Nevertheless, even among these, the specific choices are quite different.

7. Unless, of course, required reserve ratios were deliberately raised to induce a compensating increase.

8. The equation used in Table 3 is

$$\Delta R = R\frac{\Delta\rho}{\rho} + R\frac{\Delta K}{K} + R\frac{\Delta P}{P} + R\frac{\Delta Y}{Y} + I,$$

where I is the interaction term obtained as a residual. The measures used here have the advantage of being internally consistent; that is, the variables are defined so that the equation $R = \rho KPY$ is, in fact, fulfilled in any year. The measure of money income is gross national product, and this is separated into real income and price level by use of the implicit price deflator of the gross national product as prepared by the Department of Commerce. Velocity is gross national product divided by the same measure of the money supply as that used in obtaining ρ. The money supply is deposits adjusted, including both time and demand deposits, plus currency outside banks.

9. ρ is the sum of the remaining columns in Table 4. The table presents numerical values for terms in the expression given in note 2.

10. The formulation in this paragraph has much in common with that of Clark Warburto. . An important difference, however, is that Warburton would use the increase in the money supply as a central criterion in pursuing stabilization objectives, whereas I am interested here only in the implications of increase in the money supply for fiscal planning. This paper is neutral on what the role of the quantity of money can or should be in achieving stabilization objectives (see Clark Warburton, "Monetary Theory, Full Production, and the Great Depression," *Econometrica*, Vol. 13 [April 1945], 74–84; "Volume of Savings, Quantity of Money, and Business Instability," *Journal of Political Economy*, Vol. 55 [June 1947], 222–33; "The Secular Trend in Monetary Velocity," *Quarterly Journal of Economics*, Vol. 63 [February 1949], 68–91; "Banks and Business Fluctuations," *Estadistica: Journal of the Inter-American States Institute*, Vol. 3 [March 1950], 59–68).

11. It is possible for ρ to be greater than 1 because the banks and government hold reserve-using currency and deposits not considered to be part of the money supply. To calculate ρ with 100 per cent reserves, let ρ_M equal 1 in Table 4.

12. See Friedman, "A Monetary and Fiscal Framework for Economic Stability," p. 251.

13. See Mints, *op. cit.*, pp. 191–96.

14. Two main lines of argument in favor of a positive government debt are that it is an instrument of stabilization and that taxpayers as a group may rationally wish to defer tax payments.

15. One can think of a variety of reasons, of course, why the quantities of all assets might not increase just at the same rate. Secular shifts in the supply and demand for different kinds of assets are to be expected. If we assume that capitalization influences the price of interest-bearing securities, their values will be affected by changes in the rate of interest.

16. In contemplating changes in ρ, we also need to take into account the ability of the banking system to adjust to portfolio changes in an orderly manner.

17. Curiously, the literature on 100 per cent reserves—where the bank earnings and hence the service-charge problem become most acute—does not seem to contain any meaningful consideration of this question.

18. The following important assumptions underlie this scheme: (1) that reserves for deposits may be taken to include all cash assets; (2) that income associated with asset holding may be attributed entirely to non-cash assets; and (3) that assets other than reserves may be viewed as if they were all earning the average return. Obviously, the scheme can be defended only as providing a first approximation.

19. The figures given in this paragraph are derived from *Federal Reserve Bulletin*, Vol. 41 (May 1955), 564.

20. From *Federal Reserve Bulletin*, Vol. 41 (May 1955), 508 and 517.

21. This was derived on p. 398.

22. The discrepancy of 0.01 was lost in rounding.

23. Very nearly the same estimate is obtained from using data for the latest year available, 1956.

24. To note only one·of many possible qualifications, since banks probably reduce other cash assets to some extent because they hold required reserves, the charge for money may not be so greatly affected by required reserves as is assumed in the text. It may be emphasized that the admitted crudity of the estimates does not imply a corresponding lack of usefulness. For example, we can now assert that the tax in ad valorem terms must almost certainly lie somewhere between, say, 5 and 50 per cent; this was not obvious before.

25. To obtain an estimate of the tax on currency similar to that obtained above for deposits would require investigation of government expenses in providing hand-to-hand currency.

26. I believe that there would be no particular difficulty in paying interest on currency. However, no attempt has been made to explore this extreme kind of reform very deeply in this article.

27. If interest were paid on reserves, reserves might become such an attractive asset to banks that they would choose to hold substantially more than the present legal minimum reserves. For stabilization purposes, the Federal Reserve authorities might find it desirable for reserves to be near their minimum legal levels so that short-run changes in the money supply could be effected quickly if the need arose. If interest were paid on reserves, therefore, required reserve ratios might be raised to whatever level was needed to insure that banks had an incentive to stay near these ratios. The payment of interest would help to mitigate the undesirable resource-allocation effects of this procedure.

28. The accumulation of earning assets by the Federal Reserve indicates that there has in any case been more than enough debt retirement to offset gold purchases. The second alternative program discussed below seeks to make the tax on money exactly enough to cover gold acquisitions.

29. Would the best solution to this problem be to cease continuous accretions to the gold stock? Of course, another (bad?) solution to the problem would result from inflating the price level sufficiently so that increases in currency alone would be enough to offset increases in gold.

30. Other less important influences on the volume of earning assets are being neglected here.

31. This statement applies particularly to the variant in which earning assets would be left at current levels. If earning assets were to be zero, there might be a series of reductions in required reserve ratios.

Part **V**

The Rate
of Interest

The claim on the part of economics to be a quantitative science rests to a considerable degree on the existence of the concept of the rate of interest. It is the link between the flow of income and the stock of capital and, as such, it is of central importance in the calculus of economics. This crucial role of the rate of interest has long been recognized and consequently has been subjected to searching analysis for several centuries. In spite of this prolonged examination, our knowledge of the nature of the rate of interest and its role in the economy is less developed than that of many other economic factors which have not had the benefits of as long, nor as intensive, an inquiry.

The modern discussion of the rate of interest has concentrated on three areas: (1) criticism of Keynes' theory of liquidity preference; (2) the relationship between stock and flow analyses; and (3) the effectiveness of the rate of interest as a policy instrument.

Two general approaches have been followed in developing the modern monetary theory of the rate of interest. The first, the loanable funds approach developed by Wicksell and his followers, introduced financial considerations into the classical theory of the rate of interest in which the rate of interest depended essentially on the marginal productivity of capital and the time preference of income receivers. Wicksell treated the rate of interest as a price which would equate the supply of loanable funds (savings, S, and changes in the money supply, ΔM) with the demand for money (investment, I, and hoarding, H, i.e., the desired change in the community's stock of money and securities). The rate of interest would vary until it just equated the supply of and demand for loanable funds so that:

$$S + \Delta M = I + H$$

The various terms in the preceding equation were defined with differing degrees of netness and disaggregated for various sectors of the economy to produce a theory of varying degrees of complexity.[1]

[1] See Joseph W. Conard, *Introduction to the Theory of Interest* (Berkeley 1963), Chapter. 9.

The liquidity preference theory of interest made the rate of interest equate individuals' desires to divide their wealth between money and securities with the actual stock of wealth and securities. In addition, Keynes made some special assumptions concerning the demand for money at very low interest rates. We have seen that Keynes assumed that a community's preferences to hold a certain proportion of its assets in the form of money was a function of the rate of interest and that this preference schedule was relatively constant in the short-run so that the money supply which was established by the monetary authority determined the equilibrium rate of interest in the short-run.

The loanable funds theory was expressed in terms of flow variables while the liquidity preference theory was expressed in terms of the willingness to hold a particular stock of money. The conditions under which these two theories are equivalent engendered a great deal of discussion during which many new facets of the role of the rate of interest were discovered, or rediscovered and made more precise.

Hicks made an early attempt to reconcile the two theories by applying Walras' Law. He pointed out that in a general equilibrium system the demand, D, and supply, S, of goods, g, securities, s, and money, m, depend on the price of goods, P, and the price of securities, which may be expressed as the rate of interest, i. In general equilibrium there can be no excess (or deficit) demand in any of these three markets, so that the demand and supply in each market must equal one another:

$$D_g(P, i) = S_g(P, i) \qquad \text{(goods market)} \qquad (1)$$
$$D_s(P, i) = S_s(P, i) \qquad \text{(securities market)} \qquad (2)$$
$$D_m(P, i) = S_m(P, i) \qquad \text{(money market)} \qquad (3)$$

Hicks explained that, as a consequence of Walras' Law, if two of the markets are in equilibrium, there must also be an equilibrium in the third market, so that one of the equations shown above is redundant and may be omitted. The loanable funds approach omits the equation for the money market while the liquidity preference approach omits the equation for the securities market. Hicks' analysis is formally correct in that it showed that the loanable funds approach was consistent with the liquidity preference approach in Walrasian general equilibrium. The exact relevance of this type of equilibrium, however, to the Keynesian equilibrium and that of other models, and the question of the determinacy of other variables such as the general price level has engendered much discussion in recent years.

A great deal of confusion is eliminated by recognizing the three types of equilibrium to be considered. One is short-run equilibrium, where the influence of the size of the flows on the level of stocks may be regarded as negligible. This is largely the type of equilibrium Keynes had in mind (". . . in the long-run we are all dead"). The second type of equilibrium is where the flow variables have sufficient time to affect the level of stocks and vice versa but there is not sufficient time for stocks to attain equilibrium levels. This may be called the medium-run equilibrium and is largely the type of equilibrium that has caused the most problems. Last, there is the equilibrium where all the stocks and flows have attained their equilibrium levels; this may be called the classical long-run equilibrium.

Patinkin's criticism of Keynes is, in part, inappropriate in that he compares a theory which is a long-run equilibrium theory developed under the assumptions of perfect interest and price certainty with Keynes' short-run equilibrium theory in which uncertainty plays a central role. If there were no interest and price uncertainty there would be no speculative demand for money and one of the most significant differences between Keynesian and classical theory would disappear.

Although Keynes recognized the importance of changes in the stock of non-monetary financial assets on saving,[2] he chose to ignore these effects in his final analysis. From one point of view this was justified in that it was the short-run equilibrium that interested Keynes, where the magnitude of the flows was negligible relative to the stocks of existing assets (with the exception of the stock of money which was determined autonomously by the monetary authority), and the stocks of non-monetary assets could be treated as constant. However, from another viewpoint one may question this treatment of the stock problem, since the rate of interest is the yardstick by which the stock of capital is measured. Changes in the rate of interest result in changes in the real value of all income-yielding assets unless there are compensating changes in the price level to offset this effect. This effect requires little time to take place and one may question whether it is proper to ignore it, even in Keynes' short-run equilibrium. One may rationalize Keynes' position by saying that he did not feel this was important in the depression situation he was intent in analyzing, where the rate of interest was close to a minimum level set by the "liquidity trap" and the opportunity for capital gains would be small. The possibility of capital losses would only strengthen his major argument.[3] However, in growing and relatively prosperous economies, economists have rightly asked what might be the effects of the rate

---

[2] *General Theory of Employment, Interest and Money* (New York 1936), p. 92.

[3] The quotation of Fouraker, given by Shackle on page 447, on the Cambridge method is particularly relevant here.

of interest on the stock of assets and thus on consumption and investment decisions.[4]

There is disagreement as to what constitutes an "equilibrium situation." The flows may be in equilibrium in that wealthholders and investors do not wish to add to their stocks faster than they are presently adding to them though they are not satisfied with the present level. Thus it is a "desired level of stocks" only in the sense that, all other things taken into consideration, it is the highest level to which individuals believe they may raise their stocks at that moment. However, this obviously is not a stationary equilibrium since it is assumed that individuals will still add to their stocks. Only when the stocks of all assets have attained their desired levels and the levels of investment and saving have adjusted to this situation, will a stationary long-run equilibrium be attained. A good deal of controversy might have been avoided if these three equilibrium time periods were clearly distinguished and if the participants defined precisely what they meant by "stationary" and "dynamic equilibrium." It is possible in medium-run situations to have a stationary equilibrium in the flow variables and disequilibrium in the stock variables in a stationary sense, although in terms of a dynamic analysis both stock and flow variables may be in equilibrium. What has greatly hampered the discussion of the relationship between stocks and flows is that most of the controversy has taken place in the framework of models that have not specified the relationship between the level of stocks and the rate of saving which would make it possible to reconcile static and dynamic relationships.

The distinction between medium- and long-run equilibrium is very much like the distinction Wicksell made between medium-run situations where the money rate of interest differed from the "natural" rate of interest as determined by the marginal productivity of capital, and long-run situations where they were equal. In some respects the contemporary discussion of the stock and flow problem has taken on, in a highly formalized way, the problem that fascinated Wicksell a half a century ago.

The contemporary discussion, besides attempting to define what is meant by equilibrium of stocks and flows in the medium-run, has raised several other important questions. Does Say's Law hold in the medium-run when there are stocks of money in existence which may be employed to alter the level of demand? Does the rate of interest affect the rate of saving in any significant manner in the medium- and long-run? Is the rate of saving linked to the level of

[4] See Richard S. Thorn, "Long-Run Adjustments to Changes in the Capital-Output Ratio and the National Debt," *Yale Economic Essays*, Vol. 2 (Spring 1962), 247–99.

permanent income or the level of wealth? All these questions still await definitive answers.

The term structure of interest rates has attracted new attention in the postwar period. It first appeared in connection with the now discredited "bills only" doctrine of the Federal Reserve whereby monetary open market operations were confined primarily to Treasury bills in an effort to minimize the effects upon the rate of interest for long-term government debt. More recently, it was discussed in connection with the Federal Reserve's apparently successful attempt to raise short-term interest rates without substantially increasing long-term interest rates, thus reducing the strain on the balance of payments caused by the outflow of short-term funds without adversely affecting domestic investment.

Two conflicting theories of the term structure of interest rates have come into prominence. One is the "expectational theory," which maintains that the long-term interest rate is a geometric average of the expected short-term rates. The other approach may be called the "institutional theory," which maintains that institutional investors are, by and large, risk-averters and determine their holdings of debt of different maturities on the basis of liquidity, hedging, cost of acquiring and administering debt, and expectations. However, "institutional" theorists believe that the "behavior of borrowers and lenders is not ordinarily governed by the last named factor."[5] Meiselman has put the expectational hypothesis to an empirical test and found the data for the United States consistent with this hypothesis if one incorporates an error-learning mechanism (which introduces a highly flexible distributed lag) by which expectations are revised. The institutional approach has not been subject to an intensive empirical testing and it still remains to be seen if it will provide a superior empirical explanation of the data.[6]

[5] J. M. Culbertson, "The Term Structure of Interest Rates," *Quarterly Journal of Economics*, Vol. 71 (November 1957), 490.

[6] R. Kessel, *The Cyclical Behavior of the Term Structure of Interest Rates* (New York: National Bureau of Economic Research, July 1962), however, has made an extensive empirical investigation of the liquidity and expectation hypotheses and concluded that his findings supported the expectations hypothesis supplemented by liquidity considerations.

16 Recent Theories Concerning the Nature and Role of Interest

G. L. S. Shackle *University of Liverpool*

Preface

The place of interest rates in the economic process has since 1945
been mainly discussed, within the literature in English, along three
lines: first, criticism and defence of Keynes's position; secondly,
advocacy of a stock or of a flow analysis, or of the need to combine
them; thirdly, examination of the claim of interest to be a suitable
and effective regulator of the pace of growth of the nation's wealth.
The following survey tries to explain and criticise this debate and
to interject some suggestions into it, without aiming at more than
an illustrative coverage of the literature. It is earnestly hoped that
the absence of a name from this article will not be taken to imply
any judgment on the value and importance of any person's work.

Part I THE NATURE OF INTEREST

Types of Economic Theory

When we have no theory about economic affairs, no state of
those affairs and no temporal succession of states seems inconceivable. A theory restricts the conceivable states and successions
of states to those in which the relations between quantifiable things
in the economy conform to some specified rules. Theories differ

Reprinted from *Economic Journal*, Vol. 71 (June 1961), 209–54, by permission
of the author and the Royal Economic Society.

from each other in the list of quantifiable (not necessarily measurable) things to be considered, and in the precise character of the rules about their interrelations. This meaning of "economic theory" leaves unlimited the number of different theory-classifying schemes we can set up. But in historical fact the cleavages between groups of theories have run along a few clear lines, which can for practical purposes be easily defined. These lines, of course, intersect each other and yield cross-classifications.

One dichotomy is between *equilibrium* and *development* theories. Equilibrium is a test that selects for the economist one particular situation out of an infinity of situations and justifies his calling attention to it as something special. Judged by the smallness of the ratio of what it accepts to what it rejects, no other test seems able to rival its selective power. No other test, it may also be claimed, can state so sharply in what the accepted differs from the rejected situations. By contrast, no test of comparable power and conviction can be found for selecting among paths of development. On the most general grounds, equilibrium has great claims as an economiser of thought. To dispense with it has meant, in practice, to be reduced to mere factual enumeration. For ninety years few economists, save the German historical school, have based their theories upon any other principle. Even those most anxious to disparage it as a *description of what is* and, still more, of what ought to be, have nonetheless needed it as a means of understanding and of accounting for what is. Even Keynes's *General Theory of Employment, Interest and Money* [20], so strongly repudiating some of the conclusions of equilibrium theories, was itself an equilibrium theory in its method.

Theories may secondly be distinguished according to the mode of choice which faces their acting subjects. When a theory supposes the available alternatives to be perfectly known to these subjects in every respect which concerns them, I shall speak of a theory of *pure* choice. Under any other assumption the acting subject has, with greater or less freedom, to create his own list of alternatives before he can choose among them. If the alternatives are not *given* to him, or in so far as they are not given, he must necessarily produce them by his own thought, judgment and imagination. Choice of this two-stage kind I shall call *impure* choice.

A subject facing pure choice has no motive for not dealing at once with every question that arises concerning the details of the action he shall adopt. For he knows everything about the consequences of every available act. But a subject facing impure choice may elect a "simple" immediate act designed to secure freedom of deferred choice among more specialised alternatives. In fact, rather than decide what to buy, he may elect to retain money. In theories of pure choice there is thus room for money only as a unit of account and none for money as a store of value, an *asset*. But all the interesting properties of money arise from its use as an asset. Thus theories of pure choice are "non-monetary" theories.

Finally, we must make a subdivision within the equilibrium method. For this method can, paradoxically, be concerned either with *events* or with *states*. *Long-period* equilibrium is, of course, a state, and its meaning may even excuse us from asking whether it would, given stability of all the "non-economic governing conditions," eventually be attained or not. There are degrees of strictness with which long-period equilibrium may be interpreted. We may mean by it the perfect and complete adjustment of everything in the economy to everything else, a general equilibrium attained after no matter how long a time. Or we may have in mind a period sufficient for some particular impulse (such as an increase in the money stock) to have worked itself out through the system as it exists, even though that system itself may not be in complete long-period internal adjustment. Let us call this a "middle-period" equilibrium. Middle-period equilibrium is also, then, essentially a means of studying states.

When we seek to determine a state of affairs in which, if the economy ever arrived at that state, it could remain at rest, because this state is one of long-period general equilibrium, we are not concerned with the path from the existing to that ultimate state, we are not interested in the *event* or chain of events carrying the economy from one situation to the other. But in the short period the temporary and partial equilibrium, which defines as it were a gravitational force acting on the economy, serves rather to describe an event than a state. It answers the question "What will happen next to the economy?" The two meanings of equilibrium are thus rather sharply contrasted in regard to the part they play in analysis. In its short-period connotation, equilibrium can enable a dynamic tale to be told in static language.

Keynes and the Classics

If we have spent some time preparing the foregoing classificatory scheme, our reason is that theories can appear to be widely divergent and contradictory, while in fact, because they are answering different questions, they are perfectly harmonious. An example is provided by the first source we shall consider. Professor Patinkin [35] finds Keynes's interest theory wrong on almost all counts. In this criticism, however, Patinkin is setting a long-period equilibrium analysis of almost pure choice, which therefore is in

vital respects non-monetary, against Keynes's short-period equilibrium analysis of impure choice treating money in its full-
blooded sense. No reader of Keynes's article "The General Theory
of Employment" [21], published in February 1937 in answer to
critics, will be in doubt that Keynes looking back saw as the main
theme of his book the commanding importance of uncertainty and
of the conventions by which the insoluble problems it poses, and
the nonsense it makes of pure "rational calculation," can be
shelved in order to make life possible at all. Professor Patinkin, by
contrast, says: "the limited objective of this [Patinkin's] book . . .
is to understand the functioning of a money economy under perfect
interest and price certainty." And a little earlier: "Once the
Pandora box of expectations and interest and price uncertainty is
opened upon the world of economic analysis, anything can happen."
Patinkin's analysis, worked out with watch-like precision, is concerned with money as a means, merely, of meeting random demands for payment, and not as a means of speculation or of
deferring specialised decisions.

Patinkin, then, quite excludes those Bulls and Bears who would
otherwise smash up the china shop of rational economics. They are,
to a degree which Patinkin, despite an incomparable scrupulous-
ness towards his reader, does not perhaps sufficiently make clear,
the heart of Keynes's liquidity preference theory. Once the transactions motive is satisfied, all the rest of the existing money must
be held by Bears (or at least, non-Bulls), of whom there have got
to be enough for this purpose. The business of the interest rate,
qua equilibrator of liquidity preference, is to move to such a level
as will create these necessary Bears, or eliminate some of them if
there are too many. Nor are we, in this dynamic world of speculation, free to think of the speculative demand for money as depending solely on the *level* of the interest rate. At any moment this
demand may be powerfully influenced by the most recent *movement*
of the interest rate, its extent and speed. We may go farther. People
who are holding money because they think the interest rate will
rise may decide to hold it no longer if they observe the interest
rate to remain where it is. For at a constant interest rate (that is,
constant prices of bonds) they are missing an income (namely
receipt of interest) which they could have with no offsetting capital
loss. Thus if the constancy of the interest rate has been due to a
force of non-Bulls just brought to sufficiency by the presence in it
of some Bears who count on a rising rate, this constancy will soon
destroy itself by disillusioning these Bears, who will buy bonds, and
cause the rate to fall. Interest may be *inherently restless*. All this is
outside the limits of Professor Patinkin's concerns. It is, indeed,
beyond the range of the equilibrium method.

His main contention is a simple and compelling one. Money's usefulness, no matter in what context, derives ultimately from its exchangeability for goods (including factors of production) of those kinds which are wanted for their own sake or for their *technical* transformability into goods wanted for their own sake. Money by definition cannot be enjoyed, consumed or made a physical tool of; it can, ultimately, only be exchanged. It can be stored, but even then only with a view to its being in the end, at some time or other, exchanged. It can be lent, but only with the result of promising more money later on, which money will then be serviceable only by being exchanged. If you are holding money with a view to paying for things the quantity of money you need depends on the prices of the things you have contracted to pay for. The marginal utility of a given stock of money thus depends on the price level. This is true whatever the *proximate* motive for holding the money, whether it be to bridge the unforeseeable time-gap between receipts and spendings or to make the time-shape of spending different from the time-shape of income by the issue or purchase of bonds, or even (so Patinkin says, and here we are not quite so readily convinced) to make a capital gain in the bond market.

If, by government decree, the British unit of currency were altered overnight from the pound to the florin, everyone whose bank had owed him £100 would now owe him 1,000 florins. Everyone who had owed his tailor £20 would now owe him 200 florins. Everyone who had yesterday purchased a bond for £1,000 due to be redeemed in one year's time for £1,050, would now own a bond due to be redeemed in one year's time for 10,500 florins. If, in the familiar way, tastes, techniques and real resources were the same to-day as yesterday, nothing that mattered to anyone would have changed. In France the transition to the "new franc" is almost an example, in reverse, of the very thing we have supposed. Why, in either of these cases, should the interest rate change? There is no reason.

Change of the currency unit and re-expression of all prices, debts and money stocks in terms of the new unit is, in comparative statics terms, the same thing as a change in the quantity of *each person's* money and of all prices, all incomes and all debts in one and the same proportion. Can it be claimed that this is what an increase in the total money stock will in the long period achieve? If all prices and wages were flexible; if the extra money were introduced in such a manner that everybody's holdings (positive or negative) of bonds and holdings of money were increased in one and the same proportion; if expectations were inelastic; if there were nowhere any money illusion (no tendency to regard a ten-shilling note as something in itself and not merely as ten shillings' worth of purchasing power at the prices happening at any moment to prevail); then an increase in the economy's total stock of money would leave the rate of interest unchanged for the same reason that a change in the currency unit would do so. Professor Patinkin is scrupulous to point out how far from practical reality some of these necessary conditions are. But he does believe that those which are least easily accepted are also the least harmful to the long-period neutrality of money. Equi-proportionate changes in every item of a list in which every individual's money holding is an item, his bond holding is an item and his debt on bonds he has issued is an item are wildly unlikely; but if tastes are not too dissimilar this may not make much difference. Elastic expectations he dismisses as incompatible with meaningful economic analysis. And as to absence of money illusion, he seems to be in two minds whether to make it an assumption or to claim it as a consequence of rationality.

Many who have spoken of money as a veil have failed to make explicit the conditions on which this neutrality will be achieved, and have not, in particular, insisted that money balances as well as money incomes must be supposed to be multiplied by the same factor as prices. Turning this necessary condition round, Patinkin shows that money balances cannot be increased without bringing into play forces, of that utterly familiar kind consisting in the observance of the equi-marginal utility principle, which will in the long run, and unless obstructed by law or human perversity, push prices up in the same proportion as the balances have been increased. These forces will at the same time, given this price flexibility, cause the quantities of bonds issued and held by firms and individuals to be increased in yet again this same proportion. All these consequences together constitute what he calls the "real balance effect." Time will, indeed, be needed for all these changes to work themselves out through the system, and while they are doing so the rate of interest will be lower than before. But when they have done so, an increase in the stock of money will, as Ricardo [42] and Wicksell [49] said, leave the interest rate unchanged.

Keynes must be supposed, according to Patinkin, to have thought that an increase in the stock of money would permanently oversatisfy liquidity preference at the former interest rate, and would therefore lower the rate to that level where the increased transactions balances required by the increased general output or the higher prices (or both) due to the increased investment flow at the lower interest rate would soak up such of the extra money as was not wanted by the lower rate's newly created Bears. How could he believe this? By believing that asset holders as well as wage-earners were money illusioned. We may well think it natural for those who had experienced the gentle deflation of 1920–35 to be very differently conditioned towards money from those who, in 1956, had suffered fifteen years of continuous quite rapid *in*flation. Circumstances alter cases. But there is more than this. Keynes saw economic life as made up of events and not of states. His method only was an equilibrium one, the picture he sought to explain was of booms and depressions, inflations and crises, continual challenge and change. "Equilibrium is blither," he (orally) said.

Patinkin draws from his model the following conclusions on interest:

(i) In a world where each individual feels certain that he knows, for each future date within his horizon, what interest rate, what price of each good and what level of his own income will prevail (that is, a world of "interest, price and income certainty"), a greater than zero interest rate could exist, and would be accounted for by the desire of people to consume according to a different time-shape from their incomes, and by the desire of entrepreneurs to make profits by investing in equipment. (We may note that a world of "interest, price and income certainty" is by no means the same as a world of perfect foresight. In Patinkin's model expectations are held with certainty, but are in general not correct.) Not only does interest belong to a world of certainty as well as to one of uncertainty, but "a proper approach to interest differentials begins in the classical manner with the determination of the rate on long-term bonds by the basic forces of thrift and productivity, and goes down from this rate to the shorter-term ones." (The latter part of this sentence is disturbing to a reader who is basically willing to see in Patinkin's work, not a competitor to the liquidity preference or Bulls and Bears theory, but a solution of a quite different problem. That problem is indeed the "long-period" one. But what has this to do with "long-term bonds"? They are the objects of day-to-day and hour-to-hour speculation like any Stock Exchange security.)

(ii) The threefold role of the interest rate is to equalise for every individual (in his private or his entrepreneurial capacity) the utility of consuming a marginal amount now with the utility of having the prospect of consuming the compound-interest-increased equivalent of this amount in the future; to equalise for him the utility which his marginal unit of money holdings affords by its liquidity with the utility which a bond, purchased with it, would afford by promising interest; and to equalise for him the interest he could obtain (or avoid paying) on the marginal bond with the rate of profit promised by the equipment purchasable with the price of this bond. This "threefold margin" was so named by Sir Dennis Robertson [38].

(iii) An increase in the economy's total money stock does not inevitably or essentially entail a change in the long-period equilibrium rate of interest. Any such change will arise from the special *distribution* of the extra money, and not from its coming into existence. To believe otherwise it is necessary to believe in money illusion on the part of asset owners.

(iv) "The amount of money demanded depends upon the rate of interest, the rate of interest does not depend upon the amount of money." This merely means that the rate of interest does not depend only on the amount of money but also, among other things, on prices, which when time has been given following an increase in the economy's stock of money, will increase in the same proportion as the stock, thus leaving the "real" situation and the equilibrium rate of interest unchanged. When we add that the amount of money demanded also depends on prices as well as interest, the paradox vanishes.

The facts support Professor Patinkin in his chosen context. Huge increases in the British quantity of money have been accompanied over the past twenty years, not by a fall but a rise in the long-term and, far more dramatically, in the short-term interest rates. But this long period context is nothing that Keynes ever had in mind.

In his review article in the *Economic Journal* [18], Professor Hicks applies his incisive diagrammatic tests to reach much the same understanding of Professor Patinkin's book as our broader approach above had led us to. That book is concerned, Professor Hicks says, with "full equilibrium" (this appears to us identical with "long-period" equilibrium). Full or long-period equilibrium assumes that money wages, along with all other prices, are perfectly flexible downwards as well as upwards. (The question whether this flexibility requires time or not is, let us interject, inapplicable to long-period equilibrium, for whose purposes time is not scarce.) It is in assuming this downward flexibility that the full equilibrium theory, which is the "classical" theory as Keynes meant that term, differs from Keynes's theory, whose primary assumption (realistic for the 1930's but not for the early nineteenth century) is that the money wage is given and, for institutional reasons, will not fall and, for reasons of abundant unemployed resources, will not rise as employment changes. With perfect upward and downward wage flexibility, Professor Hicks shows that real income (measured in wage units) can stand at one level, and one only, given the community's income-and-consumption schedule, the marginal efficiency of capital, the quantity of money and the absence of any speculative motive for holding money. For only at one level of real income will the amount that people wish to save out of that income be equal to the investment which, given the interest rate corresponding to the given quantity of money *and that level of real income*, the entrepreneurs are willing to do. If the entrepreneurs, all taken together, tried to have a larger investment flow than this the result would be a rise of prices and money wages without any increase of employment or output, for the unique real-income point is a point both of full employment and "full unemployment." This rise in prices, in face of the fixed quantity of money, would shift the income-interest-rate schedule towards the interest-rate axis, and thus, by raising the interest rate corresponding to a given real income, drive investment down to its former level. Similarly, a too-small investment flow would lower wages and prices and reduce the interest rate corresponding to any given real income, and so push investment and income back to their former levels. In this model it is the "real" factors of productivity and thrift which determine the interest rate. If thrift were weaker the "saving gap" between production (that is, income) and consumption would be smaller, a smaller investment flow would suffice to fill it, this small investment flow (given the schedule of the marginal efficiency of capital) could be induced by a higher interest rate and prices, given the quantity of money, would adjust themselves upwards so that this quantity of money only just sufficed for the transactions and precautions needs at this higher interest rate. Or if the marginal efficiency schedule (productivity of capital) were to shift, again a different interest rate would arise just sufficient to induce the investment necessary to fill but not over-fill the saving gap. In this model it is the level of money prices and so, given real income, the level of money income, which is altered if the quantity of money is altered. In terms of Dr. Hahn's analysis, which we shall discuss below, the classical full-equilibrium economy was effectively "decomposed" into two independent sub-systems, the "real" system, which determined *everything* "real," including the rate of exchange between present and future goods, and the "money" system, which determined only the arbitrary monetary name (measure) of the real income, *etcetera*, determined elsewhere, which it was powerless to influence in any other respect.

In pointing to the absence of downward flexibility of wages as the essential difference between the full-equilibrium model and Keynes's model, Hicks neglects in the early part of his discussion, as Patinkin does throughout, a feature which is even more characteristically Keynesian, namely, the speculative motive for liquidity. For in this neglect there is involved, given the de-natured marginal efficiency schedule which in the full-equilibrium model is no more than a physical productivity schedule, the neglect of the whole matter of uncertainty of expectation. Hicks does insist, however, on the third vital difference between Keynes and all the classics, including Patinkin: the classics were concerned with the full long period, which is the same as to say, with full flexibility. Keynes was concerned with the short period, in which some things are stickier than others.

Quite at the end of his article (superb in its clarity and penetration) Hicks brings up reluctantly the speculative motive like a shameful atom bomb to settle the matter. He has shown that the question whether unemployment can be cured by monetary expansion turns on whether we assume full flexibility of the interest rate so that it can fall to whatever level may be needed for the stimulation of a full-employment-giving level of investment, or whether we assume that there is a "floor" to the interest rate, below which it cannot be forced by any ordinary expansion of the money stock:

> In order to show that we get a better understanding of these problems by considering effects [of shifts of the marginal efficiency schedule or the income-consumption schedule.—G.L.S.S.] on employment and income first, and then correcting by possible repercussions through interest, all that is necessary is to maintain that there are ranges over which the repercussions through interest will be rather insignificant. To do that no more is necessary than to emphasise the ability of speculative funds to stabilise the rate of interest against considerable disturbances. Which is effectively what Keynes did.

To treat the transactions motive as central and the speculative motive as incidental or peripheral is as though an oceanographer should study the inflow from rivers but neglect the tide. Professor Hicks has, however, preferred to defend Keynes with classical and not with Keynesian weapons, for even he, it seems, is not willing to give Keynes full applause for his great *tour de force*: the writing of *earthquake economics* within a framework of comparative statics. One more remark seems here permissible. The theory against which Keynes has to be defended is the classical theory, which shows interest to be determined by the "real forces," productivity and thrift. That theory also shows that there can be no such thing as unemployment. It was this sort of approach which, seen from the standpoint, say, of 1933, aroused his formidable contempt.

Professor Patinkin's "Rejoinder" [37] to Professor Hicks was concerned only with insisting again on the "real balance" or "Pigou" effect, whereby, it is claimed, a fall of prices, by increasing the purchasing power of people's stocks of money, will induce them to spend more (when? over how long a period? in how thin a life-long trickle? or [abandoning Patinkin's unswerving assumption of "rationality"] in how disturbing a burst of extravagance?) on commodities. The question in this regard is whether people who are saving out of income take *income* or *assets* as the proper measure of the basis of their spending power. But this whole question and Patinkin's "Rejoinder" bear on the theory of employment rather than on that of interest.

The classical case is the long-period case. In terms of comparative statics we ideally compare, not the states of one economy at two different dates, however remote from each other in time, since then one state must precede and "lead to" the other, and we are always tempted to ask about "flexibility" and other things strictly irrelevant; but we compare two structurally identical and atemporal economies (with tastes, techniques and nearly all resources identical between the two) in one of which the quantity of money, say, is larger than in the other; and we observe what other things must then also be different.

The same "classical" conclusions for the long-period (or as we should say, atemporal) case, at which Professor Hicks arrives diagrammatically, had been put forward in 1944 by Dr. Franco Modigliani [30] in an argument which, however, Dr. F. H. Hahn in 1955 [16] found self-contradictory. Dr. Hahn reports as follows Modigliani's conclusions:

> if the supply function of labour is homogeneous of degree zero in all prices including money wages [that is, if equi-proportionate changes in all prices leave unchanged the quantity of labour supplied], then
>   (i) the rate of interest is determined by investment and savings [saving?] and
>   (ii) liquidity preference determines the level of prices and *not* the rate of interest.

If, says Dr. Hahn in effect, the "real" variables (that is, relative prices, the rate of interest and the size of the general output of all goods together) form a self-contained system sufficient to determine all its own variables and impervious to any and all other influences, while the quantity of money and the level of absolute (*i.e.*, money) prices form a separate and independently self-determining system, then, if we reject Say's Law, we might have a situation where the "real" system was in disequilibrium, with total demand for commodities exceeding total supply, and yet where the "money" system was in equilibrium, with the demand for and supply of money equal to each other. But this, says Dr. Hahn, would contradict Walras's Law, according to which the total demand for all goods, *including money*, cannot fail to be (is identically) equal to the total supply, since "all goods" includes everything in terms of which demand can be exercised and likewise everything comprised in "supply." However, if we assume Say's Law, that is, *identical* (unconditional and logically inevitable) equality between total demand and total supply of all goods *other than* money, then by Walras's Law there must also be identical equality between the quantity demanded and the quantity supplied of money, so that, since this equality holds regardless of any change in the size of the money stock (the supply of money), no such change can serve to determine the absolute price level; there is no need for any particular price level to equalise the demand for and the supply of money. By this dilemma, between a contradiction if we reject Say's Law and the indeterminacy of absolute (that is, money) prices if we accept Say's Law, Dr. Hahn holds Modigliani's argument condemned.

We think that in this part of a highly ingenious article Dr. Hahn is over-subtle. No doubt it is true that unless *both* systems, real and monetary, are in equilibrium, both must be in disequilibrium: there must be excess demand in both (numerically equal and of opposite sign) or in neither; but when the "real" system is in equilibrium, this equilibrium includes a determinate interest rate, to which the given *nominal* money stock must accommodate itself by appropriate change of the absolute price level and so of the real purchasing power represented by the given nominal money stock. There is, we are assuming, equilibrium in the "real" system and so, by Walras's Law, there must be equilibrium in the money system; and this latter equilibrium can be attained because by assumption changes of the price *level* do not disturb the equilibrium of the real system.

This is the escape from Dr. Hahn's two-pronged fork, if we are prepared to reject Say's Law; and surely Say's Law, true in a *non-monetary* economy, can find no logical basis in an economy which uses money. If goods are in fact bought and sold for money, and a money stock exists in the economy, it seems plain that money can be withdrawn from the stock and used on the commodity market, thus upsetting Say's Law. But suppose, against all reason, we insist on believing in Say's Law in the "real" part of a money economy? Then surely we must ask for a *complete* money economy. What is wrong with Dr. Modigliani's model is that it makes no mention of bonds. How can money be lent except in exchange for bonds? If, then, the money system in Dr. Modigliani's model comprises money *and bonds* it can obey a "Say's Law" of its own in the sense that the total demand and supply of monetary assets (money *and* bonds) must be identically equal, and still determine the interest rate by an equilibrium money price of bonds.

Dismissing theories which make interest to depend only on productivity and thrift, or on the *ex ante* equality of saving and investment, because such theories take no account of people's decisions of what to do with their accumulations of *past* saving, which exist at all moments in various forms exchangeable for each other at prices which express the interest rate, Dr. Hahn turns to theories which do concern themselves with the prices of *old*, as well as those of *new*, bonds. These other theories are, first, the loanable-funds theory, which says that the interest rate will change unless the excess demand for bonds is zero, and secondly, the liquidity preference theory, which some have interpreted as saying that the interest rate will change unless the excess demand for money is zero. Dr. Hahn, however, rejects this latter interpretation. For people can add to their money balances by supplying, in any interval, productive services in excess of the value of goods they demand for consumption in that interval. But Keynes explained that liquidity preference enters only at the second of two decision-stages involved in the satisfaction of people's time-preferences. At the first of these stages the individual must decide how much of his income to consume or how much to save, and here there is no question of liquidity preference. At the second stage, however, he must decide in what kind of assets he shall hold the results of saving, and here alone liquidity preference is involved. A theory which says that the interest rate is what equilibrates the demand and supply of money can, therefore, in particular circumstances imply that the interest rate equilibrates *reluctance to save* with desire for liquidity. The next step of Dr. Hahn's reasoning from this consideration is not quite easy to follow. For he is not satisfied simply to accept the consideration as a necessary consequence of discussing the interest rate in terms of a model of general interdependence. On these latter lines we might be inclined to dismiss this objection against regarding the interest rate as the price which eliminates an excess demand for money. For on what *general* ground can we elect the rate of exchange between one pair of mutually exchangeable things as worthy of attention and ignore that between another pair? Sir Dennis Robertson's threefold frontier between consumption, the purchase of earning assets and the accumulation of liquid ones, and indeed the general interdependence conception as a whole, require us to look upon the desire to consume, and the desire to accumulate liquid assets, as possible direct rivals of each other. In particular circumstances the motive to save may be the desire not for wealth in general but for the security or manoeuvring power conferred by *liquid* wealth. I may be willing to forgo wine for a year in order to have one hundred pounds in the bank, but not in order to pay off one-tenth of my mortgage debt. Apparently accepting such a view, Dr. Hahn nevertheless argues that "liquidity preference must be taken as determining the *ratio* ("form") in which assets are demanded, and *not* the total quantity of assets demanded or supplied" [16]. The argument which he builds on this leads us, by an interesting fresh route, to that question and difficulty which in my own view are the supreme enigma of interest theory and the real source of all its troubles.

Let us suppose, then, (Dr. Hahn says), that at some date *ex ante* saving is less than *ex ante* investment, and that accordingly there is an excess supply[1] of bonds. Suppose also that the *ratio* in which money and bonds are demanded is the same as that in which they are supplied. In this case the loanable-funds theory predicts a rise in the interest rate, but Dr. Hahn's interpretation of the liquidity preference theory predicts no change in the interest rate. Dr. Hahn none the less reconciles the two theories. Excess demand equations, he says, are to be understood as holding *ex ante*; that is to say, the equality of the two sides is looked to be attained at the end of some still-future "planning period" (which we may distinguish as the investment planning period). His model assumes that investment plans are (objectively; presumably within the knowledge of some super-human observer) certain to be fulfilled. This in turn implies that investors will during the (investment) planning period obtain the necessary finance. Thus within that period two transactions must take place: first, bonds must be sold for money, and then this money must be used to buy investment goods (machines, etc.). Extending from the investor's "present" to some interior date of the investment planning period, therefore, there is a second and shorter period which we might call the finance planning period. There are in fact two planning periods, a shorter one concerned with obtaining finance and a longer one concerned with using it. Corresponding to *each* of these there is a pair of ratios, the ratio in which money and bonds are demanded and the ratio in which they are supplied. Between the members of one of these pairs (in particular, the one referring to the end of the investment planning period) there can be equality notwithstanding that between the members of the other pair there is inequality, an inequality caused by the intending investors' temporary need to accumulate funds ready to spend on investment goods. As soon as this spending actually takes place the equilibrium of the investment planning period will re-assert itself over the disequilibrium of the finance planning period. Both theories are right: the loanable funds theory, which says that there will be disequilibrium in the finance planning period, and the liquidity preference theory, which says that there will be equilibrium in the investment planning period (in the circumstances assumed, viz., a ratio between the supply of money and that of bonds which is correct provided demand is not distorted by the need for "finance" for investment schemes).

If, in thus reconstructing Dr. Hahn's argument, I have preserved its essence, we have, I think, to recognise two very important questions which it raises. The first is whether it is useful or appropriate to think of finance and investment not merely as distinct stages in each separate equipment-augmenting operation by each individual business-man but also as *observable* stages in the economy's aggregate flow of equipment augmentation. For surely the release of finance which occurs when one firm spends its hoard can supply the need of another firm to build up its hoard? To say this is not in the least to deny that when a *given* aggregate national income contains a large investment component there may be required a different ratio of money to bonds from what is required when the income consists wholly of consumption. For when all transactions are small no marshalling of great sums may be needed. It will also be true that when the investment flow is planned to increase, the interest rate will tend to rise because the necessary extra finance will have first to be marshalled and then later released. But, secondly, a much more interesting and radical difficulty confronts us. The length, in calendar terms, of the planning periods is not a matter of indifference, for the relative quantities of new and old bonds offered for sale during such a period will depend on it. More fundamentally, what is the meaning, in the theory, of the length of the planning period and what determines it? These questions raise a basic theoretical and methodological issue, that of the co-existence in some markets, and pre-eminently in the bond market, of two separate possible equilibria, an equilibrium of stocks and an equilibrium of flows, and that of the relation between these two and the question whether one or other is dominant or by what process they influence each other and can both be satisfied at once.

Stock Analysis or Flow Analysis?

An essential step towards answering these questions resulted from a debate in 1950 among Professors Klein [23; 24], Fellner and Somers [13; 14] and Brunner [6]. Klein sought to show that Fellner and Somers in an earlier article [12] had been wrong to treat stock analysis and flow analysis in monetary interest theory as equivalent. He asked whether they deemed the interest rate to depend, in effect, on the whole history of the demand and supply relation for securities since time was, or only on that relation in some

current period. They replied that if the whole history up to the
beginning of the current period had resulted, at that beginning,
in an equilibrium, then any divergence from equilibrium in the
current period must result from the events of that period. This
answer was rejected by Klein as question-begging. Karl Brunner,
however, carried the whole matter forward by showing that if we
opt for a stock rather than a flow theory, we have then to choose
between a liquidity preference and a securities theory, and that
different behaviour in the securities market is implied by these
two theories.

Brunner considers first whether a stock or a flow theory is
appropriate to the securities market. The contrast, we may interpolate, is between a market such as that for electricity or fresh milk,
where what is demanded from moment to moment or from day to
day must, in so far as demand is met, be produced from moment
to moment or from day to day, and a market such as that for
antique furniture, where supply is an existing and non-augment-
able quantity existing at all times. The market for securities is
evidently nearer to the antique furniture than the electricity end
of the scale. Moreover, it is one where "the decision to hold the
stock is continuously appraised in the light of current market
situations." On the implied ground that the market is dominated
by the effect of price changes in releasing a large volume of orders
to sell *from stock* or to buy from stock, a volume which is large, that
is to say, in relation to the orders which can arise from new issues,
Professor Brunner simply declares that except in a stationary state
where new issues are zero and where, accordingly, both stock
equilibrium and flow equilibrium are achieved together, we shall
find the "momentary" price to be determined by the stock relation.
In the stationary state both stock and flow relations must be
simultaneously satisfied, since the stationary state is one where the
stock relation is satisfied subject to a special condition, viz., that
flows be zero. The non-stationary heading covers the case of stock
equilibrium combined with flow disequilibrium and the case of
stock disequilibrium combined with flow equilibrium.

It is not easy to tell from what Professor Brunner writes whether
he regards the stationary state, with zero new issues of bonds per
unit of time, as the only possible double equilibrium, that is,
simultaneous equilibrium of both stock desired to be held with
stock existing, and flow desired to be issued with flow desired to be
absorbed. When I am in a moving vehicle I am at each instant at
some particular place (my "stock" situation) and moving at a
certain speed (my "flow" situation). The combination of these two
circumstances may be exactly what I desire for that instant. Were
I not moving, I might wish to be in a different place; or were I at

that instant in a different place I might desire to be moving at a different speed. Thus, it does not seem inconceivable that a particular stock of bonds and a particular pace of new issue of bonds may both be compatible with one and the same interest rate and that the combination of all three of these values of variables may satisfy everybody. In terms of our analogy, I may be moving, not because I would have preferred to be in a different place *at the given instant*, but because I aim to be in a different place at a later instant. In economic terms, wealth owners all taken together may be willing, at some particular interest rate, to increase their holding of bonds at just the pace at which borrowers wish, at that interest rate, to issue new bonds. I think that Professor Brunner does envisage this as a possible situation, since he seems in one passage to insist that, *even* in such a situation, the stock position is dominant. We must here interpolate a further passage of our own to ask whether in such a situation the stock position is indeed dominant.

The case for saying that wealth owners' and income-earners' attitude to existing stocks of "old" bonds is dominant, as compared with would-be lenders' and borrowers' attitude to new issues, rests in our judgment on the idea that *the quantity released on to the market* (by any considerable change in the interest rate) of old bonds *could* be much larger than that of new issues. A trespasser hesitates to walk through the farm-yard at night, not because he is menaced by one dog awake, but because that dog may wake the whole hostile household. But whether this will be so or not depends on how sound the household sleeps; or in our own terms, on how sensitive bond-holders, actual or potential, are to changes of price. This sensitiveness in its turn depends, we now assert, on the *uncertainty* of their price expectations. For let us consider an economy where there are no new issues or fresh borrowing nor redemption of debt, but merely a constant stock of bonds. Let us suppose that each wealth owner has in mind some specific future date (not necessarily the same for everyone) which is the nearest he cares to look to for capital gain or loss, and that each has in mind a particular price of bonds, which price he treats as *certain* to be attained on that date. Then, with due allowance for impending payments of coupon interest, any bond-holder whose expected price is higher than the current market price will be willing to hold bonds, anyone whose expected price is below the current market price will be unwilling to hold them. Using the horizontal axis of a Cartesian diagram for numbers of bonds, and the vertical axis for bond prices, we could draw a curve connecting with each present market bond price the number of bonds which, with a given set of bond price expectations (one price for each person), wealth owners would be willing to hold at that price. It would, of course, be downward sloping towards the right, since in order to find additional willing holders of bonds we should have to lower the present market price so that it sank below the expected prices of a further section of wealth owners, or in market terminology, so that it turned some more Bears into Bulls.

Now unless this curve had some actually horizontal segments, any change in the existing quantity of bonds would, so long as expectations of bond prices remained unchanged, require some change of the interest rate (that is, of the current market price of bonds). If expectations of all actual or potential bond-holders, or of all those within some range of expected bond prices, changed, the "shape and position" of the curve would change bodily, and again there would have to be some change of the current market price of bonds; that is, of the interest rate. But now let us suppose that instead of each wealth owner entertaining with certainty a unique expected bond price, he had in mind a range of prices, all of which he regarded as possible. It might then be a reasonable first-approximation hypothesis that a bond-holder would not wish to be rid of his bonds in exchange for money unless the current market price rose above the upper limit of his range of (subjectively) possible future prices, and would not wish to acquire more bonds in exchange for money unless the current market price fell below the lower limit of the range. This supposition would require us to draw two curves, one showing, for each hypothetical existing number of bonds, the price above which the current market price must not rise if that number of bonds is to find willing holders, the other showing, for each hypothetical size of the stock of bonds existing, the price below which the current market price must not fall if that number of bonds is not to fall short of the desired number. In this case the number of bonds existing could be changed within some range without necessitating a change in the interest rate (see Figure 1a) or expectations could change to some extent without necessitating such a change (see Figure 1b).

Let us turn to a more formal aspect of the determination of price in a market which can be supplied from an existing stock as well as from new production. Suppose that output of the good in question, measured as so-and-so many units of the good per unit of time, can be at all times differentiated with respect to time so that, in ordinary language, changes in its size are "smooth" and do not include jump-discontinuities. Then the quantity of the good coming on to the market from new production will, *in zero time at any instant*, be zero. Since in a market supplied *only* from new production we can suppose demand also to vanish to the same order as supply, when shorter and shorter intervals tending to zero were considered, a balance between demand and supply in every interval can be

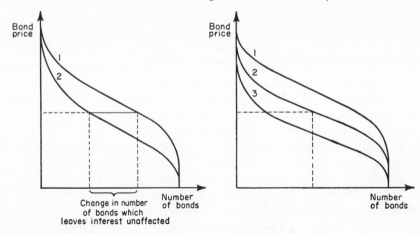

Figure 1a.

Figure 1b.

Curve 1: each ordinate shows highest bond price which will limit desired stock of bonds to that represented by the abscissa.

Curve 2: each ordinate shows lowest bond price which will make desired stock of bonds not less than that represented by the abscissa.

Curves 1 and 2: higher range of bond prices compatible with given bond stock.

Curves 2 and 3: lower range of bond prices compatible with given bond stock.

conceived, and we can perhaps further, with some artificiality, suppose such an equality *at all moments* between the demand-flow and the supply-flow to be brought about by price changes. But supply *from pre-existing stock* can be of finite amount in a zero interval of time. It is this circumstance which, in the less extreme form which it would take in reality, where flows are not "smooth" in the sense we have assumed, compels us to say that at any instant the price in such a market is dominated to some extent by the stock position. How great is this extent?

We know that except for some so-called "tap" issues of British Government securities, and any similar arrangements elsewhere, new bond issues do not conform to the smooth-stream model, but are made in large blocks by means of subscription lists which remain open for a few days, hours or minutes. There is thus much more in common between the mechanism and market impact of a new issue and that of a sale of a block of existing ("old") securities than the extreme analogy of electricity versus antique furniture would suggest. It thus appears that the most convenient way of combining the two sources of supply in one analysis is simply to regard the interest rate, in the way we were doing a few pages earlier, as the price which must stand at or move to that level at which all existing bonds, no matter whether they have existed for a century or have only this moment been put upon the market, can find willing holders. A new issue is thus incorporated into the analysis, not as something separate which influences matters *qua* "flow," but simply as what brings about a change in stocks and requires additional willing bond-holders to be found.

This leads to one final aspect of our interpolation. An equilibrium in the bond market may be looked on as having, possibly, two stages. There may at some instant, and some interest rate, be equality between the number of bonds requiring to be held and the number for which there exist willing holders. But the bonds existing may not be all in the hands of those willing to hold them. Thus sales must, or can, take place *at the current interest rate* (*i.e.*, bond price inverted) in order to bring about a complete matching of desired with actual individual holdings, this state of affairs being the second stage to which we referred above. It thus follows that the occurrence of bond sales and purchases is not an infallible sign of stock disequilibrium in the aggregative sense.

In the second part of his article Professor Brunner shows that even when we have accepted the appropriateness of a "stock" approach to the bond market, we have still to choose between a "liquidity" theory and a "securities" theory. The former declares that the rate of interest will change unless the existing stock of *money* is equal to the desired stock of money; the latter declares that the rate of interest will change unless the existing stock of *bonds* is equal to the desired stock of bonds. Further, the liquidity theory makes the speed of change of the interest rate to depend on the size of the difference between the existing and the desired stock of money, while the securities theory makes the speed of change of interest to depend on the size of the difference between the existing and the desired stock of bonds. The securities theory embodies Professors Fellner and Somer's belief that "in a multidimensional system there are a great many factors which affect the interest rate. However, in *any* system, these factors can affect the market rate of interest only through their effect on the demand and supply of interest-bearing securities." One thing, it appears, Professors Fellner and Somers have overlooked, although it fits without difficulty into their formula just quoted. Anything which affects *equally and simultaneously* the stock of bonds desired and the stock existing, and which *also* at the same time has its own independent effect on the thoughts, feelings or mental attitudes which underlie the desire for a given stock of bonds, so as to make this desire compatible with a different interest rate, can cause the rate to change *without* upsetting the equality of the desired and the existing stock of bonds. Indeed, what economist would not be willing to draw a diagram in which the demand and the supply curve of some commodity had each shifted in just such a way as to intersect at a different price but an unchanged quantity?

What thoughts, feelings or attitudes could change in such a way as to lead to such a shift? Professor Brunner's equations of the liquidity theory include among the independent variables, on which the speed of change of the interest rate might be supposed to depend, the speed of change of other prices in the system. We should ourselves prefer to say that the most relevant such influences are plainly *expectations* of price changes rather than observed, that is, *ex post* changes. Professor Brunner, however, does not refer, in his article, to expectations. In the specific mathematical form which Professor Brunner gives to it the securities theory gives no explicit place to the influence of any thoughts except those which can be resolved into functions of public *ex post* quantities.

The dilemma we found in Professor Brunner's article, which he himself seems to sweep aside, the dilemma that if there are two distinct mechanisms or sets of influences bearing on the interest rate, each by itself capable of attaining an equilibrium of its own, these two must in some way be mutually reconciled if they both bear on one and the same rate, may find a solution along lines which, for a different purpose, Mr. A. Llewellyn Wright [50] has most ingeniously suggested. The essence of Mr. Wright's proposal is that in an economy with *changing* income, and so with changing amounts per unit of time by which equipment and aggregate idle balances ("reserve," "speculative" or "pure liquidity" balances, as they might alternatively be called) are being augmented, the requirement of equality between the number of dependent variables and the number of mutually independent equations (which equality Mr. Wright, reasonably as we think, seems still prepared to accept as the equivalent of determinateness in many circumstances) allows *two* interest rates to operate simultaneously and separately on the market, the essential explanation being that their respective levels control the speeds of growth, respectively, of the saving-investment flow and of the hoarding or dishoarding flow. This, if in presenting it I have properly interpreted Mr. Wright, seems a most fertile suggestion. It means that a person's or a firm's affairs can be in equilibrium even when, for example, he is paying one rate of interest to borrow money and receiving a different one for lending it, not essentially because of any differences in risk or other such circumstances, but because he thus achieves the desired changes in the respective speeds of growth of his accumulated stocks of assets of different kinds. He ought, according to static analysis, to borrow just so much at any time that the rate of interest he pays on his marginal borrowing equals the rate he receives on his marginal lending. In a dynamic system the loss he appears to suffer by this failure to observe an equi-marginal rule may be the price he pays for, or the loss which is compensated by, the desired changes between one period and the next of the amounts added per period to his stocks, respectively, of equipment and of money.

The foregoing is my own statement of what Mr. Wright's article suggests to me. He, at least, proposes that there are two interest rates differing in their role and in the influences determining them; differing, that is to say, more essentially than in merely being "short-term" and "long-term" rates, although they may fall under these respective headings. One of these rates, called the "money rate of interest," is determined on a market which is almost literally the money market: "It can be regarded as the average rate of interest charged on bank overdrafts in any period; or, better still, it can be regarded as the Bank Rate." The other, called the "investment rate of interest," is "the rate which rules in the investment market proper, the market where the demand for investible funds is brought into equality with the supply of investible funds." His purpose in distinguishing, even in fundamental theory, two interest rates is to find for his lagged Keynesian model an extra variable unencumbered by an extra equation, since he believes the model otherwise to be over-determinate. As to the fitness of his device for its purpose, we are bound to ask whether this is not an example of that very disaggregation which Mr. Wright in his article recognises as ineffective, and Professor Brian Tew [45] has put forward the objection which must occur to every reader: can we conceptually split the loan market into halves so independent of each other that we need not have any equation connecting the prices which reign in them? We think, nonetheless, that Mr. Wright's work may yet be found to bear usefully upon our own problem, which, if the rate of interest has really to equilibrate both stock held with stock existing, and the *time-constricted* acts of offering bonds and money for mutual exchange, is also one of over-determinateness.

The problem of how "stock" influences and "flow" influences upon bond prices are related to each other can perhaps be put as follows. At any instant a stock of bonds exists. The change in the size of this stock in a short enough time interval is negligible, and thus, it appears, the bond price at any instant must be determined by those influences which make people willing or unwilling to hold a stock of bonds. Against this argument, however, the following may occur to us: in the market for such a good as electricity there is at no time any stock. The *quantity existing* at any instant is zero. Yet there is a price, validly looked upon as depending on the confrontation of supply conditions and demand conditions. Evidently a price can be determined by the comparison of the potential sizes of two flows, each depending on this price, which must be such as to equalise them. Yet is it not true that the quantity supplied in any interval tends to zero with that interval, just as the growth of a stock in some time interval becomes negligible if that interval is taken short enough? The answer plainly is, that when we are simply concerned with two flows, both the quantity supplied and the quantity demanded vanish to the same order, and thus, in a familiar way, we can think of the ratio of these two flows as remaining finite while we carry to the limit the shortening of the interval of measurement. In the measurement of a stock, of course, no time interval is in any way relevant, and thus a flow which requires some finite lapse of time to be accumulated into some finite quantity cannot influence the size or price of a stock *at some instant*.

It is an argument of this sort which I take to underlie Mr. R. W. Clower's [8] disposal of the problem:

> The aggregate quantities of various assets existing in an economy in any given period of time are inherited from the past. These quantities can be altered only gradually as a result of future economy decisions, so that if we consider appropriately short time periods, current additions to (or depletions of) aggregate asset stocks can be ignored.

Mr. Clower's purpose is to show that productivity and thrift do play an essential role in the interest rate's historical course. By regarding the rate at any moment as depending purely on the stock situation at that moment, namely the size of the bond stock, the expectations of individuals about future bond prices, the current prices of other assets, Mr. Clower can maintain that new issues of bonds, and retirements of existing bonds, occurring to-day, do not affect the rate to-day, unless they alter expectations. But when we look at two dates separated in time, the interest rate at the later date will be what it proves to be partly because of the change in size of the bond stock which new issues and retirements in the interval have brought about. The time rate at which such new issues and retirements will have taken place will be influenced by changes in productivity and thrift.

Changes in productivity may arise, as Mr. Clower points out, from inventions or other sources, and thrift also is subject to many influences. Indeed, we may say that these are in a sense only names for certain superficial aspects of the whole complex course of economic history, and Mr. Clower's aim is not, I think, to isolate productivity and thrift because they are more important than other strands in that skein, but because he wishes to get these recurrently self-assertive explanations of interest permanently filed away in the right box.

Despite the solutions to which we may resort for a practical means of handling, in our theoretical discussions, the co-existence of a "stock" mechanism and a "flow" mechanism in the market where money and bonds are exchanged for each other, this co-existence remains the most serious theoretical problem concerning the interest rate. In his article "The Equivalence of the Liquidity Preference and Loanable Funds Theories and the *New* [italics in original] Stock-flow Analysis" [27], Mr. Cliff Lloyd concludes that it is at present unsolved. He presents the matter formally, in the frame of Professor Hicks's demonstration that the liquidity preference and loanable funds theories are equivalent:

> In a consistent *n*-good system, two of the goods being bonds and money, if any $n - 1$ excess demand equations are satisfied, the *n*th must also be satisfied, thus the *n*th may be dropped .... The loanable funds theory drops the money equation, the liquidity preference theory drops the bond equation, but the two are equivalent .... This is quite a simple and clear-cut proof, provided that each of the goods in the system is represented by only one excess demand equation, but ... in an explicit stock-flow theory any stock-flow good will be represented by two excess demand equations [27].

A stock-flow good is one whose quantity, existing as a stock at each instant, can be different at different instants because a flow of the good is produced and another flow consumed, and because these flows, each measured as so-and-so many units per time-unit, can differ from each other. By equilibrium in respect of such a good, Mr. Cliff Lloyd means constancy of the stock. However, a price for the good which makes equal the stock existing and the stock desired to be held is not necessarily the same as the price which makes equal the flow produced and the flow consumed. The difference between the desired and existing stocks, considered as a function of price, gives as an excess stock demand equation, the difference between desired consumption flow and flow of production forthcoming, considered as a function of price, gives us the excess flow demand equation. Unless the difference between production and consumption is zero, the stock will be changing; that is to say, the market for the good will not be in equilibrium. The converse, however, is not true. Equality between the flows of production and consumption does not imply equality between the desired and the existing stocks. "Thus according to the 'new' stock-flow economics a stock-flow good, that is, one which is produced, consumed and held, must be represented in a general equilibrium system not with one but with two excess demand equations" [27].

Hence Mr. Cliff Lloyd infers that, whether or not in fact the liquidity preference and loanable funds theories are one and the same, Professor Hicks's proof that they are so does not hold in regard to a good which is produced and consumed as well as being held in stock. He is careful *not* to infer that no proof can ever be found.

Mr. Cliff Lloyd's argument calls for one or two comments. He does not appear to be justified in saying that Clower and Bushaw [9] were the first to study the equilibrium of a good which is produced and consumed as well as held in stock. Contrary to his assertion, Karl Brunner's article [6] referred to above deals with this case. Mr. Cliff Lloyd's particular problem is the same as that posed by Mr. Llewellyn Wright [50], but Mr. Cliff Lloyd sees no *general* solution. He shows that special assumptions will give us a model where the two excess demand equations are in effect one and the same, so that Professor Hicks's proof would apply. His way of specifying the two excess demand equations of the general case appears to us to be open to criticism. In our paraphrase of his argument we have been speaking, first, of an excess flow demand equation (as he does), but secondly, of an excess stock demand equation (as he does not). He prefers to add together the stock and flow demands and so define his second equation as "the market excess demand equation which shows the total market demand, both stock and flow, for the good." All the difficulties we have referred to in earlier pages, of justifying any particular choice of the length of the period of measurement of the flow, and, more fundamentally, the doubtful propriety of adding together two quantities of different dimension, a stock with no time-denominator and a flow which is necessarily expressed as so much per unit of time, are involved in Mr. Cliff Lloyd's method, which we have therefore chosen to re-express.

In an article [36] later than his book Professor Patinkin has argued as follows: each individual has some stock of money "now," and desires the prospect of having some particular stock at the "next" date when the matter will arise, which date we may (by a usual convention) take to be the same for everyone. Thus each individual's attitude may be *alternatively* expressed, either as a desire for some future *stock* or as a desire for some particular *change*, between now and then, in his existing stock. Dividing this change by the number of time units in the interval, we have a flow. (Professor Patinkin in this particular article does not make explicit the need for this latter step.) Thus, says Professor Patinkin, stock analysis and flow analysis are alternative ways of looking at the matter, and we have not two equations, but one.

This argument seems to us fallacious. The size which a thing has at some instant and its speed of change at that instant are two distinct things, each separately subject to choice. If Professor Patinkin prefers to regard the individual as choosing the size that his money stock shall have at the "next" date rather than "now" he must allow him to choose *also* the speed at which that money stock shall be growing, or about to grow (or decline) at that next date. However, he writes:

> Before concluding this part of the paper, I should like to re-state its general argument in the following way: Stock analysis, as well as flow analysis, pre-supposes a period of time: namely the period between the moment *at* which the individual is making his plans, and the moment *for* which he is making them. Hence if the periods pre-supposed by the analysis are the same, the excess-demand function of stock analysis must be identical with that of flow analysis. This proposition holds also in the limiting case where the period is an instantaneous one.

Why does Professor Patinkin think that the individual, in making his plans *for* a particular moment, must only concern himself with the change which will then *have occurred* and not with the one which will then be about to occur? Why, in other words, should the individual concern himself only with *one* future moment? Is it because Professor Patinkin is in this passage concerned only with "static equilibrium"? But in static equilibrium analysis do we speak of plans and distinguish the moment when they are made from the moment when they apply? The really essential point, however, is that stock equilibrium can be achieved *instantaneously* by *price changes*, *e.g.*, of bonds, without the price which effects this equality between desired and *existing* stocks necessarily bringing about an equality between the stocks desired for the "next" relevant date and the stocks which, comprising existing stock and impending "production," will exist on that next date.

Patinkin's position of 1958 [36] has been criticised by Mr. Hugh Rose [41], who refers in a short note published in 1959 to a 1957 article [40] of his own. In that earlier article Mr. Rose interprets and contrasts the Keynesian and loanable funds theories of interest. Professor H. G. Johnson [19] had suggested that the Keynesian theory is "static," seeking only to explain the state of affairs in a short-period equilibrium and how changes in circumstances will alter the equilibrium values, while the loanable funds theory is dynamic and seeks to explain precisely how interest and income move from one equilibrium to another when circumstances have changed. In contrast with this position of Professor Johnson's, Mr. Rose sees Keynes's theory also as dynamic.

In Mr. Rose's general dynamic model (providing a formal frame within which both Keynesian and loanable funds theories can be dynamically interpreted) it is assumed that the expenditure plans of both households and business are always realised, any discrepancy between the total of these plans, on one hand, and current production, on the other, falling on the buffer stocks of finished goods held by producers. Such a discrepancy is the excess demand (positive or negative) for goods. The excess demand for money is the difference between the stock of money which the public desires to hold and the stock which exists. The loanable funds theory says that the interest rate will change if the sum of the two excess demands is other than zero. The Keynesian theory (in Mr. Rose's view) says that the interest rate will change if, and only if, the excess demand for money is other than zero. If then, we believe that the excess demand for loans is the sum of the excess demands for goods and for money, Keynes appears to be maintaining that the interest rate can change even if the excess demand for loans (the excess supply of securities) is zero, and remain constant even when the excess demand for loans is not zero. Mr. Rose's solution of this dilemma is two-fold. First, he rejects "Walras's Law" that the algebraic sum of the excess demands for goods, money and securities is zero. Secondly, he shows that in Keynes's construction the excess demand for loans is always equal to the excess demand for money.

This latter result arises in the simplest fashion. Producers finance the whole of their production (of consumption goods and investment goods taken together) by sales, made concurrently with the production itself, of consumers' goods and securities. If the total of consumers' goods and securities which income receivers want to buy is smaller than the total that producers want to sell the difference is plainly an excess demand for money, and this excess demand for money is exactly the excess of the securities offered by producers over the securities demanded by income receivers: the excess demand for money and the

$$\begin{pmatrix} \text{excess supply of securities} \\ \text{excess demand for loans} \end{pmatrix}$$

are equal. An even simpler statement of the matter is as follows: In the Keynesian system the excess demand for goods *in any one period* is identically zero; for we are to conceive of decisions how much of this and that good to produce within, say, the coming month being taken at the beginning of that month and always adhered to. When goods have been produced someone has in a sense bought them, whether they wanted to or not; for someone has done the work and has a claim to the result. The lack of sufficient effective demand shows itself, in the minds of enterprisers, *before* they make their decisions as to how much to produce in the coming month; and naturally they are much influenced in their production decisions by reflecting on how much of last month's production has been left, contrary to their plans, on their own hands and been "bought" by themselves.

There is no doubt in the present writer's mind that Keynes thought of the interest rate as adjusting itself to the nut-cracker squeeze of the quantity of money existing and the quantity desired, by changes in the price of fixed-interest securities, as these were offered or demanded by those who wished for extra money or had more money than they wanted. Liquidity preference can, of course, be influenced by very many circumstances and considerations, including the prices and price changes of consumers' goods or producers' goods: all markets are in some degree inter-dependent. But it is on the securities market that the interest rate actually *emerges* as, *e.g.*, the quotient of Consol coupon rate over Consol market price.

None the less, we must maintain that it is an essential part of Keynes's vision that the interest rate *can* change without any transactions in bonds at all, and without any emergence on the Stock Market of an excess demand or supply of bonds. If it happened that every holder of bonds or money said to himself at some moment: "If the rate of interest were one point higher, my present holding would be just what I should choose to have" and if a testing of the market revealed this consensus of opinion, then the rate might be found to have moved up one point without any transactions. That is made virtually explicit in the *Treatise on Money*.

Professor H. G. Johnson's highly condensed and wide-ranging survey article on "Some Cambridge Controversies in Monetary Theory" [19] is remarkable for the contrast between the ease with which he is able, on Keynesian lines largely made explicit by Mrs. Joan Robinson, to handle every kind of shift in the macro-economic situation and show what sequence of changes will be undergone by the interest rate, the net investment flow, income and the rest, when some autonomous psychological, technical or political transition disturbs an equilibrium, on one hand; and on the other, the awkward and artificial air of his account of them in terms of a Robertsonian dynamics. Professor Johnson says that "The Keynesian theory . . . is a static theory; it is not concerned with the succession of changing [partial] equilibrium positions but only with the position which represents an equilibrium of all the forces at work." This may be formally true; I am sure it does not represent the spirit or purpose of Keynes's thought. To be formally correct, Keynes ought, no doubt, to have carefully specified the precise character and mode of operation of the influence exerted by prosperous conditions on the inducement to invest, and to have pointed out in so many words that prosperous conditions arise when, for any reason, employment, output and income are increased; and so on. He did not do so. The accelerator, the "investment coefficient" and all such are markedly absent from the *General Theory* (though not, in substance, from the *Treatise on Money*). In Chapter 22 of the *General Theory*, however, Keynes indicates plainly his conception of the way in which wide shifts of the *schedule* or curve of the marginal efficiency of capital induce abrupt and great changes in investment and hence in all its dependent variables.

Is it then better to have highly special, arbitrary and clanking mechanical systems, in which our assumptions single out one or two variables, make expectations, confidence and the whole gossamer fabric of investment-incentive to depend on these alone, and tell us precisely what effect a change in these variables will have on investment; or is it better to recognise that the inducement to invest is influenced by countless subtle aspects of the recent past and the "news" (all taking colour and meaning, of course, from the historical background which has conditioned men's minds and bequeathed them their resources) and leave ourselves freedom to analyse these from case to case as best we may by *formally* treating (as Keynes did in effect) the inducement to invest as autonomous or exogenous? Again, when we try to understand the effects of changes in the quantity of money, is it better to chase packets of money in and out of the labyrinth of balances held or spent at different times for different kinds of purposes, at the greatest risk of muddling the identities of the various packets and the dates of the various transactions, or is it better to consider a *stock* of money, existing at a particular moment and matching or failing to match the stock desired at that moment; desired for a list of motives which we can make short or long at convenience: payments reserve, speculative asset, "finance" marshalled for impending investment or what you will; and thus to show what market forces, at that same moment, will bear on the prices of bonds and thus push up or down the rate of interest? Keynes's critics have discussed whether his system is static or dynamic: they have not seen that it is *dramatic*, and that this quality arises from his method of cornering many problems and complications in one concept and dealing with them by a radical simplification. That this is the true Cambridge secret has been well understood by Mr. Lawrence E. Fouraker [15]. Writing of Marshall and Keynes he says:

> Their intellects were too proud, resourceful and thorough to go on with the thesis without firmly establishing the connections. Having satisfied themselves, however, they employed a curious

device when it came to recording the results of their pursuits. Instead of leading the reader through the intricate analytical processes that their own minds had recently traversed, they would provide a short cut, in the form of an assumption whose purpose was to eliminate consideration of the difficult problem they had faced and solved.

If all Keynes's critics had possessed Mr Fouraker's insight, what seas of ink could have been saved.

The Classical System: Incomplete or Over-determined?

The question "What determines the interest rate?" has been in postwar years one of a group of intimately linked problems which in the course of debate have seemed to swing round each other continually in a sort of whirlpool, now one, now another becoming central as article succeeds article from writers with different viewpoints. Among these problems is the question, discussed with brilliant clarity by Becker and Baumol [1], whether, as Lange [26] and Patinkin [31, 32, 33, 34] have maintained, the Lausanne School and other neo-classicals so defined their systems that *either* these systems were incomplete through asserting the *identical* equality of total commodity demand and supply (Say's *identity*) and thus being able to show only how inter-commodity exchange rates are determined and unable to show how absolute money prices are determined, or *else* that they were self-contradictory through assuming, in addition to Say's identity, that stocks of money are wanted for their own sake, so that the total stock of money can be other than just what, at given money prices of commodities, is desired, and can thus affect the demand for these commodities and make it other than equal to the supply. In brief, are the commodity market and the money market entirely separate from each other, so that the one determines in a wholly self-contained manner the *relative* prices of commodities and the other determines nothing because there is in it only one good, and this is always available (being not a real money but a mere *numéraire*) in just the quantity required, just as runs in cricket are available to the man in the scorer's box in just the quantity he requires for recording the events in the field of play? Or, on the contrary, are the markets connected so that when there is an excess supply of money there is *ipso facto* an equal excess demand for goods?

Becker and Baumol argue (with the support of much evidence by quotation) that what the classicals had in mind was not Say's identity but Say's *equality*. At first sight we might be inclined to think that Say's equality is a mere definitional truism to the effect that in equilibrium demand and supply are equal. But Becker and

Baumol mean by it the assertion that if an equilibrium is disturbed, as by an arbitrary increase or reduction in the existing quantity of money, a new equilibrium will be found through such changes in the price level as will make the new quantity of money just sufficient. For if the desired and existing money stock are unequal, people will offer a greater, or smaller, total money value of commodities than they demand, in order to acquire, or dispose of, stocks of money. When money prices of commodities have been given time to adjust themselves to this pressure the desired stock of money, which depends on the prices of commodities, will have adjusted itself to the quantity existing.

The question which here interpolates itself is this: If we add to the assumed system a bond market, will a change in the price of bonds, that is, a change of the interest rate, help to adjust the desired to the existing money stock? From Ricardo to Patinkin, some have said that the long-period *equilibrium* interest rate will be unaffected, and will therefore have no effect on the equilibrium of the rest of the system. Keynes, being uninterested in the long period (in which, by definition, all prices including those of productive factors are perfectly flexible), said nothing about long-period equilibrium, but said instead, like Ricardo, that in the short period the interest rate will be different and will affect other things.

Becker and Baumol do not themselves consider any role of an interest rate, but conclude that the neo-classicals did not treat the economic system as divided into two entirely separate enclaves, the non-monetary and the monetary, but instead believed, as Becker and Baumol express it, that "money derives a 'utility' from the goods it can buy, it is true, but because it can buy them at the moment the buyer considers convenient."

From a conventionally simplified frame for the question whether or not an economic system, given time, will adjust itself to any change in the size of its money stock so as to reach a new equilibrium not differing in essentials from the old, the ripples have spread out towards answers based on more and more subtle and complex assumptions. Mr. E. J. Mishan [29] distinguishes between a "cash balance effect" and an "asset-expenditure effect," and charges Patinkin with having treated them as one, at first under the name "Pigou effect" and later as "real balance effect." When the price level falls, even a person who happens at that moment to have no cash balance may feel a desire or a freedom, because his assets are now worth more in terms of the kinds of goods he desires, to spend more per time-unit on such goods. If, however, his assets consist partly in cash, he will have an additional incentive to increase his expenditure per time-unit. For now he has in hand a larger stock of cash than is needed for convenience in bridging the time gap between receipts and outgoings of cash, and so it will be natural to get rid of some of the surplus cash. Once we introduce bonds and a bond market into our system, it is plain that surplus cash may be spent either on commodities (encouraging their output and raising their prices directly) or on bonds (lowering the interest rate and encouraging investment, and so other output, *indirectly*). Because of such considerations, it is exceedingly difficult to justify any particular line of separation between monetary theory and interest theory.

In the brilliant article of 1956 by S. C. Tsiang [46] we find carried a stage further the policy of generalising the analysis so as to embrace the mutual influence of interest, employment, output, income and velocity of circulation. Mr. Tsiang's first purpose is to show, in a manner quite different from that of Walras's Law, that the liquidity preference and loanable funds theories of the determination of interest are identical "in the sense that the two sets of demand and supply functions, *i.e.*, the demand for and the supply of loanable funds, and the demand for money to hold and the stock of money in existence, would determine the same rate of interest in all circumstances, if both sets of demand and supply functions are formulated correctly in the *ex ante* sense."

Mr. Tsiang rejects the approach via Walras's Law on the ground that it links interest no more intimately with money than with any of the other multifarious goods of the general equilibrium system. Walras's Law, which simply says that the demand for everything, including money, is necessarily identical with the supply of everything, including money, shows that in the general equilibrium system we have one redundant demand and supply equation which follows from all the rest, and that accordingly some one equation, *no matter which*, may be dropped. Such an argument leads to no more explicit theory of interest than the mere statement that interest is included in the general determinate equilibrium. To invoke the Law is, says Mr. Tsiang, to use an *ex post* definition of the demand and supply of money.

Mr. Tsiang's criticism of Fellner and Somers [12] concerns the very fundamental question of how to combine stock and flow demand in one analysis. Fellner and Somers, he says, define the total supply of money as total money expenditures on goods and services as well as on the purchases of "claims" plus the amount of money held unspent.

> This total of the so-called "supply of money," the main components of which are flows over time, does not necessarily equal the total stock of money in existence (which is the usual meaning of the supply of money in the liquidity preference theory) unless the period of time over which the flows of money expenditures are measured is so defined as to make them equal.

Mr. Tsiang in his positive analysis does in fact define a "period" with this special purpose in view. But his "period" is in effect an instant, his payments are merely the allocation to various uses, by each holder of money, of all the money he possesses at that instant. In fact, Mr. Tsiang is simply adopting that definition [22] of the total quantity of money in existence, which says that it equals the total of all payments that can be made by all money holders *simultaneously*. By compelling all the economic subjects in his system to make payments at such discrete instants, Mr. Tsiang combines the notion of stock of money existing *at* an instant, with flow of payments made during some time *interval*, viz., the interval separating two of his discrete instants. Thus he shows that when people want to hold money, *for whatever reason*, and there is in total only just so and so much money for them all to hold, something must adjust their desires to this circumstance. That something is the rate of interest, and it is a matter of indifference whether we call his system a liquidity preference or a loanable funds system.

We said, however, that Mr. Tsiang's construction allows people to desire to hold money "for any reason." This, in his view, is the crux of the matter and the point on which he thinks liquidity preference theorists took a distorted view. Perhaps he is doing them an injustice. His starting-point (where surely everyone can agree) is that demand and supply schedules are *ex ante* concepts. It is indeed obvious that, since they express potential reactions, conditional decisions as to what will be done should this or that circumstance arise, they must refer to intended, future action; they are descriptions of people's forward-looking states of mind, even if we happen to be studying those states of mind from a viewpoint which places them in our past. Now Mr. Tsiang fastens upon Keynes's admission, in his article called "Alternative Theories of the Rate of Interest" [22], that intended acts of large-scale investment may provide a special motive for liquidity preference, that is, for desiring to accumulate or marshall large money balances ready for the execution of these investment schemes. Such mobilising of money "at the ready" for investment, Keynes called the motive of "finance." It was, in his view, just one more source of a desire to hold money rather than to be the possessor of someone else's I.O.U.s. Now Mr. Tsiang says that this "finance" motive is merely a part of the ordinary "transactions demand" for money. We can wholeheartedly agree with him, and so would Keynes have done, and so does Professor Hicks in his famous "Suggestion for Simplifying the Theory of Money." Professor Hicks says, in effect, that when your desire for money arises from the transactions motive, it is a desire to have money *ready* to make payments, because the time which will elapse between your receipt of the money and the need to pay it out is, or may be, too short to make the lending of a small sum worth while. Of course, the transactions motive is an *ex ante* motive. Whoever said it was not? Only proponents of a mechanical quantity theory of money.

Mr. Tsiang concludes his sections on interest with these words:

> All the disagreements between the loanable funds and liquidity preference theories on practical issues seem to arise from the failure on the part of liquidity preference theorists themselves to perceive the dependence of the aggregate liquidity preference (or demand for money) function upon the consumption and investment functions.

We feel bound to say that this statement betrays a misunderstanding of the *methodology* of the liquidity preference theory. That theory elects to concentrate on the question: Given the expectations, plans, uncertainties, hopes and fears, as well as the distribution of resources, which exist *at some moment*, where must the price of bonds stand to equilibrate the resulting market impulses? Those expectations and plans have been shaped by past history and by the most recent "news," but they have been so shaped by an inter-play so complex and subtle as to defy explicit analysis. We can, if we wish (and Mr. Tsiang is one among many who have wished), make assumptions which will enable us to trace explicitly the emergence of to-day's market situation from yesterday's. Such a model will be a mind-clearing stereotype of certain aspects of how things happen in the economic world. But in what sense, or under what conditions, can they serve as predictive models?

Mrs. Joan Robinson introduces her article on "The Rate of Interest" [39] with a definition of "a dynamic analysis" which will surely never be bettered. Its characteristic is, she says, "that it cannot explain how an economy behaves, in given conditions, without reference to past history; while static analysis purports to describe a position of equilibrium which the system will reach no matter where it started from." She further explains the paradox of Keynes's *General Theory*: "Short-period analysis is concerned with the equilibrium of a system with a given stock of capital and with given expectations about the future. Past history is thus put into the initial conditions, so that the analysis is static in itself, and yet is part of a dynamic theory." Thus we have, from Cambridge itself, a sanction and confirmation of Mr. Fouraker's thesis [15].

Disposing first of the role of productivity and thrift, Mrs. Robinson shows that these govern the answer to the question "What rate of interest will bring about full employment?" For a fall of the interest rate stimulates investment, and the degree to which investment needs stimulation, in order to make employment full, depends on the size of the saving-gap to be filled, and this gap itself is, if anything, made smaller by a fall in the interest rate. If the market rate of interest ever stands below the full-employment rate there will be inflation which will drive the market rate up to equality with the full-employment rate. The latter thus provides a "floor" for the market rate.

Turning to the short period, Mrs. Robinson ascribes the relation between the income expected from each kind of asset, and the price of that kind, to the varying types and degrees of illiquidity which those kinds involve. These types of illiquidity she distinguishes as *inconvenience, capital uncertainty, lender's risk* and *income uncertainty*. Inconvenience is the lack of a perfect market, depriving the asset-holder of "the power to realise its value in cash, whatever the value may be at the moment." Here we have perhaps some ambiguity about the meaning of "the" value. This sounds like "market value"; but the market value *at any moment* is what can *immediately* be obtained, and if the market is limited and imperfect this may be nothing. It might be better to define inconvenience as the asset-holder's lack of assurance that whatever (now unknown) value he shall attach to his asset at some future moment he will be able at that moment without delay or cost to sell it for that price. Uncertainty concerning future capital value can be otherwise expressed as uncertainty about what rate of interest will rule at future moments. Keynes, Mrs. Robinson says, "regards the rate of interest primarily as a premium against the possible loss of capital if an asset has to be realised before its redemption date." Lender's risk is the fear of the borrower's default. Income uncertainty exists for the lender when he lends on short term and will have soon to relend at he knows not what rate of interest.

Different assets, Mrs. Robinson says, are affected in different degrees by each of these qualities. Bills are very little, and bonds very much, subject to capital uncertainty, while the case is reversed for income uncertainty. Thus the relative prices and yields of bills and bonds will depend, given the supply of each, on the relative (weighted) number of "widows and orphans" who desire certainty of *income* and financial institutions who set great store by their balance sheets and desire certainty of capital values. "The general pattern of interest rates depends on the distribution of wealth between owners with different tastes, relatively to the supplies of the various kinds of assets."

On this basis Mrs. Robinson discusses the kinds of ripples or of permanent changes of level which will occur in the interest-rate pond when various disturbing events, such as changes in the quantity of money, in expectations, in thriftiness, in the size of the investment flow, and such as the adoption of a cheap-money policy, are thrown into it. Far the most intractable of these influences is expectations, and these she treats by a masterly and highly realistic *tour de force*, that of assuming that at all times, with greater or less conviction, people assume that interest rates will sooner or later return to some "normal" level which more or less recent experience has established in their minds. This accepted "norm" can itself be changed, and a cheap-money policy ill-timed or too recklessly pursued, which has therefore to be abandoned, may strengthen the general belief in a norm which is higher than the one that might have been established by a more canny approach.

There was, until 1930 or thereabouts, a "Cambridge" approach to monetary theory, in which the names of Marshall, Lavington, Robertson and Keynes suggested distinct but harmonious variants. In 1926, indeed, Sir Dennis Robertson's *Banking Policy and the Price Level* lit up the horizon of professional economics and heralded the great era of monetary theory that lasted until the War. The generous acknowledgment it made of suggestive discussions with Keynes promised a Cambridge school as closely knit as the Vienna or the Stockholm school. Unhappily the cave was not big enough to hold two giants. Sir Dennis's apparatus, with its refreshing terminology of "splashing," "lacking" and so forth, was aimed at a careful unravelling of the monetary skein. It has its lasting place in the history of thought, it typically illustrates its inventor's ingenious power to match the closest analysis with the freest fancy, and it explains the delight which his style has given to thousands of hearers and readers. Keynes's ultimate method, by contrast, was the sword of Alexander. He cut, not unravelled, the monetary tangle of ideas.

The Cambridge concert of ideas was split by the *General Theory*, and even Professor Hicks's powerful synthesising habit of mind has been unable to close the gap. That gap, we are therefore entitled to assume, is unclosable. We cannot here avoid an expression of view. The Keynesian whale under Mrs. Robinson's management can swallow with ease all fish which come to its jaws. To play them with Robertsonian hook and line, with no matter what ingenious shifts and stratagems, is much more laborious.

In his review [2] of Maurice Allais' *Economie et Intérêt*, Professor Kenneth Boulding has shown with what brevity and verve the heart of interest may be penetrated:

> What is determined in the market [he writes] is not strictly the rate of interest but the price of certain "property rights" . . . stocks, bonds or items of physical property. Each of these . . . represents to an individual an expected series of future values, which may be both positive and negative. If this expected series of values can be given some "certainty equivalent" . . . then the market price of

the property determines a rate of interest on the investment. This rate of interest, however is essentially subjective and depends on the expectations of the individual; the objective phenomenon is the present market price of the property.

As basic theory this, we think, is irreproachable. It is true too, as Boulding later hints, that nothing in life can in strictness be justifiably taken as certain: for what sort of guarantees does the human situation offer? None the less, we must qualify Boulding's position, for the practical necessities of life drive us to accept some things as unquestionable: sunrise and sunset, eventual personal dissolution and the payment of due interest by the British Government! The series of future payments to which a gilt-edged security gives the right is still, and with entire good sense, *treated in practice* as certain, even though the whole civilised fabric to which such arrangements belong is now destructible. Thus the yields of gilt-edged securities of various terms, short, medium or long, come very near to being "objective" interest rates. Professor Boulding has, strangely, omitted to mention the basic uncertainty which afflicts even the holder of gilt-edged securities, and which ultimately explains the very need for positive interest, namely, the impossibility of knowing *when and at what price* he will be driven by circumstances to sell his security. His main contention surely is invincible: the search for a "pure" interest rate in abstraction from "risk, liquidity, convenience, etc." is meaningless, "a search [in a dark room] for a black cat that isn't there."

In the foregoing we have tried to illustrate, by a commentary on selections from the post-1945 literature, those of the central problems in the determination of interest which have mainly engrossed attention since wartime preoccupations receded. In addition to this debate on fundamentals, there have been a number of more special contributions. Mr. F. P. R. Brechling [3], Dr. Börje Kragh [25] and Mr. Ralph Turvey [47], to mention them in alphabetical order, have pointed out that "the amount of money which people desire to hold as a store of wealth depends not only on the rate of interest but also on the *total* amount of wealth available." Thus in order to describe the effect of an increase in the existing quantity of money, two kinds of "reaction curves" are needed, one showing the reaction of the rate of interest to increases in the money stock effected by open-market operations which merely *exchange bonds for money* and leave the total stock of wealth unchanged, and the other showing the reaction of the rate of interest to *ceteris paribus* changes in the money stock. "The two curves will co-incide if the marginal propensity to hold money is zero."

Upon the results of his skilful empirical research into the finance of small businesses, Mr. N. J. Cunningham [10] has built a theoretical analysis of great ingenuity. His first basic finding is that the opportunity cost to a firm of investing its own ploughed-back reserves in the purchase of equipment is, for a variety of reasons, less than the cost of borrowing funds for the purpose. The most important of these reasons is that, by borrowing, an entrepreneur endangers his firm in a manner, and to a degree, which does not arise when he lays out his own undistributed profits which have been held in the form of cash or easily marketable securities. It is impossible in a few lines to do justice to Mr. Cunningham's subtle and thoroughgoing discussion, but he points mainly to the fact that, so far from being able to borrow unlimited funds at a constant market interest rate, the entrepreneur is acutely aware that the cost per unit of his borrowings will increase with the size of his total debt and that these borrowings will eventually reach an absolute limit, which will, moreover, become narrower at those very times of difficulty for the firm when borrowing may be most necessary to it. This power to borrow, Mr. Cunningham urges, is looked upon by the business-man, and should be treated by the economist, as a form of liquid reserve, a means of satisfying his precautionary and speculative motives for desiring liquidity. The "subjective" cost to the entrepreneur of using borrowed funds for the purchase of durable equipment must therefore reflect a *double illiquidity*. It requires the lender to substitute an illiquid asset (viz., an I.O.U.) in his portfolio, for a liquid asset, viz., cash; and it deprives the borrower of one possible source of liquid funds which he could otherwise resort to in emergency or in face of an unforeseen profit opportunity. The consequence of this difference of implication between owned and borrowed funds is that the curve of *marginal cost of funds for investment* is likely to have a step or jump-discontinuity at the point where "owned" funds are exhausted and resort must be had to borrowing. This vertical segment of the curve is the most striking of several features of the situation, all of which lead, in one set of circumstances or another, to the conclusion that changes of the market interest rate may quite visibly leave the firm's inducement to invest in equipment unaffected. These considerations are an important theoretical complement to the argument advanced on pages 419-21 of this article.

Mr. George Clayton [7] has considered the very interesting problem of the *velocity of circulation of real balances*. When the velocity of circulation of money is slow, as in a business depression, can the banking system of its own power do anything to increase the frequency with which given quantities of *real purchasing power* change hands? His article points out how in some circumstances the public's desire for larger nominal balances regardless of the loss of income involved, with the resulting divorce of the long-term from the short-term interest rate, added to the insensitiveness of investment to any fall of the long-term rate which may be achieved, can frustrate the speeding up of the "real" velocity of circulation even in a depression with heavy unemployment of resources. When there is full employment the banks' attempt to increase their outstanding loans merely results in higher prices. One way of expressing these well-recognised facts is to say that the banking system's power to increase the nation's nominal stock of money is by no means necessarily a power to increase the nation's money income, still less its real income. In introducing the notion of "real velocity of circulation" Mr. Clayton has, we think, greatly contributed to ease of discourse on these matters.

Mr. J. K. Eastham, in a very valuable article [11], has traced the fluctuating historic distinctions between the interest and the profit components of the earnings of "capital," and has shown the importance, for a theory of accumulation, of keeping interest among the obstacles and profit among the inducements to investment, that is, to the construction of specialised, concrete equipment.

From this survey of recent tendencies in the theory of how interest is determined, we turn now to consider the state of opinion, and to make some suggestions of our own, about the role of interest in the theory of the inducement to invest.

Part II THE ROLE OF INTEREST

The Investment Horizon

A change in an interest rate can, like a change in any other economic variable, transmit with more or less effect, and more or less delay, an impulse from one part of the economic system to another. Theory suggests that its more powerful effects are likely to be upon the demand for durable goods and upon the balance of payments. Demand for durable goods, whether by producers or householders, is investment, and the question whether interest-rate changes do or do not appreciably affect investment has been actively studied by observation, question and analysis from the 1938 attempt by the Oxford Economists' Research Group onwards.

A necessary tool for any such study is a clear conception of the *formal* role of the interest rate in the *formal* structure of a profitability calculation. Since money in hand can be lent at positive interest wherever an organised loan market exists, money in hand is equivalent on to-day's market to a larger sum of deferred money. Expected instalments of profit, or of services (such as enjoyment of a house) having a market value, are deferred money, and in order to find to-day's market worth of a series of such instalments, each must be adjusted for its deferment and, in some cases, also for its uncertainty. Any such instalment which is treated as free from uncertainty must accordingly be divided by: one plus the annual interest rate: and must be thus divided once for each year of deferment.

Since the interest rate thus occurs in the denominator of a fraction, this fraction, which is the "present" or "discounted" value of a deferred, but certain, unit instalment, will be smaller, the larger the interest rate. Thus to-day's demand price for any asset or object which is counted upon with certainty to yield specified deferred instalments will be lower, the higher the interest rate. If other relevant circumstances are unchanged, and if in particular the cost of production of such an asset is independent of the interest rate, fewer such assets will be demanded in each time-unit after than before a rise of the interest rate.

This scheme of analysis can be refined. We can suppose that the supply price of any type of equipment (any "machines") rises as the number of units ordered per time-unit increases. We can suppose that the series of deferred instalments attributed to the asset is a different one in the minds of different individuals, each relying upon some information, and some interpretive background of experience, private to himself. Each will then have his own demand price and, we may suppose, his own convenient number of machines which he will order per time-unit provided the supply price is less than his demand price. When the number of machines being supplied per time-unit is such that the corresponding supply price is just low enough to evoke that number of orders per time-unit we have an equilibrium.

But suppose that we wish to express such an equilibrium as consisting in the equality of a "rate of return," on one hand, and the loan interest rate, on the other? The appropriate formal algebraic equation looks exactly like the one by which, given the loan interest rate, we calculate the present value of a given series of annual deferred instalments. The meaning of the letters in this equation, however, is different. Instead of a present value or *demand price* we now have on the left-hand side a *supply price,* and instead of the loan interest rate prevailing in the market, we have on the right-hand side an *unknown* whose numerical value is to be determined by solving the equation. This unknown percentage, or, if we prefer, vulgar fraction or decimal fraction, is the marginal efficiency of capital. In equilibrium, the marginal (or "lowest effective") demand price of each sort of machines, and their supply price, will have been driven to equality by the search for profit. In equilibrium, therefore, the marginal efficiency of capital will have been driven, by rising supply price, to equality with the interest rate on loans. This means that, in equilibrium, the personal demand price entertained by the least sanguine of those business-men from whom an order for machines is actually elicited, will be equal to the supply price, and that therefore the percentage per annum at which this marginally sanguine placer of orders must discount his expected profits, to make their present value equal to the supply price of machines, is equal to the loan rate he must pay on money borrowed to buy these machines.

We need not, however, suppose that there are any intra-marginal investors. If we assume that the series of deferred instalments, which a machine is counted on, by the potential investor, to yield to him if he buys it, depends itself upon the number of machines ordered, and that each of these instalments is a decreasing function of that number, we can suppose *each* business-man to carry the number of orders he gives per unit of time up to that level where his own ("personal") demand price for machines is no greater than their supply price. Thus a much more interesting sense is given to the word "marginal" when we speak of the marginal efficiency of capital. If, in this case, we cease to assume implicitly that loans of no matter what term carry one and the same rate of interest, and suppose instead that each deferred instalment of profit or service is discounted at the particular rate appropriate to its own deferment, then we can accommodate in our scheme of thought the idea that some business-men will value more highly than others the prospect of recovering relatively early the money they propose to invest in machines. Such men will direct their orders to machines of types which offer an *early* concentration of instalments, each large relatively to the total amount of the whole series of instalments promised by such a machine.

In all this there has been no mention of depreciation or amortisation. Have those notions any relevance for investment decisions? Depreciation is loss of value or prospective earning power by a durable good. When a potential buyer of such a machine looks forward to a date at which some particular set or portion of the deferred instalments which it promises will have been obtained from it he will see it as destined to have, at that future date, a lesser value than it has now, and a value which he can reckon on the basis of the deferred instalments lying *beyond* that date and the interest rates which, by inference from the rates prevailing *now* for loans of various terms, he can reckon to prevail on that future date. This gradual ebb of value, as it occurs, will have to be somehow reflected in the book-keeping of his business and in the published condensations of those accounts, and for this purpose it may suit him to represent this decay by a conventional "depreciation allowance" whose annual amount may be a constant or a term of a geometric series or what not. What has this convention of book-keeping to do with the basic profitability or non-profitability of the investment? Nothing.

It is a pity that a number of writers on the question whether the size of the investment-flow is responsive to changes of interest rates, or not, still feel it necessary to encumber their analyses with ir-relevant discussions of amortisation. An interesting debate followed the publication of the evidence obtained on that question by Professors M. D. Brockie and A. L. Grey [4], who had concluded therefrom that the interest-elasticity of firms' demand for equip-ment was low. Dr. W. H. White [48] interpreted their figures differently, but failed to convince them, and the debate must be called inconclusive. It did, however, raise the exceedingly interest-ing question of the lengthening which Brockie and Grey [5] believe to have occurred in the "pay-off period." If the yearly profit which a proposed investment is counted upon to earn is taken as con-stant for all years there will be some number of years such that the total profits of those years equals the first cost (construction cost) of the investment. As a more refined definition, we may take the pay-off period to be that number of years whose total *discounted* profits equal the construction cost of the investment. In the Oxford Economists' 1938 study [28] business-men were often heard to say that they would not order equipment unless it promised to "pay for itself in 3 (sometimes even 2) years." Grey and Brockie [4] found that 85% of their respondents used either the "pay-out period" method or "an alternative formulation amounting to virtually the same thing (the percentage of initial cost of the in-vestment recovered out of earnings each year) . . . for evaluating prospective investments." White [48] comments upon this:

> Because the pay-out-period method requires that initial cost be recovered during a very small number of years, it connotes very short economic horizons, very high required rates of return and unscientific investment planning; consequently, the investment plans of 85% of large firms may be assumed unaffected by the cost of capital.

Any economic theoretician will readily sympathise with Dr. White's attitude. Nevertheless, we must beware here of letting pure theory kick aside too much of practical realism. Can it be truly called scientific to base profitability estimates on years too far ahead for knowledge about the observable *present* to throw any light upon their circumstances? Dr. White is correct, as we showed many years ago [43], in saying that interest-rate changes will be almost powerless to change the inducement to invest, when the planning horizon is only two or three years into the future. But this is not a reason for pretending that we can see beyond the horizon.

Why do [43, 44] business-men place their horizon at only two or three years ahead, and *ignore* deliberately the possibility that their proposed equipment may still, in the years beyond that horizon, prove capable of making goods which will sell for more than the running-costs of the machines? It is because they cannot be *sure* that these profits will be earned, they cannot brush aside the threat that newer inventions will enable their rivals to undercut them or to oust their product with a better one. The present throws light on the immediate future, but that light dims rapidly as we peer farther ahead. The business-men are not "unscientific," they are cautious. Now plainly no equipment is worth buying if the money to be spent on it will not be recovered, let alone any return for "enterprise," "decision-making," "risk-taking" or the general services of the enterpriser. If only three years' profit can be counted on, that profit must be at a rate equal to one-third, at the very least, of the first cost of the machine. A minimum requirement of 34% per annum may seem, at first glance, to be a deliberate rejection of countless profit opportunities which might yield, say, 20 or 15%, still much in excess of the *loan interest rate*. In such an argument two wholly different ideas are being utterly confused. To spend £1 million and to get back £150,000 in each of three years, and then nothing, is not to make a profit.

The true relation between the crude annual profit, assumed to be the same from year to year and to be earned for just so-and-so many years and then to relapse to nothing, and treated as a proportion of the first cost of the equipment, on the one hand; and the rate of return which can be legitimately compared with the loan rate of interest, on the other; is simply the following. Each year's assumed profit is to be divided by: one plus an "unknown" fraction: divided once, for each year of deferment; the answers thus obtained are to be summed, and their sum is to be set equal to the machine's first cost. The resulting equation is then to be solved for the "unknown" fraction, and the numerical value obtained is the "marginal efficiency of capital" which can be compared *meaningfully* with the interest rate. There is still no mention of amortisation. An example [43] will illustrate the matter. Let the first cost of a machine be 100, and the assumed earnings (excess of sale proceeds of product over *running* costs, no mention of amortisation) in each of the next three years be 40, with nothing thereafter. Then the marginal efficiency of capital is 10% per annum, and it *will not pay* to buy this machine with loaned money on which a rate of interest of more than 10% per annum has to be paid, notwithstanding the appearance that the machine is going to earn "40% per annum" of its first cost.

In any such calculation the air of precision and certainty are entirely bogus. We have deliberately spoken of "assumed" profits.

What is in question here is the need for some basis of argument, something to be set against the background of fact, news, experience and technical knowledge which the business-man has at command. We have avoided speaking of expected profits, for the reason that "expected" can cover everything from a feeling of conviction to the merest toying with a wild hope. The business-man who resolves to count on nothing beyond three years ahead is well aware of the open door to good fortune which he will thus offer. If all goes well, the machine which has earned 40% of its first cost in each of the first three years of its life may continue to do so, thus realising a larger overall gain.

By contrast with these uncertainties, the powerlessness [43] of interest rates, within the ordinary range of 2–8% per annum, to influence the demand price of *near horizon* equipment by undergoing any change of a size which may be supposed to occur within months, is a matter of plain arithmetic. It is plain for anyone to see what kind of difference is involved when we divide the supposed profit of three years hence by $\left(\frac{104}{100}\right)^3$ instead of by $\left(\frac{105}{100}\right)^3$, that is by $\frac{225}{200}$ instead of by $\frac{232}{200}$. This is the sort of difference made when the interest rate changes by a whole percentage point, from 5 to 4% per annum.

The ineradicable uncertainty of enterprise, the nearness of the horizon thus imposed, the powerlessness of interest rate changes, are all intimately bound together. Where this uncertainty is less (it is, of course, a subjective thing, a judgment or a state of mind, we are not called upon to justify a feeling that some forms of durable goods are more confidently counted on then others to yield profits in the distant future) the interest rate may have a powerful leverage. A house which is counted on to yield £100 per annum for eighty years has, at an interest rate of 4% per annum, a present value of £2,400; at 2% per annum it has a present value of £4,000. Upon which of the equal annual instalments, counted upon with certainty to be received from some durable good, does a small change of the interest rate used for discounting have the largest *absolute* effect in altering the present value of that instalment? The answer [43] may at first surprise a reader who has not come across it. The greatest absolute change in the present value of any one equal instalment affects that instalment whose deferment, in years, is equal to the reciprocal of the annual interest rate. Thus if that rate is 3% per annum the largest gain in present value, due to a change to $2\frac{7}{8}$% per annum, will be achieved by the instalment due in thirty-three years' time. It would be for our children or our children's children to say whether or not we should allow a change in the yield of Consols to tempt us to build houses for them, could we but consult their future knowledge now!

Harrodian Dynamics

We turn to a broader canvas. Sir Roy Harrod's *Towards a Dynamic Economics* [17] reverts in its broad style and spirit to the classic models, where the whole darkling plain of human affairs was in view, but its economic features were emphasised by the lamps of settlement. A different metaphor suggests its character in detail.

Rivers, tides and ocean currents irresistibly present themselves as an image and analogy of the economic process. There are the short-period waves and the idiosyncratic storms, there are tides and more constant, oneway currents acting slowly over great stretches of time. This picture is brought to mind by the view of interest which underlies Sir Roy's economics of long-period growth or decline. No one better understands Keynes's short-period pre-occupations or his view of interest as the hourly and momently fluctuating equilibrator of Bull and Bear expectations. Yet in his *Towards a Dynamic Economics*, written immediately after the War, Harrod is concerned with the slowest, most deep-seated and steady forces which bear upon, and are transmitted by, the rate of interest. The view that liquidity preference and expectations (the specula-tive motive), however important and spectacular their effects, are waves on the surface of a deep tide representing the "real" forces of thrift and productivity, is one shared in some degree by writers as widely separated as Sir Dennis Robertson and Mrs. Joan Robinson. Like Mrs. Robinson, Harrod in discussing the long-term forces, reverts in effect to the older usage whereby "interest" covered any gain due to the possession of a stock of wealth, other than the market appreciation of the assets themselves. Saving is the continual or repetitive act by which wealth is permitted to ac-cumulate. What considerations in the income-receiver's mind must be overcome by a positive interest rate, in this older sense, if he is ever to save?

> There are two quite distinct reasons for spending now rather than waiting for a larger sum later. One is that the larger sum may veritably have less utility than the smaller sum now, the other the lack of telescopic faculty whereby we fail to estimate justly the utility that the larger sum will have.

In the secure and virtually tax-less Victorian world the well-to-do no doubt looked upon "the family" and its "fortune" as ever-lasting, only provided each successive generation took seriously its duty of maintenance and improvement. But can we, even so, argue as though life were a space within which there is free movement for the human individual; as though he were provided with some sort of fix-point and a mental theodolite, by which he can survey the country of life and make some objective comparison of the utility a given expenditure would give him at different parts of that life?

> A man may choose to sacrifice 2 units of utility—of utility not money—in 20 years from now for the sake of 1 unit now; but in 20 years' time he will presumably regret having done so.

At the later date, we might by this reasoning equally well argue, he will regret not having lived for twenty years at subsistence level in order at last to be rich. In so far as *any* current consumption impoverishes my later years, I ought to live in a garret in order to be buried in a Pharaoh's tomb. But in what sense can the actual, experienced and not merely imagined utility of one moment be compared with that of a different moment? What common ground, what fix-point is there, in the time not of the sophisticated outsider but of the living individual in his moment-to-moment experience? Every comparison of *my own* utility (not that of the "economic subject" under my microscope) which I can *in fact* make is inevitably made at some one moment. Who has the right to tell me that this comparison is ill-judged? What sense will it make, in forty years' time, if my then self says, "That young man ought to have saved for my old age instead of spending to enjoy his youth"?

These are intensely difficult matters and we may perhaps be forgiven for taking an unusual view of them. In doubting the meaningfulness of that sort of inter-temporal comparisons which underlie Böhm-Bawerk's "first ground" for the existence of interest we are saying only that a man cannot stand outside of time and of his own immediate present, and weigh the relative expediency, by some objective, impersonal, omni-temporal standard, of this act or that. Comparisons of "then" and "now" are made *now*. There is no "third point" in time, no neutral, a-temporal common ground, from which the comparison can be made so as to leave the individual still free to act "now" in whatever way that comparison suggests.

The central and continuous theme of *Towards a Dynamic Economics* is the search for those various sets of circumstances, any one set among which, once attained, would carry the economy on a path of steady enrichment of each and all of its subjects; and if such circumstances seem too precarious or elusive, then a search for the policy and means by which the economy can be consciously held to such a path. Sir Roy looks upon a steady, slow secular fall of the interest rate as able, to some extent, to take the place of the accelerator in providing an inducement to invest strong enough to keep the economy at full employment along a rising ceiling of output. The accelerator, if relied upon alone to maintain full employment, might require a pace of growth of output *greater* than the upward slope of the ceiling; a pace of growth, that is to say, which it would be impossible to maintain. Therefore the rate of interest must be pushed ever downward in order that a steady *deepening* of the structure of capital equipment may reinforce the *widening* induced by the growth of output. Besides the problem of a chronic tendency to under-employment equilibrium there is, however, a second problem, that of the business cycle, and here Sir Roy regards the interest rate as wholly ineffective. He compares as follows the two problems:

> While the fall in the long-term rate may not produce any strong immediate effect by making entrepreneurs reconsider their productive methods or by making durable goods more attractive to the consumer, it is not inconsistent with this to hold that in due time, that is after there has been time for the lower rate to sink in and become part of the furniture of the mind of entrepreneurs and others, the various adjustments consequent upon it may add up to a sizeable amount.

But—

> This does not help us with our trade cycle problem. What we there want is responsiveness preferably within a few months, but, at the very worst, within a year or two. . . . I am inclined to attach great weight to the views of those who urge us not to expect a very great increase of capital outlay in the period immediately following a change in the long-term rate of interest.

Interest is the most paradoxical of all economic quantities. At first sight it seems to present us with the opportunity of doing calculations, and of obtaining in this way results which are at once quantitatively exact, logically inescapable and theoretically interesting. It is one of the main pillars of the claim of economics to be Queen of the Social Sciences, the only one of those sciences reducible to mathematical statement and analysis. It runs in an unbroken thread through the whole theory of accumulation of wealth, both on the saving and on the investment side, and thus seems to reign over the theories of employment, of money, of growth, of the general price level and of the balance of payments. It can appear, from this viewpoint of pure theory, as the pivot of the entire system, the sun in the midst of its planets. Yet when examined closely, these claims dissolve. It has been admitted from Marshall's time at least that the influence of the interest rate on saving is doubtful even as to its algebraic sign. More recently its influence on investment has been denied on the basis of business-men's own testimony. Bank rate is still nominally the Bank of England's leading-rein for the commercial banking system, but it has had to be reinforced by "directives," special deposits, hire-purchase regulations and what not. It seems likely that the interest rate, or the system of rates, will continue to receive from theoreticians the homage due to a ceremonial monarch, without in fact counting for more than such a monarch in the real affairs of western nations.

NOTE

1. By a slip Dr. Hahn's article refers to an excess *demand* for bonds.

REFERENCES

1. Becker, G. S., and W. J. Baumol, "The Classical Monetary Theory: The Outcome of the Discussion," *Economica*, 19 (November 1952).

2. Boulding, K. E., "M. Allais' Theory of Interest," *Journal of Political Economics*, 59 (February 1951).

3. Brechling, F. P. R., "A Note on Bond Holding and the Liquidity Preference Theory of Interest," *Review of Economic Studies*, 24 (1956–57).

4. Brockie, M. D., and A. L. Grey, "The Marginal Efficiency of Capital and Investment Programming," *Economic Journal*, 66 (December 1956).

5. ———, "The Rate of Interest, the Marginal Efficiency of Capital and Investment Programming—A Rejoinder," *Economic Journal*, 69 (June 1959).

6. Brunner, K., "Stock and Flow Analysis: Discussion," *Econometrica*, 18 (July 1950).

7. Clayton, G., "A Note on the Banking System's Power to Lend," *Metroeconomica*, 7 (1955).

8. Clower, R. W., "Productivity, Thrift and the Rate of Interest," *Economic Journal*, 64 (March 1954).

9. ———, and D. W. Bushaw, "Price Determination in a Stock-flow Economy," *Econometrica*, 22 (July 1954).

10. Cunningham, N. J., "Business Investment and the Marginal Cost of Funds," *Metroeconomica*, 10 (1958).

11. Eastham, J. K., "A Redefinition of the Boundary between Interest and Profit Theories," in J. K. Eastham (ed.), *Dundee Economic Essays* (Dundee, 1955).

12. Fellner, W., and H. M. Somers, "Note on 'Stocks' and 'Flows' in Monetary Interest Theory," *Review of Economics and Statistics*, 31 (May 1949).

13. ——— "Stock and Flow Analysis: Comment," *Econometrica*, 18 (July 1950).

14. ——— "Stock and Flow Analysis: Note on the Discussion," *Econometrica*, 18 (July 1950).

15. Fouraker, L. E., "The Cambridge Didactic Style," *Journal of Political Economy*, 66 (February 1958).

16. Hahn, F. H., "The Rate of Interest and General Equilibrium Analysis," *Economic Journal*, 65 (March 1955).

17. Harrod, Sir Roy, *Towards a Dynamic Economics* (London, 1948).

18. Hicks, J. R., "A Rehabilitation of 'Classical' Economics?" *Economic Journal*, 67 (June 1957).

19. Johnson, H. G., "Some Cambridge Controversies in Monetary Theory," *Review of Economic Studies*, 19 (1951–52).

20. Keynes, J. M., *The General Theory of Employment, Interest and Money* (London, 1936).

21. ———, "The General Theory of Employment," *Quarterly Journal of Economics*, 51 (February 1937).

22. ———, "Alternative Theories of the Rate of Interest," *Economic Journal*, 47 (June 1937).

23. Klein, L. R., "Stock and Flow Analysis in Economics," *Econometrica*, 18 (July 1950).

24. ———, "Stock and Flow Analysis: Further Comment," *Econometrica*, 18 (July 1950).

25. Kragh, B., "Two Liquidity Functions and the Rate of Interest: A Simple Dynamic Model," *Review of Economic Studies*, 17 (1949–50).

26. Lange, O., "Say's Law: A Restatement and a Criticism," in O. Lange, F. McIntyre, and T. O. Yntema (eds.), *Studies in Mathematical Economics and Econometrics*, in memory of Henry Schultz (Chicago 1942).

27. Lloyd, C. L., "The Equivalence of the Liquidity Preference and Loanable Funds Theories and the *New* Stock-flow Analysis," *Review of Economic Studies*, 27 (June 1960).

28. Meade, J. E., and P. W. S. Andrews, "Summary of Replies to Questions on Effects of Interest Rates," *Oxford Economic Papers*, No. 1 (October 1938).

29. Mishan, E. J., "A Fallacy in the Interpretation of the Cash Balance Effect," *Economica*, 25 (May 1958).

30. Modigliani, F., "Liquidity Preference and the Theory of Interest and Money," *Econometrica*, 12 (1944).

31. Patinkin, D., "Relative Prices, Say's Law and the Demand for Money," *Econometrica*, 16 (April 1948).

32. ———, "The Indeterminacy of Absolute Prices in Classical Economic Theory," *Econometrica*, 17 (January 1949).

33. ———, "A Reconsideration of the General Equilibrium Theory of Money," *Review of Economic Studies*, 18 (1949–50).

34. ———, "The Invalidity of Classical Monetary Theory," *Econometrica*, 19 (April 1951).

35. ———, *Money, Interest and Prices* (Evanston, Ill., 1956).

36. ———, "Liquidity Preference and Loanable Funds: Stock and Flow Analysis," *Economica*, 25 (November 1958).

37. ———, "Keynesian Economics Rehabilitated: A Rejoinder to Professor Hicks," *Economic Journal*, 69 (September 1959).

38. Robertson, Sir D., "Mr. Keynes and the Rate of Interest," in *Essays in Monetary Theory* (London, 1940).

39. Robinson, J., *The Rate of Interest and Other Essays* (London, 1952).

40. Rose, H., "Liquidity Preference and Loanable Funds," *Review of Economic Studies*, 24 (February 1957).

41. ———, "The Rate of Interest and Walras's Law," *Economica*, 26 (August 1959).

42. Sayers, R. S., "Ricardo's Views on Monetary Questions," *Quarterly Journal of Economics*, 67 (February 1953).

43. Shackle, G. L. S., "Interest-rates and the Pace of Investment," *Economic Journal*, 56 (March 1946).

44. ———, "Business and Uncertainty," *Bankers' Magazine*, 189 (March 1960).

45. Tew, B., "Sequence Analysis and the Theory of the Rate of Interest," *Economic Journal*, 66 (September 1956).

46. Tsiang, S. C., "Liquidity Preference and Loanable Funds Theories, Multiplier and Velocity Analyses: A Synthesis," *American Economic Review*, 46 (September 1956).

47. Turvey, R., "Consistency and Consolidation in the Theory of Interest," *Economica*, 21 (November 1954).

48. White, W. H., "The Rate of Interest, the Marginal Efficiency of Capital and Investment Programming," *Economic Journal*, 68 (March 1958).

49. Knut Wicksell, *Interest and Prices*, trans. R. F. Kahn (London 1936).

50. Wright, A. L., "Sequence Analysis and the Theory of the Rate of Interest," *Economic Journal*, 65 (December 1955).

17 *Alternative Monetary Approaches to Interest Theory*

William Fellner *Yale University*
and Harold M. Somers
University of California, Los Angeles

This article is concerned with the relation between the loanable-funds theory of interest and the liquidity-preference theory of interest. In part one we consider briefly some of the main points discussed by those who have taken part in the current controversy on this subject. Part two contains our attempt to represent graphically the relation between the two approaches, and part three deals with the conclusions derived therefrom.

Some Remarks on the Current Controversy

According to the loanable-funds theory of interest, the rate of interest is determined by the interaction of the demand for, and the supply of, loanable funds. This theory (sometimes called the "credit" or "claims" theory of the rate of interest) has been advocated in recent years as a two-dimensional approximation to reality—through the particular equilibrium approach—by Professors Haberler, Ohlin, Robertson, and Viner, among others. According to the liquidity-preference theory of interest, the rate of interest is determined by the interaction of the demand for, and

Reprinted from *Review of Economic Statistics*, Vol. 23 (Cambridge, Mass.: Harvard University Press, February 1941), 43–48, by permission of the authors and publisher. Copyright, 1941, by the President and Fellows of Harvard College.

the supply of, money. This is the Keynesian interest theory as presented in the *General Theory of Employment, Interest and Money* and in Mr. Keynes' more recent writings.

The distinctive feature of the liquidity-preference theory does not lie in the fact that it takes account of "hoarding." The loanable-funds theory takes account of this phenomenon as well. Yet the loanable-funds theory assumes that the desire to "hoard" (or to "dishoard") is one of the factors influencing the demand for and the supply of loans, and that the rate of interest is determined by this demand and supply; while the liquidity-preference theory assumes that the demand for and the supply of money are the direct determinants of the interest rate.

The belief that the techniques suggested by the two theories respectively yield identical results became rather general among economists who expressed their views on the subject,[1] although a well-known sentence in one of Mr. Keynes' articles might convey the impression that he regards the loanable-funds approach to be completely incorrect.[2] Keynes' argument, however, is directed, throughout his writings, against the proposition that the rate of interest equates Savings and Investment, and never *really* against the proposition that it equates demand and supply on the loanable-funds market. Even in the article referred to, his objection to the loanable-funds theory seems to spring from his contention that this theory is but a new name for the old Savings-Investment doctrine.[3] Ohlin (temporarily) gave rise to this misunderstanding by holding in an article published earlier than that of Mr. Keynes that, "*Ex post* one finds equality between the total quantity of new credit during the period, and the sum total of positive individual savings. (Of course, a person who uses his own savings is then said to give credit to himself; . . .)."[4] This statement was erroneous and was withdrawn readily by Ohlin after Keynes had derived conclusions from it.[5] Keynes did not explicitly revise his statement on this question, but a number of passages in the *General Theory* and in his various articles can hardly be interpreted in any other way than to mean that he, too, believes both methods lead to the same result,—as against the Savings-Investment theory, which he considers to be fallacious.[6]

We must, therefore, turn our attention to the nature of the technique by which these two apparently different theories are able to derive "one and the same" rate of interest in any particular set of circumstances; and then we shall be able to consider how the fundamental statements of the two theories compare with each other. The fact that this question has a direct bearing on problems of general price theory has been emphasized by Messrs. Hicks,[7] Fleming,[8] and Millikan[9] (although it has not, of course, been overlooked by the other authors involved in or commenting on the controversy). Professor Hicks' presentation is essentially as follows: The rate of interest "is a price like other prices and must be determined with them as part of a mutually inter-dependent system." If we are given all demand and supply functions in terms of money, Hicks states, we have for *money*, *claims*, and $n - 1$ *"other"* commodities, a total of $n + 1$ equations. This follows from the fact that we have n single equations expressing the equality of demand and supply in terms of money for the n commodities (including claims) and we also have an equation expressing the equality of total money receipts and money outlays. This system of equations is over-determined, since the equality of total money receipts and outlays follows from the n other equations. Hence we must eliminate one equation; which one we eliminate depends upon which "theory of interest" we favor. The loanable-funds theory of interest makes the money equation unnecessary, for this theory fits into a theoretical framework within which all demands and supplies are represented as functions of all commodity prices (including the price of claims and thus the interest rate). The liquidity-preference theory, on the other hand, implies the elimination of the equation for claims. Thus the liquidity-preference theory leads to a system in which the demand and supply of the $n - 1$ "other" commodities, together with the demand and supply of money, are related to all prices, inclusive of the interest rate. Hicks holds that the choice between the two methods is a matter of convenience. The Keynesian method has the advantage of stressing more explicitly the close connection between the concepts of money and interest, whereas the other, more usual, method has the advantage of lending itself more readily to a discussion of the interest-rate structure.

We believe, however, that two questions here must be clearly distinguished: what these theories suggest as two-dimensional approximations to reality; and how they may be fitted into a multi-dimensional theory by the addition of commodity prices as further variables. Professor Hicks is concerned mainly with the latter aspect of the problem, but we shall be concerned with the former aspect because the verbal formulation of both theories, as well as the formal descriptions of them (with the help of curves), are those of two-dimensional approximations. From which of the two propositions one *starts* does not matter if one *adds* all commodity prices as further variables. Hicks, of course, is right in holding that in both cases one arrives at one and the same theory stating that all demands and all supplies are simultaneously determined by all prices. But this fact has no direct bearing on the question of what is meant in saying (a) that interest equates demand and supply on the loan market and (b) that interest equates the demand for money with the supply of money, *instead of* saying that the interest rate and all commodity prices together perform the function of equating all demands with all supplies. After all, both of the two former propositions are two-dimensional in character. They attribute to the rate of interest some particular role, which in a theory of the "general" (multi-dimensional) type is attributed in a somewhat neutral way to the "entire price system"; and although a particular role can be attributed to any single variable in the first approximation only, the characteristic feature of both theories lies just in this first approximation. A theory holding that the price of automobiles equates the demand for shoes with the supply of shoes could also be transformed into the same general theory by the addition of $n - 1$ other variables, but the argument that for this reason such a statement is an equivalent alternative to the usual particular equilibrium theory of the automobile price would be rather far-fetched.

Thus we shall be mainly concerned with the suggestion contained in these "two-dimensional" propositions respectively and not with the general theory into which all special theories can ultimately be resolved. Of what nature are these two approximations and what do they suggest?

Simultaneous Representation of the Two Approaches

The following model seems suitable for a comparative analysis of the loanable-funds and the liquidity-preference theories.[10] During any period of time the total demand for money may be divided into three parts from the point of view of what the economic subjects demanding the money are supplying in order to acquire it. They are supplying either (a) commodities other than claims;[11] or (b) their own money, by the non-spending of which they help to satisfy their demand for money;[12] or (c) claims.[13]

This division of the demand for money is represented in Figure 1 where the second and third of these components are made interest-elastic while the first component (L_a) is not. The reasons for these assumptions will be discussed below, but we may provisionally say that the interest-inelasticity of the first component is essentially an expression of the fact that the liquidity-preference curve must apply to a given level of income.[14] Interest rates are measured on the ordinate, and amounts of money on the abscissa. We may designate the three divisions of the demand for money by L_a, L_b, and L_c, respectively, so that the total demand for money, L, is the sum of these three. In Figure 1, the horizontal distance between the L_c curve and the vertical axis represents L_c; the horizontal distance between the $L_b + L_c$ curve and the L_c curve represents

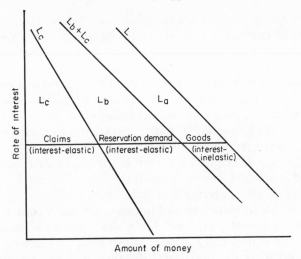

Figure 1. *Demand for Money*

L_b; and the horizontal distance between the $L(= L_a + L_b + L_c)$ curve and the $L_b + L_c$ curves represents L_a.

An analogous division may be made with respect to the supply of money at any moment, which may be divided according to what the economic subjects wish to acquire for their money. They wish to acquire either (a) commodities other than claims;[15] or (b) their own money, by the non-spending of which they supply it to themselves;[16] or (c) claims.[17] These three parts may be designated by M_a, M_b, and M_c, respectively, and the total by M. These parts are represented in Figure 2, where, again, the last two compo-

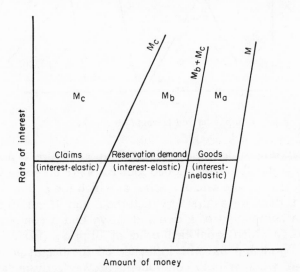

Figure 2. *Supply of Money*

nents are made interest-elastic while the first (M_a) is not. The total supply curve is made upward sloping to the right, as this might perhaps be considered the more "general" case. The result is not, however, affected by this assumption.[18]

The two sets of curves have been drawn to satisfy four conditions, two of which have already been mentioned, and all of which will be justified in the course of the discussion:

1. L_a($=$ the horizontal distance between the L curve and the $L_b + L_c$ curve) is interest-inelastic;

2. M_a($=$ the horizontal distance between the M curve and the $M_b + M_c$ curve) is interest-inelastic;

3. $L_a = M_a$ for every rate of interest;

4. $L_b = M_b$ for every rate of interest, although both L_b and M_b are interest-elastic (i.e., the horizontal distance between the $L_b + L_c$ curve and the L_c curve is different for different rates of interest and so is the horizontal distance between the $M_b + M_c$ curve and the M_c curve; but the two horizontal distances *equal each other* for every rate of interest).

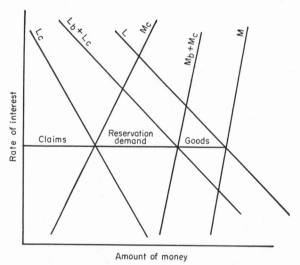

Figure 3. *Supply of and Demand for Money*

We may now superimpose Figure 2 upon Figure 1, and obtain Figure 3. If the above-mentioned four rules are observed when the curves are drawn, the rate of interest at which the L_c and M_c curves intersect is the same as that at which the L and M curves intersect; because a component of a demand curve and a component of a supply curve which equal each other at all prices (like L_a and M_a, or like L_b and M_b) have no influence on the height of the price, *regardless* of whether both components are perfectly inelastic with respect to that price (like L_a and M_a), or whether both have a finite elasticity (like L_b and M_b).

Now before discussing these conditions (or "rules" of the graph), we must consider whether our Figure 3 actually represents the two interest theories under discussion. With respect to the loanable-funds theory the answer is obvious: The rate of interest is determined by the L_c curve and the M_c curve. With respect to the liquidity-preference theory, however, the answer is not so obvious. Mr. Keynes and his followers generally state that the rate of interest equates the demand for cash with the supply of cash. The liquidity-preference theory would then be represented by the L and M curves in Figure 3. But in one of his articles Mr. Keynes says, "If we mean by 'hoarding' the holding of idle balances, then my theory of the rate of interest might be expressed by saying that the rate of interest serves to equate the demand and supply of hoards. . . ."[19] In the Keynesian terminology this amounts to saying that interest equates the demand for M_2 with the supply of M_2. However, the "demand and supply of M_2" are concepts presupposing the knowledge of the total demand for money and of the total supply of money. It is impossible to distinguish on the supply side an *ex ante* supply of M_2.[20] There *is* such a thing as paying an individual a certain amount of money, on condition that he deliver a certain quantity of shoes, but there is no such thing as paying an individual a certain amount of money on condition that he increase his speculative balances with it and does not spend it. To Keynes' distinction between different components on the demand-for-money side, an analogous distinction on the supply side does not correspond, since the motive with which the money is demanded is the principle on which his distinction is based. Hence, the so-called supply of M_2 is a residual, which can only be derived by subtracting the demand for M_1 (and that for "finance") from the *total* supply of money. The liquidity-preference technique must necessarily employ the total demand and supply of money, inclusive of our L_a and M_a.

We may now turn to a discussion of the four conditions which, we believe, have to be satisfied when the graph is drawn. Condition 4 ($L_b = M_b$ for every rate of interest) follows from the fact that L_b and M_b are essentially different designations for one and the same thing; both represent that part of the demand for money which the economic subjects satisfy by supplying themselves with their own money. Conditions 1–3 (interest-inelasticity of L_a and M_a, and $L_a = M_a$ for every rate of interest) might require a few words.

The L curve and the M curve must necessarily be construed as *ex ante* functions, in the sense that they must be definable without yet knowing what the interest rate is actually going to be.[21] The approximation suggested by the proposition that the rate of interest equates L with M is characterized by the assumption that the values of the other variables of these functions, i.e., the commodity prices, are given. Now, obviously, the suggestion that commodity prices play a subordinate part in equating commodity demands with commodity supplies is not intended. Yet interest-elastic L_a and M_a functions would suggest this, because they would imply that it is profitable to regard, in the suggested first approximation, the commodity prices as given independently of commodity demands and supplies. Since this obviously is not the intention, the simplifying assumption of given commodity prices is identical with that of given commodity demands and supplies and thus of a given level of income.

To say that commodity prices have determined commodity demands and supplies implies, of course, that these demands and supplies equal one another ($L_a = M_a$) for all conceivable rates of interest. From the point of view of our conclusions this condition ($L_a = M_a$ for all interest rates) is significant, and not the interest-inelasticity of both of these functions. The condition $L_a = M_a$ for all rates is quite sufficient to show that in this model L_a and M_a do not affect the level of the interest rate. And the coincidence of this latter condition with the simplifying assumption of given commodity prices may even be termed as "self-evident."

The reader must be reminded that we do not mean to hold that any theorist expressing himself in two-dimensional terms (such as "the rate of interest equates the demand for loans with the supply of loans" or "the rate of interest equates the demand for money with the supply of money") has really in mind that some function in the economic system is *exclusively* performed by one factor. But while "two-dimensional" statements are not intended to be taken at their face value, their content is intended to suggest something with respect to the relative significance of different variables in performing some specific function. To say that the interest rate equates the demand for money with the supply of money suggests that in the first approximation it is helpful to conceive of the demand for money and the supply of money as functions of the interest rate, with given commodity prices and hence with given commodity supplies and demands which are equated by other variables.

Implications of the Two Approaches

Professor Hicks has pointed out, quite truly, that both expository devices—that of the loanable-funds approach and that of the liquidity-preference approach—can be transformed into the identical multi-dimensional device. In fact Professor Lange in his highly interesting article, "The Rate of Interest and the Optimum Propensity to Consume,"[22] has interpreted the Keynesian system essentially in this manner, and Lange's interpretation was approved by Keynes.[23] The question is not settled, however, as to the meaning of attributing to the rate of interest the role of equating the demand for loans with the supply of loans, or that of equating the demand for cash with the supply of cash. By transforming either of the two devices into a general equilibrium theory one immediately minimizes the significance of the propositions themselves, which, although they are not intended to be taken literally, are undoubtedly meant to express something.

Now the "suggestion" of the loanable-funds theory has the well-known advantages and defects of the particular equilibrium approach, the defects being in this case even aggravated by the circumstance that the state of the loan market is especially closely interwoven with that of certain commodity markets. As against this, the suggestion that the rate of interest equates the demand for money with the supply of money is difficult to interpret and probably does not convey the precise meaning intended.

Hicks contends that the Keynesian proposition suggests a close connection between money and interest. But is anything apart from pure algebra suggested by holding that, in a system in which $n - 1$ variables have equated considerable portions of the demand for and the supply of money, the nth variable can be said to equate not only the remainder of the demand and of the supply, but *thereby* also to equate the whole demand with the whole supply? Can any worth-while suggestion be contained in directing the reader's interest to the intersection of our L and M curves as against that of our L_c and M_c curves, if we are told at the same time that we must consider $L_b = M_b$ and $L_a = M_a$ for all conceivable interest rates?

Keynes and the Keynesian school obviously intend to suggest that the demand for idle deposits is a highly significant determinant of the interest rate. Whether this is or is not true must be considered a controversial issue, but the suggestion undoubtedly has content. This suggestion is not, however, expressed in the statement that the interest rate is determined by the demand for and the supply of cash, because this latter statement is true only in a sense in which it would be just as true if no idle deposits existed. Even in the absence of idle deposits, once one has conceived of a large portion of the demand for and the supply of money as being equated by $n - 1$ commodity prices, the nth variable can arbitrarily be said to equate not merely the remainder but *thereby* also the whole demand and supply. The formal "correctness" of this procedure does not depend on the relative significance of idle balances, but neither does its arbitrariness. It will always remain arbitrary, and for this reason confusing, to express the working hypothesis according to which $n - 1$ variables are regarded as already having equated $n - 1$ demands and supplies by saying that the nth variable equates an aggregate consisting of the n demands and supplies.

The rate of interest equates demand and supply of cash only in the sense in which the shoe price can also be said to perform this function if all other prices are given. *This proposition in itself is entirely empty and contains no more than the methodological suggestion of the loanable-funds theory in disguise; this suggestion is merely that commodity prices (and the level of income) might be considered given in the first approximation.* Techniques of approximation can be judged only by their ability to express essential propositions. And the essential suggestion of the Keynesians, that the desire to hoard is a significant determinant of the interest rate, does not justify the unusual procedure of adding the same constant to both sides of an equation. This suggestion must be introduced into either of the two theories by a special assumption. It can, of course, easily be introduced into the loanable-funds theory. The assumption that the elasticity of the loanable-funds curves mainly depends on the public's desire to hoard might lack realism, but it does not lack clarity.

Postscript of The Authors

The foregoing argument was developed in a framework in which it was assumed, as it was in the Keynesian as well as in the loanable-funds framework, that prices and the interest rate actually equate demands with supplies in the commodity markets and in the security market. But we believe that we have demonstrated subsequently, in an exchange of views in which Lawrence R. Klein, Karl Brunner, and ourselves participated,[1] that our proposition concerning the equivalence of the liquidity-preference theory with the loanable-funds theory holds also in any acceptable "dynamic" model in which the *changes* of prices and of the interest rate from one period to the next are represented as functions of always existing *excess demands* (positive or negative). In such models stock theories do become different from flow theories in that the magnitude of the excess demands is different on the stock level from what it is on the flow level. But whether our models are static or dynamic, they must take account of the fact that the interest rate can move only under the influence of excess demand in the security market (excess demand for stocks *or* for flows of claims, as the case may be). This is because both Keynes and the loanable-funds theorists *defined* the interest rate as the price of claims. Hence any interest theory that attributes a role to excess demands other than the excess demand for securities must recognize that those other excess demands can change the interest rate only to the extent that they do not offset each other, i.e., to the extent that they become equivalent to excess demand in the security market. A "dynamic" liquidity-preference model not recognizing this is inconsistent with the definition of the interest rate which Keynes and the loanable-funds theorists had in common. Whether we prefer to use the liquidity-preference theory or the loanable-funds theory, we must of course be aware of the fact that in a general equilibrium model all demands and supplies become interrelated.

W. F.
H. M. S.
May 1965

NOTES

1. See, for instance, D. H. Robertson, *Essays in Monetary Theory* (London 1940), p. 9: "Essentially they are two different ways of saying the same thing."

2. Keynes, *Economic Journal*, Vol. 47 (1937), 241 *et seq.*

3. "Thus we are completely back again at the classical doctrine" (*ibid.*, p. 245).

4. *Ibid.*, p. 224.

5. *Ibid.*, p. 425.

6. We may refer to two rather conclusive statements by Keynes. When arguing against a passage in Marshall's *Principles*, where Marshall holds that the rate of interest equates the demand for capital with the aggregate stock of capital forthcoming in the market, Keynes says, "It is equality between the demand and supply of loans of money, i.e., of debts, which is brought about by the rate of interest" (*General Theory*, p. 186, note 1). Later he says, "The rate of interest . . . equalises the advantages of holding actual cash and a deferred claim on cash" (*Economic Journal*, Vol. 47 [1937], 245).

7. Hicks, *Value and Capital* (Oxford 1939), Chapter 12. See also Hicks' first review of the *General Theory*, "Mr. Keynes' Theory of Employment," *Economic Journal*, Vol. 46 (1936), 238–53.

8. Fleming, "The Determination of the Rate of Interest," *Economica*, New Series, Vol. 5 (1938), 333–41.

9. Millikan, "The Liquidity-Preference Theory of Interest," *American Economic Review*, Vol. 28 (1938), 247–60.

10. In his interesting article, "Alternative Formulations of the Theory of Interest" (*Economic Journal*, Vol. 48 [1938], 211–30), Mr. Lerner has two diagrams—Figures 2 and 3—which simultaneously represent the

loanable-funds and the liquidity-preference theories of interest. Neither of these is, however, suitable for our purpose since neither shows the component parts of the demand for and supply of cash. Figure 2, moreover, contains—as Professor Haberler has pointed out (*Prosperity and Depression* [Geneva, 1939 edition], p. 189 n.)—an incorrect representation of the loanable-funds theory because *ex post* Savings and Investment are added to the increase in the amount of money during the period and the net (Keynesian) "hoarding," respectively, while the functions of the loanable-funds theory are of an *ex ante* character.

11. Hicks' $n - 1$ "other" commodities.

12. This is "reservation demand," the inclusion of which is optional in any analysis, provided that it is also included on the supply side. See part (b) in the division of the supply of money. We include the item since it plays an important part in the current discussion.

13. The definition of claims is admittedly arbitrary and must depend on what we want to call "the rate of interest" (i.e., on what we want to include, by definition, in the interest-structure). But once we have decided on any definition of "claims," we must, of course, be consistent in what we regard as "the rate of interest," since the latter is but a slightly different expression for the price of claims. The "reservation demand" (outstanding claims which do not change hands) is not included here, since the representation becomes clearer if we deal only with components of the demand for and the supply of money. Yet it is self-evident that the "gross" version of *any* price theory (gross of reservation demand) always determines the same price as its "net" version (net of reservation demand).

14. The same holds for the supply curve of money. (See the explanation of Figure 2.)

15. See footnote 11.

16. See footnote 12.

17. See footnote 13.

18. An M curve perfectly inelastic to interest would imply that the policy of the banking system is such as to provide the economy with a certain amount of money regardless of the demand curve (and thus, regardless of the interest-rate). This special assumption is not quite so strict as the assumption of a constant money supply, since the former permits of shifts of the M curve, while the latter does not. Our model is not based on either of these special assumptions, but the conclusions hold for these cases as well.

19. Keynes, *Economic Journal*, Vol. 47 (1937), 250.

20. See Professor Shaw's graphical representation (*Journal of Political Economy*, Vol. 46 [1938], 838–56), which illustrates the point very clearly.

21. This is the sense in which Professor Ohlin uses the term "*ex ante*" in one of his later articles (*Economic Journal*, Vol. 47 [1937], 423–27), and in which we use it throughout this article. In previous articles, Ohlin seems to have used the term in a different sense, namely in that of a planned *magnitude*, not function (*ibid.*, pp. 53–69).

22. Lange, *Economica*, New Series, Vol. 5 (1938), 12–32.

23. Keynes, *Economic Journal*, Vol. 48 (1938), 321, note.

NOTE TO POSTSCRIPT

1. For the exchange of views referred to see *Econometrica*, Vol. 18 (July 1950), 236–252. For earlier discussions of the problems raised in the authors' article see Abba P. Lerner, "Interest Theory—Supply and Demand for Loans or Supply and Demand for Cash," *Review of Economics and Statistics*, Vol. 26 (May 1944), 88–91; Lawrence R. Klein, *The Keynesian Revolution* (New York 1947), pp. 121–22; and William Fellner and Harold M. Somers, "Note on 'Stocks' and 'Flows' in Monetary Interest Theory," *Review of Economics and Statistics*, Vol. 31 (May 1949), 145–46. [Editor]

18 Expectations, Errors, and the Term Structure of Interest Rates

John H. Wood *University of Birmingham, England*

The expectations hypothesis concerning the determination of relationships among interest rates on default-free securities that differ only with respect to maturity[1] has come under frequent attack in recent years.[2] Writers have become fond of statements such as "an unfortunate lacuna still exists between the writings of economic theorists and the practices of bond traders and institutional investors,"[3] and "the influence of the expectational theory seems to have been confined mainly to academic economists."[4] These writers, unable to attack successfully the logical structure of the expectations theory, have based their criticisms on empirical grounds.[5] It is stated or implied that, while some investors might possibly manage their security holdings on the basis of expectations, the overwhelming majority of investors are risk-averters and determine their relative holdings of securities of different term-to-maturity on the basis of hedging, liquidity, and other "institutional" considerations. Another obstacle is then placed in the path of the expectations hypothesis by the consideration that borrowers, also, are not indifferent between issues of short- and long-term debt.[6]

Reprinted from *Journal of Political Economy*, Vol. 71 (April 1963), 160–71, by permission of the author and The University of Chicago Press. Copyright 1963 by The University of Chicago Press.

A review article of David Meiselman's *The Term Structure of Interest Rates* (Englewood Cliffs, N.J.: Prentice-Hall, 1962). Page numbers in parentheses in the text refer to this work.

However, without exception until the appearance of the work under review, there has not been advanced a rigorous empirical test of any of the alternative theories, expectational or otherwise,[7] of the determination of the interest-rate structure. Earlier tests of the expectations hypothesis have been cursory and highly inadequate. These tests may be grouped into three categories.

1. According to the expectations hypothesis, long-term rates are modified geometric averages of current and expected short-term rates. Therefore, if expected future short rates exceed current short rates (that is, if short-term rates are expected to rise), current long rates will exceed current short rates. Conversely, if short-term rates are expected to fall, current long-term rates will lie below current short rates. If short-term interest rates are expected to remain unchanged over the relevant horizon, current long and short rates will be equal (that is, the yield curve will be horizontal). Since, during the recovery phase of the business cycle, interest rates are generally expected to rise, the yield curve, in order to be consistent with the expectations theory, should be positively sloped. By the same reasoning the yield curve should have a negative slope during recessions and should be approximately horizontal during periods of relative calm. Lutz and others,[8] after casual examinations of the data, have concluded "that the relationship between interest rates on different maturities is determined in the main by the expectations as to the future course of interest rates."[9]

2. Another type of test of the expectations hypothesis, described by Meiselman (pp. 11–12 n.), was a survey conducted by Donald Woodward during the mid-1940's, in which "two hundred 'experts' in various fields were polled and asked to express their best judgment on the average rate of interest on Treasury obligations which might prudently be relied upon by a life insurance company for the next two decades." There was substantial difference of opinion in the 105 forecasts received in reply. "The modal forecast was that yields would not differ from the then current Treasury long-term yield of 2.5 per cent . . . and the mean expected rate was 2.78 per cent." The yield curve in 1943 had a positive slope, but was more steeply inclined than indicated by the gradual increase in the mean expected rate of the survey. Meiselman concludes that "expectations of higher rates suggested by the survey are consistent with the shape of the prevailing yield curve"[10] (pp. 11–12 n.).

3. Several tests have been conducted of what may be termed the perfect-foresight version of the expectations hypothesis. Since expectations are not directly observable, the analyst substitutes the rate actually prevailing in period $t + n$ for the short rate expected in period t to prevail n periods in the future. Then, if long rates in period t are found to be approximately equal to the geometric

average of current and (correctly) expected short rates, the expectations theory is regarded as being substantiated; if not, the expectations hypothesis is rejected.

Macaulay concluded from such a study that "the forecasting of short-term interest rates by long-term interest rates is, in general, so bad that the student may well begin to wonder whether, in fact, there really is any attempt to forecast."[11]

Meiselman is correct when he points out that this does not constitute a valid test of the expectations hypothesis as conceived by Hicks and Lutz.[12] "Anticipations may not be realized yet still determine the structure of rates in the manner asserted by the theory" (p. 12).

It is in this atmosphere of extremely perfunctory or misdirected empirical work and fuzzy thinking with regard to the effects of expectations vis-à-vis institutional factors that Meiselman provides us with (1) a rigorous test of the expectations hypothesis, the major contribution of his book, and (2) a reconciliation of the expectations hypothesis and the so-called institutional theories of the rate structure. Since the latter contribution provides much of the theoretical foundation for Meiselman's empirical work, it will be discussed first.

A Reconciliation of Expectations and Institutional Theories of the Rate Structure

There appears to have become imbedded in the literature the view that expectations will fail to determine the structure of rates in the presence of investors who allocate their holdings of securities of different term-to-maturity on the basis of considerations other than expectations regarding future rates of interest. The clearest statement of this position comes from Lutz:

> Certain institutional factors also influence the structure of interest rates. American banks look upon Government bonds and notes with maturities up to five years as eligible for holding in their "secondary reserve." This creates a strong demand for such bonds, and we may presume that this factor by itself makes for lower interest rates on investments with maturities up to five years than on those with longer maturities. . . . English banks aim at keeping a certain relatively fixed percentage of their assets (the 30 per cent ratio) in the form of cash and short material. There is therefore a relatively fixed supply of funds whose owners are not prepared to shift them into the long market, even if the rate there is higher. This makes it possible for the Treasury to cause the short rate to fall below the long rate, simply by curtailing the issue of Treasury bills. This discrep-

ancy will last as long as the shortage of Treasury bills continues, and it is one which cannot be explained in terms of expectations.[13]

But Meiselman points out that there is no contradiction between the expectations hypothesis, according to which short- and long-term securities may be treated as if they were perfect substitutes, and the fact that individual investors speculate or hedge on the basis of risk aversion (p. 10).

> There appear to be a great many overlapping areas of the yield curve in which important transactors tend to specialize. At the shortest end are the commercial banks; somewhat longer are savings banks and savings and loan associations, and at the very longest end of the yield curve are life insurance companies. The market is given even more continuity by security dealers and professional short-period traders. In addition, there are also speculators who trade in commodity futures or the equity markets on a non-professional or non-specialized basis. Taken together, the transactors who specialize in coping with uncertainty in one part of the yield curve and act to reduce the variance of expected returns, plus others who need not have such preferences or restraints imposed by legal and institutional requirements, give the market a continuity that is not apparent from observing the narrow range of choice of any one large transactor group [p. 53].

Actually, this chain of reasoning is not necessary to the expectations hypothesis. All that is required is that one group of speculators, indifferent to uncertainty and having similar expectations, be sufficiently well financed, and these speculators will offset disturbances to the yield curve brought about by the institutional investors (p. 54). Thus, the expectations hypothesis implies

> that market excess demand schedules of securities of given maturities tend to be infinitely elastic at rates consistent with current and expected short-term rates. Of course, it is not necessary that all transactors have infinitely elastic schedules in order that the market schedules be infinitely elastic. It is only necessary that one class of adequately financed transactors have an infinitely elastic excess demand schedule. . . . Speculators with given expectations adjust quantities of securities taken from or supplied to the market in order to maintain the structure of rates consistent with expectations [p. 57].

Meiselman's empirical work is a test of the hypothesis that, "as a matter of descriptive reality, individual transactors may still speculate or hedge on the basis of risk aversion, but the speculators who are indifferent to uncertainty will bulk sufficiently large to determine market rates on the basis of their mathematical expectations alone" (p. 10).

A Test of the Expectations Hypothesis

THE MODEL

Rigorous testing of the expectations hypothesis has in the past been hindered by the unavailability of independent evidence of interest-rate expectations. Meiselman asserts, however, that:

> The expectations hypothesis need not be tested by relating yield curves to contemporaneous expectations. Instead, *changes* in, rather than *levels* of interest rates can be related to factors which systematically cause *revisions of expectations* . . . . Recent research in a wide variety of behavioral contexts has indicated that hypotheses which assert that expectations tend to be related to past experience, often a weighted average of past experience, are consistent with the data. Further, these hypotheses state that expectations tend to be systematically altered on the basis of new experience whenever unfolding events differ from what had been anticipated [pp. 18–19].

Meiselman applies the same sort of reasoning to expectations of interest rates and points out that "the task of estimating expectations for purposes of testing the expectations hypothesis is made easier because, according to the theory we seek to test, expectations are already impounded and discounted in the term structure" (p. 19). That is, assuming the expectations hypothesis to hold, given current rates of interest, we can derive current expectations of future rates of interest. The relationship between current rates and expectations of future short rates may be expressed as

$$(1 + R_{n_t}) = [(1 + {}_t r_{1_t})(1 + {}_{t+1} r_{1_t}) \cdots (1 + {}_{t+n-1} r_{1_t})]^{1/n},$$

where $R_{1_t}, R_{2_t}, \ldots, R_{n_t}$ are rates of interest prevailing at time t on securities maturing at the ends of years $t, t + 1, \ldots, t + (n - 1)$, and ${}_{t+1} r_{1_t}$ is the rate on a one-year security that is expected at the beginning of time t to prevail during the period $t + 1$.[14] Current rates of interest are, of course, directly observable, and, given these rates prevailing at time t, we can solve for the expected rates. For example, the rate on a one-year security expected in period t to prevail in period $t + 1$ is

$$_{t+1} r_{1_t} = \frac{(1 + R_{2_t})^2}{(1 + R_{1_t})} - 1.$$

Meiselman's model is based upon this relationship between current and expected rates implied by the expectations hypothesis. His model is succinctly stated (p. 20), and it may be worthwhile to give it in full here:

> At the beginning of the year t one can look back at the market rates prevailing one year earlier. From these rates one can derive

the one-year rate that had been expected to prevail at the beginning of year t. The expected rate can then be compared with the actual market rate on one-year loans at the beginning of year t. If actual rates are higher than had been anticipated, then the market may systematically revise upward expectations of what short-term rates in the future are likely to be. Similarly, if actual rates are lower than had been anticipated, then the market may also systematically revise downward expectations of future short-term rates.

We therefore have the substantive hypothesis that forward short-term rates change on the basis of errors made in forecasting the current short-term rate,

$$_{t+n}r_{1t} - {}_{t+n}r_{1t-1} = f(R_{1t} - {}_{t}r_{1t-1})$$

or,

$$\Delta_{t+n}r_{1t} = g(E_t),$$

where E_t is the forecasting error $(R_{1t} - {}_{t}r_{1t-1})$, the difference between the actual one-year rate and the one-year rate which had been expected to prevail. If we assume that the functional relationship is linear it may be expressed as

$$\Delta_{t+n}r_{1t} = a + bE_t.$$

TESTS OF THE ERROR-LEARNING MODEL

Meiselman tests his model with annual data on the basic yields of corporate bonds compiled by Durand and Winn,[15] and finds that "changes in forward one-year rates classified by maturity are, in fact, highly correlated with the forecasting error for the fifty-four annual observations covering the 1901–1954 period" (p. 21). The results of eight regressions are presented in which $\Delta_{t+n}r_{1t}(n = 1, 2, \ldots, 8)$ is the dependent variable and E_t is the independent variable. These results contain four principal characteristics.

First, the correlations between the first differences in the future rates and the forecasting error are high and positive. . . . Second, the correlation coefficient tends to vary inversely with the maturity of the dependent variable [being, for example, .95 for $n = 1$ and .59 for $n = 8$]. Third, the regression coefficient and hence the sensitivity of forward rates to forecasting errors also tends to vary dependably and inversely with the maturity of the dependent variable [from .7 when $n = 1$ to .2 when $n = 8$]. Fourth, none of the constant terms of the regression equations differs significantly from zero [pp. 21–22].

The regression equation for $n = 1$, for example, is[16]

$$\Delta_{t+1}r_{1t} = .00 + .703E_t.$$
$$(.02)$$

Meiselman's results may be interpreted as follows. First, the high correlation coefficients obtained indicate that a significant part of the movements of forward rates, or the expectations that are implied by the expectations hypothesis, can be explained by errors in forecasting the rate on one-year securities. That is, the expectations hypothesis, supplemented by the error-learning mechanism for the revision of expectations, is supported by the data. Second, the performance of this model declines as the expectations that comprise the dependent variable increase in maturity. This result should not be at all surprising. It is reasonable to suppose that investors will have fairly firm expectations regarding the level of rates one year from the present and will formulate their decisions on the basis of these expectations, whereas expectations of what rates will be several years into the future are likely to be at best hazy and, as a consequence, investors are likely to determine their holdings of one-year relative to, say, eight-year securities to a large extent on the basis of considerations other than expectations of future short rates. Third, since investors are likely to take their short-term forecasts more seriously than long-term forecasts, they will revise the former to a greater degree when their expectations of the previous period prove to be incorrect. The fourth characteristic of Meiselman's results also makes good economic sense. A constant term significantly different from zero would indicate that speculators, even when expectations proved to be correct, revise their expectations either upward (in the event of a positive constant term) or downward (in the case of a negative constant term). A constant term equal to zero, suggested by the data, means that investors leave their expectations unrevised when the expectations of the preceding period are realized.

Meiselman also tests the hypothesis that "because a long-term rate is an average of current and forward short-term rates . . . unanticipated changes in the long-term rate are . . . based on errors made in forecasting short-term rates" (pp. 20–21, 24–29). Here, as in the results discussed above, the correlation coefficients are significant and vary inversely with maturity, and the constant terms are not significantly different from zero at the 5 per cent level.

Meiselman considers the possibility that "if long-term rates are revised on the basis of unanticipated changes in short-term rates, then these revisions may be related to errors made in previous periods $t - 1$, $t - 2$, etc., as well as contemporaneous errors" (p. 29). The correlation coefficient increases only from .82 to .84 when E_{t-1} and E_{t-2} are added as explanatory variables, and the values of the coefficients of E_{t-1} and E_{t-2} do not differ significantly from zero at the 15 per cent level.

When Meiselman experiments with estimating the regression coefficients using data from various subperiods of the 1901–54 period, the coefficients associated with the error term, E_t, do not change much, but the constant term becomes positive and significantly different from zero in several cases, notably the 1930–54 subperiod (pp. 39–40).

These results imply that, during the 1901–29 period, speculators did not revise their expectations of future rates when past estimates proved to be correct, but, when anticipations were realized in the 1930–54 period, speculators nevertheless revised their expectations upward. This is consistent with the fact that rising yield curves have been much more prevalent since 1930 than before.

Tests of Alternative Theories of the Term Structure of Interest Rates

THE HICKSIAN LIQUIDITY-PREMIUM MODEL

Meiselman devotes a substantial portion of his last chapter to tests of liquidity and hedging theories of the term structure of interest rates (pp. 43–52). The Hicksian liquidity-premium model differs from the expectations hypothesis in that speculators are assumed to be risk-averters. Hicks contends that the forward rate implied by the expectations hypothesis is higher than the expected rate by some risk or liquidity premium because lenders are speculators who are not indifferent to risk.[17] They can be induced to face uncertainty as holders of claims that fluctuate in price only by the payment of a risk premium. This model can be expressed as

$$(1 + R_n) = [(1 + R_1)(1 + r_2 + L_2) \ldots (1 + r_n + L_n)]^{1/n},$$

where $r_2, r_3, \ldots, r_n$ are expected one-period interest rates in periods 2, 3, ..., n, and $L_2, L_3, \ldots, L_n$ are the Hicksian liquidity premiums for periods 2, 3, ..., n. The forward short-term rate for period n will be $F_n = r_n + L_n$. Meiselman regards the constant term of the regression equation $\Delta_{t+n}r_{1_t} = a + bE_t$ as a measure of the liquidity premium (p. 45). Consider the regression equation $\Delta_{t+8}r_{1_t} = .01 + .2E_t$. The estimated values of the coefficients in this equation indicate that, when $E_t = 0$ (that is, the actual one-year rate at time t is equal to the forward rate observed at time $t - 1$), the forward rate will rise by 0.01 percentage points. This suggests to Meiselman that "the forward one-year rate is typically greater than the expected one-year rate" so that, when expectations are realized, expectations of future rates will nevertheless be revised upward. But, as we have already seen, the constant terms do not differ significantly from zero (when the entire 1901–54 period is considered). Meiselman interprets these results as not contradicting "the assumption of the expectations hypothesis that the risk premium on default-free claims is zero" (p. 46).

Implicit in Meiselman's test of the liquidity-premium model is the assumption that speculators, whether risk-averting or risk-indifferent, will revise expectations of future rates only when expectations of the preceding period turn out to be wrong. That is, $_tR_{1_t} - _{t'}r_{1_{t-1}} = 0$ implies $_{t+n}r_{1_t} - _{t+n}r_{1_{t-1}} = 0$. If this is the case, then in the expectations hypothesis *sine* liquidity premiums, the constant term, a, must of necessity equal zero. Thus, Meiselman's results are consistent with the expectations hypothesis. It can, however, be shown that a zero value for the constant term may reasonably exist in the presence of positive liquidity premiums and still be consistent with the assumption of no revision of future expectations when past expectations have proved correct.

The Hicksian liquidity-premium model is presented in the framework of Meiselman's error-learning model in the following equation:

$$_{t+n}F_{1_t} - _{t+n}F_{1_{t-1}} = a + b(R_{1_t} - _tF_{1_{t-1}}),$$

where $_{t+n}F_{1_t} = _{t+n}r_{1_t} + _{t+n}L_{1_t}$ and the prescripts and subscripts are defined as on pages 486–87 above. Substituting expected rates and liquidity premiums for the forward rates, we get

$$(_{t+n}r_{1_t} + _{t+n}L_{1_t}) - (_{t+n}r_{1_{t-1}} + _{t+n}L_{1_{t-1}})$$
$$= a + b(R_{1_t} - _{t'}r_{1_{t-1}} - _tL_{1_{t-1}}).$$

Rearranging,

$$(_{t+n}r_{1_t} - _{t+n}r_{1_{t-1}}) + (_{t+n}L_{1_t} - _{t+n}L_{1_{t-1}})$$
$$= a + b(R_{1_t} - _{t'}r_{1_{t-1}}) - b(_tL_{1_{t-1}}).$$

Meiselman distinguishes between the risk-indifferent and Hicksian liquidity-premium models on the basis of the value taken by the constant term, a, under the assumption that $_tR_{1_t} - _{t'}r_{1_{t-1}} = 0$ implies $_{t+n}r_{1_t} - _{t+n}r_{1_{t-1}} = 0$. If we let these two differences be equal to zero (that is, assume expectations to be realized), the above equation becomes

$$_{t+n}L_{1_t} - _{t+n}L_{1_{t-1}} = a - b(_tL_{1_{t-1}}).$$

Meiselman asserts that $a = 0$ is inconsistent with the liquidity-premium theory. This thesis can be tested by letting a be equal to zero and noting whether the equation remains consistent with the liquidity-premium model. When $a = 0$ and expectations are realized,

$$_{t+n}L_{1_t} - _{t+n}L_{1_{t-1}} = -b(_tL_{1_{t-1}}).$$

The terms $_{t+n}L_{1_t}$, $_{t+n}L_{1_{t-1}}$, and $_tL_{1_{t-1}}$ are the liquidity premiums for n, $n + 1$, and 1 periods into the future, respectively. If we assume, as does Meiselman, that the Hicksian model implies higher liquidity premiums for more remote future periods,[18] then it will be true that $_{t+n}L_{1_t} - {}_{t+n}L_{1_{t-1}} < 0$. This is consistent with a negative term on the right-hand side of the equation, which is the case since both b and $_tL_{1_{t-1}}$ are positive.

Thus, a constant term equal to zero, although necessary to the expectations hypothesis under Meiselman's assumptions, is also consistent with the liquidity-premium theory under the same assumptions.[19]

THE HEDGING THEORY

The hedging theory of the structure of rates asserts that hedgers—investors who manage their portfolios so that the maturity distributions of their assets and liabilities are similar—rather than speculators dominate the market. Meiselman examines the implication of the hedging theory that the structure of interest rates is related to the maturity structure of the debt outstanding (pp. 48–52). He finds that, "during the 1917–1956 period, changes in maturity composition were unrelated to changes in the relationship between short- and long-term rates. The correlation coefficient of first differences in the ratio of total short- to total long-term debt outstanding and first differences in the spread between short- and long-term interest rates is but +.05" (pp. 49–50).[20] The correlation coefficient is +.71 when the original data are used. The tactic of lagging interest rates one year behind the debt ratio did not change the results.

Even aside from the fact that the data used by Meiselman are extremely crude in many respects,[21] this test is unsatisfactory from a theoretical standpoint. Important aspects of both supply and demand are neglected. The supplies of securities of different term-to-maturity are dependent upon, among other things, the relation between short-term and long-term interest rates, so that the direction of causation between the variables used by Meiselman works both ways. Thus one of the basic assumptions of classical least-squares regression, which states that the disturbance terms must be independent of all the explanatory variables, is not satisfied.[22] Further, substantial shifts in the aggregate demand function for short-term relative to long-term securities took place during 1917–56, as a result of redistribution of total liabilities between hedgers issuing mainly short-term liabilities and hedgers issuing mainly long-term liabilities. Such shifts will arise, for example, from increases in the public's demand for, say, life-insurance policies relative to its demand for deposits in commercial banks. If life-insurance companies and commercial banks are hedgers, the result will be an increase in the demand for long-term relative to short-term securities, causing a decline in the ratio of long- to short-term interest rates even though the ratio of long-term to short-term debt used by Meiselman remains unchanged. It is evident from the data that such shifts in demand did occur during the period 1917–56. For example, the ratio of total loans and investments of commercial banks to total loans and investments of life-insurance companies increased from 4.1 in 1917 to 5.0 in 1920, declined to 1.4 in 1940, increased to 2.7 in 1945, and declined again to 1.7 in 1956.[23] The loans and investments of commercial banks and life-insurance companies comprised approximately 40 per cent of total holdings of private and government debt in 1950, indicating that shifts in aggregate demand for long-term relative to short-term debt arising from shifts in the total debt holdings of commercial banks relative to those of life-insurance companies constitute an important consideration left out of Meiselman's test of the hedging theory.[24]

A Test of the Liquidity Preference Theory

Meiselman's test of the Keynesian liquidity preference theory is based upon the following hypothesis (p. 54): The liquidity preference theory of interest implies that rates of return on default-free securities are directly related to their proximity to money, and since their proximity to money is in turn directly related to maturity, "this implies that an increase in the demand for money proper will be associated with (1) an increase in the demand for money relative to other assets and (2) a corresponding increase in the illiquidity premium on long-term securities." Therefore, "the liquidity gap between money and bonds will widen as transactors attempt to move towards money along the continuum of liquidity."

From this, I think, accurate interpretation of the liquidity preference theory, Meiselman concludes:

> We should find that fluctuations in income velocity are directly related to changes in the spread between short-term and long-term rates. When the demand for money increases (velocity falls), the short-term rate should fall relative to the long-term rate; and when there is a decline in the demand for money (velocity rises), the short-term rate should rise relative to the long-term rate [p. 54].

But the correlation of changes in velocity with changes in the differential between long- and short-term rates does not constitute a sound test of the liquidity preference theory unless changes in velocity during the period under consideration come about solely as a result of shifts in the demand for money. If velocity changes as the result of variations in output or the money supply, we cannot expect velocity to be correlated with short- and long-term interest rate differentials. For example, the initial consequences of a decrease in the stock of money, according to the liquidity preference theory, are increases in interest rates and velocity.[25] But, in the instance of a change in the money supply, although liquidity preference shifts as a result of the change in real balances, there has occurred no change in the "illiquidity premium" on long-term securities and there is, consequently, no reason to expect a change in interest-rate differentials. Thus, changes in the money supply, although inducing changes in velocity, do not induce corresponding changes in interest-rate differentials. Since there is no reason to suppose that changes in interest rates have come about more often as a result of shifts in liquidity preference than because of changes in the stock of money, one should not expect, on the basis of the liquidity preference theory, changes in velocity to be generally associated with changes in the spread between short-term and long-term rates.

Implications of the Expectations Hypothesis for the Supply of Liquidity

Meiselman attempts to draw implications from the results of his tests of the expectations hypothesis for the controversy stemming from arguments that "money is but the starting point of a continuum of assets yielding a corresponding continuum of liquidity services, and that banks are but one among many institutions creating liquid assets" (pp. 57–59). If

> holders of short-term claims essentially view them as composite commodities, part debt and yielding explicit pecuniary returns, part money and yielding implicit liquidity services . . . holders of claims (lenders) can be in equilibrium when market long-term rates are higher than averages of expected short-term rates because the liquidity component must be added to the expected pecuniary returns. If net lenders are in equilibrium when forward rates are higher than expected rates, net borrowers with the same expectations would not be in equilibrium unless there is a stream of illiquidity costs to them which exactly match the corresponding stream of liquidity returns to lenders [pp. 57–58].

And, "borrowers' illiquidity costs are excluded by the considerations of the expectations hypothesis that imply the infinitely elastic excess demand schedules just discussed" (p. 58). That is, the expectations hypothesis implies that, when net lenders are in equilibrium in the presence of liquidity returns, the excess demand schedules of net borrowers are sufficiently (perhaps infinitely) elastic at rates consistent with current and expected short-term rates to cause long-term rates to be averages of these current and expected rates in the manner described by the theory.[26] Therefore, under these assumptions and "abstracting from transactions costs, marginal liquidity returns tend to be driven to zero if the adjustments between expectations and market rates are complete in the sense that each long-term rate is an average of expected short-term rates" (p. 58). Consequently, "the liquidity or 'moneyness' component of short-term or other non-demand obligations has essentially zero marginal content in equilibrium" (p. 58).

It is Meiselman's contention that "the maturity continuum in this analysis does not extend to demand obligations, debts which are typically employed as money" (p. 58). Whereas "private profit seeking transactors can generally issue desired quantities of obligations of any maturity without institutionally imposed limits, . . . the stock of demand obligations is limited by well-known institutional factors" (p. 58). Rates on long-term securities may not, in equilibrium, be higher than averages of current and expected rates on short-term securities because of the existence of perfectly elastic excess demand functions on the part of expectationally oriented net borrowers. However, rates of return on securities may exceed current and expected rates of return on demand deposits by the amount of a liquidity premium because no excess demand function of infinite elasticity exists on the part of suppliers of demand obligations because of institutional constraints. According to Meiselman, "it is this difference in supply conditions" that separates "money from other claims which may appear to be close substitutes for money" (p. 59).

The distinction between money and other assets asserted by Meiselman depends upon two assumptions: (*a*) the dominance of the excess demand schedules of risk-averting lenders over the excess demand schedules of risk-indifferent lenders, and (*b*) the dominance of risk-indifferent borrowers over the combined influence of risk-averting borrowers and risk-averting lenders. It should be pointed out that, although these assumptions are consistent with the expectations hypothesis, there is nothing in Meiselman's empirical results to indicate that these assumptions reflect the actual workings of the securities markets. Meiselman's findings are equally consistent with (1) infinitely elastic excess demand schedules on the part of risk-indifferent net borrowers, (2) infinitely elastic excess demand schedules on the part of risk-indifferent net lenders, and (3) infinitely elastic excess demand schedules on the parts of both net borrowers and net lenders, who are indifferent as to risk and share the same expectations. Meiselman's discussion of the supply of liquidity implies that only (1) is true.

If assumption (*a*) is dropped (that is, if we allow the excess demands of risk-indifferent net lenders to be infinitely elastic), then the infinitely elastic excess demand functions of the risk-indifferent lenders are the mechanism through which the expectations hypothesis is satisfied with respect to the structure of rates on securities. These lenders will, despite the imperfectly elastic excess demands of suppliers of demand obligations, exchange money for securities up to the point where there is no liquidity component influencing spreads between rates of return on money and securities. If assumption (*a*) is retained and the converse of (*b*) is assumed (that is, if we suppose borrowers to be risk-averters), then long rates will in equilibrium differ from the average of current and expected short rates.[27] Thus, if either of these two assumptions is dropped, the distinction between money and other assets fades away. When assumption (*a*) is dropped, there is no liquidity component affecting the spread between rates, either between securities or between securities and money. When assumption (*b*) is dropped, a liquidity component is always present in the spread between rates, both among rates on securities and between rates on securities and money.

Thus, although the distinction between money and other claims stemming from differences in supply conditions, asserted by Meiselman, is consistent with certain assumptions that are, in turn, consistent with the data, there is in this data nothing that prevents us from choosing other assumptions not consistent with a distinction between money and other claims of the character suggested by Meiselman.

Summary and Implications of Meiselman's Results

Meiselman has explained how, despite the existence of "institutional" demands, the expectations hypothesis may constitute a valid descriptive theory of the structure of interest rates on default-free securities that are identical in all respects except term-to-maturity. He has then shown that annual data taken from the 1901–54 period are consistent with the expectations hypothesis when combined with the assumption that revisions of expectations of future short-term rates are linear functions of past errors in predicting short-term rates. Meiselman has, in effect, thrown the burden of proof onto the critics of the expectations theory. They must show that the data are at least as consistent, in some sense, with alternative theories of the term structure of rates if they hope to lend credulity to their condemnations of the expectations hypothesis.

Meiselman's attempts to utilize his results for the testing of alternative theories and related fields of monetary economics, however, are unimpressive. He is incorrect when he states that his empirical results are inconsistent with the Hicksian liquidity-premium model; the test of the liquidity preference theory is invalid. While his empirical findings are consistent with the implications of the expectations hypothesis which he draws for the supply of liquidity, the findings are equally consistent with implications which are precisely the opposite of those which Meiselman asserts. Finally, his test of the hedging theory of the structure of rates is based on such rough data and leaves out so many considerations implicit in this theory that the results of this test cannot be construed to contradict the theory.

These failures must not, however, be allowed to obscure the very substantial accomplishments, summarized in the first paragraph of this section, of the book under review.

It may, in closing, be useful to note an important implication of Meiselman's results. Exponents of the expectations hypothesis, including Meiselman (p. 49), state that actions on the part of the Treasury or the Federal Reserve which affect the maturity composition of outstanding debt will not affect the term structure of interest rates unless such actions also influence expectations of future rates. Meiselman's model provides us with the description of a mechanism by which such government activities *must* affect expectations and therefore the structure of rates. If the Federal Reserve performs a swapping operation whereby long rates are driven upward and short rates driven downward, Meiselman's error term (p. 20) will be affected, causing a different revision of expectations than would have been the case in the absence of government activities and thereby inducing a different relation between long and short rates than would have existed had the swapping operation not occurred. Consequently, although the expectations hypothesis does not imply as great or as reliable an effect on the structure of rates due to government operations as is implied by the hedging theory, the expectations hypothesis, incorporating the error-learning mechanism by which expectations are revised, does *not* imply that changes in the maturity composition of outstanding debt will have no influence on the term structure of interest rates.

NOTES

1. The expectations hypothesis asserts that securities of different maturity are perfect substitutes in the eyes of a significant portion of investors, that these investors maximize the present value of expected receipts on the basis of confidently held single-valued expectations with respect to future rates of interest, and that investors operating on the basis

of expectations control a sufficiently large proportion of total investible funds to bring long-term rates plus unity into equality with geometric averages of current and expected short-term rates plus unity. Alternative formulations of the expectations hypothesis are given in J. R. Hicks, *Value and Capital*, 2nd ed. (Oxford: Oxford University Press, 1946), pp. 144–45; and Friedrich A. Lutz, "The Structure of Interest Rates," *Quarterly Journal of Economics*, Vol. 60 (1940–41), 36–63 (reprinted in William Fellner and Bernard Haley (eds.), *Readings in the Theory of Income Distribution* [Philadelphia: Blakiston Co., 1946], pp. 499–529).

2. For example, J. M. Culbertson, "The Term Structure of Interest Rates," *Quarterly Journal of Economics*, Vol. 71 (November 1957), 485–517; and D. G. Luckett, "Professor Lutz and the Structure of Interest Rates," *Quarterly Journal of Economics*, Vol. 73 (February 1959), 131–44.

3. B. G. Malkiel, "Expectations, Bond Prices, and the Term Structure of Interest Rates," *Quarterly Journal of Economics*, Vol. 76 (May 1962), 197.

4. Culbertson, *op. cit.*, p. 487.

5. An exception is Luckett, *op. cit.*, pp. 131–44.

6. See Culbertson, *op. cit.*, pp. 489–504, for a discussion of these considerations.

7. For discussions of the various theories of the interest structure see Joseph Aschheim, *Techniques of Monetary Control* (Baltimore: Johns Hopkins Press, 1961), pp. 55–60; and Ralph Turvey, *Interest Rates and Asset Prices* (New York: The Macmillan Co., 1961), pp. 91–93.

8. See Lutz, *op. cit.*, pp. 521–25; W. L. Smith, *Debt Management in the United States* (Study Paper No. 19 for Employment, Growth, and Price Levels, Joint Economic Committee [Congress, January 1960]), pp. 82–83; and J. W. Conard, *An Introduction to the Theory of Interest* (Berkeley: University of California Press, 1959), p. 328.

9. Lutz, *op. cit.*, pp. 528–29.

10. H. C. Wallich, on the other hand, deduced that, because the incline in the yield curve was less than that implied by the theory, the predictions received in reply to the survey contained "little or no evidence that the course of short-term rates was regarded as determining the prospect for long rates" ("The Current Significance of Liquidity Preference," *Quarterly Journal of Economics*, Vol. 60 [August 1946], 493).

11. F. R. Macaulay, *The Movements of Interest Rates, Bond Yields and Stock Prices in the United States since 1856* (New York: National Bureau of Economic Research, 1938), p. 33.

W. B. Hickman, in an unpublished study, tested the perfect-foresight version of the expectations theory in a manner similar to that of Macaulay and concluded that there did not exist a "close correspondence between the historical pattern of short rates and the forecasts of short rates expected on the basis of the theory" ("The Term Structure of Interest Rates: An Exploratory Analysis" [New York: National Bureau of Economic Research, 1943]), pp. iii–3.

In the Macaulay-Hickman tradition, Culbertson (*op. cit.*, pp. 508–9) concludes that, because expectations implied by the structure of rates have been so incorrect, "speculative activity . . . does not determine the broad course of interest rates or of interest-rate interrelationships."

12. Lutz drops the assumption of correct expectations very early in his analysis and Hicks does not rely on it at all.

13. Lutz, *op. cit.*, pp. 519–20, note. For additional expressions of this view see Culbertson, *op. cit.*, pp. 488–90; and C. E. Walker, "Federal Reserve Policy and the Structure of Interest Rates on Government Securities," *Quarterly Journal of Economics*, Vol. 68 (February 1954), 22–23.

14. Meiselman uses the following notation: capital letters represent actual market rates; lower-case letters represent expected rates; the duration of the loan is given by the first subscript; the prescript is the period in the beginning of which the rate in question becomes applicable (Meiselman uses the prescript in conjunction with both actual and expected rates, but the prescript will be used only in connection with expected rates for the purposes of this review); the second subscript gives the period at the beginning of which the rate is recorded in the market. For example, R_{30t} refers to the actual current market rate of interest on a security maturing in thirty years, while $_{t+3}r_{1t}$ refers to the forward rate on a one-year loan starting at the beginning of period $t + 3$ that is implied by the market rates existing at the beginning of period t.

15. David Durand, *Basic Yields of Corporate Bonds, 1900–1942* (Technical Paper No. 3 [New York: National Bureau of Economic Research, 1942]), pp. 5–6, Table 1; and David Durand and Willis J. Winn, *Basic Yields of Bonds, 1926–1947: Their Measurement and Pattern* (Technical Paper No. 6 [New York: National Bureau of Economic Research, 1947]).

Estimates for years subsequent to 1947 appeared in *The Economic Almanac.*

16. Meiselman fails to record the standard errors for many of his estimated regression coefficients and the standard errors of estimate of any of his regression equations. This, of course, hinders our analysis of his results.

17. Hicks, *op. cit.*, pp. 145–47.

18. Hicks (*ibid.*, p. 146) states that, "other things being equal, a person engaging in a long-term loan contract puts himself in a more risky position than he would be in if he refrained from making it." Meiselman explicitly agrees with this view that liquidity premiums increase with the maturity of the future payment (p. 45).

19. It has come to my attention that Reuben Kessel has independently and previously arrived at precisely the same conclusion with respect to the implications of the value of the constant term for the liquidity-premium model (cf. Kessel's *The Cyclical Behavior of the Term Structure of Interest Rates* [New York: National Bureau of Economic Research, July, 1962], pp. 29–33). Kessel's manuscript also presents the results of additional empirical investigation of the expectations and liquidity hypotheses (pp. 66–80) as well as an interesting and informative discussion of the early empirical work on the term structure (pp. 17–25). He interprets his findings as supporting the expectations hypothesis supplemented by liquidity considerations.

20. This test is very similar to those employed by Conard (*op. cit.*, pp. 335–37) and Turvey (*op. cit.*, p. 99), both of whom interpret their results as being consistent with the hedging hypothesis.

21. The boundary between short- and long-term debt is taken to be one year to maturity. The allocation of outstanding debt into these two categories should be based on current maturity. However, since 1937, corporate debt has been reported on an original maturity basis. Some state and local government debt and some mortgage debt have current maturities of less than one year, but both have been allocated to long-term debt. Also, some private non-corporate non-mortgage debt has a current maturity of more than one year but all debt in this category has been treated as short-term (p. 66).

The inability to break private debt down into more than two categories is a serious deficiency. Changes in the maturity composition of these categories will undoubtedly, according to the hedging theory, influence the rate structure.

22. The satisfaction of this assumption is necessary if we are to obtain consistent estimates of the structural coefficients.

23. These ratios are based on data from the *Federal Reserve Bulletin* and the *Life Insurance Fact Book*.

24. In fairness to Meiselman, it should be pointed out that he recognizes many of the shortcomings in his analysis indicated here.

25. We must distinguish between the initial impact of a shift in liquidity preference, which results in interest-rate movements, and the new equilibrium that is reached subsequently to the disturbance, in which the new rate of interest may be equal to the equilibrium rate that prevailed prior to the disturbance (cf. George Horwich, "Real Assets and the Theory of Interest," *Journal of Political Economy*, Vol. 70 [April 1962], 157–69).

26. It is awkward to speak of "net lenders" or "net borrowers" as having perfectly elastic excess demand functions because such demand functions imply that certain individuals or groups stand ready to become either net lenders or net borrowers (up to an infinite quantity) in response to an infinitesimal change in relative prices.

27. Unless the illiquidity costs to borrowers exactly match liquidity returns to lenders.

Part **VI**

Monetary Policy

The conduct of monetary policy and the development of monetary theory followed largely independent paths in the immediate prewar and postwar periods. The theorists directed their energies toward developing Keynesian analysis leaving monetary policymakers for the most part to their own devices in solving the monetary problems of the wartime and immediate postwar periods, or, in many cases, became policy-makers themselves. This situation was sharply reversed first by the Patman Hearings in 1951 and later as the result of the two major inquiries into the operation of the monetary system on both sides of the Atlantic, conducted by the Radcliffe Committee, which published its findings in 1959, and the Commission on Money and Credit, which issued its report in 1961.

The three groups conducted a sweeping inquiry into the goals of monetary policy, the institutional arrangements employed in monetary decision-making, the effectiveness of existing institutions in the choice of policy instruments and in the diagnosis of the economic situation, and the possible need for new policy instruments. The two latter Reports received poor marks at the hands of the academicians which, in a way, was inevitable since they were grading the current unsettled state of monetary theory and policy according to standards upon which they themselves hardly agreed even with regard to fundamental issues. Under these conditions it was unreasonable to expect the two broadly composed inquiring groups to resolve the wide range of open issues. In one way however, the inquiries were a success. They confronted policy-makers with the theoretical issues that were involved in their decision-making and theoreticians with the practical issues that their theories had to answer if they were to affect policy. This confrontation gave a new impetus to the study of monetary problems as may be witnessed by the selections and bibliography of this book. But, what was, perhaps, most important of all, these inquiries gave rise to the empirical testing of theoretical and pragmatic hypotheses concerning the operation of the monetary system.

In the end, it is this testing that must winnow out the false from the valid doctrines and produce an accepted core of theory which will provide a guide to policy-makers in the future.

Tinbergen called attention to the logical truth that in order to achieve a set of policy objectives simultaneously, one must have at one's disposal as a minimum, an equal number of policy instruments.[1] The traditional objective of monetary policy was to maintain the internal and external value of the currency. The policy instruments placed at the disposal of the monetary authority were adequate to achieve these objectives. In recent years, however, the number of objectives the monetary authority has been asked to take into consideration, among them full employment and an adequate rate of growth, has increased considerably. The responsibility for achieving these objectives is shared with other branches of government and new policy instruments have been devised, most importantly, fiscal policy. It appears likely, however, that the policy objectives of British and American governments exceed the number of feasible policy instruments at their disposal, and, consequently, economic authorities are forced to maintain a changing hierarchy of objectives. Which economic objectives are to be assigned to the monetary authority and how the priorities assigned to these goals are to be revised is still an unsolved problem as revealed by the two aforementioned Reports.

Mundell suggests the principle of Tinbergen needs to be supplemented for policy purposes by what he calls the principle of effective market classification whereby policy instruments would be paired with the objectives upon which they have the most influence. If this principle is violated, Mundell cautions, what may appear to be stabilizing policies may actually have the contrary effect.

Aside from these general problems, there exists the question whether instruments of monetary policy can significantly influence the course of the economy in a desired direction. This problem is discussed in several of the selections. The question may be broken down into three parts: (1) diagnosis—can the economic situation be determined early and with sufficient reliability to employ discretionary policies; (2) selection and use of policy instruments— which existing or new policy instruments should be applied and in what magnitude in order to achieve desired objectives in particular economic situations; (3) effectiveness—assuming the correct policy instruments are applied to achieve their maximum effectiveness, will they be able to make a significant contribution toward achieving the desired objectives.

Roosa attempted to answer the critics of monetary policy who maintained that the limited changes in the rate of interest ex-

[1] Jan Tinbergen, *On the Theory of Economic Policy* (Amsterdam 1952).

perienced in the early postwar period had little influence on either borrowers or savers, by pointing out that the major impact of interest rate changes lies with the reactions of *lenders* who influence directly the "availability of credit" and that lenders were sensitive to even small changes in the rate of interest and the uncertainty that those changes generated.

Mayer raises the question whether the lags in monetary policy may be so great from the time the economic situation is diagnosed until the Federal Reserve changes its policy fully, and until this policy is felt in the credit market, and reflected in investment decisions, and then in actual investment, output and consumption, as to cast serious doubt on the usefulness of discretionary monetary policy as a counter-cyclical policy instrument. White, however, challenges Mayer's results and argues that he has seriously over-estimated the average lag. He believes a correct estimate of the lag would find it short enough for a counter-cyclical monetary policy to be effective.

The monetary authorities on both sides of the Atlantic, although placed on the defensive largely as a result of the critical nature of contemporary analysis of monetary policy, have not let the developments of the past fifteen years go unheeded. In a slow, deliberate manner many basic changes are being wrought in the operations of the central bank. One of the most important is the gradual integration of monetary policy into the total framework of economic policy, including fiscal policy, with an improved coordination between the central bank and other branches of government. Nevertheless, the most pressing general issue yet to be resolved is whether monetary rules, discretionary policy, or some mix of the two would be the best possible course for future monetary policy.

19 *The Radcliffe Report and Evidence*

John G. Gurley *Stanford University*

A drama critic recently wrote of an evanescent Broadway play: "It was paved with good intentions, and, like most pavements, it was trodden underfoot." While for myself, I hesitate to call this an epitaph to the Radcliffe *Report*, it describes pretty well the initial responses of the *Report's* horde of critics, some of whom judged it the most monumental flop of the 1959 season, and most of whom felt that it had nice stage settings and all that, but was terribly weak in the theme.

These judgments are understandable and probably not grossly unfair. Nevertheless, I believe that they are based on the worst the *Report* has to offer and not on the best. At its worst, the *Report* is full of exaggerations, errors, confusions, conflicting statements, and careless writing. These no doubt represent, as the critics suggest, the "real" *Report*. But, if one attributes the exaggerations to a desire to escape the conventional, the conflicting and hazy statements to the task of achieving unanimity among diverse committee members, the confusions and errors to deadlines—if, in short, one excuses the weaknesses—and chooses the very best from its pages, the *Report* has much to recommend it.

In this idealized form, the *Report* presents a pioneering analysis of Britain's financial system, in which the monetary system and money are considered as only part of a complex, but integrated,

Reprinted from *American Economic Review*, Vol. 50 (September 1960), 672–700, by permission of the author and the American Economic Association.

structure of financial institutions, assets, and markets, and in which monetary policy, debt management, and fiscal policy are treated as coordinating techniques of a general financial policy aimed at regulating spending through this financial structure. In the underlying theme of the *Report*, all issuers of financial assets are relevant to financial policy; the private sectors issuing their debts and equities; the Treasury issuing various forms of government securities; the monetary system creating money and other claims; and nonbank intermediaries creating liquid claims. The idealized *Report* sees the level and structure of interest rates, which are the immediate targets of financial policy, determined partly by the whole range of financial assets—the level by the relation of liquid assets, including money, to holdings of financial and physical assets, and the structure to the composition of financial assets and demands for these components, with expectations playing their role in both cases. It sees money as only one asset among many, banks as only one type of institution among many, and the control of money as only one aspect of an over-all financial policy. This is the *Report* at its best.

The Committee on the Working of the Monetary System, known as the Radcliffe Committee, was appointed by the Chancellor of the Exchequer in May 1957 "to inquire into the working of [Britain's] monetary and credit system, and to make recommendations." The Committee was composed of the chairman, Lord Radcliffe, two businessmen, two bankers, two trade union leaders, and two academic economists, the latter being Professors A. K. Cairncross and R. S. Sayers. During the fifty-nine days of hearings, scattered from July 1957 to April 1959, evidence was obtained from the Treasury, the Bank of England, clearing banks and other financial institutions, dozens of trade associations, business leaders, and many economists. In addition, the Committee received memoranda from many of these witnesses and from others, including the National Institute of Economic and Social Research, the Central Statistical Office, and, inevitably, a few monetary cranks.

The unanimous *Report* of the Committee was published in August 1959. This was followed in March 1960 by four volumes of evidence.[1] The first of these, *Minutes of Evidence*, is a huge, 980-page, double-column tome of the hearings. The other three volumes—*Memoranda 1, 2,* and *3*—contain 142 papers submitted by various groups and individuals. As a rough guess, the *Report* and four volumes of evidence are packed with upwards of $3\frac{1}{2}$ million words, a fact that I must note because it is possible that I have inadvertently slid over a hundred thousand or so here or there, and by so doing have done less than full justice either to the Committee or to some of its contributors.

I begin with a brief outline of the Committee's principal views on monetary theory and policy. I shall then discuss these views, in about the same order, supplementing the discussion with material from the oral and written evidence.[2] Since this procedure misses three areas that occupied much of the Committee's time—international finance, the status of the Bank of England, and financial statistics—I touch upon these briefly at the end.

The Report's Monetary Theory and Policy: An Outline

The following appear to qualify as the Committee's dominant views on monetary theory and policy:

1. The money supply has been largely uncontrolled during the postwar period; neither the banks' cash ratio nor their liquidity ratio has placed an effective upper limit on monetary growth.

2. But the money supply is of no great concern. First, it is incidental to the level of interest rates. These rates, though affected by liquidity, are determined largely by the expectations and confidence of the public, which in turn are determined by what the monetary authorities say. Second, there is virtually no direct relationship between the money supply and spending.

3. Interest rates, in and of themselves, have had little or no direct effect on spending decisions.

4. While spending is not directly affected by interest rates, it is affected by liquidity, which is composed of the money supply and the money people can get hold of. The private sector's liquidity is increased by the lending of commercial banks and other financial intermediaries, because such lending increases the supply of loanable funds ("the money people can get hold of"), and the growth of liquidity stimulates spending. The important thing about financial institutions is not the liquid liabilities (monetary or otherwise) they create but the lending they do—the assets they purchase.

5. The lending of all financial institutions can be indirectly controlled through changes in the level and structure of interest rates. A rise in interest rates will slow down their lending by imposing capital losses on their security holdings. Thus, while a rise in interest rates has little direct effect on spending, it depresses spending indirectly by reducing the lending of financial institutions and so the public's liquidity.

6. This means that the "centre-piece" of monetary action is the level and structure of interest rates, and not the money supply. The structure of rates can best be influenced by debt management policy working on the composition of the national debt. Since, however, it is not a good thing to have highly fluctuating interest

rates, and since the lending of financial institutions in ordinary times should not be directly controlled, more emphasis should be placed on fiscal policy as a short-run stabilizer, leaving monetary policy to set the tone of longer-run developments.

7. But, during emergency situations, when runaway inflation threatens, monetary policy should be used vigorously. In these cases, lending should be restricted directly, by controls on commercial-bank lending, perhaps by the extension of such controls to other intermediaries, by consumer credit regulations, and by restrictions on issues of long-term securities.

Control of the Money Supply

DEFINITION OF MONEY

The Committee regards the money supply as consisting of notes[3] (but evidently not coins!) outside of banks plus net deposits, the latter being liabilities of London clearing banks and of Scottish and Northern Irish banks.[4] However, nowhere in the *Report*—and, indeed, nowhere in the *Minutes of Evidence* or the three volumes of *Memoranda*—is there an extended series of the money supply in accordance with this definition.[5] Bank deposits comprise not only current accounts, which earn no interest and are repayable on demand, but also deposit accounts, which are similar to our time deposits, not subject to check, and hence, strictly speaking, not used as money by the public.[6] The Committee recognizes that deposit accounts are not quite the same as current accounts, but nevertheless they are counted as money. The reason seems to be that they are easily exchangeable for money.[7] The inclusion of these accounts raises the question of why other highly liquid claims, such as deposits in acceptance houses, in hire-purchase companies, in Trustee Savings Banks, and so on, are excluded.[8] While the Committee does lay down an explicit definition of money, at other times it goes out of its way to "fuzz up" the concept, by placing the supply of money in quotation marks, followed by "however that is defined," "whatever that may be made to mean," and similar derogations.[9]

CASH AND LIQUIDITY RATIOS OF BANKS

The Bank of England normally attempts to control the volume of bank deposits in the traditional way—by controlling the supply of certain bank assets which are held, by convention and not by statute, in fairly constant proportions to deposit liabilities. The conventional cash ratio is 8 per cent, with cash consisting of vault cash and deposits at the Bank of England. Deposit expansion is also limited potentially by a conventional 30 per cent liquidity ratio, where liquid assets for this purpose include cash, Treasury bills, call loans, and commercial bills.[10] There has been a spirited debate in recent years concerning which ratio, if either, is the effective one.

To reduce bank deposits, the Bank of England can decrease the banks' cash and thus their liquid assets by selling securities in the market. To regain liquidity, the banks can sell short-dated bonds, which do not count as liquid assets, to the discount houses, the latter financing the bonds by borrowing at call from the banks, with call loans counting as liquid assets. Or the banks may sell bonds and buy Treasury bills or commercial bills. It has been easy enough for banks to get liquid assets, but none of these operations replenishes their cash. For this purpose the banks must borrow from (or sell something to) the central bank. In the United States, borrowing is done directly; in Britain it is done indirectly through the discount houses. These houses hold Treasury bills, short-dated government bonds, and commercial bills, and they borrow at call from London clearing banks and other banks. In addition, they and not the clearing banks are permitted to borrow from the Bank of England. When the clearing banks lose cash, therefore, they may call some loans from the discount houses. Under pressure, these houses may then either sell Treasury bills to or borrow from the Bank of England, and in these ways restore to the clearing banks the cash initially lost.[11] But, as the Bank explained to the Committee:

> It should be noted that the creation of a cash shortage is not without effect. For, particularly, if it is such as to compel borrowing from the Bank of England, which is relatively expensive to the Discount Houses, they will try to reduce such borrowing so far as possible by raising their bids for money [that is, selling bills or short bonds], thus causing short-term interest rates to rise.[12]

This was further explained, in response to a question from the Committee, as follows:

> If we wanted to raise interest rates, then we would give less or possibly no help in the ordinary way [by purchasing bills from the discount houses], and we would say: "If you want cash you must come to the Discount Office for it." And moreover we could if need be so arrange things that the market needed a great deal of cash. . . .[13]

This is the familiar process by which open-market sales of a central bank reduce the "cash" of commercial banks and force them to reduce earning assets and the money supply, raising market rates of interest. Commercial banks can get more cash from the central bank any time they want to, but they presumably have a demand schedule for cash that is negatively related to its price. Hence, if the central bank raises the price, the banks will demand less cash, and so less earning assets and less monetary liabilities.

The Committee seems to have misunderstood this evidence, taking it to mean that, since banks could get more cash at any time, the cash ratio was therefore ineffective in limiting the money supply. This confusion appeared several months later when the Committee was again questioning spokesmen for the Bank. The latter stated that during times of inflationary pressure it would be better for the government to finance a deficit by selling Treasury bills to the market than by borrowing from the central bank (by Ways and Means advances), inasmuch as, though either measure could increase the liquid assets of banks, the latter would raise their cash base. This prompted the following exchange:[14]

> I understood their policy of increasing deposit liabilities would be determined by their total of liquid assets, not the amount of cash?
> ——The two things come out to the same, in the sense that the total of liquid assets in either case is affected in the same way; but the composition of their liquid assets would be different. With the Bank of England making Ways and Means Advances, their cash would be inflated. It would be inflated to a point beyond the 8 per cent they require, and to that extent they would be looking round for earning assets. . . .
>
> Is not this a different doctrine from what we have been told hitherto?——I do not think so. . . .
>
> We are now back on the question of the whole control of the volume of bank deposits; we have been taught hitherto that it is the liquid assets ratio that matters?——Surely we have said there are two aspects of this control. . . .[15]

Passing over this and other evidence, the Committee in its *Report* states that the cash ratio was ineffective.[16] Nevertheless, at other times, the Committee seems to recognize that this is incorrect, for it is stated, in substance, that the cash ratio would be ineffective only if the Bank of England set out to stabilize the Bill rate (which it generally has not done); otherwise, it would be effective.[17] But it is the former view that carries the day. In the Committee's eyes, the more effective ratio is the liquidity ratio, though it is stressed that banks have found it comparatively easy to evade this, through the mechanism described above, and that it has been thirty years since bank lending has been restrained by liquidity considerations.[18] In the end, one gathers that the Committee believes that the money supply has been largely uncontrolled.

These views are not easily reconciled with the fact that interest rates have increased sharply during the last decade in Britain, unless of course it is held that the money supply has nothing to do with the level of interest rates, a proposition I turn to in a moment. The banks have been subject, it is true, to requests to hold the line on or to reduce their advances (loans and overdrafts), but these restrictions have been short-lived, and in any case the banks could always purchase other earning assets and so increase their deposit liabilities.[19] In view of all the evidence, it seems more reasonable to conclude that there has been more or less effective control of the money supply, at least since 1951, and that this control has probably operated primarily through the cash base of the banks, as described by Bank officials.

Interest Rate Determination

At one point in its *Report*, the Committee presents an admirable account of the determination of the level of interest rates. After extolling the role of liquidity in economic analysis, the statement continues:

> We would nevertheless emphasize that the amount of money . . . is of considerable significance. The other classes of liquid assets . . . are inferior, in convenience to the holders, and this inferiority has to be compensated by the payment of interest. If there is less money to go round, in relation to the other assets (both physical and financial), it will be held only by people willing to make a greater sacrifice in order to hold it: that is to say, rates of interest will rise. But they will not, unaided, rise by much, because in a highly developed financial system . . . there are many highly liquid assets which are close substitutes for money, as good to hold and only inferior when the actual moment for a payment arrives . . . (i.e., the more efficient the financial structure, the more can the velocity of circulation be stretched without serious inconvenience being caused).[20]

Unfortunately, this statement is in sharp conflict with what appears to be the Committee's principal view of this subject. While it can be reasonably argued that the *Report* does not in fact present a theory of interest rate determination—or, perhaps better, that it obliquely presents several—it is fair to say, I think, that the Committee looks upon "expectations and confidence" of the public as the chief determinant of rate levels—though lip service is paid now and then to the role of liquidity. And these expectations are greatly affected by what the authorities say, by the public's interpretation of their mood. That is, expectations are molded by the "faces" made by the authorities; presumably, a squinty-eyed look might raise interest rates, a vapid stare maintain them, and an ebullient expression lower them. When this theory takes over, the authorities never change interest rates by operating on the money supply or on liquidity generally; rather: "The authorities must seek . . . to influence the general liquidity situation by operating on rates of interest."[21] It is even stated that the money supply is incidental to interest rate policy.[22] It is for this reason that the Committee can properly hold the view that the money supply has been largely uncontrolled in the face of sharp changes in levels of interest rates; for after all money has little or nothing to do with interest rates.[23]

The theory that interest rates are determined by words and faces is indicated repeatedly in the *Minutes of Evidence*.[24] As an example, consider this exchange with Winfield Riefler, then assistant to the chairman of the Board of Governors of the Federal Reserve System:

> Then is not much the most important thing you do not the buying and selling of Bills, not the raising or lowering of [discount] rates, but what you *say*?——No.
>
> Why do you have to operate in the market as well as telling the market what you think about things?——Our operations in the market actually determine the funds available.[25]

This evidently left the Committee incredulous. Though there are some indications that it was not willing to accept wholeheartedly the dominance of expectations in interest rate determination,[26] the truth is that this factor, by elimination, becomes the only solid explanation of rate movements in the *Report*, a theory which suggests that bond markets in Britain are peopled by a lot of nervous wrecks. The Committee was also influenced in this view by R. F. Kahn,[27] to whom I shall return later.

The Committee landed in this position despite the fact that F. W. Paish and others presented data to show the very close post-war relationship between the ratio of money to national income and bond rates,[28] and despite Paish's excellent testimony about this relationship. Here is a sample of it:

> During the period up to 1956 during which there was this tremendous drop in the ratio of bank deposits to national income, was there not considerable liquidity in business?——If there is so much liquidity, why are firms willing to pay very high rates of interest for raising long-term loans on the London market?
>
> They may expect prices to rise?——It is liquidity in relation to what they want to do. I would say that the long-term rate of interest is the inverse of liquidity.
>
> Would this mean that you would feel that if you knew the ratio of bank deposits to net national money income you could predict what the rate of interest would be?——So long as the conditions remain, I would say almost exactly.

The point you are putting to us is that there is an inverse relation-ship between the liquidity of the system and the rate of interest, liquidity being defined not just in the terms of the money supply, but to include near-money?——I would put it in terms of the money supply. One would expect the amount of near-money to affect the shape of the curve. . . .

The issue is whether the relationship is sufficiently close and the lags sufficiently limited to allow of operational application?——I would say that in the short run one can get it down to pure expec-tations if one can persuade people that long-term rates are going to fall and that they will have a heavy capital appreciation. There could be very marked temporary shifts on those expectations; but if the authorities wanted to stabilize the long-term rate round about $4\frac{1}{2}$ per cent, they would have to allow the ratio of bank deposits to national income to rise to more nearly 40 per cent than 35 per cent.[29]

And in response to an additional question about the effects of near-money, he answered:

I would say that whereas they could get a given rate of interest with a 40 per cent ratio of bank deposits to national income if there was not very much near-money in the system, they might need 35 per cent to get the same rate if there was a lot of near-money in the system. They would have to set off the increased liquidity due to large holdings of near-money by having less real money, in order to get the same effect on total liquidity.[30]

Excellent memoranda and testimony were also submitted on this question by many others. Altogether, there seems to be an im-pressive body of evidence to support the view that the money-income ratio, modified by the presence of other liquid assets, and within the context of "real" variables, was the principal deter-minant of the level of interest rates in Britain during the postwar period.[31] But, for some reason, the Committee chose to ignore this evidence.[32]

The Direct Effects of Interest Rates on Spending

The Committee adopts a "three-gears" view of interest rates. At any time, people believe that interest rates are either in low, middle, or high gear. Any play of rates within a given gear is not likely to have much, if any, direct effect on spending. If people "are to be shaken into some change of course, the gear must be changed."[33] A rise in the Bank Rate from $4\frac{1}{2}$ per cent to 7 per cent, for example, would generally be regarded as a shift from middle to high gear.

Nevertheless, though such upward shifts have occurred in post-war Britain, and so might have produced downward pressure on spending through the "interest rate effect," the Committee states that it found very little evidence that this has in fact happened.[34] According to the Committee, it found no evidence that higher interest rates, in and of themselves, reduced consumption; there was practically no indication that interest rates were important to large firms with respect to investment in either inventories or fixed capital; expenditures of the nationalized industries were also largely impervious to changes in interest rates; the same was true for local authorities' expenditures; and spokesmen for the smaller firms treated the interest rate effect with general skepticism.[35] "It has become clear that, as the system works at present, changes in rates of interest only very exceptionally have direct effects on the level of demand. . . ."[36] If we accept these statements, they would seem to dispose once and for all of the subject, as it relates to postwar Britain up to 1959.

But, from other material presented to the Committee by witnesses and others,[37] it is doubtful that the statements can be accepted in their present extreme form. When this evidence is compared with the conclusions of the Committee, it is hard to escape the feeling that its final appraisal should have been more guarded.

There is, first of all, the survey made by the Federation of British Industries of its manufacturing members with respect to the impact of higher interest rates in early 1955 on their investment decisions. Among the questions, was: "Was the rise in Bank Rate from 3 to $4\frac{1}{2}\%$ during January and February, 1955 a *major* factor in taking your business decisions?" (Their italics.) Almost 12 per cent (179) of the firms answering (1526) said that it was. Of these 179 firms, 40 per cent were in the engineering, shipbuilding, electrical, and textile industries. The rest were found among more than a dozen other industries. These firms reported deferment or reduction of investment projects, or reduction or deferment of inventory purchases, or other action.[38]

The Committee, in commenting on this survey in its *Report*, states:

> The response rate . . . was relatively low, and it may well be that answers came for the most part from those who had some positive reaction to report . . . in discussions with us representatives of the Federation were not confident that these figures could be regarded as firm enough to be the basis for general conclusions.[39]

The first part of this statement suggests that those who did not answer the survey may have had a lower ratio of yes-to-no answers than those who did. This may well be: but it should be noted that the questionnaire contained dozens of questions on other subjects, so that the nonrespondents could have had many other reasons for not participating.

As to the second part of the statement, I can find nothing in the *Minutes of Evidence* to support it. What I do find is a continual "hounding" of the witnesses, a barrage of counterarguments and suggestions from the Committee, until finally the witnesses wilt under extreme pressure and state that "it might not be so." First of all, the Committee made it quite clear to the witnesses that it considered the figure of 179 out of 1595 "astonishingly high" and "most surprising," especially in view of the fact that the firms at the time probably anticipated inflation. The witnesses, after some hesitation, finally agreed that the figure might indeed be surprising. The Committee then asked them whether such expectations of inflation might not swamp the effect of higher rates [yes], whether other measures that accompany the higher rates might not be responsible for reduced spending [very likely], whether the interest rate can be isolated from other influences [yes], and whether the interest rate is really a factor taken into account before investment is made [not a principal factor]. Having prodded the witnesses into saying that interest rates are relatively unimportant, the Committee next asked them how, in view of that, the interest rate came to be a major factor with 179 firms. The answer and the Committee's response to it follow:

> [First witness:] I am becoming nervous about how well the question was understood by these 179 people. [Second witness:] I do not think the 179 merely took account of the rise in interest rates alone; they took it in the context of the other measures. It is not explicit in the answers. [First witness:] We could go back to these 179 firms, and cross question them about this, and perhaps get more information.
>
> It is rather vital to our discussions. We have had so many people tell us over so many years that, at any rate in the manufacturing industries, the rate of interest hardly affects these decisions at all, and one has come to think that whatever else Bank Rate changes can do they cannot do anything much about investment in the manufacturing industries.——[Answer not relevant.]

And, finally, after the witnesses agreed that the factor of uncertainty in investment projects diminished the importance of interest rates—still another observation having nothing directly to do with the survey results—we find:

> That is exactly what the university lecturer says when he is lecturing. He is describing the position correctly when he says that?——
> In my limited experience, yes.

You will see why, after having had years of that, one finds these figures so surprising?——It is a complex of factors, and this expectation of inflation has, I am sure, been a very prominent consideration in that complex.

My experience as a partner in an issuing house is relevant [to what has just been said]. I cannot remember a case where a company has come to my firm, and asked what the cost of money would be.——[Answer not relevant.]

Is there not another aspect to this? A great deal of capital expenditure so classified is in fact a total of a very large number of small decisions taken throughout the period; in relation to those decisions all sorts of practical considerations of the market such as have been mentioned are really far more relevant and major considerations than the cost of money?——Yes.[40]

Well, the theory of the university lecturer won out over the facts. "In discussions with us," the Committee said—and I come back to this without further comment—"representatives of the Federation were not confident that these figures could be regarded as firm enough to be the basis for general conclusions."

Another survey in March 1958 was taken by The Association of British Chambers of Commerce, inquiring about the effects of the credit squeeze after September 1957 on a wide range of companies. 16,000 questionnaires were sent out, but there were only 3404 usable responses. Of those stating that they had, since September 1957, experienced reductions in their turnover or in investment programs, only 4 per cent said they were due to the higher cost of borrowing, though 20 per cent attributed them to that plus tight money and restrictions of bank credit. And 30 per cent of those firms said that they had taken steps to reduce or pay off their bank borrowing because of increased costs.[41] After noting this, the Committee throws doubt on the results in this way:

> ... but it may well be that the dramatic rise in cost, which certainly attracted much attention, was being blamed for reductions many of which were in fact dictated much more by expectations of a decline in the level of activity than by the rise in the rate of interest.[42]

Its concluding remarks about these two surveys are also interesting:

> The results of these questionnaires add up to substantial evidence that a proportion, big enough to be relevant to policy, of business firms were vaguely discomforted by the changes in monetary conditions in 1955–57, and especially in September 1957; but we have not found sufficient evidence to justify a conclusion that in the conditions of the 1950s the rise in interest rates would by itself have directly provoked a worthwhile curtailment of demand.[43]

Aside from what is "worthwhile," the last part of this statement is necessarily true because the surveys did not seek to determine the amount of reduction in demand due to higher interest rates but only the number of firms reporting such a reduction.

A third survey was carried out, in October 1957, by the Birmingham Chamber of Commerce; questionnaires were sent to 3,400 member firms, and 610 responded. 185 firms reported that they had postponed or cancelled plans after 1955 for new factory or office buildings, extensions to existing buildings, replacement of machinery or equipment, or orders for new machinery or equipment. Of these, almost 40 per cent attributed such reductions to the increase in interest rates on borrowed capital.[44]

During the hearings with the representatives of The Association of British Chambers of Commerce, this was brushed aside rapidly, in the following way:

> In the Birmingham inquiry about 40 per cent of those who postponed or cancelled plans attributed this to an increase in interest rates. That is a very high proportion. Did it not surprise you?—— I have no explanation of the results. It may be something that was peculiar to Birmingham. I wonder whether this may have had something to do with the recession in the motor industry.
>
> If we leave the Birmingham inquiry aside for the moment, and concentrate on your own much more elaborate inquiry. . . .[45]

As it turned out, the "moment" proved to be of infinite duration.

That is by no means all of the evidence submitted to the Committee that ran contrary to its general conclusions. Not all of the following evidence is clear-cut; in fact, much of it is at best sketchy, but all of it stood up under sharp questioning.

For example, representatives of the British Engineers' Association stated that higher interest rates increased their costs and so hurt their business;[46] those of the Country Landowners' Association testified that higher interest rates had cut back farm improvement projects substantially;[47] The Scottish Landowners' Federation had essentially the same story, claiming that capital expenditures in agriculture and forestry had been reduced by higher interest rates and would almost certainly be stimulated if credit became easier;[48] for this reason capital expenditures were also reduced by wholesalers, and their demand for inventories was curtailed;[49] it was the opinion of representatives of The Association of Investment Trusts that higher rates had cut back business spending all along the line;[50] a furniture dealer said that the rise in rates in September 1957 caused him to reduce capital expenditures, and that an increase in the Bank Rate "does come very much into our planning for the present and for the future";[51] a dealer in wine and spirits offered similar testimony;[52] witnesses for the Association of Municipal Corporations knew of several instances, involving water projects, housing programs, and so on, where expenditures were cut back because of higher interest rates;[53] a small amount of local authority's expenditures was said to be affected by a change in rates;[54] there is some evidence, though not much, that rubber merchants reduced inventories because of higher rates;[55] a survey carried out by the Council of Scottish Chambers of Commerce found that one-third of those firms replying stated that they had taken steps after September 1957 to reduce bank loans because of the higher cost;[56] the Committee heard that the high cost of money was a factor in reducing inventories of automobile dealers;[57] it also heard that retail chemists reduced or postponed capital expenditures and inventory purchases partly because of higher borrowing costs, though this was qualified in response to questioning;[58] a representative of the North of Scotland Hydro-Electric Board stated that higher rates undoubtedly slowed down their program for distributing electricity;[59] the building of a hotel was deferred partly because of higher borrowing costs;[60] evidence was put forth that some wholesale tobacconists, timber people, and others reduced inventories because rates went up;[61] two bankers stated that the higher rates after September 1957 caused some businesses to reduce overdrafts;[62] the same was reported by other bankers, who further claimed that merchants, and to a lesser extent, industrial concerns reduced inventories and that some capital expenditures were curtailed for interest-rate considerations, though this view was modified under questioning;[63] London clearing bankers, too, reported that bank loans probably fell after September 1957 due to higher borrowing rates.[64] The Committee also had the opinions of several economists that a change in interest rates was effective in altering spending throughout the economy;[65] and the Bank of England concurred with this.[66]

It is far from certain, of course, what all this adds up to, especially since an equally impressive list could be produced for the other side. But, as a minimum, it would seem that the Committee's extreme conclusions are presumptuous in view of the evidence it heard.

Liquidity and Financial Institutions

As I have noted, the Committee all but eliminates the money supply as a factor in the determination of interest rate levels; it believes that changes in these rates have had little direct effect on spending; and it does not think that there is any direct, close connection between the money supply and spending. But, while money is shoved out of the house through the front door, for all to see, it does make its reappearance surreptitiously through the back as a part of general liquidity: and the most important source of liquidity is the large group of financial institutions.[67]

This is the reason the Committee devotes much space in its *Report* not only to the monetary system but also to the large number of nonbank financial intermediaries. The more important of these intermediaries are the discount houses, hire-purchase companies, insurance companies, superannuation and pension funds, Post Office Savings Bank, building societies, and investment trusts. At the end of 1958 the assets of this group exceeded those of the monetary system by about 60 per cent.[68]

It is no simple matter to discover in the *Report* by what process the intermediaries alter liquidity, for the Committee shifts around from one point of view to another and never does get down to definitions. But its principal view seems to be that the public's liquidity is composed not only of the money supply but of the amount of money it can get hold of; at one point, the matter is put in even vaguer terms when it is stated that liquidity in the broad sense depends on "the amount of money people *think* they can get hold of."[69] Since people can get hold of money from financial institutions, liquidity is increased when such additional borrowing sources become available: the greater the number of potential lenders, especially institutional lenders, the greater is the public's potential liquidity, because it is then easier to raise funds.[70]

Put somewhat differently, the notion is that the proliferation and growth of financial intermediaries increase the demand for "bonds," which "makes money more available" and stimulates spending for current output, even though the banking system is tightly controlled. With one possible exception, nowhere in the *Report* is there a statement as explicit as that, and nowhere does the Committee attempt to explain the process just described.[71] The reader is simply left with the thought that if a new intermediary comes along, or if an old one grows, the aggregate demand for "bonds" is somehow increased—there is an increase in the supply of loanable funds, and more money is made available to potential spenders.

The Committee fails to note that the extent to which this is true depends on whether the growth of intermediaires reduces the public's demand for money—and so money becomes vital to the analysis. This may be illustrated as follows. Assume that there are three financial assets—bonds, money, and savings deposits—which are liabilities of the public, the monetary system, and nonbank intermediaries, respectively. Assume, further, for simplification, that the assets of all financial institutions consist only of bonds. Then, in the usual definition, the supply of loanable funds is defined:

(1) Supply of Loanable Funds $=\begin{cases} & \text{Planned saving by public} \\ + & \text{Increase in stock of money} \\ - & \text{Increase in demand for money} \\ & \text{(hoarding).} \end{cases}$

To simplify further, assume that saving and investment are done by different groups and that savers do not repay debts. Then planned saving is equal to the public's increase in demand for bonds, money, and savings deposits; the public's increase in demand for savings deposits is equal to nonbank intermediaries' increase in demand for bonds; and the increase in the stock of money is equal to the monetary system's increase in demand for bonds. Hence,

(2) Supply of Loanable Funds $=\begin{cases} \text{Increase in demand for bonds by} \\ \text{the public, nonbank intermediaries,} \\ \text{and the monetary system.} \end{cases}$

It may be seen, then, that an increase in demand for bonds by nonbank intermediaries will increase the supply of loanable funds only if it is not accompanied by an equivalent or greater decrease in demand for bonds by the public and the monetary system. Suppose the public increases its demand for savings deposits, enabling nonbank intermediaries to increase their demand for bonds. Given the public's propensity to save, this means that there is a reduction in the public's demand for either money or bonds. If bonds, then the reduction in demand for bonds by the public is exactly offset by the increase in demand for bonds by nonbank intermediaries, and so the supply of loanable funds remains the same. On the other hand, if the shift is away from money, then the public does not reduce its demand for bonds, and neither does the monetary system reduce its demand for bonds (because a decrease in demand for bank liabilities will not alter the monetary system's outstanding liabilities and so will not change its bond assets). Hence, in this case, there is a net increase in the supply of loanable funds.

It is possible, therefore, that the purchase of bonds (lending) by nonbank intermediaries will not increase the supply of loanable funds. If it does not, then the public's increase in demand for money and savings deposits is matched exactly by the increase in the stock of these assets. There are more "liquid assets" in the economy, but there is also an equivalent increase in demand for them. The amount of funds made available to the public, at given interest rates and other terms of lending, is exactly the same as before; the growth of nonbank intermediaries has not changed the over-all situation.

It follows that the extent to which the growth of nonbank intermediaries will increase the supply of loanable funds (or "liquidity"
in the Committee's terms, i.e., the excess stock of liquid assets) depends on the degree of substitutability between savings deposits
and money, so that an answer to this question requires an analysis
of the types of claims issued by the intermediaries. By concentrating
on the asset side of the intermediaries' balance sheet, and neglecting the liability side, the Committee fails to come to grips with the
problem. Its failure to compare what is being withdrawn from the
market with what is being issued to the market—or, put another
way, its failure to consider the demand for liquid assets as well as
the supply of them—is at the heart of the difficulty. This one-sided
view is reflected in many conclusions in the *Report:* that nonbank
intermediaries are important only because they lend; that banks are
important not because they create money but because they make
loans; that it is not the money supply that should be controlled but
bank advances; and so on.[72]

I cannot say that the Committee is wrong in stating that nonbank
intermediaries have increased liquidity and the supply of loanable
funds, and have done this in such a way as to exert a destabilizing
influence on spending. These views may well be correct as applied
to postwar Britain. The point is that the analysis leading to these
conclusions is faulty, which not only leaves the reader unconvinced
of them but leads the Committee down some wrong policy paths.

The Committee raises the question of whether the destabilizing
activities of nonbank intermediaries should be controlled as the
banks' are. On this it states:

> If we are right in believing that the level of total demand is in-
> fluenced by the lending behaviour [the asset side again!] of an in-
> definitely wide range of financial institutions, and not just by the
> supply of money, it might be supposed that we should substitute
> for the traditional control of the supply of money a complex of
> controls of that wide range of financial institutions. Such a prospect
> would be unwelcome except as a last resort, not mainly because of
> its administrative burdens, but because the further growth of new
> financial institutions would allow the situation continually to slip
> from under the grip of the authorities.[73]

The *Report* later adds that:

> Any severely restrictive control of [bank] operations is certain, over
> a period of time, to be defeated by the development of rival insti-
> tutions; during the interim, the community will have suffered loss
> by interference with the most efficient channels of lending. We
> therefore begin with some presumption against discriminatory con-
> trol of banks, at any rate in ordinary times.[74]

In principle, then, there should be no discriminatory controls on
banks in ordinary times; but only as a last resort should controls

be imposed on other financial institutions; and whether they are imposed solely on banks or on a wider range of institutions they are bound to be undermined in the long run by the development of rival institutions. Leaving this somewhat ambiguous principle, which, not surprisingly, was endorsed unanimously by the Committee, it is stated that when you get right down to it the banks must be controlled.[75] However:

> If, in the light of future experience, it should appear desirable to reinforce the authorities' power by raising the minimum liquidity ratios of the banks appreciably above their present levels, the practicability of imposing comparable restraints on other groups of financial institutions should be considered.[76]

The question of controlling other financial institutions was raised with several witnesses, and other individuals expressed their opinions (or those of their organizations) in memoranda to the Committee. The most extensive discussion of this was carried on with M. H. de Kock, Governor of the South African Reserve Bank. Here is how a small part of it went:

> Does it follow from [your] argument . . . that there is a danger that when you operate on the quantity of money the banks as particular financial institutions may be penalized, and that, if you are going to operate a credit squeeze, it should if possible operate widely over the whole field of finance and not narrowly on one set of institutions?——Yes. Years ago, when commercial banks were the main financial intermediaries, the authorities could by contracting bank credit achieve all that they wanted to achieve. In the thirties we considered that that was all that was necessary. Since that time the development of these other financial institutions has been far more active than that of the banks, and they are encroaching more and more on the field of the banks in all sorts of little ways; and today the banks are hampered in their attempts to follow the requests of the central bank.[77]

Roughly similar views were expressed by T. Balogh and by representatives of the Trades Union Congress.[78] There were of course many dissenters, among whom was Winfield Riefler, who was torn between two opposing views: that nonbank intermediaries, when borrowing funds from the public, have no effect on monetary equilibrium; and that such intermediaries, when creating money substitutes, do upset monetary equilibrium.[79] He was not asked to reconcile these views. Others, including M. W. Holtrop, president of The Netherlands Bank, were on the same side. Holtrop stated that, inasmuch as nonbank intermediaries simply redistributed the community's savings, there was no reason to believe that they would create a monetary disturbance, but that his bank, nevertheless, collected data on their activities—why, he did not say.[80]

Debt Management and Monetary Policy

The Committee's views up to this point seem to leave us in a box. The money supply has little to do with the determination of interest rates; changes in these rates have had little direct effect on spending; spending is instead influenced by liquidity, which is increased when financial institutions lend; but only as a last resort should lending by nonbank intermediaries be directly controlled, and only in emergency situations (as we shall see) should bank lending be so controlled. How is spending, then, to be regulated effectively by monetary techniques?

The answer is that the authorities can *indirectly* control the lending of financial intermediaries, and, hence, the liquidity and spending of the public, by changing the level and structure of interest rates. A rise in interest rates, for example, will slow down lending by these intermediaries to the private sector by imposing capital losses on their security holdings. Or, as Sayers put it during the hearings, "you insert the gelatine of uncertainty into their liquidity."[81] Moreover, if the national debt is lengthened at the same time, the liquid-asset base of commercial banks will be limited and thus their lending depressed.[82]

This brings debt management to the head of the class, because it is the principal means of affecting the level and structure of interest rates, and the rate structure should be considered "the centre-piece of monetary action." It is through this mechanism that regulation is exerted on the lending ability of banks and other financial intermediaries and on the public's ability to spend.[83] The authorities, in managing the debt, should not concentrate exclusively on short rates but should give a lead to the market on long rates as well; it is this structure of rates they should keep their eyes on and not "some notion" of the money supply.[84] In principle, during inflationary periods, the debt should be lengthened and interest rates raised: during deflation, the opposite policies should be followed.[85]

Thus the national debt, and not the money supply, becomes the focal point in the economy for the control of interest rates, and through these rates, for the control of institutional lending and thus the economy's liquidity and spending. In this set-up, banks are important because they are key lenders:

> It is the level of bank advances rather than the level of bank deposits that is the object of this special interest; the behaviour of bank deposits is of interest only because it has some bearing, along with other influences, on the behaviour of other lenders.[86]

In looking upon the national debt as the focal point of financial control, the Committee claims that it is following the evidence submitted to it by Kahn.[87] But, when one looks at this evidence, it is apparent that the Committee has gone somewhat further than Kahn did. Kahn stated his main thesis on this point in the following way:

> Within wide limits it is possible to achieve any desired structure of interest rates *by a suitable combination* of monetary policy with management of the National Debt. The Exchequer, by issuing short-dated securities in the place of long-dated, or *vice versa*, can secure the desired shift in relative rates of interest *against the background of a monetary policy which operates on rates in general*.[88]

Now Kahn further added that the authorities, in conducting a monetary policy, should not control the money supply *"as an end in itself"* but only because the money supply, other things given, determines the general level of interest rates.[89] He underlined this by saying:

> It is the lower level of interest rates, not the larger quantity of money, which exercises an expansionist influence . . . it is immaterial what changes in the quantity of money have to occur as part of the process of securing a particular desired behaviour of rates of interest.[90]

Kahn is clearly advocating a monetary policy that controls the money supply for the purpose of setting the general level of rates, and a debt policy that controls the composition of debt for the purpose of setting the rate structure. But, presumably because of Kahn's oft-repeated assertion that the money supply is not important as an end in itself, the Committee seems to have been misled into believing that he was de-emphasizing the link between money and interest rates, and thus removing money from any central role in policy decisions, that he was putting all of his eggs into the debt-management basket, and that he was advocating the structure of rates as the "centre-piece" of monetary action. In any case, the Committee in its *Report* and in its questioning of witnesses seems obsessed with the idea of debt managers "doing something" about the structure of rates, while control of the money supply as a means of influencing the level of rates, or the price level, receives only passing mention, and then usually for the purpose of ridiculing the notion.

Presumably, then, debt management should operate in this way: the managers set the general level of interest rates by forcibly playing on the expectations and confidence of the public; they then go to work on the structure of rates by manipulating the composition of debt. In pursuit of this policy, debt managers may be called upon at times to change the level and structure of interest rates markedly. Also, in view of the record of the 1950's, rates would have to fluctuate very widely to affect spending directly. Are such fluctuations desirable? In answering this, the Committee states that if the wide fluctuations could be confined to the short-end of the rate structure the case for this policy would be fairly strong. But, since movements in short-term rates cannot much influence spending, either directly or indirectly, it is the long-term rates that must move. And there are three reasons why this policy should be rejected. First, while long-term rates can be raised quite high, the reverse policy of lowering them sharply during recessions would require a flood of liquidity into the economy that would play havoc with attempts at stability when the economic climate reversed itself;[91] and this liquidity would at the same time inspire a speculative swing against sterling. Second, widely fluctuating long-term rates would gravely weaken the foundations of financial institutions, by involving them, when rates are rising sharply, in capital losses on large blocks of securities.[92] Third, changes in long-term rates, no matter how marked, probably have little direct impact on spending in the short run.

Inasmuch as short-run movements in interest rates, in the Committee's opinion, can get at spending only through imposing capital losses on financial institutions' security holdings, and inasmuch as this policy is rejected partly because it would "gravely weaken" the foundations of these institutions, where do we go from here? Well, the Committee states, interest rates do have a direct effect on spending in the long run, and they do influence institutional lending in the long run, so they should be used carefully and slowly in a way to set the general long-term tone of the economy.[93]

> Our conclusions on rate of interest policy are therefore that, while there can be no reliance on this weapon as a major short-term stabilizer of demand, the authorities should think of rates of interest—and particularly long rates—as relevant to the domestic economic situation. The authorities should not aim at complete stability of interest rates, but should take a view as to what the long-term economic situation demands and be prepared by all the means in their power to influence markets in the required direction.[94]

To fill the policy gap in the short run, the Committee would like to see more use made of fiscal policy, as a short-run stabilizer (after some of its present defects are corrected), leaving monetary policy to act on the longer-term situation.[95] Thus, the standard policy prescription is turned on its head; it now reads: Use fiscal policy to iron out short-run fluctuations and monetary policy to guide the economy for the longer period.[96]

So much for poor old monetary policy in ordinary times. However, during an emergency, when the danger is that of "headlong inflation," monetary measures should be used vigorously. This does not mean restriction of the money supply—for that is not important—but rather striking "more directly and rapidly at the liquidity of spenders."[97] Now, since most of us are immediately inclined to identify the money supply as a major part of liquidity, these pronouncements seem contradictory, until we remember that, for the Committee, liquidity often refers only to lending (or borrowing). So it comes as no surprise that the monetary measures the Committee has in mind in such an emergency are direct controls of capital issues, bank advances, and consumer credit—and perhaps the control of lending by nonbank intermediaries.[98]

The role envisaged for monetary policy, in ordinary times, as modest as it may be, nevertheless requires that the authorities take positive action from time to time to influence the level and structure of interest rates. The Committee notes that during most of the 1950's the monetary authorities concentrated on short-term rates and were unwilling to admit "there was much scope for the exercise of official influence over long-rates"; it recommends that the authorities give a more positive lead in the long-end of the market.[99]

This seemingly innocent recommendation was actually the upshot of a running debate between representatives of the Bank of England and the Committee that was one of the hottest of the hearings, rivaling even those of recent years in this country between the Federal Reserve and its Nemesis in Congress. The Bank authorities defended, with the greatest of moral fervor, the doctrine that they do not, and most certainly should not, influence in any direct way the level of long-term rates; and, moreover, at times they argued that they should not exert such influence, except on a very temporary basis, in any indirect way, such as by operating at the short-end of the market. They simply "follow the market," permitting the natural forces of supply and demand to determine the level of rates. Spokesmen of the Bank were never ready to concede that operations at the short-end were meant to influence the entire rate structure, though they did think that at times their operations probably did have some impact on long-term rates, undesirable and annoying as that may have been.[100]

At one stage, Bank officials were asked why, in view of strong inflationary pressures, they did not act more energetically in getting long-term rates higher. The answer and subsequent exchange follow:

> I want it to be quite clear that we do not set out to intervene in a trend.
>
> Even though it was reasonably plain that the reason for the action was to establish a long-term rate of interest that was needed to the

general economic health of the country?——Yes, even doing one's best to make it plain that "it hurts me more than it hurts you."[101]

Bank officials felt that their operations had not in fact pushed up long rates, that these rates had increased because of the public's fear of inflation,[102] and that it was really the impersonal forces of supply and demand that had "a pretty big influence" on long-term rates.[103] Under questioning, however, it was admitted that the Bank could affect both supply and demand, but the officials made it clear that under no conditions would they wish to do this in any direct way, because such a policy would lead the public to cry "stinking fish" at government securities and would damage Her Majesty's Government's credit. But the officials were hard put to defend this position:

> When you say that "it would greatly damage the Government's credit," what effect have you in mind there?——Put briefly, that if we have just issued a new stock at, let us say, 100, and we then proceed actively to sell it down ourselves to 95, we have largely by our own direct actions on that security forced a book loss of five points on the people who took the security at 100.

> It operates in a similar way in your sales of Treasury Bills from day to day; the Bank Rate will very definitely affect the Treasury Bill rate. You impose a loss on all holders of Treasury Bills?——I accept that, but that is the recognized play of the money market.

> Why is the one transaction objectionable and the other not?—— The Treasury Bill and short bond market is a technical market, where these things are clearly understood ... [The institutional market is different]; if, shortly after you bought [a security] at 100, you found someone else buying it at 92 or 93 your confidence would be very seriously reduced. We cannot afford to impair people's confidence. . . .[104]

The Bank's Status, Sterling, and Statistics

In the foregoing, I have neglected several areas that received much attention in the *Minutes of Evidence* and that were dealt with at some length in the *Report*. There is space only to skip across the high points of three of these areas.

THE STATUS OF THE BANK OF ENGLAND

The Committee rejects the theory that the Bank of England should be completely independent of political influence.[105] It believes that the function of the Bank "is to act as a highly skilled executant in the monetary field of the current economic policy of the central Government," and that "the policies to be pursued by the central bank must be from first to last in harmony with those avowed and defended by Ministers of the Crown responsible to Parliament."[106] The Bank should generate advice, views, and proposals of its own, but the will of the government should be paramount.[107]

The Committee's opinions on the status of a central bank were not shared by Riefler, whose comments on this subject prompted the Committee to ask:

> This means, leaving Congress on one side, that, as between the Administration and the Federal Reserve on an issue of policy, the initiative and the last word rest with the Federal Reserve? Suppose that the Administration want a certain economic climate to be created, they can merely discuss their desires with the Federal Reserve?——The only question that comes up relates to the reading of the business and credit situation. Sometimes there are differences of view. The question then is whose judgment is going to prevail. Our position is that obviously the people who are more specialized in reading the business and credit situation have to make the judgment. It would make no sense to have us try to make a judgment on what the business and credit demand is, and then have somebody else super-imposing another judgment. It ought to be made by whoever is most capable of making it.[108]

Riefler returned to the point later:

> If the System is in this way by statute independent of the executive, and therefore from direct political pressure, and also independent of private interest, is the argument ever heard that, by being so insulated, they are in an ivory tower and out of touch with what is going on in the length and breadth of the United States?—— Yes, Mr. Elliott Bell does say that in *Businessweek* [sic]; anyone wishing to criticize the system is very likely to say that. I do not think it is taken very seriously. The system, through the directors of the Banks and the branches, and through its contacts, is intimately bound into the structure of the economy. In a sense it is the most important recorder of the state of the economy of the country; often the same people who are opposed to some action taken and who raise the cry of the "ivory tower" rush to us to corroborate any judgment they have on economic questions.[109]

The *Report* recommends the formation of a Standing Committee which would be advisory in character; it proposes that changes in the Bank Rate be made in the name of the Chancellor; and that part-time directors of the Bank be retained, a subject that had been discussed at length before the Parker Tribunal.[110]

INTERNATIONAL ASPECTS

The Committee says nothing in this portion of the *Report* that will upset foreign confidence, steps gingerly around many touchy issues, and generally approves of official postwar policy toward sterling.

It has little confidence in the ability of changes in short-term rates to correct balance-of-payments difficulties. "We have had little evidence of actual movements of funds in response to changes in short-term rates . . . ," though it adds that there is some indication that a rise in long-term rates has induced purchases of long-term securities in London. However, "the fact that changes in rates have had only a limited effect on the movements of funds in a period when sterling was weak does not imply that they will be correspondingly ineffective if sterling is strong." Rather than relying on movements of interest rates, it perhaps would be better at times to support the forward rate of exchange, though many weaknesses of this proposal are noted.[111] The Committee favors a fixed parity for sterling, rejecting freely fluctuating exchange rates, which were advocated by James E. Meade, and devaluation as a policy, "though as a way of escape it cannot be excluded."[112]

Despite the recent improvement in reserves, the Committee states that they are still far from adequate; but it is noted that the U.K.'s problem in this respect is really part of a world-wide "shortage" of international reserves relative to levels of trade.[113] This raises the question of whether there should be a substantial increase in the world price of gold, a proposal that is rejected by the Committee as not "immediately necessary [nor] the most helpful approach to the problem of international liquidity." Moreover, an increase in the price of gold would alter the existing distribution of reserves "very much in favour of the countries that are most amply provided."[114]

It is felt that this problem can best be attacked by utilizing existing international machinery, such as the International Monetary Fund, but the Committee believes that in its present form the IMF has many defects. Several suggestions are offered to remedy these defects, including relaxing the requirements on drawing rights, but the Committee seems more enthusiastic in suggesting that the IMF might be turned into an international central bank, with its own unit of account, along the lines originally suggested by Keynes.[115]

The Committee approves the steps taken toward convertibility and nondiscrimination in trade. It is hopeful about the international position of the United Kingdom, and believes that the dollar problem "is likely to be more intermittent and less intractable than is sometimes supposed, and that it has already changed in character, and is likely to continue to do so."[116] It is reported that the Treasury is looking ahead to a larger current account surplus in the early 1960's.[117] This is all to the good, because it is necessary "to maintain a balance of payments sufficiently favorable to leave a margin for loans and other investments. This margin must be correspondingly widened to allow of grants in aid of colonial development." Since, however, it is better for the United Kingdom to use its surplus more to build up reserves than long-term assets, other sterling countries should be encouraged to borrow more in other areas of the world.[118] But the United Kingdom should remain a major source of capital to the Commonwealth even if it has to borrow abroad for this purpose.[119]

FINANCIAL STATISTICS*

Although many trade associations, the Bank of England, the Treasury, and others submitted economic data to the Committee that had not previously been published,[120] the Committee was frequently handicapped by a lack of information on matters into which it was inquiring. The Committee discussed this problem in its *Report* at some length and carefully pointed out the means of correcting it.[121] As anyone who is at all familiar with the paucity of British economic data might guess, the *Report* called for more reporting and publishing of statistical series in almost every field of conceivable interest to the authorities and the informed public.

*   *   *

Finally, for anyone interested in further pursuit of this matter of statistics, he could do no better than follow the Committee in its quest for the marketable security holdings of the Exchange Equalization Account in 1939, a real thriller with a surprise ending.[122]

Concluding Remarks

An English visitor here, when asked what he thought of the Radcliffe *Report*, replied that it was "woolly." He undoubtedly meant that it was confused and hazy. But there is a colloquial meaning of the word, which is "attended with unusual excitement," as a woolly melodrama. The *Report* is certainly woolly in both senses.

* This section has been abridged by the editor. [R.S.T.]

It is exciting because the Committee's undertaking was hazardous from the very beginning, being nothing less than the development of a general theory of finance that would explain the impact of financial variables on the postwar British economy. And it must be said, considering the string of celebrated witnesses that paraded before it, that the Committee received surprisingly little help in its main task. In view of all this, not to mention time limitations, the *Report* it turned out, for all its deficiencies, is remarkable. The macrocosmic view the *Report* gives of the world of finance will leave many monetary theorists and policymakers uneasy in their self-imposed exile to a small corner of this world. If it does nothing more than open up this larger world to them, it will have served a worthy purpose.

But at the same time, in its analysis of this wide, wide world there seems to be confusion everywhere—in the role of the money supply, in the concept of liquidity, in the analysis of nonbank intermediaries, in the discussion of interest rate determination, in the exalted role assigned to debt managers, and so on. Even so, though this is the *Report* at its worst, it can still be judged an honorable failure. "Honorable" because, as Zarathustra reminded the dying rope-dancer, there is nothing contemptible in making danger one's calling, nor in perishing in that calling. Nothing contemptible; but still, in the way it all ended, something distinctly sad.

NOTES

1. The five volumes of the Committee on the Working of the Monetary System are: (1) *Report* (London 1959), pp. viii, 375; (2) *Minutes of Evidence* (London 1960), pp. ix, 980; (3) *Memoranda 1* (London 1960), pp. vi, 308; (4) *Memoranda 2* (London 1960), pp. vi, 227; (5) *Memoranda 3* (London 1960), pp. vi, 251.

2. Unless otherwise indicated, footnote references have the following meanings: R, 000 refers to the *Report* and its paragraph number; MinE, 000 refers to *Minutes of Evidence* and the number of the question-answer; M-1, 000 refers to the first volume of *Memoranda* and its page number; and similarly for M-2, 000 and M-3, 000.

3. Most of them issued by the Bank of England but some by Scottish and Northern Irish banks. R, 347, 349.

4. R, 388, 478.

5. Partial series, which are either inconsistent with one another, refer to different things, or are for different dates, are scattered around like Easter eggs. The *Report* shows total deposits of London clearing banks (R, 134) and of Scottish banks (R, 149), but only for 1958; net personal deposits in London clearing banks for four postwar years (R, 478);

and a chart of the ratio of the money supply to national income for 1946–58 (R, 478). Elsewhere, data are presented for currency with the public and net deposits of clearing banks (M-3, 69), note circulation and clearing bank deposits (M-3, 184), in chart form the ratio of the money supply (currency with the public and net deposits of clearing banks) to GNP (M-3, 102), note issues and deposits of all reporting banks and acceptance houses, with intergroup items not omitted (M-2, 202–3), and in chart form the ratio of net bank deposits to national income (MinE, 10433).

6. R, 128–31.

7. R, 131. The Scottish banks appear to treat their deposit accounts somewhat differently. See R, 153.

8. For example, see MinE, 8033–35 and 8132 for evidence that deposits in Trustee Savings Banks are more and more being used as current accounts.

9. R, 125, 504; also 395, 523.

10. R, 143–48, 351; M-1, 9–10.

11. R, 175, 355–58; M-1, 9–10; MinE, 183–89, 1568–96.

12. M-1, 10.

13. MinE, 98. For a similar statement, see MinE, 421, which the Committee quotes in R, 360.

14. In this and subsequent exchanges quoted here, the first part of each paragraph is a question from some member of the Committee, and the second part, after the dash, is the answer by one of the witnesses. I have not thought it necessary most of the time to identify the interrogators and respondents.

15. MinE, 2262–70. It should be noted, though, that at times even the Bank argued that the cash ratio was largely ineffective because it had to act as a lender of last resort to the discount market (M-1, 38). However, it was brought out in testimony that this meant only that the Bank, as lender of last resort, would give the market, *at a price*, all the cash it wanted; it did not mean that the Bank, as lender of last resort, relinquished all control over interest rates (MinE, 94–101).

16. R, 120, 376, 430, 583. In fact, in direct opposition to the above evidence, the *Report* says: "But now that the credit-creating capacity of the banks is limited by the 30 per cent liquid assets' convention, an increase in cash precisely balanced by a decrease in the Treasury Bill issue has become irrelevant to the credit-creating power of the banks" (R, 167).

17. R, 376. See also R, 121, 355, 357.

18. R, 120, 167, 175, 505–7. For further discussion of the weaknesses of the liquidity ratio, see MinE, 183–89, 1568–96, 1654–58, 1909–13, with supplementary notes to 1909 on pp. 952–54, and 3738–65.

19. R, 411, 417, 422; MinE, 2677 ff., 3265–72, 3523–3645; and M-1, 40. However, if the control over bank advances forces the banks to purchase other earning assets that are more liquid than those they would have purchased, a given money supply is likely to be associated with a higher interest rate structure, other things the same.

20. R, 392 and footnote.

21. R, 504; also 385, 397 ff.

22. R, 397. This is also suggested in R, 394.

23. In other words, while there may be a liquidity-preference schedule, drawn against interest rates, the schedule is subject to such wide shifts, as expectations change, that interest rates are in fact little influenced by the amount of liquidity in the system.

24. I admit that it is a tricky business to impute views to the Committee from questions asked and statements made by it during examination of witnesses. But I have done this only when such evidence seems consistent with the final views of the Committee as stated in its *Report*.

25. MinE, 9760–61; also 10220, 10236. My emphasis.

26. See, for example, R, 563, as modified by 565. Note also the Bank's stress on confidence as the prime determinant of interest rates in MinE, 2398–99, qualified slightly in supplementary notes of the Bank, pp. 955–56.

27. R, 395. For Kahn's opinions on this, see M–3, 144.

28. MinE, 10433; M–3, 102, 184–85.

29. MinE, 10431–32, 10434, 10436, 10438.

30. MinE, 10441. See also MinE, 10443–53 for further discussion of these points.

31. See M-3, 66, 179, 183–85, 85, 113, 146–48; and MinE, 10425–512. Outstanding memoranda on this subject were produced by James V. Morgan and J. C. R. Dow.

32. For one flagrant example, see R, 570, where the Committee presents three reasons for the rise in bond rates without once mentioning the money supply or national income.

33. R, 442–43.

34. R, 386.

35. R, 450–51, 489, 495.

36. R, 487. Sayers kept pressing the view on witnesses that an increase in interest rates will raise actual investment in the short run. His theory was that higher rates will lower consumption and so leave more room for investment, given aggregate demand. No witness accepted this, and it does not show up in the *Report*. See, *e.g.*, MinE, 4189–92, 5656–61.

37. Some of this material appears in the *Report*, R, 452–53.

38. M-2, 118-22.

39. R, 453.

40. This is part of the full exchange found in MinE, 5566–5617.

41. M-2, 88–96; R, 453; MinE, 11119 (and footnote).

42. R, 453.

43. R, 453.

44. M-2, 87–88.

45. MinE, 11169–70.

46. MinE, 6266–69.

47. MinE, 6427–29.

48. MinE, 6490–93, 6499.

49. MinE, 6734–47.

50. MinE, 7568–79.

51. MinE, 8149, 8155–67, 8171–75, 8178.

52. MinE, 8188, 8206.

53. MinE, 8263–66, 8276. But see 8279 where this view seems to be modified.

54. MinE, 8544.

55. MinE, 8583–85.

56. MinE, 8918.

57. MinE, 11360–62, 11414.

58. MinE, 11605, 11618–28.

59. MinE, 11726.

60. MinE, 12287.

61. MinE, 12992–96.

62. MinE, 12952–55.

63. MinE, 4976–86.

64. MinE, 3617, 3646.

65. M-3, 178–82, 182–88, 95, 213.

66. M-1, 35–38.

67. R, 125, 389.

68. The monetary system is composed of the Bank of England, the London clearing banks, and the Scottish and Northern Irish banks. The assets of the separate financial institutions for several postwar years are given in the memorandum of the Central Statistical Office (M-1, 130–41), but the most recent data are in the *Report*, Table 20, and referred to in R, 313.

69. R, 390. My italics.

70. R, 316, 389, 390.

71. The possible exception is R, 392.

72. On this last point, the basic difficulty with the Committee's approach stands out most clearly. It is stated that "regulation of the banks is required not because they are 'creators of money' but because they are the biggest lenders at the shortest (most liquid) end of the range of credit markets" (R, 504). That banks lend at the "most liquid end of the range of credit markets" is an argument against controlling them. The more the assets purchased by a financial institution resemble the liabilities it creates, the less need is there to control that institution. An institution, for instance, that purchased money and created money would not have to be controlled. (In another context, the Committee comes to this conclusion with respect to the note issues of Scottish banks which are backed by Bank of England notes.) Nor would one that purchased bonds and issued what the market considered to be identical bonds need to be controlled. Financial intermediaries become potentially more dangerous to the stability of the economy the more illiquid their assets are relative to their liabilities, given the rate and pattern of their growth.

73. R, 394.

74. R, 504.

75. R, 505.

76. R, 509. See also R, 510–11, 527.

77. MinE, 9377. For de Kock's full views on this, see M-1, 289–90.

78. M-3, 37; MinE, 10172–80.

79. This testimony is in MinE, 9822–27. Riefler also dealt with this problem in his memorandum, in which he stated that nonbank inter-

mediaries play a neutral role in the saving-investment process and that control of the money supply has pervasive influences throughout the whole financial structure. See M-1, 301.

80. MinE, 11812–18. For similar, though milder, statements, see the memorandum of The Bank of Australia, M-1, 249, and the British Treasury's statements, MinE, 1607–11.

81. MinE, 9366.

82. R, 374, 393.

83. R, 395, 514, 603.

84. R, 499, 395.

85. R, 562.

86. R, 395.

87. R, 393.

88. M-3, 145. My emphases.

89. M-3, 145. His emphasis.

90. M-3, 144. See also Kahn's testimony, MinE, 10983–87.

91. This statement recognizes the connection between liquidity (lending) and the level of interest rates, and it is therefore in opposition to what I have called the dominant view of the *Report* on this matter.

92. R, 487–91. N. Kaldor, in his memorandum, advanced an additional argument against highly fluctuating rates: namely, that the average rate over time would then be higher, due to risk considerations, which would push the economy more toward consumption and away from investment, and so slow down its growth rate. He also felt that saving, under these conditions, would be allocated less efficiently to investment alternatives. M-3, 148.

93. R, 492–97.

94. R, 498.

95. R, 516–17. See also the Committee's discussion of this with the Treasury, MinE, 13311–22.

96. Along these lines, for what is probably the most extreme statement ever made on the relative merits of fiscal and monetary policies, see the memorandum by I. M. D. Little, R. R. Neild, and C. R. Ross, M-3, 159–67.

97. R, 524.

98. R, 520–29.

99. R, 428.

100. This is noted in R, 428, 552, 583. The Committee states that "we were sometimes assured that the bill rate has practically no connection with long rates."

101. MinE, 1884, 1887. See also MinE, 1792, 1796, 1804, 1845.

102. MinE, 1849–51.

103. MinE, 1870.

104. MinE, 1849, 1855–60. For a fuller discussion of these questions, see MinE, 1762–63, 1792–1805, 1841–98. The Committee's views are in R, 551, 575–76. The Treasury's position was much the same as the Bank's; see MinE, 2387–98, 2953–72, 2799–2995.

Subsequently, the Bank did use open-market operations to influence long-term rates. For a justification of this and a slight modification of its initial position, see MinE, 11919, 12000–01, 12008–14, 13416, 13453. This change is discussed by the Committee in R, 341, 428, 553.

105. R, 768.

106. R, 767, 769.

107. R, 761–62. See also MinE, 256–58.

108. MinE, 9407.

109. MinE, 9454. Compare Riefler's statement with that of the Governor of the Bank of England, who said in part: "I have no doubt that in modern conditions it is proper that Government should have the final word on policy and that the central bank should not be free to pursue a completely independent line." MinE, 12813.

110. R, 771, 773, 778–87; MinE, 262–63, 269. A similar body has been suggested here many times in recent years, but the proposal has been attacked partly because it would jeopardize the independence of the Federal Reserve. Four years ago, before the Joint Economic Committee, Elliott Bell submitted a remedy:

> If . . . it is felt that the Federal Reserve Board is so sensitive that contact with the President would corrupt it, then I suggest there might usefully be formed a National Economic Council without regular representation by the Federal Reserve Board. In this event, the Fed might be invited to send an observer with the express understanding that he could sit near an open door ready to fly to the sanctuary of Constitution Avenue if he felt the danger at any point of political contamination.

See *Hearings before the Subcommittee on Economic Stabilization of the Joint Economic Committee*, on December 10–11, 1956, p. 7.

The Committee received and heard an unusually large amount of evidence concerning the status of the Bank. For the Bank's views, see M-1, 5–9; MinE, 249–86, 752–60, 12813–900. For opinions of part-time directors of the Bank, see M-1, 44–45; MinE, 12066–188. Riefler's statements are found in MinE, 9395–9407, 9422–36, 9452–54. The views of former Chancellors and others are found in M-3, 47–48, 70–71, 207–11, 248–49; MinE, 11250–99, 12301–640.

111. R, 695–702, 703–07. See the Treasury's spirited objection to the support of the forward rate in M-1, 121–22.

112. R, 716, 719–22, 728.

113. R, 670–71; MinE, 2531.

114. R, 672–74.

115. R, 678.

116. R, 684.

117. R, 630, 734.

118. MinE, 2492–2507, and p. 956.

119. R, 741–47. The Bank's views on the international aspects in M-1, 13–17, 34–35; MinE, 833–947, 948–71; the Treasury's in M-1, 105, 112–22; MinE, 2483–2615, 3211–22, 9695–9734. Economists addressed themselves to these issues in M-3, 71–76, 132–36, 243.

120. The Bank presented a memorandum on the current sources of banking statistics (M-1, 66–70); the Central Statistical Office prepared

data on sources of financial and economic statistics relating to the monetary system and on assets of financial institutions (M-1, 129–62); The National Institute of Economic and Social Research presented a comprehensive memorandum on financial and economic statistics (M-3, 3–27); and the many data presented by trade associations are found throughout the evidence.

121. The recommendations are found principally in Chapter 10 of the *Report*; but see also R, 366–67, 580, 582, 629.

122. MinE, 2848–55, 3223.

20 *The Report of the Commission on Money and Credit*

Karl Brunner *Ohio State University*

*The Commission**

*   *   *

The Commission on Money and Credit[1] was formed in 1958 . . . [Its] mandate implied the following specific obligations:

1. A consensus on economic goals and criteria for an evaluation of the economy's aggregate performance had to be worked out. Ideally, this task required the specification of a social utility function.

2. With the goals accepted, or a social utility function more or less vaguely outlined, a re-evaluation of the existing institutional arrangements became necessary. Different arrangements impose different restrictions on the social goals. The choice of institutions may significantly affect the economy's performance. One might formalize the specific problem faced by the Commission as an optimal choice of restrictions on the social utility function. This task may be broken into four parts: (*a*) evaluation of institutions bearing on policy-making processes; (*b*) assessment of institutions bearing on operation of financial markets and behavior of eco-

Reprinted from *Journal of Political Economy*, Vol. 69 (December 1961), 605–20, by permission of the author and The University of Chicago Press. Copyright 1961 by The University of Chicago Press.

* The part of this section dealing with the organization and background of the Commission has been omitted. [Editor]

nomic units; (*c*) choice of policy variables, that is, of economic magnitudes which are directly and immediately controlled by actions of responsible authorities; (*d*) choice of economic signals associated with specific operations on selected policy variables.

3. Optimal choice of institutional arrangements relative to a specified social valuation presupposes a rational foundation. The goals on the one side and the appraisal of institutions on the other are linked by our systematic knowledge of the financial environment. A more assured, less speculative, and better validated explicit theoretical comprehension of the financial system's mode of operation in the United States and its connection with the behavior of employment and price was required. The development of theory would appear to form the third major task for a Commission on Money and Credit.

* * *

The Report

The report's political impact will be determined by its more than eighty recommendations bearing on the Federal Reserve, the Treasury, commercial banks, thrift institutions, federal credit programs, international arrangements, and the relation between the Congress and the Executive branch of the government. These proposals are accompanied by descriptions and summaries evidently emanating from the contributions made by the staff and numerous subcontractors who submitted research material. Whatever the underlying analysis and substantive contributions may have been, this purely cognitive aspect of the Commission's work is unavoidably muted and appears only in summarized and sketchy form. Still, the report reveals some excellent underlying pieces of research.[2] But it also contains symptoms of thoroughly inadequate analysis and worn-out textbook legends.

The proposals appear, on balance, well conceived. The Commission avoids an easy and fascinating gamesmanship with dubiously founded and obscurely justified institutional innovations. In particular, the Commission shows commendable intellectual self-discipline by avoiding impressionistic recommendations for new controls simply because the morphology of the financial system has changed. The recommendations exhibit a refreshing attempt to question and appraise existing monetary and financial institutions. They effectively point to ill-conceived and redundant arrangements imposed on our financial system. Numerous regulations on the asset portfolios of financial institutions or on the geographic distributions of their operations impair the rational use of our resources and contribute little to an effective monetary policy.[3] The Commission's determined effort to evaluate institutions in terms of their contribution to an efficacious policy mechanism is highly significant. It underscores the importance of appropriate analysis and empirical investigation which provide the necessary foundation for the Commission's judgments.

Numerous recommendations, particularly those on the structure and organization of Federal Reserve authorities and the coordinative machinery, are designed to improve the efficacy of the institutional frame within which policy-making proceeds.[4] These proposals, though not unimportant, will not be discussed further here. Their meaning depends on the systematic and validated comprehension of our financial environment.

The core of other proposals is more closely associated with the system's mode of behavior. These recommendations refer to institutional arrangements that influence the choice of policy variables or that affect the *modus operandi* of the financial process. A vast range is covered, including the host of federal credit programs and non-bank financial intermediaries. The subsequent discussion selects some broad problems for more detailed consideration.

The Commission's discussion of national economic goals reveals an ample consensus in the choice of the rate of price change, the rate of economic growth, and the rate of unemployment as major arguments of the social utility function.[5] However, a potentially serious cleavage appears in the mode of evaluating unemployment. The report specifies the volume of unfilled vacancies as setting the tolerance level for unemployment. Expansionary policy would not be applied until the number of those seeking jobs exceeded the number of available jobs. Ruttenberg, on the other hand, insists on 3 per cent unemployment as the tolerance level.[6]

This disagreement in the specification of the social utility function has important ramifications. The two formulations tend to be associated with sharply divergent policy conceptions. A definite percentage for tolerable unemployment focuses attention on inflationary monetary and fiscal policies combined—or compensated—with a complex arrangement of selective controls. The other formulation directs attention to the allocative mechanism and the government's responsibility for the deliberate fostering of an appropriate institutional frame which minimizes the size of the tolerance level.

The Commission seems at least partly aware of this implication of its evaluation of unemployment. On various occasions the report expresses concern for a properly functioning (relative) price mechanism and the suitable discharge of governmental obligations with respect to the construction of an adequate institutional environment.[7] However, the awareness seems spotty and the discussion of the issue uneven. The impact of important legal institutions, for example, the pattern of court decisions on labor issues and the minimum wage laws, is not even mentioned.[8]

The emerging unemployment pattern and the prospect for economic growth are, of course, related to market institutions. The Commission notes the persistent rise in the rate of unemployment. Two factors are adduced in the report to partially explain observed and expected unemployment behavior, namely, (1) the additional load imposed on the absorptive capacity of the allocative mechanism by accelerated rates of introducing new technologies and (2) rates of entry into the labor market. The increase in such load factors raises the level of structural unemployment. This effect is compounded by institutional restrictions, in the form of stiffer union conditions and higher legal minimum wage levels, impairing the mechanism's absorptive capacity. Sustained pockets of unemployment, particularly among Negroes, women, the young, and the old are thus created.[9] A proper identification of the prevalent types of unemployment is of decisive importance for effective policy action. If the analysis briefly summarized above is correct, additional doses of inflationary policy would have a marginal effect on the average rate of unemployment. When the problem is one of structural unemployment a closer attention to our labor-market institutions would assume considerable urgency.

The report conveys an ambivalent impression with respect to economic growth. Some thoughtful passages evidently summarize systematic studies on the relation between growth and inflation, and the Commission specifically disposes of the contention that inflation is a necessary condition for growth.[10] The relation between the performance of the allocation mechanism and economic growth, however, remains shaded in doubt and confusion. Some statements clearly specify lower barriers to resource mobility as a prerequisite to satisfactory growth and may be understood to emphasize the dependence of economic growth on the quality of the allocation process.[11] Other passages, and particularly comments by individual members, refer to growth as an entity determined by processes unrelated to the manner in which markets operate to adjust to new labor entries, to new technologies, and to new demand patterns induced by our rising wealth.[12] Such notions suggest that "dynamic adjustments" are eased and "structural unemployment" removed by sufficient "growth."

The Commission emerges as a strong advocate of monetary and fiscal policies. It suggests that intelligent use of available instruments would substantially moderate economic fluctuations. The

Commission evidently feels that we possess a satisfactory cognitive foundation to formulate a reliable guide for intelligent policy. The report asserts, in particular, that "there is fairly general agreement about the nature of the processes through which monetary policy affects economic activity."[13]

I submit that this is a pleasant delusion and seriously misrepresents our actually established, systematic knowledge. Do we have a widely accepted workable demand function for money which clarifies the effects of wealth, windfalls, income, other transactions, interest rates, and the composition of wealth on the demand for money? Or do we have an adequate and reasonably useful formulation of the supply mechanism which explains the major determinants of the money supply, its response to particular policy changes, and the orders of magnitudes of their effects? Is there useful knowledge of the position of interest rates in this mechanism and the role of feedback from income, together with the meaning for money-supply behavior of a variety of institutional detail? Most important, do we have a satisfactory explanation of the connection between monetary variables and current output and price level? Is the connection dominated by a few interest elasticities, in the tradition of orthodox Keynesianism? Do we mind Patinkin and incorporate a real balance effect? Are there processes associated with the composition of wealth and the relation between wealth and output, vaguely known but not formally developed, which determine the position of monetary variables with respect to the pace of economic activity?

A glance at the literature reveals the existence of two barely connected worlds of intellectual endeavor in the monetary field. In one we find the textbooks on money and banking, where empirical concern is restricted to the description of institutional detail and analysis is replaced most often by a few numerical examples and graphical exercises. In the other we notice a learned pursuit of the esoterica of formal models with no concern for their possible cognitive significance. This description is not fundamentally unfair, since the test is provided, after all, by our list of well-established empirical hypotheses on money demand, money supply, and aggregate demand for output. Yet the description overlooks the developing pattern in recent research activities, to which the Commission itself signally contributed. For some years through systematic investigations researchers have formulated and assessed hypotheses in the field of money demand and money supply. In the field of aggregate demand theory, differently motivated considerations simultaneously suggest a useful reformulation which incorporates stock (wealth) and flow (new production flows) variables with an explicit description of their interrelation.

Money is a component of wealth with two specific properties: it has the smallest transaction costs and, in our contemporary civilization, the smallest ratio of marginal cost to market price. Both costs nearly vanish when compared to the exchange price of money. The first property explains the existence of a positive demand for this asset; the second property explains the government's responsibility for "maintaining the value of money." Money appears thus as an asset competing with other assets, financial and real, for a place in the balance sheet of economic units. These units are usefully visualized as optimizing their balance-sheet positions— subject to some institutional or technological restrictions. This conception evolves into an explanation of the desired balance-sheet position in terms of prevailing market conditions and the inherited position. Such a framework promises to provide new insights into monetary processes and the nature of the connection between policy variables (that is, reserve requirements, Federal Reserve portfolio, and rediscount rate) and the rate of current output or the price level.

Variations in policy variables induce a reallocation of assets (or liabilities) in the balance sheets of economic units which spills over to current output and thus affect the price level. Injections of base money (or "high-powered" money) modify the composition of financial assets and total wealth available to banks and other economic units. Absorption of the new base money requires suitable alterations in asset yields or asset prices. The banks and the public are thus induced to reshuffle their balance sheets to adjust desired and actual balance-sheet position.

The interaction between banks and public, which forms the essential core of money-supply theory, generates the peculiar leverage or multiplier effect of injections of base money on bank assets and deposits and, correspondingly, on specific asset and liability items of the public's balance sheet. The readjustment process induces a change in the relative yield (or price) structure of assets crucial for the transmission of monetary policy-action to the rate of economic activity. The relative price of base money and its close substitutes falls, and the relative price of other assets rises.

The stock of real capital dominates these other assets. The increase in the price of capital relative to the price of financial assets simultaneously raises real capital's market value relative to the capital stock's replacement costs and increases the desired stock relative to the actual stock. The relative increase in the desired stock of capital induces an adjustment in the actual stock through new production. In this manner current output and prices of durable goods are affected by the readjustments in the balance sheets and the related price movements set in motion by the injection of base money. The wealth, income, and relative price effects involved in the whole transmission process also tend to raise demand for non-durable goods.

The above discussion is the barest outline of a promising approach in monetary theory. The Commission contributed to the exploration of these ideas in some of the underlying study papers.[14] The report itself contains partial glimpses at best. Analysis along the lines indicated still needs considerable tightening, suitable formalizations, and empirical evaluation. Still, it seems sufficiently developed to permit a tentative appraisal of a variety of issues presented in the report.

The report discusses in some detail the effect of interest rates on spending decisions, particularly on investment expenditures. It concludes that the irrelevance of interest rates has often been overstated and cautiously admits that interest rates may very likely exert some significant effect on investment expenditures. The survey presented by the Commission appropriately emphasizes the inadequacy of available evidence. It seems worth pondering whether the tenuous character of this evidence partly reflects some unresolved analytical problems.

The usual evidence derives from econometric studies and questionnaires or interviews. The latter evidence is usually caught in a whirlpool of dubious meanings. If we admit the results at face value, they could hardly be interpreted to deny the influence of interest rates on spending decisions.[15]

Econometric studies of investment behavior have usually been of the pure-flow variety with the accumulated capital stock perhaps intruding. Most statistical estimations yield poor results for the interest variables. The regression coefficient is small, even vanishes, relative to its standard error. The portfolio-balance analysis, outlined above, explains this result and clarifies the place of interest rates in the transmission mechanism. The association of some market rates of interest with investment expenditures in the context of a pure-flow analysis, modified at best by the incorporation of the accumulated capital stock (measured at cost), does not provide an adequate test for the significance of interest rates.

A generalized stock-flow analysis would reveal that in the case of new issues of government securities, or improved expectations concerning the rate of return from real capital, the relative price of government securities falls and the relative price of real capital rises. This means that a positive correlation between market rates and investment expenditures is generated by the process. The previous example of base money injection indicated a negative correlation. Isolation of the cost aspect of interest rates with respect to purchases of new durable goods in econometric studies thus requires an appropriate specification of the stock-flow interrelations centered on real capital. An omission of this mechanism makes the interest rate in the standard flow formulation reflect two opposite forces—cost and wealth effect—which tend to cancel each other in the statistical estimation based on this formulation.[16]

The portfolio-balance analysis may resolve an issue between traditional money and banking analysis and monetary theory mirrored to some extent in the report. The "new skepticism" gave new impetus to the controversy over "credit" *versus* "money supply." Monetary processes have often been described as operating essentially on aggregate demand for current output through a magnitude called "credit." This magnitude seems at times to be a stock variable (portfolio of loans, or portfolio of total earning assets of banks) and at times it occurs as a flow variable (rates of change of the above stock variables).[17] "Credit" as a stock variable appears jointly with the components of the money supply in a complete portfolio analysis; "credit" as a flow is simply the by-product of the adjustments in the balance sheets to modifications in "initial" positions.

The report's description of monetary policy lays particular stress on the importance of lenders' reaction as a crucial link in the transmission of policy actions. This emphasis is subsequently qualified by stressing the importance of a sufficiently large borrowers' demand.[18] The discussion is rather confused, but two strands of thought seem to merge in the report's summary. It appears, first, that only "lending flows" (that is, the rate of change in the banks' loan portfolio) matter and, second, that the borrowers' demand for loans is practically insensitive to interest variations. The second point can be reformulated by saying that changes in market conditions will not induce the public to readjust liabilities and assets.

The general balance-sheet analysis immediately disposes of the first point, but a decision on the second requires a detailed empirical investigation. This issue is closely related to another assertion made by the report, namely, that "excess liquidity" endangers the effectiveness of monetary policy. This notion of a "liquidity trap" has been with us for some time and is still expounded occasionally.

A detailed appraisal of monetary developments in the thirties strongly confirms both the absence of a liquidity trap in the banking system's operation and the public's continued willingness to readjust balance-sheet position to new situations.[19] The results also confirm the existence of a marked non-linearity between periods of low excess reserves and high interest rates, and periods of large excess reserves and low interest rates. The operation of this non-linearity generates the asymmetry between the impact of a restrictive policy in a high-interest regime and the impact of expansionary policy in a low-interest regime asserted by the report. However, the evidence assembled emphatically underscores that such asymmetry is accompanied by a sustained efficacy of monetary policy in a deflationary environment. The report's rather tenuous description of these policy mechanisms leads to a strange and very dangerous formulation. Having asserted that "excessive liquidity" impairs monetary policy, the report suggests that in the case of a downswing the authorities should remove such "excess liquidity" and simultaneously accelerate the reduction in interest rates.[20] Portfolio analysis should reveal the stark inconsistency of the two actions and indicate that the removal of "excess liquidity" inserts an amplifying feedback into the mechanism generating fluctuations of economic activity. The very notion of "excess liquidity"—in the absence of price controls—should be clearly understood as a result of inadequate analysis.

The report is permeated by the awareness that institutional reform does not proceed without costs. This awareness prevented recommendations of radical changes where the possible gains to be expected from the modified arrangements are minute. The report should be commended for this balanced appraisal; yet in the case of discount policy some safeguarding qualifications need to be added. These explicit safeguards can be subsumed under the report's general admonition to the Federal Reserve authorities to adjust policies to the maximization of the "social utility function" specified.

The report recommends that discount facilities be continued and that the associated policies and administrative procedures be uniform in the system. Discount facilities have traditionally been conceived as the means of establishing the essential link between a central bank and the commercial banks. This arrangement was supposed to enable the central banker to gauge the varying demand-and-supply pressures on the loan markets. Such a conception may have prompted the Federal Reserve authorities on occasions in the past to prescribe "continued maintenance of contact with the money market" as a guide in policy considerations. The context of these declarations indicates that policy should be adjusted so as "to keep banks closely tied to the central bank," in other words, so that asset and deposit expansion depend on additional reserve funds being made available by the authorities. This conception may be properly conceived in terms of a continuously effective discount policy, particularly if the banks' demand for cash assets is comparatively insensitive to variations in the discount rate. However, such a policy involves a serious confusion of means and ends and endangers the stabilization desired by the Commission.

In the case of a deflationary process, the policy guide inspired by the conception of a "sustained contact with the money market" leads the central bank to sell on the open market or raise reserve requirements in order to force the "market into the bank." Continuation of existing discount facilities, to be compatible with stabilization, requires recognition by our monetary authorities that an effective monetary policy may involve a breakdown in the operation of discount policy.[21]

Open-market policy and changes in reserve requirements are advocated by the report as major policy variables, with the qualification that only sparing use should be made of the second instrument. It is suggested that reserve requirements against demand deposits be imposed on all insured banks, whereas requirements against time and savings deposits should be abolished.

It can be shown that reserve requirements on time deposits do not raise the authorities' degree of control over the money supply. Abolition of differential requirements would undoubtedly simplify our arrangements and probably raise the authorities' degree of control over the money supply. However, I suspect that the Commission exaggerates the expected gain in the precision of monetary control.[22] Still, differential requirements have no pertinent function either, and a uniform requirement is therefore a move in the proper direction.

The report also notes that changes in reserve requirements and open-market operations appear equally effective in shaping the money supply.[23] The comparatively frequent changes in requirement over the postwar period permit an evaluation of this statement. Our investigation determined that injection of a billion dollars of base money or liberation of a billion dollars of reserves by a reduction in the requirements generates on the average the same money-supply reaction. These results suggest the need for a reconsideration of the specific contribution made to monetary control by the Federal Reserve's discretionary power over reserve requirements. The Commission offers no justification for this power. More fundamentally, while it dismisses reserve requirements on time deposits, it presents no case for the continued adherence to a system of fractional requirements against demand deposits.

A possible rationale for the existence of requirements or the institution of discretionary power with respect to the level of requirements may be formulated either in terms of the degree (or precision) of control over the money supply or in terms of the Treasury's net interest cost. Discretionary requirements were granted in the thirties as a means of increasing Federal Reserve power. The Federal Reserve's portfolio was small relative to excess reserves. It was alleged that open-market operations could not prevent serious inflation in these circumstances. However, such discretionary power over requirement ratios is not a necessary condition for preventing inflation.

Maximization of the degree of control and minimization of net interest costs are equally unable to justify the Federal Reserve's discretionary power. Examination of the money-supply mechanism assigns the same degree of control whether the money-supply reaction is generated by variations in reserve requirements or by changes in the monetary base. Minimizing net interest cost could always rationalize a higher, but never a lower, requirement ratio. On what grounds then should the discretionary powers be continued?

The report is equally mute concerning the existence of fractional requirements. An empirical appraisal indicates that elimination of reserve requirements would lower the precision of control, but probably by a comparatively small margin. In the absence of requirements, the possible gain in the degree of control attributable to their introduction would barely balance the social cost of allocating administrative efforts and legislative energies to their establishment. The existence of reserve requirements necessitates a greater injection of base money than would occur in the absence of requirements to obtain a given secular growth rate in the money supply. Gradual elimination of requirements would generate an increase in the money supply of approximately 15 per cent without a change in the base; subsequent changes in the base would have a greater leverage (30 per cent greater). The greater injection of base money under the existing reserve requirement is accompanied by a correspondingly smaller average volume (over a decade) of Treasury debt outside the government sector. This lower volume compresses the net interest cost. Some computations based on the assumption of a 4 per cent growth in the money supply over the past decade yield an annual saving of approximately $50 million a year attributable to the existence of present requirements. Is this the rationale for reserve requirements, and if it is, why not a 100 per cent requirement?[24]

The report is quite explicit as to the basic identity of debt management and monetary policy. In both cases the authorities modify the existing composition of the government sector's outstanding debt; in both cases the transmission mechanism outlined by the balance-sheet equilibrating process operates in the same manner. The Commission is here again consistent with its basic purposes when it recommends the abolition of statutory limitations on debt volume and interest rates.

Awareness of the identity between the Treasury's debt management and the Federal Reserve's open-market operations uncovers the problem of effective policy co-ordination. The report strongly opposes any merger of the two institutions or concentration of all the government's debt-issuing activities in the Federal Reserve Board.

The report makes a variety of recommendations concerning technical points related to the Treasury's debt operations. Among the points mentioned is the appropriate spacing and regularization of the Treasury's debt issues. I suspect that this suggestion is worth serious exploration. A regular spacing of Treasury debt combined with larger and more homogeneous issues would lead to smaller time intervals between outstanding issues. This might be expected to improve significantly the operation of the longer term market and create the environment for smoother arbitrage. A set of rules would have to be formulated to regulate the Treasury's refunding, issuing, and retirement operations according to the specification of a definite debt structure. Among the major advantages to be gained by this institutional reform are the elimination of the Treasury's guessing game with respect to the issuing conditions. The near continuous yield curve determined by the spacing provides a close guide for the new issues. Extended application of auction techniques, as suggested by the report, would be unnecessary to avoid the price-setting problem. Furthermore, market uncertainty would be reduced and the frequency of the Treasury's operations on the market with their attendant restrictions on Federal Reserve policy lowered. Most important, perhaps, long-term market operations would approximate in efficiency short-term operations.

A market structure is likely to emerge which would tend to increase the efficaciousness of the transmission of monetary policy through the financial markets to the stock of real capital and current output. Under such an arrangement no conflicts between debt-management policy and the Federal Reserve's policy could arise. The Treasury would operate within a fixed refunding or issuing procedure and the Federal Reserve Board would change the composition of the government's outstanding debt according to the indications of stabilization policy. This suggestion of a regularized debt structure is not advanced in a spirit of contention, but the report does touch on it, and the arrangement might render most other technical modifications superfluous and contribute significantly to creating an institutional framework that would raise the effectiveness of policy mechanisms.[25]

Most of the institutional recommendations made in the report are quite sensible in terms of the outlined monetary analysis. The liberalizing of branching and investment regulation, a basic feature of the proposals, would improve the allocative efficiency of credit markets and be likely to raise the sensitivity of the transmission process to policy action. Similar properties hold for numerous aspects of the federal credit programs. Insurance and guarantee features seem to make a decisive difference in allocative efficiency at a vanishing social cost.

The report's discussion of fiscal policy is in some respects less detailed and more general than the survey of monetary and credit arrangements. Two considerations dominate the Commission's proposals in the fiscal field. The report notes that discretionary fiscal policy "was hardly ever used as a stabilizer"[26] and stabilizing processes were restricted to the operation of the "built-in automatic stabilizers." The Commission is, therefore, concerned both with strengthening automatic stabilization devices and with achieving proper timed flexibility of discretionary tax and expenditure policy.

The central proposal emerging under the Commission's scrutiny is for changes in the first bracket rate of the personal income tax according to a predetermined formula (the recommendation of "formula flexibility") or according to discretionary judgment. The report justifies this proposal on the basis of its efficacy in affecting the short-run spending decisions of the public.

Unfortunately, recent developments in the theory of the consumption-function associated with the work of Modigliani and Friedman—which contribute to the systematic incorporation of wealth into monetary analysis—give little support for the report's confidence. Short-run changes in the first bracket rate of personal income tax exert a minor effect on a unit's wealth position, and if wealth dominates consumers' expenditure, formula flexibility and discretionary bracket changes, while not useless, could not be expected to make the contribution asserted by the Commission. The case for short-run adjustments in the first bracket rate would improve if windfalls could be shown to exert some effect on consumers' demand. So far analysis and evidence are inconclusive. We have to know considerably more before the report's major fiscal proposal can be properly assessed.[27]

A major aspect of monetary policy is covered implicitly rather than explicitly by the report, namely, the choice of signals for the policy-making bodies to watch. The original mandate given to the Federal Reserve System has a tenuous relation to the goals formulated by the Commission and a reformulation of the mandate in terms of our major economic goals is certainly appropriate. It could be expected to remove some old conceptions which might otherwise confuse public attention. In this manner we might replace the old concern for an "elastic currency" with a clearly defined responsibility with respect to the "general protection of liquidity." A carefully stated mandate aids in resolving the choice of appropriate signals and policy-indicators but cannot determine this choice by itself.

The Federal Reserve authorities have assigned indicative importance to a variety of magnitudes in the past: the index of consumers' prices, interest rates, the volume of free reserves, and "credit." The discussion in a previous section also noted the volume of banks' indebtedness to the Federal Reserve banks among the signals to be considered. The contribution of monetary policy to economic stabilization depends both on the effectiveness of the transmission mechanism and the manner in which the policy function is discharged. The performance of the policy function is crucially determined by the choice of signals.

Are these signals approximately optimal? The report expresses serious doubt with respect to the consumer price index. It observes that this index is substantially lagged relative to the major cycle movement. Close attention to such an index would delay appropriate policy action in a major downswing. Serious reservations also apply to the choice of interest rates, free reserves, and "credit." These indicators do not suitably mirror the policy requirements imposed by growth and stabilization. Linking policy to some of these indicators may well, under quite general circumstances, generate an amplifying feedback endangering our fundamental goal of stabilization.

The choice of a set of rules is an alternative to the choice of signals. Policy action involves *some* choice and we might just as well try to be deliberate and rational about it. This rationality involves the full utilization of our systematic and validated knowledge. The choice of signals or rules, or the choice between the two alternatives, is not an issue which we can safely leave to the limbo of arts, feelings, and flairs. There is a significant theoretical or cognitive component in this issue and no intelligent choice can deny this component. The issue is still unresolved and pressing, and it seems that both monetary authorities and economists should be concerned with obtaining a firmer cognitive base for judging the decision.

Concluding Remarks

This review article has concentrated attention on our domestic institutions and monetary mechanism. One chapter of the report surveys the United States economy's international position.

The nature of contemporary balance-of-payments problems is discussed and solutions considered. The provision of adequate international "liquidity" and the development of an adjustment mechanism are the report's dominant concern in the field of international policy.

The Commission recommends explicitly that restrictive monetary and fiscal policies should not be used to correct a balance-of-payment deficit. Flexible exchange rates are not even mentioned as a possible alternative and exchange or quantitative trade control is evidently undesirable. But the Commission hopefully explores a host of institutional devices. Some unilateral arrangements, mostly dealing with possible information, insurance, and credit programs for United States exporters, are casually indicated. A variety of complex multilateral institutions requiring concerted action and policies is discussed in more detail. These institutions would also supply additional international "liquidity," balancing the increase in demand associated with expanding world trade under a regime of fixed exchange rates. A (more or less) uniform rise in the price of gold as a means of enlarging the trading nations' "liquidity base" is explicitly rejected by the report because of the unequally distributed benefits and the resulting allocation of resources to (an apparently useless?) gold production. The Commission's suggestions in the field of international finance require some critical analysis. It is quite possible that the political collaboration between debtor and creditor countries necessary to work the institutions proposed (for example, an international central bank) may actually emerge. It also may be the case that flexible exchange rates are definitely a suboptimal arrangement. Still, the judgments should rest on explicit analysis and adequate evidence. In particular, gold might appear as a (no doubt costly) substitute for political collaboration (not necessarily costless) and flexible exchange rates (*horribile dictu!*) a conceivably cheap substitute for gold which simultaneously solves the problems of international liquidity and adjustment.

The Commission's central contribution deals with the financial structure of the domestic economy. Most significant in the longer run is the deliberate appraisal of institutions in terms of their effect on the operation of the market mechanism and the economy's aggregative performance. Institutional innovations proposed for their own sake, or simply because "1960 is not 1920," are successfully resisted. Furthermore, the report does not hesitate to recommend the elimination of arrangements with no essential monetary function.

The systematic evaluation of our financial structure depends on a firm cognitive foundation. Intelligent judgment presupposes validated theoretical work, the construction and assessment of meaningful theories incorporating or bearing on important institutional detail. The Commission appears to have been aware of this. A large number of study papers covering many facets of our financial system have been prepared. Ultimate judgment of the Commission's contribution is therefore unavoidably suspended. But if the discussion presented in the report sharpens our awareness of the awkward situation in contemporary monetary theory and simultaneously awakens our appreciation of the potential power of systematic analysis we need not wait for the study papers to express our satisfaction with the Commission's achievements.

NOTES

1. *Money and Credit: Their Influence on Jobs, Prices, and Growth* (a report of the Commission on Money and Credit) (Englewood Cliffs, N.J.: Prentice-Hall, Inc., 1961).

2. A biased selection would be: (1) the section on differential effects of monetary policy (pp. 57–60, esp. the short summary on the lower half of p. 59); (2) the section on non-banking intermediaries (pp. 78–81); (3) the essentially descriptive section on the Treasury securities market (pp. 115–20); (4) the concise description of the working of political institutions in the last chapter.

3. The recommendations on pp. 69, 77–79, 113, 161–68, 204 refer to the Commission's most significant ideas relating to the improvement of the financial structure.

4. Examples of such recommendations are on pp. 87–89, 90, 174, 263, 272–73, 277, 281.

5. See Chapter 2.

6. The disagreement may be formalized as follows: Let p be the numerical value of the rate of change in the price level, $u =$ the rate of unemployment, $v =$ unfilled vacancies as a percentage of the labor force, $g =$ the growth rate; then we may write, for Ruttenberg,

$$U(p, u, g)$$
$$U_p < 0;\ U_u < 0 \equiv u > 3 \text{ per cent};\ U_g > 0;$$

for the Commission,

$$U(p, u - v, g)$$
$$U_p < 0 \qquad U_{u-v} < 0 \equiv u > v; \qquad U_g > 0.$$

7. See pp. 12, 35–39, 40.

8. Shuman [who is president of the American Farm Bureau Federation] comments on this point on p. 25.

9. An excellent analysis of the problem and the reason for the pattern of "structural unemployment" appears in Harold Demsetz, "Structural Unemployment: A Reconsideration of the Theory and the Evidence," *Journal of Law and Economics* (October 1961). Demsetz analyzes the data

made available by the Council of Economic Advisers and concludes that the data support the contention of structural unemployment and are not consistent with the C.E.A.'s interpretation, which asserts that this type of unemployment is negligible.

10. The report contains a short survey of inflation analysis (pp. 13–21). I wish to make two points with respect to this passage. First, the report grants entirely too much intellectual respectability to the notion of a "cost push." Reference to the Schultze hypothesis, particularly in connection with structural unemployment, is well conceived. Second, I find the discussion of the effects of inflation underlying the assumed negative social marginal utility of inflation quite unconvincing. Until some pertinent evidence has been exhibited, I doubt that the net debtor position of economic units is highly correlated with their total wealth. Without such correlation, inflation would not induce a regressive wealth redistribution. The report also mentions a wasteful allocation of resources. It would be useful to know more precisely what the Commission means by this. One possible interpretation refers to an inflation with a high degree of anticipation. In such a case economic units to a considerable extent will substitute real resources with a positive marginal opportunity cost for money balances with a negligible (social) marginal opportunity cost. Experience indicates that inflation must be quite substantial—and not of the 3–6 per cent variety—before anticipations emerge definitely enough to induce the above substitution process. Finally, the report mentions that inflation "tends to feed on itself." The only systematic study available on this problem, Cagan's analysis of hyperinflation, makes me rather skeptical of this beloved textbook formula.

11. Pages 32–33.

12. See p. 30, both text and notes.

13. See p. 54. The report contains some conflicting pieces of underlying analysis which exemplify the gaps and tenuous aspects of our cognitive comprehension. On pp. 78–81 the position of non-bank financial intermediaries in the financial nexus is appraised. The report considers particularly the notion of "offsetting velocity behavior" allegedly shaped by the evolving financial patterns. Evidently, some detailed empirical investigation led the Commission to reject the idea that non-bank financial intermediaries impair monetary policy by generating an offsetting velocity behavior. In the discussion of the Treasury's debt structure (pp. 102–3) the notion of an offsetting velocity behavior reappears. A high proportion of short debt is alleged to introduce destabilizing processes. Interest elasticity of money demand seems to be higher (numerically) with such a debt structure, and offsetting velocity behavior appears therefore more pronounced. It would be useful to have these ideas adequately explicated in a manner capable of empirical testing.

14. I had the opportunity to read preliminary drafts of two underlying study papers published subsequently by the Commission. One was M. Friedman and D. Meiselman, "The Relative Stability of Monetary Velocity and the Investment Multiplier in the United States, 1897–1958" [*Stabilization Policies* (Englewood Cliffs, N.J. 1963)]; section 6 of this study deals with "The Channels through Which Monetary Policy Works." The other paper was J. Tobin's "Essay on the Principles of Debt

Management" [*Fiscal and Debt Management Policies* (Englewood Cliffs, N.J. 1963)]. Both papers discuss various aspects of the balance-sheet reaction process or of the "portfolio-balance" analysis. See also the paper by P. Cagan which develops an analysis clearly moving in the same direction ("Why Do We Use Money in Open Market Operations?" *Journal of Political Economy*, Vol. 66 [February 1958]). Note also the following papers in the *Papers and Proceedings of the American Economic Association, 1961:* K. Brunner, "Some Major Problems in Monetary Theory"; H. G. Johnson, "The *General Theory* after Twenty-five Years"; J. Tobin, "Money, Capital and Other Stores of Value."

15. The issue turns on a *slope* property, that is, a reaction at the margin. Thus, if five out of one hundred interviewees say they react to interest-rate variations (accepting whatever is said at face value), then the results could hardly be construed to deny the existence of the slope property at issue.

16. The studies published in A. C. Harberger (ed.), *The Demand for Durable Goods* (Chicago: University of Chicago Press, 1960) bear significantly on the discussion in the text. I concur thoroughly with the report's declaration: "Unfortunately, studies of the actual behavior of business investment and interest rates have not reliably isolated the effects of monetary policy from shifts in other determinants of investments" (p. 52).

17. See pp. 48–49 of report. When the effect of a restrictive policy is discussed "credit" appears to play a crucial role in the transmission mechanism. At other places the money supply moves into the center of the policy considerations. See also p. 50.

18. See pp. 52–54.

19. To be published in two forthcoming papers: "The Structure of the Monetary System and the Supply Function of Money" and "Money Stock and Credit Market."

20. See p. 57. "If excessive liquidity positions of banks . . . and the public are not allowed to develop, and if the Federal Reserve and the Treasury take direct action to speed the adjustment process of long-term and short-term interest rates, the impact of monetary policy should be felt sooner." This passage of the report evidences no understanding of the connection between "excess liquidity" and the operation of the interest mechanism.

21. The second paper mentioned in note 19 develops a detailed analysis of the problem discussed in the text. It should be noted that Tobin's proposal to grant interest on excess reserves equal to the discount rate would help to some extent to remove the problem. Still, in the absence of a clear recognition of the problem there remains a good case for the abolition of discount facilities, particularly as "flexible adjustments of reserve positions" do not appear to hinge decisively on the discounting mechanism. Tobin's proposal could still be useful in the absence of discounting facilities.

22. See p. 68.

23. See p. 67. The report's formulation is indirect: "There is little clear evidence to indicate that the effects of open market operations are slower than those following reserve requirement changes."

24. The results concerning reserve requirements and the precision of control are based on an extensive discussion of the problem in the first paper mentioned in note 19. It should be noted that the Commission dismisses secondary reserve requirements and velocity requirements.

25. I was introduced to this idea by A. H. Meltzer, who presented it in an unpublished paper, "Monetary Policy, Debt Management, and the Dealers Market in Treasury Securities." He also referred to T. C. Gaines's *Techniques of Treasury Debt Management* (New York 1962), which appears to develop a similar proposal.

26. See p. 122.

27. It should be noted that the essential point is not affected by the choice of interpretation for Friedman's exponentially weighted average of past incomes, whether we understand it as an index of wealth or, as Klein insists, simply as a distributed lag in the influence of past income on current consumers' demand. The Modigliani-Friedman notion of wealth-dominated consumers' demand has an interesting implication with respect to a possible interpretation of the "burden of the debt," a problem considered by the Commission. A larger debt means a correspondingly large wealth position of the public—assuming that tax liabilities corresponding to the larger debt are not imputed in the wealth evaluations of the public. The greater wealth shifts output absorption from investment to consumption. The discounted yield stream associated with the resources reallocated from investment to consumers' goods may be understood as *some* measure for the burden of the debt.

The report's discussion of automatic stabilizers contains a strange assertion not justifiable in terms of standard (linear) models of income analysis. It is asserted that the strength of the built-in stabilizers depends on the ratio of government expenditures or taxes to national product. What is the base for this assertion—some peculiar non-linearities not considered in standard models?

21 Interest Rates and the Central Bank

Robert V. Roosa

Brown Brothers Harriman and Co., New York

Two decades ago it still bordered on heresy to suggest that central bank control over interest rates was useless as a restraint upon cyclical swings in the American economy. Today that heresy has become widely accepted as dogma.[1] But paradoxically the dominant importance acquired by the public debt in World War II has, at once, confirmed the adherents of the new dogma in their views, and raised new prospects for strengthening contra-cyclical credit policy in the United States through variations in interest rates. To those who already believed that guided variation in interest rates was largely futile, it was but a final, clinching development that an enlargement of the public debt should seem to narrow the range of permissible rate movement. Yet is may be precisely the conditions that now make it desirable, and possible, to limit rate variation which at the same time offer the central bank an opportunity for effective action.

Presumably, a limitation on the range of interest rate fluctuations is implied by the existence of a large public debt because the rate variations typical in the twenties and earlier would, in the new circumstances, set off a cumulative unloading or acquisition of debt instruments that would have harmful repercussions throughout the economy, and might perhaps (in the event of unloading) impair the

Government's credit. It is this fundamental concern, rather than the effect of rate changes on the Treasury's outlays for debt service, that makes a return to widely fluctuating rates unlikely. However, is this not merely to say, when examined in another light, that the securities and credit markets have become much more susceptible than they were years ago to any given change in interest rates? May it not also be significant that the presence of a substantial volume of Government securities in the debt structure, at all maturity periods, gives the central bank a medium through which it can directly influence the prices and yields on securities and credits of all terms? Is it not possible now that relatively small changes in interest rates, initiated or permitted by a central bank capable of reaching any segment of the rate structure, may give general credit policy an influence which it could not exert in the past?

These questions cannot, of course, be answered categorically, but the present paper aims deliberately at exploring the possibilities of an affirmative reply. For this purpose, administrative questions are not relevant; attention centers on the potential applications of central banking policy, not on whether that policy should in practice be administered by the Treasury, the Federal Reserve, or shared between them. It is relevant, but will not be labored here, that the great emphasis of the postwar years upon sustaining high levels of output and employment may itself produce an economic environment with a high susceptibility to inflationary distortions, and their aftermath—an environment in which the marginal influence of changes in credit availability may assume critical importance in finding a balance, from year to year, somewhere between the extremes of rigidity and instability.[2] This paper will limit itself, however, to a re-examination of some of the avenues for influencing economic activity through changes in market rates of interest, as these changes may be guided or controlled by the central bank.

At one time it was thought that changes in market rates of interest provided a satisfactory explanation—and central bank control over rates an adequate corrective—for cyclical economic disturbance. But experience proved disappointing. In part, the failings of earlier analysis and policy may be attributed to a misdirection of emphasis. Economists and central banking theorists long believed that the significance of market rates of interest, and of central banking efforts to vary these rates, lay in the effects produced upon *borrowers*, and upon *savers*. Little if any attention was given to *lenders*; their function was considered that of automatic response to central bank action, without any meaningful independent influence on economic behavior. Insofar as writers did attach some importance to changes in the "availability of credit," they failed to see that any general control over changes in credit availability was inseparably linked to changes in interest rates. Consequently, as experience and direct investigation revealed a rather wide range of indifference to rate changes among borrowers, and suggested that saving was closely related to such other factors as changes in income, there was an understandable slackening in the enthusiasm for central bank control over rates as a positive method of moderating cyclical fluctuation.

In part, too, environmental changes can account for the failure of interest rates to arouse the expected response from borrowers and savers during the twenties and thirties. Although both may have been more responsive to interest rate fluctuations in an earlier day, changes were taking place in the debt structure, and in the flow of loanable funds through institutional intermediaries, which increased the independent significance of the lending function in the financing mechanism of the American economy. There was, in effect, a cultural lag between the development of the theory of interest rates and of central banking, on the one hand, and the changing characteristics of the money markets, on the other. Moreover, since the shifts in credit availability which rate changes reflect can be only one of many influences upon the stability of the economy, the significance of changes in lender behavior might well have gone unnoticed by those earlier students who were hoping to find in rate movements and central bank action a complete solution to the problem of cyclical fluctuations.

Now that the leavening phases of exaggerated emphasis, and of reaction and disillusionment, have been passed, it should be useful to attempt a fresh review of the part which interest rate variations effected by the central bank can play in moderating cyclical swings in the American economy, to see where we have come out. This will be attempted here, first, by reviewing a few of the landmarks in the vast literature that has appeared on this question during the first half of the present century; second, by describing the major institutional changes affecting the flow of lendable funds and the money markets in the United States, particularly those occurring since the establishment of the Federal Reserve System in 1914; and third, by discussing the substance of central bank rate action, as applied to short-term rates, long-term rates, and the interrelations between them.

The Development of Concepts[3]

From the Wicksell of *Interest and Prices*[4] to the Keynes of the *General Theory*,[5] despite the twists and turns of interest rate and central banking theory at other hands over the intervening years, the main stream of analysis implicitly accepted three underlying propositions. First, a change in rates at the central bank would actually assure a roughly corresponding change at the commercial banks. Second, by focusing attention on "the" interest rate, most writers assumed a synchronous movement throughout the rates on comparable debt instruments of all maturities; that is, a change at the commercial banks was expected to spread throughout the short-term market and on through all other maturities. Third, once rate changes were achieved through central bank action, they would be followed by appropriate action on the part of borrowers (and, most writers would have added, on the part of savers). Only if all three of these presumed relationships were to hold would it be possible to go on further to accomplish precise objectives in terms of the money supply, the price level, and the control of the business cycle.

During the first and second decades of Federal Reserve operations, most American writers supported doctrines similar to those of Wicksell. There was little awareness of the three underlying assumptions implied by such doctrines, nor of possible gaps between concept and reality at any of these three critical stages in the credit process. Such writers as Irving Fisher, having developed the equation of exchange into the quantity theory of money, devoted themselves instead to clarifying the purposes for which the presumably powerful central bank controls should be used. Only the Federal Reserve System itself, facing the concrete problems of implementation, saw the possible gaps and entertained a genuine skepticism over the feasibility of bridging them.

When the reaction against central banking and the significance of interest rates began in the mid-twenties, two writers with broad backgrounds of experience within the System undertook some clarification. Pointing out the exaggerated nature of the claims that had been made for central banking, Burgess in 1927 and Riefler in 1930 showed the limitations existing at each of the three stages which separate central bank action from its end results. A change in discount rate, even when reinforced by the newly discovered use of open market operations, would not automatically induce corresponding rate changes among the commercial banks. Moreover, interest rate changes themselves (once achieved in the market) were regarded as important chiefly "as the outward evidence of changes in underlying credit conditions."[6] Burgess pointed out that ". . . the importance of a change in the discount rate lies principally in its being a public recognition by a group of responsible and well-informed people of a change in the credit situation."[7] Riefler also found that rate changes by the central bank or the commercial banks (appropriately confined to short-term debt by the traditions of the "commercial loan theory") might extend with diminished force, if at all, into the long-term segment of the debt structure.[8]

But the most important controversy appeared at the third stage—the effects of rate changes upon borrowing and saving. Keynes, for example, held in the *Treatise* that only the long-term rate could be effective in bringing saving and investment into equilibrium.[9] And in the *General Theory*, having discovered the tautology which relieved him of concern over a divergence between saving and investment, he still regarded "the" interest rate as the determinant (in conjunction with the marginal efficiency of capital) of private investment.[10] Hawtrey was most prominent among those who placed reliance on the short-term rate, which influenced the working capital investment of traders, and affected saving primarily through the resulting effects of the traders' actions upon the price level.[11] The eventual reaction of many writers to the disputes between "the short-enders and the long-enders" was to disown both. Hicks, for one, had by 1939 come to the position that rate movements within the "ordinary range (say between 2 per cent and 7 per cent per annum) . . . ." could have at best only a slight effect upon short-term borrowers; while the longer-term borrowers, who should find their capitalized present values more sharply affected by interest rate changes, would discover that their necessary "risk-allowance will become so large as to wipe out any possible gains."[12]

The Oxford surveys of 1938 and 1940, questioning businessmen concerning the importance of interest rates in their decisions, reinforced Professor Hicks' iconoclasm.[13] But the later of the two questionnaires, better devised and reaching a wider sample of respondents, showed the door opening upon what has become, at least in the United States since World War II, the dominant significance of interest rates and of central bank controls. Roughly a quarter of the replies indicated that the *availability* of bank credit, or of funds obtained through the securities markets, affected businessmen's decisions to make (or the *timing* of their decisions to make) expenditures upon new plant, or upon repairs and maintenance, or upon inventories.[14] It follows, although the Oxford writers did not draw this conclusion from their own data, that if changes in various market rates of interest exert an important influence upon the extent to which *lenders* make funds available, those rates will have some appreciable influence upon economic activity.

Although Burgess and Riefler both saw that rates and credit availability were reflections of each other, rather than separate compartments of the financial mechanism, it was not until 1941 that the full relevance of this fact to monetary policy began to emerge in published discussion, notably in Professor Williams' address at the annual meetings of the American Economic Association.[15] From that point on, largely through an oral medium, without benefit of a published written record, Williams has taken the leadership in focusing attention on the lenders, and on the significance of interest rates as a symptom of the factors causing a tightening or loosening in the new credit made available by lenders.[16] In essence, it is not necessarily interest rates as a cost to the borrower, nor as an inducement to the saver, but rather interest rates as a reflection of underlying changes in credit availability, that have an important (though certainly not always a decisive) impact upon the generation of business cycles. The changed character of the debt and the changes in the flow of loanable funds—which have raised this aspect of interest rates to new prominence and have created a high degree of market sensitivity to influences reflected in relatively slight movements of rates—are described in the following section.

Changing Characteristics of the Credit System

The fundamental structural changes affecting the significance of central bank control over interest rates have themselves, in turn, resulted from many causes. For present purposes those causes are not relevant. What matters is that the size and composition of the net debt of the economy, the institutional channels through which resources pass into the holdings of that debt, and the organization of the markets in which debt instruments are bought and sold, have all changed considerably since the Federal Reserve System began operations in 1914. It is important to identify the major developments, and to interpret their consequences for effective central bank action.

THE MAJOR DEVELOPMENTS[17]

1. *The "supply" of debt instruments.* In 1914, it was roughly correct to say that all of the ultimate net debt of the economy embodied some degree of credit risk.[18] The general public could choose between holding cash and holding risk assets; and the commercial banks in turn held risk assets, in large measure, as the collateral supporting the bank deposits which represented most of the cash. The calculus of the choice between cash (or idle reserves) and risk assets involved not only liquidity preference (with its complex of determining motives), but also an allowance for credit risk. Yet it was the "pure" rates with which the prevailing theory, and the prescriptions for central bank action, were concerned. Not until a form of debt instrument free of credit risk should become a dominant part of the total debt, extending through a representative

selection of all maturities, would it be possible to distinguish sharply the effects of time and liquidity preference (net of the credit risk factors) for a given money supply at a given point in time. Moreover, only then would it be possible for market forces to reveal unambiguously (through comparison with the schedule of rates free of credit risk) the magnitude of risk differentials among various types of debt, and perhaps to point up the significance of efforts to influence the risk premium itself.

By the end of World War II, such an environment had been created as a result of the enormous growth of the public debt. Total net debt in the United States, both public and private, was roughly 65 billion dollars in 1914. It had doubled by 1919; tripled by 1929; emerged about the same as a decade earlier by 1939; and was more than six times the 1914 figure by 1948. Meanwhile the proportion of Federal Government securities in the total had grown from 1.5 per cent in 1914 to 50.4 per cent in 1948. Short-term debt, which the traditions of the commercial loan theory made the special province of commercial banks, had shrunk from 40.9 per cent of total net debt in 1914 to 30.0 per cent in 1948; and the proportion of Government securities in the total of short-term debt had risen from a negligible figure to nearly one third.[19] Among the short-term debt instruments used actively for bank reserve adjustments in the New York money market, Government securities had risen from a volume of virtually no significance in 1914 to about one sixth of the total in 1924, and to more than nine tenths of the total in 1948.

2. *The "demand" for debt instruments.* By 1948, the choice confronting any lender was no longer between cash and the short- or long-term debt instruments of private borrowers, but among cash, Government securities of all practicable maturities, and the debt of private individuals or corporations. And certain institutional changes, marked by the channeling of loanable resources into highly specialized investment concerns, had made lenders acutely sensitive to slight changes in the yield differentials among alternatives, both short and long. A steadily growing popular insistence on "security"—the avoidance of loss, at the expense of accepting lesser yields—had favored the growth of conservative intermediary institutions, operating on relatively narrow margins, and alert to small changes among the yields on debt instruments that would have been considered trivial a few decades earlier. While statistical pitfalls in double-counting challenge any effort to describe accurately the growing "institutionalization of savings" in the United States, there is a basis for very rough generalization. It appears that in 1914 more than one half of the ultimate net debt was held directly by the corporations or individuals providing the

resources. By 1948, barely one quarter of the ultimate debt was held directly; the remainder was held through financial intermediaries.

3. *Organization and mechanics of the money market.*[20] The changing composition of the debt and the shifting distribution of debt holding were accompanied by a third set of changes of major significance. The organized markets through which issuers or sellers and purchasers or holders of debt were brought together also adapted themselves to the altered character of the supply and demand for debt instruments. During the twenties and thirties, trading in Government securities became increasingly specialized in an over-the-counter market among dealers, and transactions through the stock exchange dwindled to insignificance. By the middle thirties the principal dealers themselves had become part of an informal market organization in which the Federal Reserve Bank of New York, as agent for the Federal Open Market Committee, exerted an increasingly influential role. And as the market demand became more and more sensitive to slight changes in rates, both as among various types of Government securities and between Governments and the debt instruments (including loans) of the private sector, the mechanics of market quotation also reflected the change.

For example, throughout the twenties (and until they disappeared temporarily from use in 1934) certificates, the Government's one-year debt instrument, were traded in terms of price per 100 dollars of par value, just as bonds are traded today. The unit of price change was in thirty-seconds, that is, roughly equivalent to 3 cents per 100 dollars of par value. And the spreads between bid and offer quotations, representing the cost of turn-around sale and repurchase, were rarely less than $\frac{2}{32}$ (or 6 cents per 100 dollars), often rising to $\frac{10}{32}$ (about 30 cents per 100 dollars). Month-to-month variations in effective yield were frequently $\frac{1}{2}$ of 1 per cent even during relatively tranquil periods, becoming much greater in the event of disturbance. Having been reintroduced as a market instrument in 1942, certificates are no longer quoted on a price basis but in fine graduations of yield. Use is now made of "basis points" of $\frac{1}{100}$ each (corresponding to one cent per 100 dollars). Price spreads, instead of ranging from 6 cents to 30 cents, are usually about 2 cents on the longer certificates; in actual trading, markets are often narrowed to one.[21] The month-to-month yield variation in placid periods is now customarily in the neighborhood of $\frac{1}{16}$ of 1 per cent, or even less, instead of $\frac{1}{2}$, with other fluctuations correspondingly narrowed.

Changes of comparable significance have occurred in the bond market over this same period, and have been reflected as well in the market which grew up for Treasury bills (i.e., three-month instruments) after they were first introduced in the United States at the end of 1929. As a corollary of these changing characteristics in the market pricing of Governments, underwriters' bidding and the sale of new issues of corporate and municipal bonds or debentures during recent years have also developed a sensitivity to very small changes. Successful bidding has, since the end of the war, often depended on differences in the third decimal place of an intended yield.[22] It is such changes in customary market practices which indicate, more convincingly than abstract analysis, that the increasing relative importance of Government securities, and the growing concentration of investible funds in the hands of yield-conscious institutions, have made the money markets highly susceptible to slight changes in interest rates.

THE CONSEQUENCES FOR CENTRAL BANK ACTION

The paradoxical result of the major developments just described has been to create an environment in which the three unstated premises of Wicksellian theory became, with important modifications, finally fulfilled. These premises, as noted above, fitted the three stages between action by the central bank and eventual reaction by the economy: (1) the direct effect of central bank action upon commercial banks and their loan rates; (2) the fluidity between short-term banking rates and long-term rates; and (3) the influence of the tightening or loosening of credit, as reflected in market rate changes, upon significant economic decisions—to borrow for capital expenditure, to save, or to lend. These developments also raise new questions concerning possible limitations on the effectiveness of central bank action, and alter materially the use which can be made of changes in reserve requirements to affect the availability of bank credit.

1. *The direct impact of central bank action.* While the central bank has used, and continues to use, the discount rate as a direct influence upon the cost of credit at commercial banks, and as a symbol to the economy of a general change in the economic weather and of central bank policy, the new environment now provides the central bank with direct access to the going rate structure as well. It is no longer sufficient to consider the effects of the discount rate upon commercial bank borrowing from the central bank, the effects of that borrowing upon bank rates and the money supply, and the effects of those in turn upon the entire level and structure of interest rates.[23] For open market operations in Government securities bring the central bank into contact not only with the volume of available bank reserves, but also with the portfolios of all classes of lenders. Open market purchases may not only increase the primary reserves of the commercial banking system, but

also the loanable funds of private investors who have sold Governments; and as a counterpart of such a change in the volume of funds potentially available for new commitments, some or all interest rates may decline. Conversely, System sales, or merely an unwillingness to purchase, may drive down the prices of Government securities as potential lenders attempt to acquire fresh funds by unloading Governments, and the associated rise in rates will signify a growing tightness in credit availability.

2. *Interrelations between short-term and long-term rates.* Because of the relatively high proportion of Government debt to total debt, at all relevant maturities, the behavior of prices for Government securities will directly influence the actual availability of credit for alternative uses (at each maturity) and virtually determine the approximate level of "basic" yields, as well as the direction of change in yields. And the prices of all Governments can be reached (or allowed to move without offsetting interference) through the System's open market operations. Effective central bank action is no longer limited to the roundabout results achieved through influencing the indebtedness of commercial banks (or the reverse— the volume of their excess reserves). Moreover, there is no longer any impediment to a substantial flow of resources back and forth between the short-term and long-term markets. Such switches, compounded of judgments concerning both the economic situation and the market intentions of the System authorities, have not only become a commonplace, they have actually degenerated into a disruptive "playing the pattern of rates" on several occasions during and following World War II.

Moreover, the commercial banks themselves are no longer confined to short-term obligations; more than one half the earning assets of the member banks in 1948 carried maturities beyond one year, while the estimated proportion in 1914 was one sixth. Not only longer-term Government securities, but also term loans and amortized mortgages, accounted for this shift in the direct impact of the banks upon the longer-term market.

Clearly, through the medium of Government securities and the lengthened term distribution of "bankable" private debt, a real fluidity is imparted to movements between the short-term and long-term markets. And while it may generally be expected that longer-term yields will not shift as swiftly as the shorter-terms in response to the changes in credit availability associated with day-to-day variations in the economic outlook, the long-term market will definitely be influenced by any sustained ease or tightening in the short-term market. The first two of Wicksell's implicit premises have, therefore, been reasonably well satisfied.

3. *Rate changes and the decisions to borrow, to save, or to lend.* There is little doubt that Wicksell, his contemporaries, and his followers

exaggerated the direct significance of market rates of interest as cost elements affecting decisions to borrow for investment; the niceties of logical refinement, in isolating any one variable for marginal analysis, frequently result in an excess of zeal for the influence of the variable studied. Nonetheless, Wicksell had more on his side than recent critics have allowed. Interest rates do have some importance as a cost factor, particularly with respect to the timing of decisions concerning changes in inventory or plant where the ratio of stocks to sales, or of equipment to sales, is relatively high.

So far as saving is concerned, it may well be income and a host of other factors that dominate the decisions of individuals, rather than changes in the inducement offered by interest rates. But a phenomenon little noticed by the Wicksellians has come to overshadow personal savings in importance in the United States. Business savings, gross or net, have generally exceeded personal savings in recent years. And the critical decision as to whether or not to pay out dividends, or retain profits for internal use, may be materially affected by changes in interest rates. In general, rising rates encourage a greater financing of internal expansion through retained earnings; that is, rising rates tend to increase savings.

But it is the lender, neglected by the monetary theorists, who does most to put new substance in the older doctrine. As pages 572–79 will indicate in further detail, rate changes brought about by the open market operations of the central bank influence the disposition or the ability of lenders to make funds available to borrowers, either for the continuation of outstanding indebtedness or for incurring new debt to finance expansion.

4. *Limitations upon central bank action.* In addition to the obvious fact that interest rates and credit availability alone cannot determine the level of economic activity, and can at best exert but one set of pressures among many, there are two major limitations upon the use which can be made of central bank control over rates. First, the Treasury has an inevitable bias toward low, and relatively constant, interest rates on the Government debt; it faces both the budgetary necessity of holding down the aggregate burden of debt service, and the managerial responsibility for continually refinancing annual maturities that now constitute about $\frac{1}{5}$ of the outstanding public debt. Second, although business decisions to retain earnings may to some extent be indirectly influenced by changes in interest rates (as already noted), the secular growth in internal financing (particularly among manufacturing corporations) tends to insulate many businesses from the direct effects of changes in credit availability.

Neither need be a debilitating limitation, however. So far as the Treasury is concerned, it can give up the comforts of low and constant yields in periods when these are attainable only by releases of

Federal Reserve credit that would result in inflationary expansion and a sustained depreciation in the purchasing power of the dollar. Moreover, with the money markets sensitive to small changes in interest rates, it is not likely that the Treasury would ever have to face wide swings in its issuing rates. Whatever swings occur may, furthermore, offset each other over time. A rise in rates associated with tighter credit will presumably be followed by rate reductions in periods of ease, so that although the Treasury's interest charge on current refinancing may vary from year to year, the long-time average of the debt burden need not necessarily be altered materially under a flexible program of central banking control over credit and rates.

While some segments of the economy may be more nearly independent of outside financing than was true in the earlier years of this century, the influence of changes in credit availability for the economy as a whole remains significant. There probably is, as suggested earlier, some marginal interrelationship between the current behavior of the money markets and business decisions to retain profits; in general, rising rates (or a heightened state of uncertainty) should stimulate the retention of earnings. Even if there were no such relationship, the implied market judgment of the business outlook, associated with changes in interest rates and credit availability, will itself (along with other factors) exert some influence upon business decisions to expand capacity or output, or to postpone such action. Further, there still remain large sectors of the economy which depend heavily upon the credit available from lenders. Much of the construction industry, and a high proportion of railroad and public utility investment, for example, require substantial outside financing;[24] the same is true for most wholesalers and retailers.

5. *Interest rates and changes in reserve requirements.* There is another implication for credit control in the widespread holding of the public debt—an implication which has not yet been fully appreciated. That is, changes in reserve requirements have now become a poor substitute for open market operations in exerting a contra-cyclical influence upon the availability of bank credit. For when all banks hold large portfolios of Government securities, which they regard as the closest substitute for excess reserves, a change in requirements may have no more than a moderate psychological effect upon the bank credit extended to private borrowers. Instead, a higher requirement, for example, may lead mainly to a shift of Governments from the banks into the Federal Reserve, *unless* interest rates on the Governments are allowed to rise as the Federal Reserve "backs away" from the securities being offered to it. Because of the large volume of Government securities

now wedged between bank reserve balances and their private credits, open market operations, rather than the blunt impact of changes in reserve requirements, provide the most flexible and effective method for bringing about changes in the availability of credit in the highly sensitive money markets that have evolved over recent years.

Thus, it is a mistake to suppose that changes in the reserve requirements applicable to member banks can, in the new environment created by a large public debt, effectively accomplish a material change in the availability of short-term (or of long-term) bank credit without affecting interest rates.[25] If reserve requirements are raised while at the same time the central bank is attempting to hold the interest rates on Government securities constant, there will be an ample flow of new central bank credit to absorb all of the Governments which the banks wish to unload; there must be, to prevent a price decline. In that event, there will simply be a reduction in the volume of bank-held Government securities (corresponding closely to the amount of the added reserve requirements) and a parallel rise in central bank purchases, without any necessarily significant effect upon the extension of private credit. Tightening can only be achieved through an increase in reserve requirements if that action is carried out as a form of open market operations, with the Federal Reserve, in effect, forcing the banks to meet the requirement either by selling their Government securities to nonbank investors, or by curtailing their private credits. To do that, the Federal Reserve must be able to lower the prices at which it purchases Government securities. The desired degree of tightness can no doubt be obtained with a relatively small price (rate) change—so small, perhaps, as superficially to appear trivial. But the potency of such a change comes from the impact of "uncertainty" upon markets dominated by sensitive investors; and there can be no uncertainty if the central bank is committed in advance to pegged support of Government securities at the prices and rates attached to those securities when they were issued in the past.

Nor can the inevitable link between changes in credit availability and changes in interest rates be broken by a compromise approach—compelling member banks to hold interest-earning Government securities instead of additional reserve balances, in the event of a rise (for example) in reserve requirements. For so long as banks hold a substantial volume of Government securities outside the security-reserve, marginal changes in the credit available at the banks will depend on possible shifts between their "free" Government securities and other debt instruments. Only if rates are permitted to rise, can credit extension based on the funds obtained through sale of the "free" Government securities be restrained. The effective restraint would still be that imposed by the rate changes (and by expectations of rate changes). To attempt to avoid the fundamental interrelationship between rates on Government securities and the general availability of bank credit by freezing *all* bank holdings of Governments into such reserves would be impractical and grossly inequitable. The proportions of Government securities held by the various individual banks differ widely, ranging roughly from 20 per cent to 80 per cent of total deposits. Even if such a freeze were feasible, fresh credit could still be provided by all lenders other than member banks so long as the Federal Reserve were purchasing freely the Government securities offered for sale by other lenders. And each sale of Governments to the central bank by nonbank lenders would, in turn, increase the reserves of the banking system—permitting multiple bank credit expansion upon these reserves unless the central bank could re-absorb them through open market sales (an unlikely expedient if short- and long-term security prices were being supported).

It appears impossible, therefore, to use reserve requirements (whether applied to reserve balances or to a security-reserve) as an effective direct control over credit availability, *unless* interest rates can move to express the intended tightening (or loosening) of credit. Any effective control must always come back to interest rates. No mechanical contrivance, aimed at immobilizing a part of commercial bank portfolios, can effect a short-cut around the variable interest rates which accompany changes in credit availability. The place for changes in reserve requirements, under postwar conditions, would seem to be largely that of effecting long-run structural adjustments in the ultimate reserves of the banking system, not in independently attempting the contra-cyclical regulation of credit availability, a function better served by open market operations (with changes in the discount rate giving emphasis to particular market developments).

The Scope of Central Bank Action

The views expressed in this paper represent a reaction against a reaction; they do not by any means, however, imply a return to the original conception of central bank rate policy as the touchstone of economic stability. Through its effects upon lenders, and in lesser measure through its effects upon borrowing and upon saving, the central bank action that is possible through interest rate flexibility can, however, exert some moderating restraint upon cyclical swings in the economy. The possibilities for purposeful action may conveniently be considered under three headings: short-term rates, long-term rates, and the relationship between short- and long-term rates.

SHORT-TERM RATES

Because short-term securities and loans usually comprise the greatest proportion of resources "on move the," central bank action will generally be concentrated on short-term rates. For the same reason, changes in the behavior and expectations of lenders will most frequently be reflected in the short-term sector. Short-term rates will, therefore, customarily be the first to register a change in the underlying credit situation—whether that change has originated with the Federal Reserve or with the private sector, or both. Fluctuations in the short-term rates on Government securities are consequently important not only for their effect in increasing or decreasing the attractiveness of alternative short-term loans or investments, but also as a signal of possible further changes throughout longer-term segments of the rate structure. A decline, however slight, if sustained for any appreciable length of time will create uncertainty over the possibility that credit may be turning generally easier, and that other rates may also fall. A rise may set off an opposite chain of expectations. And oftentimes the mere indication of a change in the direction of rate movements may be enough to transform many of the dominant institutions from willing to reluctant lenders, or the reverse. Or, given a gradual development of small rate changes, in an upward direction for example, one more slight twist of the screw may be sufficient to deter a lender's commitment of funds, turning him toward the relative security of a short-term Government issue until the growing uncertainty shall have cleared away.

The pattern of lender reactions need not necessarily be the same for a change of the same direction, or the same magnitude, at two different points in time. The one assured fact is that lenders will always be sensitive to slight changes, careful to balance the possible capital loss (or gain) resulting from a rise (or reduction) in rates against the possibilities of a greater (or lower) yield. But because lenders cannot always be expected to take the same steps following a given rate change, the System's open market account cannot be operated according to a formula. Operations must instead be based on continuous close study of the money markets. Achievement of a desired degree of ease or of restraint will depend heavily on the ability of the central bank officials to "play by ear." And the supreme advantage of open market operations for this purpose is that they can proceed in small steps,[26] where appropriate; they need not be accompanied by formal announcements of intentions, with the rigidity and the possible exaggerated emphasis inherent in such announcements; and they can be readily reversed if the desired response is attained more quickly than expected, or in the event of a subsequent change in the underlying market situation. When emphasis upon a particular rate change is required, both for its direct market impact and its psychological repercussions, the Reserve Banks can complement the effect of their open market operations upon short-term rates by changing their discount rates.

The effects of these short-rate changes are threefold. First, they enable the central bank to absorb or to release reserve funds on its own initiative, thereby altering the general supply of funds available for credit expansion. Second, they cause a change in the willingness of lenders to make funds available for short-term private credits—not, for example, because a rise of $\frac{1}{8}$ of 1 per cent in the bill rate will shut off all other loans being made at 2, or 3, or 4 per cent, but because the uncertainty over further rises will cause hesitation, an unwillingness to go all the way in a new commitment if rates may be generally higher a few weeks later on, a shortening in commitment terms, and a general desire "to wait and see." Third, short-rate changes immediately affect expectations concerning the long-term market, and carry over directly into that market if they are sustained, thereby exerting an important effect upon the timing of lenders' long-term commitments (and of lenders' decisions to switch between long-term Governments and private issues).

LONG-TERM RATES

In addition to influencing the movement of long-term rates, and expectations concerning the future behavior of long rates, through changes in the short-term sector, the central bank may also exert its influence directly upon the prices of long-term securities. Prices were, of course, effectively pegged by the support program initiated during the last war. The measures since taken to unloosen these rigid pegs have themselves resulted, in effect, in central bank guidance of the rate levels. Moreover, it seems inevitable that rate changes in the long-term sector, just as in the short, must henceforth be a reflection of central bank policy, regardless of the actual factors setting off such change, and regardless of any desire there might be to avoid placing such rate responsibility in the central bank.

The choice is not between central bank control and reliance upon "free market prices," but among alternative uses of the inherent power imposed upon the central bank by the existence of the large public debt. That power will be exercised, whether consciously or unconsciously; and whether by the Treasury or the Federal Reserve. The need is for purposeful direction, based upon an understanding of the influences which changes in long-term rates may bring about.

Already the postwar experience suggests that yield changes of scarcely $\frac{1}{8}$ of 1 per cent for the longest-term bonds have considerable market effects.[27] A rise in long-term rates, initiated to reinforce a tightened credit policy, tends to exert a restraining influence upon the lending policies of banks and other lenders, particularly with respect to term loans, thereby slowing up the business expansion dependent upon longer-term financing. The market pricing of new security issues is also immediately affected, and new issues may for a time be held back, leading in some cases to indefinite postponement. As dealers encounter difficulty in retailing issues already "on the shelves," their receptiveness to new issues is notably chilled. At the very least, a greater "spacing-out" of new issues results, in comparison to the flow that would otherwise have occurred. An even sharper effect is exerted upon lenders' attitudes toward mortgages. With most mortgages now carrying conventional interest rates, kept in place by the influence of various guarantee arrangements, any appreciable evidence of an upward trend in long-term rates is associated with an immediate tightening in the availability of mortgage credit. Moreover, any resulting rise in effective mortgage rates (outside the relatively rigid guarantee programs) will raise the total costs of new building to the borrower considerably, since the financing cost is normally a high proportion of the total. Potential borrowers and builders may, therefore, also be discouraged by the rise in (unguaranteed) mortgage rates which usually follows an increase in yields on Government securities, as well as by the reduced availability of mortgage funds.

Conversely, a lowering of yields on long-term Government securities has appreciably stimulative effects. Banks are encouraged to take some of the resulting capital gains on their long-term Government bonds, placing the proceeds in credits to private borrowers. The impetus to the desired bank action may be somewhat weaker in the case of rate reductions than of rate increases, particularly after very low rates have been in effect over a long period. But the initial effect at the time of the rate reduction (provided the economy is not in a state of panic, or utter collapse) can be important. A yield reduction will also usually lead to aggressive purchases of non-Government securities by most lenders, clearing the dealers' shelves of old issues that may have been hard to sell previously, and opening the way for ready financing of newly arising (or previously postponed) issues, as the carrying capacity of dealers is increased by their unloading of old inventories. A comparable stimulus will be given to mortgage financing.

The market conditions governing such changes in yields, so long as the direction and extent of further change is uncertain, will alternately discourage or encourage potential borrowers, who depend upon receptive and favorable markets for obtaining the outside debt financing which their new undertakings require.[28]

The calculus confronting conservative lenders, alert to fractional differences in their portfolio earnings and portfolio values, can be readily illustrated by a few simple computations in investment mathematics. Suppose, for example, that a term structure of rates on Government securities roughly comparable to the 1948 yield curve had been prevailing for some period of time. That is, yields would have been running from $1\frac{1}{4}$ per cent on Government bonds within one year of call date to $2\frac{1}{2}$ per cent on similar issues extending 20 years to call. A uniform rise of $\frac{1}{8}$ of 1 per cent in the market yields throughout this curve would present lenders with the following typical calculations. A newly issued 20-year Government bond, bearing a coupon rate of $2\frac{1}{2}$ per cent, would drop $1\frac{15}{16}$ per cent below par; the capital loss on sale would be about $19.40 per $1,000. A similar bond with the same coupon, purchased on the old yield curve when it had 15 years to run, would fall about $15.60 per $1,000 (par value). The same type of bond, purchased at the previous rates with 10 years to run, would fall $12.50 per $1,000 (par value). These capital losses would be roughly doubled if the yield curve rose by $\frac{1}{4}$ of 1 per cent instead of by $\frac{1}{8}$, and would be nearly four times as great with an upward shift in the yield curve of $\frac{1}{2}$ of 1 per cent. The capital losses on the 20-year bond, for example, would be approximately 4 and 8 per cent, respectively, of the principal amount.

To shift from such bonds into a higher yield (and presumably relatively safe) short-term private loan would require a rate differential sufficiently large to absorb this capital loss, with something left over to make the shift attractive. Or to shift into an alternative long-term private investment would require a yield sufficiently high, after allowance for a necessary risk differential, to cover the writing-off of the capital loss on the lender's sale of his Government bond, and to produce a gain in average net income over time.[29]

Of course, the converse also follows: a stimulus to sales, and to the transfer of resources into other alternatives, would be provided by reductions in the yields on Government bonds. For simplicity, it may be sufficient to consider the capital gain on a 20-year ($2\frac{1}{2}$ per cent) Government bond, following yield reductions from the original yield curve described above. A yield decline of $\frac{1}{8}$ of 1 per cent would provide a capital gain of nearly 2 per cent; a decline of $\frac{1}{4}$, a gain of 4 per cent in sale price; and a decline of $\frac{1}{2}$, a gain of about $8\frac{1}{2}$ per cent in price over the principal amount of the original purchase. Lenders may, of course, when confronted by such prospects, merely sell long Governments to obtain the capital gain and go back into short Governments to await better yields in the long-term sector, with no apparent increase in the credit currently available to the private economy. This is one form of the possible abuses of "rate playing"; but undesirable rate playing can be checked (if it should occur in more than a few isolated instances) by encouraging wider fluctuations in short rates, thereby injecting greater uncertainty into the short end of the yield curve. Moreover, this is not a usual phenomenon. The actual result, if declining rates are at all likely to continue, will no doubt be that many lenders tempted to unload their long Governments will switch into another block of long-term debt instruments—real estate mortgages, utility bonds, term loans (and direct placements), or the bonds of manufacturing and trade corporations. Moreover, a freshening of demand for these issues creates a favorable climate for the offering of more, and even borrowers who may consider interest rates of no significance to their own decisions will be activated by the evidence of an increased availability of long-term funds.

No doubt the restraint or the stimulus provided to credit expansion through changes in long-term rates will never turn the course of economic activity alone. But rate changes can certainly exert some influence upon the flow of funds and the timing of new undertakings. If not consciously controlled, or worse still, if irrevocably "pegged," the long-term market will inevitably add cumulative force to any major cyclical swings of the economy. Properly guided—not with central bank pinpointing of rates, but with central bank action at critical junctures to bring about changes in the direction and pace of rate movements—the long-term market can, by spacing the flow of funds into longer-term investment opportunities, make a positive contribution toward lessening the amplitude of booms and depressions.

THE RELATION BETWEEN SHORT- AND LONG-TERM RATES

Most of the interrelations between short- and long-term rates that would affect the decisions of lenders have necessarily been described in the preceding sections; neither end of the rate structure can be discussed as a closed compartment. There is, however, another important aspect of the interrelationship which remains to be clarified. Emphasis has been placed throughout this analysis upon the great significance of small changes—the creation of some uncertainty, a simple reversal in direction of change, or a small change in magnitude—as influences upon lender behavior. The implications of such an analysis for changes in long-term rates may be intuitively convincing, for their effects upon capital values are demonstrable and impressive; and the great pressure of demand from the dominant lenders (many of whom must satisfy an actuarial type of income requirement) will create a keen sensitivity to slight variations in yield. But granting that only moderate changes in long rates are, in present circumstances, likely to be permitted, and that within this range an effective influence can be exerted upon lenders through small rate changes, does this not also imply a low ceiling on possible fluctuations of short-term rates? And if so, will not the principal lenders soon come to realize that the range of movement for short-term rates is very narrow indeed, and that the significance of any uncertainty arising from changes within this slender band is relatively trivial?

Such skepticism is prompted, of course, by the characteristic yield curve to which lenders became accustomed over the decade of the forties, when the gently upward sloping schedule that was frozen in by central bank action at the beginning of the war eventually acquired in some circles the status of "natural" permanence. But there is no necessity for maintaining the differentials of the recent past. The differentials suitable for bringing about a change in the market will depend upon the underlying supply and demand for funds, and upon the intensity and speed of the central bank's action to tighten or loosen credit. There is no inherent structural reason why short-term rates should not reach or exceed the long-terms in periods that require a vigorous tight money policy; the short-term nature of such a rise would deter any wholesale unloading of longs by investors who would like to "cash in" on a brief period of high short rates. Moreover, changes in the spread between the shortest and longest rates can, in appropriate circumstances, be as much a part of the central bank's rate policy as the individual changes of such rates themselves. And in general, of course, so long as short rates remain below the long, the narrower the spread between them the less will be the inducement for lenders to commit funds for a long period.

Furthermore, the shape of the yield curve extending from the shortest to the longest yields may be expected to vary with the effects of tighter or easier credit conditions. One of the first effects of a vigorous tight money program might, for example, be a flattening of the yield curve. That would, if brought about rapidly, make intermediate bonds somewhat more attractive than longer issues to investors disposing of newly arising funds, thereby rendering credit unavailable to some potential long-term borrowers. It would at the same time tend to "block in" existing holders of the intermediate Governments by eliminating the large appreciation in capital value which such bonds would otherwise acquire through the passage of time under the typical sloping yield curve.

So far as the effectiveness of central bank action upon short-term rates is concerned, the relative constancy of the long-term market yields imposes no constraint. The significance of the interrelationship between long and short rates actually runs in the opposite direction. It is the greater sensitivity of the long market to small changes in short-term rates that gives added impact to any change in short rates. Thus, while short rates can be permitted to vary over a rather wide range, they will probably not have to do so in the interest of an effective credit policy. Short-term rates can certainly fluctuate over a sufficient range to make uncertainty concerning possible changes in these rates a powerful tool of central bank control over the availability of credit.

Conclusions

Central banking and interest rate control have passed through two extremes of public favor and disfavor during the past half-century, and now appear to be settling themselves somewhere in between. First they were seized upon as panaceas; then shunted aside in favor of another panacea, fiscal policy; and now they are being rediscovered, are recognized as more delicate and flexible than fiscal policy for early action against cyclical swings, and are accepted as one among a number of sets of influences that may be helpful in attempting to stabilize over-all economic activity. This paper has been concerned mainly with the changing theory and application of central bank control over interest rates through these three phases, with emphasis upon the scope of action that has ultimately emerged.

The growth of a large public debt, providing a medium for effective central bank influence upon the interest rate structure, has coincided with an increased channeling of investable resources into lending institutions which have, by their nature, a high sensitivity to small changes in yield among alternative debt instruments. Through its guidance of prices in the Government securities markets the central bank can, therefore, exert a powerful influence upon the volume and timing of changes in the general availability of credit. It is principally through effects upon the position and decisions of lenders, and only secondarily through effects upon the decisions of borrowers and savers, that central bank action affecting interest rates achieves its significance.

There are, of course, many aspects of these relatively recent developments which have been ignored by this paper in focusing attention upon the potentialities of central bank control. Treasury debt management, particularly the term distribution and the offering rates of the large annual volume of refinancing, pose related problems; so do the Treasury's current surpluses or deficits, arising from the Government's over-all fiscal policy. Conceivably, Treasury action could, for example, by shifting drastically the proportions of debt in long-term and short-term form, raise or lower the "permanent" level of yields on long-term securities which, for the present analysis, has been accepted as given. But whether the average level of long-term rates should eventually shift, or remain where it is, the major impact of central bank policies at any given time will be produced by the effects on the current prospects of lenders of changes in the availability of Federal Reserve credit, and the accompanying relatively small changes within the existing rate structure—primarily upward or downward changes in the rates on Government securities.

While still immediately concerned with the commercial banks, and bank reserves, the central bank has now been brought closer to other lenders. For virtually all lenders have a substantial proportion of Government securities in their portfolios, and the general availability of credit to the private sector of the economy is determined in large measure by the willingness and the ease with which lenders can shift into or out of Government securities, at the margin. Since the central bank, because of the immensity of the public debt, cannot avoid a controlling responsibility for the prices (and yields) of these securities, its influence at the critical margin of lender's decisions is similarly unavoidable. If diverted solely to the rigid support of Government security prices, central bank action can be prevented from exerting any effective contra-cyclical control over the availability of credit—no device can be substituted for, or employed successfully to suppress, the inherent causal relationship between a guided variation in credit availability and variation in interest rates. Carefully exercised, through selective operations in the open market, central bank influence can effect a meaningful restraint upon, or inducement toward, the readiness of lenders to extend private credit.

As had been generally accepted in earlier periods, any central bank action in the modern setting is likely to be most powerful in restraining excessive credit expansion, somewhat less powerful in reversing a credit contraction during its early stages, and relatively weak in stimulating credit expansion in the more severe stages of cyclical depression. In any of these situations, the extent of the influence will depend upon early timing, and require the use of delicate (and readily reversible) instruments. But there is clearly a useful contribution to be made—through the creation of market uncertainty over rate movements, through a simple reversal in the direction of rate movements, and through small and successive rate changes in a consistent direction. The central bank can now reach directly into the short-term and the long-term money markets, serving through the impersonal mechanism of these markets as the arbiter of general credit availability.

NOTES

1. For example, see President's Council of Economic Advisers, "Comment Submitted to the Joint Congressional Committee on the Economic Report," *Hearings before the Joint Committee, January 17–20, 1950* (Washington: U.S. Government Printing Office, 1950), especially pp. 63–68. The present writer has commented on the Council's expression of views in "The Revival of Monetary Policy," in *Review of Economics and Statistics*, Vol. 33 (February 1951), 29–37.

2. Cf. Richard A. Musgrave, "Credit Controls, Interest Rates, and Management of the Public Debt," *Income, Employment and Public Policy* (New York: W. W. Norton & Co., 1948), p. 253.

3. Dr. Clifton H. Kreps, Jr., of the Research Department of the Federal Reserve Bank of New York, has contributed greatly to this summary of the literature on interest rate and central banking theory.

4. Knut Wicksell, *Interest and Prices* (London: Macmillan & Co., 1936), a delayed translation of *Geldzins und Guterpreise* (Jena: Gustav Fischer, 1898).

5. J. M. Keynes, *The General Theory of Employment, Interest and Money* (New York: Harcourt, Brace & Co., 1936).

6. W. R. Burgess, *The Reserve Banks and the Money Market*, 1st ed. (New York: Harper & Bros., 1927), p. 276. Cf. W. W. Riefler, *Money Rates and Money Markets* (New York: Harper & Bros., 1930), p. xv, ". . . the importance of changes in money rates lies in the underlying readjustments which they connote."

7. Burgess, *op. cit.*, p. 185. Cf. also the 2nd ed., 1936, p. 221.

8. Riefler, *op. cit.*, especially pp. 116–123, and p. 218 where he says, "whether the effect of credit policy on money rates . . . could ever seriously affect the level of bond yields . . . raises a question . . . that does not lend itself either to categorical affirmation or denial." The firm position taken by Keynes in *A Treatise on Money*, Vol. 2 (New York: Harcourt, Brace & Co., 1930), especially pp. 352–362, presents an interesting contrast, since Keynes relies upon Riefler's work for much of his statistical evidence.

9. Keynes, *Treatise*, Vol. 2, *op. cit.*, p. 348, and pp. 352–364.

10. Keynes, *General Theory, op. cit.*, especially Chapters 13 through 17.

11. R. G. Hawtrey, *Currency and Credit* (London: Longmans, Green and Co., 1919), presents in Chapter 13 the earliest form of these views;

his subsequent development of them continued through a number of volumes. The latest thorough treatment is in *Capital and Employment* (London: Longmans, Green and Co., 1937).

12. J. R. Hicks, *Value and Capital* (Oxford: Oxford University Press, 1939), pp. 225–226. Hicks' doubts were anticipated earlier in Williams' review of Keynes' *Treatise*, cf. J. H. Williams, "The Monetary Doctrines of J. M. Keynes," *Quarterly Journal of Economics*, Vol. 45 (August 1931), especially pp. 575–584.

13. H. D. Henderson, "The Significance of the Rate of Interest," *Oxford Economic Papers*, Vol. 1 (October 1938), 1–13; J. E. Meade and P. W. S. Andrews, "Summary of Replies to Questions on Effects of Interest Rates," same volume, pp. 14–31. And R. S. Sayers, "Business Men and the Terms of Borrowing," *Oxford Economic Papers*, Vol. 3 (March 1940), 23–31; P. W. S. Andrews, "A Further Inquiry into the Effects of Rates of Interest," same volume, pp. 32–73.

14. Andrews, "A Further Inquiry," *op. cit.*, pp. 35–37; cf. also Sayers, *op. cit.*, pp. 23 and 28.

15. J. H. Williams, "The Implications of Fiscal Policy for Monetary Policy and the Banking System," *Proceedings of the American Economic Association*, Part 2, Vol. 32 (March 1942), reprinted in *Postwar Monetary Plans and Other Essays*, 3rd ed. (New York: Alfred A. Knopf, Inc., 1947), especially pp. 98–103.

16. One of the few published expressions of this same point of view appears in F. A. Lutz, "The Interest Rate and Investment in a Dynamic Economy," *American Economic Review*, Vol. 35 (December 1945), especially pp. 828–830. Professor Paul McCracken, formerly Director of Research, Federal Reserve Bank of Minneapolis, developed similar views in his paper, "The Present Status of Monetary and Fiscal Policy," *The Journal of Finance*, Vol. 5 (March 1950), 24–39.

17. The data used in this section on changes in the composition of total debt and in the distribution of debt holdings are derived from an unpublished study of the American debt structure from 1914 to 1948 by A. J. R. Smith of Harvard University.

18. Only 1.5 per cent of total net debt was in U.S. Government securities, and most of these securities were lodged in the reserves held by national banks against their note issues.

19. For technical reasons, Smith has defined short-term debt as that with original maturity under one year. The well-known defects of such a definition for current money market analysis do not apply, however, in the study of long-run trends.

20. Arthur Willis, Special Assistant in the Securities Department, Federal Reserve Bank of New York, contributed greatly to the preparation of this section and of pages 574–77.

21. Of course, the spread and the customary quotation changes continue to increase with wider market swings (and greater uncertainty), but the range of variation has shrunk to an order of magnitude fundamentally different from that of the period 1917–32, when certificates were first in use on a substantial scale.

22. One bidding early in 1950 for some short-term bonds went to the

fourth decimal place. A bid at net interest cost to the borrower of 1.7181 was successful over a bid of 1.7184, *The New York Times*, March 22, 1950, p. 39. And there have been several similar cases.

23. Moreover, the influences resulting from changes in the discount rate itself can no longer be limited to this causal sequence. Discount rate changes serve, in effect, to signal a change in the boundaries upon fluctuations in short-term open market rates, and in the prices of Federal Funds, thereby giving particular emphasis when necessary to developments associated with open market operations.

24. Cf. A. G. Hart, *Money, Debt and Economic Activity* (New York: Prentice-Hall, Inc., 1948), p. 181, where he says that the direct influence of interest rates as costs is significant in these industries, and adds that "these lines almost always account for well over one-half of investment."

25. Contrast the view expressed in President's Council of Economic Advisers, *op. cit.*, p. 68.

26. There are a number of technical devices which may strengthen the effect of a simple change in rates. For example, a mere widening of the spread between the System's buying and selling rates on bills may discourage sales to the System Account from lenders' portfolios. But such devices, while essentially corroborating the thesis of this paper, involve details of market mechanics that are outside the scope of this discussion.

27. For a review of the actual experience in a limited use of the new central bank influence since World War II, see Mr. Sproul's article, "Changing Concepts of Central Banking," in this [original] volume.

28. A brief market note in *The New York Times* for January 28, 1950, p. 20, clearly illustrates the possibilities of this modest type of influence: "Market uncertainties have held hazards for the flotation of new issues of both bonds and stocks this week and sentiment in Wall Street is on the cautious side for the period immediately ahead. The continued drift in the prices of Government securities, with several of the shorter-term obligations hovering around 'par' has taken from the bond market much of the buoyant character of a couple of weeks ago. Two substantial issues of securities had to be repriced by underwriting syndicates this week to get by the 'no sale' block."

29. There is also a widespread phobia concerning capital losses on security sales that is of some significance currently, although it may eventually disappear. In numerous instances, even among large lending institutions, a mathematical demonstration of the long-run gain from such switches is rejected because the impact of the capital loss on current income is considered too great. Thus a slight rise in yields on Governments may "freeze in" many current holders who would readily have shifted from Governments into new loans or investments had the yield on Governments been pegged.

22 *The Availability Doctrine: Theoretical Underpinnings*

Ira O. Scott, Jr. *Long Island University*

The availability doctrine has been cited in defense of monetary policy when the latter's efficacy has been questioned on the ground that borrowers may be insensitive to the cost of borrowing. According to the availability doctrine, a restrictive monetary policy may cause a reduction in the quantity of credit supplied private borrowers by private lenders irrespective of the elasticity of demand for borrowed funds. This result would evidently imply a perfectly inelastic schedule of the supply of loanable funds and a shift of that schedule to the left.[1] The purpose of this paper is to formalize certain institutional factors which may explain the characteristics of supply implied by the availability doctrine.

The pressures exerted by monetary policy upon lenders according to the availability doctrine may be described in the following way. First, monetary policy may change the degree of uncertainty in the Government securities market and hence affect the liquidity of the lender's portfolio. Secondly, there is the competitive effect upon the demand for private securities of changes in the prices of Government securities. The following model depicts a particular equilibrium theory of assets suggested by these two aspects of the availability doctrine.

Reprinted from *Review of Economic Studies*, Vol. 25 (October 1957), 41–48, by permission of the author and publisher.

Assume two kinds of fixed-interest-bearing securities of equal maturity and given denomination to be available for selection, Government and private securities represented by g and p, respectively. Let X_g stand for the proportion in par value terms of the portfolio composed of Governments, X_p the proportion in private securities. Assume the investor remains fully invested; that is, cash is zero. Also exclude short positions. These constraints thus imply:

$$1 - X_g - X_p = 0$$

and:

$$X_g \geq 0, \qquad X_p \geq 0.$$

Let r_g and r_p be the rates of return on g and p, respectively. The expected yield of the portfolio is:

$$E = X_g \epsilon_g + X_p \epsilon_p$$

where ϵ_g and ϵ_p are the expected values of r_g and r_p, respectively.[2] The variance of the expected yield of the portfolio is:

$$V = X_g^2 \sigma_g^2 + 2 X_g X_p \rho \sigma_g \sigma_p + X_p^2 \sigma_p^2$$

where σ_g and σ_p represent the standard deviations of r_g and r_p, respectively, and $\rho \sigma_g \sigma_p$ their covariance.[3]

Two kinds of risk will dominate the formation of the probability beliefs represented by the σ's. First, there is uncertainty with respect to the prices at which the securities can be sold before maturity. Secondly, there is the degree of certainty with which the investor may expect interest payments to be made and principal to be repaid. The first may be designated as *market risk*, the second as *credit risk*. Private securities are subject to both kinds of risk. Government securities are not subject to credit risk. The degree of market risk to which they are subject depends upon monetary policy. The fact that Governments are not subject to credit risk implies, however, a greater market risk for private than for Government securities. Because of these uncertainty characteristics, the following condition obtains:

$$\sigma_g - \sigma_p < 0.[4]$$

It may also be assumed that:

$$\epsilon_g - \epsilon_p < 0[5]$$

and:

$$0 < \rho < 1.[6]$$

Finally, static probability beliefs are postulated; that is, the ϵ's and σ's are constant.

After $(1 - X_g)$ is substituted for X_p, the model consists of the following equations and side conditions:

$$E = (\epsilon_g - \epsilon_p)X_g + \epsilon_p \tag{1}$$

$$V = (\sigma_g^2 - 2\rho\sigma_g\sigma_p + \sigma_p^2)X_g^2 + 2(\rho\sigma_g\sigma_p - \sigma_p^2)X_g + \sigma_p^2 \tag{2}$$

$$0 \leq X_g \leq 1 \tag{3}$$

$$\sigma_g - \sigma_p < 0 \tag{4}$$

$$\epsilon_g - \epsilon_p < 0 \tag{5}$$

$$0 < \rho < 1. \tag{6}$$

Equation (1) is linear in E and X_g. Its slope, $\epsilon_g - \epsilon_p$, is negative due to (5). Because of (3), the greatest value of E is ϵ_p, the smallest value, ϵ_g. Equation (2) gives V as a parabolic function of X_g, where V attains a minimum. The maximum value of V is σ_p^2, when $X_g = 0$. When $X_g = 1$, $V = \sigma_g^2$. These results are presented diagrammatically in Figure 1. Both E and V are measured on the vertical axis. X_g is measured on the horizontal axis. Given X_g, the variance and expected yield of the portfolio are determined.

Since there are two equations, (1) and (2), and three unknowns, E, V, and X_g, there is not a sufficient number of conditions to deter-

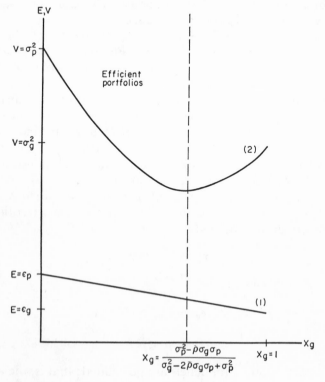

Figure 1.

mine the composition of the portfolio. However, the "expected returns-variance of returns" $(E - V)$ rule may be applied in order to identify those security combinations which are *efficient*.[7] According to the $E - V$ rule, the investor chooses those combinations of securities with a "minimum V for a given E or more and maximum E for given V or less."[8] An *efficient mix*, then, may be defined as an $E - V$ combination not dominated by any other $E - V$ combination. An *efficient set* is composed of all efficient mixes. In the model at hand, the efficient set evidently consists of all portfolios lying within the range:

$$0 < X_g < \frac{\sigma_p^2 - \rho\sigma_g\sigma_p}{\sigma_g^2 - 2\rho\sigma_g\sigma_p + \sigma_p^2}.^9$$

What can be said about the choice of a specific portfolio from the efficient set? Typically, investment officers attempt to earn the highest possible return consistent with minimum liquidity requirements.[10] In terms of the model, this means there is some maximum level of V, or riskiness, which the financial committee will tolerate. This value of V will thus determine the choice of a specific portfolio. A final condition must, therefore, be added to the model:

$$V - k = 0.^{11} \tag{7}$$

The essence of the availability argument is then:

$$\frac{dX_g}{d\sigma_g} > 0.$$

That this condition obtains in the case of the model may be seen intuitively.[12] Increased uncertainty is injected by the central bank into the Government securities market. At first glance, it appears that the investor should go out of Governments into private securities. However, the relative variance and risk constraints, (4) and (7), force the opposite reaction. The riskiness of the portfolio is increased by the change in monetary policy. In order to maintain his minimum liquidity standard, the investor must move into Governments. This follows from the fact that Governments are still relatively less risky than private securities. Thus, the investor must have recourse to Governments if he is to repair his liquidity position. A reduction in the availability of credit to the private sector ensues. If, at the time of the change in monetary policy, the investor were engaged in the process of unloading Government securities, the action of the central bank would either halt the unloading altogether or reduce the extent to which Governments could be sloughed off without endangering the investor's liquidity position. Hence, there is a reduction in the amount of credit which would otherwise have been made available to private borrowers.[13]

These results are shown diagrammatically in Figure 2. The initial solution, $\overline{X}_g$, is determined by the intersection of $V = k$ with the variance function, equation (2), in the efficient portfolio range. With the increase in σ_g following a change in monetary policy, the variance schedule shifts upward, as shown by curve (2'). $\overline{X}_g$ then shifts to the right to give the new solution. Should the latter solution represent the investor's initial position, the upward shift in the variance function would eliminate his incentive to move toward a higher yield combination.

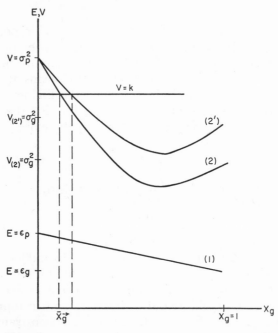

Figure 2.

This model highlights the theoretical implications of institutional restraints upon the degree of substitutability between risk and yield manifest in references to "minimum liquidity requirements," "portfolio balance," and the like, by bank examiners and the financial press. Nevertheless, an alternative solution may be obtained along marginal lines by substituting for the minimum liquidity constraint a utility function depicting the investor's preferences with respect to variance and expected yield. This utility function, combined with the transformation function in variance and expected yield, gives the marginal solution.

This solution may be obtained in the following manner. The basic equations of the original model were:

(1) $\quad E = (\epsilon_g - \epsilon_p)X_g + \epsilon_p$

(2) $\quad V = (\sigma_g^2 - 2\rho\sigma_g\sigma_p + \sigma_p^2)X_g^2 + 2(\rho\sigma_g\sigma_p - \sigma_p^2)X_g + \sigma_p^2.$

From (1), $X_g = \dfrac{E - \epsilon_p}{\epsilon_g - \epsilon_p}$.

Substituting for X_g in (2), the following transformation function in V and E is obtained:

$$V = (\sigma_g^2 - 2\rho\sigma_g\sigma_p + \sigma_p^2)\left[\frac{E^2 - 2E\epsilon_p + \epsilon_p^2}{(\epsilon_g - \epsilon_p)^2}\right]$$

$$+ 2(\rho\sigma_g\sigma_p - \sigma_p^2)\left[\frac{E - \epsilon_p}{\epsilon_g - \epsilon_p}\right] + \sigma_p^2.$$

This gives V as a parabolic function of E.[14]

The model now consists of the following relationships:

(i) $\quad t(V, E) = 0$

(ii) $\quad u(V, E) = c$

where (ii) is a hypothetical utility function and c is the parameter denoting various degrees of ophelimity.

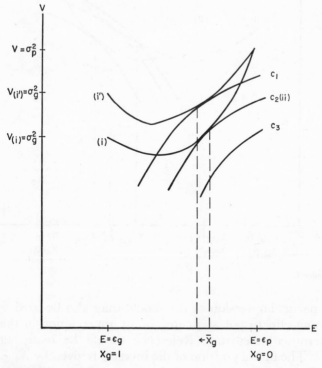

Figure 3.

The revised model is presented in Figure 3. [The relationship] (i) is shown with the earlier constraints upon X_g. The indifference curves are assumed to be of the normal shape, that is, concave to the E-axis, and $c_1 < c_2 < c_3$. The marginal solution is then given by $\overline{X}_g$.[15]

The effect of an increase in σ_g is also illustrated in Figure 4. The initial solution is given by $\overline{X}_g$. Following the change in σ_g, (i) shifts up to (i′). $\overline{X}_g$ shifts to the left, leaving the investor on a lower indifference curve. Thus, a lower yield-higher risk combination is chosen, with the proportion in Governments increasing.[16]

Next, the model may be adapted to illustrate the competitive effect of a change in the prices of Government securities. The effect of an increase in ϵ_g is shown in Figure 4.[17] [The relationship] (i) now shifts to the right to (i′) putting the investor on a higher indifference curve. Again X_g increases.[18]

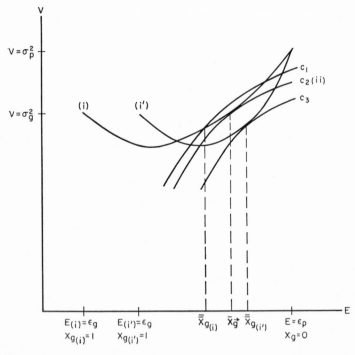

Figure 4.

This particular version of the model may also be used to show dampening effect upon switching of an appreciation in the yields of Government securities. Reference should be made again to Figure 4. The initial position of the investor is given by $\overline{\overline{X}}_{g(i)}$. Here, the additional risk which the investor would be willing to accept in exchange for a given increase in yield is greater than that required by the market. Thus it would "pay" the investor to move along (i) to the more attractive position on c_2. [The value of] ϵ_g increases, however, shifting (i) to the right to (i'). This leaves $\overline{\overline{X}}_{g(i')}$ as the best attainable portfolio combination.[19]

In actual practice, changes in σ_g and ϵ_g are likely to occur simultaneously. In this event, the liquidity and yield effects reinforce one another. Hence, this case need not be analyzed separately. Of course, additional dimensions must be added to the basic model in order to provide a more realistic range of maturities from which the investor may choose. The desired degree of liquidity may be achieved through shortening the portfolio as well as through improving the quality of given maturities. An increase in the liquidity of an investor's portfolio will, in any case, have a deflationary effect.[20]

NOTES

1. In other words, if the schedule of supply is perfectly inelastic and if it shifts to the left, the elasticity of demand will not affect the extent to which the flow of funds is reduced. This will be true even if demand is perfectly inelastic, for in that case supply takes precedence over demand. *Cf.* Richard A. Musgrave, "Credit Controls, Interest Rates, and Management of Public Debt," in *Income, Employment and Public Policy*, Essays in Honor of Alvin H. Hansen (New York: W. W. Norton & Co., 1948), pp. 229–30.

2. r_g and r_p are assumed to be random variables. *I.e.*, the investor is assumed to act as though he has probability beliefs concerning these variables. The expected return from the portfolio is thus a weighted sum of random variables where the weights are determined by the investor.

3. ρ is their coefficient of correlation. These formulae for the expected value and variance of a weighted sum of random variables may be found by consulting an introductory text in mathematical statistics.

4. Thus, a fundamental assumption of the model is that, while changes in risk factors may affect the expected values of the distributions of yields, they will always lead to changes in the dispersion of those distributions, and, since risk must always be present to a greater degree in the private securities market, that the dispersion of this distribution will always exceed that of the yield distribution for Governments.

Although it is logically possible for changes in risk to affect only the mean value of the yield distribution, realistically the possibility of this seems nil. For example, while the lessening of the credit risk on a given security, say by the guarantee of principal and interest of the obligation of a smaller corporation by a large company, would lead to an upward shift in capital value and consequent downward shift in yield, it would also decrease the anticipated range of fluctuation about that yield. To the extent, therefore, that credit risk affects dispersion in this manner, only in its total absence would its impact on dispersion be zero. Hence, it seems reasonable to assume that, because of its presence in the private security market, the above condition will hold.

Lastly, to the extent that investors expect central banks to put a floor and/or ceiling to fluctuations of Government security values, this conclusion is given further support from a direct truncation of the dispersion of the Government security distribution.

5. These conditions appear to be justified by the historical relationship among the yields of fixed-interest-bearing securities. The yields of equities, on the other hand, may bear a different relationship in a bull market.

6. The formal proof of this contained in a footnote in the original article is omitted. [Editor]

Although the model is presented diagrammatically in its more general form, *i.e.*, with $\rho\sigma_p < \sigma_g$, the uncertainty characteristics of Government securities and the pervasive influence of these securities upon the capital market, implying a high ρ when the cause-and-effect relationship runs from Government to private securities, suggest $\rho\sigma_p \geq \sigma_g$. The latter condition, of course, eliminates the possibility of gain in liquidity through diversification, *per se*.

7. See Harry Markowitz, "Portfolio Selection," *Journal of Finance*, Vol. 7 (March 1952), 77–91. Also *Portfolio Selection*, Part III (New York 1959). [Editor]

8. *Ibid.*, p. 82. In the two-security case, this rule degenerates into a "maximum E for given V," since a single V is attainable for a given E.

9. This follows from the fact, as shown above, that minimum V occurs when $X_g = \dfrac{\sigma_p^2 - \rho\sigma_g\sigma_p}{\sigma_g^2 - 2\rho\sigma_g\sigma_p + \sigma_p^2}$ and that for each portfolio with $X_g > \dfrac{\sigma_p^2 - \rho\sigma_g\sigma_p}{\sigma_g^2 - 2\rho\sigma_g\sigma_p + \sigma_p^2}$ another portfolio exists with a greater E for the same V. This result, of course, is based upon the assumption that $\rho\sigma_p < \sigma_g$. Otherwise, all possible portfolios are efficient.

10. These will depend upon institutional liabilities to meet unpredictable contingencies which may arise because of unforeseen regional shifts, cyclical disturbances, or foreign drains. In addition to the internal provision of liquidity, minimum liquidity requirements may be imposed externally by legislative enactment, supervisory authority, or examiner.

11. $k > \sigma_p^2$ exerts no influence upon the selection. $k < V_{min}$ prevents the formation of the portfolio. Realistically, $\sigma_p^2 > k > V_{min}$.

12. The formal proof given in a footnote in the original article is omitted. [Editor]

13. *Cf.* Reply by the Chairman of the Board of Governors of the Federal Reserve System, *Monetary Policy and the Management of the Public Debt, Their Role in Achieving Price Stability and High-Level Employment, Replies to Questions and Other Material for the Use of the Sub-Committee on General Credit Control and Debt Management*, Joint Committee on the Economic Report, 82nd Congress, 2nd Sess. (Washington: United States Government Printing Office, 1952), pp. 371, 372, 380.

14.

$$\frac{dV}{dE} = \left[\frac{\sigma_g^2 - 2\rho\sigma_g\sigma_p + \sigma_p^2}{(\epsilon_g - \epsilon_p)^2}\right] 2(E - \epsilon_p) + \frac{2(\rho\sigma_g\sigma_p - \sigma_p^2)}{\epsilon_g - \epsilon_p}$$

$$\frac{d^2V}{dE^2} = \frac{2(\sigma_g^2 - 2\rho\sigma_g\sigma_p + \sigma_p^2)}{(\epsilon_g - \epsilon_p)^2}$$

The denominator of the second derivative is positive. It can be shown that the numerator is also positive. Thus, the transformation function attains a minimum rather than a maximum.

15. Note that the efficient set of portfolio combinations now lies to the right of V_{min}.

16. A necessary condition for this result is that the indifference curves are not parallel in a vertical direction. (*Cf.* Marcel K. Richter, "Cardinal Utility, Portfolio Selection and Taxation," *Review of Economic Studies*, Vol. 27 [June 1960], 154, note 4.) Such a condition may be provided by postulating a utility function of the third degree with a third moment equal to zero. The author is indebted to Jacob Mincer for this suggestion.

17. ϵ_p, it will be recalled, remains constant, representing, *e.g.*, the stickiness in customer loan rates or legal limitations on the yields of guaranteed mortgages and state and local obligations.

18. X_g increases even though the shift in $\overline{X}_g$ is to the right. This follows from the fact that the shift of (i) to (i') involves a corresponding shift of the X_g associated with a given E on the horizontal axis. *I.e.*, if X_g were to decrease in magnitude, it would have to move to the right of the E given by the intersection with (i') of a line drawn parallel to the E-axis through the point of the initial tangency.

19. *I.e.*, $\overline{X}_g(i) = \overline{X}_g(i')$. See footnote 18.

20. Even in the case where the investor in question repairs his liquidity position by substituting short-term Governments or cash for long-term Governments, there is the deflationary effect of the greater illiquidity that is imposed upon other portfolios.

23 *The Inflexibility of Monetary Policy*

Thomas Mayer *Michigan State University*

The view is widely held that monetary policy is a fast and flexible tool. According to the Federal Reserve System, ". . . monetary policy is flexible. It can be applied rapidly, it can be applied gradually in experimental doses and it can be easily reversed."[1] Similarly, the 1956 *Economic Report of the President* stated that monetary policy "can be adjusted gradually, and if need be promptly reversed,"[2] and the C.E.D. believes that "monetary policy can take some risk of being wrong because it can reverse itself quickly."[3] Although this view has been questioned by Milton Friedman,[4] A. G. Hart,[5] G. L. Bach,[6] and others, few attempts have been made to test it statistically. This paper describes such a test. It shows that monetary policy is much too slow to be reversed quickly and that it cannot offset more than 10 per cent of the fluctuation in industrial production during most business cycles.

There are, however, two major limitations in the study. Monetary policy has two significant functions. At the least, monetary policy can be used to prevent the occurrence of a liquidity crisis. More ambitiously, monetary policy can be used to limit inflation during a boom, and to stimulate investment during a depression. This paper deals only with the second of these two functions. There

Reprinted from *Review of Economics and Statistics*, Vol. 40 (Cambridge, Mass.: Harvard University Press [November 1958]), 358–74, by permission of the author and publisher. Copyright, 1958, by the President and Fellows of Harvard College.

is little question that the Federal Reserve can fulfill its minimal function of making sufficient funds available to the market at very little notice. The second limitation is that nothing is said directly about the strength of monetary policy. This paper is concerned only with *timing* and not with the question of how strong monetary policy is. But, as will be shown later, it is possible to conclude from a study of the *timing* of monetary policy that, regardless of its potential strength, it cannot very effectively offset the business cycle.

i. *Method*

In view of the dangers of time series correlation it was decided to estimate the lags of investment directly for major sectors of the economy. The sectors studied here accounted for over 70 per cent of the sum of all domestic investment (excluding investment by the federal government) plus consumer credit in the period 1953–55.[7]

Much of the information used in this study consists of approximations. For some sectors of the economy, such as consumer credit and inventories, it was not possible to obtain reliable estimates. In these cases a minimum lag was used, instead of the most likely lag.[8] The conclusions reached are therefore biased on the low side. Since the purpose of this paper is to show that monetary policy is not flexible, the benefit of the doubt was given to the proposition that monetary policy *is* flexible—hence, weaknesses in the data used are unlikely to be responsible for the conclusions.

The time between the beginning of the need for a new monetary policy and its effects on GNP can be divided into four lags. First, there is the policy inauguration lag. This is the time between the occurrence of the need for a new policy and the time it is adopted. The second lag is the time it takes to apply the policy. Third, some time may pass before the new monetary policy changes the availability of credit to the borrower. Finally, there is the lag between changes in the availability of credit and changes in GNP. This paper is primarily concerned with the last of these lags. The other lags are, to a considerable extent, policy variables, and hence are unstable. They will therefore be discussed only briefly. The fourth lag, however, depends to a considerable extent upon partially technological factors, and hence can be estimated statistically.

The first three lags are discussed in sections two to four. Then, in sections five and thirteen the fourth lag is taken up for each of the eight sectors studied. The fixed investment sectors are dealt with first (sections six to eleven), and next inventory investment and consumer credit are considered (sections twelve and thirteen).

Sections six to thirteen are somewhat technical, and readers interested only in the results of the study may wish to skip them. In the next two sections delivery dates are translated into production dates, and the data for the various sectors are combined. The implications of the results are then discussed in section sixteen.

II. *Policy Inauguration Lag*

There is normally a lag between changes in business conditions and the adoption of a new monetary policy. This lag has two components. First, information on current conditions become available only with a lag; and second, some time is needed to evaluate this information and to decide upon a new policy. The former component is relatively stable, but the second varies, depending upon such factors as the sharpness of the turning point,

TABLE 1   *Lag of Monetary Policy Changes behind Business Cycle Turning Points, 1921–39 and 1949–52*

(Number of Months)

Date of monetary policy adoption	LAG BEHIND CYCLICAL TURNING POINTS	
	Expansionary policy	*Restrictive policy*
1921	15	
1922		9
1923	7	
1924		4
1927	7	
1928		1
1929	4	
1937	3	
1939		17
1949	4 to 6*	1
1952	−2 to 0†	

Note: Criteria used in deciding when a new monetary policy was adopted may have changed over time.

* One expansionary policy was adopted 4 months after the cyclical turning point, another 6 months afterward.

† One expansionary policy was adopted 2 months prior to the cyclical turning point, another in the same month as the cyclical turning point.

Sources: Joint Committee on the Economic Report, *Monetary Policy and the Management of the Public Debt*, Part 1, 82nd Cong., 2nd Sess.; "Use of Monetary Instruments Since Mid-1952," *Federal Reserve Bulletin* (December 1954); W. C. Mitchell, *What Happens During Business Cycles*, National Bureau of Economic Research, *32nd Annual Report*.

the immediately preceding history of the economy, and the political attitudes of the policy makers. An idea of the length of this lag can be obtained, however, by comparing business cycle turning points with turning points in monetary policy (see Table 1).

III. *Policy Period*

Although the Federal Reserve has the power to tighten or ease credit suddenly, monetary policy generally proceeds by small steps spread over several months (see Table 2). As Chairman Martin has explained, this is due to the uncertainties involved in monetary policy actions.[9]

IV. *Credit Market Lag*

Once a new monetary policy has been adopted there is some lag until the money market is affected. This lag depends upon the type of monetary policy used, the magnitude of the new policy, and on current money market conditions. All of these factors may differ at different times and hence this lag may be quite variable. For example, if the Federal Reserve follows the "bills only" doctrine there *may* be a much longer lag than if it operates in all sections of the market.[10] Two studies of the speed of bank reactions are available. First, George Horwich found that in 1953–55 "the response of bankers to changes in effective reserves was fairly immediate; it usually occurred in an interval which is no greater than a month, and probably much less ..."[11] Similarly, Robert P. Black's study of the reaction of Richmond District member banks to changes in reserve requirements found that: ". . . the expansionary process is very quick, reaching almost its full limits within the first [semi-monthly] reserve period."[12] For non-bank lenders, however, the lag may be much longer.[13]

V. *Output Lag*

This lag is here estimated separately for a tight money policy and for an easy money policy. Since it depends, to some extent at least, on economic conditions, the conditions assumed for the model must be specified.

For a tight money policy it is assumed that the policy is strong enough to make banks limit new commitments, but not powerful enough to make banks abandon previous informal commitments.

TABLE 2   Duration of Monetary Policy Actions, 1919–39, 1946–49, and 1952–53

(Number of Months)

YEAR POLICY STARTED	EXPANSIONARY POLICY	RESTRICTIVE POLICY
1919		17
1921	16	
1922		13
1923	10	
1924		6
1925		2
1926	1	1
1927	6	
1928		16
1929	22	1
1932	7	
1933	7	
1934	15	
1936		2
1937	8	
1939		3
1946		11
1948		8
1949	6	18*
1952		9
1953	17	
Mean	10	8
Median	8	8

Note: If two policies followed each other with a gap of no more than 2 months they were counted as one policy. If one policy was adopted while a similar policy was already in effect, it was not counted as a separate policy.

* Computed only to April 1951.

Sources: Joint Committee on the Economic Report, *Monetary Policy and the Management of the Public Debt*, Part 1, 82nd Cong., 2nd Sess.; "Use of Monetary Instruments Since Mid-1952," *Federal Reserve Bulletin* (December 1954).

It is also strong enough to make businessmen revise their programs, but not strong enough to make them cancel programs for which funds have already been obtained, or to cancel equipment orders already placed.[14] A high level of economic activity is assumed, which has not yet reached the stage where expectations turn inflationary, or where orders are "backed up" abnormally at the manufacturers' level.[15] The easy money policy model, on the other hand, assumes a mild recession unaccompanied by a liquidity crisis.

Finally, it is assumed that there is no change during this period in the *relative* effects of monetary policy on the different sectors. Thus, for a tight money policy it is assumed that banks reduce commitments to all the sectors *at the same time.*[16]

It should be noted that the model understates the lag for an easy money policy in one important respect. Some of the investment caused by easier credit conditions occurs only during the upswing when expectations improve. In another respect, however, it may overstate the lag. If monetary policy is eased after a period of tight money, investment may increase substantially at first, as the pent-up demand for investment is met, and then level off. This tends to shorten the lag for the average unit of investment.

vi. *Residential Construction*

To estimate the length of time monetary policy takes to affect non-farm residential construction, the largest sector, information is needed on (1) the lag between the increased availability of funds and the start of construction, for an easy money policy; (2) the lag between the lender's commitment of funds and the start of construction, for a tight money policy;[17] and (3) the timing of expenditures after construction has started.

At a recent Congressional Hearing two industry witnesses respectively estimated the lag between the easing of credit and the start of construction as six months and as six to eight months.[18]

To supplement this information several industry specialists were interviewed by the author. Their comments suggested a lag of about five months between the easing of credit and the start of construction.[19]

No information is available on the lag between changes in the availability of credit and the start of maintenance and repair construction. This lag may well be shorter than for new construction. But since maintenance and repair construction is probably less affected by monetary policy than is new construction, a lag of five months was used for both new construction and maintenance and repair construction together.[20]

Regarding the lag of housing starts behind the lender's commitments of funds, statistical data are available only for F.H.A. financed construction. For such construction, which accounts for about one fifth of total residential housing starts, the lag from the F.H.A.'s commitment to the start of construction has averaged two and a half months in the period 1953–55.[21] For Savings and Loan Associations the lag between the commitment of funds and the start of construction was estimated at two to three months by

the Chairman of the Home Loan Bank Board, Mr. Walter Mc-
Allister.[22] Conversations with industry specialists provided estimates ranging up to 12 months for large builders, with a median of
three to four months.[23] Again, no data on repair and maintenance
construction are available. But even if it is assumed that the lag for
repair and maintenance is quite short, it appears that the average
lag for residential construction is about three months.

Finally, data on the time pattern of expenditures subsequent to
the start of construction were obtained through the courtesy of the
U.S. Bureau of Labor Statistics.[24] These data, for new construction, are shown in Table 3. In the absence of other data it was

TABLE 3   Value Put in Place During Each Month of Construction

(As a Per Cent of Value of Complete Project)

MONTH OF CONSTRUCTION	NEW NON-FARM RESIDENTIAL CONSTRUCTION (1)	INDUSTRIAL PLANTS (CONSTRUCTION ONLY) (2)	STATE AND LOCAL GOVERNMENT CONSTRUCTION (3)*	PRIVATE NON-RESIDENTIAL BUILDING CONSTRUCTION (4)†
1	13.1	6	2	8
2	29.4	6	6	11
3	25.0	7	7	13
4	15.6	9	9	15
5	8.4	16	9	14
6	4.2	9	9	10
7	2.2	10	9	8
8	1.0	4	8	5
9	0.5	3	7	5
10	0.3	3	6	4
11	0.2	4	5	4
12	0.1	4	5	3
13		5	4	
14		7	3	
15		7	3	
16			2	
17			2	
18			2	
19			1	
20			1	

* Data relate to contracts let, rather than to complete projects, and are averages
for different types and sizes of projects weighted by average contract size and by bond
flotations between July 1952 and July 1954. Not all types of construction are included.
The highway construction data exclude winter shutdowns and similar delays.
    † Excludes farm construction and industrial plant construction.
    Sources: Col. (1) unpublished U.S. Bureau of Labor Statistics data; col. (2)
estimated from unpublished U.S. Department of Commerce data; col. (3) estimated
from unpublished data obtained through the courtesy of the U.S. Bureau of Labor
Statistics, Board of Governors of the Federal Reserve System, and U.S. Bureau of
the Census, *Survey of Construction Plans of State and Local Governments*; col. (4) estimated
from unpublished U.S. Department of Commerce data.

assumed, on the basis of discussions with Bureau of Labor Statistics specialists, that maintenance and repair expenditures have the following pattern: 20 per cent is put into place the first month, 55 per cent the second, 20 per cent the third, and 5 per cent the fourth month. The time patterns for new construction and for repair and maintenance were combined, by giving new construction a weight of 90 per cent.

VII. *Industrial Plant and Equipment*

This sector consists of new industrial plants or plant additions equipped either with new machinery or with equipment moved from other plants. Purchase of equipment for use in already existing buildings is excluded.

Monetary policy can affect such industrial plant and equipment purchases at any stage prior to completion. But in order to construct a statistical model it is necessary to use specific "cut off" points after which monetary policy can no longer affect such investment.

There are several possible cut off points which could be used in the case of an easy money policy. Thus, an easy money policy may cause businessmen to start considering the purchase of new plant and equipment. In this case the relevant lag is quite long, being the time from the *start* of consideration to the start of construction. On the other hand, an easy money policy may cause businessmen to approve projects which otherwise would have been rejected. The relevant lag, in this case, is the time between the final decision (i.e. the *end* of the consideration period) and the start of construction. Finally, an easy money policy might affect investment at an even later stage by preventing the cancellation of previously approved projects. In order to select an intermediate case as an "average" of these possibilities, the time of the final approval was chosen.

For a tight money policy, too, there are several possibilities. Thus, at one extreme, a tight money policy can discourage the *start* of consideration of new projects; in this case there is a long lag until expenditures are affected. Or, to take a less extreme case, it can prevent the final approval of some previously considered projects. At the other extreme, some companies probably ignore a tight money policy until they reach the stage of trying to obtain external financing for the project, and in this case the lag is quite short. The completion of financing data is probably an extreme limit; in most cases after financing has been obtained for a project it is unlikely to be cancelled because credit is tightened.[25] Since an average of these possibilities is needed as a cut off point, an intermediate case was taken, namely the point half-way between the date of the decision to undertake the project, and the date when external financing is completed.

The information needed consists, therefore, of the lag between the final decision and the start of construction and the lag between external financing and the start of construction. In addition, an estimate of the length of the construction period itself is needed. These data were obtained by sending questionnaires to 276 companies building new industrial plants or electric power stations.[26] Although the questions dealt with confidential material, returns with meaningful data were received from about 40 per cent of the sample. In order to avoid hypothetical and attitudinal questions, neither the questionnaire nor the covering letter mentioned monetary policy.[27]

The results of the survey are shown in Table 4.[28] On the basis of the decision and financing dates shown in this table, a six months lag will be used for an easy money policy, a four months lag for a tight money policy, and a fifteen months lag will be used for the construction period itself.[29]

It remains to determine the distribution of expenditures during the construction period. Estimates of the percentage of construction and equipment put into place during each month of the construction period were obtained by interpolating unpublished data for complete plants provided through the courtesy of the Department of Commerce. Since the data related to a 13.1 months construction

TABLE 4   Timing of Industrial Plant, Investment-Weighted Means

TIME FROM:	NUMBER OF MONTHS	NUMBER OF CASES
Start of consideration to start of construction:	23	64
Start of drawing of plans to start of construction:	7	61
Final decision to build to start of construction:	6	36
Placing of first significant orders to start of construction:	2	70
Start of financing to start of construction:*	4	19
Completion of financing to start of construction:†	3	12
Start of construction to completion:	15	77

* Excludes 5 companies starting construction prior to start of financing.
† Excludes 7 companies starting construction prior to completion of financing.

period, they had to be "stretched out" over fifteen months. The equipment inputs were distributed on the basis of data for nine industries.[30] Again a twelve months pattern had to be stretched out over fifteen months and interpolated. These equipment figures shown in Table 3 are only crude approximations, and very little accuracy can be claimed for them.[31]

VIII. *Manufacturers' Independent Equipment Purchases*

The previous sector comprised industrial equipment bought in conjunction with new plants; this, the third of the fixed investment sectors, deals with equipment bought for installation into old plants, and hence completes the manufacturing segment of the model.

The available data come from a study by the National Industrial Advertisers Association of equipment purchases in manufacturing plants with over 500 employees. According to this study there are, on the average, about two months between the realization of the need for a piece of equipment and date of the purchase order.[32] Although monetary policy can have its effects at any time in this period, from stimulating the discovery of a "need" to facilitating the final approval, it is best to assume that, *on the average*, monetary policy exerts its effects halfway through this process; hence, a one month lag will be used.

After the order is placed there is an additional lag until the equipment is delivered.[33] This lag can be estimated by taking the ratio of unfilled machinery orders to monthly sales. In the two boom years, 1953 and 1955, unfilled orders represented five months sales, and in the two recession years, 1949 and 1954, four months sales.[34] A total lag of six months will therefore be used for a restrictive credit policy inaugurated during a boom and a total lag of five months for an easy money policy during a recession.[35]

IX. *State and Local Government Construction*[36]

This fourth sector comprises new construction by states, municipalities, school districts, and special authorities.[37] Counties were not included since they accounted for less than 5 per cent of total state and local government bond flotations in 1953.[38]

Questionnaires were sent to all the states. Replies with useable data were received from sixteen states, while ten others replied that they had no, or only very infrequent, bond issues for public works.[39] Questionnaires were also sent to all cities with a population of over 250,000 and to a stratified sample of smaller cities.[40] A random sample of fifty-two school districts advertising bond or note sales in the 1955 *Commercial and Financial Chronicle* was used.[41] Replies with useable data were received from half. No attempt was made to secure a fully representative sample of special authorities. Most special authorities are quite small, and a large proportion of their borrowing consists of issues of less than one million dollars. On the other hand, a few very big authorities, such as toll road commissions, float very large issues—the New Jersey Turnpike, for instance, sold a single bond issue of $220 million. Questionnaires were therefore sent only to authorities floating issues of ten million dollars or more.[42]

The results of the survey are shown in Table 5. A combined average was obtained by weighting all types of governments in proportion to their long term bond sales in the period January 1953–June 1954.[43]

The model used for state and local construction differs from that for industrial plants. Since it is unlikely that a tight money policy

TABLE 5   *Decision and Financing Lags for State and Local Government Construction*

(Number of Months)

	Time from decision to build to start of construction	Time from obtaining funds to start of construction	NUMBER OF CASES Decision	NUMBER OF CASES Financing	Bond flotations June 1953–54 as per cent of total[a]
States[b]	9.7	3.7	13	15	20.7
Municipalities[c]	6.0	2.5	41	42	24.2
School districts[d]	8.1	3.3	24	24	16.4
Special authorities[e]	11.5	5.6	12	12	38.7
All state and local governments combined[f]	9.2	4.1	90	93	100.

  [a] Excludes issues of less than $500,000 and refunding issues. Data obtained through the courtesy of the Board of Governors of the Federal Reserve System.

  [b] Mean weighted by personal income of each state in 1954.

  [c] Unweighted means for cities of 500,000–1,000,000, 250,000–500,000, 100,000–250,000, 50,000–100,000, and urban places below 50,000 combined with weights equal to the population of each of these groups. Cities with a population of over 1,000,000 are excluded.

  [d] Weighted by cost of facility. One very large case was excluded.

  [e] Mean weighted by cost of project. Distinction between states and special authorities is arbitrary and does not correspond exactly to the distinction made in the bond flotation data used as weights.

  [f] Mean weighted by bond flotations June 1953 to June 1954.

affects *legislative* considerations or approval of a project,[44] it is best to assume that a tight money policy affects such investment, not half-way between the approval and the financing dates, but only at the financing date. Hence, the lag used is the time between the security sale and the start of construction.

For an easy money policy there is an additional complication. Some of the public works stimulated by an easy money policy are not new projects, but are projects which were deferred during a preceding period of tight credit.[45] For such a project the lag between the original decision to undertake it and the start of construction is not relevant. It will be assumed, as a working hypothesis, that for such deferred projects there is a one month lag between the easy money policy and the re-offering of the bonds.[46]

Unfortunately, no information is available on the relative importance of new and deferred projects. But since the purpose of this paper is to make a minimum estimate of the lag of monetary policy this problem can be solved by assuming that all projects affected by an easy money policy are previously deferred projects. On this assumption the average lag for an easy money policy becomes five months.[47] Fortunately, the relative weights given to the two cases are not very critical. If it is assumed instead that half of the affected projects are new projects, the average lag is increased only two months.

Data on the time pattern of expenditures during the construction period for various types of construction contracts were obtained through the courtesy of the Bureau of Labor Statistics.[48] The patterns for the different types of projects were combined and are shown in Table 3.

x. *Agricultural Investment*

There are four major components of agricultural investment: equipment purchases, construction, livestock, and inventories. Due to the absence of other information only equipment purchases and construction will be considered here.

Since farmers are generally less aware of monetary policy than manufacturers, the best assumption is that a tight money policy affects, not the farmer's *decision* to purchase, but rather his ability to obtain financing when he attempts to purchase equipment or finance construction. Since there is no significant lag between financing and the purchase of equipment or the start of construction, no lag at all is used for a tight money policy.

The lag for an easy money policy is a composite of those cases where the farmer's *decision* to purchase is influenced, and those cases where the farmer who previously would have been turned down is now granted credit. In the former case the lag is probably quite substantial, since it takes farmers some time to hear about easier credit conditions. In the second case, the lag is again zero. No data on the relative importance of these two cases are available, but again, to make a minimum estimate, a one month lag can be used.[49]

The construction period itself is three to four months. A three months period will be used to give the benefit of the doubt to the view that monetary policy is fast. No data on the time pattern of construction are available, but since construction inputs are frequently bunched in the middle of the period, a 25 per cent, 50 per cent, and 25 per cent pattern will be used.

There remain the relative weights of equipment and construction. Although in the period 1948–52, equipment purchases accounted for only 40 per cent of the total investment in construction and equipment,[50] equipment is given a weight of two thirds, since monetary policy is more likely to influence agricultural equipment purchases than construction.

xi. *Nonresidential Construction*

The last of the fixed investment sectors is private nonresidential construction.[51] The same methods were used for this sector as for plant and equipment. The cut off point for an easy money policy is again the date of the final decision to build, and the cut off point for a tight money policy is taken as half-way between the decision date and the completion of financing date. The relevant data, shown in Table 6, were obtained by sending questionnaires to a sample of nonresidential building projects listed

TABLE 6   *Decision and Financing Lags of Private Nonresidential Construction**

NUMBER OF MONTHS BETWEEN:	WEIGHTED MEAN (Number of Months)	NUMBER OF CASES
Final decision and start of construction	8†	35
Obtaining of commitments for external funds and start of construction	5	15

* Excludes farm construction and industrial plant construction.

† One case was excluded since it was so large and had such a long decision period that, if included, it would have dominated the mean. Even then one case accounted for one quarter of the total weight. If this case had been excluded the mean would have become 6 months.

in the *Engineering News Record* between March 1954 and March 1955.[52] Replies with useable data were received from one third of the 109 projects canvassed.[53] Estimates of the value put in place each month of construction (Table 3) were obtained by interpolating unpublished estimates provided through the courtesy of the Construction Statistics and Economics Branch of the Department of Commerce.[54]

XII. *Consumer Credit*

Data on the impact of monetary policy on consumer credit, the seventh sector, were obtained for commercial banks and for sales finance companies. These two lender groups accounted respectively for 35 and 20 per cent of total consumer credit outstanding at the end of each month in the period 1953–55.[55] The lags for these lenders were estimated through interviews with officials in two large sales finance companies and several banks in Indiana and West Virginia. In addition inquiries were sent to four large banks, two in New York and two in California. The replies show that when credit is tightened sales finance companies require, on the average, two months until they can reduce credit extension, but that banks can do so at once.[56]

No information is available for retailers and for other consumer lenders. But if a lag of one or two months is assumed for retailers and other lenders, the total lag for all lenders becomes one month. Hence, in the absence of other information, a one month lag will be used.[57]

Little information is available for an easy money policy. For sales finance companies the relevant lag is about three months, but for banks the lag varies from time to time and place to place since it depends upon the size of the unsatisfied fringe of borrowers. However, since it takes longer to obtain new customers than to turn away existing customers, a two months lag will be used for an easy money policy. This is most unlikely to be an overstatement.[58]

XIII. *Inventories*

There are four major ways in which a tight money policy can discourage the final sector, inventory investment. First, it prevents banks from renewing some lines of credit; second, it limits banks in granting new take-out commitments; third, it discourages banks from granting other types of inventory loans. Finally, a tight money policy reduces the entrepreneur's incentive to borrow. In the first case, there is probably a quite substantial lag. Lines of credit usually run for a year or less,[59] and hence at the time credit is tightened the average credit line will still have six months or less to run.[60] No information is available on the average duration of take-out commitments. For other types of inventory loans, however, the lag is likely to be short. The effects on the entrepreneur's investment decisions may also take place rapidly, perhaps within a month or two, since inventory budgets are reviewed frequently.[61] Similar considerations govern the lags of an easy money policy.

Although no precise information is available on the relative importance of these four cases, it appears likely that the weighted mean is at least one month, and probably longer.[62] A one month lag is therefore used in the model, not because this is the most likely lag, but because this is a minimum estimate. To this must be added two months for the lag between the placing of the order for inventory and its delivery.[63]

xiv. *Production Dates*[64]

The installation and delivery date information of the preceding sections has to be translated into production dates. For construction, labor and similar inputs occurring each month of the construction period were first estimated separately for each sector. A materials industry accounting for 73 per cent of all building materials was then synthesized by combining primary metals, fabricated metal products, lumber, and stone, clay and glass products. Comparisons of sales and production in these industries showed that, on the whole, production and sales occurred in the same months. Building materials were therefore "passed through"[65] this materials industry without a lag. Since a significant proportion of the inputs into the materials industry originate themselves in this industry, the remainder was passed through twice more,[66] and the final remnant was distributed proportionally.[67]

Equipment is primarily custom-made, and the value added in the equipment producing industries was allocated over the production period. A significant proportion of the inputs into the equipment industries originate in the materials industries—hence these inputs were passed three times through the materials industries. Inventories were treated similarly, except that for the first pass through the value added in the inventory producing industries was used. Consumer durables (from the consumer credit sector) and agricultural equipment were first passed through a retail sector, and their production timing was obtained through discussion and correspondence with manufacturers.

xv. *Combination of Sectors*

The eight sectors discussed above must now be combined. Unfortunately, no unique set of weights can be used, since the relative effect of monetary policy on the different sectors varies at different times.

The weights used are shown in Table 7, together with a set of *proportional weights*. The proportional weights were obtained by allocating, arbitrarily, 70 per cent of the total weight to the six fixed investment sectors, and distributing this weight among them in proportion to their relative size. These proportional weights are shown only as a standard of reference and are not used in any model.

A set of *intermediate weights* was then prepared on the basis of what is known about the effects of monetary policy on various types of investment.[68] These intermediate weights were then used in turn to prepare two sets of extreme weights; a set of *short weights* placing heavy weight on the sectors in which monetary policy is relatively fast, and a set of *long weights* emphasizing the sectors in which monetary policy is relatively slow. These two models represent rather extreme limits; at most times the true weights probably lie somewhere between these two extreme cases.

xvi. *Conclusion*

The lag obtained by combining these sectors is substantial (see Table 8).[69] Looking at the intermediate weights, which are the most realistic, a restrictive policy reaches only half its effectiveness five months after the change in credit availability and reaches three quarters effectiveness only after nine months. An expansionary policy takes even longer—seven months to reach the 50 per cent level and ten months to reach the 75 per cent level. Even the short weights, biased downward as they are, show a substantial lag; four months to reach half the effect and six months to reach three quarters of the effect of a restrictive policy. And these are only the effects on investment; to obtain the effects on income the multiplier lag must still be added to these figures.

These figures can be used to see whether the effect of monetary policy can be "reversed promptly."[70] For this it is necessary to apply multipliers to determine when the total effects of monetary policy on income take place. Since the income velocity is an unreliable guide to the length of this period,[71] it was decided to use not only a four months lag but a series of lags ranging from zero up to six months. Several other assumptions had to be made too.

TABLE 7   Weights of Sectors

	AVERAGE ANNUAL EXPENDITURE 1953–55		Proportional weight^a (3)	WEIGHTS		
	Billions of dollars (1)	Per cent of total fixed investment (2)		Short^b (4)	Intermediate (Per Cent) (5)	Long^c (6)
Fixed investment:						
Residential construction^d	19.6	41	29	30	28	25
Industrial plant and equipment	11.4	24	17	5	13	20
Manufacturers' independent equipment purchases				3	2	2
State and local government construction	8.4	17	12	5	15	20
Nonresidential building (except farm and industrial buildings)	4.3	9	6	5	7	15
Farm equipment and construction	4.2	9	6	7	5	3
Total fixed investment	42.2	100	70			
Other:						
Change in inventories (nonfarm)	n.a^e			20	15	10
Consumer credit (average of year-end figures)	34.0			25	15	5
Grand total				100	100	100

a Weight proportional to each sector's share of all fixed investment expenditures.
b Weights emphasizing sectors with short investment lags.
c Weights emphasizing sectors with long investment lags.
d Repair and maintenance expenditures for 1955 taken as equal to 1954 level.
e Gross figures not available due to cancellation of investment and disinvestment figures.
Sources: "National Income and Product in 1955," *Survey of Current Business* (February 1956); "National Income and Product of the United States, 1955," *Survey of Current Business* (July 1956); *Construction Review* (January 1956); *Construction Review* (January 1957); *Economic Report of the President* (January 1957); *Construction Volume and Costs 1915–1954* (Statistical Supplement to *Construction Review*); "Revision of Consumer Credit Statistics," *Federal Reserve Bulletin* (October 1956); "Higher Investment Programmed for Third Quarter," *Survey of Current Business* (June 1956).

TABLE 8   Percentage of Full Effectiveness Reached by Monetary
Policy at Different Times—Three Illustrative Projections

(Per Cent of Full Effectiveness Reached Each Month)

Number of months after change in credit availability	RESTRICTIVE POLICY			EXPANSIONARY POLICY		
	Inter-mediate weights	Short weights	Long weights	Inter-mediate weights	Short weights	Long weights
1	2	2	1	0	0	0
2	15	22	7	5	6	3
3	27	41	13	19	28	10
4	41	58	24	34	51	18
5	52	70	34	37	54	20
6	61	78	43	44	62	27
7	67	84	51	54	72	37
8	73	87	59	63	79	46
9	78	90	66	70	85	55
10	82	92	72	75	88	62
11	85	94	77	80	91	70
12	88	95	81	84	93	76
13	90	96	84	87	95	80
14	92	97	87	89	96	84
15	93	97	90	91	96	86
16	95	98	93	93	97	89
17	97	99	95	94	98	92
18	98	99	97	96	98	94
19	99	100	98	97	99	96
20	99	100	99	98	99	98
21	99	100	99	99	100	99
22	100	100	100	100	100	99
23	100	100	100	100	100	100

First, a specific multiplier coefficient of 2.5 was used.[72] Second, since the effects of easy and tight money policies are being compared, their relative strength has to be known, and it was assumed, for illustrative purposes, that both policies affect GNP by an equal amount when each is operating at 100 per cent effectiveness. This assumption is not crucial. If a tight money policy is stronger than an easy money policy it takes less time to reverse an easy money policy, but it then takes longer to reverse a tight money policy. Moreover, the model can easily be modified for any given combination of strengths of the two policies by using the data shown in Table 8. Third, the accelerator and the Pigou effect were assumed away; this, of course, tends to understate the time taken by monetary policy.

Given these assumptions, two figures can be computed. First, to take the example of an easy money policy, is the time required for the increase in income caused each month by an easy money policy to equal the income reduction caused in *that* month by the former tight money policy. In the early months of the easy money policy, it has as yet little effect on income, the main monetary influence is still the "tailing off" of the tight money policy. But eventually the "balance point" is reached; in that month the easy money policy raises income by as much as the previous tight money policy is still lowering it. From this month on the easy money policy has a greater effect than the previous tight money policy. But more time must pass until the damage done in previous months has been made up.[73] This point is called the "compensation point." At this point the easy money policy has raised income by as much as the tight money policy has reduced income over the whole period after the policy was changed.

TABLE 9   *Illustrative Projections of the Time Required to Reverse the Effects of Monetary Policy*

(Number of Months after Change in Credit Availability)

	BALANCE POINT			COMPENSATION POINT		
*Model**	*Per cent of full effect reached by previous monetary policy*					
	100	75	50	100	75	50
Intermediate weights (See Table 10)						
0 month	6	4–5†	4	12	9	6
2 months	9	7	6	17	13	9
4 months	11	8	7	22	16	11
6 months	13	10	7	26	19	13–12†
Short weights						
0 month	4	4	3–4†	9	6	4
2 months	7	6	4	14	10	7
4 months	9	7	5	18	13	9
6 months	10	8	5	22	15	10
Long weights						
0 month	8	7	5	16	12	9
2 months	11	9	7	21	16	12
4 months	13	10	8	26	19	14
6 months	15	11	9	30	22	16

Note: Unless otherwise indicated figures are the same for both a tight and an easy money policy.

* Number of months refers to length of multiplier round.

† First number is the time required by an easy money policy to offset a previous tight money policy, the second is the time required by a tight money policy to offset the effects of an easy money policy.

Source: Table 8.

Although a monetary policy itself may be quickly reversed, its *effects* may not. Thus, taking the intermediate weights and a four months multiplier period, Table 9 shows that if a tight money policy has reached its full effectiveness, it takes eleven months, almost a year after it is reversed, until the balance point is reached. And twenty-two months must pass until the new policy has fully offset the damage of the previous policy. *This is just one month less than the average length of the expansion or contraction phase of the interwar National Bureau cycles.*[74] It should be noted that this does not even allow for the policy inauguration lag, the policy period itself, and for the credit market lag. For example, if monetary policy is changed two months after the cyclical turning point and the policy period is eight months, with half the effect occurring half way through the policy period, and there is no credit market lag at all, then it takes seventeen months before the new monetary policy affects income as much as the old monetary policy still does. And the damage done by the old monetary policy when it is no longer applicable will not have been made up for two years and four months.[75]

Even if a monetary policy reaches only half its effectiveness before it is reversed it cannot be offset quickly. With intermediate weights and four months lags, for example, it takes seven months to reach the balance point and eleven months to reach the compensation point, quite apart from the policy inauguration lag, the policy period, and the credit market lag.

This inflexibility limits monetary policy in offsetting industrial fluctuations. Friedman has shown that the percentage of the standard deviation of a series which can be offset by a countercyclical policy of optimum size can be measured if one knows the coefficient of correlation between the series (in the absence of the policy) and the time-path of the policy itself.[76] Any attempt to do more actually leads to a smaller offset and may even *increase* the fluctuation. Friedman's formula was used to see what percentage of the standard deviation of industrial production could be eliminated by monetary policy. The standard deviation is a measure of the proportion of the fluctuation which can be eliminated, since business fluctuations can be treated as deviations from a trend.[77] The percentage of the fluctuations which can be eliminated expressed in standard deviation units differs, to some extent, from a straight percentage, since the squaring process gives heavy emphasis to large deviations. This is not necessarily bad, since a single large fluctuation may have greater repercussions than a large number of small fluctuations. In any case, experiments with random numbers indicate that the difference between the percentage of standard deviations and the percentage of pure numbers is usually quite small for small percentages of standard deviations. For most cycles the standard deviation ratios can therefore be treated as a first approximation to straight percentages of industrial production.

In addition to using industrial production, another test using the wholesale price index was undertaken. The preliminary results of this test indicate that monetary policy is less troubled by inflexibility in offsetting fluctuations in prices than in industrial production. This difference, it should be noted, results purely from the time shape of the production index and the wholesale price index—it is not at all connected with the point that it takes a stronger policy to influence prices than production.

To use the Friedman test the various lags must be combined. As stated above, the policy inauguration lag, the policy period, and the credit market lag are quite variable. But reasonable assumptions can easily be made to obtain illustrative projections. First, for the policy inauguration lag the second shortest lag shown in Table 1 is used, i.e., three months for an easy money policy and one month for a tight money policy. Since monetary policy is generally applied fairly evenly over the policy period, it is assumed that half its effects are felt halfway through the period, and hence half the median shown in Table 2 (i.e., four months) is used for the policy period.[78] This is quite favorable for a tight money policy since its later stages probably have more effects than the earlier ones.[79] Finally, the credit market lag is taken as half a month. The assumptions made for Table 9 are used again.

To show that the results reached here do not depend on the special assumptions used, three variants of the basic model were run. First, for two models, the percentages were recomputed using a multiplier coefficient of 1.5. As could be expected the percentages generally increased, but even on the basis of these figures monetary policy could not offset much. Second, the assumption was removed that a tight money policy and an expansionary policy are equally strong. As can be expected on *a priori* grounds, this assumption makes almost no difference except for one cycle.[80] Finally, in the models the beginning and terminal months are both included in the cycle so that the cycles overlap by one month. Two models were therefore recomputed excluding the starting and terminal months of each cycle. Again the conclusions survive the removal of the assumption.[81]

Turning to the results, the six cycles in Table 10 fall into three clearly defined groups.[82] In two of them, the 1921 and 1927 cycles, a monetary policy of optimum strength could have offset a substantial proportion of the fluctuation in industrial production. In these two cases monetary policy was probably limited more by lack of strength than by inflexibility. In the 1933 cycle a monetary policy of optimum strength could have offset 10 to 20 per cent of

TABLE 10 *Per Cent of the Standard Deviation of Industrial Production Which Could Be Eliminated by a Monetary Policy of Optimum Size*

(Per Cent)

	CYCLES STARTING IN:					
	1919	1921	1924	1927	1933	1945
Intermediate weights[a]						
0 month	25[b]	68	17	46	14	13
1 month	14	63	10	46	14	9
2 months	10[c]	56	6	49	15	7
3 months	10	50	5	53	17	5
4 months	10[d]	48	4	56	19	4
Short weights						
0 month	35	65	24	41	13	16
1 month	22	69	16	42	13	12
2 months	16	66	11	45	14	10
3 months	15	61	9	50	16	8
4 months	15	57	7	55	17	6
Long weights						
0 month	11	59	7	47	15	8
1 month	4	50	4	47	16	5
2 months	3	44	2	49	16	4
3 months	3	40	5	52	18	3
4 months	4	38	1	55	19	2
	SPECIAL COMPUTATIONS (INTERMEDIATE WEIGHTS)					
Multiplier value of 1.5						
2 months	17	65	11	47	15	10
4 months	16	61	9	51	16	8
Easy money policy taken as half as effective as a restrictive policy; multiplier value of 1.5; 4 months	6	62	9	50	16	7
Excluding initial and terminal months of cycle (other conditions as in immediately preceding cycle);	4	63	10	59	14	7
Multiplier value of 2.5; 0 month	21	68	16	46	12	13

a Number of months refers to length of the multiplier rounds.

b Becomes 14 per cent if it is assumed that the easy money policy is half as effective as the restrictive policy.

c Becomes 3 per cent if it is assumed that the easy money policy is half as effective as the restrictive policy.

d Becomes 3 per cent if it is assumed that the easy money policy is half as effective as the restrictive policy.

Sources: Based on Table 8 and "1953 Revision of the Monthly Index of Industrial Production," *Federal Reserve Bulletin* (December 1953).

the standard deviation, and in the 1919 cycle it could also have offset about that much too, given an easy money policy as strong as the tight money policy.[83] But given an easy money policy only half as strong as the tight money policy (which is much more realistic) then, except in the zero month case, monetary policy could have offset only 3 to 6 per cent. In the two remaining cycles (leaving aside certain improbable cases) a monetary policy of optimum size could have offset very little of the fluctuation.

But even these figures overstate the effectiveness of monetary policy because it is impossible to achieve just the right degree of strength in a policy. To determine the optimum size of a monetary policy the Federal Reserve would have to be able to forecast accurately the length, amplitude, and shape of the cycle, the relevant multiplier lags, and the correct sector weights, as well as the effectiveness of its own operations. Clearly, the monetary policy used will always differ from the optimum, and hence could offset less of the fluctuations than is shown in Table 10. While it is not possible to make an exact allowance for this factor, it is highly probable that it reduces the effectiveness of monetary policy significantly, probably by a third or more. If some rough adjustment of this order is made to the figures shown in Table 10, it appears that in two of the cycles monetary policy was not inhibited by inflexibility; in one cycle it could have reduced the standard deviation of industrial production by only about 10 per cent and in three cycles by only about 5 per cent.[84] To summarize these results by taking a median of the cycles: monetary policy is too inflexible to reduce the fluctuation of industrial production by more than about 5 to 10 per cent on the average.[85]

Are there any qualifications? First, there is the weakness of some of the data. But, as pointed out above, these inaccuracies are much more likely to have raised the effectiveness of monetary policy then to have lowered it. Second, this study did not consider the "first aid" an easy money policy can provide by preventing a liquidity panic. In this respect monetary policy is probably quite flexible. Third, the study did not deal with the use of monetary policy against "speculative fever." Fourth, the effectiveness of monetary policy was measured with reference to the industrial production index; had wholesale prices been used instead monetary policy would have seemed more flexible. In a subsequent paper the author hopes to combine production data for the recession phase with price data for the boom phase into a "general fluctuation index" and to test the flexibility of monetary policy against this more relevant index. Fifth, it was assumed that we will have the same type of cycles in the future as in the past.[86] Sixth, the only function of monetary policy analyzed was that of evening out the cycle. Monetary policy may still be flexible enough to deal with long-run unemployment problems such as occurred in the 1930's.[87] But even if allowance is made for all of these qualifications, one can hardly agree with the Macmillan Report that monetary policy is "a most delicate and beautiful instrument."[88]

NOTES

1. Address of Governor Szymczak printed in U.S. Congress, Joint Committee on Defense Production, *Hearings*, December 6–8 and 11, 1949 (*Defense Production Act, Regulation W—Automotive*), 81st Cong., 2nd Sess., pp. 122–23. For a similar statement see "Monetary Policy in a Free Economy," *Federal Reserve Bulletin* (September 1950), p. 1112: In its reply to the Patman Committee, however, the Board of Governors did not commit itself. (U.S. Congress, Joint Committee on the Economic Report, *Monetary Policy and the Management of the Public Debt*, 82nd Cong., 2nd Sess., p. 383. This report will henceforth be called the *Patman Compendium*.)

It is not quite clear what Federal Reserve spokesmen mean when they speak of flexibility. If they mean merely that monetary policy changes can be instituted rapidly, or that the money market will frequently react rapidly, then they are clearly right. But this type of flexibility is unimportant; the important question is how long it takes monetary policy to affect GNP. In at least one place ("Federal Financial Measures for Economic Stability," *Federal Reserve Bulletin* [May 1953], pp. 457–59), the impression is given that the term flexibility is being used in this latter, more important, sense.

2. *Economic Report of the President* (Washington 1956), p. 29.

3. U.S. Congress, Joint Committee on the Economic Report, Subcommittee on Monetary, Credit and Fiscal Policies, *Hearings*, September 23–December 7, 1949 (*Monetary, Credit and Fiscal Policies*), 81st Cong., 1st Sess., p. 277.

4. Milton Friedman, "A Monetary and Fiscal Framework for Economic Stability," *American Economic Review*, Vol. 38 (June 1948), 254–58; "The Effects of a Full-Employment Policy on Economic Stability: A Formal Analysis," reprinted in his *Essays in Positive Economics* (Chicago 1953), pp. 117–32.

5. A. G. Hart, *Money, Debt and Economic Activity*, 2nd ed. (New York 1953), p. 489.

6. G. L. Bach, "The Economics and Politics of Money," *Harvard Business Review* (March–April 1953), p. 89.

7. The types of investment excluded from the model were, however, analyzed as closely as the available data would permit. This analysis suggested that there is not enough difference between the average lags of the types of investment included and that excluded from the model to upset the conclusions of the paper. Mimeographed copies of this analysis are available upon request from the author. The major excluded sectors are: privately-owned public utilities; railroads; road transportation; shipbuilding; nonresidential maintenance and repair; equipment expenditures of trade, finance, and service industries; and investment by

the construction industry. Other omitted areas are the effects of monetary policy on the capital intensity of investment, on foreign investment, on saving, and on working capital.

8. The sectors for which no adequate estimates are available are sectors where the lag must in any case be relatively short, and hence only relatively small (absolute) errors are introduced by using minimum estimates in the place of accurate figures.

9. U.S. Congress, Joint Committee on the Economic Report, Subcommittee on Economic Stabilization, *Hearings*, December 6 and 7, 1954 (*United States Monetary Policy: Recent Thinking and Experience*), 83rd Cong., 2nd Sess., p. 25.

10. See Deane Carson, "Recent Open Market Committee Policy and Techniques," *Quarterly Journal of Economics*, Vol. 69 (August 1955), 335–39; Alvin H. Hansen, "Monetary Policy," this *Review* [*Review of Economics and Statistics*], Vol. 37 (May 1955), 110–11, and the literature cited therein.

11. George Horwich, "Elements of Timing and Response in the Balance Sheet of Banking, 1953–1955," *Journal of Finance* (May 1957), p. 254.

12. Robert P. Black, "An Analysis of the Impacts of the 1953 and 1954 Reductions in Federal Reserve Member Bank Reserve Requirements" (unpublished Ph.D. dissertation, University of Virginia, 1955), p. 280.

13. E. Sherman Adams, "Credit Policies and Economic Stability," American Economic Association, *Papers and Proceedings* (1957), p. 135. For a good discussion of the credit market lag see also W. L. Smith, "On the Effectiveness of Monetary Policy," *American Economic Review*, Vol. 46 (September 1956), 588–606. Moreover, there is a lag in the regional transmission of the effects of monetary policy, but it is not clear how this affects the average for the country. Cf. Ira O. Scott, Jr., "The Regional Impact of Monetary Policy," *Quarterly Journal of Economics*, Vol. 69 (May 1955), 269–84.

14. It is also assumed that a tight money policy does not cause borrowers to accelerate their borrowing (and hence expenditures) in order to "beat the gun" on expected further increases.

15. If expectations are inflationary, monetary policy may be faster than at other times, if it can change these expectations. On the other hand, if there is a large order backlog, then monetary policy is slower than otherwise, since new orders would not have gone into production for some time.

16. The data used here can, however, be adapted to other cases if it is known which loans banks will reduce first. In any case the results reached below are valid unless there is a systematic bias toward reducing credit first to those sectors where monetary policy is faster than average.

17. It is assumed that once a borrower has obtained a firm commitment for his mortgage funds and construction loans, a tight money policy cannot affect him. It is, of course, possible that a builder already assured of his funds may decide not to build if his expectations turn pessimistic as credit is tightened. However, this is unlikely, since a reduced availability of credit strengthens the competitive position of a builder whose mortgage funds are already assured.

18. U.S. Senate, Committee on Banking and Currency, Subcommittee on Housing, *Hearings*, November 28 and 29, 1955 (*Mortgage Market Problems*), 84th Cong., 1st Sess., pp. 34 and 76.

19. Five separate estimates were obtained ranging from three months to "over six months," with a median of five months. These estimates are much lower than that of Charles Roos. According to Roos the lag of housing starts behind credit easing is two to four years (*Dynamic Economics* [Bloomington, Ind. 1934], pp. 81–89).

20. An average lag of five months is obtained if new construction (with a five and a half month lag) is given 90 per cent of the weight, and maintenance and repair construction (with a lag of anywhere from zero up to five and a half months) is given a weight of 10 per cent. Repair and maintenance expenditures accounted for 31 per cent of total residential construction expenditures in the period 1952–54 (U.S. Department of Commerce and Labor, *Construction Volume and Costs, 1915–54* [statistical supplement to *Construction Review*], Vol. 1, pp. 2, 10). It is probable, however, that monetary policy has much less effect upon maintenance and repair expenditures than upon new construction. Much maintenance and repair construction consists of relatively small items which are less likely to be financed by credit than is new construction. Moreover, interest changes are less important for this type of construction since the maturity of the loan is generally shorter.

21. The lag was 2.6 months in 1953, 1.8 months in 1954, and 3.3 months in 1955. The author is indebted to the Division of Research and Statistics of the F.H.A. for these data.

22. Savings and Loan Associations accounted for 37 per cent of the value of home mortgages recorded in the United States in 1955 (Savings and Loan League, *Savings and Loan Fact Book, 1956* [Chicago 1956], p. 31).

23. A survey of several savings banks, however, found a six months lag between the bank's commitment and the actual making of the mortgage loan (Paul Nadler, "Home Loan Mortgages Sighted for Savings Banks," *Journal of Commerce* [September 23, 1955]). This leaves two months for the commitment-to-start-of-construction lag, if it is assumed that a house takes four months to construct and is sold at the time of completion.

24. It should be noted that the time pattern may vary with economic conditions. Thus, in 1931 one-family frame houses took 10 per cent less time to complete than in 1929. It is not known to what extent this variation is due to changes in the product mix, the efficiency of labor, or the use of more machinery ("Elapsed Time in Building Construction," *Monthly Labor Review* [January 1933], pp. 162–64).

25. This date, three months prior to the start of construction, is probably also fairly close to the latest date at which a tight money policy is likely to affect internally financed projects. At this time plans have been in preparation four months already and the first significant orders will be placed the next month (see Table 4).

26. For reasons explained in the mimeographed material mentioned below, the electric power company data could not be used in the model.

27. There are two other reasons for not asking questions specifically about monetary policy. First, most companies would probably have replied that monetary policy does not affect them and would not have provided any data. Second, since businessmen may prefer monetary policy to fiscal policy, there was the danger of introducing a bias if the purpose of the study were known. To save space the details of the survey have been described in a mimeographed appendix which can be obtained from the author. In this appendix unweighted means are given for complete plants, large plant additions, small plants, and plants using a new technology or producing a new product. Since the means for these different plants are, by and large, quite similar, all plants were combined in Table 4.

28. Table 4 contains some material which was not used in the model. At the time the survey was made no definite decision about the structure of the model had been made. This material is presented here since it may be of interest for its own sake.

29. These estimates are not in disagreement with the findings of Gehrels and Wiggins, "Interest Rates and Fixed Investment," *American Economic Review*, Vol. 47 (March 1957), 79–92, that there is a lag of one year between interest rate changes and plant and equipment investment. The average lag between changes in monetary policy and the start of construction is five months, and it takes six months until half the expenditures are made, assuming that payment occurs on the completion or delivery date. The Gehrels and Wiggins estimate includes manufacturers' independent equipment purchases, which, as is shown in the next section, have a shorter lead time than complete plants. But their estimate is in terms of half yearly intervals, so that a one year lag means a lag of somewhere between nine and fifteen months. Even if manufacturers' independent equipment is given 35 per cent of weight (which is probably too high) the two estimates are in agreement.

30. Thomas Mayer, *Input Lead Times for Capital Coefficients* (Interindustry Research Item Number 52, U.S. Bureau of Mines [Washington 1953], mimeo.), Table 2. The industries used were: sawmills; planing and veneer mills; plywood, paper, and board mills; industrial organic chemicals; plastics materials; copper rolling and drawing; nonferrous metal rolling, n.e.c.; primary aluminum; and power transmission equipment.

31. For reasons explained in the source the original data are subject to a large margin of error. Further inaccuracies were introduced here by the use of unweighted figures for only nine industries, by the stretching-out process, and by the interpolation of the quarterly figures to obtain monthly estimates. The stretching-out process consisted of reducing the inputs in each month proportionately.

32. National Industrial Advertisers Association, *Survey of Industrial Buying Practices* (New York 1949), p. 55. The estimate derives some support from the conclusion of Walter Heller than "firm capital investment plans are typically limited to a few months" ("The Anatomy of Investment Decisions," *Harvard Business Review* [March 1951], p. 99). But it *may* be an understatement. George Terborgh estimated that there is a lag of "not more than a month or two" between the authorization for an

equipment purchase and the receipt of the order by the supplier (Joint Committee on the Economic Report, Subcommittee on Economic Statistics, *Hearings*, July 19 and 26, October 4 and 5, 1955, 84th Cong., 1st Sess., p. 44). But there is surely some lag between the change in monetary policy and the authorization of the expenditure, particularly since "most medium-sized and larger companies now follow the practice of drawing up capital budgets for at least a year in advance" (*ibid.*).

33. In order to maintain comparability between the various sectors it is necessary to use the delivery date of the equipment rather than the fabrication date. Manufacturers' independent equipment was treated as being put in place in a single period of time rather than over a period of time, as in the case of equipment put into new plants.

34. Data were obtained from the U.S. Department of Commerce, *Business Statistics, 1955* (Washington 1955), pp. 14–22; *Business Statistics, 1953* (Washington 1953), pp. 17–22; and *Survey of Current Business* (February and April 1956), pp. S-4 and S-5. The figures used in the text contain two upward biases. First, the unfilled orders series contains some duplication, since orders for the same piece of equipment are sometimes placed with several suppliers. Second, some equipment which is to be placed in newly built plants will be ordered ahead of the normal "order lead time." Hence, newly received orders can be given priority over it, and the true lag for new orders is less than is indicated by backlog data. However, since the data used above are rounded to the nearest month, these biases are of no significance if they amount to less than half a month. While no information on their magnitude is available, it was assumed that they do amount to less than half a month, and hence no adjustment was made for them.

35. While the data relate only to plants with over 500 employees, it is likely that the inclusion of smaller plants would not affect the results, since lags are rounded to the nearest month. Thus, if it is assumed that three quarters of the effects of monetary policy in this sector occur in plants with fewer than 500 employees and that for such plants the lag between the recognition of the need and the placing of the order is 0.4 months, the average for both types of plants would still be one month.

36. The author would like to express his gratitude to Mr. D. F. Herrick, Executive Director of the American Public Works Association, for useful information on the characteristics of this sector.

37. Regarding other types of state and local government investment, purchases of land and existing structures are excluded since they are not part of GNP. Equipment expenditures are excluded because they accounted for only 7 per cent of total state and local government capital outlays in the period 1953–55 (U.S. Bureau of the Census, *Summary of Government Finances in 1955* [Washington 1956], p. 29).

38. Based on unpublished tabulations provided through the courtesy of the Board of Governors of the Federal Reserve System. Issues of less than $500,000 were excluded.

39. Several states indicated that they had only relatively minor construction programs financed through borrowing, and some others confined their replies to an example of one specific bond issue. In both of these cases the data given were included in the general average. It should

be noted that there is a two year seasonal variation here since in many states the legislature meets only every two years.

40. It was not possible to include in the model cities with a population of over one million. These cities, which in 1955 accounted for 42 per cent of all borrowing by cities of over 25,000 population (U.S. Bureau of the Census, *Compendium of City Government Finances in 1955* [Washington 1956], p. 12), frequently do not borrow for specific projects, but use a general construction fund which is replenished by bond flotations either when new funds are needed or else at fixed intervals. Thus, if a particular bond issue is prevented by a tight money policy, it is not possible to determine which particular construction project is affected.

41. School corporations and similar institutions were not covered in the survey.

42. Since the size of the sample had to be kept relatively small the inclusion of small issues would most probably not have affected the results. In the weighting process the small issues would have been swamped by the few large ones. It was not possible to avoid this difficulty by using a stratified sample since no weights were available. The sample was taken from the 1955 *Commercial and Financial Chronicle*. It is possible that some of the special authorities included are so closely related to their state government that they should not have been included. The amount of error, if any, resulting from this is probably minor, and hence it was not considered worth while to study the relation between each of the special authorities and its state government.

43. These weights are unpublished Federal Reserve tabulations of data published in the *Bond Buyer*. Issues for less than $500,000 are excluded from the tabulation.

44. Such an attitude is not irrational since money market conditions may change between the time of approval and the time the securities are floated.

45. Thus, the Board of Governors in its discussion of the effects of a tight money policy on state and local government expenditures referred to the timing rather than to the volume of such expenditures. "Financing cost and the general availability of credit, particularly in the long-term capital market, has an influence on the *timing* of State and local government outlays which require credit" (italics added) (*Patman Compendium, op. cit.*, p. 378).

46. The existence of a lag is indicated by the fact that bond advertisements should be published about two weeks in advance of the bond sale (Carl H. Chatters and A. M. Hillhouse, *Local Government Debt Administration* [New York 1939], p. 41).

47. The same result is obtained with the alternative assumptions that three quarters of the effect of monetary policy consists of previously deferred projects and that, in view of the previous planning, there is only a three months lag between bond flotation and the start of construction.

48. Nearly all types of public works are included in these unpublished tabulations. The major exclusions are residential construction, military construction, and conservation and development construction. Some of

the components had to be obtained by using unweighted means of the subcomponents. The estimates used for highways do not include winter and similar close-downs, and hence understate the true lag to some extent. No information is available on the lag between the start of construction and the letting of the *average* contract. Some contracts are, of course, let right away, but others are let only later in the construction period. Due to the absence of information this lag will be ignored, and the length of time monetary policy takes to influence state and local government construction is therefore, to some extent, understated.

49. The total weight given to farm investment is relatively small, varying from 3 per cent (of the weight of all sectors together) in one model to 7 per cent in another. In view of the number of guesses it was necessary to make in this section, this low weight is indeed fortunate.

50. Department of Commerce and Labor, *op. cit.*, p. 4; and J. W. Kendrick and Carl E. Jones, "Farm Capital Outlays and Stock," *Survey of Current Business* (August 1953), p. 18.

51. Nonresidential construction as defined by the Department of Commerce comprises industrial and office buildings, warehouses, stores, restaurants and garages, religious and educational buildings, hospitals and institutional buildings, and social, recreational and miscellaneous nonresidential buildings (Department of Commerce and Labor, *op. cit.*, p. 54). The definition used here is similar except that industrial buildings were excluded.

The assumption is made here, as throughout this paper, that investment in each of the sectors is independent of investment in other sectors. In a paper published after the present study was well along, John Mattila and Wilbur Thompson pointed out that a significant part of nonresidential construction is induced by residential construction ("Residential-Service Construction: A Study of Induced Investment," this *Review* [*Review of Economics and Statistics*], Vol. 38 [November 1956], 465–73). The failure to include such repercussions imparts a downward bias to the lags shown in this paper.

52. Unfortunately, this source excludes nonresidential buildings costing less than $93,000.

53. In addition, another 6 per cent replied that they could not provide data for various reasons; some, because they decided not to build. Not all the replies received were used in Table 6, since some respondents did not reply to the two questions shown in this table, but only to some of the other questions which were not used. One very large observation had to be excluded to prevent it from dominating the weighted mean.

Only sixteen useable replies are available for the financing date. They show a much longer lag than that for industrial plant and equipment. Fortunately, there is other evidence that the lag between financial commitments and the start of construction is quite long for commercial construction. (See Consultant Committee on Business Plant and Equipment Expenditure Expectations, *Statistics on Business Plant and Equipment Expectations*, in U.S. Congress, Joint Committee on the Economic Report, Subcommittee on Economic Statistics, *op. cit.*, p. 26.)

54. The various types of nonresidential construction were combined on the basis of their 1954 volume ("National Income and Product of the United States, 1954," *Survey of Current Business* [July 1955], p. 20).

55. Paul F. Smith, "Revision of Consumer Credit Statistics," *Federal Reserve Bulletin* (October 1956), pp. 1038 and 1039. Single payment loans of sales finance companies were excluded from the above estimate due to the lack of data.

56. This statement is, of course, an average concealing wide disperpersion. Small sales finance companies can react faster than large ones, and some banks would experience a lag.

57. This is unlikely to be an overstatement; if no lag at all is assumed for retailers and other lenders, the total becomes zero months—but not by much (0.4 months). On the other hand, if the lag for retailers and other lenders is taken as three months, the total lag becomes two months, but again not by much (1.7 months). It is most unlikely that retailers and other lenders react with no lag at all. Retailers in particular might react slowly, waiting until they have difficulty in negotiating bank loans. Hence, the combined lag used above may well be an understatement. As pointed out in the beginning, in cases of doubt a minimum lag is used.

58. It is quite possible, however, that this lag may change over time. Our financial institutions have so far had little time to learn (or rather to relearn) how to operate in a world with an active monetary policy. As they become more accustomed to it, their reactions may quicken. For the fixed investment sector, however, the opposite may be true. As borrowers become more aware of monetary policy they may seek more forward commitments and hence slow down the effects of monetary policy.

59. Caroline H. Cagle, "Credit Lines and Minimum Balance Requirements," *Federal Reserve Bulletin* (June 1956), p. 575.

60. However, if the use of these lines tends to be unevenly distributed over their life, the relevant lag would not be equal to half the life of the line.

61. A recent survey (primarily of large firms) found that inventory budgets were reviewed frequently, "with weekly or monthly reviews being the most common" (Business Executives Research Group, *The Strategic Role of Inventories* [Wharton School of Finance and Commerce, University of Pennsylvania, Philadelphia, n.d.], p. 40).

62. Since the data used in the model were rounded to the nearest month, any figure in excess of half a month results in a one month estimate. Only one of the cases, loans made without lines of credit or take-out commitments, may have a lag of less than half a month.

63. This figure was obtained by taking the ratio of manufacturers' unfilled orders to sales (U.S. Department of Commerce, *Business Statistics, 1955, op. cit.*, pp. 13 and 22; *Survey of Current Business* [March 1956], pp. S-3 and S-5).

64. A mimeographed appendix giving a full description of the methods and sources used in this section can be obtained from the author.

65. A "pass through" consists of multiplying the shipments of an industry by its ratio of value added to shipments. The product is the activity generated in this industry.

66. Since commodities spend on the average one month in raw material inventories, a one month lag was used between pass throughs.

67. For all the construction sectors except residential construction, the figures thus obtained were very similar to the original "put in place" figures.

68. The main source of information is the Federal Reserve's statement to the Patman Committee (*Patman Compendium, op. cit.*, pp. 373–78, 413–14, 689). See also United States Senate, Committee on Banking and Currency, *op. cit.*, pp. 17–18; Saul B. Klaman, "The Effects of Credit and Monetary Policy on Real Estate Markets: 1952–54," *Land Economics* (August 1956), pp. 239–49. This article also found that there is a lag of several months. Investment Bankers Association of America, "A Survey of the Municipal Bond Market," *Statistical Bulletin*, Number 1 (October 1956), p. 8; J. W. Kendrick and C. E. Jones, *op. cit.*, pp. 17–19; Federal Reserve Bank of Philadelphia, "Prosperity on the Installment Plan," *Business Review* (January 1956), p. 7; Board of Governors of the Federal Reserve System, *Consumer Installment Credit* (Washington 1957), Vol. 1, Part 1, pp. 276 and 279; Vol. 2, pp. 41–140; Vol. 1, Part 2, pp. 403 and 298–313.

69. The figures are, for illustrative purposes, shown to the nearest per cent. The reader must, of course, be aware that no such high degree of accuracy can be claimed for them. Rather they should be taken as indicative of the general order of magnitude involved.

70. In addition to measuring the reversibility of monetary policy and the percentage of the business cycle it could offset, an attempt was made to compare the speed of monetary policy with discretionary tax policy. While no definite conclusion could be reached it appears that tax policy frequently takes as long, or longer, than monetary policy, though not necessarily in all cases.

71. See Gardner Ackley, "The Multiplier Time Period: Money, Inventories, and Flexibility," *American Economic Review*, Vol. 41 (June 1951), 350–68; William L. Miller, "The Multiplier Time Period and the Income Velocity of Active Money," *Southern Economic Journal* (July 1956), pp. 74–79 and the literature cited therein. The multiplier used here was truncated after the fifth round when it had reached 95 per cent of its full effect.

72. This is, of course, an arbitrary value; at certain times the true value will be greater and at other times less, and it is likely to be different in different phases of the cycle. Clearly this problem cannot be solved within the confines of this paper.

73. The damage referred to above is measured simply by the initial impact. The total damage done to the economy may differ from this due to differences in the susceptibility of the economy to monetary measures at different times. Thus, a perverse monetary policy in the early stages of the cycle may have a greater effect than an equally strong monetary policy later on.

74. Wesley C. Mitchell, *What Happens During Business Cycles* (New York 1951), p. 12.

75. This has an interesting implication. Monetary policy may have greater potential *strength* than is apparent. In many cases monetary

policy may seem to be weak because of the partial cancellation of the effects of two opposite policies.

76. Friedman, "The Effects of a Full-Employment Policy on Economic Stability: A Formal Analysis," *op. cit.*, pp. 117–32.

77. Alternatively the variance could have been used as the basic measure. Monetary policy can offset a much greater percentage of the variance than of the standard deviation. The standard deviation was used because it is numerically much closer to a simple percentage than is the variance. The seasonally adjusted industrial production index was taken from Board of Governors of the Federal Reserve System, *Federal Reserve Monthly Index of Industrial Production* (Washington n.d.), p. 86, and was adjusted for trend by use of a semilogarithmic trend of yearly data with linear interpolations of natural numbers used to obtain the monthly data. The trend was fitted for the period 1919–55.

78. The policy period is treated differently from the policy inauguration lag. The latter has undergone a secular decline and hence a median would overstate the probable lag in the future. The policy period, however, shows no trend. The median is used rather than the mean to give the benefit of the doubt to the view that monetary policy is fast.

79. Cf. Edward S. Shaw, *Money, Income and Monetary Policy* (Chicago 1950), p. 408.

80. Reducing the effectiveness of a restrictive policy amounts primarily to shifting the axis, and this does not affect the correlation coefficient. There is *some* difference because the tailing off of the former tight money policy is not affected by the reduction in the effectiveness of the expansionary policy, but this does not change the results much. The reason the 1919 cycle changed substantially is that this cycle was started from a *tabula rasa*, and hence, for the first few months there is no monetary policy at all. Therefore, when the axis is shifted the y's for these months change their position relative to the other y's. For this reason several other models were recomputed on the half-strength assumption for this cycle.

81. Since correlation coefficients are sensitive to errors in the data little weight should be attached to any single percentage shown in Table 10. It is the over-all results shown in this table which are significant, not any single figure.

82. In addition to the over-all picture two peculiarities of the results may be noticed. First, there are substantial variations among the different cycles. The percentage of each cycle which can be offset depends in an intricate way upon the peculiarities of the cycle. Thus, an optimum monetary policy could have been quite effective in the 1927 cycle, apparently because of its length (65 months, counting both the starting and terminal months). But in the 1933 cycle, which is almost as long (64 months), monetary policy would have done much less. The shape as well as length of the cycle is relevant. For example, a substantial offset could have been obtained in the relatively short 1921 cycle (37 months) apparently because the cycle started from a deep depression and had a relatively minor contraction phase.

Second, in some models the percentages which could have been offset do not decrease as the multiplier lags increase. This is so probably because the longer the lags, the smaller is the percentage of full effectiveness reached by a policy at a given time and hence, there is less of it to be reversed by a later policy.

83. This first cycle was started from a *tabula rasa*—it was assumed that there was no previous monetary policy to be offset. This tends to impart an upward bias to the figures in Table 10.

84. This statement is based primarily on the intermediate weight cases. With a multiplier of 2.5 and lags of two to four months only about 3 per cent could be offset; with a multiplier coefficient of 1.5 the offset rises to about 6 per cent.

85. The median is a better measure than the mean in this case. The two large observations should not be allowed to dominate the average since monetary policy is not likely to be strong enough to offset 40 or 50 per cent of the standard deviation of industrial production. Thus, to offset 50 per cent of the standard deviation of industrial production, monetary policy would have to be strong enough to affect industrial production with a force equal to 85 per cent of the original fluctuation as measured by the standard deviations. The fact that monetary policy can affect a few percentage points of the fluctuation does not mean that only a weak monetary policy is needed. It requires a strong monetary policy to reduce the *net* fluctuation by a small amount, since monetary policy both adds to and subtracts from the fluctuation. For example, to offset 9 per cent of the standard deviation of industrial production, monetary policy would have to be over 40 per cent as strong as the original fluctuations. The basic formula for the optimum strength is given by Friedman, "The Effects of a Full-Employment Policy on Economic Stability: A Formal Analysis," *op. cit.*, p. 125.

86. The past cycles used were, of course, influenced by the then prevailing monetary policy. In this respect the conditions specified by Friedman's formula were not met. Put more precisely, it is assumed that future fluctuations in industrial production (before the applications of monetary policy) will be similar to past fluctuations which were influenced by monetary policy. Only National Bureau cycles were used. If Juglars had been used instead monetary policy would probably seem less effective. If Juglar cycles had been used as a basis of measurement, but monetary policy turning points had been based on National Bureau cycles, then perhaps monetary policy would appear more effective since the two cycles where monetary policy was not limited by inflexibility would be averaged with other cycles, hence reducing the number of cycles in which monetary policy could have little effect. But this would be an illusion since in these two cases monetary policy would not be strong enough to offset as much as its flexibility would allow.

87. Thus, monetary policy may attempt to raise over-all demand for the average of the cycle rather than to average out the fluctuations. But a tight money policy has at times been applied shortly after the lower turning point. This suggests that in the past the Federal Reserve has been more concerned with offsetting fluctuations than with raising the level of demand generally.

88. Committee on Finance and Industry, *Report*, Cmd. 3897, (London 1931), p. 97. This phrase was used in reference to bank rate policy.

24 *The Flexibility of Anticyclical Monetary Policy*

William H. White *International Monetary Fund*

Anticyclical monetary (and fiscal) measures achieve their effects on total money demand only after a lag. There has been growing concern about the length of this lag among economists, and this may have been a consideration deterring the authorities from administering full-strength doses of anticyclical medicine. These lags are said to be so great that anticyclical measures would have to be reversed far in advance of reversals in current movements in economic activity. Building on the model presented in one of the most important sources of this skepticism about anticyclical measures—Professor Milton Friedman's well-known *a priori* arguments for expecting aggravation more often than moderation of the cycle,[1]—an important recent study by Professor Thomas Mayer has now provided a set of empirically-determined reaction lags and multiplier lags in the realization of anticyclical effects.[2] This valuable, almost encyclopedic, contribution to knowledge about the potentialities of monetary policy makes possible an approach to quantification of the actual lag and of the limits to the stabilizing

Reprinted from *Review of Economics and Statistics*, Vol. 54 (Cambridge, Mass.: Harvard University Press [May 1961]), 142–47, by permission of the author and publisher. Copyright, 1961, by the President and Fellows of Harvard College.

The views expressed are the writer's own and do not represent those of the writer's employer, the International Monetary Fund.

This paper is a slightly expanded version from that originally published. [Editor]

effects of monetary measures. As published, the findings confirm suspicions at least about the feebleness of the results that can be expected: the probable reduction in the amplitude of the typical short cycle is merely five to ten per cent.[3]

The present article proposes modification of Mayer's empirical evidence and of his model, modifications which may yield the conclusion that the lag problem in anticyclical policy is too small to require hesitancy in using, or abandonment of, cycle stabilizing measures.

Professor Mayer finds that under the most plausible assumptions (aside from some gift of benefit of doubt to monetary policy when evidence for a single quantitative value was lacking), the effects of a new monetary policy on the current income level would require eleven months to grow to the point where they could outweigh the persisting opposite effects of the opposite monetary measures applied in the previous cycle phase (expansion or contraction).[4] This lag is the resultant of several underlying lags: the lag from change in monetary conditions to effects on investment decisions, the lag from investment decision to start of investment project plus the lag from start to completion of project (projects already under way or close to initiation being assumed immune to the effects of change in monetary conditions), the lag in working out the multiplier effects of such investment changes, and the resulting persistence of the effects of prior investment changes on current GNP levels even after the prior monetary measures have been reversed.

In addition to these structural lags, Mayer found a two-month delay after cycle turning points for cancellation of the old monetary policy and eight more months for gradual intensification of the new measures (which could be treated as equivalent to half-strength measures adopted four months after the new policy's actual introduction). Allowance for these led to a finding that anti-recession measures would start to raise current income after seventeen months after the cycle peak and that anti-inflationary measures would start to restrain income seventeen months after the cycle trough.[5] Given the National Bureau average contraction and expansion periods of twenty-three months, anticyclical measures would therefore begin to work only six months before the trough or peak of the cycle. This starting date of anticyclical benefits was considered rather late for important effects in cycle stabilization; applied to the six National Bureau cycles starting in the years 1919 through 1945, it yielded a median reduction in cycle amplitude of perhaps ten to fifteen per cent. This result is achieved only if measures of the optimum strength for the given reaction lags and impending cyclical movements are applied. Allowance for inability to determine the optimum leads Mayer to conclude that only five to ten per cent of the cycle amplitude could have been expected to be cancelled by anticyclical monetary policy. He mentions similar results (not yet published) for anticyclical fiscal policy also.[6]

1. Anticyclical monetary measures have two objectives: smoothing the cycle by transferring demand from the vicinity of the peak to the vicinity of the trough, and preventing the excess, in-real-terms unsatisfiable part of demand from expressing itself in pushing up prices. The multiplier model employed in the derivation of Mayer's results makes provision only for the former effect and disregards the fact that some of the frustrated investment demand (and, via the multiplier, consumption demand) could not have been realized even in the absence of tight money. Because such investments would not have been made in any case, their absence as a sustaining force in the earlier stages of the recession should not be treated as an offset to the early effects of the easy money measures adopted after the beginning of the downturn. (Specifically, these forestalled investment demands could not have led to the starting of plant construction projects, spending on which would have had to go on after the recession began until completion of the plants.) Thus, given strong prosperity movements wherein a major part of the forestalled spending would have led to price increases, the anticyclical program achieves net effects on current (real) income levels much earlier in the recession than appears from a model that ignores the major, anti-inflationary function of restrictive monetary policy.[7]

2. That part of inventory investment which is subject to monetary influences (and is not provided for elsewhere in Mayer's very thorough model) is primarily a stock variable which can undergo fairly rapid, once-and-for-all adjustment fairly early in the life of the newly-adopted monetary program. It should not be treated as a flow variable (like fixed investment) on which the current monetary policy exerts pressure for as long as it continues.[8] Concentration of the inventory reaction in the earlier stages of a new monetary program leads to an important amount of shock treatment which rapidly cancels persisting effects of the old monetary policy and therefore yields attainment of the appropriate net effects of GNP in appreciably less than seventeen months.

Because stocks of inventory holdings are so large relative to the annual flow of gross fixed investment (including housing and state and local investment), plausible inventory reactions to monetary conditions must be large relative to what the total plausible fixed investment reaction of a one-year period would be (even after fixed investment reactions had grown to their maximum level). Because [the] inventory reaction is concentrated toward, say, the first half of the first year in which a new monetary policy begins affecting expenditure, we find that the lag in the building-up of the total investment response to monetary measures is much shorter than was estimated with Mayer's model. Important reductions of the seventeen-month lag in achieving net monetary effects of proper sign are therefore to be expected.

3. A major factor in the finding of a lag as long as seventeen months appears to be the use of a very long period of construction (fifteen months) for construction expenditures by manufacturers.[9] With this much time required for completion of factories, (more than) fifteen months of tight money must elapse before the old, pre-tight-money projects have been completed and all of the current plant investment spending can have been subjected to tight money measures. The fifteen-month period is the weighted average found by a survey (covering firms reported as undertaking construction projects), which all but excluded the less ambitious plant repair, modernization, and expansion projects in favor of expenditures for complete new plants.[10] The former projects presumably have shorter construction periods than complete new plants; and the construction periods for projects costing under about $90,000, which could not be given any representation in the survey sample at all,[11] should be particularly short. Strong evidence of the unimportance of complete plant projects in manufacturers' total construction investment is provided in the annual reports to the Census Bureau by manufacturers doing the greater part of manufacturers' fixed investment: these firms' total investments in entire new plants that were not completed during the report year were only 7–10 per cent of their total construction outlays for the year.[12] Now even with plant construction periods shorter than Mayer's fifteen months, the year's spending on entire new plants that *are* completed during the year should not be greater than the amount spent on entire new plants that are not completed during the year.[13] It follows, therefore, that on the average complete new plant spending should be only 14–20 per cent of total construction outlays, so that over 80 per cent of manufacturers' construction expenditures should be on less ambitious projects, which presumably have construction periods well under fifteen months. In fact, the 1954 *Census of Manufacturers* provides some evidence that the greater part of building investment is made up of the very-small-scale and presumably rapidly-completed projects costing under $90,000, which were not covered at all in the survey of plant construction periods. For plants with 100–200, 200–500, and 500–1,000 employees, the data yield average total capital spending per plant of $71,000, $160,000, and $390,000, respectively.[14] In view of the fact that the plants involved made 40 per cent of total capital ex-

penditure, it is clear that the exclusion of separate construction projects costing under $90,000 seriously distorted the results.

Evidence that large firms' smaller projects—including new plant projects—have short construction periods is provided by the chairman of the Board of Directors of General Electric. He reported a lag of two or more years from investment decision to completion of project in the case of "a large project such as the turbine building." This is similar to the twenty-one month time lags used by Mayer for all kinds of construction projects: six months from final decision to start of construction, and fifteen more months to completion of construction.[15] But General Electric has much shorter construction periods for less ambitious projects: "In other instances a project may be planned, approved, and completed within the same calendar year." "A facility for the manufacture of small appliances may be in production within a matter of a few months from the date on which the commitment is made for the capital expenditure."[16]

Mayer provides some breakdown of his survey findings on plant construction periods. Comparison of the separate average periods found for complete new plants (70 per cent of the cases) and plant "additions" (30 per cent) suggest that perhaps only a one-month reduction in the plant construction period might be justifiable if complete new plants were reduced from their over-70 per cent weight in the weighted average to the appropriate under-20 per cent weight. Even that shortening of lag could increase the prospects of sufficiently prompt anticyclical effects. And introduction of a suitably large proportion of the disregarded group of projects costing under $90,000 would doubtless shorten the average construction period, and hence the lag, still more. Moreover, the Mayer survey evidence that only a one-month reduction in construction period would be justified is questionable; that evidence is based on the several unweighted average construction periods presented for various components of the sample, all of which are close to eleven (rather than fifteen) months. The weighted average period for the entire sample of fifteen months used in the lag estimates presumably diverges from the eleven-month figure primarily because the cases of complete new plants—which presumably have longer than average construction periods and cost much more than the average of other construction projects—are given much greater influence than their 70 per cent numerical share by the introduction of weighting. (In particular, "Bias may have resulted . . . from the heavy weight given the two large observations in Table 4.")[17]

From these considerations, it seems safe to assume that the actual weighted average time taken to complete manufacturers' building projects should be markedly reduced below the fifteen-month period built into the Mayer model. This shortening of the plant construction period has two and one-half times as much effect on the aggregate monetary policy lag as the volume of manufacturers' building investment might suggest, for the equipment outlays linked to (the later stage of) a plant construction project are assumed to cost fifty per cent more than the plants themselves.

The same bias from overweighting complete new plants (and large plants) appears to be present in the estimate of the cut-off point after which introduction of tight money cannot prevent subsequent start of construction projects. The cut-off point leads the start of construction by the average between the lead of final decision to invest and the lead of completion of financing for the investment. In the case of manufacturing investment, the weighted average for the former lead is six months.[18] No unweighted average is presented, but for the lead of start of drawing plans over start of construction, the weighted average is seven months, whereas the unweighted average is six months. More important, the unweighted averages for three components of plant investment are: seven months for complete new plants, five months for large additions to existing plants, and three months for small additions.[19] Given the dominance of the latter types of project in total plant expenditure, an additional reduction of at least one month in the reported lag in achievement of full effects on plant spending seems justified.

The other of the two leads over start of construction used as cut-off point is also open to question. It is now reported that in addition to the twelve companies having a three-month weighted average lead of completion of financing over start of construction, there were seven companies that had negative values for this lead.[20] These seem properly included in the average, with zero leads assigned, since the project is presumably started on the assumption that the financing problems to be met will be roughly the same as those existing at the start of construction.[21] This should justify a further one-month reduction of the plant-spending effect's lag.

4. A further basis for shortening the lag seems to exist in Mayer's assumption that the estimated third of machinery and equipment that is not associated with plant investments—the fastest-responding investment category after inventory—is only half as vulnerable to monetary measures as are plant and associated equipment. The reasons given—relatively more self-financing of independent equipment; its relatively greater role in routine, mechanical replacement outlays; its lesser sensitivity to interest rate changes because of relatively short economic life[22]—seem far from sufficient to demonstrate the halved sensitivity. The probable extent of greater ex-

ternal financing of plant investments shrinks when it is recognized that eighty per cent or more of plant spending is *not* for complete new plants; in any case the frequent statements that plant investments are made "to meet demand," whereas independent equipment investments are relatively more likely to be made on the basis of profit calculations, should make it likely that those using external finance for plant outlays would often consider their independent equipment outlays the ones that would have to justify themselves against the cost of outside funds (see, for example, J. Duesenberry, *Business Cycles and Economic Growth*, pp. 62–63). Mayer himself must give little weight to the lesser interest-rate sensitivity argument, since his study apparently assumed that monetary measures operate primarily through money availability rather than money cost,[23] and in any case, as the writer intends to show elsewhere, shortening economic life reduces interest sensitivity far less than customarily supposed.

Professor Friedman's reasoning that the impossibility of sufficiently good forecasting of the next cycle turning point and cycle shape made cycle aggravation likely on the average was subjected to a partial test by Professor Mayer's dry runs with the six actual cycles starting during 1919–45. Mayer's results contradict Friedman's expectations in two respects: (a) benefits could be secured on the average even though the monetary policy change was assumed to have occurred (and then to have been made strong only gradually) *after* the turn in the business cycle,[24] and (b) in no instance was the *aggravation* of particular cycles foreseen by Friedman found. Even lengthening the "normal" seventeen-month lag in achievement of effects on income of the proper sign to nineteen months[25] did not lead to a finding of increase in cycle amplitude for any of the six cycles (although for two of them the maximum reduction in amplitude was cut to one per cent and two per cent). It is true that the avoidance of any instance of cycle aggravation is conditioned on the employment of anticyclical measures that are not too much stronger than the optimum levels; and in the two extreme instances just cited, and in some of the other cases of little scope for cycle stabilization, excessively strong anticyclical measures might be expected. However, the danger that the anticyclical efforts may occasionally prove excessively strong seems less than Mayer's results for the seventeen-month lag would indicate: the more recent of the observed cycles tested may already reflect the application of anticyclical measures which were already achieving a portion of the reduction in cycle amplitude that optimum measures could produce. In that situation the achievements found for Mayer's *additional* anticyclical measures must have underrepresented the true potentialities for anticyclical policy.[26]

Important further enlargement of the potentialities is provided by the various reasons offered above for expecting less of a lag in achieving GNP effects of proper sign than Mayer's seventeen months: freedom from deflationary hangovers into the recession insofar as restrictive measures merely prevent price inflation; concentration of inventory effects into a period shortly after the monetary policy change begins to be felt rather than even distribution of inventory effects over the policy's existence; marked reduction in the reaction lag of Mayer's slowest-responding sector—manufacturers' plant and associated equipment investment; and an increase in the role assigned the fast-reacting independent equipment sector. These adjustments seem sufficient both to compensate for whatever (unjustified) benefit of doubt was given to monetary policy in instances where quantitative lag information was lacking and to produce an important reduction in the seventeen-month monetary effects lag. With a twelve-month lag the ideal one (given the twenty-three month cycle expansions and contractions used by Mayer), these adjustments should yield a close to ideal timing for changes in monetary policies first begun two months after the cycle turning point and cautiously intensified over a period of eight months more; there is no logical barrier under these conditions to (almost) complete smoothing out of the business cycle. The fact that anticipatory and/or rapid changes in anticyclical monetary (or fiscal) policy are not necessary for success in management of the cycle means that the dangers of making a (strong) change in policy that is later proved unjustified by erratic cycle behavior need not be serious.

If the twenty-three month contraction phase should be displaced by the twelve-month or shorter contractions recently experienced (and assuming that the shortening of the observed contractions would prove *not* to be simply the consequence of anticyclical policies), the chances for levelling up the trough of the cycle would be reduced. The shortening of the seventeen-month lag proposed above might be insufficient to prevent a slight deepening of the trough. Even here anticyclical measures seem worthwhile, for substantial additions to the depressed income levels still experienced after the trough had been passed could be expected, and the long recovery and boom period would provide ample time for appropriate anticyclical effects in the prosperous stages of the cycle.

The preceding defense of anticyclical policy has disregarded attacks from another direction: Where the accelerator is important in the causation of the cycle, proper timing of stabilizing measures will be extremely difficult.[27] The difficulties seem to have been greatly exaggerated, however. The fact of long and variable distributed lags of capital expenditures after the spending decision has been made does not greatly complicate anticyclical policy. All that is required for stabilization is that policy measures can be taken in time to affect the investment decision which is going to be distorted by accelerator variables. Sufficient promptness of policy might be possible if the changes in GNP or in capacity utilization affected decisions after the same lapse of time that policy measures require for their effects. It would certainly be possible if policy variables have lags a little shorter than those of accelerator variables.[28]

Even with somewhat longer delays in making policy changes and achieving effects on decisions, there would still be substantial scope for smoothing the pure accelerator cycle. The investment decision leads, on the average, to a sequence of investment expenditures distributed over at least four quarters. Given a distribution that is not too different from rectangular, the four-quarter pattern permits substantial counteracting of the accelerator cycle if the policy measures are tardy in affecting investment decisions by one quarter, and some benefit may be attained even when they are tardy by two quarters.

Finally, in the case of anticyclical monetary policy, the nonlinearity of the accelerator (investment being little affected by changes in capacity utilization while utilization is low) is likely to be matched by non-linearity of the effects of monetary policy because the desire to make enough investments to need external financing is also low when capacity utilization is low.

Subject to confirmation of Professor Mayer's important empirical findings[29] and of the validity of the various modifications in details of these findings here proposed—and subject to whatever modifications are required by the counteracting influences of the accelerator and the lead of the income-stimulating effects of new orders over production of the ordered goods—the arguments for aggressive use of anticyclical measures must now be considered persuasive.[30]

NOTES

1. Milton Friedman, "The Effects of a Full-Employment Policy on Economic Stability: A Formal Analysis," reprinted in his *Essays in Positive Economics* (Chicago 1953), pp. 117–32.

2. Thomas Mayer, "The Inflexibility of Monetary Policy," this *Review* [*Review of Economics and Statistics*], Vol. 40 (November 1958), 358–74 [reprinted in this volume—Ed.].

3. Mayer, *loc. cit.*, p. 374 (p. 616).

4. Mayer, *loc. cit.*, p. 371 (p. 612).

5. Mayer also gives attention to another lag that is eleven months longer than this one—the lag until the perverse effect on income levels first experienced is compensated by later net beneficial effects—called

the lag to the "compensation point" [*loc. cit.*, pp. 371–72 (pp. 612–14)]. The "perverse" effect is merely a symptom of change in the cycle's *timing*, and the lag in "compensation" for it is therefore of no concern and will not be discussed here. Even in the absence of a timing shift, only the small segment of the compensation that took place toward the extreme of the next contraction or expansion phase, if any, could constitute unfavorable evidence against monetary measures, and such evidence would not be conclusive.

6. Mayer, *loc. cit.*, pp. 370, 371, 374 (pp. 611, 612, 616). The benefit was, of course, increased by the contribution of monetary measures toward avoidance of "speculative fever" in boom and liquidity crisis in recession [p. 374 (p. 616)].

7. This discussion is not much affected by introduction of wage (profit) inflation that is accepted as a necessary price for the prime objective of full employment. In a full employment investment boom there will exist demand for loanable funds beyond what is necessary to handle the wage-induced rise in prices. Money then is "tight" when it tends to deny financing to this surplus amount of excess demand.

8. That inventory is treated, like fixed investment, as a flow variable is shown by the mimeographed Appendix supplied by Mayer, *loc. cit.*, pp. 17–18, Table 3.

9. Mayer, *loc. cit.*, p. 363 (p. 601). Plant construction and association equipment investment is the slowest to respond of all sectors he analyzed.

10. Mayer, *loc. cit.*, mimeographed Appendix, p. 8, Table 1, shows that 70 per cent of the cases in the survey sample were new plants, 20 per cent were "plant additions so large they took as long to plan or construct as a new plant," and 10 per cent were more rapidly completed "plant additions."

11. Mayer, *loc. cit.*, Appendix, p. 5.

12. U.S. Bureau of the Census, *Annual Survey of Manufactures 1952, 1953, 1955, 1956* and *1957*, pp. 105, 114, 118, 119, and 112, respectively; and *Census of Manufactures 1954*, Vol. 1, pp. 206–12. In the first *Annual Survey* to carry such information, the ratio was 13 per cent (*Annual Survey of Manufactures, 1951*, p. 117).

13. Thus, given certain reasonable simplifying assumptions of stable expenditure rates, even a twelve-month construction period would raise the year's spending on plants completed during the year only to equality with the amount of spending on plants that were not completed during the year.

14. *Census of Manufactures*, Vol. 1, p. 203–1. The data exaggerate the amount of plant spending per project in existing plants because they combine plant and equipment (plant being for the aggregate only one-third of the total—pp. 206–12), and because they combine a single plant's separate projects into one total; on the other hand, because of the inclusion of all plants, many of which did no plant spending in a recession year, they understate the average expenditures per project. In this connection it may be noted, however, that 1954 plant expenditures were not smaller than in the prosperous year 1955 and only one-fifth smaller in real terms than in the investment boom years 1956–57 (cf. *Survey of Current Business* [July 1959], p. 31).

Mayer notes that the $90,000 minimum for the sample led to some bias from under-sampling of small *plants* but evidently set this bias off against other biases of opposite direction that he also noted. With the demonstration above that most spending was for plant repairs and additions rather than for new plants, and that most construction probably involved projects of whatever sort costing under $90,000, it becomes clear that plants of all sizes, as well as large companies who own plants of all sizes, are involved. The bias thus must be assumed to outweigh greatly the counterbiases set off against it.

15. Mayer, *loc. cit.*, p. 364, Table 4 (p. 602).

16. See statements by Philip D. Reed in Joint Committee on the Economic Report, *Hearings, Volume and Stability of Private Investment*, Part 2 (Washington 1950), p. 531.

17. Mayer, *loc. cit.*, Appendix, p. 6, note 1. The direction of the possible bias is not given, but it is hardly likely that weighting could raise the average from eleven to fifteen months if these two influential cases had construction periods as short as fifteen months. The closeness of cluster of the unweighted averages for two sets of four sub-categories presented by Mayer makes it even more likely that additional over-weighting of complete new plants was the cause of the rise from an un-weighted figure of eleven months to the weighted average figure of fifteen months.

18. Mayer, *loc. cit.*, p. 363 (p. 602).

19. Mayer, *loc. cit.*, p. 364 (p. 602), Table 4, and Appendix, p. 8.

The order-placing and plans-drawing leads, which are also presented in both weighted and unweighted form, show similar biases from improper weighting.

20. T. Mayer, "Plant and Equipment Lead Times" *Journal of Business of the University of Chicago* (April 1960), p. 128.

21. These negative financing leads should perhaps be counted at their actual negative values (rather than being valued at zero leads), for projects are sometimes slowed or scaled down when tight money is introduced *after* their financing has been obtained; the tight money conditions may justify diversion of part of the funds obtained to later, more lucrative projects which the necessity of financing in tight money conditions would otherwise restrict.

22. Mayer, "The Inflexibility of Monetary Policy," Appendix, p. 20.

23. Anticyclical monetary measures are identified throughout the study as "easy money" and "tight money," except in Table 3 of the Appendix, p. 17: "Percent of Full Effectiveness Reached by Monetary Policy in Various Months . . ." The first column of this table is labeled "Number of months after change in credit availability." Interest rates are also mentioned [p. 361, note 20 (p. 599)], in the same deprecatory way as used for independent equipment, in connection with housing repair loans.

24. The two-month delay after the cycle turning point used might still be too brief to permit confidence that the turning point really had occurred. The assumption of gradualness in intensification of the new monetary measures makes this reservation of limited importance, however.

25. The points where benefit of doubt was given to monetary policy aside, Mayer considers this an extreme limit for the lag [Mayer, "The Inflexibility of Monetary Policy," p. 370 (p. 609)].

26. This assumes that the actual lags were not much larger than those used by Mayer and that the actual anticyclical policies were not misconceived. Mayer notes that the test should ideally have been applied to the policy-free, pure cycles but only in a way indicating that merely a loss of realism rather than that a systematic bias could have resulted ["The Inflexibility of Monetary Policy," p. 374, note 89 (p. 617)].

27. See, for example, W. J. Baumol, "Pitfalls in Countercyclical Policies: Some Tools and Results," *Review of Economics and Statistics*, Vol. 43 (February 1961), 21–26.

28. See W. H. White, "Inventory Investment and the Rate of Interest," *Banca Nazionale del Lavoro Quart. Review*, No. 57 (June 1961), 147–148 (Brookings Institution Reprint No. 57, 9–10).

29. Tentative evidence found by the writer that financing in advance of need in anticipation of the tightening of money is not important suggests that the financing lead Mayer derived from a recession-time survey would require only minor adjustment.

30. Professor Friedman recently presented a new kind of argument against anticyclical monetary policy: from statistics showing that the peak in the rate of change of the money supply leads by a large but variable number of months the cyclical peak in industrial production, he has inferred that the decline in the rate of money expansion causes (after an unpredictable delay) the subsequent decline in production (Joint Economic Committee, *Hearings, Employment Growth and Price Levels*, Part 4, "The Influence on Prices of Changes in the Effective Supply of Money" [Washington 1959], p. 639, Chart 2; pp. 661, 615–16). With the rate of change in industrial production itself reaching a peak before the peak in industrial production and with rising velocity of circulation in cyclical expansions elsewhere explained by Professor Friedman as a consequence of cyclical expansion rather than a cause of later contractions (*The Demand for Money, Some Theoretical and Empirical Results*, Occasional paper No. 68 [New York: National Bureau of Economic Research, 1959]), publication of a fuller description of the relationships inferred must be awaited. [See M. Friedman and A. Schwartz, *A Monetary History of the United States, 1867–1960* (Princeton, N.J. 1963)—Ed.]

25 *Free Reserves, Total Reserves, and Monetary Control*

William G. Dewald *Ohio State University*

Most textbooks and presumably money and banking courses present a fairy tale about Federal Reserve open-market operations. As the story goes, open-market transactions are made (1) to offset random or regular disturbances in the sources and uses of member-bank *reserves* or (2) to change member-bank reserves and permit monetary expansion or contraction. This is not just an over-simplification. It is wrong. The truth is that the Federal Reserve carries on open-market operations to cushion the money market from a variety of shocks that would, in the absence of offsetting actions, cause member-bank *reserve positions* to change from a policy-determined target level. The *reserve position* is defined as member-bank excess reserves less their borrowings from the Federal Reserve. It is termed free reserves when positive and net borrowed reserves when negative.

I

Behind the walls of the Reserve banks, the reserve position approach to monetary control is the dominating theme. Outside, a chorus of financial reporters and money marketers sing along in close harmony. The accepted approach has its origin in the work

Reprinted from *Journal of Political Economy*, Vol. 71 (April 1963), 141–53, by permission of the author and The University of Chicago Press. Copyright 1963 by The University of Chicago Press.

of Burgess and Riefler about thirty-five years ago.[1] Since then the principal change is that the reserve positions member banks want are no longer assumed to be always zero but to be a function of such factors as market rates of interest, the discount rate, and the distribution of funds among banks in various size classes.[2]

$$* \quad * \quad *$$

II

. . . [As] a framework for comparing the currently used reserve position guide to monetary control with the alternative of a total reserves guide, I hypothesize various supply-and-demand functions upon which the supply of money depends.

SUPPLY OF BORROWED RESERVES:

$$r = r_o$$

In Figure 1a the supply of Federal Reserve discounts and advances to member banks (B) appears as a perfectly elastic function at the prevailing discount rate (r). Though each Reserve bank administers discounting as it interprets the governing regulations, the fact is that borrowers are almost always accommodated with no questions asked.

DEMAND FOR BORROWED RESERVES:

$$B_d = B(r, i); \qquad \frac{\partial B}{\partial r} < 0, \qquad \frac{\partial B}{\partial i} > 0$$

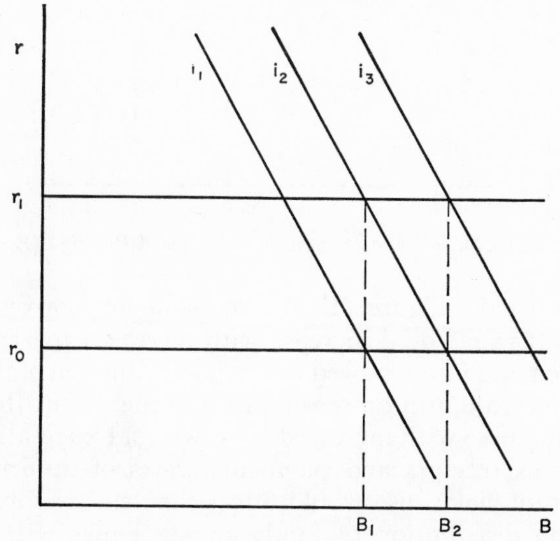

Figure 1a. *Supply and Demand for Borrowed Reserves* (B)

Figure 1a also shows the demand for borrowings as a down-sloping function of the discount rate. The explanation of banks not borrowing indefinitely as long as the discount rate is less than the market rate (i) may be partly the result of official or unofficial ceilings on individual bank borrowing. For a particular market rate, as the discount rate is reduced an increasing number of banks might be willing to approach their limit. Part of the explanation may be that portfolio risks of capital losses increase with increased borrowings. Bankers are presumed to attract deposits or borrow and to buy investments or make loans so as to attain a maximum of expected utility that depends on their subjective evaluation of expected earnings and associated portfolio risk and their preferences with respect to risk and return. It may take a reduction in costs of borrowing, for given market rates, to prompt utility-maximizing bankers to increase their borrowings when not just expected earnings but risks of capital loss are thereby increased.

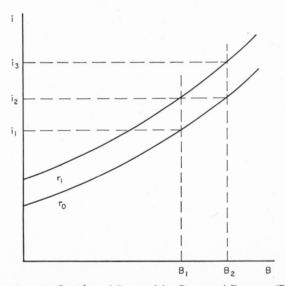

Figure 1b. *Supply and Demand for Borrowed Reserves* (B)

As diagramed in Figure 1b, the demand for borrowings at a given discount rate would increase with increased market interest rates. The demand for borrowed reserves as a function of the market rate would increase at a decreasing rate to the extent that risks of capital loss increase with increased borrowings. Expectations about such factors as receipts and payments, rates of return, and the term pattern of yields also would affect the demand for borrowed reserves. The distribution of funds among banks with different propensities to borrow is another relevant factor.

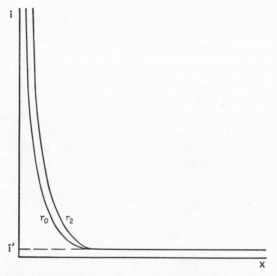

Figure 2. *Demand for Excess Reserves* (X)

DEMAND FOR EXCESS RESERVES:

$$X_d = X(r, i); \qquad \frac{\partial X}{\delta r} > 0, \qquad \frac{\partial X}{\partial i} < 0$$

The demand for excess reserves (X) similarly may be expected to be a function of the discount and market rates, as indicated in Figure 2. There should be an inverse relationship between the interest and the demand for excess reserves for at least three reasons. First, banks hold idle funds for many of the same reasons that non-bank investors hold money for other than transaction purposes. Accordingly increasing interest rates may be expected to lead banks to substitute earning assets for excess reserves up to the point where the added return is not worth the added risk.[3] Second, because there are transaction costs of investing temporarily idle balances, rising interest rates would provide the incentive to reduce any excess reserves that might be held for transaction purposes.[4] Third, the fact that the banks have demand obligations (withdrawal risks) partly accounts for a decrease in excess reserves as interest rates rise.[5] Such risks would account for an increase in demand for excess reserves as deposits rise, a factor ignored in this analysis.

If there is a liquidity trap for banks at some low interest rate (i'), the slope of the demand for excess reserves with respect to the interest rate would decline as the rate fell. A minimum of excess reserves might be approached with increasingly high interest rates. That minimum would depend on such factors as size distribution of banks, length of reserve periods, deposit turnover, speed of communication, and development of money markets. There is evidence that the minimum level of excess reserves is virtually zero for large money-market banks, while it may be a very considerable magnitude for small banks.[6]

To the extent that borrowings and excess reserves are substitute buffers against portfolio and withdrawal risks, the discount rate could also affect the demand for excess reserves. At a given market rate of interest, an increase in the discount rate would be associated with an increased demand for excess reserves.

DEMAND FOR FREE RESERVES:

$$F_d = X_d - B_d$$

For a given discount rate, the demand for free reserves is simply the sum of excess reserves less borrowings at each market rate. Such a summation is shown on the left-hand side of Figure 4a (see below)—a graph where positive units are measured from the origin in every direction except from the origin down (south). Increases in the discount rate could be expected to increase the demand for excess reserves and decrease the demand for borrowed reserves and, hence, increase the demand for free reserves on both counts. Changes in such factors as the distribution of funds, the state of expectations, and the pattern of rates could also shift the demand for free reserves as a function of the market rate of interest.

SUPPLY OF EXCESS RESERVES:

$$X_s = R - qM; \quad 0 < q \leq 1$$

Though ordinarily not identified as such, the supply of excess reserves is a concept on which a great deal of academic energy in the money and banking field has been spent. Consider a simple example. Suppose that net demand deposits (D) are the only bank liability upon which required reserves are figured and that the required-reserve ratio is q. Required reserves are defined, $Q = qD$. Total reserves (R) are given, $R = R_o$. As a parallel to the consumption function of national income analysis, the banking system is presumed to have a behavior pattern such that $E = (1 - q)D$, where $(1 - q)$ is the "marginal propensity" to acquire earning assets (E). Imposing the equilibrium condition that assets equal liabilities, $E + R = D$, one obtains the familiar solution that $D = (1/q)R_o$. Alternately $Q = qD$ can be considered as a parallel to the saving function and $R = R_o$ as comparable to exogenous spending in a simple national income determination illustration.

Imposing the equilibrium condition that $Q = R$ the identical solution is obtained.

This model can be expressed in terms of the demand and supply of excess reserves. The demand is $X_d = 0$; the supply, $X_s = R_o - qD$ for given total reserves. Imposing the equilibrium condition that $X_s = X_d$ one again obtains $D = (1/q)R_o$. A graphical solution to this problem is shown in Figure 3. $\overline{D}$ is the equilibrium amount of net demand deposits.

The supply of excess reserves in the upper right-hand quadrant of Figure 4a is expressed as a function of the money supply as a whole. The slope of the function is the negative of a kind of average member-bank required-reserve ratio. It equals the ratio of member-bank required reserves to the total money supply and can be thought of as a weighted average of the various member-bank required-reserve ratios. The weights depend on the fraction of money held by the public in currency, the amount of non-member-bank deposits, and the relation between the monetary liabilities of member banks and the liabilities upon which their required reserves are figured.[7] Zero excess reserves, the intercept on the horizontal axis, would be associated with a volume of money supply that can be termed the maximum potential money supply. Maximum excess reserves would be total reserves, which in turn equal the sum of borrowed reserves (B) and unborrowed reserves (U). Under the reserve position guide to monetary control presently employed, one may think of unborrowed reserves as a magnitude that is determined by open-market operations—it is policy controlled.

I shall now show how the demand for free reserves affects the money supply. For given discount rate and unborrowed reserves,

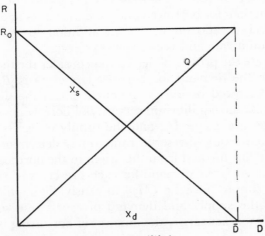

Figure 3. *Excess Reserves Equilibrium*

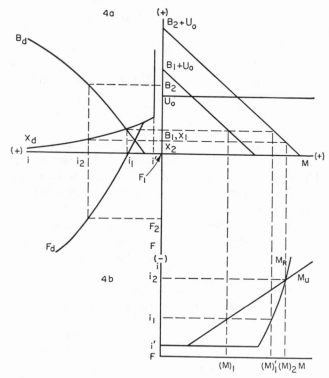

Figures 4a. and 4b. *Supply of Money* (M)

the money supply (M) at each market rate of interest (i) is an amount such that the demand and supply of borrowed reserves are equal and the demand and supply of excess reserves are equal. The money-supply function (M_U), given the particular values of r_o and U_o, is derived in Figure 4a and recorded as a function of market rates of interest in Figure 4b. The function depends on the demand functions for borrowed and excess reserves and the average required-reserve ratio on money in addition to the policy-controlled discount rate and unborrowed reserves.

To illustrate the process of derivation consider the market rate i_2. At this rate the demand for borrowed reserves is B_2. Since the supply of borrowed reserves is independent of the discount rate, B_2 will also be the equilibrium quantity of borrowings at i_2. Hence total reserves are $B_2 + U_o$, and the supply of excess reserves for given average required-reserve ratio (q) is determined. It is the downsloping line furthest from the origin in the northeast quadrant of Figure 4a. At i_2 the demand for excess reserves is X_2. Therefore the money supply must be $(M)_2$ to satisfy the equilibrium condition that the supply and demand of excess reserves be equal. At the lower market rate i_1 the amount of borrowing is reduced to

B_1 and the supply of excess reserves shifts down to intercept the vertical axis at $B_1 + U_o$. The demand for excess reserves at i_1 rises to X_1, which only coincidentally would be equal to B_1 as indicated in the diagram. Equating supply and demand for excess reserves, one obtains a money supply of $(M)_1$ that is smaller than $(M)_2$. In general, a reduction of the market interest rate, given the discount rate, level of unborrowed reserves, and relevant behavioral relations would be associated with a reduced money supply because there will be (1) a decrease in borrowed reserves that will reduce total reserves and hence the supply of excess reserves and (2) an increase in the demand for excess reserves. In Figure 4b the money supply (M_U) for given r_o and U_o is depicted as a function of market rates of interest. M_R will be discussed below. An increase in unborrowed reserves would shift the supply of excess reserves to the right; this would be reflected in a comparable shift of the money-supply function. For a given interest rate and hence given borrowed and excess reserves, this would lead to a multiple increase in the money supply. In this case $\partial M / \partial U = 1/q$. A decrease in the discount rate would increase the amount of borrowed reserves at each market rate and similarly be associated with an increase in total reserves, an upward shift in the supply of excess reserves, and thus an increase in the amount of money supplied at each market rate of interest.

Presuming in Keynesian fashion that money is demanded for investment (M_2) and transaction purposes (M_1) and imposing the equilibrium condition that money supply and demand be equal, one obtains the familiar relationship between money national income and the market rate of interest. This may be termed the money-equilibrium relation (ME_U) associated with a money-supply function for given discount rate and unborrowed reserves. In Figure 5a a market rate i_2 would be associated with demand for idle balances $(M_2)_2$ and money supply $(M)_2$. If the total money demand and supply are equal, transactions demand must be $(M_1)_2$, that is, $(M)_2 - (M_2)_2$. Only if money income is Y_2 will transactions balances of $(M_1)_2$ be demanded. Hence, for given r_o and U_o, one has the point (Y_2, i_2) on the money equilibrium relation as depicted in Figure 5b. It is associated with particular underlying behavioral relations and policy-controlled magnitudes. At a lower market interest rate i_1 the demand for idle balances increases and the supply of money decreases. On both counts one has lower market rates associated with lower money income on the money-equilibrium curve. The money-equilibrium curve will be more elastic, the more elastic is the investment demand for money and the more elastic is the supply of money. A liquidity trap in either the investment demand or the demand for excess reserves is

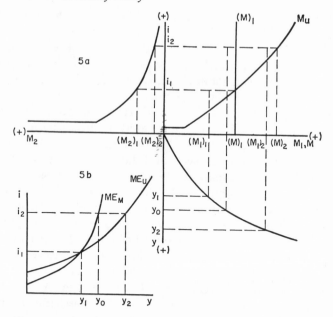

Figures 5a. and 5b. *Money Equilibrium*(M)

sufficient to cause the money-equilibrium relation to be perfectly elastic with respect to the market rate of interest.

III

In Figure 6 a relation between the rate of interest and money income such that income and expenditure are equal is recorded. This is the familiar commodity-equilibrium relation (CE) or investment-equals-saving relation. Ignoring considerations of the price level and aggregate supply, the market rate ($\bar{\imath}$) and money income level ($\bar{Y}$) such that both commodity (CE) and money equilibrium (ME) obtain may be termed their equilibrium levels. Should the commodity-equilibrium curve shift to the right (CE') for some reason, the resulting increase in equilibrium income and interest rate will depend on the money-equilibrium relation. Three basic varieties of such relations are depicted in Figure 6: ME_M, ME_R, and ME_U. ME_U represents a money-equilibrium relation associated with a money-supply function for given discount rate, unborrowed reserves, and relevant behavioral relations. Moving along ME_U a shift from CE to CE' will increase the equilibrium interest rate from $\bar{\imath}$ to $\bar{\imath}_U$ and the level of money income $\bar{Y}$ to $\bar{Y}_U$. This increase in the interest rate will have increased the profitability of making loans and investments and will have prompted utility-maximizing bankers to lend and invest increased amounts;

as a result, when they are "surprised" by withdrawals or additional loan demand they will reduce their excess reserves and/or be "forced" to the Federal Reserve "discount window" to borrow reserves. The increase in the money supply that results dampens the effect of a change in the commodity-equilibrium curve less than would be the case if the money stock were given as is so often assumed in theoretical and econometric studies of national income determination.

In Figures 5b and 6, ME_M is the money-equilibrium relation for a quantity of money fixed at $(M)_1$. It is less elastic than ME_U because rising interest rates are associated with higher income only to the extent that a decline in the demand for idle balances frees money to be held for transaction purposes. ME_R, the money-equilibrium curve associated with the money-supply function for given total reserves, will be discussed in a later section.

At the open-market trading desk of the Federal Reserve Bank of New York, an increase in the commodity-equilibrium curve such as has been hypothesized would be reflected in a money market that feels increasingly tight. Interest rates would rise and free reserves fall in the absence of changes in the behavioral relations governing the supply and demand for money. If the level of free reserves falls below the desired level as he interprets the minutes and off-the-record comments of the last Federal Open Market Committee meeting, the manager of the Open Market Account would purchase sufficient securities to increase free reserves to the

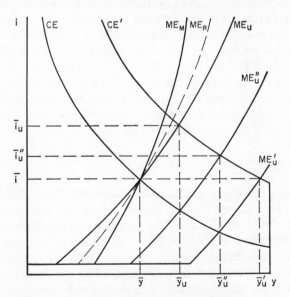

Figure 6. *Income and Interest-Rate Equilibrium*

desired magnitude. The consequence of making the proper amount of purchases is that unborrowed reserves would increase and as a result the money-supply function would move to the right sufficiently to shift the money-equilibrium curve far enough (ME'_U) to reduce the level of the interest rate to its initial level $(\bar{\imath})$ and thereby attain the associated desired level of free reserves. Given the relevant behavioral relations and policy-determined magnitudes, maintaining a free-reserve target in the face of an increased desire to spend prevents rising interest rates from dampening increased spending at all. In the opposite circumstances a cut in planned spending would not be offset at all by a decline in interest rates.

Of course, the target level of free reserves is not permanently fixed. Rather it is increased when the Open Market Committee perceives that an expansionary policy is desirable and vice versa. Of exceedingly great significance is the fact that the Committee often interprets a decline in free reserves and/or an increase in the rate of interest as a contractionary policy, and the reverse developments as expansionary. Whether tight money is contractionary, and easy money expansionary, depends critically on the extent to which economic instability results from instability in investment demand and other determinants of the commodity-equilibrium relation. In response to a destabilizing increase in the commodity-equilibrium curve, there is a substantial danger that the level of unborrowed reserves would not be decreased to offset increased borrowed reserves and, to a lesser extent, decreased excess reserves. In Figure 6 discount and open-market policies that shift the money-equilibrium curve from ME_U to ME''_U are not countering an increase in spending stemming from a shift in the commodity-equilibrium curve from CE to CE' but are contributing to its force in spite of the fact that the rate of interest rises. There is evidence that the Open Market Committee has sometimes not distinguished between tight and contractionary policies or between easy and expansionary policies.

IV

*   *   *

Without question monetary policy aimed at easing money conditions and increasing the supply of money and bank credit through the first half of 1960. The means by which this was to have been accomplished was through an increase in the level of free reserves. Yet the money supply declined substantially—about $4 billion in the year ended in mid-July, 1960. In fact, though free reserves were increased even further during the second half of 1960 the seasonally adjusted average money supply in the second half of November was but a half billion over the minimum value it touched during June and July. Subsequently relatively rapid monetary expansion occurred. But this did not happen until there was a change in required reserve ratios and total reserves; and then it occurred almost simultaneously with a turn in the level of economic activity. This pattern is not a coincidence. It is a natural result of pursuing a reserve position guide to monetary control on the one hand, and on the other of establishing a reserve position target on the basis of what happened in the immediate past.

Though the economic record is most discouraging, it would be possible for the Federal Reserve to vary free reserves and/or interest rates sufficiently to permit money-supply changes to be counter-cyclical even within the framework of the means of monetary control now used. What is required is that reserve positions be increased by sufficient purchases of securities to cause money-supply increases to bolster expenditure when this is less than desired, and vice versa. Despite this fact, a case can be made for an alternative method of monetary control.

V

An alternative to using the presently employed reserve position guide to monetary control is to conduct open-market operations to hit a total-reserves target. Each day the manager of the Open Market Account would consider the same kind of information as he presently does. He would have projections of each of the uncontrolled sources and uses of member-bank reserves and, most important, he would have the reserve-balance data for the portion of the reserve period that had already elapsed. He would authorize sales if the accumulated average of reserves was above the target level for the reserve period and if non-controlled factors were not expected to absorb a sufficient volume of reserves in the remainder of the period to bring about the desired level. By such responses, there is little question that the average level of reserves over a two- or three-week period could be controlled within narrow limits.

To see the implications of manipulating total reserves for monetary control, consider again the demand and supply of excess reserves in Figure 4a. Total reserves are to be considered not a variable but a particular policy-determined amount, say R_o. The interest rate does not affect total reserves now but only the fraction that is borrowed. Let R_o be equal to $B_2 + U_o$ in Figure 4a. In this case $B = B_2$ and $U = U_o$ only coincidentally. At i_2 the quantity of money supplied will be $(M)_2$, a quantity such that the supply and demand for excess reserves are equal as recorded in Figures 4a and 4b. The associated money supply is labeled M_R. The supply and demand for borrowed reserves would also be equal, but this would no longer influence the supply of money. Whatever borrowed reserves are, open-market operations would adjust unborrowed reserves so that $U + B = R_o$. At i_1 the demand for excess reserves would rise and, when equated with the supply of excess reserves, be associated with a decrease in the supply of money to $(M)_1$. This decrease would result only from an increase in the demand for excess reserves, in contrast to the unborrowed reserve case, where a decrease in interest rates not only increased excess reserve demand but also decreased excess reserve supply because of a cut in borrowed reserves.

The supply of money for given discount rate and total reserves is $1/q$ times as responsive to interest-rate changes as is the demand for excess reserves, while the supply of money for given discount rate and unborrowed reserves has that response plus $1/q$ times the increase in borrowed reserves resulting from an increase in interest rates. At a high interest rate, the presumed inelasticity of the demand for excess reserves results in comparable inelasticity in the money supply for given total reserves. At rates above the rate at which the minimum level of excess reserves is reached, the money-supply function would be perfectly inelastic.

Derivation of the money-supply function for given total reserves has not established that total reserves control is preferable to free-reserves control. That argument rests on the proposition that one random variable can be predicted more accurately than a function of that random variable and another one as well. Since the money supply for given total reserves is independent of borrowed reserves, to predict what the money-supply function will be, one only needs predictions of the supply and demand for excess reserves and not predictions of borrowed reserves as is the case under the reserve position alternative. The entire argument is summarized in the following algebraic expressions of the alternative models that have been discussed. $\sigma^2(M_R)$ is necessarily less than $\sigma^2(M_U)$ as long as $2\sigma(BX)$ is smaller than $\sigma^2(B)$ or negative. In the absence of more vigorous discount-rate policy than has been observed in this country $\sigma(BX)$ would in all probability be negative, thus insuring that $\sigma^2(M_R) < \sigma^2(M_U)$.

MONEY SUPPLY WITH DISCOUNT RATE AND

TOTAL RESERVES GIVEN

$$
\begin{aligned}
q &= q_o \\
R &= R_o \\
r &= r_o \\
X_s &= R - qM \\
X_d &= X(r, i) \\
X_d &= X_s
\end{aligned}
$$

$$
\begin{aligned}
M_R &= 1/q_o[R_o - X(r_o, i)] \\
\sigma^2(M_R) &= 1/q_o^2 \sigma^2(X)
\end{aligned}
$$

MONEY SUPPLY WITH DISCOUNT RATE AND

UNBORROWED RESERVES GIVEN

$$q = q_o$$
$$U = U_o$$
$$r = r_o$$
$$R = U + B$$
$$B_d = B(r, i)$$
$$B_d = B_s$$
$$X_s = R - qM$$
$$X_d = X(r, i)$$
$$X_d = X_s$$

$$M_U = 1/q_o[U_o + B(r_o, i) - X(r_o, i)]$$
$$\sigma^2(M_U) = 1/q_o^2[\sigma^2(B) + \sigma^2(X) - 2\sigma(BX)]$$

The variance terms found above may be modified to account for borrowed and excess reserves being estimated more accurately than by their means. If one assumes that $B_d = B(r, i) + v$ and $X_d = X(r, i) + w$ where v and w are dependent random disturbances with zero expected values and finite variances and covariance, then $\sigma^2(M_R) > \sigma^2(M_U)$ only if $\sigma^2(v) < 2\sigma(vw)$.

Meigs has examined evidence leading to the conclusion that a small part of the variation of changes in member-bank net deposits is accountable to variation in the demand for free reserves as a function of market interest rates and the discount rate.[8] Rather, the bulk of the variation in member-bank deposits is due to variation in unborrowed reserves. My own empirical work has established that variation from one semimonthly period to the next in the average required-reserve ratio on member-bank net demand deposits is over 99 per cent accountable to seasonal factors and changes in required-reserve ratios.[9]

VI

In conclusion, there is a substantial case both theoretically and empirically against the presently employed means of monetary control in the United States; I believe that actions of the Federal Reserve Open Market Committee have been conceived and executed with the highest possible motives about the welfare of the American people. But easy and expansionary policies (or tight and contractionary policies) have often been confused because of the free-reserve guide. Certainly the frequently observed slowdown in monetary growth or monetary contraction as the level of economic activity peaks out and begins to fall is not desirable, especially if there is a lag in the impact of money-stock changes on the level of expenditure.

These recommendations follow from the preceding analysis. First, the Open Market Committee should be persuaded to distinguish between easy and expansionary policies, and tight and restrictive policies. Second, the manager of the Open Market Account should be educated to stop forcing cuts in the money stock when the Open Market Committee calls for monetary expansion and vice versa. Third, the Open Market Committee should direct the manager of the Open Market Account to try to achieve a target level of daily average total reserves (or money supply) during the interim between its meetings.

These recommendations are intended to make monetary policy stabilizing, in contrast to present guides for policy, which often have had destabilizing effects. Stabilizing monetary policy may not achieve the best of all possible worlds, but there is good reason to think that the conduct of monetary policy could bring us closer than it has.

NOTES

1. W. R. Burgess, *The Reserve Banks and the Money Market* (New York: Harper & Bros., 1927); and W. W. Riefler, *Money Rates and Money Markets in the United States* (New York: Harper & Bros., 1930).

2. P. D. Sternlight and R. Lindsay, "The Significance and Limitations of Free Reserves," *Monthly Review, Federal Reserve Bank of New York* (November 1958), pp. 162–67.

3. A. D. Roy, "Safety First and the Holding of Assets," *Econometrica*, Vol. 20 (July 1952), 391–405; and J. Tobin, "Liquidity Preference as Behavior towards Risk," *Review of Economic Studies*, Vol. 25 (February 1958), 65–86 [reprinted in this volume—Ed.].

4. W. J. Baumol, "The Transactions Demand for Cash: An Inventory Theoretic Approach," *Quarterly Journal of Economics*, Vol. 66 (November 1952), 545–56 [reprinted in this volume—Ed.]; and J. Tobin, "The Interest-Elasticity of Transactions Demand for Cash," *Review of Economics and Statistics*, Vol. 38 (August 1956), 241–47.

5. D. Orr and W. J. Mellon, "Stochastic Reserve Losses and Bank Credit," *American Economic Review*, Vol. 51 (September 1961).

6. W. Dewald, "Money To Spare: Excess Reserves," *Monthly Review, Federal Reserve Bank of Minneapolis* (August 1961), pp. 2–7.

7. W. Dewald, "Monetary Control and the Distribution of Money" (unpublished Ph.D. dissertation, University of Minnesota, 1963).

8. A. J. Meigs, *Free Reserves and the Money Supply* (Chicago: University of Chicago Press, 1962).

9. Dewald, "Monetary Control and the Distribution of Money."

26 The Appropriate Use of Monetary and Fiscal Policy for Internal and External Stability

Robert A. Mundell *University of Chicago*

This paper deals with the problem of achieving internal stability and balance of payments equilibrium in a country which considers it inadvisable to alter the exchange rate or to impose trade controls. It is assumed that monetary and fiscal policy can be used as independent instruments to attain the two objectives if capital flows are responsive to interest rate differentials, but it is concluded that it is a matter of extreme importance how the policies are paired with the objectives. Specifically, it is argued that monetary policy ought to be aimed at external objectives and fiscal policy at internal objectives, and that failure to follow this prescription can make the disequilibrium situation worse than before the policy changes were introduced.

The practical implication of the theory, when stabilization measures are limited to monetary policy and fiscal policy, is that a surplus country experiencing inflationary pressure should ease monetary conditions and raise taxes (or reduce government spending), and that a deficit country suffering from unemployment should tighten interest rates and lower taxes (or increase government spending).[1]

Reprinted from *Staff Papers* (March 1962), pp. 70–77, by permission of the author and the International Monetary Fund.

The Conditions of Equilibrium

Internal balance requires that aggregate demand for domestic output be equal to aggregate supply of domestic output at full employment. If this condition is not fulfilled, there will be inflationary pressure or recessionary potential according to whether aggregate demand exceeds or falls short of, respectively, full employment output. It will be assumed here that, during transitory periods of disequilibrium, inventories are running down, or accumulating, in excess of desired changes, according to whether the disequilibrium reflects a state of inflationary or recessionary potential.

External balance implies that the balance of trade equals (net) capital exports at the fixed exchange parity. If the balance of trade exceeds capital exports, there will be a balance of payments surplus and a tendency for the exchange rate to appreciate, which the central bank restrains by accumulating stocks of foreign exchange. And likewise, if the balance of trade falls short of capital exports, there will be a balance of payments deficit and a tendency for the exchange rate to depreciate, which the central bank prevents by dispensing with stocks of foreign exchange.

In what follows it is assumed that all foreign policies and export demand are given, that the balance of trade worsens as the level of domestic expenditure increases, and that capital flows are responsive to interest rate differentials. Then domestic expenditure can be assumed to depend only on fiscal policy (the budget surplus) and monetary policy (the interest rate) at the full employment level of output. The complete system can thus be given a geometric interpretation in the two policy variables, the interest rate and the budget surplus[2] (Figure 1).

In the diagram, the *FF* line, which will be referred to as the "foreign-balance schedule," traces the locus of pairs of interest rates and budget surpluses (at the level of income compatible with full employment) along which the balance of payments is in equilibrium. This schedule has a negative slope because an increase in the interest rate, by reducing capital exports and lowering domestic expenditure and hence imports, improves the balance of payments; while a decrease in the budget surplus, by raising domestic expenditure and hence imports, worsens the balance of payments. Thus, from any point on the schedule an increase in the rate of interest would cause an external surplus, which would have to be compensated by a reduction in the budget surplus in order to restore equilibrium. Points above and to the right of the foreign-balance schedule refer to balance of payments surpluses, while points below and to the left of the schedule represent balance of payments deficits.

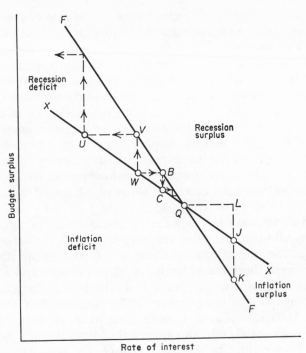

Rate of interest

Figure 1.

A similar construction can be applied to the conditions representing internal balance. The XX line, or "internal-balance
schedule," is the locus of pairs of interest rates and budget surpluses which permits continuing full employment equilibrium in
the market for goods and services. Along this schedule, full employment output is equal to aggregate demand for output, or,
what amounts to the same condition, home demand for domestic
goods is equal to full employment output less exports. There is,
therefore, only one level of home demand for domestic goods consistent with full employment and the given level of exports, and
this implies that expenditure must be constant along XX. The
internal-balance line must therefore have a negative slope, since
increases in the interest rate are associated with decreases in the
budget surplus, in order to maintain domestic expenditure constant.

Both the internal-balance and the foreign-balance schedules
thus have negative slopes. But it is necessary also to compare the
steepness of the slopes. Which of the schedules is steeper?

It can be demonstrated that FF must be steeper than XX if
capital is even slightly mobile, and by an amount which depends
both on the responsiveness of international capital flows to the rate
of interest and on the marginal propensity to import. The absolute
slope of the internal-balance schedule XX is the ratio between the

responsiveness of domestic expenditure to the rate of interest and the responsiveness of domestic expenditure to the budget surplus. Now, if it is assumed for a moment that capital exports are constant, the balance of payments depends only on expenditure, since exports are assumed constant and imports depend only on expenditure. In other words, if capital exports are constant, the slope of FF also is the ratio between the responsiveness of domestic expenditure to the rate of interest and the responsiveness of such expenditure to the budget surplus. Therefore, apart from the effects of changes in capital exports, the two slopes are the same. It is then possible to see that the responsiveness of capital exports to the rate of interest makes the slope of FF greater in absolute value than the slope of XX.[3]

Consider, for example, what happens to an initial situation of over-all equilibrium at Q as this equilibrium is disturbed by an increase in the rate of interest equal to QL. Because of the higher rate of interest, there would be deflationary pressure and a balance of payments surplus at the point L. If the budget surplus is now lowered, the deflationary pressure can be eliminated at a point like J on the internal-balance schedule. But at J, expenditure is the same as it was at Q, and this means that imports, and hence the balance of *trade*, must be the same as at Q. The balance of *payments* is therefore in surplus at J because of capital imports attracted by the higher rate of interest; this makes necessary a further reduction in the budget surplus in order to bring the balance of payments again into equilibrium. It follows, then, that the point K on the foreign-balance schedule is below the point J on the internal-balance schedule, and that FF is steeper than XX. It can then also be concluded that the absolute difference in slopes is greater, the more mobile is capital (because this causes a larger external surplus at J) and the lower is the marginal propensity to import (because this necessitates a larger budget deficit to correct any given external surplus).[4]

In Figure 1, the two schedules separate four quadrants, distinguished from one another by the conditions of internal imbalance and external disequilibrium. Only at the point where the schedules intersect are the policy variables in equilibrium.

Two Systems of Policy Response

Consider now two possible policy systems determining the behavior of fiscal policy and monetary policy when internal and external balance have not been simultaneously achieved. The government can adjust monetary policy to the requirements of internal stability, and fiscal policy to the needs of external balance, or it can use fiscal policy for purposes of internal stability and monetary policy for purposes of external balance.

It will be demonstrated first that the policy system in which the interest rate is used for internal stability, and fiscal policy is used for external equilibrium, is an unstable system. Consider, for example, a situation of full employment combined with a balance of payments deficit, represented by the point W. To correct the deficit by fiscal policy, the budget surplus must be raised from that indicated by W to that given by V. At V there will be equilibrium in the balance of payments, but the increased budget surplus will have caused recessionary pressure. If now the threatening unemployment is to be prevented by monetary policy, the rate of interest must be lowered from that indicated by V to that described by U. But at U there is again a balance of payments deficit, which in turn necessitates a further increase in the budget surplus. The process continues with the interest rate and the budget surplus moving ever further from equilibrium.[5]

To show formally that the system is unstable, it is sufficient to note that the payments deficit at U, after the first round of policy changes, exceeds the deficit at W. This is evident since it is known that the balance of *trade* at U and W is the same but, because of the lower rate of interest, the balance of *payments* at U is worse. It follows that this type of policy reaction is unstable.

On the other hand, the opposite type of policy response is stable. Suppose that the authorities adjust the interest rate to correspond to the needs of external equilibrium and adjust fiscal policy to maintain internal stability. Then from the same disequilibrium point W, the rate of interest would be raised to B, thereby correcting the external deficit. But the tendency toward unemployment generated by the restrictive credit policy must now be corrected by a reduction in the budget surplus or increase in the budget deficit. At C there is again internal balance and a balance of payments deficit, as at W. But it is now possible to see that the deficit at C is *less* than the deficit at W. This follows, as before, because the balance of *trade* at C is identical with that at W but, since the rate of interest is higher at C, the balance of *payments* deficit must be less. The system is therefore stable.

The diagrammatic argument can be absorbed at once when it is realized that at W—or anywhere in the quadrant representing a deficit and recession—the interest rate is lower, and the budget surplus is higher, than is appropriate to the over-all equilibrium at Q. The use of fiscal policy for external balance, and monetary policy for internal balance, drives the interest rate and budget surplus further away from equilibrium, while the alternative system moves the instruments closer to equilibrium.

The same argument applies to an initial disequilibrium in the opposite quadrant, representing inflationary pressure and external surplus. To restore equilibrium, the interest rate must be reduced, and fiscal policy must be made more restrictive. Only if monetary policy is used for the external purpose, and fiscal policy for the internal purpose, will correction of the disequilibrium automatically ensue.[6]

In the other two quadrants, monetary and fiscal policies will be moving in the same direction under either system of policy response, because both tighter monetary policy and an increased budget surplus correct inflationary pressure and external deficit, and both easier monetary policy and a reduced budget surplus tend to alleviate recession and external surplus. The distinction between the two policy systems appears less important in these phases of the international trade cycle; it nevertheless remains, since inaccurate information about the exact location of the point Q could propel the situation into one of the quadrants involving either recession and deficit or inflation and surplus.[7]

Conclusions

It has been demonstrated that, in countries where employment and balance of payments policies are restricted to monetary and fiscal instruments, monetary policy should be reserved for attaining the desired level of the balance of payments, and fiscal policy for preserving internal stability under the conditions assumed here. The opposite system would lead to a progressively worsening unemployment and balance of payments situation.

The explanation can be related to what I have elsewhere called the Principle of Effective Market Classification: policies should be paired with the objectives on which they have the most influence.[8] If this principle is not followed, there will develop a tendency either for a cyclical approach to equilibrium or for instability.

The use of fiscal policy for external purposes and monetary policy for internal stability violates the principle of effective market classification, because the ratio of the effect of the rate of interest on internal stability to its effect on the balance of payments is less than the ratio of the effect of fiscal policy on internal stability to its effect on the balance of payments. And for precisely this reason the opposite set of policy responses is consistent with the principle.

On a still more general level, we have the principle that Tinbergen has made famous: that to attain a given number of independent targets there must be at least an equal number of instruments.[9] Tinbergen's Principle is concerned with the *existence* and location of a solution to the system. It does not assert that any given set of policy responses will in fact lead to that solution. To assert this, it is necessary to investigate the stability properties of a dynamic system. In this respect, the Principle of Effective Market Classification is a necessary companion to Tinbergen's Principle.

NOTES

1. This possibility has been suggested, and to a limited extent implemented, elsewhere. See, for example, De Nederlandsche Bank N.V., *Report for the Year 1960* (Amsterdam 1961).

2. The assumptions could be made less restrictive without detracting from the generality of the conclusions. Thus, an assumption that capital imports directly affect domestic expenditure, as in theoretical transfer analysis, would tend to reinforce the conclusions. Even the (plausible) assumption that, in addition to capital flows, capital indebtedness is responsive to the rate of interest (to take account of the "stock" nature of much of international floating capital) would not change the conclusions, although it may affect the quantitative extent of the policy changes required.

Notice, however, that I have implicitly assumed away strong "Pigou" effects, speculation on international markets that is related to the size of the (positive or negative) budget surplus, forward rate movements that more than offset interest-rate-differential changes (an unlikely occurrence), and concern about the precise composition of the balance of payments; the last assumption may mean that the method of achieving equilibrium suggested below is desirable only in the short run.

3. Both the absolute and relative values of the slopes depend on the particular fiscal policy in question. The discussion in the text applies to income tax reductions because that instrument tends to be neutral as between home and foreign spending. The conclusions would be strengthened or weakened, respectively, as the particular fiscal policy was biased toward or against home goods; the more the change in the budget surplus results from a change in spending on home goods, the greater is the difference between the slopes of XX and FF.

4. The assumption that imports depend only on expenditure, while the latter depends partly on the rate of interest, means that imports are affected by the rate of interest, although the *share* of imports in expenditure is not. This assumption could be relaxed without fundamentally altering the results, although an exception—remote in practice but possible in theory—does arise, if import goods are highly responsive to the rate of interest while home goods are not, capital flows are only slightly responsive to the rate of interest, and the marginal propensity to buy imports is high relative to the marginal propensity to buy home goods. Under these conditions, it is possible that XX may be steeper than FF.

More formally, then, it is necessary to limit the present conclusions to countries in which the ratio of the effect of budget policy on the balance of payments to its effect on domestic excess demand is less than the ratio of the effect of the interest rate on the balance of payments to its effect on excess demand.

5. It need hardly be mentioned that the demonstration of instability in this instance (or of stability in the subsequent analysis) is not dependent upon the particular assumption that the government corrects imbalance first in one sector and then in the other, an assumption which is made only for expositional convenience. The conclusions follow, for example, even if the authorities simultaneously adjust fiscal and monetary policies.

6. Even if the authorities do not wish to pair instruments and targets, they can use the information provided by the analysis to determine the relation between *actual* policies and *equilibrium* policies. Thus, situations of deficit and recession imply that the budget surplus is too high and the interest rate is too low, while situations of surplus and inflation imply the opposite. In this manner, appropriate policies can be determined by observable situations of target disequilibria.

7. The system can be generalized for a two-country world by assuming that the other country adjusts fiscal policy to maintain internal stability. The only difference in the conclusion is that the conditions of dynamic stability of the adjustment process are slightly more restrictive, requiring that the marginal propensities to import be, *on the average*, no greater than one half; this is the usual assumption necessary to rule out any "reverse transfer" that is due to policies affecting expenditure.

8. "The Monetary Dynamics of International Adjustment Under Fixed and Flexible Exchange Rates," *Quarterly Journal of Economics*, Vol. 74 (1960), 249–50.

9. J. Tinbergen, *On the Theory of Economic Policy* (Amsterdam 1952).

Selected Bibliography

This classified bibliography covers the articles and books on monetary theory and policy for the period 1960 to 1964 with some exceptions. Articles in English appearing before 1964 may also be found in the *Index of Economic Journals, 1896–1963* (Homewood, Ill.: 1962, 1965), prepared by the American Economic Association. For books before 1963 see the *Economics Library Selections: Cumulative Bibliography Selections, Series I and II, 1954–1962* (New York 1965). For an unclassified bibliography for the period 1950–1965, see *Monetary Theory and Policy: A Bibliography* (Board of Governors of the Federal Reserve System [Washington: 1965]). Certain items in this *Selected Bibliography* may cover a wider area than the particular subheading may indicate.

Monetary Theory and Value Theory

1. Botha, D. J., *A Study in the Theory of Monetary Equilibrium* (Leiden: 1959).
2. Friedman, M. (ed.), *Studies in the Quantity Theory of Money* (Chicago: 1956).
3. ———, and A. J. Schwartz, *A Monetary History of the United States, 1867–1960* (Princeton: 1963).
4. Gurley, J. and E. Shaw, *Money in a Theory of Finance.* With a mathematical appendix by A. E. Enthoven (Washington, D.C.: 1960).
5. Johnson, H. G., "The General Theory after Twenty-five Years," *American Economic Review Proceedings* 51: 1–17 (May 1961). Reprinted in H. G. Johnson, *Money, Trade and Economic Growth* (London: 1962).
6. Keunne, R. E., "Keynes's Identity, Ricardian Virtue and the Partial Dichotomy," *Canadian Journal of Economics and Political Science* 27: 323–36 (August 1961).
7. Lindbeck, A., *A Study in Monetary Analysis* (Stockholm: 1963).
8. Meinich, P., "Money Illusion and the Real Balance Effect," *Statsekonomisk Tidsskrift* 78: 8–33 (March 1964).

9. Negishi, T., "Conditions for Neutral Money," *Review of Economic Studies* 31: 147–48 (April 1964).

10. Patinkin, D., *Money, Interest, and Prices*, 2nd Edition (New York: 1964).

11. Thorn, R. S., "Long-Run Adjustments to Changes in the Capital-Output Ratio and the National Debt," *Yale Economic Essays* (Spring 1962).

12. Tobin, J., "Money, Capital and Other Stores of Value," *American Economic Review* 51: 26–37 (May 1961).

The Demand for Money

1. Axilrod, S. H., "Liquidity and Public Policy," *Federal Reserve Bulletin* 47: 1161–77 (October 1961).

2. Bloch, E., "Short Cycles in Corporate Demand for Government Securities and Cash," *American Economic Review* 53: 1058–77 (December 1963).

3. Bronfenbrenner, M. and T. Mayer, "Liquidity Functions in the American Economy," *Econometrica* 28: 810–34 (October 1960).

4. Brunner, K. and A. H. Meltzer, "Predicting Velocity: Implications for Theory and Policy," *Journal of Finance* 18: 17–54 (May 1963).

5. Ellis, H. S., "Notes on the Demand for Money," *Kyklos* 15: 216–230 (1962—No. 1).

6. Feige, E. L., *The Demand for Liquid Assets: A Temporal Cross-section Analysis*. Ford Foundation Doctoral Dissertation Series, 1963 award winner (Englewood Cliffs, N.J.: 1964).

7. Fleming, M., "The Timing of Payments and the Demand for Money," *Economica* 31: 132–57 (May 1964).

8. Freeman, J. F., "Liquidity Preference *v.* Loanable Funds: A New Approach to the Problem," *Economic Journal* 73: 681–88 (December 1963).

9. Friedman, M., "The Demand for Money," *American Philosophical Society Proceedings* 105: 259–64 (June 1961).

10. Fujino, S., "The Permanent Income and the Transactions Demand for Money by Households," *Hitotsubashi Journal of Economics* 5: 37–51 (June 1964).

11. Guthrie, H. W., "Consumers' Propensities to Hold Liquid Assets," *Journal of the American Statistical Association* 55: 469–90 (Summer 1960).

12. Johnson, H. G., "Notes on the Theory of Transactions Demand for Cash," *Indian Journal of Economics* 44: 1–11 (July 1963).

13. Juster, F. T., "Consumer Sensitivity to the Price of Credit." Discussion by T. Smith and R. W. Johnson. *Journal of Finance* 19: 222–39 (May 1964).

14. Latané, H. A., "Individual Risk Preference in Portfolio Selection," *Journal of Finance* 15: 45–52 (March 1960).

15. ———, "Portfolio Balance—The Demand for Money, Bonds and Stocks," *Southern Economic Journal* 28: 71–77 (October 1962).

16. Lee, T. H., "Income, Wealth and the Demand for Money: Some Evidence from Cross-Section Data," *Journal of the American Statistical Association* 59: 746–62 (September 1964).

17. Lloyd, C. L., "The Equivalence of the Liquidity Preference and Loanable Funds Theories and the *New* Stock-Flow Analysis," *Review of Economic Studies* 27: 206–9 (June 1960).

18. Matthews, R. C., "Expenditure Plans and the Uncertainty Motive for Holding Money," *Journal of Political Economy* 71: 201–18 (June 1963).

19. Meltzer, A. H., "The Demand for Money: A Cross-Section Study of Business Firms," *Quarterly Journal of Economics* 77: 405–22 (August 1963).

20. ———, "The Demand for Money: The Evidence from the Time Series," *Journal of Political Economy* 71: 219–46 (June 1963).

21. Ohlin, B., "The Quantity Theory in Swedish Literature," *Economic History* 2: 3–18 (1959).

22. Pesek, B. P., "Determinants of the Demand for Money," *Review of Economics and Statistics* 45: 419–24 (November 1963).

23. Pratt, J. W., "Risk Aversion in the Small and in the Large," *Econometrica* 32: 122–36 (January–April 1964).

24. Rakshit, M. K., "Invariance of the Demand for Cash and Other Assets: A Comment," *Oxford Economic Papers* 16: 291–98 (July 1964).

25. Reierson, R. L., "New Forces in the Money Market," *Journal of Finance* 17: 220–29 (May 1962).

26. Schmolders, G., "The Liquidity Theory of Money," *Kyklos* 13: 345–60 (1960—No. 3).

27. Selden, R. T., "The Postwar Rise in the Velocity of Money: A Sectoral Analysis," *Journal of Finance* 16: 483–545 (December 1961).

28. U.S. Congress, *Liquidity and Financial Institutions in the Postwar Economy*, by John G. Gurley. Study paper No. 14, Joint Economic Committee, 86th Congress, 2nd Session (Washington: 1960).

The Supply of Money

1. Alhadeff, D. A., "Credit Controls and Financial Intermediaries," *American Economic Review* 50: 655–71 (September 1960).

2. Argy, F., "Non-Banking Financial Intermediaries and the Process of Credit Creation," *Economic Record* 36: 530–41 (December 1960).

3. Bach, G. L. and C. J. Huizenga, "The Differential Effects of Tight Money," *American Economic Review* 51: 52–80 (March 1961).

4. Basevi, G., "Vault Cash and the Shift in the Desired Level of Free Reserves," *Journal of Political Economy* 71: 408–12 (August 1963).

5. Baxter, N. D. and H. T. Shapiro, "Compensating-Balance Requirements: The Results of a Survey," *Journal of Finance* 19: 483–96 (September 1964).

6. Black, R. P., "The Impact of Member Banks Reserves upon the Money Supply," *Southern Economic Journal* 29: 199–210 (January 1963).

7. Brunner, K., *The Structure of the Monetary System and the Supply Function for Money.* Unpublished dissertation (University of California: 1961).

8. ——— and A. H. Meltzer, "The Place of Financial Intermediaries in the Transmission of Monetary Policy," *American Economic Review* 53: 372–82 (May 1963).

9. ——— and ———, "Some Further Investigations of Demand and Supply Functions of Money," *Journal of Finance* 19: 240–83 (May 1964).

10. Cagan, P., *Determinants and Effects of Changes in the Stock of Money, 1875–1960.* National Bureau of Economic Research (New York: 1965).

11. Carson, D., "The Differential Effects of Tight Money: A Comment." Reply by G. L. Bach and C. J. Huizenga. *American Economic Review* 51: 1039–43 (December 1961).

12. Clayton, G., "British Financial Intermediaries in Theory and Practice," *Economic Journal* 72: 869–86 (December 1962).

13. Coppock, D. J. and N. J. Gibson, "The Volume of Deposits and the Cash and Liquid Assets Ratio," *Manchester School of Economics and Social Studies* 31: 203–22 (September 1963).

14. Cramp, A. B., "Financial Intermediaries and Monetary Policy," *Economica* 29: 143–51 (May 1962).

15. Dacey, W. M., "Treasury Bills and the Money Supply," *Lloyds Bank Review* 70: 1–16 (January 1960).

16. Davis, R. G. and J. M. Guttentag, "Balance Requirements and Deposit Competition," *Journal of Political Economy* 71: 581–85 (December 1963).

17. Dewald, W., "Free Reserves, Total Reserves and Monetary Control," *Journal of Political Economy* 71: 581–85 (December 1963).

18. Ettin, E. C., "The Growth of Non-Bank Financial Intermediaries and the Interest Rate Determination," *Quarterly Journal of Economics* 78: 649–52 (November 1964).

19. Friend, E., H. P. Minsky, and A. L. Andrews, *Private Capital Markets.* Prepared for the Commission on Money and Credit (Englewood Cliffs, N.J.: 1964).

20. Klein, J., "Price Level and Money-Denomination Movements," *Journal of Political Economy* 71: 369–78 (August 1960).

21. Marty, A. L., "Gurley and Shaw on Money in a Theory of Finance," *Journal of Political Economy* 69: 56–62 (February 1961).

22. McLeod, A. N., "Credit Expansion in an Open Economy," *Economic Journal* 72: 611–40 (September 1962).

23. Meigs, A. J., *Free Reserves and the Money Supply* (Chicago: 1962).

24. Miller, H. L., Jr., "Stochastic Reserve Losses and Bank Credit." Reply by D. Orr and W. G. Mellon. *American Economic Review* 52: 1118–22 (December 1962).

25. Netzler, D. and A. D. Goldstine, "Types of Money in Use in the 1950's," *Journal of Finance* 17: 606–21 (December 1962).

26. Newlyn, W. T., "The Supply of Money and Its Control," *Economic Journal* 74: 327–46 (June 1964).

27. Orr, D. and W. G. Mellon, "Stochastic Reserve Losses and Expansion of Bank Credit," *American Economic Review* 51: 614–23 (September 1961).

28. Patinkin, D., "Financial Intermediaries and the Logical Structure of Monetary Theory," *American Economic Review* 51: 95–116 (March 1961).

29. Ritter, L. S., "The Structure of Financial Markets, Income Velocity and the Effectiveness of Monetary Policy," *Schweizerische Zeitschrift für Volkswirtschaft und Statistik* 98: 276–89 (September 1962).

30. Rousseas, S. W., "Velocity Changes and the Effectiveness of Monetary Policy, 1951–1957," *Review of Economics and Statistics* 40: 27–36 (February 1960).

✓ 31. Shearer, R. A., "The Expansion of Bank Credit: An Alternative Approach," *Quarterly Journal of Economics* 77: 363–77 (August 1963).

32. Torrance, C. M., "Gross Flow of Funds Through Savings and Loan Associations," *Journal of Finance* 15: 140–56 (May 1960).

33. U.S. Congress, *Increased Flexibility for Financial Institutions*. Hearings before the House Committee on Banking and Currency, 88th Congress, 1st session (Washington: 1964).

✓ 34. Wicker, E. R., "The Behaviour of the Consumer Money Supply since World War II," *Journal of Political Economy* 69: 437–46 (October 1961).

35. Willis, J. B., "Gross Flow of Funds Through Mutual Savings Banks," *Journal of Finance* 15: 170–90 (May 1960).

36. Wright, K. M., "Gross Flow of Funds Through Life Insurance Companies," *Journal of Finance* 15: 140–56 (May 1960).

✓ 37. Yohe, W. P., "Financial Institutions in Aggregative Models," *Statsøkonomisk Tidsskrift* 77: 205–33 (December 1963).

The Rate of Interest

1. Axilrod, S. H. and R. A. Young, "Interest Rates and Monetary Policy," *Federal Reserve Bulletin* 48: 1110–37 (September 1962).

2. Bojt, A., "Real Bond Holdings and the Rate of Interest," *Economia Internazionale* 13: 1–24 (February 1960).

3. Conard, J., *Introduction to the Theory of Interest* (Berkeley and Los Angeles: 1963).

4. Gray, H. P., "Some Evidence on Two Implications of Higher Interest Rates on Time Deposits," *Journal of Finance* 19: 63–75 (March 1964).

5. Guttentag, J. M., "Credit Availability, Interest Rate and Monetary Policy," *Southern Economic Journal* 27: 219–28 (January 1960).

6. Horwich, G., "Real Assets and the Theory of Interest," *Journal of Political Economy* 70: 157–69 (April 1962).

7. Juster, F. T. and R. P. Shay, *Consumer Sensitivity to Finance Rates: An Empirical and Analytical Investigation*. National Bureau of Economic Research, Occasional Paper No. 88 (New York: 1964).

8. Kessel, R. A., *The Cyclical Behavior of the Term Structure of Interest Rates*. National Bureau of Economic Research, Occasional Paper No. 91 (New York: 1965).

9. Latané, H. A., "Income Velocity and Interest Rates: A Pragmatic Approach," *Review of Economics and Statistics* 42: 445–49 (November 1960).

10. Laudadio, L., "Size of Bank, Size of Borrower and the Rate of Interest," *Journal of Finance* 18: 20–28 (March 1963).

11. Levenson, A. N., "Interest Rate and Cost Differentials in Bank Lending to Small and Large Business," *Review of Economics and Statistics* 44: 190–97 (May 1962).

12. Malkiel, B. G., "Expectations, Bond Prices, and the Term of Structure of Interest Rates," *Quarterly Journal of Economics* 76: 197–218 (May 1962).

13. Meiselman, D., *The Term Structure of Interest Rates* (Englewood Cliffs, N.J.: 1962).

14. Mundell, R. A., "The Public Debt, Corporate Income Taxes, and the Rate of Interest," *Journal of Political Economy* 68: 622–26 (December 1960).

15. Smith, P. F., "Optimum Rate on Time Deposits," *Journal of Finance* 17: 622–33 (December 1962).

16. Turvey, R., *Interest Rates and Asset Prices* (London: 1960).

17. U.S. Congress, *Interest Rates on Foreign Official Time Deposits*. Hearings before the Senate Committee on Banking and Currency, 87th Congress, 2nd Session (Washington: 1962).

18. White, W. H., "The Structure of the Bond Market and the Cyclical Variability of Interest Rates," *IMF Staff Papers* 9: 107–47 (March 1962).

19. Wood, J. H., "Expectations, Errors, and the Term Structure of Interest Rates," *Journal of Political Economy* 71: 160–71 (April 1963).

20. ———, "The Expectations Hypothesis, the Yield Curve, and Monetary Policy," *Quarterly Journal of Economics* 78: 457–70 (August 1964).

Monetary Policy

1. Alhadeff, D., *et al.*, "The Commission on Money and Credit's Research Studies: A Collective Review Article," *Journal of Finance* 19: 497–533 (September 1964).

2. Anderson, L. C., "The Incidence of Monetary Measures on the Structure of Output," *Review of Economics and Statistics* 46: 260–68 (August 1964).

3. Anderson, R. B., "Financial Policies for Sustainable Growth," *Journal of Finance* 15: 127–39 (May 1960).

4. Arndt, H. W., "Radcliffe Monetary Theory: A Comment," *Economic Record* 38: 341–51 (September 1962).

5. Aschheim, J., *Techniques of Monetary Control* (Baltimore: 1961).

6. Auten, J. H., "Monetary Policy and Forward Exchange Market," *Journal of Finance* 16: 546–58 (December 1961).

7. Bach, G. L., "Process and Responses in Monetary Control," *Review of Economics and Statistics*, Supplement 45: 129–31 (February 1963).

8. Baumol, W. J., "Pitfalls in Contracyclical Policies: Some Tools and Results," *Review of Economics and Statistics* 43: 21–26 (February 1961).

9. ———, R. W. Clower, and M. L. Burstein, F. H. Hahn, R. J. Ball and R. Bodkin, G. C. Archibald and R. G. Lipsey, "A Symposium on Monetary Policy," *Review of Economic Studies* 28: 29–56 (October 1960).

10. Bell, J. W. and W. E. Spahr (eds.), *A Proper Monetary and Banking System for the United States* (New York: 1960).

11. Bronfenbrenner, M., "Statistical Tests of Rival Monetary Rules," *Journal of Political Economy* 69: 1–14 (February 1961).

12. ——, "Statistical Tests of Rival Monetary Rules: Quarterly Data Supplement," *Journal of Political Economy* 69: 621–25 (December 1961).

13. Christ, C. F., "On the Report of the Commission on Money and Credit," *Review of Economics and Statistics* 44: 418–27 (November 1962).

14. Commission on Money and Credit, *The Federal Reserve and the Treasury: Answers to Questions from the Commission on Money and Credit* (Engelwood Cliffs, N.J.: 1963).

15. ——, *Federal Credit Agencies.* A series of research studies prepared for the Commission on Money and Credit (Englewood Cliffs, N.J.: 1963).

16. ——, *Federal Credit Programs,* by S. Johnson *et al.* Prepared for the Commission on Money and Credit (Englewood Cliffs, N.J.: 1963).

17. ——, *Fiscal and Debt Management Policies,* by W. Fellner, *et al.* Prepared for the Commission on Money and Credit (Englewood Cliffs, N.J.: 1963).

18. ——, *Impacts of Monetary Policy.* Prepared for the Commission on Money and Credit (Englewood Cliffs, N.J.: 1964).

19. ——, *Inflation, Growth, and Employment.* A series of research studies prepared for the Commission on Money and Credit (Englewood Cliffs, N.J.: 1964).

20. ——, *Money and Credit: Their Influence on Jobs, Prices and Growth* (Englewood Cliffs, N.J.: 1961).

21. ——, *Private Financial Institutions.* A series of research studies prepared for the Commission on Money and Credit (Englewood Cliffs, N.J.: 1964).

22. ——, *Stabilization Policies.* A series of research studies prepared for the Commission on Money and Credit (Englewood Cliffs, N.J.: 1964).

23. ——, *Monetary Management,* by F. M. Tamanga, *et al.* Prepared for the Commission on Money and Credit. (Englewood Cliffs, N.J.: 1963).

24. Cox, A. H., Jr. and R. F. Leach, "Defensive Open Market Operations and the Reserve Settlements Periods of Member Banks," *Journal of Finance* 19: 76–93 (March 1964).

25. Culbertson, J. M., "Friedman on the Lag in Effect of Monetary Policy," *Journal of Political Economy* 68: 617–21 (October 1960).

26. ——, "The Use of Monetary Policy," *Southern Economic Journal* 27: 130–37 (October 1961).

27. ——, "The Lag in Effect of Monetary Policy: A Reply," *Journal of Political Economy* 69: 467–77 (October 1961).

28. Dewald, W., *Monetary Control and the Distribution of Money.* Unpublished Ph.D. dissertation (University of Minnesota: 1963).

29. ——, "Money to Spare: Excess Reserves," Federal Reserve Bank of Minneapolis *Monthly Review* 2–7 (August 1961).

30. Dorrance, G. S. and W. H. White, "Alternative Forms of Monetary Ceilings for Stabilization Purposes," *IMF Staff Papers*-9: 317–42 (November 1962).

31. Friedman, M., "The Lag in the Effect of Monetary Policy," *Journal of Political Economy* 69: 447–66 (October 1961).

32. ———, *A Program for Monetary Stability* (New York: 1960).

33. Gibson, N. J., "Special Deposits as an Instrument of Monetary Policy," *Manchester School of Economics and Social Studies* 32: 239–59 (September 1964).

34. Gray, H. P., "The Effects on Monetary Policy of Rising Costs in Commercial Banks," *Journal of Finance* 18: 29–48 (March 1963).

35. Harris, S. E., J. W. Angell, W. Fellner, A. H. Hansen, A. G. Hart, H. Neisser, R. V. Roosa, P. A. Samuelson, W. L. Smith, W. Thomas, J. Tobin, and S. Weintraub, "Controversial Issues in Recent Monetary Policy: A Symposium," *Review of Economics and Statistics* 42: 245–82 (August 1960).

36. Henderson, J. M., "Monetary Reserves and Credit Control," *American Economic Review* 50: 348–60 (June 1960).

37. Hodgman, D. R. "Credit Risk and Credit Rationing," *Quarterly Journal of Economics* 74: 258–78 (May 1960).

38. ———, "The Deposit Relationship and Commercial Bank Investment Behaviour," *Review of Economics and Statistics* 43: 257–68 (August 1961).

39. Iengar, H. V. R., *Monetary Policy and Economic Growth* (Bombay: 1962).

40. Jasay, A. E., "The Workings of the Radcliffe Monetary System," *Oxford Economic Papers* 12: 170–80 (June 1960).

41. Johnson, H., *Alternative Guiding Principles for the Use of Monetary Policy*. Essays in International Finance No. 40 (Princeton: 1963).

42. ———, "Objectives, Monetary Standards and Potentialities," *Review of Economics and Statistics*, Supplement 45: 137–44 (February 1963).

43. Kavesh, R. A. and J. Mackey, "A Financial Framework for Economic Growth," *Journal of Finance* 16: 202–25 (May 1961).

44. Lipsey, R. G. and F. P. Brechling, "Trade Credit and Monetary Policy," *Economic Journal* 73: 618–41 (December 1963).

45. Luckett, D. G. " 'Bills Only': A Critical Appraisal," *Review of Economics and Statistics* 42: 301–6 (August 1960).

46. Lundberg, E., "Economic Stability and Monetary Policy," *Skandinavian Bank Quarterly Review* 42: 9–18 (1).

47. ———, "What Do We Know about the Efficacy of Monetary Policy?" *Skandinavian Bank Quarterly Review* 42: 107–16 (1962).

48. Martin, W. McC., Jr., "Monetary Policy and International Payments," *Journal of Finance* 18: 1–10 (March 1963).

49. Meltzer, A. H., "Public and Private Financial Institutions: A Review Article from Reports of Two Presidential Committees," *Review of Economics and Statistics* 46: 269–78 (August 1964).

50. ———, "Mercantile Credit, Monetary Policy and the Size of Firms," *Review of Economics and Statistics* 42: 429–37 (November 1960).

51. Miller, E., "Monetary Policies of the United States since 1950: Some Implications of the Retreat to Orthodoxy," *Canadian Journal of Economics and Political Science* 27: 205–22 (May 1961).

52. Morgan, E. V., *Monetary Policy for Stable Growth*. Institute for Economic Affairs, Hobart Paper No. 27 (London: 1964).

53. Mundell, R. A., "The Monetary Dynamics of International Adjustment under Fixed and Flexible Exchange Rates," *Quarterly Journal of Economics* 74: 249–50 (1960).

54. Noyes, G. E., "Short-Run Objectives of Monetary Policy," *Review of Economics and Statistics*, Supplement 45: 147–48 (February 1963).

55. Olakanpo, J. O., "Monetary Management in Dependent Economies," *Economica* 28: 395–408 (November 1961).

56. Pesek, B. P. and T. R. Saving, "Monetary Policy, Taxes and the Rate of Interest," *Journal of Political Economy* 71: 347–62 (August 1963).

57. Piggott, W., "Federal Reserve Open Market Policy 1952–61: The 'Bills Only' Era," University of Washington *Business Review* (February 1963).

58. Porter, R. C., "A Model of Bank Portfolio Selection," *Yale Economic Essays* (Fall 1961).

59. Reuber, G. L., *The Objectives of Monetary Policy*. A working paper prepared for Royal Commission on Banking and Finance. Canada: Royal Commission on Banking and Finance (1962).

60. Roosa, R. V., "Reconciling Internal and External Financial Policies," *Journal of Finance* 17: 1–16 (May 1962).

61. Saulnier, R. J., *Recent Studies of Our Financial System*. Bureau of Business Research, Business Paper No. 9 (Bloomington: 1964).

62. Smith, W. L., "The Instruments of Monetary Control," *National Banking Review* 47–76 (September 1963).

63. Tarshis, L., "Money and Credit." A review article. *American Economic Review* 52: 472–80 (June 1962).

64. Teigen, R. L. A., "A Structural Approach to the Impact of Monetary Policy." Discussion by C. F. Christ and D. Hester. *Journal of Finance* 19: 284–312 (May 1964).

65. Thorn, R. S., "Nonbank Financial Intermediaries, Credit Expansion, and Monetary Policy," *IMF Staff Papers* 6: 369–83 (November 1958).

66. Tucker, D. P., "Bronfenbrenner on Monetary Rules: A Comment," *Journal of Political Economy* 71: 173–79 (April 1963).

67. U.S. Congress, *The Prevalent Monetary Policy and Its Consequences*, by L. H. Keyserling. Analysis submitted to the Subcommittee on Domestic Finance, House Committee on Banking and Currency, 88th Congress, 2nd Session (Washington: 1964).

68. ———, *Debt Management in the United States*, by W. L. Smith. Study Paper No. 19, Joint Economic Committee, 86th Congress, 2nd Session (Washington: 1960).

69. ———, *The Federal Reserve's Attachment to the Free Reserve Concept: Staff Analysis*. Subcommittee on Domestic Finance, House Committee on Banking and Currency, 88th Congress, 2nd Session (Washington: 1964).

70. ———, *The Federal Reserve System after 50 Years*. Hearings before the Subcommittee on Domestic Finance, House Committee on Banking and Currency, 88th Congress, 2nd Session (Washington: 1964).

71. U.S. Government, *Report to the President by the Committee on Federal Credit Programs* (Washington: 1963).

72. ———, *Report of the President's Committee on Financial Institutions* (Washington: 1963).

73. Viner, J., *Problems of Monetary Control.* Essays in International Finance No. 45 (Princeton: 1964).

74. White, W. H., "The Flexibility of Anticyclical Monetary Policy," *Review of Economics and Statistics* 43: 142–47 (May 1961).

75. Yeager, L. B. (ed.), *In Search of a Monetary Constitution.* Lectures delivered at the Thomas Jefferson Center for Studies in Political Economy, University of Virginia (Cambridge: 1962).

76. Young, R. A. and C. A. Yager, "The Economies of 'Bills Preferable,' " *Quarterly Journal of Economics* 74: 341–73 (August 1960).

77. Zupnick, E., "Consumer Credit and Monetary Policy in the United States and the United Kingdom," *Journal of Finance* 17: 342–54 (May 1962).

A Note on the Type

The text of this book has been set on the Monotype in a type-face called Baskerville, a modern recutting of a type originally designed by John Baskerville (1706–75). Baskerville, who was a writing master in Birmingham, England, began experimenting about 1750 with type design and punch cutting. His first book, set throughout in his new types, was a Virgil in royal quarto, published in 1757, and it was followed by other famous editions from his press. Baskerville's types, which are distinctive and elegant in design, were a forerunner of what we know today as the "modern" group of type faces.

This book was designed by R. D. Scudellari and was composed, printed and bound by Vail Ballou Press, Binghamton, New York.

About the Author

Richard S. Thorn, Professor of Economics at The University of Pittsburgh, received his Ph.D. from Yale in 1958. He has served as an economist with the International Monetary Fund and with the Alliance for Progress. In 1964 he headed the Inter-American Development Bank Mission to Bolivia and in 1967 was advisor to the Deputy Prime Minister of Iran on budgetary matters. He has published numerous articles in leading economic journals.